# ACCOUNTING
## TO TRIAL BALANCE

CENGAGE

# ACCOUNTING
## TO TRIAL BALANCE

## MROCZKOWSKI
## FLANDERS

### Eleventh Edition

Accounting to Trial Balance
11th Edition
Nicholas Mroczkowski
David Flanders

Publishing manager: Dorothy Chiu
Senior publishing editor: Sophie Kaliniecki
Developmental editor: Tharaha Richards
Project editor: Michaela Skelly
Art direction: Olga Lavecchia
Cover designer: Leigh Ashforth
Text designer: Danielle Maccarone
Editor: Diane Fowler
Proofreader: Jamie Anderson
Permissions/Photo researcher: Debbie Gallagher
Indexer: Julie King
Reprint: Magda Koralewska
Cover: Shutterstock.com/echo3005
Typesetter: MPS Limited

Any URLs contained in this publication were checked for currency during the production process. Note, however, that the publisher cannot vouch for the ongoing currency of URLs.

The 10th edition was published in 2011

For product information and technology assistance,
in Australia call **1300 790 853**;
in New Zealand call **0800 449 725**

For permission to use material from this text or product, please email
**aust.permissions@cengage.com**

National Library of Australia Cataloguing-in-Publication Data
Author:        Mroczkowski, Nicholas A.
Title: *Accounting to Trial Balance*
               Nick Mroczkowski; David Flanders.
Edition:       11th edition
ISBN:          9780170245517 (paperback)
Subjects:      Accounting.
               Accounting--Problems, exercises, etc.
Other Authors/Contributors: Flanders, David, author.
Dewey Number: 657.044

Cengage Learning Australia
Level 7, 80 Dorcas Street
South Melbourne, Victoria Australia 3205

Cengage Learning New Zealand
Unit 4B Rosedale Office Park
331 Rosedale Road, Albany, North Shore 0632, NZ

For learning solutions, visit **cengage.com.au**

Printed in China by 1010 Printing International Limited.
8 9 10 11 12 13 24

# CONTENTS

## Contents

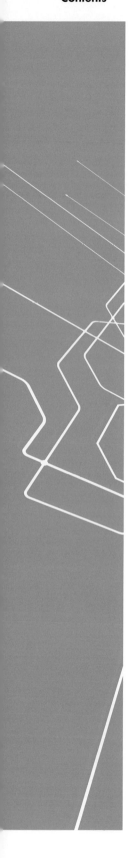

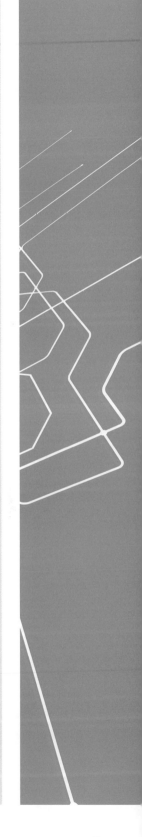

**Contents**

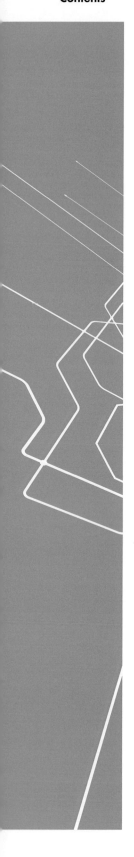

# PREFACE

*Accounting: To Trial Balance* is designed specifically for students studying introductory accounting as part of the accounting courses within the Financial Services Training Package. It is also suitable for any introductory accounting course, whether in the TAFE or secondary area. Companion texts *Accounting: Basic Reports* and *Accounting: Financial Accounting Applications* have been published for students wishing to progress to the subjects that follow introductory accounting.

In order to satisfy the requirements of the Financial Services Training Package (FNS04 and FNS10), this text follows closely the structure of the competencies. Its main emphasis is on accounting procedures up to and including the trial balance. It provides a comprehensive treatment of double-entry principles, business documents, journals, General Ledger, subsidiary ledgers for accounts receivable and accounts payable, petty cash, bank reconciliation, GST and payroll. All material has been written in strict accordance with current financial *Accounting Standards* and practice.

All units contain full topic introductions, illustrative examples, extensive questions graded in a learning sequence and solutions to some key questions. Students may purchase a workbook containing all the stationery required by the text. A solutions manual containing solutions not provided in the text is also available.

*Accounting: To Trial Balance* has been designed for students who have no prior accounting knowledge. The workbook and solutions manual will be of valuable assistance to teachers and students, particularly those who are studying introductory accounting courses by distance learning.

## Sequence of learning material

Accounting is a discipline based on logic and sound practice and, in our many years of experience, a subject that many students thoroughly enjoy and apply toward their further career development. Once the ground rules have been established, students are able to master the subject largely by themselves by completing a progression of practical exercises.

It is most important, however, that the learning material is presented in the correct sequence so that each stage in the learning process is a logical progression from the last. The authors believe that this text is presented in the most desirable sequence for learning purposes. We consider it is important, for example, that students understand the basic elements of business reports and the principles of double entry before the formal accounting process is introduced.

### Stock recording

The accounting principles presented in this text are based on the physical (periodic) method of stock (inventory) recording. This method was chosen because of its relative simplicity and because it is used by the majority of small businesses.

### Ledger format

Apart from Chapter 1, ledgers used in illustrations and solutions are in columnar format. This approach is in accordance with current accounting practice and is consistent with computerised accounting systems.

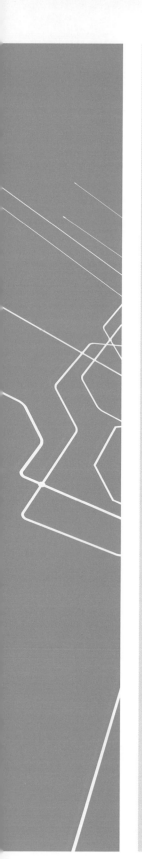

# ABOUT THE AUTHORS

### Dr Nicholas A Mroczkowski

PhD (Finance) *Monash*, MAcc (Finance) *RMIT*, BBus (Accounting) *Swinburne*, DipBus (Financial Accounting) *Ballarat*, BEd *Hawthorn Inst Ed*, FCPA, Chartered Accountant

Nick is a Senior Academic in the Faculty of Business at the Australian Catholic University, Melbourne (ACU). He has more than 30 years of professional experience in Australia and abroad, encompassing a variety of technical disciplines including auditing, financial accounting, finance and education. Prior to joining ACU, Nick was a Senior lecturer in Finance and Accounting at Swinburne University of Technology, Lecturer in Accounting and Finance at Monash University, and a Senior Lecturer in Accounting at Deakin Business School. Nick has also held senior positions in professional practice, including the position of Technical Director (Audit and Accounting) for a major chartered accounting firm for a period of 15 years. His client base included banks, non-financial institutions, governments, educational bodies and a range of medium-to-large companies in the private sector.

### David Flanders

CPA, BCom, BEd

David Flanders has been an accounting teacher at Kangan Institute for more than 20 years. His main teaching areas are computing accounting, financial accounting, budgeting and corporate governance. He has co-authored several textbooks across different accounting areas for more than 10 years and has been extensively involved in writing materials for students via distance learning.

# ACKNOWLEDGEMENTS

We would like to thank the following people for their contribution to the previous edition:

- Daryl Fleay
- Neville Poustie

Their work has provided a tremendous platform for future editions to follow. They have also assisted in reviewing and providing valuable feedback to the current edition.

We would also like to thank Silvana Disisto for completing a technical edit of the textbook.

The publisher and the authors would also like to thank the following people for reviewing the text and providing valuable feedback:

- Steven Hams – Wodonga TAFE
- Sharon Halstead – Chisholm Institute of TAFE.

# RESOURCES GUIDE

## FOR THE STUDENT

As you read this text you will find a wealth of features in every chapter to help you understand and enjoy your studies of *Accounting: To Trial Balance*.

*Learning objectives* are listed at the start of each chapter to give you a clear sense of what the chapter will cover.

*Worked examples* clearly demonstrate theory in practice so you can easily visualise concepts.

*In-chapter questions* enable you to test your comprehension of key concepts as you work your way through each chapter.

*The Workbook* for this new 11th edition of *Accounting: To Trial Balance* is specifically structured to work in combination with the text, and provides consistent and professionally presented solution templates for each chapter. The workbook is accompanied by a CD that has exercises in a MYOB format, additional exercises and UWatch demonstrations.

The CD that accompanies the Workbook includes exercises in a MYOB format, additional exercises and UWatch demonstrations.

*UWatch demonstrations* are video tutorials that give you step-by-step instructions for a range of key skills. These are available on the CD that comes with the Workbook.

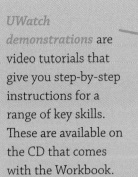

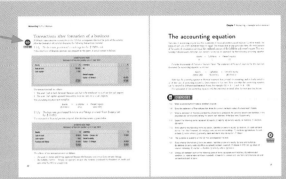

*Additional exercises* are provided in both workbook and MYOB format, allowing you to further test your understanding of key concepts.

# FOR THE INSTRUCTOR

Cengage Learning is pleased to provide you with a selection of resources that will help you prepare for your lectures. These teaching tools are available on the Instructors companion website and other resources accessible via *http://login.cengage.com.*

## Solutions manual

The *solutions manual* provides answers to all the questions in the text.

## PowerPoint™ presentations

Chapter-by-chapter *PowerPoint presentations* cover the main concepts addressed within the text and can be edited to suit your own requirements. Use these slides to enhance your lecture presentations and to reinforce the key principles of your subject, or for student handouts.

## Test bank

The *test bank* for each chapter addresses learning objectives and key topics. It can be exported into your learning management system so you can easily create, customise and deliver tests, both in print and online.

## Revision quizzes

The *revision quizzes* for each chapter allow you to test comprehension of the key concepts covered and review what has been covered in the chapter.

## Competency grids

A *competency grid* at the start of the text clearly demonstrates which elements from each competency are covered in each chapter. Please refer to the website for detailed mapping of:

- elements and performance criteria
- required skills and knowledge
- relevant chapters and specific exercises in the text.

# COMPETENCY GRID

This text covers the following competencies from the Financial Services Training Package.

- FNSACC301: Process financial transactions and extract interim reports
- FNSACC302: Administer subsidiary accounts and ledgers
- BSBFIA302: Process payroll (manual aspects only)
- FNSBKG405: Establish and maintain a payroll system (manual aspects only)

The following grids map the elements of the above units to the relevant chapters in the text.

## FNSACC301: Process financial transactions and extract interim reports

| Element | Chapter |
|---|---|
| 1. Check and verify supporting documentation | 2 |
| 2. Prepare and process banking and petty cash documents | 2, 4, 5, 6 |
| 3. Prepare and process invoices for payment to creditors and for debtors | 2, 4 |
| 4. Prepare journals and batch monetary items | 2, 5, 6, 7 |
| 5. Post journals to ledger | 3, 4, 5, 6, 7 |
| 6. Enter data into system | 2, 3, 4, 5, 6, 7 |
| 7. Prepare deposit facility and lodge flow | 2, 5 |
| 8. Extract a trial balance and interim reports | 1, 2, 3, 4, 5, 6, 7 |

## FNSACC302: Administer subsidiary accounts and ledgers

| Element | Chapter |
|---|---|
| 1. Review accounts receivable process | 4 |
| 2. Identify bad and doubtful debts | 4 |
| 3. Review compliance with terms and conditions and planned recovery action | 4 |
| 4. Prepare reports and file documentation | 4 |
| 5. Distribute creditors' invoices for authorisation | 4 |
| 6. Remit payment to creditors | 4, 5 |
| 7. Prepare accounts paid report and reconcile balances outstanding | 4, 5 |

## BSBFIA302: Process payroll

| Element | Chapter |
|---|---|
| 1. Record payroll data | 7 |
| 2. Prepare payroll | 7 |
| 3. Handle payroll inquiries | 7 |

## FNSBKG405: Establish and maintain a payroll system

| Element | Chapter |
|---|---|
| 1. Record payroll data | 7 |
| 2. Prepare payroll | 7 |
| 3. Handle payroll inquiries | 7 |
| 4. Maintain payroll | 7 |

## Online study resources

CENGAGE brain.com Visit http://www.cengagebrain.com and search for this book to access the bonus study tools on the companion website for *Accounting: To Trial Balance* (11th edition). It contains detailed mapping of:

- elements and performance criteria
- required skills and knowledge
- relevant chapters and specific exercises in the text.

# 1

# ACCOUNTING – CONCEPTS AND ENVIRONMENT

## Learning objectives

Upon satisfactory completion of this chapter you should be able to:
- outline the typical forms of business ownership in Australia
- explain the following concepts and terms:
  - accounting entity
  - legal entity
  - reporting entity
  - reporting period
  - balance date
  - owner's equity for a sole trader
  - income and income recognition
  - expense and expense recognition
  - accounting equation
  - double-entry
  - chart of accounts
  - asset and asset recognition
  - liability and liability recognition
  - accounting conventions and doctrines.

# What is accounting?

Accounting is essentially about financial information; that is, information expressed in quantitative form, such as 'dollars'. The *process* of accounting is generally concerned with collecting and recording financial information relating to a business or business activity, and then communicating relevant financial information to interested users.

Users of financial information may include a variety of stakeholders, such as owners, managers, competitors, employees, banks and other financial organisations, customers, suppliers, government agencies and the general public. Their interest will centre on the activities and financial performance of the business organisation or business venture. Businesses can be involved in many different activities, including providing services to customers, mining, manufacturing goods, buying or selling goods, providing finance, importing or exporting, or engaging in some types of not-for-profit activities (such as charities).

The business may be owned and managed by one person, or by two or more persons jointly, or owned by persons or other business concerns that have managers operating the business.

The accounting *function* is concerned with all stages of the financial information process, commencing with recording, classifying and summarising transactions of a business or a business unit, progressing through to reporting, interpreting and communicating specific financial information to interested users. An accounting *system* operating within a business consists of policies and procedures designed to facilitate all of the stages of the financial information process leading to the preparation of financial reports.

Financial reports are generally the *end product* of any accounting system. They can take many shapes and forms, ranging from a simple statement of cash flows or a sales budget through to a very complex statement of comprehensive income or statement of financial position for a business entity. Financial reports can also be used for a variety of different reasons depending on the specific needs of individual organisations and users. Consider, for example, the following groups of users:

| Users of financial information | Possible uses of information extracted from financial reports |
|---|---|
| Owners | • To determine what profit has been made for the period |
| | • To assess the current financial condition of the business |
| | • To calculate and assess whether the profit reported for the period is appropriate; that is, in proportion to the capital invested |
| | • To evaluate business strengths and weaknesses |
| | • To chart the way forward for the business |
| | • To make short-term and long-term business decisions |
| Suppliers of finance | • To determine whether the business has the ability to pay interest and the balance of debts due |
| Regulatory bodies (for example, the Australian Taxation Office) | • To review and determine whether the business has complied with statutory legislation |

It is important to recognise that the financial reports produced for one group of users may not be relevant to other users of financial information. When producing financial reports, accountants should therefore critically assess the information needs of interested users. At a minimum, most users will require information that should be understandable, relevant, reliable and timely.

The diversity of user needs in relation to financial information has led to the development of specialised fields of accounting, including some of the more typical areas of accounting listed below.

- Management accounting
- Financial accounting
- Auditing
- Public accounting
- Public sector accounting

## Management accounting

Managers are concerned with the internal operations of the business and need regular and quite detailed information relating to both current operations and future operations. Accountants will therefore need to provide managers with financial plans (referred to as budgets) relating to the future; with detailed financial information concerning each product or service that the business provides; and with regular and up-to-date information concerning what has happened in the immediate past, so that they can analyse whether the business is performing according to plan. The special field of accounting developed to meet managers' needs for information is called management accounting.

Management accounting is also concerned with costing concepts and applications. For instance, a manufacturer may wish to produce a certain product that appears to be in great demand from consumers at a certain price. Determining the cost of production will be critical for pricing the product and assessing whether the profit margin is sufficient to generate acceptable levels of profit for the firm. In this regard, accountants specialising in manufacturing operations will need to be very familiar with several accounting concepts that are specific to a manufacturing environment; for example, concepts dealing with the costing of labour, materials and other indirect costs associated with the manufacturing process.

## Financial accounting

User groups who may be interested in the operations of a business include owners, members, shareholders, employees, creditors, customers and competitors. In general, accountants will need to provide these groups with regular (usually quarterly, six-monthly or annual) reports concerning the state of affairs and the financial operations of the business. While these reports are not as detailed as the management reports which are provided to internal managers, they are often the only source of information that is available to users who have no involvement with the operations of the business. For example, an *annual report* prepared by a large company may be distributed to thousands of shareholders who are not directly involved with the company. In this sense, shareholders are considered to be external users of financial information, whereas managers involved in the operations of the business are regarded as internal users of financial information. An important point worth noting here is that since external users are not involved in the operations of the business, and given that in many cases they are also not entitled to have access to internal and detailed information, accounting standards and other rules have been established by regulatory bodies to ensure that their information needs are met. The field of accounting that has developed to meet the needs of these groups is called *financial accounting*.

The purpose of financial accounting is thus to prepare financial reports with an external focus. Accountants involved in financial accounting will often be required to have a strong understanding of accounting standards and other regulatory requirements, such as specific laws relating to particular types of entities.

# Auditing

Auditors are accountants who are independent of the internal workings of a business. Their purpose is to conduct an independent examination of the financial statements of a business so as to provide an opinion on the truth and fairness of those statements. While auditing is outside the scope of this book, it is important to note that the auditor's role is to add credibility to the external financial statements. When analysing the financial statements, users can (assuming no irregularities are reported by the auditor) have some comfort in knowing that the financial information contained therein reflects a true and fair view of the state of affairs of the company. Thus, among other things, auditors are expected to have a strong understanding of financial accounting standards, auditing standards and various other rules and regulations.

# Public accounting

Accountants involved in providing services to the public (often referred to as *clients*) are generally considered to be operating in *public practice*. The type of work performed by public practitioners includes the preparation of accounts, taxation returns, budgeting, management accounting, providing financial advice and undertaking other compliance work (for instance, preparing and lodging information with regulatory bodies such as the Australian Securities and Investments Commission). Accountants in public practice may also undertake a range of auditing duties.

# Public sector accounting

Public sector accounting is concerned with the specialised accounting responsibilities of the three levels of government, namely Commonwealth, state/territory and local governments. In addition, this includes other entities that receive government funding. These responsibilities are generally dictated by specific legislation that serves to ensure the accountability of governments.

# The accounting environment

## Business activities

The accounting process is concerned with financial information that is normally generated by some form of business activity. A business activity can be described as a commercial activity that may arise from a desire by a person or an organisation to earn a profit from the sale of goods or services, or simply as part of a normal commercial transaction in running a not-for-profit business.

Although there are many types of business activities (as briefly described opposite), this text will mainly focus on the two types of activity listed below.

1 Service activity As the name suggests, this type of business activity provides some form of service to customers; for example, a solicitor who provides legal services to clients and charges fees.

2 Wholesale/retail activity This is a business activity in which merchandise goods are bought and sold at a profit. For example, a furniture retailer buys merchandise from a wholesaler and then sells those goods to customers. Note that merchandise goods are those that are in completed form and can also be referred to as 'finished goods'.

## Business ownership (structure)

There are various ways in which a business can be owned or structured. The three most common forms of business ownership in Australia are a sole trader, a partnership and a company. Each of these forms of ownership is briefly described below.

## Sole trader

One person who owns and controls an entire business is considered to be a sole trader (or a sole proprietor). This form of business ownership is simple and generally inexpensive, and the owner is entitled to make all the decisions in the organisation and retain all the profits.

However, should the business be unable to repay its debts, then the owner may be personally liable to creditors for any unpaid amounts. The liability of the owner in this type of organisation is thus said to be unlimited.

## Partnership

A partnership is an association where two or more persons (usually a maximum of 20) own and control a business. Although partners are not legally required to have a formal agreement, this sort of organisation is usually established by a partnership deed – a written contract that discloses the rights and liabilities of each partner. The affairs of partnerships may also be regulated by government legislation; for example, the *Partnership Act* (each state of Australia has its own partnership legislation).

As is the case with a sole trader, it is normal for each partner to have unlimited liability for debts of the partnership business. This means that, if the partnership is unable to meet its debts, each partner can be personally liable for those debts. In addition, partnerships have a limited life, and can be dissolved on the death or retirement of a partner. A further feature of partnerships is that, in accordance with the legal principle of *mutual agency*, individual partners' actions are binding on all partners in the firm. Simply explained, this means that, assuming that partners act within the limits of authority conferred upon them by their fellow partners, their actions are binding upon the partnership, and thus upon all of the other partners in the business.

# Company

On a basic level, a company can be described as a body or entity created by law. When a company is formed (a process often referred to as *incorporation* or *registration*) the law creates an unnatural person that has rights and liabilities, that can sue and be sued, and that can contract in its own name. Additionally, the ability to contract allows companies to purchase and own property, such as land and buildings. Companies can also enter into debt contracts, and therefore incur liabilities that are binding on the company.

Because of their artificial nature, however, companies must rely on appointed *directors* to carry out their various business activities, including contracting. So, while companies are actually owned by shareholders who generally contribute to the capital of the company by buying shares in the company, they are mostly controlled by directors, who may not necessarily be the owners of or shareholders in the company. For example, in the case of a large company, non-shareholder directors may be appointed due to their specific industry expertise. Shares can be simply defined as units of ownership in the company. Figure 1.1 illustrates the composition of a simple company.

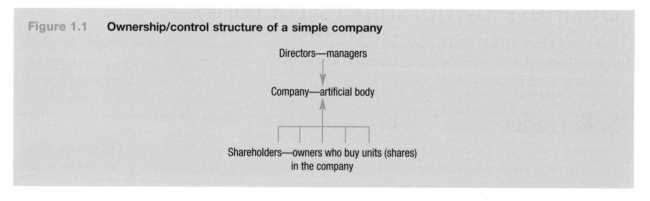

**Figure 1.1** **Ownership/control structure of a simple company**

Directors—managers

Company—artificial body

Shareholders—owners who buy units (shares) in the company

It is important to note that a company is legally separate from its shareholders. Because it is a separate entity, shareholders whose shares are fully paid have no further liability for the debts of the company. In most large companies, shareholders do not actually participate in the day-to-day management of the company. Control of the affairs of the company is maintained by a board of directors, who are elected by shareholders.

Most companies incorporated in Australia are companies limited by shares, which means that the liability of individual shareholders is limited to the amount, if any, unpaid on the value of their shares.

Companies can be classified as either *proprietary* (*private*) or *public* companies. A proprietary company must have a minimum of one shareholder and one director. The *Corporations Act 2001* (Cth) further defines a proprietary company as one that:

- restricts the rights of members (shareholders) to transfer shares to outside parties
- limits members to no more than 50
- prohibits the company from inviting the public to subscribe for shares or debentures in the company or from depositing money with the company.

The *Corporations Act 2001* also distinguishes between 'small' and 'large' proprietary companies, with small proprietary companies generally having reduced or, as in most cases, no financial reporting requirements (other than for taxation purposes).

A public company must have a minimum of one shareholder and three directors; generally, there is no limit to the number of shareholders that a public company can have. Public companies are not subject to the restrictions on share transfer and share issues etc. that are imposed on proprietary companies. Provided that certain stringent requirements are met, public companies are also able to have their shares listed on the Australian Securities Exchange. Listing on a securities exchange creates a market for the company's shares, which may be freely traded between buyers and sellers. There are many advantages to listing a company on a securities exchange, including the ability to raise large sums of capital and establishing a public profile for the company, which could increase the company's ability to generate income.

A company has perpetual succession, which means that it does not dissolve on the death or retirement of an individual shareholder, or on the transfer of share ownership, because the company is a separate legal entity with an existence independent from that of its shareholders.

Most companies are incorporated and regulated by the *Corporations Act 2001*, an Act of the federal parliament that applies uniformly in each state of Australia.

# The business operating cycle

In business, the circular flow of cash-to-goods/services-to-cash is referred to as the business operating cycle. This simple concept is illustrated in Figure 1.2.

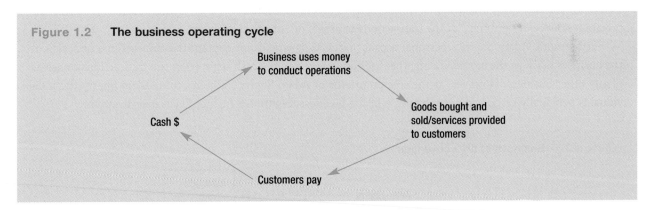

Figure 1.2 The business operating cycle

It can be seen from Figure 1.2 that at each stage of the operating cycle, goods, services or cash are exchanged. When this happens, it can be said that a transaction has occurred. An important function of the *accounting process* is to record each transaction within the operating cycle. In turn, transactions that have been duly recorded and summarised will provide the appropriate information for the preparation of financial reports for a range of interested users.

# The basic accounting framework

Before commencing a detailed analysis of the accounting process in the chapters that follow, it is important to examine the assumptions, concepts and accepted practices that provide the framework within which the accounting process operates. These are generally known as *accounting conventions* and *doctrines*, but more recently have also been described as *accounting concepts*.

## Accounting conventions

An accounting convention can be simply described as a generally accepted accounting practice that has been adopted by the accounting profession. Some of the more common conventions are listed below.

- Business entity convention
- Historical cost convention
- Monetary unit convention
- Going (or continuing) concern convention
- Accounting period convention

## Business entity convention

It is assumed for accounting purposes that each business is a separate entity from its owner(s) and from every other business.

Thus, if Adam Sherry owned and managed a liquor store, the accounting records and reports for the store would not contain either the personal transactions or assets of Adam Sherry, the owner (such as jewellery, his private residence or perfumes) or the transactions or assets of any other business.

Furthermore, Adam Sherry's personal accounting records would not contain the transactions or assets of the business (such as the store building, the cases of whisky and the cash register) or the transactions or assets of any other business. However, as the sole proprietor of Adam Sherry's Liquor Store, Adam Sherry the individual is personally responsible for the debts of the business. Figure 1.3 further illustrates this point.

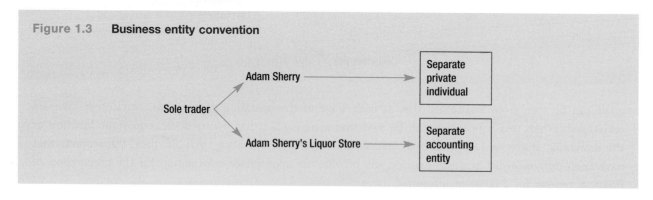

**Figure 1.3    Business entity convention**

# Historical cost convention

The historical cost convention assumes that all transactions of a business entity are recorded and shown in the financial reports at the original cost to the enterprise at the date of the transaction.

Because of this convention, financial reports are based on historical records and depict only the past happenings of a business. For example, Nick Rosas (furniture retailer) purchased premises costing $200 000 to commence operations on 1 July 2010. On 30 June 2016, the local real estate agent valued the business premises at $300 000. The premises, however, would still be shown in the financial reports at 30 June 2016 at their original cost of $200 000, if the historical cost basis of recording was used.

The historical cost convention is critical to the concept of historical cost accounting, which is based on the assumption that what was paid for an item in the past (that is, its cost) should continue to be reflected in the financial reports.

It should be noted, however, that in Australia the *modified* historical cost basis is used, which allows assets (such as buildings) to be revalued to their fair market value after acquisition. While this is an important aspect of accounting in Australia, it is an area considered to be outside the scope of this text.

# Monetary unit convention

Since accounting is concerned with financial information it must adopt a unit of measurement – which, logically, can only be the basic monetary unit of the economy concerned. In Australia, of course, this is the Australian dollar.

The monetary unit convention assumes that:

· accounting records are maintained in terms of monetary units; that is, the currency unit of the country in which the entity resides or transacts most of its business. The operating currency, which in Australia is the Australian dollar (A$), is also referred to as the *functional currency*. Legislation in Australia requires financial reports to be prepared in Australian dollars
· the monetary unit is static in terms of purchasing power (that is, the effects of inflation are not considered in measuring transactions).

# Going (or continuing) concern convention

This convention assumes that:

· the business entity will continue to operate indefinitely
· the long-term assets of the business are not available for sale
· the current (or market) values of long-term assets are ignored for the purposes of financial reports, since these assets are not available for immediate sale.

*Going concern* is a critical concept in accounting, particularly given that there is an underlying assumption that the business will continue indefinitely. For example, following the concept of *historical cost* discussed above, the assets of the business will be shown in the financial records at their historical cost (purchase) value if we can assume that the business is a going concern; that is, it will continue operations into the future without any disruption. However, if for some reason the business suddenly ceases to be a going concern – for example, the business has insufficient cash to pay for its immediate commitments – then the recorded value of the assets may be subject to considerable change. For example, if some of the assets need to be sold off in an extremely short time frame in order to raise cash to meet the outstanding commitments (this scenario is often referred to as a fire sale), then, given the difficult circumstances, the amount received for these assets will be considerably less than their historical cost. The main point here is that historical cost will only be an appropriate method of recording if it can be assumed that the firm is a going concern, and is not expected to liquidate in the immediate future.

# Accounting period convention

This convention is based on the assumption that the life of the business entity should be divided into meaningful measurement periods. This enables users to make a proper assessment of the performance of the business using a standard period of measurement, such as 12 months. A normal investment cycle in which an adequate return on invested funds can be expected ranges from about 12 to 18 months. Despite this, 12 months has traditionally been the accepted period of reporting for regulatory and investment bodies. For example, taxation authorities require reports based on a 12-month trading period. It is common, however, for owners to also require reports on a more regular basis to enable effective and regular control of the business.

On this point, we also note that the end of an accounting period is usually referred to as the balance date, or year-end date. It is on this day that the accounting records are balanced (or finalised) and financial accounting reports are prepared.

# Accounting doctrines

An accounting doctrine can be described as a belief that certain principles are desirable and should be followed by members of the accounting profession. In contrast to a convention, which is an accepted practice or procedure, a doctrine requires accountants to exercise professional judgement in applying specific principles. Five important doctrines are briefly discussed below.

# Objectivity doctrine

This doctrine requires that, wherever possible, the amounts used in recording transactions should be based upon objective evidence, rather than on subjective judgements. Accountants are also expected to prepare financial reports from a *neutral* stance and not to favour one group of report users to the detriment of others.

# Conservatism doctrine

Accountants have traditionally taken a pessimistic rather than an optimistic stance when performing their accounting tasks. This is reflected in a number of rules of accounting, the most notable of which is the *lower of cost and net realisable value* rule in relation to the valuation of inventory or stocks. This means that business entities can only disclose inventory in financial statements at the lower of the two figures (cost or net realisable value).

## Full disclosure doctrine

This doctrine requires the disclosure in the financial reports of a business of all important or material (that is, significant) information that may influence the decisions of users of these reports. For example, a change in the method of valuing assets would be of vital concern to parties providing finance to or investing in the business.

## Consistency doctrine

Accountants who prepare financial reports are expected to use the same accounting policies consistently from one period to the next. This enables a more meaningful comparison to be made of the accounting reports for successive accounting periods.

## Materiality doctrine

This doctrine requires that only material or significant information should be revealed in the preparation of financial reports. Omission of material information from the financial reports may mislead users. Similarly, the inclusion of voluminous and immaterial information in financial reports may limit the usefulness of these reports.

# Accounting standards

In Australia, the practice of accounting is generally dominated by four professional bodies: the Institute of Chartered Accountants in Australia (ICAA), the Australian Society of Certified Practising Accountants (CPA Australia), the Chartered Institute of Management Accountants (CIMA), and the Institute of Public Accountants (IPA). These bodies have been formed by accountants to foster the highest possible standards of accounting practice in Australia.

An important role played by the ICAA and CPA Australia has been their involvement and support in the development of *Accounting Standards*. These standards provide specific direction for accountants and other advisers in measurement and disclosure aspects of accounting practice.

The role of professional bodies and the accounting standard-setting process are discussed in more detail in Chapter 1 of *Accounting: Basic Reports*.

# The accounting entity and the concept of a legal entity

In accordance with the *business entity convention*, a business is treated *for accounting purposes* as a separate entity from its owner(s). This convention provides the underlying logic for the basic principles of accounting that follow in this text.

It is important, however, not to confuse this accounting convention with the legal standing of a business and its owner(s). In a sole trader or partnership form of business ownership, the owners of the business and the business itself are treated as one legal entity (see Figure 1.3). This means (as stated earlier in this text) that should such a business become insolvent, the owner(s) would be personally liable to repay the debts of the business.

It is only where a company is formed that the business becomes legally separate from its owners (shareholders).

# Reporting entity

The extent of financial and other information that is prepared by a business will depend on whether the business is a reporting or non-reporting entity. A non-reporting entity is generally a small private business entity, which prepares reports mainly for the owners of the business. Non-reporting entities usually include sole traders, partnerships and most private companies.

Reporting entities, however, are generally large business entities that are accountable to a large and diverse group of users who are dependent on financial reports for their decision-making purposes. In this regard, reporting entities must prepare comprehensive financial reports. Reporting entities include public companies, government bodies, superannuation funds, listed companies and other large business entities.

The concept of the reporting entity, which is currently under review by Australian accounting standards setting bodies, is discussed in further detail in Chapter 1 of *Accounting: Basic Reports*.

 **EXERCISES**

**Note** Suggested solutions are provided for exercises marked with an asterisk*.

1.1 Briefly outline the meaning of the term 'accounting'.

1.2 What is a business? Discuss. In your answer, briefly describe one type of business activity.

1.3 List the three most common types of business ownership and provide a brief description of each.

1.4 Distinguish between a public and a private company limited by shares.

1.5* List the advantages and disadvantages of each of the most common forms of business ownership.

1.6 Briefly explain the unlimited liability principle as it relates to the following forms of business ownership.
   a Sole trader
   b Partnership

1.7 Joe and Sam have been trading in partnership for the past four years and have decided to convert their firm to a proprietary company limited by shares. Briefly explain how this decision will affect their responsibilities for the debts of the business.

1.8     Briefly define the following terms.

    a  Business operating cycle

    b  Transaction

1.9     Laurie Driver (trading as LD Transport) operates a large interstate freight haulage business from a base in Melbourne. List two parties who would be interested in the financial affairs of the business. What financial information would they require?

1.10*   Briefly define the following terms.

    a  Basic accounting framework

    b  Accounting convention

    c  Accounting doctrine

    d  Historical cost accounting

1.11    For each of the following statements, name the relevant accounting convention or doctrine.

    a  The life of an entity can be divided into meaningful accounting periods.

    b  Accountants traditionally adopt a pessimistic rather than an optimistic stance when performing their accounting tasks.

    c  For accounting purposes, a business is treated as a separate entity from its owner(s).

    d  Amounts used in recording transactions should be based on objective evidence.

    e  When preparing financial reports, accountants are expected to use the same accounting methods consistently from one period to the next.

    f  Accounting records are maintained in terms of monetary units.

    g  The financial reports of a business should contain all important information that may influence the decisions of the users of these reports.

    h  Only material or significant information should be revealed in the financial reports of a business.

1.12    Briefly outline the nature and purpose of accounting standards.

1.13    'Every business entity is both a separate accounting entity and a separate legal entity.' Discuss the validity of this statement.

1.14    What is a reporting entity? Discuss.

 **SOLUTIONS**

1.5     **Sole trader**

*Advantages*

    –  Simple and inexpensive to form

    –  Complete control and share of profits by owner

*Disadvantages*

    –  Unlimited liability

    –  Expansion potential limited due to inability to raise large sums of capital

**Partnership**

*Advantages*

- – Ease of formation
- – Pooling of resources and special skills

*Disadvantages*

- – Unlimited liability
- – Limited life
- – Mutual agency
- – Personality clashes

**Company**

*Advantages*

- – Limited liability of shareholders
- – The potential for public companies to list on a securities exchange, which can provide enhanced financial standing and public profile, and which means that shares of the company are freely transferable
- – Perpetual succession
- – Increased availability of capital

*Disadvantages*

- – Complicated (and expensive) to form
- – Must comply with the provisions of the *Corporations Act 2001*
- – Security exchange listing can lead to loss of control by the original founders of the company and greater public scrutiny.

1.10   The *basic accounting framework* consists of the assumptions and accepted practices (accounting conventions and doctrines) that underlie the accounting process.

An accounting convention (or assumption) is a practice that has been adopted by the accounting profession as a result of a general consensus that it must be followed.

An accounting doctrine is a belief that a certain practice is desirable and should be followed by the accounting profession.

Historical cost accounting is based on the premise that what was paid for an item in the past remains representative of the value of that item forever.

# The accounting process

Having discussed some of the key assumptions and accepted practices that provide the basic framework for accounting, we can now begin to examine the nature of the accounting process itself. The principal purpose of the accounting process is to keep detailed records of the financial transactions of a business, and to provide appropriate information in the form of reports to interested parties. Figure 1.4 illustrates the manner in which transactions are processed.

The diagram in Figure 1.4 also illustrates the correct sequence in which the processing of financial transactions takes place. Although it may seem logical to structure the learning process in the same order as this diagram, this text will introduce the accounting process in a slightly different sequence. It is preferable for students to study the basic elements shown in accounting reports and the ledger (the medium in which all transactions are recorded) before attempting to study the entire accounting process.

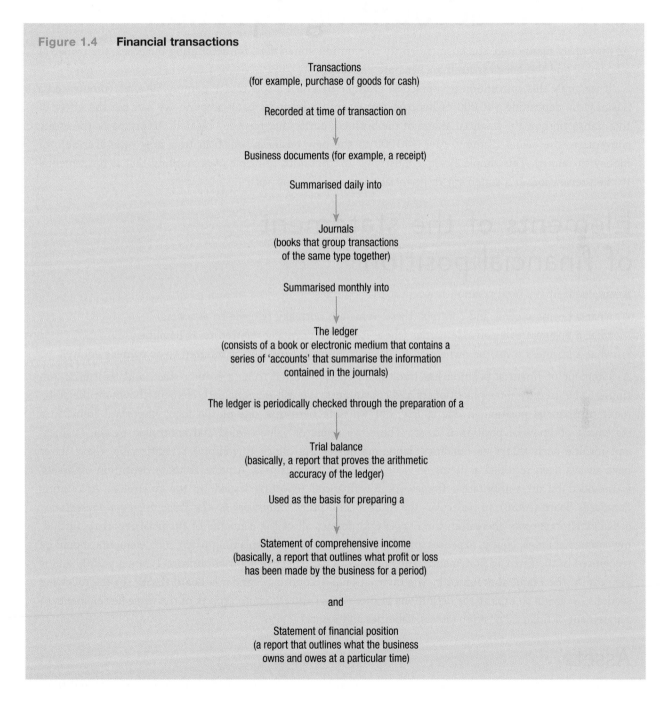

**Figure 1.4    Financial transactions**

Transactions
(for example, purchase of goods for cash)

Recorded at time of transaction on

Business documents (for example, a receipt)

Summarised daily into

Journals
(books that group transactions
of the same type together)

Summarised monthly into

The ledger
(consists of a book or electronic medium that contains a
series of 'accounts' that summarise the information
contained in the journals)

The ledger is periodically checked through the preparation of a

Trial balance
(basically, a report that proves the arithmetic
accuracy of the ledger)

Used as the basis for preparing a

Statement of comprehensive income
(basically, a report that outlines what profit or loss
has been made by the business for a period)

and

Statement of financial position
(a report that outlines what the business
owns and owes at a particular time)

# The statement of financial position and the accounting equation

As previously mentioned, the business entity convention states that, for accounting purposes, the owner of a business and the business itself are separate entities.

If we apply this convention to a practical example in which a sole trader, Sammy Silvagni, commenced a business by depositing $40 000 of his own money into a business bank account, we can see the effect of this transaction on the financial affairs of the business entity that has been created. According to the entity convention, the owner (Sammy) gave $40 000 to the new business, which in turn now owes this sum of money to Sammy. This simple example illustrates an important principle of accounting that is fundamental to the preparation of a statement of financial position for a business.

## Elements of the statement of financial position

A statement of financial position is a report that outlines:

- what a business owns and controls (these items are normally referred to as assets)
- what a business owes outside parties (these items are normally referred to as liabilities)
- what a business owes the owners at a particular point in time (this is referred to as owner's equity).

A statement of financial position has traditionally been referred to as a *balance sheet*, and this term continues to be used by some practitioners and consultants. We will examine each element shown on the statement of financial position in due course, but we note here that one of the most important items in a statement of financial position is *assets*. These are items of value owned and controlled by the business and include such things as buildings, land, machinery and stock (inventory). Traditionally, these items have always been regarded as items of value owned by the business. A more accurate definition of 'assets' is provided by an authoritative framework for financial reporting issued by the Australian Accounting Standards Board (AASB). In particular, the AASB's conceptual *'Framework for the Preparation and Presentation of Financial Statements'* (hereafter, the *Framework*) defines all of the elements of financial reporting (including assets, liabilities, equity, expenses and income), in addition to explaining when such elements should be recognised in the financial statements. The Framework had effective application from 1 January 2009 and is identical to the Framework issued by the International Accounting Standards Board (IASB). In the following sections, we begin to explore the definitions in more detail and recognise aspects of the three key elements of a statement of financial position (assets, liabilities and equity).

## Assets

The Framework defines assets as 'resources controlled by the enterprise as a result of past events and from which future economic benefits are expected to flow to the enterprise'. Put simply, this means that assets must have three basic properties.

1   An asset must be controlled by the business. In most cases control will be achieved through ownership of the asset by the business. However, there may be circumstances where the business does not own the asset but does have the ability to deny other parties the right to use the asset (for example, in certain lease arrangements or other similar contractual circumstances). These arrangements would effectively provide the business with control of an asset.

2   An asset must have been acquired as a result of past events (transactions). This is consistent with the historical cost convention, which requires that an asset be recorded at its cost price derived from the details of a past transaction. It also has an evidentiary perspective, meaning that the transaction needs to be supported by appropriate external evidence – for example, an invoice – that would provide proof of the purchase of a particular asset.

3   An asset must have future economic benefits. What this means is that assets must have the potential to provide future services (or have service potential) that will generate economic benefits. The term 'economic benefits' is used to reflect the financial aspects of assets; that is, assets must be able to provide benefits that are measurable in dollars. This, of course, is consistent with the monetary unit convention discussed on page 9. Thus, a delivery vehicle would be regarded as an asset because it has the potential to provide delivery services to customers, who will in turn pay the business for the products that are purchased.

# Liabilities

Liabilities are usually explained as amounts owed by businesses to outside parties. The definition of liabilities provided in the Framework states that 'liabilities are present obligations of the enterprise arising from past events, settlement of which is expected to result in an outflow from the enterprise of resources embodying economic benefits'. This definition appears complex at first, but it can be broken down into the following components.

1   There must be a present obligation. For instance, if the business borrows an amount of money from the local bank, it will always have an obligation to settle the loan (usually through contractual arrangements) even though repayment of the loan may be made over several years. 'Present obligation' generally means that the business must be bound in some way to repay the debt. If a liability has no requirement to be repaid (for example, a loan from a close relative), then it may not qualify as a liability because there would not be a present obligation.

2   The liability must have been created as a result of a past transaction. This is similar to the requirement above for the definition of asset. Simply put, a liability must be based on a transaction that has already occurred: in the example in point 1, the business borrows money from the local bank. The transaction would be supported by a detailed contract between the business and the bank.

3   The liability must involve a future sacrifice of economic benefits. What this relates to is the settlement of the debt and what needs to be sacrificed (given up) for the debt to finally be settled. In the above example, cash will be given up when the loan is repaid to the bank.

# Equity

Equity can be regarded as a residual item derived by subtracting liabilities from assets. Indeed the Framework defines equity as 'the residual interest in the assets of the enterprise after deducting all its liabilities'. Normally, however, equity is explained in terms of capital contributed by stakeholders (such as owners of the business and shareholders) and accumulated earnings and other gains, all of which will be explained in later sections of the text.

The example of a statement of financial position below shows the financial position of Damien's Discount Store as at 30 June 2016. This type of statement of financial position is commonly referred to as a 'T' form of statement of financial position.

**DAMIEN'S DISCOUNT STORE**
**Statement of financial position as at 30 June 2016**

| Assets | $ | Liabilities | $ | $ |
|---|---|---|---|---|
| Petty cash | 50 | Creditors | 11 000 | |
| Cash on hand | 150 | Mortgage loan on building | 220 000 | |
| Cash at bank | 1 300 | Loan from Statewide Bank | 23 000 | 254 000 |
| Building | 331 500 | | | |
| Shop fittings | 13 700 | | | |
| Equipment | 43 400 | | | |
| Furniture | 21 900 | **Owner's equity** | | |
| Debtors | 12 000 | Capital – Damien | | 200 000 |
| Stock | 26 000 | | | |
| Loan to A Smart | 4 000 | | | |
| | 454 000 | | | 454 000 |

**Explanations**

- **Petty cash** A small amount of cash kept on hand to pay for items of a minor nature
- **Cash on hand** The cash 'change float' retained in the cash register (till)
- **Cash at bank** The cash balance in the business bank account. An overdrawn bank account balance is referred to as a bank overdraft and is shown as a liability in the statement of financial position.
- **Building, shop fittings, equipment and furniture** Items of value controlled by the business
- **Debtors (also known as 'accounts receivable')** People or organisations who owe money to the business, usually because they have received goods or services and have yet to pay for them
- **Stock (also known as 'inventories')** Unused stock of goods available for sale
- **Loans to/loans from** Loans made by the business **to** persons or organisations are amounts owed to the business and are, therefore, assets. Loans received **from** persons or organisations are amounts of money owed by the business and are liabilities.
- **Creditors (also known as 'accounts payable')** People or organisations to whom the business owes money for goods or services received and not yet paid for
- **Mortgage loan** An amount borrowed to help buy an asset (in this case, buildings) and owed to the lender. A mortgage is a charge over particular assets. Explained simply, the lender will hold the ownership title of the asset as security (for example, a land title), until the debt is repaid.
- **Capital** The amount owed by the business to its owner, representing various assets that the owner has contributed to the business

# The accounting equation

The rules of accounting require that the statement of financial position must balance. In other words, the totals of each side of the statement must be equal. This means that at any particular time, the total amount of the assets of a business must equal the combined amount of the liabilities and owner's equity. This relationship between assets, liabilities and owner's equity can be expressed by the following *accounting equation*:

$$\text{Assets} = \text{Liabilities} + \text{Owner's equity}$$
$$\text{A} \qquad \text{L} \qquad \text{OE}$$

Consider the example of Damien's Discount Store. The statement of financial position for this business illustrates the accounting equation as follows:

$$\text{Assets} = \text{Liabilities} + \text{Owner's equity}$$
$$(\$454\,000) \qquad (\$254\,000) \qquad (\$200\,000)$$

Note that *the accounting equation is the most important basic principle in accounting*, and is fundamental to all of the rules of accounting studied in later sections of this text. Note also that the accounting equation can be restated in different mathematical forms; for example, $\text{OE} = \text{A} - \text{L}$ or $\text{L} = \text{A} - \text{OE}$.

The application of the accounting equation will be considered in detail after the exercises that follow.

 **EXERCISES**

1.15   What is a statement of financial position? Explain.

1.16   Does the statement of financial position show the current realisable value of a business? Explain.

1.17   When a statement of financial position for a business is prepared, the personal assets and liabilities of the proprietor are not recorded among the assets and liabilities of the business. Explain why.

1.18   Explain the following terms: (a) asset; (b) equity; (c) liability; (d) owner's equity; (e) debtors; (f) creditors; (g) capital.

1.19   State whether the following items are assets, liabilities or owner's equity: (a) debtors; (b) cash on hand; (c) loan from Vast Finances; (d) mortgage loan; (e) land and buildings; (f) creditors; (g) furniture; (h) cash at bank; (i) motor vehicle; (j) property, plant and machinery; (k) capital – P Brown.

1.20   This question is available on the CD that accompanies this text.

ADDITIONAL
EXERCISES

1.21   State whether the following items are assets, liabilities or owner's equity: (a) land and buildings; (b) debtors; (c) petty cash; (d) office equipment; (e) bank overdraft; (f) shares in XYZ Ltd; (g) stock of unused stationery; (h) capital – L Gordon; (i) delivery vehicle; (j) stocks.

1.22   Distinguish between each of the following pairs of terms: (a) assets and liabilities; (b) debtors and creditors; (c) cash at bank and bank overdraft; (d) loan to V Lawson and loan from AV Finances; (e) cash on hand and cash at bank.

**1.23** The following information relates to G Rater, retailer at 30 June 2017. You are required to:
a determine the owner's equity in the business
b prepare a statement of financial position as at 30 June 2017.

*Information*

Buildings, $30 000; creditors, $12 500; debtors, $8000; bank overdraft, $4600; loan from Never Ending Finances, $5500; stock of unsold goods, $2550; cash on hand, $100.

**1.24\*** The following information relates to Glenwood Private Hospital (manager, B Closky) at 30 June 2016. You are required to:
a calculate the owner's equity in the business
b prepare a statement of financial position as at 30 June 2016.

*Information*

Loan from Moglic Finances, $50 000; ambulance, $70 000; stock of pharmaceuticals, $35 000; premises, $700 000; beds, furniture and fittings, $200 000; bank overdraft, $36 000; creditors, $43 400; unpaid hospital debtors accounts, $155 000; capital – to be determined.

**1.25** The following information relates to E Field's Used Car Yard as at 30 June 2018. You are required to:
a calculate the owner's equity in the business
b prepare a statement of financial position as at 30 June 2018.

*Information*

Stock of cars, $320 000; premises, $350 000; creditors (for cars), $120 000; debtors, $1 250 000; stock of parts, $25 000; bank overdraft, $16 000; loan from Easy Finances, $100 000; loan to A Wheeler, $33 000; tools and equipment, $36 000; creditors (for parts), $20 000; stock of petrol and oil, $5000; capital – to be determined.

**1.26** This question is available on the CD that accompanies this text.

**SOLUTION**

**1.24** a $300 600
b

GLENWOOD PRIVATE HOSPITAL
Statement of financial position as at 30 June 2016

| Assets | $ | Liabilities | $ | $ |
|---|---|---|---|---|
| Ambulance | 70 000 | Bank overdraft | 36 000 | |
| Stock of pharmaceuticals | 35 000 | Creditors | 43 400 | |
| Premises | 700 000 | Loan from Moglic Finances | 50 000 | 129 400 |
| Beds, furniture and fittings | 200 000 | | | |
| Unpaid hospital debtors accounts | 155 000 | **Owner's equity** | | |
| | | Capital – B Closky | | 1 030 600 |
| | 1 160 000 | | | 1 160 000 |

# Business transactions

The statement of financial position for Damien's Discount Store on page 18 shows what the business owns and owes at a particular time. We will now examine the effects of business transactions and the application of the accounting equation to record these effects.

## Transactions that affect the statement of financial position

### Formation of a business

From the first day a business commences, transactions occur that affect the basic elements of a statement of financial position. For example, when Sammy Silvagni commenced his business, Sammy's Mini Mart, on 1 July 2016, he deposited $40 000 of his own money in a business bank account. If a statement of financial position for Sammy's Mini Mart was prepared at this point, it would appear as follows:

**SAMMY'S MINI MART**
Statement of financial position as at 1 July 2016

| Assets | $ | Liabilities | $ |
|---|---|---|---|
| Cash at bank | 40 000 | Nil | — |
| | | **Owner's equity** | |
| | | Capital – S Silvagni | 40 000 |
| | 40 000 | | 40 000 |

This transaction had two effects:

1 The asset *Cash at bank* was created because the business now owns a bank account with a $40 000 balance.

2 Owner's equity became $40 000 because the business now owes the owner this amount of money. This contribution of cash by Sammy is referred to as his *Capital*.

This transaction illustrates the business entity convention: the business and its owner are treated as separate entities. If the accounting equation was applied to the above statement of financial position, it would appear as follows:

$$\begin{array}{ccc} \text{Assets} & = & \text{Liabilities} & + & \text{Owner's equity} \\ \text{(Cash at bank \$40 000)} & & \text{(Nil)} & & \text{(Capital \$40 000)} \end{array}$$

The above transaction and those that follow are referred to as *statement of financial position transactions*. You will see that after each of these transactions has been recorded, the statement of financial position remains in balance.

# Transactions after formation of a business

UWATCH 1.1

A UWatch demonstration is available on the CD that accompanies this text for parts of this activity. After the formation of Sammy's business, the following transactions occurred:

1 July   *The business purchased a cash register for $1000 cash*

If the statement of financial position was prepared at this point, it would appear as follows:

| SAMMY'S MINI MART | | | |
|---|---|---|---|
| Statement of financial position as at 1 July 2016 | | | |
| **Assets** | **$** | **Liabilities** | **$** |
| Cash at bank | 39 000 | Nil | — |
| Cash register | 1 000 | | |
| | | **Owner's equity** | |
| | | Capital – S Silvagni | 40 000 |
| | 40 000 | | 40 000 |

The transaction had two effects:

1   The asset *Cash at bank* decreased because cash had to be withdrawn to purchase the cash register.
2   The asset *Cash register* appeared because the business now owns a cash register.

The accounting equation now would be:

$$\text{Assets} \quad = \quad \text{Liabilities} \quad + \quad \text{Owner's equity}$$
$$(\$40\,000) \qquad \quad (\text{Nil}) \qquad \qquad (\$40\,000)$$

2 July   *The business purchased furniture and fittings on credit from Snappy Ltd for $10 000*

The statement of financial position prepared after this transaction appears below.

| SAMMY'S MINI MART | | | |
|---|---|---|---|
| Statement of financial position as at 2 July 2016 | | | |
| **Assets** | **$** | **Liabilities** | **$** |
| Cash at bank | 39 000 | Creditor – Snappy Ltd | 10 000 |
| Cash register | 1 000 | **Owner's equity** | |
| Furniture and fittings | 10 000 | Capital – S Silvagni | 40 000 |
| | 50 000 | | 50 000 |

The effects of the transaction were as follows:

- The asset *Furniture and fittings* appeared because the business now owns furniture and fittings.
- The liability *Creditor – Snappy Ltd* appeared because the business purchased the furniture on credit and now owes $10 000 to Snappy Ltd.

Although the furniture and fittings were purchased on credit (which means 'buy now, pay later'), they are still considered to be owned by the business. Note that the asset *Cash at bank* did not change, because no cash has been paid yet for the furniture and fittings.

The accounting equation now would appear as:

$$\text{Assets} \quad = \quad \text{Liabilities} \quad + \quad \text{Owner's equity}$$
$$(\$50\,000) \qquad (\$10\,000) \qquad (\$40\,000)$$

## 3 July   *The business paid Snappy Ltd $1000 cash as part payment of the amount owing*

The statement of financial position would now look like this:

**SAMMY'S MINI MART**
**Statement of financial position as at 3 July 2016**

| Assets | $ | Liabilities | $ |
|---|---|---|---|
| Cash at bank | 38 000 | Creditor – Snappy Ltd | 9 000 |
| Cash register | 1 000 | | |
| Furniture and fittings | 10 000 | **Owner's equity** | |
| | | Capital – S Silvagni | 40 000 |
| | 49 000 | | 49 000 |

The transaction had two effects:

1   The asset *Cash at bank* decreased because cash had to be withdrawn to make the payment to Snappy Ltd.
2   The liability *Creditor – Snappy Ltd* decreased because the business has repaid part of the amount owing.

The accounting equation is now:

$$\text{Assets} \quad = \quad \text{Liabilities} \quad + \quad \text{Owner's equity}$$
$$(\$49\,000) \qquad (\$9\,000) \qquad (\$40\,000)$$

## 4 July   *Sammy gave the business his own vehicle (valued at $10 100) to be used for deliveries*

**SAMMY'S MINI MART**
**Statement of financial position as at 4 July 2016**

| Assets | $ | Liabilities | $ |
|---|---|---|---|
| Cash at bank | 38 000 | Creditor – Snappy Ltd | 9 000 |
| Cash register | 1 000 | | |
| Furniture and fittings | 10 000 | **Owner's equity** | |
| Delivery vehicle | 10 100 | Capital – S Silvagni | 50 100 |
| | 59 100 | | 59 100 |

The newly prepared statement of financial position showed the following information.

- The asset *Delivery vehicle* appeared because the business now owns a delivery vehicle.
- Sammy's *Capital* increased because he gave the business his own vehicle, thereby increasing the amount the business owes him.

It should be noted that this is the first time that Sammy's capital has changed since the business was formed. This transaction illustrates the business entity convention: the business and its owner are treated as separate entities.

Here is the accounting equation now:

$$\text{Assets} \quad = \quad \text{Liabilities} \quad + \quad \text{Owner's equity}$$
$$(\$59\,000) \qquad (\$9\,000) \qquad (\$50\,100)$$

### 5 July  *The business borrowed $3000 cash from Shark Finance Co and deposited the cash in the bank account*

**SAMMY'S MINI MART**
**Statement of financial position as at 5 July 2016**

| Assets | $ | Liabilities | $ | $ |
|---|---|---|---|---|
| Cash at bank | 41 000 | Creditor – Snappy Ltd | 9 000 | |
| Cash register | 1 000 | Loan from Shark Finance Co | 3 000 | 12 000 |
| Furniture and fittings | 10 000 | | | |
| Delivery vehicle | 10 100 | **Owner's equity** | | |
| | | Capital – S Silvagni | | 50 100 |
| | 62 100 | | | 62 100 |

The transaction had two effects:

1  The asset *Cash at bank* increased because $3000 cash was received on loan from Shark Finance Co.
2  The liability *Loan from Shark Finance Co* appeared because the business borrowed $3000 and now owes this amount to Shark Finance Co.

The accounting equation is now:

$$\text{Assets} \quad = \quad \text{Liabilities} \quad + \quad \text{Owner's equity}$$
$$(\$62\,100) \qquad (\$12\,000) \qquad (\$50\,100)$$

6 July   *The business discovered that some of the fittings purchased on 2 July were unsuitable. These fittings were sold for cash at their cost price of $500 in total*

**SAMMY'S MINI MART**
Statement of financial position as at 6 July 2016

| Assets | $ | Liabilities | $ | $ |
|---|---|---|---|---|
| Cash at bank | 41 500 | Creditor – Snappy Ltd | 9 000 | |
| Cash register | 1 000 | Loan from Shark Finance Co | 3 000 | 12 000 |
| Furniture and fittings | 9 500 | | | |
| Delivery vehicle | 10 100 | **Owner's equity** | | |
| | | Capital – S Silvagni | | 50 100 |
| | 62 100 | | | 62 100 |

The two effects of the transaction were as follows.

1   The asset *Cash at bank* increased because $500 cash was received from the sale of fittings.

2   The asset *Furniture and fittings* decreased because some of the fittings have been sold.

Here is the accounting equation:

$$\begin{array}{ccccc} \text{Assets} & = & \text{Liabilities} & + & \text{Owner's equity} \\ (\$62\,100) & & (\$12\,000) & & (\$50\,100) \end{array}$$

7 July   *Further fittings were sold on credit to A Digger at cost ($300). The amount owed by Digger is to be paid in three months*

**SAMMY'S MINI MART**
Statement of financial position as at 7 July 2016

| Assets | $ | Liabilities | $ | $ |
|---|---|---|---|---|
| Cash at bank | 41 500 | Creditor – Snappy Ltd | 9 000 | |
| Cash register | 1 000 | Loan from Shark Finance Co | 3 000 | 12 000 |
| Furniture and fittings | 9 200 | | | |
| Delivery vehicle | 10 100 | | | |
| Debtor – A Digger | 300 | **Owner's equity** | | |
| | | Capital – S Silvagni | | 50 100 |
| | 62 100 | | | 62 100 |

The transaction had two effects:

1 The asset *Furniture and fittings* decreased because some were sold.
2 The asset *Debtor – A Digger* appeared because the fittings were sold by the business to A Digger on credit (sell now, receive money later). A Digger now owes $300.

The asset *Cash at bank* did not change, because no cash has been received yet from this transaction.

The accounting equation would now appear as:

$$\text{Assets} \quad = \quad \text{Liabilities} \quad + \quad \text{Owner's equity}$$
$$(\$62\,100) \qquad (\$12\,000) \qquad (\$50\,100)$$

## 8 July   *Sammy withdrew $1000 cash from the business bank account to purchase a birthday present for his friend*

**SAMMY'S MINI MART**
**Statement of financial position as at 8 July 2016**

| Assets | $ | Liabilities | $ | $ |
|---|---|---|---|---|
| Cash at bank | 40 500 | Creditor – Snappy Ltd | 9 000 | |
| Cash register | 1 000 | Loan from Shark Finance Co | 3 000 | 12 000 |
| Furniture and fittings | 9 200 | | | |
| Delivery vehicle | 10 100 | | | |
| Debtor – A Digger | 300 | **Owner's equity** | | |
| | | Capital – S Silvagni | 50 100 | |
| | | *less* Drawings – S Silvagni | 1 000 | 49 100 |
| | 61 100 | | | 61 100 |

The effects of the transaction were as follows.

- The asset *Cash at bank* decreased because cash was withdrawn by Sammy.
- A new item called *Drawings* appeared in the owner's equity section as a deduction from Sammy's capital. The deduction was made because Sammy took some of the business's cash for his own use, thereby decreasing the amount the business owes him. It is traditional to show drawings as a separate figure, rather than just decreasing the capital figure.

This transaction further illustrates the effect of the business entity convention, where the owner and the business are treated as separate entities.

The accounting equation is now:

$$\text{Assets} \quad = \quad \text{Liabilities} \quad + \quad \text{Owner's equity}$$
$$(\$61\,100) \qquad (\$12\,000) \qquad (\$49\,100)$$

9 July   *The business purchased refrigeration equipment on credit from Fridges Ltd for $18 000. A deposit of $3000 cash was paid*

**SAMMY'S MINI MART**
Statement of financial position as at 9 July 2016

| Assets | $ | Liabilities | $ | $ |
|---|---|---|---|---|
| Cash at bank | 37 500 | Creditor – Snappy Ltd | 9 000 | |
| Cash register | 1 000 | Loan from Shark Finance Co | 3 000 | |
| Furniture and fittings | 9 200 | Creditor – Fridges Ltd | 15 000 | 27 000 |
| Delivery vehicle | 10 100 | | | |
| Debtor – A Digger | 300 | **Owner's equity** | | |
| Refrigeration equipment | 18 000 | Capital – S Silvagni | 50 100 | |
| | | *less* Drawings – S Silvagni | 1 000 | 49 100 |
| | 76 100 | | | 76 100 |

This transaction had three effects:

1   The asset *Refrigeration equipment* appeared, because the business has purchased refrigeration equipment at a total cost of $18 000. As was the case in the transaction on 2 July, this equipment is considered as belonging to the business, despite the fact that it was purchased on credit.

2   The asset *Cash at bank* decreased because the business withdrew money and paid a cash deposit on the refrigeration equipment.

3   The liability *Creditor – Fridges Ltd* appeared because the business purchased the refrigeration equipment on credit and now owes Fridges Ltd $15 000 (total cost $18 000 less $3000 cash deposit paid).

This transaction was unusual in that it had three effects on the statement of financial position, whereas most transactions only have two effects. The reason for this is that it was partly a *credit* transaction and partly a *cash* transaction.

The accounting equation would now appear as follows:

$$\text{Assets} = \text{Liabilities} + \text{Owner's equity}$$
$$(\$76\,100) \qquad (\$27\,000) \qquad (\$49\,100)$$

# The transaction analysis chart

UWATCH 1.2

A UWatch demonstration is available on the CD that accompanies this text for parts of this activity.

When examining the effects that business transactions have on a statement of financial position, it is helpful to use a *transaction analysis chart* to answer the following questions.

· Which statement of financial position items are affected by the transaction?
· Is the item affected an asset, a liability or an owner's equity item?
· Does the item increase or decrease?
· What is the amount of the increase or decrease?

Consider the following example of a transaction analysis chart, which analyses the ten transactions of Sammy's Mini Mart discussed so far in this chapter.

**SAMMY'S MINI MART**
Transaction analysis chart

| Date | Items affected | A, L or OE | Increase or decrease | Amount $ | Explanation |
|---|---|---|---|---|---|
| Formation of business | (a) Cash at bank | A | Increase | 40 000 | Sammy deposited cash in the business bank account. The business now owes this money to him. |
| | (b) Capital – S Silvagni | OE | Increase | 40 000 | |
| 1 Jul | (a) Cash at bank | A | Decrease | 1 000 | Some of the asset cash was exchanged for a cash register. |
| | (b) Cash register | A | Increase | 1 000 | |
| 2 Jul | (a) Furniture and fittings | A | Increase | 10 000 | The business bought an asset (Furniture and fittings) on credit and now owes Snappy Ltd $10 000. |
| | (b) Creditor – Snappy Ltd | L | Increase | 10 000 | |
| 3 Jul | (a) Cash at bank | A | Decrease | 1 000 | The amount owing to Snappy Ltd was decreased by $1000, which was paid from the business bank account. |
| | (b) Creditor – Snappy Ltd | L | Decrease | 1 000 | |
| 4 Jul | (a) Delivery vehicle | A | Increase | 10 100 | Contribution of an asset into the business by the owner increased his capital. |
| | (b) Capital – S Silvagni | OE | Increase | 10 100 | |
| 5 Jul | (a) Cash at bank | A | Increase | 3 000 | The business received $3000 cash as a loan and now owes Shark Finance Co this amount. |
| | (b) Loan from Shark Finance Co | L | Increase | 3 000 | |
| 6 Jul | (a) Cash at bank | A | Increase | 500 | Cash received from the sale of some of the fittings. |
| | (b) Furniture and fittings | A | Decrease | 500 | |
| 7 Jul | (a) Furniture and fittings | A | Decrease | 300 | More fittings sold (on credit). A Digger now owes the business $300 for these fittings. |
| | (b) Debtor – A Digger | A | Increase | 300 | |
| 8 Jul | (a) Cash at bank | A | Decrease | 1 000 | Withdrawal of cash from the business by the owner reduces the amount the business owes him. |
| | (b) Drawings – S Silvagni | OE | Decrease | 1 000 | |
| 9 Jul | (a) Refrigeration equipment | A | Increase | 18 000 | $3000 cash was used as a deposit for the purchase of refrigeration equipment costing $18 000. The balance of the price is still owed to the supplier, Fridges Ltd. |
| | (b) Cash at bank | A | Decrease | 3 000 | |
| | (c) Creditor – Fridges Ltd | L | Increase | 15 000 | |

# The 'narrative' statement of financial position

All of the statements of financial position shown in examples so far have been in 'T' format. Another form of presenting the statement of financial position is the narrative method. This format shows the owner's equity first, followed by assets less liabilities. It is based on the restatement of the accounting equation, so that Owner's equity = Assets – Liabilities. For example, a statement of financial position in narrative form for Sammy's Mini Mart at 9 July 2016 would appear as shown opposite.

**SAMMY'S MINI MART**
Statement of financial position as at 9 July 2016

| Owner's equity | $ | $ | $ |
|---|---|---|---|
| Capital – S Silvagni | | 50 100 | |
| *less* Drawings – S Silvagni | | 1 000 | 49 100 |
| Represented by: | | | |
| **Assets** | | | |
| Cash at bank | 37 500 | | |
| Cash register | 1 000 | | |
| Furniture and fittings | 9 200 | | |
| Delivery vehicle | 10 100 | | |
| Debtor – A Digger | 300 | | |
| Refrigeration equipment | 18 000 | | |
| Total assets | | 76 100 | |
| *less* **Liabilities** | | | |
| Creditor – Snappy Ltd | 9 000 | | |
| Loan from Shark Finance Co | 3 000 | | |
| Creditor – Fridges Ltd | 15 000 | | |
| Total liabilities | | 27 000 | |
| **Net assets** | | | 49 100 |

**Note** The term *Net assets* refers to the residual amount that is derived when total liabilities are subtracted from total assets. Note that the AASB's Framework, discussed earlier in the chapter, defines 'equity' in this manner.

## EXERCISES

1.27*   M Travelli commenced business operations as a painter and decorator on 1 June 2017. From the information below:

a   prepare a transaction analysis chart

b   prepare a statement of financial position as at 16 June 2017.

*Information*

| | | |
|---|---|---|
| 1 Jun | Travelli deposited $10 000 into a bank account styled 'Travelli – Painter and Decorator'. |
| 2 | Purchased a second-hand station wagon for $3500 cash. |
| 4 | Purchased drop sheets for $300 on credit from PQR Suppliers. |
| 6 | Purchased brushes on credit for $180 from Brush Wholesalers. |
| 10 | Paid PQR Suppliers $100. |
| 12 | Purchased ladders, trestles and planks for $600 cash. |
| 16 | Travelli deposited an extra $5000 into the business bank account from his own personal account. |

1.28 The following information relates to D Fraser, Pool Supplies. You are required to prepare a statement of financial position as at 31 August 2016.

| | | | | | |
|---|---|---|---|---|---|
| **D Fraser Pool Supplies** | | | | | |
| **Statement of financial position as at 31 July 2016** | | | | | |
| **Assets** | **$** | **Liabilities** | **$** | **$** | |
| Cash in hand | 50 | Creditors – P Filter | 750 | | |
| Cash at bank | 5 500 | – A Valve | 250 | | |
| Debtors – F Hose | 2 200 | Loan from Moula Loans | 5 000 | 6 000 | |
| – D Earth | 2 800 | | | | |
| Furniture and fittings | 7 500 | **Owner's equity** | | | |
| Stocks of pool supplies | 22 000 | Capital – D Fraser | | 34 050 | |
| | 40 050 | | | 40 050 | |

*Transactions for period 1 August 2016 to 31 August 2016*

1 Aug   Paid creditor P Filter $400.

5   Debtor F Hose paid his account.

10   Purchased computer on credit from BB Supplies $800.

18   Proprietor contributed $10 000 into the business bank account.

20   Purchased a motor vehicle for $8000 cash.

31   D Fraser withdrew $50 from the business bank account to pay her daughter's parking fine.

ADDITIONAL EXERCISES

1.29 This question is available on the CD that accompanies this text.

1.30* From the following information of R Hidaka, retailer, you are required to prepare a statement of financial position as at 16 July 2017.

| | | | | | |
|---|---|---|---|---|---|
| **R Hidaka, Retailer** | | | | | |
| **Statement of financial position as at 30 June 2017** | | | | | |
| **Assets** | **$** | **Liabilities** | **$** | **$** | |
| Bank | 21 000 | Creditor – NT Supplies | 16 000 | | |
| Debtor – J Wone | 13 500 | – FL Wholesalers | 14 000 | | |
| – P Nent | 500 | Mortgage loan | 340 000 | 370 000 | |
| Stock | 65 000 | | | | |
| Premises | 410 000 | | | | |
| Fixtures and fittings | 32 000 | **Owner's equity** | | | |
| Goodwill | 20 000 | R Hidaka – Capital | | 192 000 | |
| | 562 000 | | | 562 000 | |

*Transactions for period 1 July 2017 to 16 July 2017*

1 Jul   Repaid $2000 principal off mortgage loan.

3       Purchased delivery vehicle on credit from TZ Motors valued at $15 000; paid $5000 deposit.

5       Paid for mother's birthday present, $1000.

7       Paid FL Wholesalers $14 000.

8       Proprietor withdrew fittings for personal use, $500.

10      Proprietor introduced furniture valued at $2000 into the business.

12      Debtor P Nent paid his account.

16      Repaid $2000 principal off mortgage loan.

**Note** An arrangement has been made with the bank for overdraft accommodation up to $20 000.

 **SOLUTIONS**

1.27   a

| | | M Travelli – Painter And Decorator | | | |
|---|---|---|---|---|---|
| | | Transaction analysis chart | | | |
| **Date** | **Items affected** | **A, L or OE** | **Increase or decrease** | **Amount $** | **Explanation** |
| 1 Jun | (a) Cash at bank | A | Increase | 10 000 | Travelli deposited cash in the business bank account. The business now owes this money to Travelli. |
| | (b) Capital – M Travelli | OE | Increase | 10 000 | |
| 2 Jun | (a) Motor vehicle | A | Increase | 3 500 | Some of the asset 'Cash' was exchanged for a vehicle. |
| | (b) Cash at bank | A | Decrease | 3 500 | |
| 4 Jun | (a) Equipment (drop sheets) | A | Increase | 300 | The business bought an asset (equipment) on credit and now owes PQR Suppliers $300. |
| | (b) Creditor – PQR Suppliers | L | Increase | 300 | |
| 6 Jun | (a) Equipment (brushes) | A | Increase | 180 | The business bought more equipment on credit and now owes Brush Wholesalers $180. |
| | (b) Creditor – Brush Wholesalers | L | Increase | 180 | |
| 10 Jun | (a) Cash at bank | A | Decrease | 100 | The amount owing to PQR Suppliers was decreased by $100, which was paid from the business bank account. |
| | (b) Creditor – PQR Suppliers | L | Decrease | 100 | |
| 12 Jun | (a) Equipment (ladders, trestles & planks) | A | Increase | 600 | Some of the asset cash was exchanged for more equipment. |
| | (b) Cash at bank | A | Decrease | 600 | |
| 16 Jun | (a) Cash at bank | A | Increase | 5 000 | Travelli deposited $5000 cash in the business bank account. The business now owes this money to Travelli. |
| | (b) Capital – M Travelli | OE | Increase | 5 000 | |

b

### M Travelli – Painter And Decorator
### Statement of financial position as at 16 June 2017

| Assets | $ | Liabilities | $ | $ |
|---|---|---|---|---|
| Cash at bank | 10 800 | Creditor – PQR Suppliers | 200 | |
| Motor vehicle | 3 500 | – Brush Wholesalers | 180 | 380 |
| Equipment | 1 080 | | | |
| | | **Owner's equity** | | |
| | | Capital – M Travelli | | 15 000 |
| | 15 380 | | | 15 380 |

1.30

### R Hidaka, Retailer
### Statement of financial position as at 16 July 2017

| Assets | $ | Liabilities | $ | $ |
|---|---|---|---|---|
| Debtor – J Wone | 13 500 | Bank overdraft | 2 500 | |
| Stock | 65 000 | Creditor – NT Supplies | 16 000 | |
| Premises | 410 000 | Mortgage loan | 336 000 | |
| Fixtures and fittings | 31 500 | Creditor – TZ Motors | 10 000 | 364 500 |
| Goodwill | 20 000 | | | |
| Delivery vehicle | 15 000 | **Owner's equity** | | |
| Furniture | 2 000 | Capital – R Hidaka | 194 000 | |
| | | *less* Drawings – R Hidaka | 1 500 | 192 500 |
| | 557 000 | | | 557 000 |

# Income and expense transactions

Thus far, this chapter has examined business transactions that affect the statement of financial position. The example using Sammy's Mini Mart showed that there are generally only two types of transactions that affect the owner's capital.

1  The owner contributes assets to the business.
2  The owner withdraws assets from the business for personal use.

In the following sections, we discuss another way in which the owner's capital can change; that is, when the business makes a profit or loss from trading activities. Consider the trading process illustrated in Figure 1.5 for Sammy's Mini Mart.

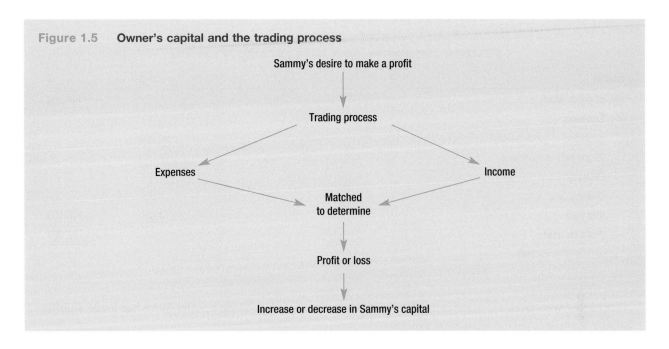

Figure 1.5    **Owner's capital and the trading process**

As shown in Figure 1.5, the trading process involves two new elements of accounting: *income* and *expenses*.

*Income* can be defined broadly as amounts earned from the sale of goods or services for cash or credit. The AASB's Framework defines income as 'increases in economic benefits during the accounting period in the form of inflows or enhancements of assets or decreases of liabilities that result in increases in equity, other than those relating to contributions from equity participants'. Applying this definition on a practical level, when Sammy's business sells groceries it will earn income that will be received in the form of cash. Similarly, when a lawyer charges a fee for work undertaken for a client, income is earned and will be received in the form of cash.

*Expenses* can be broadly defined as the costs involved in earning income. The AASB's Framework defines expenses as 'decreases in economic benefits during the accounting period in the form of outflows or depletions of assets'. What this means is that expenses are benefits that have been consumed (used up) in the income-earning process. These are normally regarded as costs of the business. Thus, Sammy's business pays wages to its employees, because the business has consumed the benefit of their labour in generating income. Wages are therefore regarded as an expense to the business.

Note, however, that an expense is not an asset. An expense could be generally regarded as a consumed benefit, whereas an asset continues to have remaining benefits that have not yet been consumed. This is a handy hint to remember when processing transactions involving the business; for example, a motor vehicle will provide benefits over several accounting periods, whereas the petrol purchased would be consumed within one accounting period.

# The statement of comprehensive income

The statement of comprehensive income is a report that shows the income of the business and the expenses involved in earning income for a specific accounting period, such as 12 months. Consider the statement of comprehensive income in the example of Mario's Super Store shown overleaf.

| MARIO'S SUPER STORE<br>Statement of comprehensive income for the year ended 30 June 2017 | | |
|---|---|---|
| **Income** | **$** | **$** |
| Sale of goods (stock) | | 140 000 |
| *less* **Expenses** | | |
| Purchases of goods (stock)* | 90 000 | |
| Wages paid to employees | 21 000 | |
| Electricity | 1 400 | |
| Cleaning costs | 1 600 | |
| Rent paid | 4 000 | 118 000 |
| = **Profit for year** | | 22 000 |
| * (assuming all stock sold) | | |

It can be seen from the statement of comprehensive income that Mario's Super Store has made a profit, because income is greater than total expenses.

If the statement of comprehensive income is expressed in equation form, it will appear as follows:

$$\underset{(\$22\,000)}{\text{Profit}} = \underset{(\$140\,000)}{\text{Income}} - \underset{(\$118\,000)}{\text{Expenses}}$$

In cases where total expenses are greater than income earned, a loss has occurred.

After the profit has been calculated (as shown in the statement of comprehensive income), it is added to the owner's equity (in the statement of financial position). Profit is added to the owner's capital because the owner is entitled to all profits made by the business. The relationship between the statement of comprehensive income and the statement of financial position is illustrated in Figure 1.6. The link between the two reports is the profit (or loss) amount – a profit increases capital whereas a loss decreases capital.

**Figure 1.6    Relationship between the statement of comprehensive income and the statement of financial position**

| Profit = Income − Expenses | | | Assets = Liabilities + Owner's equity | | | | |
|---|---|---|---|---|---|---|---|
| Statement of comprehensive income | | | Statement of financial position | | | | |
| | **$** | **$** | **Assets** | **$** | **Liabilities** | **$** | **$** |
| **Income** | | 10 000 | Bank | 5 000 | Loan from ALT | | 142 000 |
| *less* **Expenses** | | | Motor vehicle | 10 000 | | | |
| Wages | 6 000 | | Land and buildings | 200 000 | **Owner's equity** | | |
| Materials | 1 000 | | | | Capital | 70 500 | |
| Power | 500 | 7 500 | | | *plus* **Profit** | 2 500 | 73 000 |
| = **Profit** | | 2 500 | | $215 000 | | | $215 000 |

LINK

# Effect of income and expense transactions on the statement of comprehensive income and the statement of financial position

A UWatch demonstration is available on the CD that accompanies this text for parts of this activity.

Earlier in this chapter, the effect of several transactions in the first nine days of trading for Sammy's Mini Mart were examined in relation to the statement of financial position. These transactions were all *statement of financial position transactions* and thus did not involve *income* and *expenses* elements, primarily because the business had not yet commenced trading. When the business commences trading, transactions involving income and expense items will become part of the trading process. These are commonly referred to as *income and expense transactions*, or (sometimes) profit and loss transactions.

On 10 July 2016 Sammy's Mini Mart opened its doors to the public and the following *income and expense transactions* occurred on that day.

## The business purchased groceries for $4000 cash

If a statement of comprehensive income and a statement of financial position were prepared after this transaction, they would appear as follows:

**SAMMY'S MINI MART**
**Statement of comprehensive income for 10 July 2016 (incomplete)**

|  | $ | $ |
| --- | --- | --- |
| **Income** |  | Nil |
| *less* **Expenses** |  |  |
| Purchase of groceries | 4 000 |  |

**SAMMY'S MINI MART**
**Statement of financial position for 10 July 2016 (incomplete)**

| Assets | $ | Liabilities | $ | $ |
| --- | --- | --- | --- | --- |
| Cash at bank | 33 500 | Creditor – Snappy Ltd | 9 000 |  |
| Cash register | 1 000 | Loan from Shark Finance Co | 3 000 |  |
| Furniture and fittings | 9 200 | Creditor – Fridges Ltd | 15 000 | 27 000 |
| Delivery vehicle | 10 100 |  |  |  |
| Debtor – A Digger | 300 | **Owner's equity** |  |  |
| Refrigeration equipment | 18 000 | Capital – S Silvagni | 50 100 |  |
|  |  | *less* Drawings – S Silvagni | 1 000 | 49 100 |

The transaction had two effects:

1 In the statement of comprehensive income, the expense *Purchase of groceries* appeared. The groceries purchased represent the inventory/stock that will be sold to generate income for the business and is therefore shown as an expense and not as an asset.

2 In the statement of financial position, the asset *Cash at bank* decreased, because the business paid out cash for the groceries. The statement of financial position shown on page 35 commenced where the previous example using Sammy's Mini Mart left off (see page 29); that is, after 9 July.

The transaction had one effect on the statement of comprehensive income and one effect on the statement of financial position, because it was an income and expense transaction. Remember that statement of financial position transactions only affect the statement of financial position.

**Note** Both the statement of comprehensive income and the statement of financial position shown in this example will **remain incomplete** until all of the transactions for 10 July have been recorded and the profit for the day has been calculated.

## The business purchased groceries for $2500 on credit from I Koochew

After this transaction, the statement of comprehensive income and statement of financial position would appear as follows:

SAMMY'S MINI MART
Statement of comprehensive income for 10 July 2016 (incomplete)

|  | $ | $ |
|---|---|---|
| **Income** | | Nil |
| *less* **Expenses** | | |
| Purchase of groceries | 6 500 | |

SAMMY'S MINI MART
Statement of financial position as at 10 July 2016 (incomplete)

| **Assets** | $ | **Liabilities** | $ | $ |
|---|---|---|---|---|
| Cash at bank | 33 500 | Creditor – Snappy Ltd | 9 000 | |
| Cash register | 1 000 | Loan from Shark Finance Co | 3 000 | |
| Furniture and fittings | 9 200 | Creditor – Fridges Ltd | 15 000 | |
| Delivery vehicle | 10 100 | Creditor – I Koochew | 2 500 | 29 500 |
| Debtor – A Digger | 300 | | | |
| Refrigeration equipment | 18 000 | **Owner's equity** | | |
| | | Capital – S Silvagni | 50 100 | |
| | | *less* Drawings – S Silvagni | 1 000 | 49 100 |

It can be seen that this transaction had two effects:

1 In the statement of comprehensive income, the expense *Purchase of groceries* increased by $2500 because more groceries were purchased. It is important to note that the expense was recorded even though the groceries have not yet been paid for. This is because the business has already received the groceries and can begin to sell them to earn income.

This treatment is in accordance with the *accrual concept* of accounting, which states that income is recognised when it is earned and expenses are recognised when they are incurred.

2 In the statement of financial position, a liability *Creditor – I Koochew* appeared because the business purchased the groceries on credit and now owes $2500 to I Koochew.

## The business sold some of its groceries for $8900 cash

After this transaction, the statement of comprehensive income and the statement of financial position should appear as follows:

**SAMMY'S MINI MART**
Statement of comprehensive income for 10 July 2016 (incomplete)

|  | $ | $ |
|---|---|---|
| **Income** |  |  |
| Sale of groceries |  | 8 900 |
| *less* **Expenses** |  |  |
| Purchase of groceries | 6 500 |  |

**SAMMY'S MINI MART**
Statement of financial position as at 10 July 2016 (incomplete)

| Assets | $ | Liabilities | $ | $ |
|---|---|---|---|---|
| Cash at bank | 42 400 | Creditor – Snappy Ltd | 9 000 |  |
| Cash register | 1 000 | Loan from Shark Finance Co | 3 000 |  |
| Furniture and fittings | 9 200 | Creditor – Fridges Ltd | 15 000 |  |
| Delivery vehicle | 10 100 | Creditor – I Koochew | 2 500 | 29 500 |
| Debtor – A Digger | 300 |  |  |  |
| Refrigeration equipment | 18 000 | **Owner's equity** |  |  |
|  |  | Capital – S Silvagni | 50 100 |  |
|  |  | *less* Drawings – S Silvagni | 1 000 | 49 100 |

The transaction has two effects:

1  In the statement of comprehensive income, *Sale of groceries* appeared as income. Sammy's Mini Mart is in business to sell groceries, so any amounts earned in this way become income.

2  In the statement of financial position, the asset *Cash at bank* increased because cash was received from the sale of groceries.

## The business sold some of its groceries on credit to A Barclay for $100

**SAMMY'S MINI MART**
**Statement of comprehensive income for 10 July 2016 (incomplete)**

|  | $ | $ |
|---|---|---|
| **Income** | | |
| Sale of groceries | | 9 000 |
| *less* **Expenses** | | |
| Purchase of groceries | 6 500 | |

**SAMMY'S MINI MART**
**Statement of financial position as at 10 July 2016 (incomplete)**

| Assets | $ | Liabilities | $ | $ |
|---|---|---|---|---|
| Cash at bank | 42 400 | Creditor – Snappy Ltd | 9 000 | |
| Cash register | 1 000 | Loan from Shark Finance Co | 3 000 | |
| Furniture and fittings | 9 200 | Creditor – Fridges Ltd | 15 000 | |
| Delivery vehicle | 10 100 | Creditor – I Koochew | 2 500 | 29 500 |
| Debtor – A Digger | 300 | | | |
| Refrigeration equipment | 18 000 | **Owner's equity** | | |
| Debtor – A Barclay | 100 | Capital – S Silvagni | 50 100 | |
| | | *less* Drawings – S Silvagni | 1 000 | 49 100 |

- In the statement of comprehensive income, the income item *Sale of groceries* increased by $100, because the business sold more groceries. It is important to note that the income from this transaction was recorded, even though A Barclay had not yet paid the business for the groceries. Income is recorded as soon as it is earned, because realisation has occurred, generally meaning that the obligations of both parties have been met and the goods have passed between the seller and the buyer, despite the seller not receiving cash. A practical example of the concept of realisation is when a customer buys goods from the local supermarket on credit. When the customer signs the credit authority the cashier will allow the goods to pass over the counter to the customer and thus the transaction has been settled, with both parties (buyer and seller) satisfactorily performing their obligations in the trading process.

This is another illustration of the accrual concept of accounting (see additional notes following transaction 2).

- In the statement of financial position, an asset *Debtor – A Barclay* appeared, because A Barclay now owes the business $100 for the groceries sold to him on credit.

## The business paid wages of $500 in cash to its employees

**SAMMY'S MINI MART**
**Statement of comprehensive income for 10 July 2016 (incomplete)**

| | $ | $ |
|---|---:|---:|
| **Income** | | |
| Sale of groceries | | 9 000 |
| *less* **Expenses** | | |
| Purchase of groceries | 6 500 | |
| Wages paid | 500 | |

**SAMMY'S MINI MART**
**Statement of financial position as at 10 July 2016 (incomplete)**

| Assets | $ | Liabilities | $ | $ |
|---|---:|---|---:|---:|
| Cash at bank | 41 900 | Creditor – Snappy Ltd | 9 000 | |
| Cash register | 1 000 | Loan from Shark Finance Co | 3 000 | |
| Furniture and fittings | 9 200 | Creditor – Fridges Ltd | 15 000 | |
| Delivery vehicle | 10 100 | Creditor – I Koochew | 2 500 | 29 500 |
| Debtor – A Digger | 300 | | | |
| Refrigeration equipment | 18 000 | **Owner's equity** | | |
| Debtor – A Barclay | 100 | Capital – S Silvagni | 50 100 | |
| | | *less* Drawings – S Silvagni | 1 000 | 49 100 |

- In the statement of comprehensive income another expense, *Wages paid*, appeared because this payment was necessary in operating the business.
- In the statement of financial position, the asset *Cash at bank* decreased because the business paid out $500 in wages.

*The business paid rent for its shop premises by sending the landlord a cheque for $200 (the final transaction for 10 July)*

After this final transaction, the statement of comprehensive income and the statement of financial position can be completed.

**SAMMY'S MINI MART**
**Statement of comprehensive income for 10 July 2016**

|  | $ | $ |
|---|---:|---:|
| **Income** | | |
| Sale of groceries | | 9 000 |
| *less* **Expenses** | | |
| Purchase of groceries | 6 500 | |
| Wages paid | 500 | |
| Rent paid | 200 | 7 200 |
| = **Profit** | | 1 800 |

**SAMMY'S MINI MART**
**Statement of financial position as at 10 July 2016**

| Assets | $ | Liabilities | $ | $ |
|---|---:|---|---:|---:|
| Cash at bank | 41 700 | Creditor – Snappy Ltd | 9 000 | |
| Cash register | 1 000 | Loan from Shark Finance Co | 3 000 | |
| Furniture and fittings | 9 200 | Creditor – Fridges Ltd | 15 000 | |
| Delivery vehicle | 10 100 | Creditor – I Koochew | 2 500 | 29 500 |
| Debtor – A Digger | 300 | | | |
| Refrigeration equipment | 18 000 | **Owner's equity** | | |
| Debtor – A Barclay | 100 | Capital – S Silvagni | 50 100 | |
| | | *less* Drawings – S Silvagni | 1 000 | |
| | | | 49 100 | |
| | | *plus* Profit | 1 800 | 50 900 |
| | 80 400 | | | 80 400 |

- In the statement of comprehensive income another expense, *Rent paid*, appeared because this payment was necessary in operating the business.
- In the statement of financial position, the asset *Cash at bank* decreased because the business paid out $200 in rent. Payments by cheque are considered as cash payments and are therefore deducted from cash at bank.

The statement of comprehensive income for 10 July is now complete because all transactions for the day have been recorded. The day's profit of $1800, calculated by deducting the total expenses from the income earned, is then added to Sammy's capital in the statement of financial position.

The statement of financial position is also complete, following the addition of the profit to Sammy's capital in the owner's equity section. The accounting equation for Sammy's Mini Mart now would appear as follows:

$$\underset{(\$80\,400)}{\text{Assets}} = \underset{(\$29\,500)}{\text{Liabilities}} + \underset{(\$50\,900)}{\text{Owner's equity}}$$

**Note** It is not usual practice to a prepare statement of comprehensive income for only one day. The statement is normally prepared to cover a much longer period of time, most commonly 12 months. Note further that we have assumed that Sammy's Mini Mart did not have a stock of unsold goods remaining at 10 July 2016.

# Treatment of stock/inventory

Stock is a term used to describe merchandise that has been purchased for resale. Stock is also referred to as *inventory* or simply as merchandise inventory. We will use the terms 'stock' and 'inventory' interchangeably, although the term 'stock' appears to be more commonly used in Australia. Accountants have a number of choices when recording stock transactions within the accounting process. This text uses the physical method of stock recording, which requires the business to undertake a physical stocktake at year's end to determine the value of stock on hand. It also requires that all purchases of stock during the year be recorded as expenses.

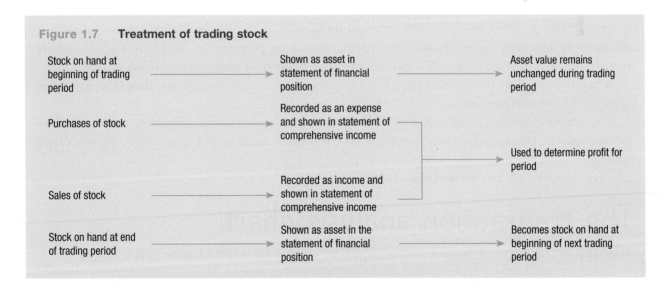

**Figure 1.7    Treatment of trading stock**

When using the physical method of stock recording, it is important to remember four points (see Figure 1.7):

1 When a business has stock of goods on hand at the beginning of a trading period, this stock is recorded as an asset in the statement of financial position. The value of this asset remains unchanged in the accounting records for the remainder of the trading period, despite subsequent purchases and sales of stock during the period.

2 Purchases of stock are not added to the asset 'Stock', but instead are recorded as Purchases expense and are shown in the income statement.

3 Sales of stock are not deducted from the asset 'Stock', but instead are recorded as Sales income and are shown in the income statement.

4 Stock on hand at the end of a trading period is determined by a physical stocktake. This figure is shown in the statement of financial position as an asset at year's end. Stock on hand at the end of one period becomes stock on hand at the beginning of the next accounting period.

This method of recording stock is known by accountants as the *physical* or *periodic method*.

**Note**  For further and more detailed discussion on the treatment of stock remaining unsold (closing stock) at the end of the trading period, additional coverage is provided in Chapters 3 and 4 of *Accounting: Basic Reports*.

# Cash and credit transactions

It is important at this point to expand on the terms *cash* and *credit* used in this text in relation to transactions.

A business receives cash in many ways, including:

- notes, coins and cheques received
- 'direct debit' (EFTPOS) sales
- electronic funds transfer (EFT) from other parties
- sales where customers use credit cards issued by major banks.

All of these situations represent cash received for accounting purposes; in some cases actual cash is received, whereas in other cases cash is transferred electronically to or from a specific bank account.

A business will make payments by cash, EFT and cheque. For accounting purposes, cheque payments are considered to be cash payments.

Credit transactions can occur as part of credit arrangements made between a business and its suppliers or, alternatively, through sales where customers use credit cards issued by financial institutions other than banks.

These concepts will be explained more fully in Chapter 2.

# The transaction analysis chart

UWATCH 1.4

A UWatch demonstration is available on the CD that accompanies this text for parts of this activity.

Earlier in this chapter, a transaction analysis chart was used to analyse the first transactions of Sammy's Mini Mart (see page 31). The following analysis chart for the six transactions that occurred on 10 July 2016 shows two additional elements: income (I) and expenses (E).

**SAMMY'S MINI MART**
Transaction analysis chart for 10 July 2016

| Transaction number | Items affected | A, L, OE, I or E | Increase or decrease | Amount $ | Explanation |
|---|---|---|---|---|---|
| 1 | (a) Purchase of groceries | E | Increase | 4 000 | The business has purchased groceries that will be used to earn income. Cash was paid for the groceries. |
| | (b) Cash at bank | A | Decrease | 4 000 | |
| 2 | (a) Purchase of groceries | E | Increase | 2 500 | More groceries have been purchased. They have been received so expense is recorded. The business now owes I Koochew $2500, as the groceries were purchased on credit. |
| | (b) Creditor – I Koochew | L | Increase | 2 500 | |
| 3 | (a) Sale of groceries | I | Increase | 8 900 | Through the sale of groceries, the business earns income. This was received in cash. |
| | (b) Cash at bank | A | Increase | 8 900 | |
| 4 | (a) Sale of groceries | I | Increase | 100 | More groceries have been sold. Income is recorded as soon as the customer receives the goods. A Barclay now owes the business $100 for groceries he received on credit. |
| | (b) Debtor – A Barclay | A | Increase | 100 | |
| 5 | (a) Wages paid | E | Increase | 500 | The payment of wages is an expense necessary in operating the business. |
| | (b) Cash at bank | A | Decrease | 500 | |
| 6 | (a) Rent paid | E | Increase | 200 | The payment of rent is an expense necessary in operating the business. |
| | (b) Cash at bank | A | Decrease | 200 | |

# Statement of comprehensive income for a service business

The example of Sammy's Mini Mart used in this chapter illustrates how profit is calculated for a *retail* business.

The profit for a service business is calculated in exactly the same way and is also reported in a statement of comprehensive income. Consider the following example of a statement of comprehensive income for a service business.

**D Simpson's Laundromat (Proprietor, D Simpson)**
Statement of comprehensive income for the month ended 31 July 2017

| | $ | $ |
|---|---|---|
| **Income** | | |
| Fees received for laundry services | | 14 000 |
| *less* **Expenses** | | |
| Wages paid to employees | 4 000 | |
| Purchase of detergents | 5 500 | |

|  | $ | $ |
|---|---:|---:|
| Electricity | 800 | |
| Rent paid | 1 000 | |
| Repairs to equipment | 700 | 12 000 |
| = **Profit** for July | | 2 000 |

The format of the statement of comprehensive income is the same as that for a retail business. Income in a service business is earned from providing a service, whereas in a retail business income is earned from the sale of goods. In a retail business, one of the main expenses is the purchase of goods for resale, whereas in a service business, the main expenses are usually the cost of materials used (such as detergents in the above example) and wages.

As is the case in a retail business, the profit of a service business is added to the owner's capital in the statement of financial position.

# Other sources of income

This chapter has considered two sources of income:

- sale of goods (retail business)
- the provision of services (service business).

Examples of other sources of income include rent received by a business that owns property, and interest received on loans or bank accounts, commissions and other investment income such as shares, which will provide dividend income. Income from these sources can vary depending on the size and nature of the business, and from time to time we have included income from these sources in some exercises in this text.

 **EXERCISES**

**1.31**  What is the purpose of a statement of comprehensive income?

**1.32**  What is an income and expense transaction? How does it differ from a statement of financial position transaction?

**1.33**  Briefly define the following: income, expense, profit, loss, drawings, on credit, the trading process.

**1.34**  Briefly outline the 'connection' between the statement of comprehensive income and the statement of financial position.

**1.35**  Classify the following items as either income or expenses: (a) sales; (b) repairs and maintenance; (c) commission received; (d) wages; (e) interest paid; (f) fees received; (g) advertising; (h) rent received; (i) interest received; (j) power; (k) rent paid; (l) accounting fees paid.

1.36 Classify the following items as assets, liabilities, owner's equity, income or expenses: (a) rent received; (b) interest paid; (c) creditor – B Brown; (d) repairs and maintenance; (e) sales; (f) cash on hand; (g) shares in PRG Ltd; (h) wages; (i) mortgage loan – land and buildings; (j) bank overdraft; (k) cash at bank; (l) debtor – S Lacy; (m) stock of unsold goods; (n) commission received; (o) government bonds; (p) creditors; (q) premises; (r) rent paid; (s) capital; (t) loan from XYZ Ltd; (u) equipment; (v) loan to V Wake; (w) fees received; (x) power and light.

1.37 Classify the following items as assets, liabilities, owner's equity, income or expenses: (a) computer; (b) materials used; (c) debtor – A Black; (d) service fees; (e) bank overdraft; (f) creditor – B White; (g) sales; (h) insurance; (i) buildings; (j) interest on bank overdraft; (k) rent paid; (l) fixtures and fittings; (m) capital; (n) stocks of goods; (o) rent received; (p) shares in AB Ltd; (q) interest on mortgage loan; (r) furniture; (s) bank charges; (t) loan from PT Finances; (u) rates and taxes; (v) dividends received; (w) loan to Ace Ltd; (x) motor vehicles; (y) mortgage loan on land and buildings; (z) interest received.

ADDITIONAL
EXERCISES

1.38 This question is available on the CD that accompanies this text.

1.39 Prepare an income statement for the year ended 30 June 2017 from the following information of G Glove, Gardener: cash at bank, $5000; gardening fees, $25 000; debtor – T Weed, $6000; petrol and oil used, $750; interest received, $250; mowers, $1500; repairs to mowers, $400; advertising, $200; wages, $3450.

1.40 Prepare an income statement for the year ended 30 June 2017 from the following information of P Ricey, retailer: debtor – T Ace, $10 000; cost of stock purchased, $120 000; cash sales, $85 000; electricity, $1200; telephone, $1500; rent paid, $15 000; wages, $22 000; motor vehicle expenses, $1750; furniture and fittings, $35 000; credit sales, $116 000.
**Note** There was no stock on hand at 1 July 2016 and all stock purchased during the year has been sold.

1.41 Prepare an income statement for the year ended 31 December 2016 from the following information of B Ryan, retailer: loan from Bank of ABC, $30 000; cost of goods sold, $64 000; cash sales, $43 000; interest on loan, $3000; wages, $25 000; electricity, $2800; advertising, $1200; rent paid, $14 000; credit sales, $57 000.
**Note** There was no stock on hand at 1 January 2016 and all stock purchased during the year has been sold.

1.42 This question is available on the CD that accompanies this text.

ADDITIONAL
EXERCISES

1.43 Prepare a transaction analysis chart to show the effects of the following income and expense and statement of financial position transactions of Pizza Land.

*2016*
1 Jul J Stewart started a pizza business by depositing $108 500 in a business bank account entitled Pizza Land.
2 The business purchased equipment for $5000 cash.
3 A delivery vehicle was purchased on credit from Shifty Motors for $25 500.
4 Stocks of food were purchased on credit from Hungry Foods for $2500.
5 Cash sales of foods, $950.

6    Credit sales of foods to F Fuller, $750.

7    Paid rent of premises, $220.

8    Paid wages, $310.

**1.44**   Using the following information relating to Piper Instrument Sales (proprietor Peter Piper), you are required to prepare:

a   a transaction analysis chart

b   a statement of comprehensive income for period ending 9 October 2018

c   a statement of financial position as at 9 October 2018.

**PIPER INSTRUMENT SALES**
Statement of financial position as at 1 October 2018

| Assets | $ | Liabilities | $ | $ |
|---|---|---|---|---|
| Debtor – Acme | 9 400 | Creditor – JBC | 10 200 | |
| Cash on hand | 200 | Creditor – XL Co | 10 000 | |
| Cash at bank | 13 000 | Mortgage loan | 286 800 | 307 000 |
| Motor vehicle | 19 400 | | | |
| Premises | 348 000 | | | |
| Furniture | 42 000 | **Owner's equity** | | |
| Equipment | 29 000 | Capital – Peter Piper | | 154 000 |
| | 461 000 | | | 461 000 |

*During the period ending 9 October 2018, the following transactions occurred.*

2 Oct   Purchased trading stock on credit from XL Co, $20 000.

3    Furniture costing $6000 was purchased for cash.

4    Cash sales of $30 000 were made.

5    Debtor – Acme paid $5100.

6    Stock was sold on credit to T Thumb for $9900.

7    Electricity bill of $4000 was paid.

8    $10 200 was paid to creditor – JBC.

9    Equipment costing $5900 was purchased for cash.

**1.45**   This question is available on the CD that accompanies this text.

**1.46**   This question is available on the CD that accompanies this text.

**1.47***   The following information relates to L Vixen, carrier. You are required to:

a   prepare a statement of comprehensive income for the month ended 30 June 2017

b   prepare a statement of financial position as at 30 June 2017.

### L Vixen, carrier
### Statement of financial position as at 31 May 2017

| Assets | $ | Liabilities | $ | $ |
|---|---|---|---|---|
| Cash in hand | 100 | Creditor – AY Garages | 2 000 | |
| Cash at bank | 5 000 | Loan from Finance Inc. | 15 000 | 17 000 |
| Debtors – P Jest | 2 000 | | | |
| – P Gost | 3 000 | | | |
| Trucks | 150 000 | | | |
| Storage yard | 50 000 | **Owner's equity** | | |
| Goodwill | 10 000 | L Vixen – Capital | | 203 100 |
| | 220 100 | | | 220 100 |

Transactions for the period 1 June 2017 to 30 June 2017 were:

| 1 Jun | Repaid $1000 principal and $100 interest to Finance Inc. |
|---|---|
| 3 | Paid $3000 repairs and maintenance. |
| 10 | Completed cartage job for L Lentil and received $5000. |
| 14 | Paid wages $300. |
| 18 | Paid petrol and oil $500. |
| 24 | Completed cartage job for B West $15 000. West agreed to pay the amount due in 60 days. |
| 28 | L Vixen contributed additional capital of $4000 cash. |
| 30 | P Jest paid his account. |
| | L Vixen cashed a cheque for personal use, $100. |

 **SOLUTION**

**1.47 a**

### L Vixen, Carrier
### Statement of comprehensive income for the month ended 30 June 2017

| Income | $ | $ |
|---|---|---|
| Fees | | 20 000 |
| *less* **Expenses** | | |
| Repairs and maintenance | 3 000 | |
| Wages | 300 | |
| Petrol and oil | 500 | |
| Interest on loan | 100 | 3 900 |
| **Profit** | | 16 100 |

b

### L Vixen, Carrier
### Statement of financial position as at 30 June 2017

| Assets | $ | Liabilities | $ | $ |
|---|---|---|---|---|
| Cash in hand | 100 | Creditor – AY Garages | 2 000 | |
| Cash at bank | 11 000 | Loan from Finance Inc. | 14 000 | 16 000 |
| Debtors – L Gost | 3 000 | | | |
|     – B West | 15 000 | **Owner's equity** | | |
| Trucks | 150 000 | L Vixen – Capital | 207 100 | |
| Storage yard | 50 000 | *add* Net profit | 16 100 | |
| Goodwill | 10 000 | | 223 200 | |
| | | *less* Drawings – L Vixen | 100 | 223 100 |
| | 239 100 | | | 239 100 |

# Ledgers and trial balance

In the preceding section of this chapter, a series of financial transactions for Sammy's Mini Mart were processed and the effects of these transactions on the five basic elements of business – income, expenses, assets, liabilities and owner's equity – were examined.

The effects of the transactions were recorded by preparing a statement of comprehensive income and a statement of financial position, and by progressively changing these reports as transactions occurred.

This approach is useful in demonstrating the changes that occur in the basic financial elements of the business, but is very complicated and tedious to use where financial transactions are numerous. For this reason, using a *ledger* is a more convenient method for recording transactions.

## The nature, purpose and format of the ledger

A ledger is a system that is used to record changes in the basic elements of a business. It consists of a number of *accounts*: one account being kept for each asset, liability, income, expense and owner's equity item. In a manual system of recording, for example, each account would consist of an appropriately ruled page or card, used to record changes (increases and decreases) in the item to which it relates (for example, cash at bank).

There are two common formats for ledger accounts:

1 'T' account format

2 columnar account format.

Initially, this chapter will focus on the 'T' account format.

# 'T' account format

As the name implies, a 'T' account is simply a card or page drawn up in the form of a 'T' as shown below.

| Cash at Bank Account (Asset*) | | | | | |
|---|---|---|---|---|---|
| Date | Particulars | Amount | Date | Particulars | Amount |
| | | $ | | | $ |
| | | | | | |
| | | | | | |

*After writing the name of an account at the top of a page, it is wise to specify what type of account it is (asset, liability etc.). Although this practice is not followed in business, it is helpful when learning the rules that apply to ledger accounts.

The left-hand side of a 'T' account is referred to as the *debit* side (usually abbreviated to the letters 'Dr'). Conversely, the right-hand side is referred to as the *credit* side (usually abbreviated to the letters 'Cr'). The two sides of each account need to be distinguished in this manner in order to process financial transactions according to the following rules:

| | Debit | Credit |
|---|---|---|
| *Increases in assets* are recorded on the *debit* side of an account. | X | |
| *Decreases in assets* are recorded on the *credit* side of an account. | | X |
| *Increases in liabilities* are recorded on the *credit* side of an account. | | X |
| *Decreases in liabilities* are recorded on the *debit* side of an account. | X | |
| *Increases in owner's equity* are recorded on the *credit* side of an account. | | X |
| *Decreases in owner's equity* are recorded on the *debit* side of an account. | X | |
| *Increases in expenses* are recorded on the *debit* side of an account. | X | |
| *Decreases in expenses* are recorded on the *credit* side of an account. | | X |
| *Increases in income* are recorded on the *credit* side of an account. | | X |
| *Decreases in income* are recorded on the *debit* side of an account. | X | |

Figure 1.8 overleaf provides a useful summary of the debit and credit rules.

**Figure 1.8**   **Summarising these important rules may help you to remember them**

| | Increase | Decrease |
| --- | --- | --- |
| **Debit** | Left-hand side of an account, abbreviated by the letters Dr. | |
| **Credit** | Right-hand side of an account, abbreviated by the letters Cr. | |
| Asset | Dr | Cr |
| Expense | Dr | Cr |
| Liability | Cr | Dr |
| Owner's equity | Cr | Dr |
| Income | Cr | Dr |

# Applying the rules

UWATCH 1.5

A UWatch demonstration is available on the CD that accompanies this text for parts of this activity.

We will now examine the recording process for a series of transactions using 'T' accounts.

The relevant ledger accounts for the following transactions of R Wells must be prepared.

*2018*

1 Jul   R Wells commenced a retail clothing business by depositing $10 000 into the business's bank account.

2        The business purchased shop fittings for $1000 cash.

3        The business purchased trading stock on credit from D Pits for $4000.

4        Trading stock was sold for $2500 cash.

5        Wages of $500 were paid.

6        Trading stock was sold for $600 cash.

When transactions were processed in earlier sections of this chapter, a transaction analysis chart was used to help answer the following questions:

- Which items (accounts) are affected by the transaction?
- Is the item (account) affected an asset, liability, owner's equity, income or expense item?
- Does the item (account) increase or decrease?
- What is the amount of the increase or decrease?

It is also helpful to use a transaction analysis chart when processing transactions in the ledger accounts. However, the analysis chart will require one more question:

- In each account affected, is the transaction recorded on the *debit* side (that is, do we debit the account?) or the *credit* side (that is, do we credit the account?)?

To answer this question, it is necessary to refer to the debit and credit rules given in Figure 1.8 above.

Having noted the five questions, the analysis chart can be prepared. (**Note** For convenience, the explanation column has been omitted.)

For each transaction, notice that there is an equal amount of debit and credit. This must always occur.

**R Wells**
**Transaction analysis chart**

| Date | Items (accounts) affected | A, L, OE, I or E | Increase or decrease | Amount | Debit or credit |
|---|---|---|---|---|---|
| 2018 | | | | $ | |
| 1 Jul | Cash at bank | A | Increase | 10 000 | Dr |
| | Capital – R Wells | OE | Increase | 10 000 | Cr |
| 2 | Shop fittings | A | Increase | 1 000 | Dr |
| | Cash at bank | A | Decrease | 1 000 | Cr |
| 3 | Purchases | E | Increase | 4 000 | Dr |
| | Creditor – D Pits | L | Increase | 4 000 | Cr |
| 4 | Sales | I | Increase | 2 500 | Cr |
| | Cash at bank | A | Increase | 2 500 | Dr |
| 5 | Wages | E | Increase | 500 | Dr |
| | Cash at bank | A | Decrease | 500 | Cr |
| 6 | Sales | I | Increase | 600 | Cr |
| | Cash at bank | A | Increase | 600 | Dr |

The accounts required to process the transactions of R Wells can now be determined from the analysis chart. These are:

Cash at Bank (asset)
Capital – R Wells (owner's equity)
Shop Fittings (asset)
Purchases (expense)

Creditor – D Pits (liability)
Sales (income)
Wages (expense).

Having established the accounts required, we can now draw up each account. It will then be necessary to record the details of each transaction on the debit or credit side of the appropriate account as indicated by the analysis chart. Carefully examine the following accounts and trace each transaction from the analysis chart to the ledger of R Wells.

| | R Wells | | | | |
|---|---|---|---|---|---|
| | Ledger (using 'T' accounts) | | | | |
| **Dr** | | | **Cr** | | |
| Date | Particulars | Amount | Date | Particulars | Amount |
| **Cash at Bank Account (Asset)** | | | | | |
| 2018 | | $ | 2018 | | $ |
| 1 Jul | Capital – R Wells | 10 000 | 2 Jul | Shop fittings | 1 000 |
| 4 | Sales | 2 500 | 5 | Wages | 500 |
| 6 | Sales | 600 | | | |
| **Capital – R Wells Account (Owner's equity)** | | | | | |
| | | | 2018 | | |
| | | | 1 Jul | Cash at bank | 10 000 |
| **Shop Fittings Account (Asset)** | | | | | |
| 2018 | | | | | |
| 2 Jul | Cash at bank | 1 000 | | | |
| **Purchases Account (Expense)** | | | | | |
| 2018 | | | | | |
| 3 Jul | Creditor – D Pits | 4 000 | | | |
| **Creditor – D Pits Account (Liability)** | | | | | |
| | | | 2018 | | |
| | | | 3 Jul | Purchases | 4 000 |
| **Sales Account (Income)** | | | | | |
| | | | 2018 | | |
| | | | 4 Jul | Cash at bank | 2 500 |
| | | | 6 | Cash at bank | 600 |
| **Wages Account (Expense)** | | | | | |
| 2018 | | | | | |
| 5 Jul | Cash at bank | 500 | | | |

The following points should be noted:

- An account only needs to be created once. For example, only one *Cash at bank* account is opened to record all cash transactions, one *Sales* account to record all sales of stock, one *Wages* account to record all wages and so on.
- Each transaction recorded in the accounts above has an equal debit and credit amount. This self-balancing mechanism used in the accounting process is referred to as 'double entry'.

- Each transaction is cross-referenced when it is recorded in the ledger; the name of the account credited appears in the Particulars column of the account debited (and vice versa). For example, the transaction on 1 July was recorded as a debit of $10 000 in the *Cash at bank* account and a credit of the same amount in the *Capital – R Wells* account, as shown:

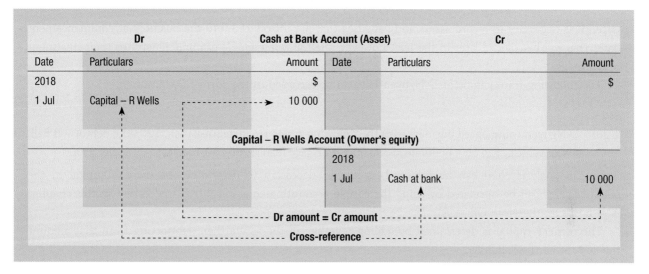

Cross-referencing is a handy learning tool because:

- it serves as a reminder of the double-entry effect of each transaction
- it provides a means of checking the accounts if errors are suspected.

Thus, ledger accounts are a means of classifying and recording transactions into specific element groups as shown in Figure 1.9.

**Figure 1.9    Classifying and recording transactions**

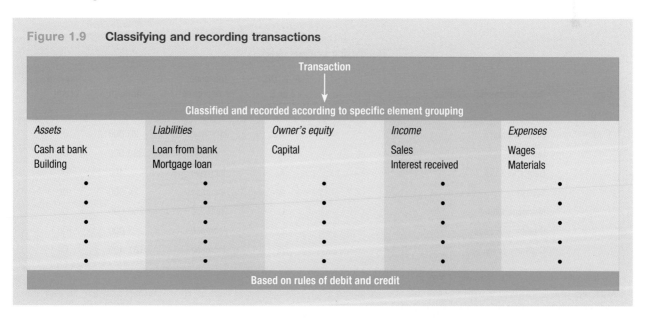

# Assets and liabilities at commencement date

Often it is necessary to record assets and liabilities that are introduced into the business at commencement date. This will be covered later in the text; however, the following simple example illustrates their treatment in the ledger.

The following transactions of D Nguyen have to be recorded in the correct accounts.

*2019*

1 Jul   D Nguyen commenced business with the following assets and liabilities: cash, $20 000; debtor – B Ball, $400; vehicle, $24 000; buildings, $390 000; mortgage loan, $250 000; creditor – E Eadie, $3000.

Before an analysis chart can be prepared, it is first necessary to determine the owner's capital in the business. This can be calculated by using the simple accounting equation introduced earlier in this chapter: A = L + OE, therefore OE = A – L.

The owner's capital is determined by adding together all the assets then subtracting from that amount the sum of all the liabilities.

$$
\begin{aligned}
\text{Owner's equity} \quad &= \quad \text{Total assets} \quad - \quad \text{Total liabilities} \\
&= \quad \$434\,400 \quad - \quad \$253\,000 \\
&= \quad \$181\,400
\end{aligned}
$$

Having established the owner's capital in the business, a simple transaction analysis chart can be prepared.

**D Nguyen**
**Transaction analysis chart**

| Date | Items (accounts) affected | A, L, OE, I or E | Increase or decrease | Amount | Debit or credit[*] |
|------|---------------------------|------------------|----------------------|--------|--------------------|
| 2019 | | | | $ | |
| 1 Jul | Cash at Bank | A | Increase[†] | 20 000 | Dr |
| | Building | A | Increase | 390 000 | Dr |
| | Debtor – B Ball | A | Increase | 400 | Dr |
| | Vehicle | A | Increase | 24 000 | Dr |
| | Mortgage loan | L | Increase | 250 000 | Cr |
| | Creditor – E Eadie | L | Increase | 3 000 | Cr |
| | Capital – D Nguyen | OE | Increase | 181 400 | Cr |

[*]The total value of debits = the total value of credits.

[†]Assets and liabilities introduced at commencement date often are referred to as starting (or opening) balances. For the purposes of applying the debit and credit rules, starting balances are recognised as increases.

From the analysis chart, the required accounts can be established and the transaction details recorded.

| | D Nguyen | | | | |
|---|---|---|---|---|---|
| | **General Ledger** | | | | |
| Date | Particulars | Amount | Date | Particulars | Amount |
| | **Cash at Bank Account (Asset)** | | | | |
| 2019 | | $ | | | $ |
| 1 Jul | Capital – D Nguyen | 20 000 | | | |
| | **Building Account (Asset)** | | | | |
| 2019 | | | | | |
| 1 Jul | Capital – D Nguyen | 390 000 | | | |
| | **Debtor – B Ball Account (Asset)** | | | | |
| 2019 | | | | | |
| 1 Jul | Capital – D Nguyen | 400 | | | |
| | **Vehicle Account (Asset)** | | | | |
| 2019 | | | | | |
| 1 Jul | Capital – D Nguyen | 24 000 | | | |
| | **Mortgage Account (Liability)** | | | | |
| | | | 2019 | | |
| | | | 1 Jul | Capital – D Nguyen | 250 000 |
| | **Creditor – E Eadie Account (Liability)** | | | | |
| | | | 2019 | | |
| | | | 1 Jul | Capital – Nguyen | 3 000 |
| | **Capital – D Nguyen Account (Owner's equity)** | | | | |
| | | | 2019 | | |
| | | | 1 Jul | Sundries* | 181 400 |

*'Sundries' means 'various other accounts'.

The analysis chart serves a useful purpose in summarising the effects of financial transactions on the various elements of a business. It is, however, only a learning technique and on gaining a thorough knowledge of the rules of debits and credits, students should automatically enter transactions into the accounts and bypass the analysis chart.

## Errors

Making errors is a problem in any recording process. It is important that errors are corrected in a proper manner. In a manual accounting system, the incorrect entry should simply be crossed out by a single stroke of the pen and the correct amount written directly above it. For example:

$86

~~$96~~

Using an eraser or correction fluid to obliterate errors is not encouraged as, for control purposes, it is usually necessary to know the original entry that was recorded.

# Balancing the 'T' account

UWATCH 1.6

A UWatch demonstration is available on the CD that accompanies this text for parts of this activity.

In the example of R Wells on pages 50–3, financial transactions were processed using 'T' accounts. To prepare financial reports for R Wells, we must determine the final balance of each account. Because this may be difficult where accounts have numerous debit and credit entries, a standard balancing procedure is adopted. We will use the *Cash at bank* account of R Wells to illustrate the balancing procedure.

| Cash at Bank Account (Asset) | | | | | |
|---|---|---|---|---|---|
| 2018 | | $ | 2018 | | $ |
| 1 Jul | Capital – R Wells | 10 000 | 2 Jul | Shop fittings | 1 000 |
| 4 | Sales | 2 500 | 5 | Wages | 500 |
| 6 | Sales | 600 | | | |

**Step 1** On the side with the greater number of entries, rule parallel lines (as shown in the next account) leaving a space between the last entry and the first ruled line. Then rule similar lines in the corresponding position on the opposite side of the account. Double-ruled lines indicate the *final total* for both sides.

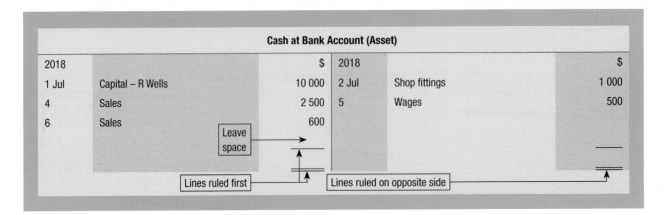

Step 2    Total the side that is the higher in value. Sometimes it may be necessary to total both the debit and credit sides to determine which is the higher. In this example, the debit side of the *Cash at bank* account has the higher value: total debits = $13 100. Enter this amount between the lines ruled in Step 1.

**Cash at Bank Account (Asset)**

| 2018 | | $ | 2018 | | $ |
|------|------|------|------|------|------|
| 1 Jul | Capital – R Wells | 10 000 | 2 Jul | Shop fittings | 1 000 |
| 4 | Sales | 2 500 | 5 | Wages | 500 |
| 6 | Sales | 600 | | | |
| | | ____ | | | ____ |
| | | 13 100 | | | 13 100 |

Value entered

Step 3    Calculate the difference between the totals on both sides and enter this amount into the side lower in value, just above the total entered in Step 2. Enter the date in the date column and the word 'Balance' in the particulars column.

**Cash at Bank Account (Asset)**

| 2018 | | $ | 2018 | | $ |
|------|------|------|------|------|------|
| 1 Jul | Capital – R Wells | 10 000 | 2 Jul | Shop fittings | 1 000 |
| 4 | Sales | 2 500 | 5 | Wages | 500 |
| 6 | Sales | 600 | | | |
| | | | 6 | Balance | 11 600 |
| | | ____ | | | ____ |
| | | 13 100 | | | 13 100 |

Calculated difference

Step 4    The amount calculated in Step 3, the date and the particulars are also entered into the side higher in value, just below the double line.

| Cash at Bank Account (Asset) | | | | | | |
|---|---|---|---|---|---|---|
| 2018 | | | $ | 2018 | | $ |
| 1 Jul | Capital – R Wells | | 10 000 | 2 Jul | Shop fittings | 1 000 |
| 4 | Sales | | 2 500 | 5 | Wages | 500 |
| 6 | Sales | | 600 | | | |
| | | | | 6 | Balance | 11 600 |
| | | | 13 100 | | | 13 100 |
| 6 | Balance | | 11 600 | | Calculated difference | |

The final balance in the *Cash at bank* account has been determined as a debit balance of $11 600.

## Example

Using the procedure outlined above, balance the *Sales* account for R Wells (see page 52).

| Sales Account (Income) | | | | | | |
|---|---|---|---|---|---|---|
| 2018 | | | $ | 2018 | | $ |
| | | | | 4 Jul | Cash at bank | 2 500 |
| | | | | 6 | Cash at bank | 600 |
| 6 Jul | Balance | | 3 100 | | | |
| | | | 3 100 | | | 3 100 |
| | | | | 6 | Balance | 3 100 |

The remaining accounts of R Wells do not require balancing because only one entry has been recorded in each. Consequently, their balances are already known. *Shop fittings*, for example, has a debit balance of $1000; *Capital*, a credit balance of $10 000, and so on.

# Columnar accounts

UWATCH 1.7

A UWatch demonstration is available on the CD that accompanies this text for parts of this activity.

The advantage of using a 'T' account is that it is easy to use and understand. The main disadvantage of this method is that balancing the accounts is laborious and time consuming. This problem can be avoided by using columnar accounts in which the process of balancing is performed after each entry. A columnar account is illustrated opposite.

| Cash at Bank Account | | | | | |
|---|---|---|---|---|---|
| Date | Particulars | | Debit | Credit | Balance |
| | | | $ | $ | $ |
| | | | | | |

The debit and credit rules used for recording transactions into 'T' accounts also apply when using columnar accounts.

# Example

Record the following transactions of A Tran into columnar accounts:

*2017*

27 Jun   Commenced business by depositing $36 000 into a bank account.
28       Bought furniture for $10 000 cash.
29       Bought computer on credit from RZ Equipment Co, $1600.
30       Paid RZ Equipment Co $400 cash.

| A Tran | | | | | |
|---|---|---|---|---|---|
| General Ledger (using columnar accounts) | | | | | |
| Date | Particulars | | Debit | Credit | Balance |
| Cash at Bank Account (Asset) | | | | | |
| 2017 | | | $ | $ | $ |
| 27 Jun | Capital – A Tran | | 36 000 | | 36 000 Dr |
| 28 | Furniture | | | 10 000 | 26 000 Dr |
| 30 | Creditor – RZ Equipment Co | | | 400 | 25 600 Dr |
| Capital – A Tran Account (Owner's equity) | | | | | |
| 2017 | | | | | |
| 27 Jun | Cash at bank | | | 36 000 | 36 000 Cr |
| Furniture Account (Asset) | | | | | |
| 2017 | | | | | |
| 28 Jun | Cash at bank | | 10 000 | | 10 000 Dr |

▶▶

| General Ledger (using columnar accounts) | | | | |
|---|---|---|---|---|
| Date | Particulars | Debit | Credit | Balance |
| **Creditor – RZ Equipment Co Account (Liability)** | | | | |
| 2017 | | $ | $ | $ |
| 29 Jun | Computer | | 1 600 | 1 600 Cr |
| 30 | Cash at bank | 400 | | 1 200 Cr |
| **Computer Account (Asset)** | | | | |
| 2017 | | | | |
| 29 Jun | Creditor – RZ Equipment Co | 1 600 | | 1 600 Dr |

**Note** After each entry in a columnar account, a balance is determined and entered in the balance column. By using the abbreviations 'Dr' and 'Cr' we can show whether the account has a debit or credit balance.

# The trial balance

The transactions of R Wells, D Nguyen and A Tran, above, were processed by using accounts ('T' and columnar account formats, respectively). One method of checking the double-entry rules (debits and credits) used to record these transactions is to prepare a *trial balance*. A trial balance is simply a statement listing each account and its balance.

For example, the following is the trial balance of R Wells as it would appear as at 6 July 2018.

| R Wells Trial balance as at 6 July 2018 | | |
|---|---|---|
| Account | Debit | Credit |
| | $ | $ |
| Cash at bank | 11 600 | |
| Capital – R Wells | | 10 000 |
| Shop fittings | 1 000 | |
| Purchases | 4 000 | |
| Creditor – D Pits | | 4 000 |
| Sales | | 3 100 |
| Wages | 500 | |
| | 17 100 | 17 100 |

The trial balance is an accounting report used for internal checking purposes. It is therefore necessary (as with most reports) to state:

- the owner's name
- the name of the report, in this case 'Trial balance'
- the period covered by the report; for the trial balance the words 'as at' should precede the appropriate date.

The trial balance does not always balance the first time it is prepared; that is, the total debits may not equal the total credits. When this problem arises, the following steps are helpful in determining the reasons for the imbalance.

- Ensure that all the accounts appear on the trial balance.
- Ensure that the balances of each account are recorded in their correct debit or credit column on the trial balance.
- Verify the additions and subtractions in the accounts.
- Look for amounts that may be transcribed incorrectly.

## Limitations of the trial balance

Although the trial balance is a useful means of checking the double-entry rules, there are some errors that the trial balance will not disclose; for example:

- transactions that were completely omitted
- transactions that were entered in the wrong accounts, such as a credit entry recorded in the *Cash at bank* account instead of the *Loan* account
- an arithmetic mistake that was compensated by another mistake of the same value.

# The General Ledger and its supporting ledgers

The General Ledger, in simple terms, is a book (or container – where cards are used – or a computer file) that houses the main accounts of the business. From the trial balance of R Wells, for example, it can be seen that the General Ledger of R Wells has these accounts: *Cash at bank*, *Capital – R Wells*, *Shop fittings*, *Purchases*, *Creditor – D Pits*, *Sales*, *Wages*.

Most businesses find it necessary to have more than one ledger. A large business, for example, would need a special ledger for all its debtors or creditors. Consider the situation where a large company is established with a General Ledger consisting of 600 assorted accounts. After two years of trading, the General Ledger doubles to 1200 accounts, most of which are debtors' accounts. It would be logical for this firm to use only one *control account* for its debtors, the balance of which would represent the combined balances of all debtors' accounts. A similar system could be used for creditors. The complete details of individual debtors and creditors would be recorded in separate, subsidiary ledgers independent of the General Ledger.

One advantage of the subsidiary ledger is that a great amount of detail is removed from the General Ledger, making the preparation of the trial balance and subsequent reports easier and quicker.

Another advantage is that subsidiary ledgers encourage control. The debtors' ledger, for example, provides complete and accurate details of each debtor, which enables a separate credit department to monitor the affairs of each debtor (particularly overdue amounts). Control accounts and subsidiary ledgers will be considered in more detail in later chapters of this book.

 **EXERCISES**

**1.48** What is a ledger account? Explain.

**1.49** For each of the following, answer True or False:
  a   Increases in assets are recorded as credits.
  b   Increases in liabilities are recorded as credits.
  c   Increases in income are recorded as credits.
  d   Increases in expenses are recorded as debits.
  e   Decreases in owner's equity are recorded as debits.
  f   Decreases in liabilities are recorded as debits.

**1.50** Outline the basic differences between a 'T' account and a columnar account.

**1.51** From the following selected transactions of Fiona Shepherd, cleaning contractor, prepare a transaction analysis chart using the headings: date, items affected, type (A, L, OE, I or E), increase/decrease and debit/credit.

  *2019*
  1 Mar   Commenced business operations by depositing $25 000 into a bank account.
  2        Bought equipment for $5000 cash.
  4        Bought cleaning materials on credit from XY Company, $1000.
  10       Received $500 for cleaning a showroom.
  12       Received $10 000 loan from Easy Finances.
  15       Received $250 for cleaning windows for an office complex.
  31       Paid $150 on account to XY Company.

**1.52** From the following selected transactions of C Capelli, motor vehicle retailer, prepare a transaction analysis chart using the headings: date, items affected, type (A, L, OE, I or E), increase/decrease and debit/credit.

  *2018*
  1 Apr   Carmel Capelli commenced business as Capelli Motors by depositing $7500 into a business bank account.
  7        The business purchased premises on credit from A Reilly for $420 000. A cash deposit of $50 000 was paid and a $370 000 mortgage loan was arranged to finance the balance of the purchase price.
  11       Motor vehicles for resale were purchased on credit from Mac & Co for $24 500.
  18       Cash sales of motor vehicles, $16 800.
  20       Paid salesperson's wages, $3500.

26       Sold a vehicle on credit to P Allen for $6500.

31       Paid advertising account with local newspaper, $250.

**Note** An arrangement has been made with the bank for overdraft accommodation up to $100 000.

1.53    This question is available on the CD that accompanies this text.

1.54    The following information relates to As Good As Mum's Laundry Service. Prepare a transaction analysis chart using the headings: date, items affected, type (A, L, OE, I or E), increase/decrease and debit/credit.

*2018*

1 Nov  Commenced business operations by contributing $25 000 into a bank account.

2       Paid a deposit of $75 000 on premises costing $500 000. Mortgage loan for the balance obtained from Bank of Geelong.

5       Purchased a washing machine for $2500 cash.

8       Completed a laundry job for $5000 cash.

12      Repaid $1000 of the mortgage loan.

13      Paid $25 000 interest on mortgage.

15      Paid wages, $2750.

18      Completed a laundry job for Getaway Motels. It was agreed that the $8000 owing would be paid in 30 days.

19      Purchased laundry detergents for $2000 cash.

20      Owner contributed additional capital of $15 000.

21      Owner took $250 of laundry detergents for use at home.

30      Purchased a clothes dryer for $2300 cash.

**Note** An arrangement has been made with the bank for overdraft accommodation up to $100 000.

1.55    Katie Green commenced a dress boutique in St Kilda on 1 January 2019. She asks you to open ledger accounts for her in 'T' form and to record the following transactions:

*2019*

1 Jan  Commenced business as Green's Fashions by contributing $5500 into a business bank account.

2       Purchased stock of dresses on credit from Fancy Dress Clothes for $1500.

3       Cash purchases of dresses, $850.

4       K Green withdrew $300 cash for her personal use.

5       Sales of dresses on credit to B Max, $1350.

6       Rent of $500 was paid in cash.

1.56    C Talimandis opened a theatre restaurant in Darwin on 1 June 2017. She asks you to open ledger accounts for her in 'T' form and to record the following transactions:

*2017*

1 Jun  Contributed $500 000 into a bank account.

2       Purchased premises for $480 000 cash.

5       Purchased equipment on credit from Movie Co., $160 000.

25      Paid advertising, $250.

26      Cash takings, $9750.

         Paid wages, $3500.

27      Paid Movie Co. $10 000 on account.

30      Paid bank charges, $200.

**1.57** In each of the following cases, identify the transaction that would result in the ledger entries given. For example, the entries, debit Cash at Bank account, credit Interest account would have resulted from the transaction: received interest in cash.

a   Debit Wages account, credit Bank account.

b   Debit Motor Vehicle account, credit Creditor – A M Motors account.

c   Debit Debtor – V Knight account, credit Sales account.

d   Debit Power and Light account, credit Cash at Bank account.

e   Debit Buildings account, credit Mortgage Loan account.

f   Debit Loan to B Murray account, credit Cash at Bank account.

g   Debit Cash at Bank account, credit Capital account.

**1.58** Record the following for D Cameron, using 'T' accounts:

*2016*

1 Jan   D Cameron commenced business with the following assets and liabilities: cash, $25 000; furniture, $10 000; delivery vehicle, $28 000; loan from E Halt, $23 000.

**1.59** Open 'T' ledger accounts for B Spender and record the following balances:

| Assets and liabilities at 1 July 2017 | | | |
|---|---:|---|---:|
| | $ | | $ |
| Bank overdraft | 5 000 | Creditor – S Haws | 2 000 |
| Debtor – G Jolly | 9 750 | Motor vehicle | 16 550 |
| Loan from AD Finance | 110 000 | Land and buildings | 284 000 |
| Capital | to be determined | | |

**1.60** Copy and balance the following 'T' accounts as at 31 July 2016.

| Cash at Bank Account | | | | | |
|---|---|---:|---|---|---:|
| **2016** | | **$** | **2016** | | **$** |
| 1 Jul | Capital | 10 000 | 3 Jul | Wages | 1 000 |
| 2 | Fees income | 5 000 | 7 | Advertising | 2 000 |
| | | | 31 | Bank charges | 50 |
| **Fees Income Account** | | | | | |
| | | | 2016 | | |
| | | | 2 Jul | Bank | 5 000 |
| | | | 26 | Debtor – A Jones | 1 130 |

**1.61** G Elliott commenced business as a tyre retailer on 1 April 2019. She asks you to open ledger accounts in columnar format and to record the following transactions.

*2019*

1 Apr  Commenced business by depositing $100 000 in a business bank account.

4      Purchased premises on credit from Carter & Co for $450 000.

       Paid a cash deposit of $50 000 and financed the remainder of the price through a mortgage loan from Donlup Finance.

9      Purchased stocks of tyres for cash, $33 750.

12    Purchased equipment on credit from Lever Co for $23 500.

14    Credit sales of tyres to R Tube, $5250.

19    Paid wages, $5500.

22    Made a mortgage loan repayment to Donlup Finance, $1000.

26    Cash sales of tyres, $17 000.

30    G Elliott withdrew $400 cash for her private use.

**1.62** G Lorry commenced business as a cartage contractor on 1 July 2017. He asks you to open ledger accounts for him in columnar form and to record the following transactions.

*2017*

1 Jul  G Lorry commenced business with the following assets and liabilities: cash, $8500; truck, $212 600; equipment, $42 500; loan from JK Loans, $50 000; premises, $545 000.

3      Completed first cartage job and received fee of $1000 in cash.

4      Completed small cartage job on credit for I Johns, $250.

9      Paid the following expenses: advertising, $200; electricity, $350; telephone, $110.

14    Completed cartage jobs: for cash, $700; on credit, $1550 for E Ham.

19    Paid wages, $2500.

23    G Lorry introduced his own computer for exclusive use by the business. Value, $600.

27    Purchased equipment on credit from Arco Ltd $3600.

31    Received payment in full from debtor I Johns.

**1.63** Refer to the ledger you completed for G Elliott in Exercise 1.61. Prepare a trial balance for the ledger as at 30 April 2019.

**1.64** Refer to the ledger you completed for G Lorry in Exercise 1.62. Prepare a trial balance for the ledger as at 31 July 2017.

**1.65** 'A trial balance is a method of checking the double-entry process of accounting.' Explain.

**1.66** What are the limitations of a trial balance? Provide at least three examples of these limitations in your answer.

**1.67*** A Cristodulou has been in business as a floor coverings retailer for several years. You are required to:
a  open a ledger in 'T' form and record the transactions listed overleaf for the business, Cristodulou Floor Coverings
b  prepare a trial balance for the business as at 31 January 2017.

*2017*

1 Jan    Cristodulou Floor Coverings has the following balances in its ledger at the beginning of the year:

|  | $ |  | $ |
|---|---|---|---|
| Cash at bank | 9 000 | Creditor – D Frost | 3 500 |
| Shop premises | 355 700 | Furniture and fittings | 31 200 |
| Trading stock | 27 600 | Debtor – S Hall | 5 400 |
| Motor vehicle | 12 800 | Capital – A Cristodulou | 438 200 |

4    $4400 was received from debtor – S Hall.

7    Purchased stock of carpets for cash, $2500.

11   Obtained a loan of $75 000 cash from Berber Finance Co.

16   Sales of floor coverings: for cash, $13 500; on credit to S Hall, $2700.

19   Paid the following expenses by cheque: wages, $2350; power and light, $120; cleaning, $570.

24   A Cristodulou withdrew $300 cash to pay his bowling club membership fee.

28   Paid creditor D Frost the balance owed to him.

31   Purchased more stock on credit from D Frost, $5000.

1.68   This question is available on the CD that accompanies this text.

ADDITIONAL EXERCISES   1.69   From the following transactions of Big Book Sales (owner, B Rowe), prepare:

a    a ledger (columnar form) for the business for June 2017.

b    a trial balance as at 30 June 2017.

*2017*

1 Jun    Commenced business with the following assets: cash, $3000; stock of books, $2800; furniture and fittings, $4000.

4    Purchased books on credit from Worm Industries, $3500.

7    Cash sales of books, $2600.

10   B Rowe introduced additional capital in cash, $3000.

13   Credit sales of books $1000 to N Cooke.

17   Sold some fittings for cash at their cost price of $200.

19   Paid the following amounts by cheque: rent, $600; wages, $750.

22   Paid Worm Industries $2000 on account.

25   Purchased shop fittings on credit from AL Design for $2600, paying a deposit of $500.

29   Received the amount owing from N Cooke.

30   Paid wages, $700.

1.70   This question is available on the CD that accompanies this text.

ADDITIONAL EXERCISES   1.71   'The General Ledger is supported by other ledgers in an accounting system.' Discuss.

1.72   What advantages do subsidiary ledgers offer in an accounting system? Discuss.

1.73    L Grass started a lawn-mowing business on 1 October 2018. He asks you to open ledger accounts for his business, to record the transactions listed below and to prepare a trial balance as at 14 October 2018.
**Note** In this exercise and the others remaining in this section, you should use columnar form ledger accounts.

*2018*

1 Oct    Commenced business operations by depositing $2000 in a bank account styled 'Grass's Mowing Service' with the Bank of Canberra.

3    Purchased two mowers for cash, $1000.
Purchased a motor vehicle for $16 000 on credit from TY Motors.

4    Purchased petrol and oil supplies from Fred's Garage of Acton on credit, $300.

5    Grass decided that his lawn-mowing business would use his personally owned trailer exclusively. Value of trailer, $600.

6    Paid $120 for advertising pamphlets.

7    Paid $200 to distribute pamphlets in Canberra.

8    Paid $100 for advertisement placed in local newspaper.

9    Mowed lawns for K Bluegrass and received $140 cash.

11    Mowed lawns for W Clover and received $40.
Purchased wife's birthday present by drawing a cash cheque on the business's bank account, $300. Paid $100 to TY Motors.

12    Purchased tools to repair mowers, $100 cash.
Cut lawns for I Couch on the understanding that Couch would pay $50 next week.

13    Paid $20 to Sam's Garage of Yass for mending a puncture to the motor vehicle.

14    Cut lawns for the local church and received $190, paying $50 to a pensioner for assisting.

1.74*    S Panda opened up a health studio called the Big Cat Studio on 1 November 2017. She asks you to open ledger accounts for her, to record the following transactions and to prepare a trial balance as at 30 November 2017.

*2017*

1 Nov    Commenced business operations by contributing $50 000 cash and a motor vehicle worth $9000.

2    Paid $50 000 deposit on premises costing $250 000. $200 000 mortgage loan obtained from Nick Finances Pty Ltd.

3    Additional cash contributed by S Panda, $20 000.
Purchased fixtures and fittings, $10 000 cash; equipment, $3000 cash.

8    Purchased computer on credit from Myroc Computers valued at $1800.

9    Received cash for services, $200.
Paid electricity, $100.
Commission paid, $50.

12    Services provided on credit to W Hip, $250; F Lash, $100.

14    Paid advertising, $120; paid office wages, $1000.

15    Paid rates, $1500.

16    Received cash for services, $3500.
Provided services on credit to F Lash, $270.

17    S Panda cashed a cheque on the business bank account and gave the money to a friend, $1750.

20    W Hip paid his account in full.

Received cash for services provided, $4500.

22    Paid White Wash Cleaners $130 for laundering expenses.

25    Paid office wages, $1000.

1.75    G Bloom is the proprietor of Bloom's Florist Shop. You are required to open a ledger to record the following transactions, and to prepare a trial balance as at 31 July 2019.

| Trial balance as at 1 July 2019 | | |
|---|---|---|
| Account | Debit | Credit |
| | $ | $ |
| Cash at bank | 29 000 | |
| Debtor – A Pansy | 16 900 | |
| Creditor – P Ivy | | 12 200 |
| Stock | 22 600 | |
| Mortgage loan | | 190 000 |
| Premises | 223 500 | |
| Shop fittings | 4 400 | |
| Equipment | 32 200 | |
| Capital – G Bloom | | 126 400 |
| | $328 600 | $328 600 |

*Transactions for July 2019 are:*

1 Jul    Cash sales, $2500.

4    Received $8200 from debtor A Pansy.

11    Credit purchases of stock from P Ivy, $4900.

13    Credit sales to A Pansy, $1900.

15    Purchased equipment on credit from Flowerquip Co for $1700. Paid a cash deposit of $500.

16    G Bloom withdrew $1000 cash to pay a gambling debt.

19    Received commission, $480.

20    Paid casual wages, $80.

24    Paid creditor P Ivy the amount owed on 1 July.

26    Cash purchases, $3400.

Paid interest on mortgage loan, $1000.

28    Cash sales, $3100.

31    Paid municipal rates, $360.

# SOLUTIONS

1.67   a

| Cristodulou Floor Coverings | | | | | |
|---|---|---|---|---|---|
| General Ledger | | | | | |
| Date | Particulars | Amount | Date | Particulars | Amount |
| Cash at Bank Account (Asset) | | | | | |
| | | $ | 2017 | | $ |
| 2017 | Balance | 9 000 | 7 Jan | Purchases | 2 500 |
| 1 Jan | Debtor – S Hall | 4 400 | 19 | Wages | 2 350 |
| 4 | Berber Finance Co | 75 000 | | Power and light | 120 |
| 16 | Sales | 13 500 | 11 | Cleaning | 570 |
| | | | 24 | Drawings – A Cristodulou | 300 |
| | | | 28 | Creditor – D Frost | 3 500 |
| | | | 31 | Balance | 92 560 |
| | | 101 900 | | | 101 900 |
| 31 | Balance | 92 560 | | | |
| Shop Premises (Asset) | | | | | |
| 2017 | | | | | |
| 1 Jan | Balance | 355 700 | | | |
| Trading Stock Account (Asset) | | | | | |
| 2017 | | | | | |
| 1 Jan | Balance | 27 600 | | | |
| Motor Vehicle Account (Asset) | | | | | |
| 2017 | | | | | |
| 1 Jan | Balance | 12 800 | | | |
| Creditor – D Frost Account (Liability) | | | | | |
| 2017 | | | 2017 | | |
| 28 Jan | Cash at bank | 3 500 | 1 Jan | Balance | 3 500 |
| 31 | Balance | 5 000 | 31 | Purchases | 5 000 |
| | | 8 500 | | | 8 500 |
| | | | 31 | Balance | 5 000 |

| Date | Particulars | Amount | Date | Particulars | Amount |
|------|-------------|--------|------|-------------|--------|
| | | **General Ledger** | | | |
| | | | | | |
| | | **Furniture and Fittings Account (Asset)** | | | |
| 2017 | | $ | 2017 | | $ |
| 1 Jan | Balance | 31 200 | | | |
| | | **Debtor – S Hall Account (Asset)** | | | |
| 2017 | | | 2017 | | |
| 1 Jan | Balance | 5 400 | 4 Jan | Cash at bank | 4 400 |
| 16 | Sales | 2 700 | 31 | Balance | 3 700 |
| | | 8 100 | | | 8 100 |
| 31 | Balance | 3 700 | | | |
| | | **Capital I – A Cristodulou Account (Owner's equity)** | | | |
| | | | 2017 | | |
| | | | 1 Jan | Balance | 438 200 |
| | | **Purchases Account (Expense)** | | | |
| 2017 | | | 2017 | | |
| 7 Jan | Cash at bank | 2 500 | | | |
| 31 | Creditor – D Frost | 5 000 | 31 Jan | Balance | 7 500 |
| | | 7 500 | | | 7 500 |
| 31 | Balance | 7 500 | | | |
| | | **Loan from Berber Finance Co Account (Liability)** | | | |
| | | | 2017 | | |
| | | | 11 Jan | Cash at bank | 75 000 |
| | | **Sales Account (Income)** | | | |
| 2017 | | | 2017 | | |
| | | | 16 Jan | Cash at bank | 13 500 |
| 31 Jan | Balance | 16 200 | | Debtor – S Hall | 2 700 |
| | | 16 200 | | | 16 200 |
| | | | 31 | Balance | 16 200 |
| | | **Wages Account (Expense)** | | | |
| 2017 | | | | | |
| 19 Jan | Cash at bank | 2 350 | | | |

▶▶

| General Ledger | | | | | |
|---|---|---|---|---|---|
| Date | Particulars | Amount | Date | Particulars | Amount |
| **Power and Light Account (Expense)** | | | | | |
| 2017 | | $ | 2017 | | $ |
| 19 Jan | Cash at bank | 120 | | | |
| **Cleaning Account (Expense)** | | | | | |
| 2017 | | | | | |
| 19 Jan | Cash at bank | 570 | | | |
| **Drawings – A Cristodulou Account (Owner's equity)** | | | | | |
| 2017 | | | | | |
| 24 Jan | Cash at bank | 300 | | | |

b

**Cristodulou Floor Coverings**
**Trial balance as at 31 January 2017**

| Account | Debit | Credit |
|---|---|---|
| | $ | $ |
| Cash at bank | 92 560 | |
| Shop premises | 355 700 | |
| Trading stock | 27 600 | |
| Motor vehicle | 12 800 | |
| Creditor – D Frost | | 5 000 |
| Furniture and fittings | 31 200 | |
| Debtor – S Hall | 3 700 | |
| Capital – A Cristodulou | | 438 200 |
| Purchases | 7 500 | |
| Loan from Berber Finance Co | | 75 000 |
| Sales | | 16 200 |
| Wages | 2 350 | |
| Power and light | 120 | |
| Cleaning | 570 | |
| Drawings – A Cristodulou | 300 | |
| | $534 400 | $534 400 |

**1.74    a**

| | | | | |
|---|---|---|---|---|
| | Big Cat Studio | | | |
| | General Ledger | | | |
| Date | Particulars | Debit | Credit | Balance |
| **Cash at Bank Account (Asset)** | | | | |
| 2017 | | $ | $ | $ |
| 1 Nov | Capital – S Panda | 50 000 | | 50 000 Dr |
| 2 | Premises | | 50 000 | Nil |
| 3 | Capital – S Panda | 20 000 | | 20 000 Dr |
| | Fixtures and fittings | | 10 000 | 10 000 Dr |
| | Equipment | | 3 000 | 7 000 Dr |
| 9 | Fees | 200 | | 7 200 Dr |
| | Electricity | | 100 | 7 100 Dr |
| | Commission | | 50 | 7 050 Dr |
| 14 | Advertising | | 20 | 7 030 Dr |
| 14 Jun | Office wages | | 1 000 | 6 030 Dr |
| 15 | Rates | | 1 500 | 4 530 Dr |
| 16 | Fees | 3 500 | | 8 030 Dr |
| 17 | Drawings – S Panda | | 1 750 | 6 280 Dr |
| 20 | Debtor – W Hip | 250 | | 6 530 Dr |
| | Fees | 4 500 | | 11 030 Dr |
| 22 | Laundering | | 130 | 10 900 Dr |
| 25 | Office wages | | 1 000 | 9 900 Dr |
| **Motor Vehicle Account (Asset)** | | | | |
| 2017 | | | | |
| 1 Nov | Capital – S Panda | 9 000 | | 9 000 Dr |
| **Capital – S Panda Account (Owner's equity)** | | | | |
| 2017 | | | | |
| 1 Nov | Sundries | | 59 000 | 5 000 Cr |
| 3 | Cash at bank | | 20 000 | 79 000 Cr |
| **Premises Account (Asset)** | | | | |
| 2017 | | | | |
| 2 Nov | Sundries | 250 000 | | 250 000 Dr |

| Date | Particulars | Debit | Credit | Balance |
|------|-------------|-------|--------|---------|
| — General Ledger | | | | |

| Date | Particulars | Debit | Credit | Balance |
|------|-------------|-------|--------|---------|
| **Mortgage Loan on Premises Account (Liability)** | | | | |
| 2017 | | $ | $ | $ |
| 2 Nov | Premises | | 200 000 | 200 000 Cr |
| **Fixtures and Fittings Account (Asset)** | | | | |
| 2017 | | | | |
| 3 Nov | Cash at bank | 10 000 | | 10 000 Dr |
| **Equipment Account (Asset)** | | | | |
| 2017 | | | | |
| 3 Nov | Cash at bank | 3 000 | | 3 000 Dr |
| **Computer Account (Asset)** | | | | |
| 2017 | | | | |
| 8 Nov | Creditor – Myroc Computers | 1 800 | | 1 800 Dr |
| **Creditor – Myroc Computers Account (Liability)** | | | | |
| 2017 | | | | |
| 8 Nov | Computer | | 1 800 | 1 800 Cr |
| **Fees Account (Income)** | | | | |
| 2017 | | | | |
| 9 Nov | Cash at bank | | 200 | 200 Cr |
| 12 | Debtor – W Hip | | 250 | 450 Cr |
| 12 | Debtor – F Lash | | 100 | 550 Cr |
| 16 | Cash at bank | | 3 500 | 4 050 Cr |
| | Debtor – F Lash | | 270 | 4 320 Cr |
| 20 | Cash at bank | | 4 500 | 8 820 Cr |
| **Electricity Account (Expense)** | | | | |
| 2017 | | | | |
| 9 Nov | Cash at bank | 100 | | 100 Dr |
| **Commission Account (Expense)** | | | | |
| 2017 | | | | |
| 9 Nov | Cash at bank | 50 | | 50 Dr |
| **Debtor – W Hip Account (Asset)** | | | | |
| 2017 | | | | |
| 12 Nov | Fees | 250 | | 250 Dr |
| 20 | Cash at bank | | 250 | Nil |

| General Ledger | | | | |
|---|---|---|---|---|
| Date | Particulars | Debit | Credit | Balance |
| **Debtor – F Lash Account (Asset)** | | | | |
| 2017 | | $ | $ | $ |
| 12 Nov | Fees | 100 | | 100 Dr |
| 16 | Fees | 270 | | 370 Dr |
| **Advertising Account (Expense)** | | | | |
| 2017 | | | | |
| 14 Nov | Cash at bank | 20 | | 20 Dr |
| **Office Wages Account (Expense)** | | | | |
| 2017 | | | | |
| 14 Nov | Cash at bank | 1 000 | | 1 000 Dr |
| 25 | Cash at bank | 1 000 | | 2 000 Dr |
| **Rates Account (Expense)** | | | | |
| 2017 | | | | |
| 15 Nov | Cash at bank | 1 500 | | 1 500 Dr |
| **Drawings – S Panda Account (Owner's equity)** | | | | |
| 2017 | | | | |
| 17 Nov | Cash at bank | 1 750 | | 1 750 Dr |
| **Laundering Account (Expense)** | | | | |
| 2017 | | | | |
| 22 Nov | Cash at bank | 130 | | 130 Dr |

b

| Big Cat Studio Trial balance as at 30 November 2017 | | |
|---|---|---|
| Account | Debit | Credit |
| | $ | $ |
| Cash at bank | 9 900 | |
| Motor vehicle | 9 000 | |
| Capital – S Panda | | 79 000 |
| Premises | 250 000 | |
| Mortgage loan on premises | | 200 000 |

| Account | Debit | Credit |
|---|---|---|
| | $ | $ |
| Fixtures and fittings | 10 000 | |
| Equipment | 3 000 | |
| Computer | 1 800 | |
| Creditor – Myroc Computers | | 1 800 |
| Fees | | 8 820 |
| Electricity | 100 | |
| Commission | 50 | |
| Debtor – F Lash | 370 | |
| Advertising | 20 | |
| Office wages | 2 000 | |
| Rates | 1 500 | |
| Drawings – S Panda | 1 750 | |
| Laundering | 130 | |
| | $289 620 | $289 620 |

# Trading entries

Figure 1.10 summarises the effect of profits and losses from trading on the owner's capital.

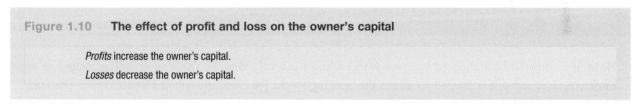

**Figure 1.10    The effect of profit and loss on the owner's capital**

*Profits* increase the owner's capital.

*Losses* decrease the owner's capital.

Both profits and losses are the result of the process of trading, which consists of buying and selling stock (in the case of a retailer) or providing services (in the case of a service business). In practice, trading is not always a simple process and for some businesses the recording of trading transactions can become quite complicated.

This section will detail the customary accounting rules required to process common trading transactions. For this purpose we will return to the example of Sammy's Mini Mart. Some of the transactions undertaken by the business during its second month of trading will be examined in the following pages.

## Purchase of stock

In this section, the physical (periodic) method of recording stock outlined on pages 41–2 will be used; thus, all purchases of stock are to be treated as expenses.

*Cash purchases of stock*

2 Aug   The business made a $2000 cash purchase of stock for resale from I Koochew.

The ledger entries for Sammy's Mini Mart would be:

| Purchases Account (Expense) | | | | | |
|---|---|---|---|---|---|
| 2016 | | $ | | | $ |
| 2 Aug | Bank | 2 000 | | | |
| **Bank Account (Asset)** | | | | | |
| | | | 2016 | | |
| | | | 2 Aug | Purchases | 2 000 |

*Purchases of stock on credit*

If the above purchase from I Koochew had been on credit, the ledger entries would be:

| Purchases Account (Expense) | | | | | |
|---|---|---|---|---|---|
| 2016 | | $ | | | $ |
| 2 Aug | Creditor – I Koochew | 2 000 | | | |
| **Creditor – I Koochew Account (Liability)** | | | | | |
| | | | 2016 | | |
| | | | 2 Aug | Purchases | 2 000 |

**Note** If Sammy had commenced business with trading stock valued at $1000, this would be treated as an asset. An asset account is created to record the opening stock. This account remains intact during the trading period. Subsequent purchases of stock are expenses. Figure 1.11 summarises the treatment of stock for accounting purposes.

Figure 1.11    **Treatment of stock for accounting purposes**

| | |
|---|---|
| To record stock brought into the business at commencement date | → Dr Stock (asset) account → Cr Capital (owner's equity) account |
| To record purchases of stock during the trading period | → Dr Purchases (expense) account → Cr Creditor (liability) account |
| | OR |
| | Cr Cash at Bank (asset) account, if cash used instead of credit |

# Example

UWATCH 1.8

A UWatch demonstration is available on the CD that accompanies this text for parts of this activity.

*2019*

1 Jun   M Amrain commenced business with the following assets: cash at bank, $20 000; stock, $4000.

2        Bought stock for resale, $2000, on credit from Ace Company.

The ledger entries for M Amrain would be:

| Stock Account (Asset) | | | | | |
|---|---|---|---|---|---|
| 2019 | | $ | | | $ |
| 1 Jun | Capital – M Amrain | 4 000 | | | |
| **Cash at Bank Account (Asset)** | | | | | |
| 2019 | | | | | |
| 1 Jun | Capital – M Amrain | 20 000 | | | |
| **Capital – M Amrain Account (Owner's equity)** | | | | | |
| | | | 2019 | | |
| | | | 1 Jun | Sundries | 24 000 |
| **Purchases Account (Expense)** | | | | | |
| 2019 | | | | | |
| 2 Jun | Creditor – Ace Co | 2 000 | | | |
| **Creditor – Ace Co Account (Liability)** | | | | | |
| | | | 2019 | | |
| | | | 2 June | Purchases | 2 000 |

## *Purchases returns and allowances*

It is not uncommon in business for goods to be purchased initially and then subsequently returned to the supplier for a variety of reasons (such as damage, oversupply etc.). Consider the following transaction:

*2016*

3 Aug   Sammy's Mini Mart returned damaged stock $400 to I Koochew. (This stock had been purchased on credit.)

The ledger entries for Sammy's Mini Mart would be:

| Creditor – I Koochew Account (Liability) | | | | | |
|---|---|---|---|---|---|
| 2016 | | $ | 2016 | | $ |
| 3 Aug | Purchases returns and allowances | 400 | 2 Aug | Purchases (previous entry) | 2 000 |
| Purchases Returns and Allowances Account (Expense offset) | | | | | |
| | | | 2016 | | |
| | | | 3 Aug | Creditor – I Koochew | 400 |

In analysing these entries, we note the following: first, Creditor – I Koochew's account was reduced because faulty stock was returned.

Second, a new account, *Purchases Returns and Allowances*, was created to record the amount of the *return*. Purchases returns and allowances effectively decrease purchases expense and are thus regarded as an offset (or contra adjustment) against purchases expense. Some accountants also refer to this account as a 'negative expense', but the more appropriate terminology in practice is an 'expense offset' or 'expense contra' account. Note also that the terms 'offset' and 'contra' mean the same thing, and it is a matter of personal choice as to which term is used (although, once selected, students should use that term consistently). Note further that while it may seem logical to directly decrease the *Purchases* account by the amount of the returns (by crediting and thus decreasing the amount in that account), it is important to establish a new account to enable specific financial information relating to purchases returns and allowances to be captured separately. In this way management will be able to assess the level of returns and make decisions accordingly. For instance, if returns were unusually high for a particular accounting period, alternative suppliers might need to be sourced. Therefore, the credit side of the *Purchases* account remains intact, and instead, a *Purchases Returns and Allowances* account is used to record all purchases returns and allowances. This procedure is demonstrated in the accounts below.

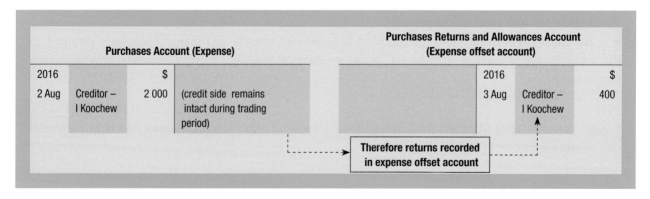

If the transactions of Sammy's Mini Mart above represented a return of goods previously purchased *for cash*, the entries required in the ledger of Sammy's Mini Mart would be as follows:

| Cash at Bank Account (Asset) | | | | Purchases Returns and Allowances Account (Expense offset account) | | |
|---|---|---|---|---|---|---|
| 2016 | | $ | | 2016 | | $ |
| 3 Aug | Purchases returns and allowances | 400 | | 3 Aug | Cash at bank | 400 |

The *Purchases Returns and Allowances* account also can be used for allowances where the price of goods is lowered as a result of damage or misdescription.

## Sale of stock

A UWatch demonstration is available on the CD that accompanies this text for parts of this activity.

UWATCH 1.9

*2016*

4 Aug   Sammy's Mini Mart sold goods on credit to A Barclay, $600.

The ledger entries for this transaction would be:

| Sales Account (Income) | | | Debtor – A Barclay Account (Asset) | | |
|---|---|---|---|---|---|
| 2016 | | $ | 2016 | | $ |
| 4 Aug | Debtor – A Barclay | 600 | 4 Aug | Sales | 600 |

Or, if the goods had been sold for cash, $600:

| Sales Account (Income) | | | Cash at Bank Account (Asset) | | |
|---|---|---|---|---|---|
| 2016 | | $ | 2016 | | $ |
| 4 Aug | Cash at Bank | 600 | 4 Aug | Sales | 600 |

## Sales returns and allowances

Just as goods purchased may be returned to the supplier, goods sold by a business may be returned by customers. This is referred to as *sales returns and allowances*.

To examine the treatment of sales returns and allowances (returns of goods sold by the business), consider two related transactions for Sammy's Mini Mart:

*2016*

5 Aug   The business sold goods for cash $4500 to Rob's Diner.

| Sales Account (Income) | | | | Cash at Bank Account (Asset) | | | |
|---|---|---|---|---|---|---|---|
| | 2016 | | $ | 2016 | | $ | |
| | 5 Aug | Cash at Bank | 4 500 | 5 Aug | Sales | 4 500 | |

*2016*

6 Aug   Rob's Diner returned goods costing $500 and was given a cash refund.

| Cash at Bank Account (Asset) | | | | | | Sales Returns and Allowances Account (Income offset account) | | | |
|---|---|---|---|---|---|---|---|---|---|
| 2016 | | $ | 2016 | | $ | 2016 | | $ | |
| 5 Aug | Sales (previous entry) | 4 500 | 6 Aug | Sales returns and allowances | 500 | 6 Aug | Cash at bank | 500 | |

For similar reasons to those described above for purchases returns and allowances, a new separate account – *Sales Returns and Allowances* – is established to record the amount of sales returns, thus keeping the debit side of the sales account intact during the year. The *Sales Returns and Allowances* account is, in effect, an account that reduces sales, and in this regard it is also an offset or contra account (see the discussion above concerning purchases returns and allowances). Indeed, establishing a separate account for sales returns and allowances will provide additional information that could be useful for management. For instance, highlighting excessive returns during the accounting period could indicate problems relating to product quality or storage and distribution, and so on. The accounting procedures for sales returns and allowances are demonstrated in the accounts below.

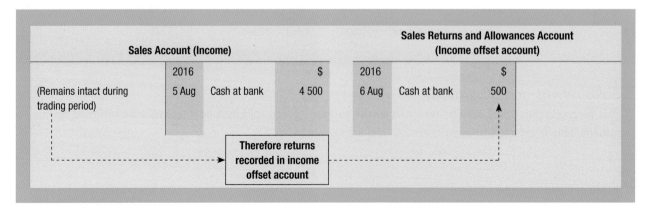

| Sales Account (Income) | | | | Sales Returns and Allowances Account (Income offset account) | | | |
|---|---|---|---|---|---|---|---|
| (Remains intact during trading period) | 2016 | | $ | 2016 | | $ | |
| | 5 Aug | Cash at bank | 4 500 | 6 Aug | Cash at bank | 500 | |

**Therefore returns recorded in income offset account**

## Credit sales returns and allowances

If the sales to Rob's Diner on 5 August had been on credit, Rob's Diner would not have been given a cash refund for goods returned on 6 August. Instead, Rob's Diner would have been allowed a reduction in the amount it owed to Sammy's Mini Mart.

In this case the ledger for Sammy's Mini Mart would have the entries shown below.

| Sales Account (Income) | | | Debtor – Rob's Diner Account (Asset) | | | | | |
|---|---|---|---|---|---|---|---|---|
| 2016 | | $ | 2016 | | $ | 2016 | | $ |
| 5 Aug | Debtor – Rob's Diner | 4 500 | 5 Aug | Sales | 4 500 | 6 Aug | Sales returns and allowances | 500 |

| Sales Returns and Allowances Account (Income offset account) | | |
|---|---|---|
| 2016 | | $ |
| 6 Aug | Debtor – Rob's Diner | 500 |

The *Sales Returns and Allowances* account also can be used for sales allowances; that is, where the price of goods is lowered as a result of damage or misdescription.

## Withdrawal of stock by the owner

Earlier in this chapter, the drawings of cash by the owner were examined. You will remember that when an owner withdraws cash from the business for personal use, this transaction is recorded as a debit entry in the *Drawings* account (owner's equity) and a credit entry in the *Bank* account. Sometimes owners withdraw stock from the business for personal use. Consider the following transaction:

*2016*
8 Aug   Sammy Silvagni took home groceries costing $200.

The ledger entries for Sammy's Mini Mart would be:

| Drawings – S Silvagni Account (Owner's equity) | | | | Purchases Account (Expense) | | | | |
|---|---|---|---|---|---|---|---|---|
| 2016 | | $ | | 2016 | | $ | 2016 | $ |
| 8 Aug | Purchases | 200 | | (previous balance) | 2 000 | 8 Aug | Drawings – S Silvagni | 200 |

As Sammy is withdrawing stock and not cash, the business's bank account is not affected.

Withdrawals of stock are not recorded in the *Stock* account; the value of stock is never altered during the year. Instead, a credit entry is made in the *Purchases* account, thereby reducing the amount of purchases expense to the business, because the goods were not in fact used by the business but by the owner. This type of transaction is the only exception to the rule of keeping the credit side of the *Purchases* account intact during the year.

UWATCH 1.10

### Discount allowed to debtors

A UWatch demonstration is available on the CD that accompanies this text for parts of this activity.

The main reason for allowing a discount to debtors is to encourage prompt payment. The effect of a discount is two-fold.

1  It reduces the amount owing by the debtor.
2  It represents an expense to the business, as it is a necessary cost of collecting debts.

*2016*

10 Aug   A Digger, a debtor to Sammy's Mini Mart, paid the amount due as follows:

| | |
|---|---:|
| Balance in account | $300 |
| *less* Discount | 20 |
| Cheque received | $280 |

The ledger entries to show this would be:

| **Debtor – I Digger Account (Asset)** | | | | | | **Cash at Bank Account (Asset)** | | | |
|---|---|---:|---|---|---:|---|---|---:|---|
| 2016 | | $ | 2016 | | $ | 2016 | | $ | |
| | (Existing balance) | 300 | | Cash at Bank | 280 | 10 Aug | Debtor – A Digger | 280 | |
| | | | | Discount expense | 20 | | | | |

| **Discount Expense Account (Expense)** | | |
|---|---|---:|
| 2016 | | $ |
| 10 Aug | Debtor – A Digger | 20 |

### Discount received from a creditor

*2016*

13 Aug   Amount owing to I Koochew (creditor) was settled by Sammy's Mini Mart as follows:

| | |
|---|---:|
| Balance in account | $4 100 |
| *less* Discount | 25 |
| Cheque drawn and sent | $4 075 |

The ledger entries to show this would be:

| Debtor – I Koochew Account (Asset) | | | | | | Cash at Bank Account (Asset) | | | |
|---|---|---|---|---|---|---|---|---|---|
| 2016 | | $ | 2016 | | $ | | 2016 | | $ |
| 13 Aug | Cash at bank | 4 075 | | (Existing balance) | 4 100 | | 13 Aug | Creditor – I Koochew | 4 075 |
| | Discount income | 25 | | | | | | | |

| Discount Income Account (Income) | | | |
|---|---|---|---|
| | | 2016 | $ |
| | | 13 Aug  Creditor – I Koochew | 25 |

Discount received from creditors is recognised as *income*, as it is an amount a business earns by paying its creditors promptly.

## Late fees charged on overdue debtors' accounts

Charging late fees on overdue debtors' accounts is another means of encouraging prompt payment. The late fee has two effects.

1 It increases the amount owing by the debtor.
2 It is income to the business.

On 15 August Sammy's Mini Mart sent a statement of account to A Barclay, which advised as follows:

| | |
|---|---|
| Amount owing 3 months overdue | $100 |
| *plus* Late fee | 10 |
| Please pay promptly | $110 |

The ledger entries for Sammy's Mini Mart would be:

| Debtor – A Barclay Account (Asset) | | | | Late Fees Income Account (Income) | | | |
|---|---|---|---|---|---|---|---|
| 2016 | | $ | | | 2016 | | $ |
| | (existing balance, including overdue amount) | 700 | | | 15 Aug | Debtor – A Barclay | 10 |
| 15 Aug | Late fees income | 10 | | | | | |

Sammy's Mini Mart also could be charged late fees on overdue accounts owing to creditors, but, of course, Sammy would ensure always that his business paid its creditors promptly!

### Bad debts

A bad debt is a defined as debt that is uncollectable – that is, where a debtor is unable to pay the balance due on an account. As soon as it is positively known that a debt has become bad (for instance, as soon as official advice has been received from an appropriate authority, such as a solicitor, that a debt is uncollectable), the debt is immediately written off by crediting the debtor's account, thus eliminating any balance remaining in that account. A bad debt represents money lost by a business and is therefore regarded as an expense. Note that another expense related to debtors is doubtful debts, which are discussed in detail in a later section of the text (page 354).

*2016*

21 Aug   Sammy's Mini Mart received notification from A Watson, solicitor, that A Barclay had become bankrupt and would be unable to pay the amount due, $710.

The ledger entries for Sammy's Mini Mart would be:

| Debtor – A Barclay Account (Asset) | | | | | | Bad Debts Account (Expense) | | | |
|---|---|---|---|---|---|---|---|---|---|
| 2016 | | $ | 2016 | | $ | 2016 | | $ | |
| | (Existing balance) | 710 | 21 Aug | Bad debts | 710 | 21 Aug | Debtor – A Barclay | 710 | |

# Goods and services tax (GST)

To this point in the text, the impact of GST on business transactions has largely been ignored. Most businesses are now required to account for GST on a wide range of transactions, which complicates the recording process.

The accounting treatment of GST will be illustrated fully from Chapter 2 onwards.

## Comprehensive example

This comprehensive example shows processing of the transactions of Jeremy's Wholesale Hardware for the month of February 2017. On the following pages you will find:

- the ledger of Jeremy's Wholesale Hardware for February 2017, commencing with the existing balances in the accounts at 1 February
- a trial balance as at 28 February 2017

*Transaction information*

*2017*

1 Feb    Jeremy's Wholesale Hardware had the following balances in its ledger, carried forward from January:

| Account | Debit | Credit |
| --- | ---: | ---: |
| | $ | $ |
| Bad debts | 1 420 | |
| Motor vans | 20 200 | |
| Cash at bank | 83 810 | |
| Office equipment | 2 000 | |
| Capital – Jeremy Jolly | | 100 200 |
| Creditor – Pots and Pans Ltd | | 18 000 |
| Creditor – Felix Supply Co | | 30 000 |
| Discount expense | 40 | |
| Discount income | | 50 |
| Drawings – Jeremy Jolly | 2 400 | |
| Furniture and fittings | 18 400 | |
| Late fees income | | 20 |
| Loan from Ladder Finance Co | | 6 000 |
| Purchases | 16 600 | |
| Purchases returns and allowances | | 800 |
| Shop equipment | 36 000 | |
| Rent expense | 400 | |
| Sales | | 28 200 |
| Sales returns and allowances | 1 000 | |
| Wages expense | 1 000 | |
| | $183 270 | $183 270 |

2 Feb    Purchased stock on credit from A Walters, $1000.

3        Cash purchases, $400.

         Sold the motor vans for cash at cost, $20 200.

4        Bought delivery truck on credit from Beta Trucks, $30 000.

5        Returned faulty stock previously bought for cash, $100.

8        Received a reduction in account from A Walters for goods damaged in transit, $40.

9        Cash sales, $400.

10      Paid wages, $900.

Paid insurance, $200.

11      Credit sales to J Martini, $4000.

19      Credit sales to A Rigosi, $1000.

20      Paid wages, $800.

J Martini returned faulty goods, $100.

21      Cash sales, $1200.

22      Jeremy Jolly withdrew for personal use: cash $200, and stock $100.

23      Paid creditor – A Walters the amount owing less 10% discount.

25      Charged debtor – J Martini $10 late fee on overdue account.

28      A Rigosi settled his account less $20 discount.

J Martini declared bankrupt. Received a final cheque for $2500 from his solicitor.

# Solution

1   The General Ledger of Jeremy's Wholesale Hardware:

| Jeremy's Wholesale Hardware Store | | | | | |
|---|---|---|---|---|---|
| **General Ledger** | | | | | |
| Date | Particulars | | Debit | Credit | Balance |
| **Bad Debts Account** | | | | | |
| 2017 | | | $ | $ | $ |
| 1 Feb | Balance | | | | 1 420 Dr |
| 28 | Debtor – J Martini | | 1 410 | | 2 830 Dr |
| **Motor Vans Account** | | | | | |
| 2017 | | | | | |
| 1 Feb | Balance | | | | 20 200 Dr |
| 3 | Cash at bank | | | 20 200 | Nil |
| **Cash at Bank Account** | | | | | |
| 2017 | | | | | |
| 1 Feb | Balance | | | | 83 810 Dr |
| 3 | Purchases | | | 400 | 83 410 Dr |
| | Motor vans | | 20 200 | | 103 610 Dr |
| 5 | Purchases returns and allowances | | 100 | | 103 710 Dr |
| 9 | Sales | | 400 | | 104 110 Dr |
| 10 | Wages | | | 900 | 103 210 Dr |
| | Insurance | | | 200 | 103 010 Dr |
| 20 | Wages | | | 800 | 102 210 Dr |

▶▶ ▶

| General Ledger | | | | |
|---|---|---|---|---|
| Date | Particulars | Debit | Credit | Balance |
| **Cash at Bank Account (continued)** | | | | |
| 2017 | | $ | $ | $ |
| 21 | Sales | 1 200 | | 103 410 Dr |
| 22 | Drawings – Jeremy Jolly | | 200 | 103 210 Dr |
| 23 | Creditor – A Walters | | 864 | 102 346 Dr |
| 28 | Debtor – A Rigosi | 980 | | 103 326 Dr |
| | Debtor – J Martini | 2 500 | | 105 826 Dr |
| **Office Equipment Account** | | | | |
| 2017 | | | | |
| 1 Feb | Balance | | | 2 000 Dr |
| **Capital – Jeremy Jolly Account** | | | | |
| 2017 | | | | |
| 1 Feb | Balance | | | 100 200 Cr |
| **Creditor – Pots and Pans Ltd Account** | | | | |
| 2017 | | | | |
| 1 Feb | Balance | | | 18 000 Cr |
| **Creditor – Felix Supply Co Account** | | | | |
| 2017 | | | | |
| 1 Feb | Balance | | | 30 000 Cr |
| **Discount Expense Account** | | | | |
| 2017 | | | | |
| 1 Feb | Balance | | | 40 Dr |
| 28 | Debtor – A Rigosi | 20 | | 60 Dr |
| **Discount Income Account** | | | | |
| 2017 | | | | |
| 1 Feb | Balance | | | 50 Cr |
| 23 | Creditor – A Walters | | 96 | 146 Cr |
| **Drawings – Jeremy Jolly Account** | | | | |
| 2017 | | | | |
| 1 Feb | Balance | | | 2 400 Dr |
| 22 | Purchases | 100 | | 2 500 Dr |
| | Cash at bank | 200 | | 2 700 Dr |

| Date | Particulars | Debit | Credit | Balance |
|------|-------------|-------|--------|---------|
| **General Ledger** | | | | |
| **Furniture and Fittings Account** | | | | |
| 2017 | | $ | $ | $ |
| 1 Feb | Balance | | | 18 400 Dr |
| **Late Fees Income Account** | | | | |
| 2017 | | | | |
| 1 Feb | Balance | | | 20 Cr |
| 25 | Debtor – J Martini | | 10 | 30 Cr |
| **Loan from Ladder Finance Co Account** | | | | |
| 2017 | | | | |
| 1 Feb | Balance | | | 6 000 Cr |
| **Purchases Account** | | | | |
| 2017 | | | | |
| 1 Feb | Balance | | | 16 600 Dr |
| 2 | Creditor – A Walters | 1 000 | | 17 600 Dr |
| 3 | Cash at bank | 400 | | 18 000 Dr |
| 22 | Drawings – Jeremy Jolly | | 100 | 17 900 Dr |
| **Purchases Returns and Allowances Account** | | | | |
| 2017 | | | | |
| 1 Feb | Balance | | | 800 Cr |
| 5 | Cash at bank | | 100 | 900 Cr |
| 8 | Creditor – A Walters | | 40 | 940 Cr |
| **Shop Equipment Account** | | | | |
| 2017 | | | | |
| 1 Feb | Balance | | | 36 000 Dr |
| **Rent Expense Account** | | | | |
| 2017 | | | | |
| 1 Feb | Balance | | | 400 Dr |
| **Sales Account** | | | | |
| 2017 | | | | |
| 1 Feb | Balance | | | 28 200 Cr |
| 9 | Cash at bank | | 400 | 28 600 Cr |
| 11 | Debtor – J Martini | | 4 000 | 32 600 Cr |

| Date | Particulars | Debit | Credit | Balance |
|---|---|---|---|---|
| **General Ledger** | | | | |
| | | | | |
| **Sales Account (continued)** | | | | |
| 2017 | | $ | $ | $ |
| 19 | Debtor – A Rigosi | | 1 000 | 33 600 Cr |
| 21 | Cash at bank | | 1 200 | 34 800 Cr |
| **Sales Returns and Allowances Account** | | | | |
| 2017 | | | | |
| 1 Feb | Balance | | | 1 000 Dr |
| 20 | Debtor – J Martini | 100 | | 1 100 Dr |
| **Wages Expense Account** | | | | |
| 2017 | | | | |
| 1 Feb | Balance | | | 1 000 Dr |
| 10 | Cash at bank | 900 | | 1 900 Dr |
| 20 | Cash at bank | 800 | | 2 700 Dr |
| **Creditor – A Walters Account** | | | | |
| 2017 | | | | |
| 2 Feb | Purchases | | 1 000 | 1 000 Cr |
| 8 | Purchases returns and allowances | 40 | | 960 Cr |
| 23 | Cash at bank | 864 | | 96 Cr |
| | Discount income | 96 | | Nil |
| **Delivery Truck Account** | | | | |
| 2017 | | | | |
| 4 Feb | Creditor – Beta Trucks | 30 000 | | 30 000 Dr |
| **Creditor – Beta Trucks Account** | | | | |
| 2017 | | | | |
| 4 Feb | Delivery truck | | 30 000 | 30 000 Cr |
| **Insurance Expense Account** | | | | |
| 2017 | | | | |
| 10 Feb | Cash at bank | 200 | | 200 Dr |
| **Debtor – J Martini Account** | | | | |
| 2017 | | | | |
| 11 Feb | Sales | 4 000 | | 4 000 Dr |
| 20 | Sales returns | | 100 | 3 900 Dr |

| General Ledger | | | | |
|---|---|---|---|---|
| Date | Particulars | Debit | Credit | Balance |
| **Debtor – J Martini Account (continued)** | | | | |
| 2017 | | $ | $ | $ |
| 25 | Late fees income | 10 | | 3 910 Dr |
| 28 | Cash at bank | | 2 500 | 1 410 Dr |
| | Bad debts | | 1 410 | Nil |
| **Debtor – A Rigosi Account** | | | | |
| 2017 | | | | |
| 19 Feb | Sales | 1 000 | | 1 000 Dr |
| 28 | Cash at bank | | 980 | 20 Dr |
| | Discount expense | | 20 | Nil |

2   The trial balance:

| JEREMY'S WHOLESALE HARDWARE STORE Trial balance as at 28 February 2017 | | |
|---|---|---|
| **Account** | **Debit** | **Credit** |
| | $ | $ |
| Bad debts | 2 830 | |
| Cash at bank | 105 826 | |
| Office equipment | 2 000 | |
| Capital – Jeremy Jolly | | 100 200 |
| Creditor – Pots and Pans Ltd | | 18 000 |
| Creditor – Felix Supply Co | | 30 000 |
| Discount expense | 60 | |
| Discount income | | 146 |
| Drawings – Jeremy Jolly | 2 700 | |
| Furniture and fittings | 18 400 | |
| Late fees income | | 30 |
| Loan from Ladder Finance | | 6 000 |
| Purchases | 17 900 | |
| Purchases returns and allowances | | 940 |
| Shop equipment | 36 000 | |
| Rent expense | 400 | |
| Sales | | 34 800 |

| Account | Debit | Credit |
|---|---|---|
| | $ | $ |
| Sales returns and allowances | 1 100 | |
| Wages expense | 2 700 | |
| Delivery truck | 30 000 | |
| Creditor – Beta Trucks | | 30 000 |
| Insurance expense | 200 | |
| | $220 116 | $220 116 |

 **EXERCISES**

**1.76** Record the following transactions in the ledger of T Chan, retailer.

*2016*

| | |
|---|---|
| 8 Jun | T Chan commenced business with the following assets: cash at bank, $5000; stock, $3000. |
| 10 | Bought stock for resale on credit from ACL Traders, $2000. |
| | Bought stock for cash, $1000 from AR Manufacturers. |

**1.77** Record the following transactions in the ledger of S Dixon, retailer.

*2017*

| | |
|---|---|
| 1 Jul | S Dixon commenced business with the following assets and liabilities: cash at bank, $8000; loan from Better Financing, $250 000; stock, $15 000; land and buildings, $460 000. |
| 3 | Purchased stock for resale on credit from BY Supplies, $5000. |
| 10 | Purchased stock for cash from NU Supplies, $2000. |

**1.78** Record the following transactions in the ledger of B Browning, retailer.

*2016*

| | |
|---|---|
| 1 May | Bought stock for $4000 cash from BH Suppliers. |
| 4 | Bought stock on credit from Murray Manufacturing, $6500. |
| 5 | Returned $1200 of damaged stock to BH Suppliers and received a cash refund. |
| 10 | Allowance of $500 given by Murray Manufacturing for damaged goods. |

**1.79** Record the following transactions in the ledger of B Arthur, retailer.

*2017*

| | |
|---|---|
| 1 Aug | Bought stock on credit from Mini Wholesalers, $5500. |
| 3 | Returned $1500 of damaged stock to Mini Wholesalers. |
| 5 | Bought stock for $7000 cash from NW Supplies. |
| 8 | Returned damaged goods to NW Supplies, $1000. |

**1.80** Record the following transactions in the ledger of A Grant, shopkeeper.

*2017*
3 Mar   Cash sales, $550.
5          Credit sales to M Ajor, $800.

**1.81** Record the following transactions in the ledger of S Short, retailer.

*2017*
4 Apr   Cash sales, $500; credit sales to G Georgiou, $400.

**1.82** Record the following transactions in the ledger of P Clements, merchant.

*2017*
1 Apr   Cash sales, $500; credit sales to T Nelson, $350.
4          Cash refund given for returns of goods previously sold for cash, $100.
5          T Nelson returned damaged goods, $50.

**1.83** Record the following transactions in the ledger of M Tan, retailer.

*2017*
1 Mar   Cash sales, $600; credit sales to D Parsons, $200.
5          Cash refund of $50 given for goods previously sold for cash.
6          D Parsons given an allowance of $80 for soiled goods.

**1.84** S Vella commenced business as a retailer on 1 July 2017. He asks you to open a ledger to record the following transactions and to prepare a trial balance as at 31 July 2017.

*2017*
1 Jul   Commenced business with the following assets: cash in bank, $5500; stocks, $3600; premises, $257 000; furniture, $2000.
4          Purchase stock for cash, $5400.
9          Sold stock on credit to J Osborne for $6300.
11        Credit purchases of stock from J Bramly, $4800.
16        Gave an allowance to J Osborne, $300, for damaged goods.
21        Cash sales of stock, $2600.
26        Received a $270 refund for returns of stock previously purchased for cash.
31        Cash sales of stock, $1200.

**ADDITIONAL EXERCISES**

**1.85** This question is available on the CD that accompanies this text.

**1.86** On 2 May 2016, J Brown, grocer, withdrew $500 worth of trading stock from his business to give to his family. On 3 May, he also cashed a cheque for $1500 on the business's bank account to pay for his son's twenty-first birthday party. Complete ledger entries for these transactions.

**1.87** D Ogg, pet-shop owner, commenced operations on 1 June 2017. She asks you to open a ledger to record the following transactions.

*2017*
1 Jun   Commenced business operations by contributing the following assets: cash, $20 000; stock, $5000.
5          Purchased stock on credit from Pet Supplies, $6000.

10      Proprietor contributed additional capital of $3000 cash.

12      Ogg gave stock costing $500 to a friend.

13      Cashed a cheque for personal use, $150.

**1.88**   Record the following transactions in the ledger of A Mahfouz.

*2017*

1 Jul    Sold goods on credit to P Lazenby, $150.

2        Cash sale to S Carter, $50.

3        P Lazenby returned $10 worth of goods.

4        S Carter was given a cash refund of $5 because the goods he received were slightly shop-soiled.

5        P Lazenby paid his account, taking 2% discount offered for prompt payment.

**1.89**   G Wills operates a soft-drink stall at the football. On 1 July 2016, her business has $500 worth of stock and $600 in the bank. Open a ledger for her and record these transactions.

*2016*

1 Jul    Purchased five crates of orange pop on credit from Harry's Drinks at $10 per crate.

2        Returned one crate of orange pop to Harry's Drinks.

9        Purchased three crates of cola from BY Drinks at $7 per crate. Paid cash.

         Paid account of Harry's Drinks, taking advantage of a 4% discount offered for prompt payment.

         Returned one crate of cola to BY Drinks. Cash refund received.

**1.90**   The following information relates to N Taylor, retailer. She asks you to copy the ledger accounts shown and to record the transactions given.

*Ledger accounts*

| General Ledger | | | | | |
|---|---|---|---|---|---|
| Date | Particulars | | Debit | Credit | Balance |
| **Debtor – H Peters** | | | | | |
| 2016 | | | $ | $ | $ |
| 1 Jul | Balance | | | | 10 000 Dr |
| 5 | Sales | | 16 000 | | 26 000 Dr |
| 6 | Sales returns and allowances | | | 5 000 | 21 000 Dr |
| **Creditor – J Downing** | | | | | |
| 2016 | | | | | |
| 1 Jul | Balance | | | | 6 000 Cr |
| 6 | Purchases returns and allowances | | 1 000 | | 5 000 Cr |
| 8 | Purchases | | | 500 | 5 500 Cr |

*Transactions*

*2016*

8 Jul    H Peters paid his account, less 5% cash discount.

12       Paid J Downing, taking 2% discount for prompt payment.

1.91    Record the following transactions on the ledger of O North, importer.

*2016*

1 May    Sold goods on credit to I Skint, $500.

1 Jul    Charged I Skint $5 late fee on overdue account.

31 Aug   Received notification that I Skint has been declared bankrupt, and that he will therefore be
         unable to repay any of his debt.

1.92    Record the following transactions in the ledger of G Big, retailer.

*2017*

1 Apr    Sold goods on credit to B Purt, $200

5        B Purt given an allowance of $50 for soiled goods.

8        Sold goods on credit to B Purt, $100.

30       B Purt declared bankrupt. $50 received as full settlement of amount owing.

1.93    J Melon has operated a greengrocery business for a number of years. Using the information below,
        prepare a ledger for March 2018 and a trial balance as at 31 March 2018.

**Melon the Greengrocer**
**Trial balance as at 1 March 2018**

| Account | Debit | Credit |
|---|---:|---:|
|  | $ | $ |
| Capital – J Melon |  | 74 000 |
| Cash at bank | 13 900 |  |
| Mortgage loan |  | 250 000 |
| Power and light | 680 |  |
| Land and buildings | 320 000 |  |
| Purchases | 48 000 |  |
| Stock | 9 800 |  |
| Fittings and equipment | 6 300 |  |
| Sales |  | 90 000 |
| Debtor – R Brown | 10 300 |  |
| Creditor – M Meyer |  | 9 800 |
| Wages | 14 820 |  |
|  | $423 800 | $423 800 |

*The transactions for March 2018 were:*

3 Mar   Cash purchases, $3480.

5       Credit sales to J Atkins, $1220.

6       Sales returns from J Atkins, $100.

11     Received $900 cash from debtor, R Brown. $30 discount was allowed.

14     Paid creditor, M Meyer, the amount owing on 1 March, less 5% discount.

15     Received a cash refund of $40 following the return of stale vegetables.

18     Cash sales, $3100.

23     Paid wages, $680.

25     Gave a refund of $110 to a customer for the return of fruit.

28     J Melon deposited $6000 of her own savings in the business bank account.

31     Made mortgage loan repayment: principal, $2000; and interest $800.

**1.94**   For each of the following transactions answer true or false to the suggested entries:

| Transaction | Entries | |
| --- | --- | --- |
| Purchase of stock on credit | Dr Stock | Cr Creditors |
| Sale of stock on credit | Dr Debtors | Cr Sales |
| Return of goods sold on credit | Dr Sales | Cr Debtors |
| Recording bad debt | Dr Bad debts | Cr Debtors |
| Charging late fee on overdue account | Dr Late fees | Cr Bad debts |
| Payment of wages | Dr Wages | Cr Cash at bank |
| Discount received from a creditor | Dr Creditor | Cr Discount income |

**1.95**   Record the following transactions in the ledger of C McReilly, building supplier, and prepare a trial balance as at 30 September 2016.

*2016*

1 Sep   Commenced business with the following assets and liabilities: cash at bank, $40 000; stock, $20 000; building, $360 000; fixtures, $2000; mortgage loan on buildings, $240 000.

2       Purchased stock, $400 cash.

3       Purchased stock on credit, $4000 from A Wily.

4       Returned stock to A Wily, $50.

5       Purchased vehicle for $10 000 paying a cash deposit of $5000; balance to be paid to Vroom Motors Ltd within 60 days.

8       Settled account with A Wily, less 2% discount.

10     Cash sales, $600.

11     Cash sales, $600.

       Credit sales to S Pooner, $400.

12     S Pooner returned faulty goods valued at $10.

13     Cash sales, $609.

Paid wages, $800.

Paid Vroom Motors Ltd $2000 of the amount owing.

17  Cash sales, $200.

Cash purchases, $200.

Credit purchases from D Brown, $2000.

20  Purchased adjoining property for storage. The terms arranged were: cash deposit, $10 000; mortgage loan (20 years), $140 000; total price $150 000.

30  Cash sales, $1000.

S Pooner settled his account less 5% discount.

Paid wages, $800.

Owner withdrew timber valued at $600 (cost) for personal use.

1.96*  From the following information relating to Roger's Deli (owner, R Williams), prepare (a) a ledger for October 2017 and (b) a trial balance as at 31 October 2017.

**Roger's Deli**
**Trial balance as at 1 October 2017**

| Account | Debit | Credit |
|---------|------:|-------:|
|  | $ | $ |
| Bank overdraft | | 30 200 |
| Capital – R Williams | | 71 500 |
| Cash on hand | 400 | |
| Delivery vehicle | 29 400 | |
| Drawings – R Williams | 1 200 | |
| Electricity | 3 480 | |
| Furniture and fittings | 32 820 | |
| Investments | 36 000 | |
| Loan from OP Loans | | 20 000 |
| Purchases | 82 100 | |
| Rent | 32 120 | |
| Sales | | 189 520 |
| Stock | 34 800 | |
| Debtor – S Fitt | 19 280 | |
| Creditor – B Broom | | 13 980 |
| Wages | 53 600 | |
| | $325 200 | $325 200 |

*The transactions for October 2017 were:*

3 Oct   Purchased new furniture on credit from Maxi Co for $8200. Paid a deposit of $1200 cash.

5       Cash sales, $3200.

7       Credit sales to S Fitt, $1900.

9       Credit purchases of stock from B Broom, $5500.

10      Received $14 520 from debtor S Fitt. Discount allowed was $480.

13      Sold investments for cash at their cost price of $16 000.

16      Cash sales, $3680.

        Paid wages, $820.

18      Returned $420 worth of stock to B Broom.

20      Made interest-only loan repayment to OP Loans, $3200.

23      R Williams withdrew stock costing $200 for his own consumption.

25      Paid for repairs to delivery vehicle, $400.

        Paid creditor B Broom, $8200, less $600 discount.

26      Paid Maxi Co the balance owing.

29      Paid the following amounts by cheque: electricity, $240; rent, $2800.

31      Cash sales, $3500.

        Received notification that debtor S Fitt had been declared bankrupt and that he would be unable to repay any of the amount owing.

1.97    This question is available on the CD that accompanies this text.

ADDITIONAL
EXERCISES

 **SOLUTION**

1.96   **a**

| Roger's Deli | | | | |
|---|---|---|---|---|
| **General Ledger** | | | | |
| **Date** | **Particulars** | **Debit** | **Credit** | **Balance** |
| **Bank Account** | | | | |
| 2017 | | $ | $ | $ |
| 1 Oct | Balance | | | 30 200 Cr |
| 3 | Furniture and fittings | | 1 200 | 31 400 Cr |
| 5 | Sales | 3 200 | | 28 200 Cr |
| 10 | Debtor – S Fitt | 14 520 | | 13 680 Cr |
| 13 | Investments | 16 000 | | 2 320 Dr |
| 16 | Sales | 3 680 | | 6 000 Dr |
| | Wages | | 820 | 5 180 Dr |
| 20 | Interest expense | | 3 200 | 1 980 Dr |

| General Ledger | | | | |
|---|---|---|---|---|
| Date | Particulars | Debit | Credit | Balance |
| **Bank Account (continued)** | | | | |
| 2017 | | $ | $ | $ |
| 25 | Vehicle repairs | | 400 | 1 580 Dr |
| | Creditor – B Broom | | 7 600 | 6 020 Cr |
| 26 | Creditor – Maxi Co | | 7 000 | 13 020 Cr |
| 29 | Electricity | | 240 | 13 260 Cr |
| | Rent | | 2 800 | 16 060 Cr |
| 31 | Sales | 3 500 | | 12 560 Cr |
| **Capital – R Williams Account** | | | | |
| 2017 | | | | |
| 1 Oct | Balance | | | 71 500 Cr |
| **Cash on Hand Account** | | | | |
| 2017 | | | | |
| 1 Oct | Balance | | | 400 Dr |
| **Delivery Vehicle Account** | | | | |
| 2017 | | | | |
| 1 Oct | Balance | | | 29 400 Dr |
| **Drawings – R Williams Account** | | | | |
| 2017 | | | | |
| 1 Oct | Balance | | | 1 200 Dr |
| 23 | Purchases | 200 | | 1 400 Dr |
| **Electricity Account** | | | | |
| 2017 | | | | |
| 1 Oct | Balance | | | 3 480 Dr |
| 29 | Bank | 240 | | 3 720 Dr |
| **Furniture and Fittings Account** | | | | |
| 2017 | | | | |
| 1 Oct | Balance | | | 32 820 Dr |
| 3 | Sundries | 8 200 | | 41 020 Dr |
| **Investments Account** | | | | |
| 2017 | | | | |
| 1 Oct | Balance | | | 36 000 Dr |
| 13 | Bank | | 16 000 | 20 000 Dr |

| Date | Particulars | Debit | Credit | Balance |
|------|-------------|-------|--------|---------|
| — **General Ledger** | | | | |

| Date | Particulars | Debit | Credit | Balance |
|------|-------------|-------|--------|---------|
| **Loan from OP Loans Account** | | | | |
| 2017 | | $ | $ | $ |
| 1 Oct | Balance | | | 20 000 Cr |
| **Purchases Account** | | | | |
| 2017 | | | | |
| 1 Oct | Balance | | | 82 100 Dr |
| 9 | Creditor – B Broom | 5 500 | | 87 600 Dr |
| 23 | Drawings – R Williams | | 200 | 87 400 Dr |
| **Rent Account** | | | | |
| 2017 | | | | |
| 1 Oct | Balance | | | 32 120 Dr |
| 29 | Bank | 2 800 | | 34 920 Dr |
| **Sales Account** | | | | |
| 2017 | | | | |
| 1 Oct | Balance | | | 189 520 Cr |
| 5 | Bank | | 3 200 | 192 720 Cr |
| 7 | Debtor – S Fitt | | 1 900 | 194 620 Cr |
| 16 | Bank | | 3 680 | 198 300 Cr |
| 31 | Bank | | 3 500 | 201 800 Cr |
| **Stock Account** | | | | |
| 2017 | | | | |
| 1 Oct | Balance | | | 34 800 Dr |
| **Debtor – S Fitt Account** | | | | |
| 2017 | | | | |
| 1 Oct | Balance | | | 19 280 Dr |
| 7 | Sales | 1 900 | | 21 180 Dr |
| 10 | Bank | | 14 520 | 6 660 Dr |
| | Discount expense | | 480 | 6 180 Dr |
| 31 | Bad debts | | 6 180 | Nil |
| **Creditor – B Broom Account** | | | | |
| 2017 | | | | |
| 1 Oct | Balance | | | 13 980 Cr |

| | General Ledger | | | |
|---|---|---|---|---|
| Date | Particulars | Debit | Credit | Balance |
| **Creditor – B Broom Account (continued)** | | | | |
| 2017 | | $ | $ | $ |
| 9 | Purchases | | 5 500 | 19 480 Cr |
| 18 | Purchases returns and allowances | 420 | | 19 060 Cr |
| 25 | Bank | 7 600 | | 11 460 Cr |
| | Discount revenue | 600 | | 10 860 Cr |
| **Wages Account** | | | | |
| 2017 | | | | |
| 1 Oct | Balance | | | 53 600 Dr |
| 16 | Bank | 820 | | 54 420 Dr |
| **Creditor – Maxi Co Account** | | | | |
| 2017 | | | | |
| 3 Oct | Furniture and fittings | | 7 000 | 7 000 Cr |
| 26 | Bank | 7 000 | | Nil |
| **Discount Expense Account** | | | | |
| 2017 | | | | |
| 10 Oct | Debtor – S Fitt | 480 | | 480 Dr |
| **Purchases Returns and Allowances Account** | | | | |
| 2017 | | | | |
| 18 Oct | Creditor – B Broom | | 420 | 420 Cr |
| **Interest Expense Account** | | | | |
| 2017 | | | | |
| 20 Oct | Bank | 3 200 | | 3 200 Dr |
| **Vehicle Repairs Account** | | | | |
| 2017 | | | | |
| 25 Oct | Bank | 400 | | 400 Dr |
| **Discount Income Account** | | | | |
| 2017 | | | | |
| 25 Oct | Creditor – B Broom | | 600 | 600 Cr |
| **Bad Debts Account** | | | | |
| 2017 | | | | |
| 31 Oct | Debtor – S Fitt | 6 180 | | 6 180 Dr |

b

**Roger's Deli**
**Trial balance as at 31 October 2017**

| Account | Debit | Credit |
|---|---:|---:|
| | $ | $ |
| Bank (overdraft) | | 12 560 |
| Capital – R Williams | | 71 500 |
| Cash on hand | 400 | |
| Delivery vehicle | 29 400 | |
| Drawings – R Williams | 1 400 | |
| Electricity | 3 720 | |
| Furniture and fittings | 41 020 | |
| Investments | 20 000 | |
| Loan from OP Loans | | 20 000 |
| Purchases | 87 400 | |
| Rent | 34 920 | |
| Sales | | 201 800 |
| Stock | 34 800 | |
| Creditor – B Broom | | 10 860 |
| Wages | 54 420 | |
| Discount expense | 480 | |
| Purchases returns and allowances | | 420 |
| Interest expense | 3 200 | |
| Vehicle repairs | 400 | |
| Discount income | | 600 |
| Bad debts | 6 180 | |
| | $317 740 | $317 740 |

# Chart of accounts

As a business expands, the number of accounts it keeps in its ledger may become quite large. When this occurs it becomes necessary to arrange the accounts in an orderly sequence so that accounts are retrieved easily. The most common system adopted is a *chart of accounts*.

A chart of accounts is essentially an index to the General Ledger. In a chart of accounts, each account in the ledger is listed under its appropriate classification (asset, liability, owner's equity, income or expense) and is assigned a number or 'code'. The coding system used must be simple, yet flexible enough to allow the insertion of additional accounts when required. Consider the examples overleaf.

## Example 1

Brian's Engineering Co uses a *block coding system* in its chart of accounts. In this system, each category or element in the ledger is assigned a block of numbers.

| BRIAN'S ENGINEERING CO Chart of accounts | | | |
|---|---|---|---|
| **Assets (1–99)** | | **Income (300–399)** | |
| 1 | Cash at bank | 300 | Sales |
| 2 | Accounts receivable control* | 301 | Sales returns and allowances# |
| 3 | Stock | 302 | Interest revenue |
| 4 | Motor vehicle | 303 | Discount revenue |
| 5 | Plant and equipment | | |
| 6 | Land and buildings | **Expenses (400–499)** | |
| 7 | Furniture and buildings | 400 | Purchases |
| 8 | Office equipment | 401 | Purchases returns and allowances# |
| | | 402 | Wages |
| **Liabilities (100–199)** | | 403 | Power and light |
| 100 | Accounts payable control | 404 | Postage and stationery |
| 101 | Mortgage loan | 405 | Advertising |
| | | 406 | Motor vehicle expenses |
| | | 407 | General expenses |
| **Owner's equity (200–299)** | | 408 | Discount expense |
| 200 | Capital – Brian | | |
| 201 | Drawings – Brian | | |

*See Debtors and creditors control accounts below.
#See Returns and allowances accounts overleaf.

## Debtors and creditors control accounts

As mentioned earlier in this chapter, a Debtors (or Accounts Receivable) Control account is normally used in the General Ledger to record *all* debtors. Individual accounts for debtors are located in the Debtors (or Accounts Receivable) Subsidiary ledger. Similarly, a Creditors (or Accounts Payable) Control account is kept in the General Ledger and individual creditors' accounts are located in the Creditors (or Accounts Payable) Subsidiary ledger.

These control accounts in the General Ledger will be used in all of the exercises that follow this section, and we will use the terms *accounts receivable* and *accounts payable* to refer to debtors and creditors for the remainder of this book. Note also that the Accounts Receivable Control and Accounts Payable Control accounts will be used to record a range of credit transactions, including sales and purchases of assets and other income and expenses, in addition to stock-related transactions.

## Returns and allowances accounts

Notice that offset accounts relating to sales returns and allowances and purchases returns and allowances are shown in the chart of accounts adjacent to the account they are intended to effectively reduce. For instance, sales returns and allowances is shown as an income (offset) account below the *Sales* account, and purchases returns and allowances is shown as an expense (offset) account below the *Purchases* account.

# Example 2

Zoe's Health Studio uses a *prefix coding system* in its chart of accounts. In this system, a prefix number, rather than a block of numbers, is assigned to each category or element (asset, liability etc.) in the ledger.

| ZOE'S HEALTH STUDIO Chart of accounts | | | |
|---|---|---|---|
| **1** | **Assets** | **4** | **Income** |
| 1.1 | Cash at bank | 4.1 | Fees income |
| 1.2 | Stock of refreshments | 4.2 | Discount income |
| 1.3 | Accounts receivable control | 4.3 | Interest income |
| 1.4 | Cash on hand | 4.4 | Sales of refreshments |
| 1.5 | Equipment | | |
| 1.6 | Furniture and fittings | **5** | **Expenses** |
| 1.7 | Motor vehicle | 5.1 | Wages |
| | | 5.2 | Electricity |
| **2** | **Liabilities** | 5.3 | Discount expense |
| 2.1 | Accounts payable control | 5.4 | Advertising |
| 2.2 | Loan from Chloe | 5.5 | Rent |
| | | 5.6 | Oils and liniments |
| **3** | **Owner's equity** | 5.7 | Purchases of refreshments |
| 3.1 | Capital – Zoe | 5.8 | General expenses |
| 3.2 | Drawings – Zoe | | |

# Example 3

John's Diner uses an *alphanumeric coding system* in its chart of accounts. In this system, an alphabetic character is assigned to each element (asset, liability etc.) in the General Ledger. Each specific account is then assigned a numeric character.

| JOHN'S DINER | |
|---|---|
| **Chart of accounts** | |

| **Assets** | | **Income** | |
|---|---|---|---|
| A1 | Accounts receivable control | I1 | Sales |
| A2 | Cash on hand | I2 | Sales returns and allowances |
| A3 | Delivery vehicle | I3 | Interest income |
| A4 | Land and buildings | I4 | Discount income |
| A5 | Stock | | |
| A6 | Fittings and equipment | **Expenses** | |
| A7 | Office equipment | E1 | Purchases |
| | | E2 | Purchases returns and allowances |
| **Liabilities** | | E3 | Wages |
| L1 | Accounts payable control | E4 | Advertising |
| L2 | Mortgage loan | E5 | Motor vehicle expenses |
| | | E6 | Power and heating |
| **Owner's equity** | | E7 | Printing and stationery |
| OE1 | Capital – John | E8 | Freight and cartage |
| OE2 | Drawings – John | E9 | Bad debts |

# Electronic coding

In computerised accounting systems, all data that is to be processed by a computer must first be abbreviated to its simplest possible form. This abbreviation is necessary to minimise the time it takes to process data, and to reduce the memory required to store the data in the computer. Abbreviation is achieved by coding all data that is to be processed.

A chart of accounts is a good example of the sort of coding that is used in computer systems. An account code number (e.g. 101) occupies a lot less memory than the name of the account (e.g. Plant and Equipment) and therefore is easier for the computer to process and store. A chart of accounts is an integral part of any computerised accounting system.

# The basic structure of an accounting system

In a business, the various records, policies and procedures used to carry out the accounting process are collectively referred to as the *accounting system*. The recording and reporting requirements of all businesses are basically similar, but the nature of the accounting systems used will vary according to several factors, including:

- *the nature of the business* – the records of a manufacturing business, for example, must provide different financial information from those of a medical clinic

- *the size of the business* – for example, a very small business that sells goods or services only on a cash basis would not require a Subsidiary Accounts Receivable ledger
- *the variety of accounting reports required* – the degree of complexity of the accounting records will be greater, for instance, for a public company listed on a securities exchange (for example, the Australian exchange), due to the stringent reporting requirements imposed by this body. In this situation, the accounting system would most likely be fully computerised, to enable prompt output of the detailed reports required.

Whatever the size or nature of an accounting system, its centrepiece is the *chart of accounts*. The chart of accounts for a business must be designed carefully to ensure that the accounting system is capable of producing suitable accounting reports.

 **EXERCISES**

1.98 Prepare a chart of accounts for Y Mitropolous, horse trainer, using a 'block' system of coding. The following are the accounts in Mitropolous's General Ledger:

| | | |
|---|---|---|
| Rent – stables | Wages – strappers | Cash at bank |
| Saddles and riding equipment | Training fees received | Prize monies received |
| Accounts receivable control | Jockey payments | Motor vehicle |
| Horse float | Motor vehicle expenses | Horse feed |
| Veterinary costs | Brooms and shovels | Loan from OZ Loans Pty Ltd |
| Capital – Y Mitropolous | Race entry fees | |

1.99 Prepare a chart of accounts for P Thomas, retailer, using a 'prefix' system of coding. The following are the accounts in Thomas's General Ledger:

| | | |
|---|---|---|
| Accounts receivable control | Advertising | Sales |
| Purchases | Capital – P Thomas | Commission received |
| Wages – salespeople | Discount allowed | Rates and taxes |
| Cash at bank | Accounts payable control | Discount received |
| Furniture and fittings | Motor vehicle | Equipment |
| Rent (shop) | Government bonds | Drawings – P Thomas |

1.100 Prepare a chart of accounts for A Fouad, gift-shop proprietor, using an alphanumeric system of coding. The following are the accounts in Fouad's General Ledger:

| | | |
|---|---|---|
| Signwriting | Office equipment | Shares in BJP Ltd |
| Accounts receivable control | Capital – A Fouad | Fittings |
| Motor vehicle | Motor vehicle expenses | Electricity |
| Telephone charges | Sales | Purchases |
| Security costs | Discount income | Discount expense |
| Sales returns and allowances | Purchases returns and allowances | Accounts payable control |
| Cash at bank | | |

1.101 From the following information relating to Chambers Canvas and Camping Gear (camping equipment retailer), prepare:

a  the General Ledger for July 2017

b  a trial balance as at 31 July 2017

c  a chart of accounts (using block coding) for the ledger you prepared in (a) above.

Chambers Canvas and Camping Gear (Owner – Paul Chambers)
Trial balance as at 1 July 2017

| Account | Debit | Credit |
|---|---:|---:|
| | $ | $ |
| Cash at bank | 21 200 | |
| Furniture and fittings | 13 050 | |
| Loan to Bruce Guyrope | 18 800 | |
| Motor vehicles | 43 520 | |
| Land and buildings | 262 430 | |
| Accounts payable control | | 55 100 |
| Accounts receivable control | 67 000 | |
| Capital – Paul Chambers | | 310 000 |
| Drawings – Paul Chambers | 14 900 | |
| Advertising | 7 500 | |
| Discount expense | 1 870 | |
| Discount income | | 1 550 |
| Power and light | 6 890 | |
| Freight and cartage | 2 400 | |
| Insurance | 2 560 | |
| Interest income | | 1 170 |
| Motor vehicle running costs | 1 710 | |
| Purchases | 127 000 | |
| Purchases returns and allowances | | 2 880 |
| Rates and taxes | 2 290 | |
| Sales | | 320 000 |
| Sales returns and allowances | 3 380 | |
| Wages | 44 200 | |
| Stock on hand | 50 000 | |
| | $690 700 | $690 700 |

*The transactions for July were:*

2017

| | | |
|---|---|---|
| 1 Jul | Cash sales, $14 300. | |
| 2 | Paid wages, $5090. | |
| | Credit sales, $8350. | |
| 5 | Cash refunds paid to customers, $450. | |
| 6 | Purchased office furniture on credit from AB Unit Co for $9600. | |
| 7 | Credit purchases, $23 360. | |
| | Freight and cartage paid, $230. | |
| 10 | Paul Chambers (the owner) withdrew a sleeping bag for his own use, cost price $185. | |
| | Returned faulty tent (cost $410 on 7 July). | |
| 12 | Paid creditors the amount owing on 1 July, deducting $1100 discount. | |
| | Advanced a further $5000 to Bruce Guyrope. | |
| 16 | Paid wages, $4760. | |
| 18 | Sales: credit, $8400; cash, $17 150. | |
| 21 | Received $47 300 from debtors, after allowing them $700 discount for prompt payment. | |
| | Bad debt written off, $5200. | |
| 25 | Sold an old office desk at cost, $1600, to John Ralph on credit. | |
| 27 | Paid the following amounts by cheque: vehicle repairs, $1150; advertising, $3600; cleaning, $550; petrol and oil, $700. | |
| 28 | Received loan repayment from Bruce Guyrope: principal, $2000; interest, $800. | |
| | Credit sales returns $1700. | |
| 29 | Paul Chambers (the owner) paid $2000 for a new set of golf clubs out of the business bank account. | |
| 31 | Cash sales, $12 350. | |
| | Credit sales, $5450. | |

**1.102** Briefly outline the factors that influence the structure of an accounting system.

# Summary

What have you covered in this chapter?

◆ Typical forms of business ownership in Australia
  - sole trader
  - partnership
  - company
◆ The following conventions
  - business entity
  - historical cost
  - monetary unit
  - going concern
  - accounting period
◆ The following doctrines
  - objectivity
  - conservatism
  - full disclosure
  - consistency
  - materiality
◆ Accounting entity versus legal entity
◆ Reporting entity
◆ The statement of financial position
  - the accounting equation: Assets = Liabilities + Owner's equity
  - assets and asset recognition
  - liability and liability recognition
  - owner's equity for a sole trader
◆ The statement of comprehensive income
  - income and income recognition
  - expense and expense recognition
◆ Double-entry recording
◆ Transaction analysis chart
◆ Chart of accounts
◆ 'T' and columnar ledgers
◆ Trial balance

# 2

# BUSINESS DOCUMENTS AND JOURNALS

## Learning objectives

Upon satisfactory completion of this chapter you should be able to:

- outline the basic features of the GST
- complete the following source documents:
    - delivery docket
    - receipt
    - tax invoice
    - adjustment note
    - cheque
    - point-of-sale daily summary
    - purchase order
    - bank deposit slip
    - remittance advice
    - statement of account

- correctly enter receipts and cash sales details into a columnar Cash Receipts Journal for a wholesale/retail business
- correctly enter payment details into a columnar Cash Payments Journal for a wholesale/retail business
- correctly enter tax invoices and credit card sales into a columnar Sales Journal for a wholesale/retail business
- correctly enter adjustment notes into a columnar Sales Returns and Allowances Journal for a wholesale/retail business
- correctly enter tax invoices into a columnar Purchases Journal for a wholesale/retail business
- correctly enter adjustment notes into a columnar Purchases Returns and Allowances Journal for a wholesale/retail business
- prepare General Journal entries for the following:
  - correction of posting errors
  - opening entries
  - bad debts written off
  - late payment accounting fees expense
  - late payment accounting fees receivable
  - withdrawal of stock by proprietor
- correctly enter source documents into journals for a service business
- correctly record EFT, EFTPOS and credit card transactions.

# Goods and services tax (GST)

Many business transactions contain an element of Goods and Services Tax (GST) and thus it is an appropriate juncture in the text to outline some of the basic features of the GST.

## What is the GST?

The GST is a broad-based consumption tax that is levied on the supply of most goods and services consumed in Australia. It is currently levied at a rate of 10%.

Figure 2.1 provides an excellent example of the way in which GST works as illustrated in the Australian Taxation Office publication 'How GST Works' (http://www.ato.gov.au > business > tax topics > GST > How GST Works).

**Figure 2.1    How GST Works: ATO example**

Collecting and paying GST on the sale of goods.

A timber merchant sells timber to a furniture manufacturer for $110 (including $10 GST). The manufacturer uses the timber to make a table, which he sells to a furniture retailer for $220 (including $20 GST). The retailer then sells the table to a consumer for $330 (including $30 GST).

| Raw materials | | Net GST to pay | |
|---|---|---|---|
| A. Timber merchant sells timber for $110, including $10 GST | GST on sale | $10 | |
| | Assume no GST credit | $0 | |
| | Net GST to pay | $10 | Timber merchant pays $10 GST to us |

A. The timber merchant needs to make $100 on the sale of the timber. So he sells the timber for $110, keeps $100 and pays $10 GST to us.

| Production | | Net GST to pay | |
|---|---|---|---|
| B. Furniture manufacturer sells table for $220, including $20 GST | GST on sale | $20 | |
| | *less* GST credit | $10 | |
| | Net GST to pay | $10 | Manufacturer pays $10 GST to us |

B. The furniture manufacturer can claim a credit for the $10 GST included in the price paid to the timber merchant. The manufacturer offsets that $10 against the $20 collected on the sale of the table to the retailer, and pays $10 GST to us.

| Distribution | | Net GST to pay | |
|---|---|---|---|
| C. Retailer sells table for $330, including $30 GST | GST on sale | $30 | |
| | *less* GST credit | $20 | |
| | Net GST to pay | $10 | Retailer pays $10 GST to us |

C. The furniture retailer can claim a credit for the $20 GST included in the price paid to the furniture manufacturer. The retailer offsets that $20 against the $30 GST collected on the sale of the table to the consumer, and pays $10 GST to us.

| Retail | | | |
|---|---|---|---|
| D. Consumer pays $330 (including $30 GST) to the retailer | | | |

D. The consumer who buys the table bears the $30 GST included in the price, as consumers cannot register for GST and cannot claim GST credits.

In general, manufacturers, wholesalers and retailers are required to pay GST on the sales ('taxable supplies') they make. Typically, a trader will add the GST payable on to the purchase price so that the trader can recover from the purchaser the GST imposed on the trader. The trader has an obligation to remit the GST it collects to the Australian Taxation Office (ATO) on a periodic basis ('tax period'). A trader may also pay GST on its business inputs (for example, GST on stock the trader acquires). The GST legislation allows for the trader to obtain a credit for the GST its pays on its business inputs ('input tax credits'). Therefore, the amount of GST payable by a trader and remitted to the ATO for a tax period is a net amount, comprising the amount of GST collected from customers less any GST paid by the trader on its business inputs. In Figure 2.1, the wholesaler collects $20 in GST when its goods are sold to the retailer but the wholesaler only remits $15 to the ATO because the wholesaler has paid GST of $5 on the stock it acquired from the manufacturer ($20 GST collected from the retailer less $5 GST paid to the manufacturer).

The example in Figure 2.1 illustrates that neither the manufacturer, the wholesaler nor the retailer bears the tax; each passes it on in the form of a higher selling price (a GST-inclusive price). The result is that GST is ultimately borne by the consumer, who is not entitled to obtain a credit for the GST paid. GST can therefore be seen as a tax on consumption. In the example in Figure 2.1, the total amount of the GST imposed on the supply is $60, which is embedded in the (final) price paid by the consumer.

# Taxable supplies

Under the GST legislation, *A New Tax System (Goods and Services Tax) Act 1999* (Cth) (the GST Act), a person must pay GST on any 'taxable supply' the person makes.

Broadly, a person makes a taxable supply if:

a   the supply is for consideration
b   the supply is made in the course or furtherance of an enterprise that the supplier carries on
c   the supply is connected with Australia, and
d   the supplier is registered, or required to be registered under the GST Act.

By way of example, a Victorian footwear retailer who is registered for GST must pay GST on the sale of each pair of shoes to a customer in Victoria, because each sale constitutes a 'taxable supply' – that is, each sale/supply is made for consideration (in other words, a purchase price is paid by a customer), and is made in the course of the retailer's business, which the retailer carries on in Australia.

# Calculating the amount of GST

Under the GST Act, the amount of GST on a taxable supply is 10% of the 'value of the taxable supply'. The value of a taxable supply is:

$$Price \times 10/11$$

Broadly, 'price' is the amount paid for the taxable supply. In the example of the Victorian footwear retailer, if a pair of shoes is sold by the retailer to a customer for $220, the price would be $220, and the GST that the retailer would be liable to pay to the ATO on the supply is $20 ($220 × 10/11).

As traders will seek to recover the GST from customers, the price the trader charges for its good or services will include GST. Therefore, to determine the GST component of a GST-inclusive price, the amount of the price is divided by 11.

# GST payable

The amount of GST payable to the ATO by an entity for a tax period is calculated as follows:

$$GST\ payable = GST\ on\ sales - Input\ tax\ credits$$

## Input tax credits

A business pays GST on goods and services (or *business inputs*) consumed in the normal course of business. The GST Act allows a credit for such GST paid; that is, an *input tax credit*.

Examples of business inputs that give rise to input tax credits are:

- purchase of trading stock
- purchase of materials and consumables
- purchase of capital assets such as land and buildings, plant and equipment, vehicles and office equipment
- utilities such as electricity, gas and water
- fees charged by accountants, solicitors, advertising agencies and the like
- rent on business premises
- consultants' fees
- insurance
- dues and subscriptions
- postage and delivery.

# GST refundable

If a business's input tax credits for a particular tax period exceed its GST liability on its taxable supplies, it is entitled to a refund of the difference from the ATO. This may occur, for example, where a business has acquired expensive new capital equipment during the relevant period and so has a high level of input tax credits.

## GST-free supplies

A supply that is 'GST-free' is not a taxable supply. The GST Act sets out categories of supplies that are GST-free; that is, the person making the supply does not have a liability to pay GST in relation to the supply.

## Food

The general rule is that food for human consumption is GST-free. However, there are a number of exceptions to this rule, including:

- restaurant and take-away food
- confectionery and snack food
- bakery products (except bread)
- prepared food
- soft drinks.

This list of exceptions is not exhaustive. The regulations covering the GST treatment of food are detailed and complex.

## Other GST-free supplies

Other items that are GST-free include:

- health services, such as those provided by doctors, hospitals, physiotherapists, chiropractors, osteopaths and other health professionals
- prescription medicines
- private health insurance premiums
- ambulance subscriptions
- course charges by educational institutions
- childcare
- religious services
- council, water and sewerage rates
- exports.

The above are only examples. A detailed analysis of GST-free supplies is not required for the purposes of this book.

Although a trader making GST-free supplies does not collect and remit GST in respect of the those supplies, the trader is entitled to claim an input tax credit for GST paid on purchases of goods and services made for the purpose of making those GST-free supplies. For example, sales of meat by a butcher shop are GST-free. The business, though, would still be entitled to claim input tax credits for GST paid on items such as electricity, rent, telephones and purchases of fixed assets. As no GST is collected, the business would receive a GST refund each tax period.

# Input-taxed supplies

Certain supplies of goods and services are *input-taxed*. This means that no GST is payable on the supply (i.e. it is not a taxable supply), but the business making the supply pays GST on its business inputs. The business is not entitled to input tax credits for GST paid on inputs used in making input-taxed supplies.

From a business perspective, services provided by banks such as loans and account facilities are input-taxed. Thus, if a business borrows money from a bank, no GST is charged by the bank on the loan or on any establishment costs or interest charges relating to the loan. The same applies to bank fees and charges relating to the business's cheque account. However, the bank must pay GST on its business inputs, for which it cannot claim input tax credits.

Conversely, a business is not required to pay GST on interest paid to it by its bank.

There are numerous other examples of input-taxed supplies.

# Combination of GST-taxable, GST-free and input-taxed sales

Accounting for GST is relatively uncomplicated where a business's sales are either all subject to GST, all GST-free or all input-taxed.

Complications arise where a business makes a combination of GST-taxable, GST-free and input-taxed supplies. For example, some products sold by supermarkets will be GST-free and others will be subject to GST. Supermarkets and other food retailers will need to be able to readily identify which items are taxable and which are not, so that the correct amount of GST is levied and paid.

As already mentioned, banking services provided by banks are input-taxed, but other services they provide, such as travel services and investment advice, are subject to GST. Input tax credits cannot be claimed for input-taxed services, so GST paid on business inputs needs to be apportioned between taxable and input-taxed supplies.

In all examples and exercises in this book it is assumed, for reasons of simplicity, that all goods and services sold are subject to GST. It will also be assumed, where it is stated that prices include GST, that the GST component is exactly $\frac{1}{11}$ of the price.

# Business transactions not subject to GST

As already mentioned, GST applies to all taxable supplies of goods and services in Australia, with the exception of GST-free supplies and input-taxed supplies.

Any transaction that does not involve a taxable supply of goods or services, then, is not subject to GST. The following is a list of some examples of business transactions not subject to GST.

- Wages, salaries, commissions, bonuses etc. paid to employees
- Superannuation contributions on behalf of employees
- Payments of taxes such as GST, income tax, payroll tax, fringe benefits tax etc.

- Drawings of cash by the proprietor for personal use
- Payments to creditors
- Receipts from debtors
- Loans and loan repayments.

# The accounting process

In Chapter 1, we outlined the sequence in which transactions are processed in the accounting system. Figure 2.2 is a brief summary of that sequence.

Recall that, before learning how to process transactions in the sequence shown in Figure 2.2, we first had to examine the basic elements of accounting reports (statement of comprehensive income and statement of financial position) and the ledger. When students become familiar with these elements, we can proceed to study the accounting process in its correct sequence.

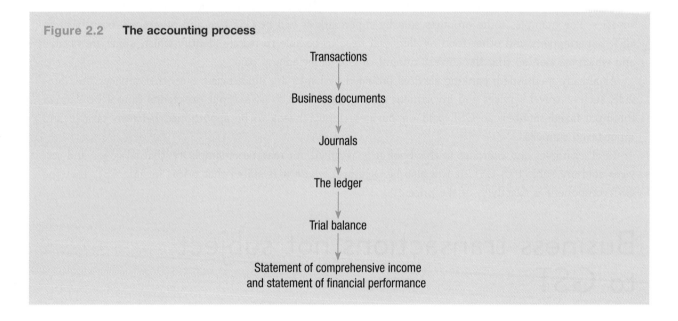

**Figure 2.2    The accounting process**

Transactions
↓
Business documents
↓
Journals
↓
The ledger
↓
Trial balance
↓
Statement of comprehensive income
and statement of financial performance

# Business documents

Whenever a financial *transaction* occurs, a *business document* is prepared. This document records all relevant details about the transaction and becomes the source of an entry in the accounting records. Business documents are the source of most entries in the accounting records.

An understanding of business documents (or 'source documents') and the transactions they represent is a very important part of the study of accounting.

# Types of business documents

In this chapter students will learn how to use the following common documents.

1  Purchase order  A written request for the supply of goods or services
2  Delivery docket  A document that accompanies goods when they are delivered
3  Tax invoice  A bill charging a customer for goods or services supplied
4  Adjustment note  A document that allows a customer a reduction in the original amount charged for goods or services supplied
5  Cheque  An order to a bank to pay a sum of money to a specified person
6  Remittance advice  A document accompanying a payment, setting out details of the amount paid
7  Receipt  A written acknowledgement of money received
8  Point-of-sale daily summary  A record of the daily takings through a point-of-sale (POS) device such as a cash register or point-of-sale computer terminal
9  Bank-deposit slip  A document prepared when depositing cash/cheques in a bank account
10  Statement of account  A monthly summary of transactions sent to a customer
11  POS receipt/tax invoice  A customer receipt prepared by a POS device after each transaction
12  Bank statement  A document that provides evidence of electronic funds transfer (EFT) transactions, direct debits, direct credits, bank charges and interest received and paid.

# Design and preparation of business documents

The examples of business documents provided below are typical of those used in business. The design of business documents will vary according to the requirements of each individual business. However, in the interests of efficiency and accurate recording, a business will develop a standardised set of documents appropriate to its needs. A business should also have in place documented policies and procedures to assist staff in the preparation of the various types of documents used in that business. When preparing documents it is important that these procedures are followed to ensure that all business transactions are properly accounted for.

# Examples of business documents

Some of the transactions of Hardware Wholesalers during October 2016 will be examined to illustrate the use of business documents.

# 1   Purchase order

This document is a formal request for the supply of goods or services. Its main purpose is to provide the supplier with instructions on the description and quantity of goods or the nature of services required, the date of delivery and an estimate of price.

The original order is forwarded to the intended supplier and a duplicate is retained by the customer for later reference.

## Example

On 2 October 2016, Hardware Wholesalers sent the following order to A Walters:

| Purchase Order | | No. 2155 |
|---|---|---|
| | **Hardware Wholesalers**<br>147 Pall Mall<br>Newville 3950<br>Tel. 9400 4120<br>ABN: 00 111 222 333 | |
| To<br>*A Walters*<br>*14 Mitchell Ave*<br>*Newville 3950* | | Date *2.10.16* |

Please supply the goods listed below, quoting our order number.

| Quantity | Description | Estimated price (inc. GST) |
|---|---|---|
| 20 | *Stainless steel saucepans, 2 litre* | *$16.50 each* |
| 20 | *Vegetable strainers* | *$1.10 each* |
| 1 | *Tool box, pressed steel, 'Ace' brand* | *Not known* |

Delivery required by *5 October*          Authorised by: *Neville Poustie*

Like all business documents, purchase orders are numbered serially to ensure that all documents are accounted for.

All details on the above order are essential to provide adequate instructions to the supplier.

# 2   Delivery docket

This document is used when goods are to be delivered to the customer by some external party, such as a general carrier. Upon receiving the goods, the customer signs the delivery docket. The carrier then provides the customer with a copy of the docket and retains the original, as evidence supporting the physical transfer of goods.

## Example

On 4 October 2016, A Walters sent the goods requested on purchase order 2155 to Hardware Wholesalers. The goods were accompanied by the following delivery docket:

| | | |
|---|---|---|
| Date  *4.10.16* | **Delivery Docket** | No. 38 |

Received from:  *A Walters, 14 Mitchell Ave, Newville 3950*

The following goods:

|  | |
|---|---|
| 20 | *Stainless steel saucepans, 2 litre* |
| 20 | *Vegetable strainers* |
| 1 | *Tool box, pressed steel, 'Ace' brand* |

in good order and condition.

Delivered to:      *Hardware Wholesalers, 147 Pall Mall, Newville*

Signature of receiver  *Neville Poustie*

As the main purpose of the delivery docket is to verify the physical transfer of goods, there are usually no prices quoted for the items delivered.

It is common practice in many businesses to prepare a *receiving report* when goods are received. This document is prepared for internal purposes and contains similar information to that contained in a delivery docket. A receiving report is prepared as goods are received into stock and has the advantage of standardising the documentation relating to goods received. The importance of the receiving report is discussed later in this text in sections dealing with *internal control*.

## 3   Tax invoice

When goods or services have been supplied, the supplier will provide a tax invoice 'charging' the customer for the goods or services. This document provides complete details of the transaction, including the price of the goods or services.

A business cannot claim an input tax credit unless it holds a *tax invoice* for the acquisition of the relevant goods or services. The supplier of the goods or services must issue the tax invoice. A tax invoice is not required (for the purpose of claiming an input tax credit) where the total value of the acquisition is $82.50 (inc. GST) or less.

The format of a tax invoice must comply with the requirements of the GST legislation. A detailed examination of these requirements is beyond the scope of this text. The example documents shown in this section comply with the GST legislation.

## Example

On 5 October 2016, A Walters forwarded the following invoice charging Hardware Wholesalers for the goods delivered on 4 October.

| Tax Invoice | | | | No. 709 |
|---|---|---|---|---|
| | **A Walters — Hardware Manufacturer/Importer** | | | |
| | 14 Mitchell Ave | | | |
| Debit to | Newville 3950 | | | |
| *Hardware Wholesalers* | ABN 00 222 333 444 | | | |
| *147 Pall Mall* | | | | |
| *Newville 3950* | | | | |

| Date  *5.10.16* | | Order no.  *2155* | Delivery Date  *4.10.16* | |
|---|---|---|---|---|
| Description | | Quantity | Unit Price inc. GST | Amount inc. GST |
| *Stainless steel saucepans* | | *20* | *$16.50 each* | *330.00* |
| *Vegetable strainers* | | *20* | *$1.10 each* | *22.00* |
| *Tool box, pressed steel, 'Ace' brand* | | *1* | *$11.00* | *11.00* |
| *Total inc. GST* | | | | *$363.00* |
| *GST included in this invoice $33.00* | | | | |

Hardware Wholesalers received the above invoice because it purchased goods from A Walters. If Hardware Wholesalers *sold* goods it would prepare a tax invoice and provide it to the customer. Consider the following transaction.

## Example

On 6 October 2016, Hardware Wholesalers sold goods on credit to A Barton and provided the following invoice to charge Barton for the goods:

| Tax Invoice | | | | No. 834 |
|---|---|---|---|---|
| | **Hardware Wholesalers** | | | |
| | 147 Pall Mall | | | |
| To | Newville 3950 | | | |
| *A Barton* | Tel (03) 9400 4120 | Date: *6.10.16* | | |
| *34 Shakespeare St* | ABN 00 111 222 333 | Order no *761* | | |
| *Newville 3950* | | Delivered *6.10.16* | | |

| Quantity | Description | Unit Price inc. GST | Amount inc. GST |
|---|---|---|---|
| *20* | *Steak knives, Nino brand* <br> *GST inc. in this invoice $14.00* | *$7.70 each* | *$154.00* |

Hardware Wholesalers would retain the invoice duplicate for later entry in the accounting records.

# 4   Adjustment note

Following the supply of goods or services, it is sometimes necessary for a business to make an adjustment to the price (and GST) charged. Circumstances that lead to such adjustments include:

- returns of goods
- reduction in the price of goods following an overcharge
- prompt payment discounts
- refund of part of the price of goods or services
- bad debts
- taking or consuming goods (originally purchased for business use) for private purposes.

In some situations where an adjustment is made to a transaction that is subject to GST, the supplier of the goods or services is required to issue an *adjustment note*. In the case of prompt payment discounts, a tax invoice that shows the terms of settlement or a statement of account may also be considered as adjustment notes. Adjustment notes are not required to substantiate bad debt adjustments.

For GST compliance purposes, there is no requirement to issue an adjustment note if the GST-inclusive amount of the adjustment is $75 or less.

Consider the following examples of adjustment notes arising from price reductions and returns of goods previously purchased or sold.

## Example

On 7 October 2016, Hardware Wholesalers advised A Walters that two of the stainless steel saucepans received on 4 October were severely dented. An allowance of $5.00 per saucepan was requested and an adjustment note was received from A Walters the following day:

| Adjustment Note | | | No. C84 |
|---|---|---|---|
| | **A Walters — Hardware Manufacturer/Importer** | | |
| | 14 Mitchell Ave | | |
| Credit to | Newville 3950 | | |
| *Hardware Wholesalers* | ABN: 00 222 333 444 | | |
| *147 Pall Mall* | | | |
| *Newville 3950* | | | |
| Date *7.10.16* | Invoice no. *709* | | |
| Description | | Price inc. GST | Amount inc. GST |
| *2    Stainless steel saucepans – dented* | | | |
| *        – credit allowance* | | *2 x $5.50* | *$11.00* |
| *GST included in this adjustment note* | | | *$1.00* |

A Walters would provide the original adjustment note to Hardware Wholesalers and retain the duplicate for later entry in his accounting records.

If Hardware Wholesalers itself allowed a credit to one of its customers, it would prepare an adjustment note for that customer. Consider the following transaction.

On 9 October 2016, A Barton returned five of the steak knives (supplied on 6 October) and requested a credit allowance for the full price of the goods returned. Barton claimed that the five steak knives were in excess of his requirements. Hardware Wholesalers prepared the following adjustment note and provided the original to A Barton.

| Adjustment Note | | | No. 246 |
|---|---|---|---|
| | **Hardware Wholesalers** | | |
| To | 147 Pall Mall | | |
| *A Barton* | Newville 3950 | | |
| *34 Shakespeare St* | ABN 00 111 222 333 | | |
| *Newville 3950* | | | |

| Date  *9.10.16* | Invoice no  *834* | | |
|---|---|---|---|
| Quantity | Description | Unit Price inc. GST | Amount inc. GST |
| *5* | *Steak knives, Nino brand* | *$7.70 each* | *$38.50* |
| | *GST inc. in this adjustment note $3.50* | | |

## 5   Cheque and cheque butt

A cheque is an order made on a bank to pay on demand a stipulated amount of money to the person named on the cheque. The *drawer* of the cheque is the person or organisation who writes out the cheque. The *payee* is the person or organisation to whom the cheque is made out. This procedure is set out in Figure 2.3.

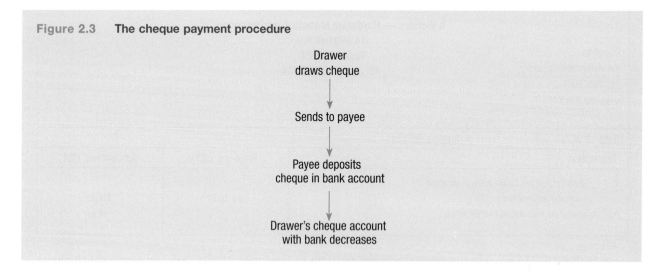

**Figure 2.3   The cheque payment procedure**

Drawer
draws cheque
↓
Sends to payee
↓
Payee deposits
cheque in bank account
↓
Drawer's cheque account
with bank decreases

Cheque books are printed by banks in standard form and consist of two parts:

1  the cheque butt, retained by the drawer for later reference
2  the cheque, received by the payee who deposits it in a bank account.

It is now common practice for banks to include a multi-page transaction record within each cheque book rather than providing a cheque butt attached to each cheque. For the purposes of this text we will utilise cheque butts as evidence of cheque payments.

## Example

On 15 October 2016, Hardware Wholesalers paid the balance owing to creditor A Walters, by preparing and forwarding a cheque. The amount of the payment was calculated as follows:

| | |
|---|---:|
| Amount charged – tax invoice 709 | $363.00 |
| *less* Credit allowance – adjustment note C 84 | 11.00 |
| = Amount owing | 352.00 |
| *less* Discount for prompt payment (inc. GST $2.00) | 22.00 |
| = Amount of cheque | $330.00 |

Cheque butt
(retained by
drawer)

Cheque
(forwarded to payee)

The cheque butt or transaction record, retained by the business that draws the cheque, provides information for subsequent entries in the accounting records. It is therefore important that full details of the payment (including any GST included in the transaction) are recorded on the cheque butt or transaction record.

# 6   Remittance advice

When a payment is made, most businesses enclose a remittance advice with the payment. A remittance advice sets out the details of the payment and is of great assistance to the payee.

## Example

When Hardware Wholesalers prepared the above cheque for payment to A Walters, it also prepared the remittance advice shown below to forward with the cheque:

| | |
|---|---|
| **Remittance Advice**<br>Hardware Wholesalers<br>147 Pall Mall<br>Newville 3950<br>ABN 00 111 222 333 | |

To
A Walters

14 Mitchell Ave

Newville 3950

Date 15.10.16

| Date | Particulars | Ref | Debit | Credit | Balance |
|---|---|---|---|---|---|
| 2016 | | | $ | $ | $ |
| 5 Oct | Purchases | Inv. 709 | | 363.00 | 363.00 Cr |
| 7 | Purchases returns and allowances | Adj. Note 246 | 11.00 | | 352.00 Cr |

Details of payment:
Balance owing          $352.00
less Discount              22.00
= Cheque amount    $330.00

As a courtesy to customers, some suppliers attach a 'tear-off' remittance slip to their invoices or statements of account. In this situation, it is not necessary for customers to prepare their own remittance advice when paying the supplier.

# 7   Receipt

This is a document used to acknowledge the receipt of money. For reasons of economy, most businesses do not issue a receipt unless specifically requested by the customer. The exception to this is the POS receipt/tax invoice (see below) that is automatically prepared by a POS device for over-the-counter and credit card transactions.

## Example

On 20 October 2016, Hardware Wholesalers received a cheque from debtor A Barton for $112.75 (being the balance owing by A Barton, less discount of $2.75), and prepared the following receipt:

| Date 20.10.16 | **Receipt** | No. 345 |
|---|---|---|
| | Hardware Wholesalers | |
| | 147 Pall Mall | |
| | Newville 3950 | |
| | ABN: 00 111 222 333 | |

Received from    A Barton

The sum of:    One hundred and twelve .......................................................................... dollars and

seventy–five .......................................................................... cents

Being for    Payment of account                                    $ 112.75

Discount $ 2.75

Authorised    Neville Poustie

Hardware Wholesalers would forward the original receipt to A Barton and retain the duplicate for entry in its own accounting records.

## 8    POS daily summary

Most businesses use POS devices to record over-the-counter transactions such as cash, EFTPOS and credit card sales. The benefits of using this method of recording are listed below.

- A daily summary is prepared by the POS device and is used as the basis for accounting entries and reconciling sales and other amounts received with the final balance of cash remaining in the cash drawer.
- The POS device provides a detailed breakdown of amounts received from various sources.
- A receipt/tax invoice is automatically prepared for the customer.

### Example

On 20 October 2016, Hardware Wholesalers had cash, EFTPOS and credit card sales totalling $1870.00 and recorded these sales through its cash register (see Figure 2.4).

**Figure 2.4    Recording sales through a POS device**

**POS receipts/tax invoices**

| Tax Invoice | |
|---|---|
| Hardware Wholesalers | |
| ABN 00 111 222 333 | |
| | $ |
| Nails 200 g | 4.40 |
| Total inc. GST | 4.40 |
| GST inc. in this total | $0.40 |
| 20/10/16    11.32 am | |

**POS daily summary**

| POS Daily | |
|---|---|
| Summary 20/10/16 | |
| | $ |
| Cash sales | 880.00 |
| EFTPOS sales* | 550.00 |
| Other credit card sales** | 440.00 |
| Total inc. GST | 1 870.00 |
| GST inc. in total | $170.00 |

*EFTPOS sales include sales by direct debit to customers' bank accounts, and sales to customers using bank-issued credit cards such as MasterCard and Visa.
**Other credit card sales include sales to customers using non-bank-issued credit cards such as American Express and Diners Club.

## 9 Bank-deposit slip (and deposit butt)

Most businesses bank all cash and cheques received on a daily basis. To assist the bank, the business will prepare a bank-deposit slip giving details of all cash and cheques included in the deposit.

Deposit books are printed by banks in standard form and consist of two parts:

1 the deposit slip, presented to the bank when the deposit is made and used by the bank to record an increase in the account of the depositor

2 the deposit butt, retained by the business (depositor) as proof of the deposit. In circumstances where the bank does not require a deposit slip, a teller's receipt is provided as a record of the deposit.

### Example

On 20 October 2016, Hardware Wholesalers deposited cash ($880 cash sales) and the cheque from A Barton for $112.75 in its bank account. It prepared the following deposit slip (and butt) to accompany the deposit:

Deposit slips issued by some banks consist of an original (presented to the bank with the deposit) and a duplicate (retained by the business for its own records). In this case, the duplicate deposit slip assumes the same purpose as the deposit butt in the above example.

Given that cash is a liquid asset and thus most likely to be susceptible to dishonest practices (compared with other, more tangible assets), strict procedures and controls must be implemented over cash receipts. At this stage of the text, however, we will defer the more detailed aspects of internal controls over cash to further discussion in Chapter 5 of the text.

## 10   Statement of account

This document is prepared by the supplier and sent to the customer, usually on a monthly basis. Its purpose is to provide the customer with a complete summary of the trading transactions that have occurred in the past month. It also highlights the total amount due (if any) at the end of the month.

### Example

On 31 October 2016, Hardware Wholesalers prepared and forwarded the statement of account (for October) shown below to A Barton.

**Statement of Account**
Hardware Wholesalers
147 Pall Mall
Newville 3950
ABN 00 111 222 333

To
A Barton
34 Shakespeare St
Newville 3950

Statement for *October 2016*

| Date | Particulars | Ref | Debit | Credit | Balance |
|------|-------------|-----|-------|--------|---------|
| 2016 | | | $ | $ | $ |
| Oct 6 | Sales | Inv. 834 | 154.00 | | 154.00 Dr |
| 9 | Sales returns | A/Note 246 | | 38.50 | 115.50 Dr |
| 20 | Bank | Rec. 345 | | 112.75 | 2.75 Dr |
| | Discount | | | 2.75 | Nil |

Terms:   2% discount if paid within 7 days
Otherwise net cash 30 days

As stated earlier, it is now more common practice to include a tear-off remittance advice at the bottom of a statement of account.

## 11   POS receipt/tax invoice

This document is prepared by a POS device and provided to the customer as evidence of the transaction. Refer to Figure 2.4 for an example of a POS receipt/tax invoice.

## 12   Bank statement

As a service to customers, a bank prepares a statement on a regular basis listing the transactions on the customer's account for a given period. In Chapter 5 of this text you will find examples of bank statements and see how they are used to reconcile the cash records of the business.

At this point it is necessary to outline the transactions revealed by a bank statement, which must be recorded in the business's accounting records. These transactions, which could be referred to as 'bank statement transactions', include the following:

- EFT transactions These represent electronic funds transfers between the business and other parties and would include the following types of transactions:
  - electronic receipts from customers and other parties
  - electronic payments to suppliers of goods and services.
- Direct debits These are automatic payments charged to a business bank account under an arrangement with the bank. Examples include loan repayments and regular payments to suppliers for such items as electricity, rent and insurance.
- Direct credits These are deposits made by customers and other parties directly into the business bank account. In these situations, the business provides its bank account details to the relevant party, who then deposits funds into the account. Alternatively, if this deposit is made electronically, it is classified as an EFT receipt.
- Bank fees and charges These represent bank fees and charges deducted directly from the business bank account by the bank.
- Bank interest received This is a periodic deposit, representing interest earned on the balance in the business bank account.
- Interest on overdraft Where the business bank account is overdrawn, the bank will deduct interest from the account.

A business is able to access details of these transactions on a regular basis via its electronic banking facilities. They can therefore be identified and recorded in the business's accounting records on a continuous basis.

## Example

On 25 October 2016, A Dalmayer, a customer of Hardware Wholesalers, paid the balance owing on her account ($375) by EFT. On 27 October, Hardware Wholesalers identified this transaction when accessing their bank account online and subsequently recorded the receipt in its accounting records.

In order to simplify the learning process, in this text, only the following types of bank statement transactions will be identified and recorded at this stage:

- electronic receipts from customers (EFT receipts)
- electronic payments to suppliers (EFT payments)
- direct debits
- direct credits.

The recording of all other bank statement transactions and other adjustments will be fully dealt with as part of the bank reconciliation process covered in Chapter 5.

The business documents illustrated above contain all of the information necessary to comply with the GST legislation. (However, students should note that simplified documents used in examples and exercises in later sections of this book will not contain all of this information.) The formats of these documents are typical of those used by most business concerns. It is important to remember, however, that the formats of documents will vary slightly from one business to another.

Figure 2.5 shows the flow of various business documents covered in this chapter.

**Figure 2.5**    **The flow of business documents**

| Transaction | Customer | Document | Supplier |
|---|---|---|---|
| Goods ordered | Retains duplicate | → Purchase order → | Receives original |
| Goods delivered | Receives duplicate with goods | ← Delivery docket ↔ | Receives original, signed by customer |
| Account sent (for goods supplied on credit) | Receives original | ← Tax invoice ← | Retains duplicate |
| Price adjustments for returns etc. | Receives original | ← Adjustment note ← | Retains duplicate |
| Payment made | Retains butt | → Cheque → | Deposits in bank |
| Details of payment (sent with cheque) | Retains duplicate | → Remittance advice → | Receives original |
| Payment acknowledged | Receives original | ← Receipt ← | Retains duplicate |
| Cash sale of goods (and EFTPOS and credit card sales) | Receives POS receipt/tax invoice | ← POS receipt/tax invoice and POS daily summary → | Retains POS daily summary |
| Cash and cheques deposited in bank | | Bank-deposit slip and butt ← | Retains butt, presents slip to bank with deposit |
| Monthly statement of account sent | Receives original | ← Statement of account ← | Retains duplicate |
| EFT transactions, direct debits, direct credits, bank fees and charges, interest received and paid | Transactions recorded | ← Bank statement ← | Customer's bank prepares bank statement |

The documents examined in this chapter are prepared by a business for use in its transactions with external parties (customers, suppliers, banks etc.). There are other documents used by businesses, mainly to record movements of stock (inventories) within the business. These documents are not illustrated in this text as they are beyond the scope of introductory accounting principles.

# Electronic funds transfer and credit card transactions

Electronic funds transfer (EFT) is a common method used by individuals and businesses to make payments for goods and services received. From a business point of view, there are two types of EFT transactions:

1  electronic funds transfer at point of sale (EFTPOS)
2  EFT using the Internet and electronic banking software provided by banks.

## EFTPOS

An electronic funds transfer at point of sale (EFTPOS) is made when a business allows a customer to use a debit card or a bank-issued credit card to purchase goods or services over the counter.

Debit card sales result in an electronic transfer of funds from the customer's bank account to the business's bank account.

Bank-issued credit cards allow customers to make purchases from a business on credit and to pay the bank (the card provider) at a later date. Well-known credit cards issued by banks in Australia include Visa and MasterCard.

When customers use debit cards or bank-issued credit cards to make purchases from a business, the proceeds from these transactions are credited to the business's bank account at the end of each day. A detailed breakdown of these transactions is provided to the business by the bank daily. A merchant fee is charged to the business's bank account monthly.

EFTPOS sales are treated by the business as cash sales for accounting purposes.

## Sales on other credit cards

Sales on other credit cards (such as American Express and Diners Club) are treated as credit sales, as the card providers do not normally settle accounts with the business until a number of days after the transaction occurs. These card providers charge a merchant fee, and this fee is deducted from payments made by the card provider to the business.

Figure 2.6 summarises the accounting treatment of EFTPOS and credit card sales.

**Figure 2.6    Accounting treatment of EFTPOS and credit card sales**

| Type of transaction | Accounting treatment |
| --- | --- |
| EFTPOS sales (debit card or bank-issued credit card) | Cash sales |
| Sales on other credit cards | Credit sales |

# Purchases using a business credit card

It is common for businesses to use credit cards as a means of payment for goods and services received. Such purchases are treated as credit purchases in the business's accounting records, regardless of the type of credit card used. The credit card provider issues the business with a monthly statement summarising all transactions for the period. The business is then required to pay at least the 'minimum payment' specified on the statement by a specified due date. If the full amount owing is not paid by this date, interest will be incurred on the balance owing.

# EFT (using the Internet and electronic banking software)

As a service to customers, banks provide Internet banking facilities to enable transfers of funds to be made electronically. Using this service allows a business to:

- transfer funds from its own bank account to the accounts of other parties
- use bill-paying facilities such as Bpay to either pay for goods and services received or allow customers to pay for goods and services supplied to them.

# Business documents that lead to entries in the accounting records

Of the twelve types of business documents outlined on page 117, only six are used to make entries in the accounting records.

1 Tax invoice Used to record purchase/sale of goods or services
2 Adjustment note Used to record transactions such as purchases returns/sales returns of goods
3 Cheque butt or transaction record Used to record cash (cheque) payments
4 Receipt duplicate Used to record money (cash/cheques) received
5 POS daily summary Used to record sales through a POS device
6 Bank statement Used to identify EFT transactions

These are the main documents that lead to entries in the accounting records. There are, however, other types of documents for certain unusual transactions that also lead to accounting entries. For example, a solicitor's letter may be used to record a bad debt in the accounting records.

The other documents outlined earlier in this chapter, although important in the trading process, do not lead to entries in the accounting records. The reasons for this are listed below.

- Purchase order  This only represents a request for goods; therefore no transaction has actually occurred.
- Delivery docket  This records the physical transfer of goods and does not contain prices of goods supplied. Therefore it cannot be used to record the transaction in the accounting records.
- Cheque  This is deposited in the payee's bank account (like cash) and cannot be retained for later entry in the accounting records. It is for this reason that the receipt (duplicate) is used to record money received.
- Remittance advice  This is only a summary of transactions already entered in the accounting records from other documents.
- Receipt (original, received by customer)  This represents a transaction already entered in the records from one of various documents when the amount was paid.
- POS receipt/tax invoice issued to customers  This is the customer's record of the transaction; from the business's point of view, the transaction would be included in the POS daily summary.
- Bank-deposit slip (and butt)  This is only a list of cash and cheques deposited, representing transactions already entered in the records from other documents.
- Statement of account  This is only a summary of transactions already entered in the accounting records from other documents.

# Documents used in a service business

All examples given so far in this chapter have related to businesses that buy and sell goods. The documents used to record transactions in a service business are the same as those illustrated in this chapter, the only difference being that tax invoices etc. are made out for services rather than for goods supplied.

## Document processing guidelines

A business will normally have documented policies and procedures relating to the authorisation, checking and processing of business documents it receives and issues. The authorisation of transactions is covered in later sections of this text, which deal with internal control procedures. At this point we will briefly outline procedures for checking the validity and accuracy of business documents processed by a business.

For documents received from suppliers and other external sources, it is common practice for the following types of checks to be made.

- Each supplier's invoices should be checked for validity against the relevant purchase order and receiving report.

- Prices and extensions on supplier's invoices should be checked for accuracy.
- Supplier adjustment notes should be matched to the original invoice and prices and extensions checked.

For documents prepared and issued by the business it is important that a thorough checking process is implemented. For example, it is desirable that the duties of clerical staff are segregated in a way that enables the work of one staff member to be checked by another. In the case of sales invoices, it is important that the details on the sales invoice (generated by the sales department) are checked by the despatch department when goods are prepared for delivery. Sales adjustment notes must be approved by authorised personnel and details checked against the original sales invoice.

Other checking processes are detailed in later chapters that deal with internal controls over accounts receivable, accounts payable and cash. A sound system of internal control over the accounting system of a business is an effective means of ensuring that errors in business documents are minimised.

## Filing of documents

After business documents have been recorded in the accounting system it is important that they are systematically filed for later reference in relation to:

- enquiries from customers, suppliers or management
- compliance requirements imposed by various taxation authorities, superannuation funds, government agencies and other external parties
- internal and external audit requirements.

Examples of the filing requirements for documents are listed below.

- Paid supplier invoices (and relevant adjustment notes, if any) should be stamped 'Paid' and could be filed in cheque number sequence. All related documents (such as purchase orders and receiving reports/delivery notes) should be attached to the relevant invoice.
- Copies of sales invoices and related adjustment notes may be filed in numerical sequence to allow easy reference. Note that where these documents are computer-generated, they should be stored securely in electronic format.
- Most other documents, including bank statements, petty cash documentation and POS daily summaries, should be filed in date sequence.

 **EXERCISES**

In all exercises, assume that GST is $\frac{1}{11}$ of the price where indicated.

2.1    What role do business documents play in the accounting process? Discuss.

2.2    Why are business documents usually pre-numbered? Discuss.

2.3    State the documents that support the following transactions of P Field:
    a    P Field ordered goods from G Brown.
    b    G Brown delivered goods to P Field.

c   G Brown sent P Field an invoice for the goods.

d   P Field used a business credit card to purchase goods from S Small.

e   P Field returned goods to G Brown and was given a credit allowance.

f   P Field settled the amount due to G Brown, paying by cheque.

2.4   State the documents that support the following transactions of Luqman Industries (owner, A Luqman).

a   Bought goods on credit from R Rolf, $130.

b   Bought goods by cheque, $600.

c   Paid creditor C Carter, $200 by EFT. Discount received, $10.

d   Sold goods on credit to R Roberts, $700.

e   R Roberts returned goods and received an allowance of $60.

f   Paid rent on premises by EFT, $120.

g   A Luqman, the owner, withdrew $200 cash for his own use, by cashing a cheque on the business's bank account.

h   Returned goods to R Rolf, $20.

i   Purchased motor vehicle costing $12 000. Paid a deposit of $4000 by cheque, the balance to be paid to AB Motors in 90 days.

j   Received $290 payment by cheque from debtor A Nelson. Discount allowed, $10.

k   Cash sales, $550 (recorded through a POS device).

2.5   Complete the appropriate document for each of the following transactions for Clarry's Cartage Service (owner, C Yalater). Clarry's Cartage Service is located at 45 Bandit Road, Shelton 3800 and uses the Shelton Branch of the Commonwealth Bank.

*2018*

1 Sep   Paid Munk Motors for vehicle repairs, $330 inc. GST (cheque no. 470).

2   Received cash from J Jackson for cartage job, $88 inc. GST (receipt no. R32).

3   Completed a cartage job on credit for B Harris (of 16 Jelly Street, Shelton 3800), $440 inc. GST (tax invoice no. 661).

4   Purchased petrol and oil on credit from Zero Oil Supplies (75 Gasoline Grove, Shelton 3800), $770 inc. GST (Order no. 700) (tax invoice no. 109).

5   Allowed B Harris a credit of $55 inc. GST (re the Sept 3 job – goods arrived 1 hour later than promised) (adjustment note no. C44).

6   Paid Zero Oil Supplies the amount owing, less 10% discount (cheque no. 471).

2.6   Complete the appropriate document for each of the following transactions for Bunny's Pet Shop (owner, Bunny Warren), 14 Ferret Drive, Jackson 5997.

*2017*

1 Jul   Supplied on credit to G Haire (4 Mary Street, Jackson 5997): 15 Siamese kittens @ $4.40 each inc. GST; 4 border collie pups @ $77.00 each inc. GST (G Haire's order no. was 2016) (tax invoice no. 331).

2   Paid electricity account to SEC, $440 inc. GST (cheque no. 4761).

3      Ordered from B Black (15 Greystone Road, Jackson 5997): 20 domestic pigeons @ $3.30 each inc. GST (order no. S232).

4      The pigeons ordered on 3 July were delivered by rail (delivery note no. D45).

5      Received an invoice from B Black for the pigeons delivered on 4 July (price was as estimated) (tax invoice no. 571).

6      Allowed a credit to G Haire. Ten of the Siamese kittens supplied on 1 July were not pure-bred and therefore were returned (adjustment note no. C55).

7      Sales, including GST (recorded through a POS device) were cash $275, EFTPOS $132, other credit cards $88 (POS daily summary).

8      Returned 5 of the domestic pigeons purchased on 3 July and was allowed a credit for the full price (adjustment note no. 7781).

9      Received the amount owing from G Haire, less $11 discount (receipt no. R55).

10     Paid the amount owing to B Black, less $2.20 discount. (Bunny's Pet Shop always sends a remittance advice when paying creditors.) (cheque no. 4762)

11     Sent a statement of account to G Haire (statement of account).

2.7*   You are working for Harfield Hardware Supply (a wholesale hardware supplier) at 1 Finch Street, Harfield 9445 (ABN 22 411 511 611). The manager, Brian Bolt, asks you to prepare the following documents:

a   A tax invoice (number 87HZ) using this purchase order:

---

**Gemini Hardware Stores**
79 Vary Street,
Harfield 9445
Tel. 3456 6543
ABN 11 011 122 233

**Purchase Order No. 66D**

Date   4.11.17

Delivery Date   6.11.17

To:   Harfield Hardware Supply
      1 Finch Street,
      Harfield 9445

| Description | Code | Quantity | Price (estimated) inc. GST |
|---|---|---|---|
| | | | $ |
| Sledge hammers, Ajax brand | S33 | 5 | 15.40 each |
| Cross saws, Ajax brand, size 2 | S41 | 3 | 25.30 each |
| Bridge spikes, 20cm | n7 | 100 | 0.55 each |

---

The prices as estimated above are correct, and the goods were delivered by the required date.

b  An adjustment note (number A4511) based on the following information:

| | |
|---|---|
| | 12 Thompson Road, |
| | Harfield 9445 |
| | ABN 77 444 111 555 |
| | 8 November 2017 |

Harfield Hardware Supply

1 Finch Street

Harfield 9445

Re Your Tax Invoice No. S311 – Goods damaged

Dear Sirs,

I am writing to request a credit allowance for the following:

Tax Invoice no. S311

Date 5/11/17

1 badly damaged wood plane – cost $24.20

I am prepared to keep the abovementioned plane, provided you allow me a suitable reduction in price.

I await your credit note at your earliest convenience.

Yours faithfully,

*I Mawinger*

I Mawinger

Brian Bolt (the manager) decided to allow Mrs Mawinger a reduction of 50% on the price of the plane (code no. H33).

c  A bank deposit slip for the following cash and cheques to be deposited in the bank on 11 November 2017:

| | | Details of cheques received: | | |
|---|---|---|---|---|
| | | Drawer | Bank | Amount |
| Notes | $1 055.00 | J Jones | New Harfield | $1 275.00 |
| Coins | 58.50 | P Allen | NSW | 845.00 |
| Cheques | 2 380.00 | T Hancock | New Harfield | 260.00 |
| Total | $3 493.50 | | | |

d  A receipt (number 751) for Mr H Poustie who paid his October account of $880.00 in cash on 14 November 2017. He was allowed 4% discount for prompt payment.

e A cheque drawn to 'Cash', to pay wages for the week ended 17 November 2017.

| Payroll summary for week ended 17 November 2017 | | | | | |
| --- | --- | --- | --- | --- | --- |
| | | Deductions | | | Net wages paid to employees |
| Particulars | Gross wages | Tax | Union | Total deductions | |
| | $ | $ | $ | $ | $ |
| Total | 3 450.00 | 1 044.00 | 86.00 | 1 130.00 | 2 320.00 |

f A statement of account for October 2017 for Mr A Tarr, using the information contained in the following simplified documents. (**Note** The balance owing by Mr Tarr on October 1 was $1500.00 Dr.)

Harfield Hardware Supply

Tax Invoice S080

4.10.17

To
A Tarr
1 Bay St
Harfield

| | $ |
| --- | --- |
| 10 tins nails | 176.00 |
| 1 chain saw | 990.00 |
| Total inc. GST | $1 166.00 |

---

Harfield Hardware Supply

R106

12.10.17

Received from: A Tarr
the sum of:
one thousand four
hundred and fifty six dollars
For: September account

$1 456.00

Discount $44.00

---

Harfield Hardware Supply

Adjustment note C902

20.10.17

To
A Tarr
1 Bay St
Harfield

| | $ |
| --- | --- |
| Overcharge on chainsaw | 154.00 |
| Total inc. GST | $154.00 |

---

Harfield Hardware Supply

Tax Invoice 165

26.10.17

To
A Tarr
1 Bay St
Harfield

| | $ |
| --- | --- |
| 2 stepladders | 198.00 |
| 10 paintbrushes | 77.00 |
| Total inc. GST | $275.00 |

A UWatch demonstration is available on the CD that accompanies this text for parts of this activity.

UWATCH 2.1

2.8 Prepare the relevant documents required to record the following transactions of A Sparks, electrical component retailer, 61 Don Street, Westville 3729, ABN 44 11 222 000.

*2016*

1 Jun    A Sparks ordered the following goods from M Abe, electrical component wholesaler, 473 Current Street, Southville 3731:

10 transistors at estimated price of $13.20 each inc. GST

40 thyristors at $3.30 each inc. GST

30 power circuit boards (price not known)

40 light-emitting diodes (price not known) (order no. P403).

2    M Abe charged A Sparks for the following goods:

10 transistors at $13.20 each inc. GST (part no. 309)

40 thyristors at $3.30 each inc. GST (part no. 607)

30 power circuit boards at $41.80 each inc. GST (part no. PC3642).

(**Note** Light-emitting diodes, part no. LED7734, out of stock) (tax invoice no. 1740). Abe's ABN is 66 000 111 999.

3    The goods charged on 2 June were delivered to A Sparks by a general carrier (delivery docket no. D36). At this time, it was discovered that one power circuit board had a major defect. M Abe agreed to allow a credit allowance of $40.70 inc. GST (adjustment note no. C79).

**ADDITIONAL EXERCISES**

2.9 This question is available on the CD that accompanies this text.

2.10* Name the document that is used to support an accounting entry for each of the following types of transactions. In each case, where appropriate, indicate which copy (that is, the original or the duplicate) would be used.

a    Credit purchase of stock

b    Wages paid by EFT

c    Cash sales of stock (through a POS device)

d    Credit purchases returns of stock

e    Services provided on credit

f    Credit sales of stock

g    Cheque received on account from a debtor

h    Credit sales returns of stock

i    A credit allowance given to a customer for unsatisfactory services provided

j    A bad debt written off

k    Withdrawal of stock by the proprietor for personal use

l    Business vehicle service paid for using a business credit card

m    A direct debit by the bank to the business bank account representing a regular monthly loan repayment

2.11    a    Briefly explain two ways in which suppliers' invoices can be checked for accuracy and validity.

b    Briefly explain the reasons for the systematic filing of all business documents.

2.12    a    Briefly outline the accounting treatment of EFTPOS and credit card sales.

b    Briefly outline how a business could utilise electronic banking facilities.

**SOLUTIONS**

2.7   a

| Tax Invoice | | | | No. 87HZ |
|---|---|---|---|---|

**Harfield Hardware Supply**
1 Finch Street,
Harfield 9445
ABN 22 411 511 611

Debit to:
Gemini Hardware Stores
79 Vary Street
HARFIELD 9445

| Date 6.11.17 | | Order no. 66D | | |
|---|---|---|---|---|
| Description | Quantity | Unit Price inc. GST | Amount inc. GST |
| | | $ | $ |
| Sledge hammers, Ajax brand (S33) | 5 | 15.40 | 77.00 |
| Cross saws, Ajax brand, size 2 (S41) | 3 | 25.30 | 75.90 |
| Bridge spikes, 20cm (N7) | 100 | 0.55 | 55.00 |
| Total (inc. GST) | | | $207.90 |
| GST included in this invoice $18.90 | | | |

b

| Adjustment Note | | | | No. A4511 |
|---|---|---|---|---|

Date 8.11.17

**Harfield Hardware Supply**
1 Finch Street
Harfield 9445
ABN 22 411 511 611

Credit to:
I Mawinger
12 Thompson Road
HARFIELD 9445

Invoice no S311
Invoice date 5.11.17

| Quantity | Description | Unit Price inc. GST | Amount inc. GST |
|---|---|---|---|
| | | $ | $ |
| 1 | Wood plane (H33) (50% credit allowed) | 24.20 | 12.10 |
| Reason for credit Damaged | | | $12.10 |
| GST included in this adjustment note $1.10 | | | |

c

| | | | |
|---|---|---|---|
| SA0162493 | Commonwealth Bank of Australia<br>ABN 48 123 123 124<br>Date *11. 11. 2017* | **Commonwealth** Bank<br>Commonwealth Bank of Australia | **Deposit** |

| Teller Use | | Date *11. 11. 2017* |
|---|---|---|
| $100 | | Notes *1 055 , 00* |
| $ 50 | | |
| $ 20 | | Coin *58 , 50* |
| $ 10 | | Credit Cards |
| $ 5 | | |
| $ | | Cheques *2 380 , 00* |
| | | Total $ *3 493 , 50* |

Account ID Number

Account Identification Number    Agent Number (if applicable)    Number of Cheques    Teller

Account Name *Harfield Hardware Supply*

$ *3 493 , 50*    Teller

*Brian Bolt*

© Commonwealth Bank of Australia

---

Please fill in the following particulars of cheques. Proceeds of cheques, whilst credited to the account, are generally not available until cleared. Please refer to your account terms and conditions for details.

**Depositor's Use**

| | Drawer | Bank | Branch | Amount | Details | Amount |
|---|---|---|---|---|---|---|
| 1 | J Jones | New Harfield | | 1 275 , 00 | J Jones | 1 275 , 00 |
| 2 | P Allen | NSW | | 845 , 00 | P Allen | 845 , 00 |
| 3 | T Hancock | New Harfield | | 260 , 00 | T Hancock | 260 , 00 |
| 4 | | | | | | |
| 5 | | | | | | |
| 6 | | | | | | |
| D 2<br>794 | | | | $ 2 380 , 00 | | $ 2 380 , 00 |

d

| | | |
|---|---|---|
| Receipt | Harfield Hardware Supply<br>ABN 22 411 511 611 | Number *751*<br>Date *14.11.17* |

Received from *H Poustie*

The sum of  *eight hundred and forty-four*                         dollars and

*eighty*               cents

For *October account*

$ *844.80*

Discount  $ *35.20*

Signed *Brian Bolt*

e

| | |
|---|---|
| Date _17. 11. 2017_ | |
| To _Cash_ | **Commonwealth** Bank |
| For _Wages_ | Commonwealth Bank of Australia |

**Commonwealth** Bank
Commonwealth Bank of Australia

Date _17. 11. 2017_

HARFIELD

Pay _Cash_

The sum of _two thousand three hundred and twenty dollars_

$ _2 320.00_

HARFIELD HARDWARE SUPPLY

_Brian Bolt_

SA0162731A

Amount _2 320.00_

Balance

000004

⑈000004⑈ 068⑈888⑆ 1002⑈1234⑈

© Commonwealth Bank of Australia

f

Statement of Account

To

_A Tarr_

_1 Bay Street_

_HARFIELD 9445_

For period ending _31/10/17_

| Date | Particulars | Ref | Debit | Credit | Balance |
|---|---|---|---|---|---|
| 2017 | | | $ | $ | $ |
| Oct 1 | Balance | | | | 1 500.00 Dr |
| 4 | Sales | Inv. S080 | 1 166.00 | | 2 666.00 Dr |
| 12 | Bank | Rec | | 1 456.00 | 1 210.00 Dr |
| | Discount | R106 | | 44.00 | 1 166.00 Dr |
| 20 | Sales returns and allowances | A/N | | 154.00 | 1 012.00 Dr |
| | | C902 | | | |
| 26 | Sales | Inv. | | | |
| | | S165 | 275.00 | | 1 287.00 Dr |

Terms

2.10    a    Invoice (original) from supplier

b    Bank statement

c    POS daily summary

d    Adjustment note (original) from supplier

e    Duplicate copy of tax invoice sent to customer

f    Duplicate copy of tax invoice sent to customer

g    Duplicate copy of receipt issued to debtor

h Duplicate copy of adjustment note sent to customer
i Duplicate copy of adjustment note sent to customer
j Letter from debtor's solicitor, advising that the debtor is officially bankrupt
k Memo from the proprietor to the accounting department
l Tax invoice (original) from supplier
m Bank statement

# General Ledger accounts for GST

Before proceeding to the next stage of the accounting process, it is important at this point to briefly discuss the General Ledger accounts required to account for GST.

In order to account for GST collected and input tax credits, two additional General Ledger accounts are required:

1 *GST Collected Account*
2 *GST Paid Account.*

The GST Collected Account is a liability account (a credit account) as it represents an amount owed to the Australian Taxation Office for GST collected on sales. The account is used to record GST collected and any adjustments relating to GST on sales, such as those relating to sales returns, allowances to customers, discounts given for prompt payment and bad debts.

The GST Paid Account is used to record all GST paid on business inputs (input tax credits). As input tax credits result in a future rebate of GST (therefore providing future economic benefits to the business) the GST Paid Account is an asset account (a debit account). The account is also used to record any adjustments relating to GST on business inputs, such as those relating to purchases returns, allowances given by suppliers, discounts received for prompt payment and goods taken for private purposes.

# Journals – books of original entry

Having examined the various types of *business documents* and the transactions they represent, we can now proceed to the next step in the accounting process – the preparation of *journals*.

## The purpose of journals

Most businesses have a large number of transactions to process during the course of trading and would therefore find it difficult and cumbersome to enter the information from business documents into the ledger on an individual transaction basis.

If business documents are to be processed rapidly and efficiently, it is necessary to use journals to summarise the information from these documents before it is entered into the ledger. This removes excessive detail from the ledger, and transaction information can be entered into the ledger in summary form.

# Data entry and occupational health and safety issues

Before entry in appropriate journals, the document(s) supporting each transaction must be examined for accuracy, completeness and appropriate authorisation. Authorisation of transactions is further discussed at the end of this chapter. It is important that journals are updated on a regular basis to ensure that timely financial information is available for reporting purposes.

As with all data entry, occupational health and safety (OH&S) considerations must be identified and addressed. Commonwealth and state legislation requires all workplaces to comply with OH&S regulations. In a data entry environment, this would encompass identification and control of hazards such as:

- lack of proper ergonomic workplace design
- physical hazards such as improper placement of electrical leads and computer cables, inappropriate room temperature, poor ventilation and excessive noise
- psychological hazards such as stress and personal threat
- inappropriate rest periods.

A detailed examination of these issues is beyond the scope of an accounting text. Further information is readily available via the websites of various workplace safety organisations in Australia, such as WorkSafe Victoria.

# Grouping of documents for entry in the ledger

As outlined above, the purpose of journals is to summarise transactions before they are entered in the ledger. To summarise the transactions, it is first necessary to sort them into *like* groups. In a *retail business*, it is customary to sort transactions into *seven* groups, and to record each group of transactions in a separate journal. The seven transaction groups and their respective journals are summarised in Figure 2.7. All journals other than the General Journal are referred to as special journals, as they are each used to summarise a special group of transactions.

Figure 2.7 summarises the accounting process when journals are used to process transactions.

**Figure 2.7    Types of journals**

| Transaction group | Journal |
| --- | --- |
| All credit sales of goods and services | Sales Journal |
| All credit purchases of goods and services | Purchases Journal |
| Credit given to customers for returns of goods or other allowances | Sales Returns and Allowances Journal |
| Credit allowed by suppliers for returns of goods or other allowances | Purchases Returns and Allowances Journal |
| All amounts received | Cash Receipts Journal |
| All payments | Cash Payments Journal |
| All transactions other than the above six groups | General Journal |

# Journal design – format and headings for retail businesses

## Preparation of journals

The coverage of journals in the following sections initially deals only with businesses that buy and sell goods. Thus, the format – the design and layout – and headings of the following journals will be covered in the sequence listed below.

- Preparation of journals to record credit transactions
- Preparation of journals to record cash transactions
- Preparation of the General Journal
- Preparation of journals for a *service* business

# Recording credit transactions

All credit transactions are recorded in one of four special journals: the Sales Journal, the Purchases Journal, the Sales Returns and Allowances Journal or the Purchases Returns and Allowances Journal. Consider Figure 2.8.

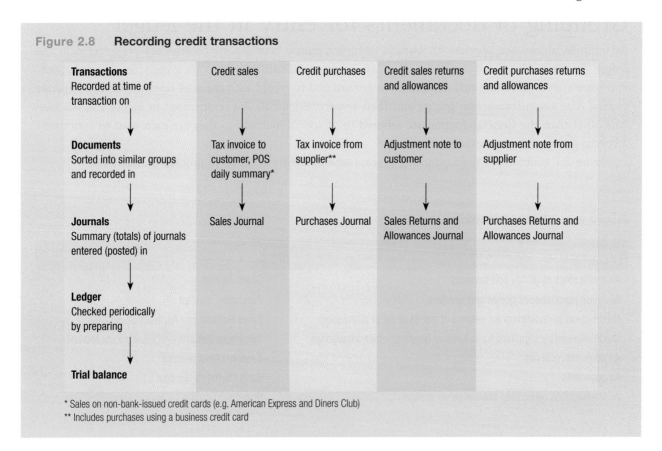

**Figure 2.8    Recording credit transactions**

| **Transactions** Recorded at time of transaction on | Credit sales | Credit purchases | Credit sales returns and allowances | Credit purchases returns and allowances |
|---|---|---|---|---|
| **Documents** Sorted into similar groups and recorded in | Tax invoice to customer, POS daily summary* | Tax invoice from supplier** | Adjustment note to customer | Adjustment note from supplier |
| **Journals** Summary (totals) of journals entered (posted) in | Sales Journal | Purchases Journal | Sales Returns and Allowances Journal | Purchases Returns and Allowances Journal |
| **Ledger** Checked periodically by preparing | | | | |
| **Trial balance** | | | | |

\* Sales on non-bank-issued credit cards (e.g. American Express and Diners Club)
\*\* Includes purchases using a business credit card

# Sales Journal

This journal is used to record credit sales of trading stock and other items. Credit sales of assets other than trading stock are also recorded in this journal. This aspect of accounting will be covered fully in Chapter 5 of the companion text *Accounting: Basic Reports*.

A UWatch demonstration is available on the CD that accompanies this text for parts of this activity.

UWATCH 2.2

## Example

Chloe's Wine Shop had the following credit sales during the first week of June 2017:

*2017*

1 Jun  Credit sales of wine to W Bates, $231 inc. GST (invoice no. S71).

Sold wine on credit to B Balmer, $330 inc. GST (invoice no. S72).

2  Wine sales on Diners Club card, $506 inc. GST (POS daily summary).

3  Sent tax invoice no. S73 to A Roberts, $3080 inc. GST for sale of excess office equipment.

4  Wine sales on American Express card, $121 inc. GST (POS daily summary).

Credit sales of wine to I Reid, $99 inc. GST (invoice no. S74).

5  Credit sales of excess office stationery to E Glover, $407 inc. GST (invoice no. S75).

The above transactions would be summarised in the Sales Journal as follows:

**CHLOE'S WINE SHOP**
**Sales Journal**

| Date | Debtor | Fol | Ref | Sales | Sundries Amount | Sundries Account | GST collected | Accounts receivable control |
|---|---|---|---|---|---|---|---|---|
| 2017 | | | | $ | $ | | $ | $ |
| 1 Jun | W Bates | | S71 | 210 | | | 21 | 231 |
| | B Balmer | | S72 | 300 | | | 30 | 330 |
| 2 | Diners Club | | POS | 460 | | | 46 | 506 |
| 3 | A Roberts | | S73 | | 2 800 | Sale of non-current assets | 280 | 3 080 |
| 4 | American Express | | POS | 110 | | | 11 | 121 |
| | I Reid | | S74 | 90 | | | 9 | 99 |
| 5 | E Glover | | S75 | | 370 | Misc. income | 37 | 407 |
| | | | | $1 170 | $3 170 | | $434 | $4 774 |

**Journal explanations**

1  The format of the Sales Journal above is designed to meet the needs of Chloe's Wine Shop.

2  Transactions must be recorded in date sequence.

3  The Debtor column records the name of the debtor involved in the transaction.

# Departmental Sales Journals

Many businesses design complex Sales Journals to cater for their particular information needs. For example, if a business is divided into several departments (each selling a separate type of product), it may design its Sales Journal to provide for divisions of sales by department. Consider the following example.

## Example

Sports Distributors (manager, Mary Docker) is a wholesale supplier of sporting equipment. Because of its large size the business is divided into two departments: 'indoors' (indoor sports equipment) and 'outdoors' (outdoor sports equipment).

The business's accountant, Fiona Fiddler, has suggested that the business should use journals to record all transactions and that these journals should record, among other items, the sales made by each of the two departments of the business. Fiona explained that recording sales, purchases and returns and allowances separately for each department would make it easier to calculate a separate profit figure for each department.

Sports Distributors had the following credit sales during the first week of November 2017:

*2017*

1 Nov   Credit sales to T Wilson: indoors, $209 inc. GST; outdoors, $198 inc. GST (invoice no. 896).

2       Sale on American Express card: outdoors, $154 inc. GST (POS).

        Sold the following on credit to P Gordon: indoors, $66 inc. GST; outdoors $77 inc. GST (invoice no. 897).

3       Credit sales to A Clayton: indoors, $187 inc. GST; outdoors, $132 inc. GST (invoice no. 898).

4       Credit sales to W Skinner: indoors, $110 inc. GST; outdoors, $44 inc. GST (invoice no. 899).

        Sold the following on credit to D Rivers: indoors, $99 inc. GST; outdoors, $132 inc. GST (invoice no. 900).

5       Sent invoice no. 901 to A Clayton: indoors, $88 inc. GST; outdoors, $209 inc. GST.

        Sent invoice no. 902 to G Piercy for hire of sporting equipment, $110 inc. GST.

The above transactions would be summarised in the Sales Journal for Sports Distributors as follows:

**SPORTS DISTRIBUTORS**
**Sales Journal**

| Date | Debtor | Fol | Ref | Sales | | Sundries | | GST collected | Accounts receivable control |
| | | | | Indoors | Outdoors | Amount | Account | | |
|---|---|---|---|---|---|---|---|---|---|
| 2017 | | | | $ | $ | $ | | $ | $ |
| 1 Nov | T Wilson | | 896 | 190 | 180 | | | 37 | 407 |
| 2 | American Express | | POS | | 140 | | | 14 | 154 |
| | P Gordon | | 897 | 60 | 70 | | | 13 | 143 |
| 3 Nov | A Clayton | | 898 | 170 | 120 | | | 29 | 319 |
| 4 | W Skinner | | 899 | 100 | 40 | | | 14 | 154 |
| | D Rivers | | 900 | 90 | 120 | | | 21 | 231 |
| 5 | A Clayton | | 901 | 80 | 190 | | | 27 | 297 |
| | G Piercy | | 902 | | | 100 | Equipment hire | 10 | 110 |
| | | | | $690 | $860 | $100 | | $165 | $1 815 |

# Purchases Journal

This journal is used to record credit purchases of trading stock and other items and services.

A UWatch demonstration is available on the CD that accompanies this text for parts of this activity.

UWATCH 2.3

## Example

Chloe's Wine Shop had the following credit purchases during the first week of June 2017:

*2017*

1 Jun    Credit purchases of wine from R Dixon, $473 inc. GST (invoice no. SC45).

2        Purchased wine on credit from B Muller, $286 inc. GST (invoice no. 502).
         Received invoice no. 151 from J Davis for consulting services costing $2200 inc. GST.

3        Purchased wine on credit from R Dixon, $308 inc. GST (invoice no. SD105).

4        Credit purchases of wine from S Turner, $638 inc. GST (invoice no. 1664).

5        Credit purchases of computer from R Dixon, $880 inc. GST using an American Express credit card (invoice no. SD264).
         Purchased wine on credit from B Muller, $407 inc. GST (invoice no. 913).

The above transactions would be summarised in the Purchases Journal as follows:

**CHLOE'S WINE SHOP**
**Purchases Journal**

| Date | Creditor | Fol | Ref | Purchases | Sundries Amount | Sundries Account | GST paid | Accounts payable control |
|---|---|---|---|---|---|---|---|---|
| 2017 | | | | $ | $ | | $ | $ |
| 1 Jun | R Dixon | | SC45 | 430 | | | 43 | 473 |
| 2 | B Muller | | 502 | 260 | | | 26 | 286 |
| | J Davis | | 151 | | 2 000 | Consultant's fees | 200 | 2 200 |
| 3 | R Dixon | | SD105 | 280 | | | 28 | 308 |
| 4 | S Turner | | 1664 | 580 | | | 58 | 638 |
| 5 | American Express | | SD264 | | 800 | Office equipment | 80 | 880 |
| | B Muller | | 913 | 370 | | | 37 | 407 |
| | | | | $1 920 | $2 800 | | $472 | $5 192 |

**Journal explanations**

1 The format of the Purchases Journal above is designed to meet the needs of Chloe's Wine Shop.

2 Transactions must be recorded in date sequence.

3 The Creditor column records the particular creditor's name stated on the invoice received.

4 The Folio column is used when posting journals to the ledger.

5 The Ref (reference) column contains a reference to the supplier invoice number.

6 The Purchases column is used to record all credit purchases of trading stock. The total of this column will be posted to the Creditors' Control Account.

7 The Sundries column is used to record credit purchases of services and items other than trading stock. It is important to record the name of the appropriate ledger account applicable to each of these transactions.

8 Each transaction is separated into its purchases and GST components. The GST Paid column is used to record the GST applicable to all business inputs, so that the business can account for the total amount of GST paid each month.

9 The business uses a creditors' control account in its ledger to record all credit purchases from suppliers. The total recorded in the Accounts Payable Control column is the amount that will be charged to the business by suppliers.

# Departmental Purchases Journals

As with the Sales Journal, it is also possible to extend the Purchases Journal for the recording of purchases for each department of a business.

# Sales Returns and Allowances Journal

This journal is used to record credit given to customers for return of goods or other allowances (for example, misdescription or overcharging on goods previously sold on credit).

UWATCH 2.4

A UWatch demonstration is available on the CD that accompanies this text for parts of this activity.

## Example

Chloe's Wine Shop had the following credit sales returns and allowances during the first week of June 2017:

*2017*

3 Jun    W Bates returned faulty wine, $77 inc. GST (issued adjustment note no. C55).

4    Allowed A Roberts for an overcharge, $44 inc. GST (adjustment note no. C56).

The above transactions would be summarised in the Sales Returns and Allowances Journal as follows:

**CHLOE'S WINE SHOP**
**Sales Returns and Allowances Journal**

| Date | Debtor | Fol | Ref | Sales returns and allowances | Sundries | | GST collected | Accounts receivable control |
|------|--------|-----|-----|------------------------------|----------|----|---------------|-----------------------------|
| | | | | | Amount | Account | | |
| 2017 | | | | $ | $ | | $ | $ |
| 3 Jun | W Bates | | C55 | 70 | | | 7 | 77 |
| 4 | A Roberts | | C56 | 40 | | | 4 | 44 |
| | | | | $110 | | | $11 | $121 |

**Journal explanations**

1    The format of the Sales Returns and Allowances Journal above is designed to meet the needs of Chloe's Wine Shop.

2    Transactions must be recorded in date sequence.

3    The Debtor column records the name of the particular debtor receiving the allowance.

4    The Folio column is used when posting journals to the ledger.

5    The Ref (reference) column contains a reference to the adjustment note number.

6    The Sales Returns and Allowances column is used to record all credit sales returns and allowances relating to trading stock.

7    The Sundries column is used to record credit sales returns and allowances relating to items other than trading stock, such as a calculation error on an invoice for the sale of excess office stationery. It is important to record the name of the appropriate ledger account applicable to each of these transactions.

8    Each transaction is separated into its sales returns (or allowances) and GST components. The GST Collected column is used to record the GST applicable to all sales returns and allowances, so that the business can account for all adjustments to GST collected each month.

9    The total recorded in the Accounts Receivable Control column is the amount that will be credited to debtors, to reduce the amount that they owe.

# Departmental Sales Returns and Allowances Journal

The Sales Returns and Allowances Journal can also be extended to record the sales returns and allowances for each department of a business.

# Purchases Returns and Allowances Journal

Credit received from suppliers for returns of goods or other allowances (for example, misdescription or overcharging on goods previously purchased on credit) is the only type of transaction recorded in this journal.

UWATCH 2.5

A UWatch demonstration is available on the CD that accompanies this text for parts of this activity.

## Example

Chloe's Wine Shop had the following purchases returns and allowances during the first week of June 2017:

*2017*

2 Jun    Received an allowance from R Dixon for faulty wine, $99 (inc. GST) on adjustment note no. RC87.

5         Returned damaged wine to S Turner and received adjustment note no. 65 for $33 inc. GST.

The above transactions would be summarised in the Purchases Returns and Allowances Journal as follows:

**CHLOE'S WINE SHOP**
**Purchases Returns and Allowances Journal**

| Date | Creditor | Fol | Ref | Purchases returns and allowances | Sundries Amount | Sundries Account | GST paid | Accounts payable control |
|------|----------|-----|-----|----------------------------------|--------|---------|----------|---------------------------|
| 2017 | | | | $ | $ | | $ | $ |
| 2 Jun | R Dixon | | RC87 | 90 | | | 9 | 99 |
| 5 | S Turner | | 65 | 30 | | | 3 | 33 |
| | | | | $120 | | | $12 | $132 |

### Journal explanations

1   The format of the Purchases Returns and Allowances Journal above is designed to meet the needs of Chloe's Wine Shop.

2   Transactions must be recorded in date sequence.

3   The Creditor column records the name of the particular creditor providing an allowance.

4   The Fol (Folio) column is used when posting journals to the ledger.

5   The Ref (Reference) column contains a reference to the adjustment note number.

6   The Purchases Returns and Allowances column is used to record all credit purchases returns and allowances relating to trading stock.

7   The Sundries column is used to record credit purchases returns and allowances relating to items other than trading stock, such as a calculation error on an invoice from a consultant. It is important to record the name of the appropriate ledger account applicable to each of these transactions.

8   Each transaction is separated into its purchases returns (or allowances) and GST components. The GST Paid column is used to record the GST applicable to all purchases returns and allowances, so that the business can account for all adjustments to GST paid each month.

9   The total recorded in the Accounts Payable Control column is the amount that will be debited to creditors, to reduce the amount owed to them.

# Departmental Purchases Returns and Allowances Journals

Like the other special journals, the Purchases Returns and Allowances Journal can be extended to allow for the recording of transactions of each department of a business.

## Comprehensive example

Sports Distributors is a business with two separate sales departments (Indoors and Outdoors). Consider the following documents relating to credit transactions for Sports Distributors for the second week of November 2017.

### Duplicate copies of sales invoices

| Tax Invoice 903 | 8.11.17 |
|---|---|
| From: Sports Distributors | |
| To: B. Wells | |
| Indoors | $110.00 |
| Total inc. GST | $110.00 |

| Tax Invoice 904 | 9.11.17 |
|---|---|
| From: Sports Distributors | |
| To: A. Clayton | |
| Indoors | $220.00 |
| Outdoors | 99.00 |
| Total inc. GST | $319.00 |

| Tax Invoice 905 | 9.11.17 |
|---|---|
| From: Sports Distributors | |
| To: T. Wilson | |
| Indoors | $198.00 |
| Outdoors | 132.00 |
| Total inc. GST | $330.00 |

| Tax Invoice 906 | 10.11.17 |
|---|---|
| From: Sports Distributors | |
| To: W. Skinner | |
| Indoors | $176.00 |
| Total inc. GST | $176.00 |

| Tax Invoice 907 | 11.11.17 |
|---|---|
| From: Sports Distributors | |
| To: P. Gordon | |
| Indoors | $99.00 |
| Outdoors | 55.00 |
| Total inc. GST | $154.00 |

| Tax Invoice 908 | 12.11.17 |
|---|---|
| From: Sports Distributors | |
| To: D Christie | |
| Sporting equipment repairs (inc. GST) | $55.00 |

## Extract from POS daily summary

| POS daily summary (extract) | 12.11.17 |
|---|---|
| Diners Club Sales Outdoors inc. GST | $132 |

## Invoices from suppliers

| Tax Invoice 200 | 8.11.17 |
|---|---|
| From: Supply Co. To: *Sports Distributors* | |

| Indoors | $143.00 |
|---|---|
| Outdoors | 66.00 |
| Total inc. GST | $209.00 |

| Tax Invoice 1094 | 10.11.17 |
|---|---|
| From: S. Tayer To: *Sports Distributors* | |

| Indoors inc. GST | $ 297.00 |
|---|---|

| Tax Invoice GC1241 | 10.11.17 |
|---|---|
| From: Golfer's Digest To: *Sports Distributors* | |

| Advertising in Oct. edition (inc. GST) | $308.00 |
|---|---|

| Tax Invoice T814 | 11.11.17 |
|---|---|
| From: Sportsrite To: *Sports Distributors* | |

| Indoors | $220.00 |
|---|---|
| Outdoors | 44.00 |
| Total inc. GST | $264.00 |

| Tax Invoice 744 | 12.11.17 |
|---|---|
| From: AD Industries To: *Sports Distributors* | |

| Indoors | $308.00 |
|---|---|
| Outdoors | 143.00 |
| Total inc. GST | $451.00 |

| Tax Invoice 1210 | 12.11.17 |
|---|---|
| From: R Wallace To: *Sports Distributors* | |

| Indoors inc. GST Paid by Visa card | $110.00 |
|---|---|

## Duplicate copies of adjustment notes sent to customers

| Adjustment Note 276 | | 9.11.17 |
|---|---|---|
| From: Sports Distributors | | |
| To: D. Rivers | | |
| Indoors returns | | $22.00 |
| Total inc. GST | | $22.00 |

| Adjustment Note 277 | | 12.11.17 |
|---|---|---|
| From: Sports Distributors | | |
| To: D. Christie | | |
| Overcharge on sporting equipment repairs | | $11.00 |
| Total inc. GST | | $11.00 |

## Adjustment notes received from suppliers

| Adjustment Note 640 | | 8.11.17 |
|---|---|---|
| From: S. Tayer | | |
| To: Sports Distributors | | |
| Returns (Indoors) inc. GST | | $33.00 |

| Adjustment Note A41 | | 11.11.17 |
|---|---|---|
| From: Golfer's Digest | | |
| To: Sports Distributors | | |
| Price rebate on advertising inc. GST | | $66.00 |

| Adjustment Note AR75 | | 12.11.17 |
|---|---|---|
| From: R Wallace | | |
| To: Sports Distributors | | |
| Price adjustment (Indoors) inc. GST Credit to Visa card | | $22.00 |

These documents would be entered in the journals of Sports Distributors as follows:

**SPORTS DISTRIBUTORS**
**Sales Journal**

| Date | Debtor | Fol | Ref | Sales Indoors | Sales Outdoors | Sundries Amount | Sundries Account | GST collected | Accounts receivable control |
|---|---|---|---|---|---|---|---|---|---|
| 2017 | | | | $ | $ | $ | | $ | $ |
| 8 Nov | B Wells | | 903 | 100 | | | | 10 | 110 |
| 9 | A Clayton | | 904 | 200 | 90 | | | 29 | 319 |
| | T Wilson | | 905 | 180 | 120 | | | 30 | 330 |
| 10 | W Skinner | | 906 | 160 | | | | 16 | 176 |
| 11 | P Gordon | | 907 | 90 | 50 | | | 14 | 154 |
| 12 | D Christie | | 908 | | | 50 | Repairs income | 5 | 55 |
| | Diners Club | | POS | | 120 | | | 12 | 132 |
| | | | | $730 | $380 | $50 | | $116 | $1 276 |

### Purchases Journal

| Date | Creditor | Fol | Ref | Purchases | | Sundries | | GST paid | Accounts payable control |
|------|----------|-----|-----|-----------|---|----------|---|----------|--------------------------|
| | | | | Indoors | Outdoors | Amount | Account | | |
| 2017 | | | | $ | $ | $ | | $ | $ |
| 8 Nov | Supply Co | | 200 | 130 | 60 | | | 19 | 209 |
| 10 | S Tayer | | 1094 | 270 | | | | 27 | 297 |
| | Golfer's Digest | | GC1241 | | | 280 | Advertising | 28 | 308 |
| 11 | Sportsrite | | T814 | 200 | 40 | | | 24 | 264 |
| 12 | AD Industries | | 744 | 280 | 130 | | | 41 | 451 |
| | Visa | | 1210 | 100 | | | | 10 | 110 |
| | | | | $980 | $230 | $280 | | $149 | $1 639 |

### Sales Returns and Allowances Journal

| Date | Debtor | Fol | Ref | Sales returns and allowances | | Sundries | | GST collected | Accounts receivable control |
|------|--------|-----|-----|------------------------------|---|----------|---|---------------|-----------------------------|
| | | | | Indoors | Outdoors | Amount | Account | | |
| 2017 | | | | $ | $ | $ | | $ | $ |
| 9 Nov | D Rivers | | 276 | 20 | | | | 2 | 22 |
| 12 | D Christie | | 277 | | | 10 | Repairs income | 1 | 11 |
| | | | | $20 | | $10 | | $3 | $33 |

### Purchases Returns and Allowances Journal

| Date | Creditor | Fol | Ref | Purchases returns and allowances | | Sundries | | GST paid | Accounts payable control |
|------|----------|-----|-----|----------------------------------|---|----------|---|----------|--------------------------|
| | | | | Indoors | Outdoors | Amount | Account | | |
| 2017 | | | | $ | $ | $ | | $ | $ |
| 8 Nov | S Tayer | | 640 | 30 | | | | 3 | 33 |
| 11 | Golfer's Digest | | A41 | | | 60 | Advertising | 6 | 66 |
| 12 | Visa | | AR75 | 20 | | | | 2 | 22 |
| | | | | $50 | | $60 | | $11 | $121 |

 **EXERCISES**

**2.13** Briefly describe the purpose of journals.

**2.14** Draw a simple diagram of the accounting process, indicating how transactions/documents are 'grouped' for entry into journals.

**2.15** a  What is a 'special' journal?
  b  Name the journals that are regarded as special journals.

**2.16** Explain the meaning of the word 'posting' in relation to journals.

**2.17** All credit transactions involving trading stock are recorded in four special journals. Name these four journals.

**2.18** Name the business documents that provide the source of information for entries in each of the following journals.
  a  Sales Journal
  b  Purchases Journal
  c  Sales Returns and Allowances Journal
  d  Purchases Returns and Allowances Journal

**2.19** Briefly distinguish between:
  a  a sales return
  b  a sales allowance.

**2.20** E Singh, used car dealer, had the following credit sales during the month of July 2019. You are required to:
  a  design a suitable Sales Journal for the business
  b  enter the transactions for July in the journal
  c  total the journal at the end of July.

  *2019*
  3 Jul  Credit sales of trading stock to H Holland, $5060 inc. GST (invoice 64).
  4     Credit sales of trading stock to H Pilcher, $3960 inc. GST (invoice 65).
  6     Sales of trading stock on American Express credit card to S Clarke, $2970 inc. GST (invoice 66).
  12    Credit sales of trading stock to S Kurske, $1980 inc. GST (invoice 67).
  31    Minor repairs for S Warren, $165 inc. GST (invoice 68).

**2.21\*** G Chapman, sporting-goods distributor, had the following credit sales during the month of August 2019. You are required to:
  a  design a suitable Sales Journal for the business
  b  enter the transactions for August into the journal
  c  total the journal at the end of August.

  *2019*
  1 Aug  Credit sales of trading stock to J Benjamin, $726 inc. GST (invoice 106).
  5     Credit sales of trading stock to J Apps, $242 inc. GST (invoice 107).

| 10 | Equipment repairs charged to L Featherstone, $363 inc. GST (invoice 108). |
| 25 | Credit sales of trading stock to D Read, $847 inc. GST (invoice 109). |
| 30 | Sales of trading stock on American Express cards, $605 inc. GST (POS). |

**2.22** This question is available on the CD that accompanies this text.

**2.23** This question is available on the CD that accompanies this text.

**2.24\*** P Searle, wholesaler, had the following credit purchases during the month of April 2016. You are required to:

a design a suitable Purchases Journal for the business

b enter the transactions into the journal

c total the journal at the end of the month.

*2016*

| 2 Apr | Credit purchases of trading stock from J Dowdle, $308 inc. GST (invoice D45). |
| 6 | Purchased shop fittings on credit from F Coyle, $407 inc. GST (invoice 622). |
| 11 | Credit purchases of trading stock from A Wheeler, $275 inc. GST (invoice 901). |
| 16 | Received invoice for insurance from Kentish Agencies, $473 inc. GST (invoice K22). |
| 24 | Purchased trading stock on credit from D Jeffrey, $297 inc. GST (invoice 442). |
| 30 | Credit purchases of trading stock from F Coyle, $385 inc. GST (invoice 709). |

**2.25** C Constantinou is the owner of Con's Menswear, a retailer of clothing for men and youths. The business is divided into two sales departments: menswear and youthwear. The business had the following credit purchases during the month of June 2019. You are required to:

a design a suitable Purchases Journal for the business

b enter the transactions for June into the journal

c total the journal at the end of the month.

*2019*

| 3 Jun | Credit purchases from P Williams: menswear, $121 inc. GST; youthwear, $77 inc. GST (invoice 296). |
| 9 | Received invoice number S428 from Teleco Ltd for $407 inc. GST for telephone and Internet. |
| 15 | Credit purchases of youthwear from Bryce & Co, $748 inc. GST (invoice K88). |
| 19 | Purchases on Mastercard from P Williams: menswear, $66 inc. GST; youthwear, $242 inc. GST (invoice 380). |
| 29 | Received invoice number 56 from Machogear for menswear, $363 inc. GST. |
| | Credit purchases from Hutchinsons Ltd: menswear, $198 inc. GST; youthwear, $165 inc. GST (invoice T031). |

**2.26** This question is available on the CD that accompanies this text.

**2.27** E Singh, used car dealer, had the following credit sales returns and allowances during the month of July 2019. You are required to:

a design a suitable Sales Returns and Allowances Journal for the business

b enter the transactions for July into the journal

c total the journal at the end of July.

*2019*

9 Jul   Debtor, H Pilcher returned damaged vehicle, $902 inc. GST (adjustment note 49).

21      Allowance given to debtor, S Kurske for an overcharge, $198 inc. GST (adjustment note 50).

2.28*   G Chapman, sporting-goods distributor, had the following credit sales returns and allowances during the month of August 2019. You are required to enter these transactions into an appropriately designed Sales Returns and Allowances Journal for the business.

*2019*

11 Aug   Allowance given to debtor L Featherstone for overcharge on equipment repairs, $121 inc. GST (adjustment note 200).

27      Debtor D Read returned damaged stock, $176 inc. GST (adjustment note 201).

2.29   Ivan's Wines and Spirits (owner, I Brown) had the following credit sales returns and allowances transactions during March 2016. You are required to enter these transactions into an appropriately designed Sales Returns and Allowances Journal for the business. (The business is divided into two departments: wine sales and spirit sales.)

*2016*

7 Mar   Debtor, P Galvin, given an allowance for damaged goods received: wine, $33 inc. GST; spirits, $44 inc. GST (adjustment note CR18).

24      B Horton returned inferior quality spirits, $55 inc. GST (adjustment note CR19).

2.30   This question is available on the CD that accompanies this text.

ADDITIONAL
EXERCISES

2.31*   P Searle, wholesaler, had the following credit purchases returns and allowances during the month of April 2016. You are required to:

a   design a suitable Purchases Returns and Allowances Journal for the business

b   enter the transactions into the journal

c   total the journal at the end of the month.

*2016*

12 Apr   Returned faulty stock purchased on credit from A Wheeler, $55 inc. GST (adjustment note 344).

26      Received an allowance from Kentish Agencies for rebate on insurance premium, $44 inc. GST (adjustment note 185).

2.32   Con's Menswear had the following credit purchases, returns and allowances during June 2019. You are required to enter the transactions into an appropriately designed Purchases Returns and Allowances Journal for the business. (Con's Menswear is a clothing retailer and is divided into two departments: menswear and youthwear.)

*2019*

5 Jun   Received an allowance from creditor P Williams for an overcharge on youthwear, $11 inc. GST (adjustment note 90).

30      Received credit for Internet overcharge from Teleco Ltd, $66 inc. GST (adjustment note R34).

2.33   This question is available on the CD that accompanies this text.

ADDITIONAL
EXERCISES

2.34 Norm Bartlett is the owner of Bartlett's Electrical, a wholesaler of electrical goods. The business had the following credit transactions during the month of May 2017. You are required to:

a design the following journals for the business: (i) Sales Journal, (ii) Purchases Journal, (iii) Sales Returns and Allowances Journal and (iv) Purchases Returns and Allowances Journal

b enter the transactions for May into the journals

c total the journals at the end of the month.

*2017*

| | |
|---|---|
| 1 May | Credit purchases of trading stock from Jason Electrical Manufacturing, $693 inc. GST (invoice 291). |
| 3 | Credit sales of trading stock to Watt Electrics, $407 inc. GST (invoice S100). |
| 6 | Credit purchases of trading stock from Electro Manufacturing using American Express credit card, $583 inc. GST (invoice 432). |
| 7 | Received invoice TR24 from Argo Ltd, $352 inc. GST for cleaning services. |
| 10 | Sent invoice no. S101 to Phillip Electrical, $374 inc. GST for sale of surplus office furniture. |
| | Credit from Argo Ltd for unsatisfactory cleaning services, $55 inc. GST (adjustment note TC105). |
| 13 | Credit sales of trading stock to Jed Industries, $264 inc. GST (invoice S102). |
| 15 | Allowance given to Jed Industries for overcharge, $44 inc. GST (adjustment note C011). |
| | Credit purchases of trading stock from Electro Manufacturing, $715 inc. GST (invoice 711). |
| 18 | Sold trading stock on credit to Watt Electrics, $143 inc. GST (invoice S103). |
| 20 | Sent adjustment note C012 to Watt Electrics for incorrect goods supplied, $44 inc. GST. |
| | Sales of trading stock on Diners Club card $506 inc. GST (POS). |
| 24 | Received invoice TR301 from Power Supply Co for electricity, $330 inc. GST. |
| 27 | Credit purchases of trading stock from Zappo Products, $99 inc. GST (invoice Z30). |
| 31 | Returned damaged trading stock to Zappo Products, $44 inc. GST and received adjustment note (ZC90). |

 **SOLUTIONS**

2.21 a, b, c

**G Chapman**
**Sales Journal**

| Date | Debtor | Fol | Ref | Sales | Sundries Amount | Sundries Account | GST collected | Accounts receivable control |
|---|---|---|---|---|---|---|---|---|
| 2019 | | | | $ | $ | | $ | $ |
| 1 Aug | J Benjamin | | 106 | 660 | | | 66 | 726 |
| 5 | J Apps | | 107 | 220 | | | 22 | 242 |
| 10 | L Featherstone | | 108 | | 330 | Repairs income | 33 | 363 |
| 25 | D Read | | 109 | 770 | | | 77 | 847 |
| 30 | American Express | | POS | 550 | | | 55 | 605 |
| | | | | $2 200 | $330 | | $253 | $2 783 |

2.24 a, b, c

**P Searle**
**Purchases Journal**

| Date | Creditor | Fol | Ref | Purchases | Sundries Amount | Sundries Account | GST paid | Accounts payable control |
|---|---|---|---|---|---|---|---|---|
| 2016 | | | | $ | $ | | $ | $ |
| 2 Apr | J Dowdle | | D45 | 280 | | | 28 | 308 |
| 6 | F Coyle | | 622 | | 370 | Shop fittings | 37 | 407 |
| 11 | A Wheeler | | 901 | 250 | | | 25 | 275 |
| 16 | Kentish Agencies | | K22 | | 430 | Insurance | 43 | 473 |
| 24 | D Jeffrey | | 442 | 270 | | | 27 | 297 |
| 30 | F Coyle | | 709 | 350 | | | 35 | 385 |
| | | | | $1 150 | $800 | | $195 | $2 145 |

2.28

**G Chapman**
**Sales Returns and Allowances Journal**

| Date | Debtor | Fol | Ref | Sales returns and allowances | Sundries Amount | Sundries Account | GST collected | Accounts receivable control |
|---|---|---|---|---|---|---|---|---|
| 2019 | | | | $ | $ | | $ | $ |
| 11 Aug | L Featherstone | | 200 | | 110 | Repairs income | 11 | 121 |
| 27 | D Read | | 201 | 160 | | | 16 | 176 |
| | | | | $160 | $110 | | $27 | $297 |

2.31 a, b, c

**P Searle**
**Purchases Returns and Allowances Journal**

| Date | Creditor | Fol | Ref | Purchases returns and allowances | Sundries Amount | Sundries Account | GST paid | Accounts payable control |
|---|---|---|---|---|---|---|---|---|
| 2016 | | | | $ | $ | | $ | $ |
| 12 Apr | A Wheeler | | 344 | 50 | | | 5 | 55 |
| 26 | Kentish Agencies | | 185 | | 40 | Insurance | 4 | 44 |
| | | | | $50 | $40 | | $9 | $99 |

# Recording cash transactions

In an earlier section of this chapter, journals were introduced and their importance in the accounting process was discussed. Of the seven journals used in a retail business, six were described as special journals, and the preparation of four of these, the Sales Journal, the Purchases Journal, the Sales Returns and Allowances Journal and the Purchases Returns and Allowances Journal, was examined.

This section examines the preparation of the other two special journals – those used to summarise all cash transactions.

The recording of cash transactions involves the use of two special journals: the *Cash Receipts Journal* and the *Cash Payments Journal*. Consider Figure 2.9.

**Figure 2.9    Recording cash transactions**

| Transaction | Document | Journal |
|---|---|---|
| Cash sales, EFTPOS sales* | POS daily summary | |
| EFT receipts | | |
| Direct credits | Bank statement | Cash Receipts Journal |
| Other amounts received | Receipt (duplicate) | |
| Payments by cheque | Cheque butt or transaction record | |
| EFT payments | | Cash Payments Journal |
| Direct debits | Bank statement | |

*Includes sales to customers who use debit cards and bank-issued credit cards

# Cash Receipts Journal

All amounts received, regardless of the source, must be recorded in the Cash Receipts Journal. Some examples of transactions recorded in the Cash Receipts Journal include EFT receipts, cash sales, EFTPOS sales, amounts received from debtors and interest received.

A UWatch demonstration is available on the CD that accompanies this text for parts of this activity.

UWATCH 2.6

## Example

Chloe's Wine Shop had the following cash receipt transactions during the first week of June 2017:

*2017*
1 Jun    Cash sales of stock $374 inc. GST (POS).
            Received interest on loan to Maggie Wilson, $50 (EFT).
2            EFTPOS sales of stock $110 inc. GST, cash sales of stock $198 inc. GST (POS).
            Received $689 from I Foster (debtor) after allowing him discount of $11 inc. GST (receipt no. R533).

3    EFTPOS sales of stock $121 inc. GST, cash sales of stock $319 inc. GST (POS).

4    Cash sales of stock $385 inc. GST (POS).

Received $393 from E Glover (debtor) after allowing her discount of $22 inc. GST (receipt no. R534).

Received commission $110 inc. GST from Wineries Ltd (DC*).

5    EFTPOS sales of stock $209 inc. GST, Cash sales of stock $187 inc. GST (POS).

The above transactions would be summarised in the Cash Receipts Journal as follows:

**CHLOE'S WINE SHOP**
**Cash Receipts Journal**

| Date | Particulars | Fol | Ref | Discount expense | | | Accounts receivable control | Cash sales | Sundries | | | Bank |
| | | | | Accounts receivable control | GST collected | Discount expense | | | Amount | Account | GST collected | |
| 2017 | | | | $ | $ | $ | $ | $ | $ | | $ | $ |
| 1 June | Cash sales | | POS | | | | | 340 | | | 34 | 374 |
| | M Wilson | | EFT | | | | | | 50 | Interest income | | 50 |
| 2 | Sales – EFTPOS | | POS | | | | | 100 | | | 10 | 110 |
| | Cash sales | | POS | | | | | 180 | | | 18 | |
| | I Foster | | R533 | 11 | 1 | 10 | 689 | | | | | 887 |
| 3 | Sales – EFTPOS | | POS | | | | | 110 | | | 11 | 121 |
| | Cash sales | | POS | | | | | 290 | | | 29 | 319 |
| 4 | Cash sales | | POS | | | | | 350 | | | 35 | |
| | E Glover | | R534 | 22 | 2 | 20 | 393 | | | | | 778 |
| | Wineries Ltd | | DC* | | | | | | 100 | Commission income | 10 | 110 |
| 5 | Sales – EFTPOS | | POS | | | | | 190 | | | 19 | 209 |
| | Cash sales | | POS | | | | | 170 | | | 17 | 187 |
| | | | | $33 | $3 | $30 | $1 082 | $1 730 | $150 | | $183 | $3 145 |

*DC = Direct Credit

**Journal explanations**

1  The format of the Cash Receipts Journal above is particularly suited to the business of Chloe's Wine Shop. Most businesses design their journals to cater for their own needs. For example, Chloe's Wine Shop has a special column for cash sales because it is a wine wholesaler and therefore has frequent wine sales transactions. It also has a separate column to record the GST applicable to all taxable supplies, so that the business can account for the total amount of GST collected each month.

2  Transactions must be recorded in date sequence.

3  The Particulars column records a description of the transaction or the name of the person or business from whom the amount was received.

4  The Fol (Folio) column is used when posting journals to the ledger (explained in Chapter 3).

5  The Ref (Reference) column contains a reference to the source of the transaction; for example, POS for POS daily summary and a receipt number for a transaction where a receipt is issued.

6  The Discount expense section is included in the Cash Receipts Journal to show, in the same record, the payment received from a debtor and the discount applicable to that payment. It is also convenient to have a discount section because discount allowed to a debtor is recorded simultaneously with the receipt of the money from the debtor. Note that it is necessary to record the GST applicable to discounts allowed to customers, as this represents an adjustment (reduction) to GST collected on sales.

7  The business uses a control account in its ledger to record all receipts from debtors (accounts receivable).

8  Where there is no special column provided for a transaction, the Sundries column is used. It is important to record the name of the appropriate ledger account applicable to each of these transactions.

9  Most businesses bank their takings daily. For this reason, entries in the Bank column represent the total of cash and cheques received each day. Note that it is necessary to enter EFTPOS sales separately in the Bank column, as the bank will credit EFTPOS takings to the business's bank account in a separate total each day. Note also that each EFT receipt must be entered separately in the Bank column as the bank credits these transactions individually to the business's bank account. As a check, the totals of the Accounts receivable, Cash sales, Sundries and GST collected columns should equal the total in the Bank column.

10  Note that it is a useful cross-check to add the totals of the accounts receivable, cash sales, sundries and GST collected columns, which should equal the total in the Bank column.

# Departmental Cash Receipts Journals

Earlier in this chapter it was explained how the Sales, Purchases, and the Returns and Allowances journals may be extended to provide for the recording of sales, purchases and returns and allowances for each department of a business. In the examples using Sports Distributors, the credit journals were designed to show the sales, purchases and returns and allowances for the Indoors and Outdoors departments separately.

In the Cash Receipts Journal for Sports Distributors, it would also be possible to record the sales of the Indoors and Outdoors departments separately.

## Example

Sports Distributors had the following cash receipts transactions during the first week of November 2017:

*2017*

1 Nov  Cash sales (inc. GST): indoors $253; outdoors $286 (POS).
       Received $389 from debtor D Costello after allowing him discount of $11 inc. GST (receipt no. 401).

2      EFTPOS sales (inc. GST): indoors $88; outdoors $55 (POS).
       Cash sales (inc. GST): indoors $253; outdoors $319 (POS).

3      EFTPOS sales (inc. GST): indoors $110; outdoors $77 (POS).
       Cash sales (inc. GST): indoors $209; outdoors $297 (POS).
       Received interest from Sportco Ltd, $70 (EFT).

4      Cash sales (inc. GST): indoors $836; outdoors $946 (POS).
       Received $358 from debtor T Wilson after allowing discount of $22 (inc. GST) for prompt payment (receipt no. 402).

5      Received $292 from Diners Club (credit card provider). A merchant fee of $33 (inc. GST) had been deducted from this payment (EFT).

These transactions would be summarised in the Cash Receipts Journal for Sports Distributors as follows:

**SPORTS DISTRIBUTORS**
**Cash Receipts Journal**

| Date | Particulars | Fol | Ref | Discount expense – Accounts receivable control | GST collected | Discount expense | Accounts receivable control | Cash sales – Indoors | Cash sales – Outdoors | Sundries – Amount | Sundries – Account | GST collected | Bank |
|---|---|---|---|---|---|---|---|---|---|---|---|---|---|
| 2017 | | | | $ | $ | $ | $ | $ | $ | $ | | $ | $ |
| 1 Nov | Cash sales | | POS | | | | | 230 | 260 | | | 49 | |
| | D Costello | | 401 | 11 | 1 | 10 | 389 | | | | | | 928 |
| 2 | Sales – EFTPOS | | POS | | | | | 80 | 50 | | | 13 | 143 |
| | Cash sales | | POS | | | | | 230 | 290 | | | 52 | 572 |
| 3 | Sales – EFTPOS | | POS | | | | | 100 | 70 | | | 17 | 187 |
| | Cash sales | | POS | | | | | 190 | 270 | | | 46 | 506 |
| | Sportco Ltd | | EFT | | | | | | | 70 | Interest income | | 70 |
| 4 | Cash sales | | POS | | | | | 760 | 860 | | | 162 | |
| | T Wilson | | 402 | 22 | 2 | 20 | 358 | | | | | | 2 140 |
| 5 | Diners Club* | | EFT | | | | | | | | | | |
| | – Gross | | | | | | 325 | | | | | | |
| | – Merchant fee | | | | | | | | | (30) | Merchant fees expense | | |
| | – GST paid | | | | | | | | | (3) | GST paid | | 292 |
| | | | | $33 | $3 | $30 | $1 072 | $1 590 | $1 800 | $37 | | $339 | $4 838 |

*The amount received from Diners Club must be recorded in four parts (gross amount received, merchant fee deducted, GST deducted and net amount received) to provide the necessary details for later entries in the ledger.

# Cash Payments Journal

All payments, for whatever purpose, must be recorded in the Cash Payments Journal. Some examples of transactions recorded in the Cash Payments Journal include cash purchases of trading stock, payments to creditors, wages paid and rent paid.

Sometimes a business will pay for goods or services at the time of purchase; for example, purchases of goods over the counter or payment immediately following the provision of a service. In these situations a business will still receive a tax invoice from the supplier but it will not be necessary to record these invoices in the Purchases Journal, as the supplier has not become a creditor. You will find examples of such transactions in the examples and exercises that follow (i.e. *cash purchases*, indicating that goods or services have been purchased and paid for at the time of the transaction). Note that in the case of payments for goods or services previously invoiced and recorded, this text will indicate that the payment was made to a creditor.

A UWatch demonstration is available on the CD that accompanies this text for parts of this activity.

## Example

Chloe's Wine Shop made the following payments during the first week of June 2017.

*2017*

| | |
|---|---|
| 1 Jun | Cash purchases of stock from Hocks Ltd, $506 inc. GST (cheque no. 705). |
| | Paid wages, $650 (EFT). |
| 2 | Paid creditor State Power Supply, $176 (EFT). |
| | Cash purchases of stock from Jasonwine Ltd, $385 inc. GST (cheque no. 706). |
| 3 | Paid creditor Golfer's Digest, $209 (cheque no. 707). |
| | Cash purchases from Acme Co $165 – cleaning ($99 inc. GST) and repairs ($66 inc. GST) (cheque no. 708). |
| | Cash purchases of stock from Leiseur Winery, $517 inc. GST (cheque no. 709). |
| 4 | Cash purchase from AC Taxi Trucks – delivery charges, $77 inc. GST (cheque no. 710). |
| | Paid creditor R Dixon $467, after deducting an allowance for discount $33 inc. GST (cheque no. 711). |
| 5 | Cash purchases of stock from Hocks Ltd, $363 inc. GST (cheque no. 712). |
| | Paid creditor B Muller $209, after deducting an allowance for discount of $11 inc. GST (EFT). |

The above transactions could be summarised in the Cash Payments Journal as shown below.

**CHLOE'S WINE SHOP**
**Cash Payments Journal**

| Date | Particulars | Fol | Ref | Discount income Accounts payable control | GST paid | Discount income | Accounts payable control | Cash purchases | Wages | Sundries Amount | Account | GST paid | Bank |
|---|---|---|---|---|---|---|---|---|---|---|---|---|---|
| 2017 | | | | $ | $ | $ | $ | $ | $ | $ | | $ | $ |
| 1 Jun | Hocks Ltd | | 705 | | | | | 460 | | | | 46 | 506 |
| | Wages | | EFT | | | | | | 650 | | | | 650 |
| 2 | State Power Supply | | EFT | | | | 176 | | | | | | 176 |
| | Jasonwine Ltd | | 706 | | | | | 350 | | | | 35 | 385 |
| 3 June | Golfer's Digest | | 707 | | | | 209 | | | | | | 209 |
| | Acme Co | | 708 | | | | | | | 90 | Cleaning | 9 | |
| | | | | | | | | | | 60 | Repairs | 6 | 165 |
| | Leiseur Winery | | 709 | | | | | 470 | | | | 47 | 517 |

**CHLOE'S WINE SHOP**
**Cash Payments Journal**

| Date | Particulars | Fol | Ref | Discount income — Accounts payable control | GST paid | Discount income | Accounts payable control | Cash purchases | Wages | Sundries — Amount | Sundries — Account | GST paid | Bank |
|------|-------------|-----|-----|-----|-----|-----|-----|-----|-----|-----|-----|-----|-----|
| 2017 | | | | $ | $ | $ | $ | $ | $ | $ | | $ | $ |
| 4 | AC Taxi Trucks | | 710 | | | | | | | 70 | Delivery expenses | 7 | 77 |
| | R Dixon | | 711 | 33 | 3 | 30 | 467 | | | | | | 467 |
| 5 | Hocks Ltd | | 712 | | | | | 330 | | | | 33 | 363 |
| | B Muller | | EFT | 11 | 1 | 10 | 209 | | | | | | 209 |
| | | | | $44 | $4 | $40 | $1 061 | $1 610 | $650 | $220 | | $183 | $3 724 |

**Journal explanations**

1 The format of the Cash Payments Journal above has been designed to suit the particular needs of Chloe's Wine Shop. A column is provided for each of the most commonly occurring transactions. It also has a separate column to record the GST applicable to all business inputs, so that the business can account for the total amount of GST paid each month.

2 Transactions must be recorded in date sequence.

3 The Particulars column records a description of the transaction or the name of the person or business to whom the payment was made.

4 The Fol (Folio) column is used when posting journals to the ledger (its use will be explained in Chapter 3).

5 The Ref (Reference) column contains a reference to the source of the transaction, such as the cheque number for cheque payments or EFT for electronic payments.

6 The Discount income section is included in the Cash Payments Journal to show, in the same record, the payment made to a creditor and the discount applicable to that payment. It is also convenient to have a discount section because discount from a creditor is recorded simultaneously with the payment of the money to the creditor. Note that it is also necessary to record the GST applicable to discounts received from creditors, as this represents an adjustment (reduction) to GST paid on business inputs.

7 The business uses a control account in its ledger to record all creditors (accounts payable).

8 Where there is no special column provided for a transaction, the Sundries column is used. It is important to record the name of the appropriate ledger account applicable to each of these transactions.

9 The total amount of each payment is recorded in the Bank column. As a check, the totals of the Accounts payable, Cash purchases, Wages, Sundries and GST paid columns should equal the total in the Bank column.

10 Note that it is a useful cross-check to add the totals of the accounts payable, cash purchases, wages, sundries and GST paid columns, which should equal the total in the Bank column.

# Departmental Cash Payments Journals

Earlier, this chapter showed how a Cash Receipts Journal could be extended to provide for the recording of sales of each department of a business. In the example for Sports Distributors, the Cash Receipts Journal was designed to show the sales for the indoors and outdoors departments separately.

In the Cash Payments Journal for Sports Distributors, it would also be possible to record the purchases of the indoors and outdoors departments separately.

## Comprehensive example

Below are shown all documents relating to cash transactions for Sports Distributors for the second week of November 2017.

## POS daily summaries

| 8/11/17 | $ |
|---|---|
| EFTPOS sales: | |
| Indoors | 55.00 |
| Outdoors | 88.00 |
| Cash sales: | |
| Indoors | 110.00 |
| Outdoors | 44.00 |
| Total inc. GST | 297.00 |

| 9/11/17 | $ |
|---|---|
| EFTPOS sales: | |
| Indoors | 66.00 |
| Outdoors | 99.00 |
| Cash sales: | |
| Indoors | 55.00 |
| Outdoors | 121.00 |
| Total inc. GST | 341.00 |

| 10/11/17 | $ |
|---|---|
| EFTPOS sales: | |
| Indoors | 110.00 |
| Outdoors | 88.00 |
| Cash sales: | |
| Indoors | 66.00 |
| Outdoors | 132.00 |
| Total inc. GST | 396.00 |

| 11/11/17 | $ |
|---|---|
| EFTPOS sales: | |
| Indoors | Nil |
| Outdoors | Nil |
| Cash sales: | |
| Indoors | 594.00 |
| Outdoors | 583.00 |
| Total inc. GST | 1 177.00 |

| 12/11/17 | $ |
|---|---|
| EFTPOS sales: | |
| Indoors | 198.00 |
| Outdoors | 176.00 |
| Cash sales: | |
| Indoors | Nil |
| Outdoors | 682.00 |
| Diners Club sales (out-doors) | 132.00 |
| Total inc. GST | 1 188.00 |

## Receipt duplicates

| Sports Distributors | |
|---|---|
| Receipt 405 | 11.11.17 |
| Rec. from: B. Wells | |
| For: Payment of a/c | |
| The sum of $89.00 | |
| Discount $ 11.00 inc. GST | |

| Sports Distributors | |
|---|---|
| Receipt 406 | 12.11.17 |
| Rec. from: Motti's | |
| For: Refund on goods (Ind.) returned | |
| The sum of $11.00 inc. GST | |
| Discount $ — | |

## Cheque butts

| Chq no. 022 | |
|---|---|
| | 9.11.17 |
| To: Phil's Newsagency | |
| For: Cash purchases (Advertising) $33 inc. GST Postage $11 inc. GST | |
| This chq | $44.00 |

| Chq no. 023 | |
|---|---|
| | 9.11.17 |
| To: Wheato Ltd | |
| For: Cash purchases (Indoors) inc. GST | |
| This chq | $407.00 |

| Chq no. 024 | | Chq no. 025 | | Chq no. 026 | |
|---|---|---|---|---|---|
| | 11.11.17 | | 12.11.17 | | 12.11.17 |
| To: Supply Co. (creditor) | | To: Motti's | | To: Worths | |
| For: Payment of account (disc. $11 inc. GST) | | For: Cash Purchases (outdoors) (inc. GST) | | For: Cash purchases (Stationery) (inc. GST) | |
| This chq | $189.00 | This chq | $154.00 | This chq | $44.00 |

## Summary of EFT transactions extracted from electronic banking facility

8 Nov   Wages paid $360.00

9        Received commission from Ace Sports $66.00 inc. GST.

10       Paid creditor Powercorp $143.00.

12       Drawings (M Docker) $100.00.

All of these documents would be entered in the cash journals of Sports Distributors as follows:

**SPORTS DISTRIBUTORS**
**Cash Receipts Journal**

| Date | Particulars | Fol | Ref | Accounts receivable control (Discount expense) | GST collected | Discount expense | Accounts receivable control | Indoors (Cash sales) | Outdoors (Cash sales) | Amount (Sundries) | Account | GST collected | Bank |
|---|---|---|---|---|---|---|---|---|---|---|---|---|---|
| 2017 | | | | $ | $ | $ | $ | $ | $ | $ | | $ | $ |
| 8 Nov | EFTPOS sales | | POS | | | | | 50 | 80 | | | 13 | 143 |
| | Cash sales | | POS | | | | | 100 | 40 | | | 14 | 154 |
| 9 | EFTPOS sales | | POS | | | | | 60 | 90 | | | 15 | 165 |
| | Cash sales | | POS | | | | | 50 | 110 | | | 16 | 176 |
| | Ace Sports | | EFT | | | | | | | 60 | Commission income | 6 | 66 |
| 10 | EFTPOS sales | | POS | | | | | 100 | 80 | | | 18 | 198 |
| | Cash sales | | POS | | | | | 60 | 120 | | | 18 | 198 |
| 11 Nov | Cash sales | | POS | | | | | 540 | 530 | | | 107 | |
| | B Wells | | 405 | 11 | 1 | 10 | 89 | | | | | | 1 266 |
| 12 | EFTPOS sales | | POS | | | | | 180 | 160 | | | 34 | 374 |
| | Cash sales | | POS | | | | | | 620 | | | 62 | |
| | Motti's | | 406 | | | | | | | 10 | Purchases returns (indoor) | | |
| | | | | | | | | | | 1 | GST paid | | 693 |
| | | | | $11 | $1 | $10 | $89 | $1 140 | $1 830 | $71 | | $303 | $3 433 |

167

Note that Diners Club sales on 12 November have not been included in the Cash Receipts Journal because sales on credit cards not issued by banks are treated as credit sales. This transaction was recorded in the Sales Journal of Sports Distributors (refer to the comprehensive example on pages 162–3).

**SPORTS DISTRIBUTORS**
**Cash Payments Journal**

| | | | | Discount income | | | Cash purchases | | | | Sundries | | | |
| | | | | Accounts payable control | GST paid | Discount income | Accounts payable control | Indoors | Outdoors | Wages | Amount | Account | GST paid | Bank |
|---|---|---|---|---|---|---|---|---|---|---|---|---|---|---|
| Date | Particulars | Fol | Ref | | | | | | | | | | | |
| 2017 | | | | $ | $ | $ | $ | $ | $ | $ | $ | | $ | $ |
| 8 Nov | Wages | | EFT | | | | | | | 360 | | | | 360 |
| 9 | Phil's Newsagency | | 022 | | | | | | | | 30 | Advertising | 3 | |
| | | | | | | | | | | | 10 | Postage | 1 | 44 |
| | Wheato Ltd | | 023 | | | | | 370 | | | | | 37 | 407 |
| 10 | Powercorp | | EFT | | | | 143 | | | | | | | 143 |
| 11 | Supply Co | | 024 | 11 | 1 | 10 | 189 | | | | | | | 189 |
| 12 | M Docker | | EFT | | | | | | | | 100 | Drawings – M Docker | | 100 |
| | Motti's | | 025 | | | | | | 140 | | | | 14 | 154 |
| | Worths | | 026 | | | | | | | | 40 | Stationery | 4 | 44 |
| | | | | $11 | $1 | $10 | $332 | $370 | $140 | $360 | $180 | | $59 | $1 441 |

You could now refer back to the comprehensive example on pages 165–7, which shows how the credit transactions of Sports Distributors were entered into the credit journals for the second week of November 2017. Together, these comprehensive examples show how all of the special journals for Sports Distributors were prepared for that week.

# Payment of GST to the Australian Taxation Office

At the end of each tax period, a business that is registered for GST must submit a Business Activity Statement (BAS). It should be noted that most businesses submit their BAS statement either monthly or quarterly, depending on their size. At this time, the business may be required to remit GST to the ATO, or it may receive a refund of GST from the ATO.

Consider the following examples. A UWatch demonstration is available on the CD that accompanies this text for parts of this activity.

UWATCH 2.8

# Example 1

For the quarter ended 31 March 2016, Tommy's Clothing Company collected $4000 GST from supplies of its goods, and paid $2500 GST on business inputs. The business was therefore required to pay the ATO a net amount of $1500 in GST ($4000 collected minus $2500 paid).

The business paid the amount on 28 April 2016 (EFT). This payment would be recorded in the Cash Payments Journal as follows:

**TOMMY'S CLOTHING COMPANY**
**Cash Payments Journal (extract)**

| Date | Particulars | Fol | Ref | Discount income | | | Accounts payable control | Cash purchases | Wages | Sundries | | | GST paid | Bank |
| | | | | Accounts payable control | GST paid | Discount income | | | | Amount | Account | | | |
|---|---|---|---|---|---|---|---|---|---|---|---|---|---|---|
| 2016 | | | | $ | $ | $ | $ | $ | $ | $ | | | $ | $ |
| 28 April | ATO | | EFT | | | | | | | 4 000 | GST collected | | | |
| | | | | | | | | | | (2 500) | GST paid | | | 1 500 |

A UWatch demonstration is available on the CD that accompanies this text for parts of this activity.

UWATCH 2.9

# Example 2

For the quarter ended 31 March 2016, Willy's Video Sales collected $3000 GST from supplies of its goods, and paid $4000 GST on business inputs. The business therefore received a GST refund of $1000 from the ATO ($4000 paid minus $3000 collected).

The refund was received from the ATO on 14 April 2016 by EFT. This would be recorded in the Cash Receipts Journal as follows:

**WILLY'S VIDEO SALES**
**Cash Receipts Journal (extract)**

| Date | Particulars | Fol | Ref | Discount expense | | | Accounts receivable control | Cash sales | Sundries | | | GST collected | Bank |
| | | | | Accounts receivable control | GST collected | Discount expense | | | Amount | Account | | | |
|---|---|---|---|---|---|---|---|---|---|---|---|---|---|
| 2016 | | | | $ | $ | $ | $ | $ | $ | | | $ | $ |
| 14 April | ATO | | EFT | | | | | | 4 000 | GST paid | | | |
| | | | | | | | | | (3 000) | GST collected | | | 1 000 |

## EXERCISES

Note that in all future exercises and examples, transactions described as 'sales' and 'purchases' refer to sales and purchases of trading stock, unless indicated to the contrary.

**2.35**  In which journals are cash transactions involving trading stock recorded?

**2.36**  Name the business document or documents that provide the source of information for entries in:
   a  the Cash Receipts Journal
   b  the Cash Payments Journal.

**2.37**  The following cash receipts transactions relate to the business of E Singh, used car dealer, for the month of July 2019. You are required to:
   a  design a suitable Cash Receipts Journal for the business
   b  enter the transactions for July in the journal
   c  total the journal at the end of July 2019.

*2019*
   5 July  Cash sales $231 inc. GST (POS).
   7        Received $300 from debtor S Busch (receipt 012).
   12       EFTPOS sales $187 inc. GST (POS).
            Singh contributed additional capital, $4000 cash (EFT).
            Cash sales $209 inc. GST (POS).
   15       Received $389 from debtor T Reeves, after allowing discount of $11 inc. GST (receipt 013).
   20       Commission received from Cars Inc. $110 inc. GST (EFT).
   31       EFTPOS sales $121 inc. GST (POS).
            Cash sales $209 inc. GST (POS).

**ADDITIONAL EXERCISES**

**2.38**  This question is available on the CD that accompanies this text.

**2.39**  I Brown is the owner of Ivan's Wines and Spirits, a liquor retailing business. The store has two departments: wine sales and spirit sales. Below are shown his cash receipts transactions for March 2016. You are required to:
   a  design a suitable Cash Receipts Journal for the business
   b  enter his transactions for March in the journal
   c  total the journal at the end of the month.

*2016*
   2 Mar  Cash sales (inc. GST): wine, $374; spirits, $550 (POS).
   4       EFTPOS sales (inc. GST): wine, $88; spirits, $99 (POS).
           Cash sales (inc. GST): wine, $253; spirits, $363 (POS).
           Received $793 from debtor R Jimby, after allowing discount of $22 inc. GST (receipt 45).
   10      Brown contributed additional capital, $5000 cash (EFT).
           Cash sales (inc. GST): wine $484; spirits, $682 (POS).

| 16 | Received $1256 from debtor P Falls, after allowing discount of $44 inc. GST (receipt 46). |
| 20 | EFTPOS sales (inc. GST): spirits, $165 (POS). |
| | Cash sales (inc. GST): wine, $363; spirits, $308 (POS). |
| | Rent received from A Jacobs $220 inc. GST (direct credit). |
| 21 | EFTPOS sales (inc. GST): wine $121; spirits, $319 (POS). |
| | Cash sales (inc. GST): wine $594; spirits, $462 (POS). |
| | Sold printer to D Hall for $110 inc. GST (receipt 47). |
| 30 | Received $1000 from debtor J Chambers (EFT). |

**2.40**  This question is available on the CD that accompanies this text.

**2.41**  The following transactions relate to the business of P Searle, wholesaler, for the month of April 2016. You are required to:

a  design a suitable Cash Payments Journal for the business

b  enter the transactions in the journal

c  total the journal at the end of the month.

*2016*

| 1 Apr | Cash purchases $220 inc. GST (cheque 101). |
| 4 | Paid wages, $440 (EFT). |
| 5 | Cash purchases from NewsWorks – advertising, $132 inc. GST (cheque 102). |
| 8 | Paid creditor Bendigo Council, $318 (EFT). |
| 9 | Paid creditor J Chellew $189, after deducting an allowance for discount $11 inc. GST (cheque 103). |
| 10 | Cash purchases, $517 inc. GST (cheque 104). |
| 15 | Paid wages, $440 (EFT). Paid creditor OZ Insurance, $242 (EFT). |
| 25 | Paid creditor S Hafagee $89, after deducting discount of $11 inc. GST (cheque 105). Searle withdrew $300 for his personal use (EFT). |
| 26 | Paid N Barr $143 for cash purchases – office expenses ($121 inc. GST) and cleaning ($22 inc. GST) (cheque 106). |
| 28 | Paid ATO $760 for net GST payable (GST collected $1060, less GST paid $300) (EFT). |

**2.42**  This question is available on the CD that accompanies this text.

**2.43**  W Gillies is the owner of Billie's Pastry Shop, a business that is divided into two separate departments: pie sales and cake sales. The documents shown below relate to the payments of the business for the month of July 2017. You are required to:

a  design a suitable Cash Payments Journal for the business

b  enter the transactions for July in the journal

c  total the journal at the end of the month.

## Cheque butts

| Chq no. 015 | Chq no. 016 | Chq no. 017 | Chq no. 018 |
|---|---|---|---|
| 4.7.17 | 11.7.17 | 19.7.17 | 24.7.17 |
| To: *Bruce's Ltd* | To: *Arnold & Co.* | To: *Bert's News* | To: *Bruce's Ltd* |
| For: *Cash purch. (inc. GST) pies $253 cakes $132* | For: *Cash purch. (inc. GST) pies $308 cakes $198* | For: *Stationery $33 inc. GST Postage $11 inc. GST* | For: *Cash purch. (inc. GST) pies $429 cakes $363* |
| This chq *$385.00* | This chq *$506.00* | This chq *$44.00* | This chq *$792.00* |

| Chq no. 019 | Chq no. 020 | Chq no. 021 |
|---|---|---|
| 26.7.17 | 31.7.17 | 31.7.17 |
| To: *D Berry* | To: *Maggies Pies* | To: *N Wills* |
| For: *Payment to creditor (disc. $11 inc. GST)* | For: *Cash purchase of pies (inc. GST)* | For: *Payment to creditor (disc. $11 inc. GST)* |
| This chq *$279.00* | This chq *$308.00* | This chq *$89.00* |

## Summary of EFT transactions

*2017*

| | | |
|---|---|---|
| 2 Jul | Paid wages $345. |
| 7 | Drawings by W Gillies $100. |
| 14 | Rent paid to AC Realty $407 inc. GST. |
| 21 | Paid wages $355. |

2.44* C Nguyen is the owner of Mac's Cameras, a wholesaler of photographic equipment. The documents shown below relate to the cash transactions of Mac's Cameras for the month of December 2018. You are required to:

a  design suitable cash journals for the business

b  enter the appropriate transactions for December in the journals

c  total the journals at the end of the month.

## POS daily summaries

| 2/12/18 | $ |
|---|---|
| EFTPOS sales | 495.00 |
| Cash sales | 990.00 |
| | |
| Total inc. GST | 1 485.00 |

| 9/12/18 | $ |
|---|---|
| EFTPOS sales | 550.00 |
| Cash sales | 1 056.00 |
| Diners Club sales | 209.00 |
| Total inc. GST | 1 815.00 |

| 16/12/18 | $ |
|---|---|
| EFTPOS sales | 715.00 |
| Cash sales | 825.00 |
| | |
| Total inc. GST | 1 540.00 |

```
23/12/18            $
EFTPOS sales     418.00
Cash sales     1 485.00
Total inc. GST 1 903.00
```

```
30/12/18            $
EFTPOS sales   1 078.00
Cash sales       770.00
Total inc. GST 1 848.00
```

## Receipt duplicates

Mac's Cameras

1.12.18

Receipt A31

Rec from R. Cusack

For Payment of account

The sum of $347.00

Discount $33.00 inc. GST

Mac's Cameras

20.12.18

Receipt A32

Rec from A Sainsbury

For Payment of account

The sum of $89.00

Discount $11.00 inc. GST

## Cheque butts

Cheque 5120

4.12.18

To: R. Neumann

For: Cash purchases – Car repairs (inc. GST)

This chq          $88.00

Cheque 5121

7.12.18

To: G Mannering

For: Payment of account (disc. $11 inc. GST)

This chq         $169.00

Cheque 5122

17.12.18

To: Cash

For: Drawings $50 Postage $33 inc. GST

This chq          $83.00

Cheque 5123

22.12.18

To: R Lamm

For: Cash purchase of stock (inc. GST)

This chq         $627.00

Cheque 5124

31.12.18

To: Photo Co

For: Cash purchase of stock (inc. GST)

This chq         $165.00

## Summary of EFT and bank statement transactions

*2018*

7 Dec   Paid wages $450 (EFT).

12        Paid Pines Golf Club for membership fee – C Nguyen $150.00 (direct debit).

16        Commission received from P Hunt & Co $77.00 inc. GST (direct credit).

26        Paid creditor G Jorgens $339.00 after receiving discount of $11.00 inc. GST (EFT).

30        Received interest on loan to T Caruso $20.00 (EFT).

2.45    R Ratnayake is the owner of Happy Hardware, a wholesale hardware store that is divided into two departments: kitchenware and crockery. (Kitchenware includes such items as saucepans, cutlery, utensils etc.) The documents shown below relate to the cash transactions of the business for the month of May 2019. You are required to:

a   design suitable cash journals for the business

b   enter the appropriate transactions for May in the journals

c   total the journals at the end of the month.

(Abbreviations used: KW = kitchenware, CR = crockery)

## Documents relating to cash transactions

| Chq no. 001 | |
|---|---|
| | 1.5.19 |
| To: G Frilay | |
| For: Cash purchases inc. GST | |
| KW $165.00 | |
| CR $154.00 | |
| This chq | $319.00 |

| 3/5/19 | $ |
|---|---|
| EFTPOS sales: | |
| KW | 77.00 |
| CR | 132.00 |
| Cash sales: | |
| KW | 121.00 |
| CR | 187.00 |
| Total inc. GST | 517.00 |

| Happy Hardware | |
|---|---|
| 3.5.19  Rec no. 740 | |
| Rec from: R. Barry | |
| For: Payment of account | |
| The sum of: $89.00 | |
| Discount: $11.00 inc. GST | |

| 7/5/19 | $ |
|---|---|
| EFTPOS sales: | |
| KW | 110.00 |
| CR | 154.00 |
| Cash sales: | |
| KW | 143.00 |
| CR | 242.00 |
| American Express sales (KW) | 198.00 |
| Total inc. GST | 847.00 |

| Chq no. 002 | |
|---|---|
| | 8.5.19 |
| To: L Williams | |
| For: Payment of account (disc. $22 inc. GST) | |
| This chq | $178.00 |

| 12/5/19 | $ |
|---|---|
| EFTPOS sales: | |
| KW | 99.00 |
| CR | 132.00 |
| Cash sales: | |
| KW | 187.00 |
| CR | 308.00 |
| Total inc. GST | 726.00 |

| 16/5/19 | $ |
|---|---|
| EFTPOS sales: | |
| KW | 66.00 |
| CR | 209.00 |
| Cash sales: | |
| KW | 220.00 |
| CR | 275.00 |
| Total inc. GST | 770.00 |

Chq no. 003

22.5.19

To: *L Hester*

For: *Cash purchases —*
*Cleaning $88*
*Repairs $66*
*(both inc. GST)*

| This chq | *$154.00* |
|---|---|

Chq no. 004

23.5.19

To: *G Kidman*

For: *Cash purchases (inc. GST);*
*KW $198*
*CR $242*

| This chq | *$440.00* |
|---|---|

| 25/5/19 | $ |
|---|---|
| EFTPOS sales: | |
| KW | 209.00 |
| CR | 308.00 |
| Cash sales: | |
| KW | 88.00 |
| CR | 110.00 |
| Total inc. GST | 715.00 |

Happy Hardware

*25.5.19* Rec no. 741

Rec from: *D Miller*

For: *Payment of account*

The sum of: *$443.00*

Discount: *$22.00 inc. GST*

Chq no. 005

28.5.19

To: *H Gill*

For: *Payment of account*

*(no discount)*

| This chq | *$400.00* |
|---|---|

```
┌─────────────────────────────┐
│  30/5/19              $      │
│  EFTPOS sales:              │
│  KW              132.00     │
│  CR              418.00     │
│  Cash sales:                │
│  KW              308.00     │
│  CR              231.00     │
│  Total inc. GST  1 089.00   │
└─────────────────────────────┘
```

```
┌──────────────────────────────┐
│  Chq no. 006                 │
│                     31.5.19  │
│  To: EB Crockery             │
│                              │
│  For: Cash purchases (CR)    │
│  inc. GST                    │
│  ─────────────────────────   │
│  This chq          $143.00   │
└──────────────────────────────┘
```

## Summary of EFT transactions

*2018*

| | | |
|---|---|---|
| 8 May | Paid wages $555. |
| 11 | Received loan repayment from A Tran $1000.00. |
| 12 | Drawings by R Ratnayake $300.00. |
| 19 | Received rent from V Batchelor $264 inc. GST. |

2.46   During June 2017, Bartlett's Electrical (electrical goods wholesaler) had the transactions listed below. You are required to:

a   design the following journals for the business: (i) Cash Receipts Journal, (ii) Cash Payments Journal, (iii) Sales Journal, (iv) Purchases Journal, (v) Sales Returns and Allowances Journal and (vi) Purchases Returns and Allowances Journal. (If you completed Exercise 2.34, which related to the same business, use the same journal formats for (iii), (iv), (v) and (vi).)

b   enter the transactions for June into the journals

c   total the journals at the end of the month.

*2017*

1 Jun   The owner, Norm Bartlett, withdrew $300 for his own use (EFT).

3   Credit purchases from Electro Manufacturing, $528 inc. GST (invoice 966).

4   Cash sales, $605 inc. GST (POS).
    Credit sales to Watt Electrics, $583 inc. GST (invoice S104).

6   Received $577 from Diners Club for payment of amount owing. Merchant fee deducted, $33 inc. GST (EFT).

9   Credit sales to Phillip Electrical, $407 inc. GST (invoice S105).
    Cash sales, $748 inc. GST (POS).

10   Received invoice TR90 from Argo Ltd for purchases, $396 inc. GST.

12   Allowance given to Phillip Electrical for overcharge, $55 inc. GST (adjustment note 401).

13    Paid the following amounts: Cash purchases – advertising, $88 inc. GST (cheque 113); wages, $280 (EFT); cash purchases, $297 inc. GST (cheque 114).

15    Credit purchase of delivery vehicle from Jackson Automotive, $8690 inc. GST (invoice 450).

16    Jackson Automotive allowed Bartlett Electrical a price adjustment for faulty air conditioner on delivery vehicle, $440 inc. GST (adjustment note 14).
      Cash sales, $209 inc. GST (POS).

19    Paid creditor Zappo Products, $67. Discount received was $11 inc. GST (EFT).

22    Sales on Diners Club card, $385 inc. GST (POS).

23    Invoiced Watt Electrics for delivery charges $121 inc. GST (invoice S106).

25    Watt Electrics returned damaged goods, $66 inc. GST (adjustment note 402).

26    Cash purchases from Manulec Ltd, $209 inc. GST (cheque 115).

29    Cash sales, $176 inc. GST (POS).
      Received interest on loan $50 from AB Investments (EFT).

30    Credit purchases from Argo Ltd using American Express card, $77 inc. GST (invoice TS006).

2.47   This question is available on the CD that accompanies this text.

ADDITIONAL
EXERCISES

## Revision – GST and double entry

2.48   Provide brief answers to each of the following questions relating to the GST:
   a   What is GST? Explain.
   b   What is an input tax credit? Explain.
   c   How does a business calculate the amount of GST payable to (or refundable by) the Australian Taxation Office at the end of each tax period?
   d   List four examples of business transactions that are not subject to GST.

2.49   Discuss the nature and purpose of each of the following ledger accounts:
   a   GST Collected account
   b   GST Paid account.
   **Note** In your answer, clearly describe the types of transactions that are recorded in each account.

2.50   Answer True or False to each of the following statements:
   a   To increase an asset account, you credit the account.
   b   To increase an owner's equity account, you credit the account.
   c   To decrease a liability account, you debit the account.
   d   To increase an expense account, you credit the account.
   e   To decrease an owner's equity account, you debit the account.
   f   To increase a income account, you debit the account.

**SOLUTION**

2.44

**MAC'S CAMERAS**
**Cash Receipts Journal**

| Date | Particulars | Fol | Ref | Discount expense Accounts receivable control | GST collected | Discount expense | Accounts receivable control | Cash sales | Sundries Amount | Account | GST collected | Bank |
|---|---|---|---|---|---|---|---|---|---|---|---|---|
| 2018 | | | | $ | $ | $ | $ | $ | $ | | $ | $ |
| 1 Dec | R Cusack | | A31 | 33 | 3 | 30 | 347 | | | | | 347 |
| 2 | EFTPOS sales | | POS | | | | | 450 | | | 45 | 495 |
| | Cash sales | | POS | | | | | 900 | | | 90 | 990 |
| 9 | EFTPOS sales | | POS | | | | | 500 | | | 50 | 550 |
| | Cash sales | | POS | | | | | 960 | | | 96 | 1 056 |
| 16 | EFTPOS sales | | POS | | | | | 650 | | | 65 | 715 |
| | Cash sales | | POS | | | | | 750 | | | 75 | 825 |
| | P Hunt & Co | | DC | | | | | | 70 | Commission income | 7 | 77 |
| 20 | A Sainsbury | | A32 | 11 | 1 | 10 | 89 | | | | | 89 |
| 23 | EFTPOS sales | | POS | | | | | 380 | | | 38 | 418 |
| | Cash sales | | POS | | | | | 1 350 | | | 135 | 1 485 |
| 30 | EFTPOS sales | | POS | | | | | 980 | | | 98 | 1 078 |
| | Cash sales | | POS | | | | | 700 | | | 70 | 770 |
| | T Caruso | | EFT | | | | | | 20 | Interest income | | 20 |
| | | | | $44 | $4 | $40 | $436 | $7 620 | $90 | | $769 | $8 915 |

**MAC'S CAMERAS**
**Cash Payments Journal**

| Date | Particulars | Fol | Ref | Discount income Accounts payable control | GST paid | Discount income | Accounts payable control | Cash purchases | Wages | Sundries Amount | Account | GST paid | Bank |
|---|---|---|---|---|---|---|---|---|---|---|---|---|---|
| 2018 | | | | $ | $ | $ | $ | $ | $ | $ | | $ | $ |
| 4 Dec | R Neumann | | 5120 | | | | | | | 80 | Vehicle repairs | 8 | 88 |
| 7 | G Mannering | | 5121 | 11 | 1 | 10 | 169 | | | | | | 169 |
| | Wages | | EFT | | | | | | 450 | | | | 450 |

**MAC'S CAMERAS**
**Cash Payments Journal**

| Date | Particulars | Fol | Ref | Discount income | | | Accounts payable control | Cash purchases | Wages | Sundries | | GST paid | Bank |
| | | | | Accounts payable control | GST paid | Discount income | | | | Amount | Account | | |
|------|-------------|-----|-----|--------|--------|--------|--------|--------|--------|--------|---------|--------|--------|
| 2018 | | | | $ | $ | $ | $ | $ | $ | $ | | $ | $ |
| 12 | Pines Golf Club | | DD | | | | | | | 150 | Drawings – C Nguyen | | 150 |
| 17 | Cash | | 5122 | | | | | | | 50 | Drawings – C Nguyen | | |
| | | | | | | | | | | 30 | Postage | 3 | 83 |
| 22 | R Lamm | | 5123 | | | | | 570 | | | | 57 | 627 |
| 26 | C Jorgens | | EFT | 11 | 1 | 10 | 339 | | | | | | 339 |
| 31 | Photo Co | | 5124 | | | | | 150 | | | | 15 | 165 |
| | | | | $22 | $2 | $20 | $508 | $720 | $450 | $310 | | $83 | $2 071 |

# The General Journal

As stated earlier in this chapter, journals are used to summarise transactions before they are entered into the ledger. So far, the preparation of the following six *special journals* has been examined.

1 Cash Receipts Journal Records all amounts received
2 Cash Payments Journal Records all payments
3 Sales Journal Records all credit sales
4 Purchases Journal Records all credit purchases
5 Sales Returns and Allowances Journal Records all credits given to customers for returns of goods or other allowances
6 Purchases Returns and Allowances Journal Records all credits allowed by suppliers for returns of goods or other allowances.

These six special journals record the most commonly occurring transactions in a business; that is, the vast majority of transactions. There are, however, certain other uncommon transactions that cannot be recorded in any of the special journals. These unusual transactions are recorded in another journal called the *General Journal*.

The General Journal is a 'general purpose' journal that is used to record any transaction that cannot be recorded in any of the six special journals. An example of such a transaction is a bad debt, which is neither a cash transaction nor a credit transaction.

The recording of transactions in the General Journal requires the application of the *rules of debit and credit*. These rules, which were introduced in Chapter 1, are reproduced in the following table:

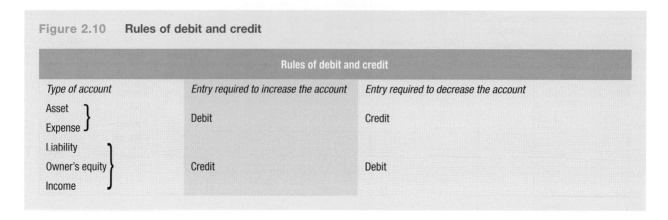

Figure 2.10    **Rules of debit and credit**

| Rules of debit and credit | | |
|---|---|---|
| *Type of account* | *Entry required to increase the account* | *Entry required to decrease the account* |
| Asset<br>Expense | Debit | Credit |
| Liability<br>Owner's equity<br>Income | Credit | Debit |

# Format of the General Journal

The format of the General Journal is very simple:

| | General Journal | | | | |
|---|---|---|---|---|---|
| **Date** | **Particulars** | **Fol** | **Debit** | | **Credit** |
| | | | $ | | $ |

When recording a transaction in the General Journal, simply indicate which ledger account/accounts are to receive a debit entry and which are to receive a credit entry, and the amount of the entry in each case. A suitable narration is added on the next line to describe what the entry is about. Some examples would include: 'Assets and liabilities introduced by owner at commencement of business' or 'Owner contributed van'. Typically, every entry would be followed by a simple narration explaining the nature for the transaction, which is useful for audit purposes. Consider the following simple example.

## Example

*2017*

3 Jun    Leanne's Hairdressing Supplies decided to 'write off' the amount owing by debtor P Wave ($407 inc. GST) as a bad debt.

This transaction would be entered in the General Journal as follows:

**LEANNE'S HAIRDRESSING SUPPLIES**
**General Journal**

| Date | Particulars | Fol | Debit | Credit |
|------|-------------|-----|-------|--------|
| 2017 | | | $ | $ |
| 3 Jun | Bad debts | | 370 | |
| | GST collected | | 37 | |
| |     Accounts receivable control | | | 407 |
| | *Amount owing by debtor P Wave written off as a bad debt* | | | |

**Journal explanations**

1 Most businesses use a standard format as shown above.

2 Each entry in the General Journal must be recorded in date sequence.

3 The Particulars column records:
   - the names of the particular ledger accounts debited or credited
   - a brief explanation ('narration') of each entry, quoting document numbers where possible.

4 Note that it is customary, when recording the names of accounts, to name the account/accounts to be debited before naming those to be credited, and to indent the name of the account/accounts to be credited (in our example, 'Accounts Receivable Control' is set in from the margin).

5 The Fol (Folio) column is used when posting the journal to the ledger and its use will be explained in Chapter 3.

6 The debits and credits for each transaction entered must be equal.

7 After each entry, a brief explanation (a 'narration') is added, including reference numbers if possible.

8 It is customary to rule a line across the Particulars column after each complete entry in the journal.

Where a debtor fails to pay for goods or services supplied on credit, the resultant bad debt written off will normally include an element of GST. In this case, this constitutes a reduction in the GST charged on the original sale. Therefore, an adjustment must be recorded to reduce the amount of GST collected. This has been achieved in the above journal entry by a debit to the GST Collected account.

# General Journal transactions

As stated above, the General Journal is used to record those transactions that cannot be recorded in any of the six special journals. We have seen how to use the General Journal to record bad debts; now we will look at other transactions that are recorded in the General Journal.

# Introduction of assets and liabilities by the owner at the commencement of business

The first transaction that occurs when a business commences is the introduction of assets and, where appropriate, liabilities by the owner. This necessitates an entry in the General Journal, sometimes referred to as an *opening journal entry*. The General Journal entry required is:

| Debit | | Each asset introduced by the owner. |
|---|---|---|
| Credit | 1 | Each liability introduced by the owner. |
| | 2 | The owner's capital; the capital figure would be calculated as follows: |

| Total assets introduced by owner | minus | Total liabilities introduced by owner | = | Capital |
|---|---|---|---|---|

A UWatch demonstration is available on the CD that accompanies this text for parts of this activity.

## Example

**General Journal**

| Date | Particulars | Fol | Debit | Credit |
|---|---|---|---|---|
| 2017 | | | $ | $ |
| 1 Jul | Cash at bank | | 5 000 | |
| | Stock | | 3 500 | |
| | Motor vehicle | | 9 500 | |
| | Bank loan | | | 8 000 |
| | Capital – A Smith | | | 10 000 |
| | *Assets and liabilities introduced by the owner at commencement of business* | | | |

Note that there are possible GST implications where the proprietor contributes assets to the business. This is a complex area of GST legislation and is beyond the scope of an introductory accounting text. It has therefore been ignored in this book.

# Additional capital contributions by the owner

During the life of a business, it is quite common for the business owner to make additional capital contributions. These may constitute one of the following:

* contributions of cash
* contributions of other personal assets
* payments made by the owner on behalf of the business.

## Contributions of cash

The owner could contribute additional cash to the business via cash, cheque or electronic funds transfer (EFT). In each case, this constitutes a receipt of money by the business, which is recorded in the Cash Receipts Journal. The Cash Receipts Journal was covered earlier in this chapter.

## Contributions of other personal assets

Where the owner contributes personal assets other than cash to the business, this transaction must be recorded in the General Journal.

This transaction results in an increase in the relevant asset account of the business and a corresponding increase in owner's equity, recorded in the owner's Capital account. The General Journal entry required is:

| | | | | |
|---|---|---|---|---|
| | | | | General Journal |
| **Date** | **Particulars** | **Fol** | **Debit** | **Credit** |
| 2017 | | | $ | $ |
| 15 Aug | Office equipment | | 2 000 | |
| | Capital – A Smith | | | 2 000 |
| | *Owner contributed his own personal computer system to the business* | | | |

As stated earlier, there are possible GST implications where the proprietor contributes assets to the business. This is a complex area of GST legislation and is beyond the scope of an introductory accounting text. It has therefore been ignored in this book.

## Payments by the owner on behalf of the business

Sometimes the owner of a business will make business payments from his/her personal funds. Examples include payments of business expenses, purchase of assets on behalf of the business and payments to business creditors. Such payments represent an additional capital contribution by the owner and must be recorded in the General Journal. Consider the following General Journal entries:

| | | | | |
|---|---|---|---|---|
| | | | | General Journal |
| **Date** | **Particulars** | **Fol** | **Debit** | **Credit** |
| 2017 | | | $ | $ |
| 20 Aug | Power and lighting | | 400 | |
| | GST paid | | 40 | |
| | Capital – A Smith | | | 440 |
| | *Payment of business electricity account by the owner* | | | |

| General Journal | | | | |
|---|---|---|---|---|
| **Date** | **Particulars** | **Fol** | **Debit** | **Credit** |
| 2017 | | | $ | $ |
| 23 Aug | Office equipment | | 300 | |
| | GST paid | | 30 | |
| | Capital – A Smith | | | 330 |
| | *Computer printer for business use purchased by the owner* | | | |

| General Journal | | | | |
|---|---|---|---|---|
| **Date** | **Particulars** | **Fol** | **Debit** | **Credit** |
| 2017 | | | $ | $ |
| 31 Aug | Accounts payable control | | 500 | |
| | Discount income | | | 10 |
| | GST paid | | | 1 |
| | Capital – A Smith | | | 489 |
| | *Payment to business creditor (G Black) by the owner* | | | |

The treatment of discount income in the above journal entry is consistent with that illustrated in the Cash Payments Journal earlier in this chapter.

# Non-cash drawings by the owner

UWATCH 2.11 A UWatch demonstration is available on the CD that accompanies this text for parts of this activity.

## Withdrawal of stock

Because of the periodic method of stock recording (the method adopted in this text), all purchases of trading stock have been treated as expenses of the business. If the owner withdraws stock for personal use, the owner's interest or investment in the business must be reduced (by the use of a Drawings account) and purchases for the period must also be reduced.

As the stock is not to be used for business purposes, an adjustment must also be made to reduce any input tax credit related to the original purchase of this stock. Consequently, a credit entry is made to the GST Paid account. The General Journal entry required is:

| General Journal | | | | |
|---|---|---|---|---|
| **Date** | **Particulars** | **Fol** | **Debit** | **Credit** |
| 2017 | | | $ | $ |
| 8 Sept | Drawings – A Smith | | 1 100 | |
| | Purchases | | | 1 000 |
| | GST paid | | | 100 |
| | *Withdrawal of stock by the owner* | | | |

## Withdrawal of other items

Where a business owner withdraws items other than stock, these transactions must also be recorded in the General Journal. Such transactions also involve an adjustment to GST paid. For example, if the owner takes business stationery for personal use, the General Journal entry required is:

| General Journal | | | | |
|---|---|---|---|---|
| **Date** | **Particulars** | **Fol** | **Debit** | **Credit** |
| 2017 | | | $ | $ |
| 9 Sept | Drawings – A Smith | | 55 | |
| | Stationery expense | | | 50 |
| | GST paid | | | 5 |
| | *Withdrawal of stationery by the owner* | | | |

Sometimes a business will pay personal expenses, such as club membership fees, on behalf of its owner. This also constitutes 'Drawings'; however, as this transaction involves a payment it is recorded in the Cash Payments Journal.

# Late payment accounting fees charged to a debtor on an overdue account

A UWatch demonstration is available on the CD that accompanies this text for parts of this activity.

UWATCH 2.12

Apart from offering cash discounts, another means of encouraging prompt payment by trade debtors is to charge late payment accounting fees on overdue accounts. When the next statement of account is forwarded to the relevant debtor, an entry is made charging the debtor with the late fee on the overdue account.

The Accounts Receivable Control account must be increased, and late fees (income) earned must be recorded. The General Journal entry required is:

| | General Journal | | | | |
|---|---|---|---|---|---|
| **Date** | **Particulars** | **Fol** | **Debit** | **Credit** |
| 2017 | | | $ | $ |
| 11 Nov | Accounts receivable control | | 10 | |
| | Late fees income | | | 10 |
| | *Late payment accounting fee charged on overdue account* | | | |

Note that GST is not charged on late payment accounting fees. In accordance with GST legislation, these are treated as consideration for a separate input-taxed supply by the supplier.

# Late payment accounting fees charged by a creditor on an overdue account

UWATCH 2.13

A UWatch demonstration is available on the CD that accompanies this text for parts of this activity.

If an account for credit purchases is not paid by the due date, a creditor may charge late payment accounting fees on the overdue account. An expense (late fees) has been incurred for the amount of late fees charged and the Accounts payable Control account must be increased.

The General Journal entry required is:

| | General Journal | | | | |
|---|---|---|---|---|---|
| **Date** | **Particulars** | **Fol** | **Debit** | **Credit** |
| 2017 | | | $ | $ |
| 30 Nov | Late fees expense | | 20 | |
| | Accounts payable control | | | 20 |
| | *Late payment accounting fee charged by creditor* | | | |

Note that, as is the case with late fees charged to debtors, GST is not charged on late payment accounting fees charged to a business by a creditor.

# Correction of errors in the accounting records

Even though an accountant may take great care, errors will still be made in the accounting records. Most of these errors will be discovered quickly and can be corrected easily by a simple cross-out and re-entry of the correct figure. However, some errors may be discovered after the completion of the accounting tasks for a period, when it is too late to make a simple correction. In such a case it is necessary to correct the error through an entry in the General Journal.

A UWatch demonstration is available on the CD that accompanies this text for parts of this activity.

UWATCH 2.14

## Example

On 31 December 2017, N Muddle discovered that he had forgotten to record an invoice (number 342 for $165 including GST) in the Sales Journal two months ago. The General Journal entry required is:

| Date | Particulars | Fol | Debit | Credit |
|------|-------------|-----|-------|--------|
| | General Journal | | | |
| 2017 | | | $ | $ |
| 31 Dec | Accounts receivable control | | 165 | |
| | Sales | | | 150 |
| | GST collected | | | 15 |
| | *Correction of error – omission of invoice no. 342* | | | |

When correcting an error through the General Journal, it is important to remember the GST implications, if any, that arise from the entries made. In the above entry, for example, the GST collected must be properly accounted for.

## Comprehensive example

Barbara Brusher commenced business as a paint and wallpaper retailer on 1 May 2017. The transactions that require recording in her General Journal during the first month of operations follow.

*2017*

1 May   Commenced business with the following assets and liabilities: cash at bank, $4500; equipment, $7100; premises, $320 000; loan from RT Bank, $25 000.

9   Barbara Brusher gave some paint (which was purchased by the business for $110 inc. GST) to her mother-in-law.

12   Barbara Brusher paid the business buildings insurance premium $495 inc. GST using her personal credit card (invoice 107).

16   Charged late payment accounting fee $20 on overdue account to debtor M Burgess.

21   M Burgess declared bankrupt. Debt of $438 (inc. GST $38) to be written off as bad.

27     P Salmon (creditor) charged Brusher a late payment accounting fee $10 on her overdue account.

31     Brusher discovered that she had made an error in her ledger recording at the end of the month. An amount of $200 was incorrectly debited to the Rates account instead of the Rent account. (Note that GST relating to this transaction has been recorded correctly.)

These transactions would be entered in Barbara Brusher's General Journal as follows:

**Barbara Brusher**
**General Journal**

| Date | Particulars | Fol | Debit | Credit |
|---|---|---|---|---|
| 2017 | | | $ | $ |
| 1 May | Cash at bank | | 4 500 | |
| | Equipment | | 7 100 | |
| | Premises | | 320 000 | |
| |    Loan from RT Bank | | | 25 000 |
| |    Capital – Barbara Brusher | | | 306 600 |
| | *Assets and liabilities introduced by owner to commence business* | | | |
| 9 | Drawings – Barbara Brusher | | 110 | |
| |    Purchases | | | 100 |
| |    GST paid | | | 10 |
| | *Withdrawal of stock by owner* | | | |
| 12 May | Insurance | | 450 | |
| | GST paid | | 45 | |
| |    Capital – Barbara Brusher | | | 495 |
| | *Payment of business expense by owner* | | | |
| 16 | Accounts receivable control | | 20 | |
| |    Late fees income | | | 20 |
| | *Late payment accounting fee charged to M Burgess on overdue account* | | | |
| 21 | Bad debts | | 400 | |
| | GST collected | | 38 | |
| |    Accounts receivable control | | | 438 |
| | *Bad debt written off – M Burgess* | | | |
| 27 | Late fees expense | | 10 | |
| |    Accounts payable control | | | 10 |
| | *Late payment accounting fee charged by creditor P Salmon* | | | |
| 31 | Rent | | 200 | |
| |    Rates | | | 200 |
| | *Correction of error – incorrect account debited* | | | |

## EXERCISES

2.51    List the seven types of journals and briefly describe the types of transactions recorded in each journal.

2.52    Briefly explain the relationship between the journals and the ledger.

2.53    What is the purpose of the General Journal? In your answer, provide three examples of transactions that are recorded in the General Journal.

2.54    Name the journal used to record each of the following transactions:
   a    credit sales of trading stock
   b    purchase of a motor vehicle for cash
   c    bad debt written off
   d    introduction of assets and liabilities by owner at commencement of business
   e    discount received from a creditor
   f    late payment accounting fee charged to a debtor
   g    sale of office equipment on credit
   h    payment of wages by EFT
   i    correction of an error in the ledger
   j    cash sales of trading stock
   k    received an invoice for insurance
   l    purchase of stock using a business credit card.

2.55    a    Wally Crump commenced business as Wally's Sales on 1 January 2019. He asks you to prepare a General Journal entry recording his assets and liabilities (and capital) at commencement of business. He introduced the following assets and liabilities: cash at bank, $1000; delivery vehicle, $9000; stock of goods for resale, $2500; shop premises, $30 000; and mortgage loan on premises $20 000.
   b    On 7 January 2019 Wally Crump purchased office equipment for the business $2200 inc. GST, using funds from his personal cheque account (invoice 247).

2.56    Record the following transaction in the General Journal for Ivan's Wines and Spirits.

*2016*
26 Mar   I Brown withdrew a carton of white wine for his own consumption. The cost of the wine was $55 inc. GST.
28       I Brown took cleaning materials costing $55 inc. GST for his own personal use.

2.57    Record the following transaction in the General Journal for Con's Menswear.

*2016*
16 Jun   Charged late payment accounting fee $40 on overdue account to debtor T Chan.

**2.58**  Record the following transaction in the General Journal for E Singh.

*2017*

4 Jul    Received a statement of account from creditor J Taylor, charging a late payment accounting fee of $20. The account in question had been inadvertently overlooked by Singh's accountant, Ivor Got.

**2.59**  Record the following transaction in the General Journal for G Chapman.

*2019*

31 Aug  Received notification from a solicitor that a debtor, N Poustie, had been declared bankrupt. It was decided to write off the amount owed by Poustie ($407 inc. GST) as a bad debt.

**2.60**  I Muffdit has made an error in her ledger recording, having debited a purchase of stock, $2650, to the Equipment account instead of the Purchases account. She asks you to correct the error by preparing a General Journal entry dated 31 May 2017. (Note that the GST relating to this transaction has been recorded correctly.)

**2.61**  Complete entries to record the following information in the General Journal of K Desanges.

*2019*

1 Jul    Creditor B Simmons charged Desanges a late payment accounting fee of $20 for non-payment of last month's account.

3         Desanges introduced his personal motor vehicle valued at $10 000 into the business.

5         Desanges withdrew stock costing $1980 (inc. GST) from the business.

12        Debtor A Douglas declared bankrupt (owes $220 inc. GST). $44 received as full settlement.

17        A credit sale of trading stock, $2310 inc. GST to D Rawson (invoice no. 375) was overlooked in May.

28        Charged debtor B Reynolds a late payment accounting fee $30 on overdue account.

**2.62***  Complete entries to record the following information in the General Journal of I Jenkins.

*2017*

9 Apr    Jenkins commenced business as a retailer with the following assets and liabilities: bank, $8500; furniture and fittings, $5200; and loan from JK Loans, $5000.

1 Jun    Jenkins withdrew stationery for own use, $198 inc. GST.

4         Debtor E Wust declared bankrupt. Only $55 of his total debt of $220 (inc. GST) will be received. The balance of his debt is to be written off.

15        Jenkins introduced his own stereo system valued at $4200 into the business.

29        Charged debtor L Brereton a late payment accounting fee $50 on overdue account.

ADDITIONAL EXERCISES

**2.63**  This question is available on the CD that accompanies this text.

**2.64**  This question is available on the CD that accompanies this text.

2.65 Stewart Bishop commenced trading as a retailer of electrical goods on 1 July 2017. The following are his transactions for the first month's operations. You are required to enter the transactions in appropriately designed journals.

*2017*

1 Jul    Bishop commenced business with the following assets and liabilities: stock, $3000; cash at bank, $100 000; premises, $50 000; mortgage loan on premises, $40 000; loan from B Burns, $20 000.

14    Stewart Bishop paid $10 000 off the business mortgage loan via EFT from his personal bank account.

15    Purchased office equipment on credit from Hoon Ltd for $3080 inc. GST (invoice 600).

     Credit purchases from Young & Co, $6050 inc. GST (invoice 15214).

16    Cash sales, $2420 inc. GST (POS).

     Credit sales to F Farrer, $1210 inc. GST (invoice 301).

17    Cash purchases from Tab Electrics, $4070 inc. GST (chq 001).

18    Bishop withdrew stock costing $440 inc. GST (memo).

19    Credit purchases from Top Electrics, $4950 inc. GST (invoice PO516).

     Credit sales to G Neale, $715 inc. GST (invoice 302).

     Credit sales to H Brown, $1210 inc. GST (invoice 303).

20    Received invoice from Bendigo Daily for advertising, $330 inc. GST (invoice BD7051).

     Returns by F Farrer, $605 inc. GST (adjustment note 101).

22    Sent invoice no. 304 to S Walls for sale of surplus office equipment, $495 inc. GST.

     Returns to Young & Co, $1980 inc. GST (adjustment note 599).

24    Paid wages, $800 (EFT).

26    F Farrer paid his account of $600, deducting discount of $33 (inc. GST) for prompt payment (receipt 401).

30    Paid Young & Co $3900. Discount received was $110 inc. GST (chq 002).

     Bishop cashed cheque no. 003 for $100 to take his wife out to dinner.

31    Received commission from Top Electrics, $220 inc. GST (EFT).

     Cash sales, $4840 inc. GST (POS).

     Cash refund, $1210 inc. GST, paid to S Tumpy for goods previously sold for cash (chq 004).

2.66* The documents shown below relate to the transactions of Mac's Cameras, photographic equipment wholesaler, for the month of January 2019. C Nguyen, the owner, asks you to enter the information contained in the documents into appropriately designed journals.

(This exercise is also available in a MYOB format on the CD that accompanies the workbook.)

ADDITIONAL EXERCISES

## POS daily summaries

| 4/1/19 | $ |
| --- | --- |
| EFTPOS sales: | 440.00 |
| Cash sales: | 1 540.00 |
| Total inc. GST | 1 980.00 |

| 16/1/19 | $ |
| --- | --- |
| EFTPOS sales: | 770.00 |
| Cash sales: | 1 870.00 |
| Total inc. GST | 2 640.00 |

| 26/1/19 | $ |
| --- | --- |
| EFTPOS sales: | Nil |
| Cash sales: | 1 980.00 |
| American Express sales: | 330.00 |
| Total inc. GST | 2 310.00 |

## Receipt duplicates

```
                    Mac's Cameras

26.1.19                              Receipt A33
Rec from: P Hunt & Co
For: Interest
The sum of: $60.00
Discount: $ —
```

## Cheque butts

```
Cheque 5125              Cheque 5126
7.1.19                   19.1.19
To: R Lamm               To: C Nguyen

For: Cash purchase of    For: Drawings
     stock inc. GST

This chq:     $572.00    This chq:     $100.00
```

```
Cheque 5127              Cheque 5128
21.1.19                  28.1.19
To: Fristo               To: Insurers Ltd
    Manufacturing
For: Payment of          For: Payment of
     account (disc.           account
     $33 inc. GST)

This chq:   $1 097.00    This chq:     $165.00
```

## Duplicate copy of adjustment note sent to customer

```
            MAC'S CAMERAS

Adjustment Note MC83              17.1.19

Credit to: M Robins

                                    $
Stock returned                    66.00
Total credit inc. GST             66.00
```

## Duplicate copies of invoices sent to customers

```
          MAC'S CAMERAS                    MAC'S CAMERAS

Tax Invoice M37          6.1.19    Tax Invoice M38          14.1.19
Sold to: A Sainsbury               Sold to: M Robins
Stock              $770.00         Stock              $143.00
Total inc. GST     $770.00         Total inc. GST     $143.00
```

| MAC'S CAMERAS | |
|---|---|
| Tax Invoice M39 | 22.1.19 |
| Sold to: M Hunter | |
| Stock | $209.00 |
| Delivery | $33.00 |
| Total inc. GST | $242.00 |

## Invoices from suppliers

| 1.1.19 | Tax Inv no. 97 |
|---|---|
| PHOTOGRAPHICS LTD | |
| Sold to: Mac's Cameras | |
| Stock inc. GST | $407.00 |

| G MANNERING | |
|---|---|
| Tax Invoice 344 | 28.1.19 |
| Charge: Mac's Cameras | |
| Stock inc. GST | $143.00 |

## Adjustment notes from suppliers

| Adj Note no. C13F | 2.1.19 |
|---|---|
| FRISTO MANUFACTURING | |
| Credit: Mac's Cameras | |
| Returns of stock (inc. GST) | $110.00 |

| 4.1.19 | Adjustment C740 |
|---|---|
| PHOTOGRAPHICS LTD | |
| Credit: Mac's Cameras | |
| Overcharge (inc. GST) | $66.00 |

## Other documents

| MAC'S CAMERAS — MEMO |
|---|
| From: C Nguyen                 1.1.19 |
| To: Accountant |
| Subject: Debtor D. Rongo's account is now 90 days overdue. Late payment accounting fee of $20 to be charged. |

| MAC'S CAMERAS — MEMO |
|---|
| From: C Nguyen                 10.1.19 |
| To: Accountant |
| Subject: Please note that I have taken a camera out of stock for my daughter's birthday (Value $330 inc. GST.) |

LARRY, CURLY & PHIL
Solicitors

31/1/19
The Manager
Mac's Cameras

Dear Sir,

I refer to your debtor, Derek D Rongo, who has an account of $680.00 (inc. GST $60) outstanding with your business.

We hereby officially advise that Mr Rongo is now bankrupt and will therefore be unable to repay any of his debt to you.

Please direct any enquiries on this matter to me.

Yours faithfully

*C Curly*
C Curly

## Summary of EFT transactions

*2019*

12 Jan   Paid wages $460.00

15   Received $493.00 from American Express for payment of account, after deducting merchant fee of $22.00 inc. GST

2.67   During July 2017, Bartlett's Electrical (electrical goods wholesaler) had the following transactions. You are required to enter the transactions in appropriately designed journals.
(This exercise is also available in a MYOB format on the CD that accompanies the workbook.)

*2017*

1 Jul   Cash sales, $660 inc. GST (POS).

2   Purchased shop fittings on credit from Fitto Co using Visa business credit card, $990 inc. GST (invoice 08).
Cash purchases from Manulec Ltd, $440 inc. GST (cheque 116).

4   Sales on Diners Club cards, $473 inc. GST (POS).
Cash sales, $770 inc. GST (POS).

7   Paid Jack's News $330 inc. GST for cash purchases – stationery (cheque 117).
Paid creditor Argo Ltd $453 on account. Discount received $22 inc. GST (EFT).

8   The owner, Norm Bartlett, withdrew business stationery costing $110 inc. GST for his own use.
Norm Bartlett also withdrew stock worth $110 (inc. GST) for his own use.

| | |
|---|---|
| 9 | Bad debt to be written off – S Simpson, $1430 inc. GST. |
| | Cash sales, $880 inc. GST (POS). |
| 14 | Received $660 on account from Diners Club. Merchant fee deducted, $22, inc. GST (EFT). |
| | Paid wages, $310 (EFT). |
| | Cash sales, $583 inc. GST (POS). |
| 17 | Received invoice no. TS300 from Argo Ltd for purchases, $440 inc. GST. |
| | Sent sales invoice no. S107 to Phillip Electrical, $770 inc. GST. |
| | Received interest on loan, $50, from AB Investments (EFT). |
| 18 | Cash sales, $660 inc. GST (POS). |
| 19 | Sent adjustment note no. 403 to Phillip Electrical for return of goods, $165 inc. GST. |
| | Credit purchases from Electro Manufacturing, $715 inc. GST (invoice 1411). |
| 22 | Sold office computer on credit to A Dargo, $330 inc. GST (invoice S108). |
| 23 | Cash sales, $770 inc. GST (POS). |
| | Received invoice from H Andyman for repairs, $66 inc. GST (invoice HA107). |
| | Received payment on account from debtor Phillip Electrical, $470. Discount allowed was $11 inc. GST (receipt R55). |
| 24 | Paid GST for June quarter to ATO (GST collected $1800, GST paid $600) (EFT). |
| 25 | Received adjustment note no. 010 from Electro Manufacturing for an overcharge on goods, $220 inc. GST. |
| 28 | Credit sales to Watt Electrics, $836 inc. GST (invoice S109). |
| 30 | A journal entry is required to correct a ledger error made in June. $90 was debited to the Wages account instead of the Advertising account. (**Note** No GST correction is required.) |
| 31 | Received a statement of account from creditor, Electro Manufacturing, including a charge of $10 (inc. GST) for a late payment accounting fee on an overdue amount. |

2.68 This question is available on the CD that accompanies the workbook. It is also available on the CD in a MYOB format.

ADDITIONAL
EXERCISES

 **SOLUTIONS**

2.62

**I Jenkins**
**General Journal**

| Date | Particulars | Fol | Debit | Credit |
|---|---|---|---|---|
| 2017 | | | $ | $ |
| 9 Apr | Cash at bank | | 8 500 | |
| | Furniture and fittings | | 5 200 | |
| |     Loan from JK Loans | | | 5 000 |
| |     Capital – I Jenkins | | | 8 700 |
| | *Assets and liabilities introduced by owner to commence business* | | | |

▶▶

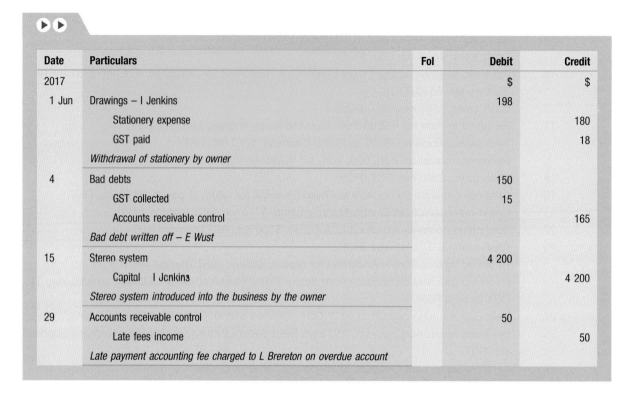

| Date | Particulars | Fol | Debit | Credit |
|------|-------------|-----|-------|--------|
| 2017 | | | $ | $ |
| 1 Jun | Drawings – I Jenkins | | 198 | |
| | Stationery expense | | | 180 |
| | GST paid | | | 18 |
| | *Withdrawal of stationery by owner* | | | |
| 4 | Bad debts | | 150 | |
| | GST collected | | 15 | |
| | Accounts receivable control | | | 165 |
| | *Bad debt written off – E Wust* | | | |
| 15 | Stereo system | | 4 200 | |
| | Capital    I Jenkins | | | 4 200 |
| | *Stereo system introduced into the business by the owner* | | | |
| 29 | Accounts receivable control | | 50 | |
| | Late fees income | | | 50 |
| | *Late payment accounting fee charged to L Brereton on overdue account* | | | |

2.66

**MAC'S CAMERAS**
**General Journal**

| Date | Particulars | Fol | Debit | Credit |
|------|-------------|-----|-------|--------|
| 2019 | | | $ | $ |
| 1 Jan | Accounts receivable control | | 20 | |
| | Late fees income | | | 20 |
| | *Late payment accounting fee charged to D Rongo on overdue account* | | | |
| 10 | Drawings – C Nguyen | | 330 | |
| | Purchases | | | 300 |
| | GST paid | | | 30 |
| | *Withdrawal of stock by owner* | | | |
| 31 | Bad debts | | 620 | |
| | GST collected | | 60 | |
| | Accounts receivable control | | | 680 |
| | *Bad debt written off – D Rongo* | | | |

## MAC'S CAMERAS
### Cash Receipts Journal

| Date | Particulars | Fol | Ref | Discount expense | | | Accounts receivable control | Cash sales | Sundries | | GST collected | Bank |
|---|---|---|---|---|---|---|---|---|---|---|---|---|
| | | | | Accounts receivable control | GST collected | Discount expense | | | Amount | Account | | |
| 2019 | | | | $ | $ | $ | $ | $ | $ | | $ | $ |
| 4 Jan | EFTPOS sales | | POS | | | | | 400 | | | 40 | 440 |
| | Cash sales | | POS | | | | | 1 400 | | | 140 | 1 540 |
| 15 | American Express | | EFT | | | | | | | | | |
| | – Gross | | | | | | 515 | | | | | |
| | – Merchant fee | | | | | | | | (20) | Merchant fees expense | | |
| | – GST paid | | | | | | | | (2) | GST paid | | 493 |
| 16 | EFTPOS sales | | POS | | | | | 700 | | | 70 | 770 |
| | Cash sales | | POS | | | | | 1 700 | | | 170 | 1 870 |
| 26 | Cash sales | | POD | | | | | 1 800 | | | 180 | |
| | P Hune & Co | | A36 | | | | | | 60 | Interest income | | 2 040 |
| | | | | | | | $515 | $6 000 | $38 | | $600 | $7 153 |

### Cash Payments Journal

| Date | Particulars | Fol | Ref | Discount income | | | Accounts payable control | Cash purchases | Wages | Sundries | | GST paid | Bank |
|---|---|---|---|---|---|---|---|---|---|---|---|---|---|
| | | | | Accounts payable control | GST paid | Discount income | | | | Amount | Account | | |
| 2019 | | | | $ | $ | $ | $ | $ | $ | $ | | $ | $ |
| 7 Jan | R Lamm | | 5125 | | | | | 520 | | | | 52 | 572 |
| 12 | Wages | | EFT | | | | | | 460 | | | | 460 |
| 19 | C Nguyen | | 5126 | | | | | | | 100 | Drawings – C Nguyen | | 100 |
| 21 | Fristo Manufacturing | | 5127 | 33 | 3 | 30 | 1 097 | | | | | | 1 097 |
| 28 | Insurers Ltd | | 5128 | | | | 165 | | | | | | 165 |
| | | | | $33 | $3 | $30 | $1 262 | $520 | $460 | $100 | | $52 | $2 394 |

### Sales Journal

| Date | Debtor | Fol | Ref | Sales | Sundries Amount | Account | GST collected | Accounts receivable control |
|------|--------|-----|-----|-------|--------|---------|---------------|-----------------------------|
| 2019 | | | | $ | $ | | $ | $ |
| 6 Jan | A Sainsbury | | M37 | 700 | | | 70 | 770 |
| 14 | M Robins | | M38 | 130 | | | 13 | 143 |
| 22 | M Hunter | | M39 | 190 | 30 | Delivery income | 22 | 242 |
| 26 | American Express | | POS | 300 | | | 30 | 330 |
| | | | | $1 320 | $30 | | $135 | $1 485 |

### Purchases Journal

| Date | Creditor | Fol | Ref | Purchases | Sundries Amount | Account | GST paid | Accounts payable control |
|------|----------|-----|-----|-----------|--------|---------|----------|--------------------------|
| 2019 | | | | $ | $ | | $ | $ |
| 1 Jan | Photographics Ltd | | 97 | 370 | | | 37 | 407 |
| 28 | G Mannering | | 344 | 130 | | | 13 | 143 |
| | | | | $500 | | | $50 | $550 |

### Sales Returns and Allowances Journal

| Date | Debtor | Fol | Ref | Sales returns and allowances | Sundries Amount | Account | GST collected | Accounts receivable control |
|------|--------|-----|-----|------------------------------|--------|---------|---------------|-----------------------------|
| 2019 | | | | $ | $ | | $ | $ |
| 17 Jan | M Robins | | MC83 | 60 | | | 6 | 66 |
| | | | | $60 | | | $6 | $66 |

| | | | | Purchases returns and allowances | Sundries | | GST paid | Accounts payable control |
|---|---|---|---|---|---|---|---|---|
| Date | Creditor | Fol | Adj | | Amount | Account | | |
| 2019 | | | | $ | $ | | $ | $ |
| 2 Jan | Fristo Manufacturing | | C13F | 100 | | | 10 | 110 |
| 4 | Photographics Ltd | | C740 | 60 | | | 6 | 66 |
| | | | | $160 | | | $16 | $176 |

Purchases Returns and Allowances Journal

# Journals for a service business

This chapter has examined the use of journals by a sole-trader business engaged in the buying and selling of trading stock. The use of journals by a sole trader engaged in a service business will now be illustrated.

Unlike the retail and wholesale business, service businesses do not have standard headings for their journals, and the number of journals used may vary considerably between businesses. For example, the journal headings used by a rubbish removalist would be inappropriate for a sole trader operating a crèche. Many service businesses also trade on a cash basis only, thus reducing the number of journals required. Therefore, before journals can be prepared for a service business, it is necessary to decide upon:

- the journals that are required
- the rulings and headings that are appropriate for each particular journal selected.

## Types of journals

In this section, the use of the following journals for a service business will be demonstrated (see Figure 2.11).

### Figure 2.11    Journals for a service business

| Journal | Function |
|---|---|
| General Journal | Records all transactions that cannot be entered in any of the journals below; for example, entries recording the commencement of a business, additional capital (except for cash) contributed by the owner, allowances given to debtors, allowances received from creditors for supplies or materials, drawings of supplies or materials by the owner for personal use, bad debts and correction of errors. |
| Cash Receipts Journal | Records all amounts received. |
| Cash Payments Journal | Records all payments. |
| Sales and Services Journal | Records all sales and services provided on credit. |
| Purchases and Supplies Journal | Records all credit purchases of supplies or services. |

Note the following important points:

1  A service business does not normally have an equivalent to the Sales Returns and Allowances Journal as used by a sole trader buying and selling stock. Thus, any allowances given to debtors would be recorded in the General Journal. If allowances to debtors were frequent transactions in a service business, a separate Allowances Journal should be used.

2  If a service business purchases supplies or materials on credit and later receives an allowance from the supplier, this allowance would normally be recorded in the General Journal. It is not necessary to create a separate Allowances Received journal as such transactions are not likely to occur frequently.

3  If a business provided its services on a cash basis only, a Sales and Services Journal would not be required.

4  In many cases, service businesses pay cash for any supplies or materials purchased, eliminating the need for a Purchases and Supplies Journal.

# Journal design – format and headings for each journal selected

This section will be illustrated by using an example.

## Example

The following transactions relate to the service business of Theresa Green, gardener and odd-job person, for the month of May 2019. You are required to:

·  prepare suitable journals with appropriate format and headings for her business

·  enter her transactions for May in the journals and total the journals (where necessary) at the end of the month.

*Transactions for May 2019*

1 May  Owner deposited $5000 into a bank account for the business (EFT).

2  Owner contributed her personal motor vehicle (valued at $6000) into the business.

3  Purchased two lawnmowers from Lawn Pro for $880 inc. GST (cheque 500).

  Purchased a trailer on credit from Excel Trailers, $902 inc. GST (invoice 213).

4  Purchased tools from Tool Co, $154 inc. GST (cheque 501).

  Purchased petrol and oil supplies from the Good Oil Co, $110 inc. GST, on business Mastercard (invoice 964).

  Paid Ace News for advertising, $55 inc. GST (cheque 502).

6  Received $220 (inc. GST) from T Perry for cutting lawns (receipt 001).

  Paid casual wages, $50 (EFT).

8  Received invoice from Moto Reg for registration and insurance on motor vehicle, $440 inc. GST (invoice 7865).

10  Lawnmowing services, $88 inc. GST, provided on credit to J Cook (invoice 101).

  Tip fees to Environmental Services, $11 inc. GST paid by owner from personal funds.

11 Received $66 inc. GST from T Railer for carting rubbish (receipt 002).

Owner used petrol worth $22 (inc. GST) for personal use (memo 1).

12 Received $220 inc. GST from J Brumby for cutting lawns (EFT).

Paid casual wages, $60 (EFT).

13 Tip fees to Environmental Services, $11 inc. GST (cheque 503).

Paid Ace News for advertising, $55 inc. GST (EFT).

14 Paid M Ellis for motor vehicle repairs, $77 inc. GST (cheque 504).

Paid Lawn Pro to replace blades on mowers, $33 inc. GST (cheque 505).

15 Mowed lawns for A Phillip $33 (inc. GST) on account (invoice 102).

16 A Phillip allowed reduction of $11 (inc. GST) in his account for forgetting to mow part of his lawns (adjustment note 001).

20 Received $66 inc. GST from J Lenders for lawnmowing (receipt 003).

21 Received $69 from debtor J Cook, allowing him discount of $11 (inc. GST) for prompt payment (receipt 004).

Repaired a set of garden gates for A Bennett and received $44 inc. GST (receipt 005).

Mowed lawns for W Bass $44 (inc. GST) on account (invoice 103).

22 Purchased petrol and oil supplies $110 (inc. GST) on business Visa card from Acme Oil Co (invoice 46).

23 Returned two cans of oil to Acme Oil Co purchased for $22 inc. GST (adjustment note 149).

Paid creditor Good Oil Co, $110 (cheque 506).

Paid Ace News for advertising, $55 inc. GST (cheque 507).

Debtor W Bass paid his account, taking discount of $11 (inc. GST) for prompt payment (EFT).

28 Paid casual wages, $20 (EFT).

30 Paid tip fees to Environmental Services $11 inc. GST (cheque 508).

Repaired a garage door for T Caruso on account, $154 inc. GST (invoice 104). Caruso paid by American Express credit card.

31 Sold second-hand mower on credit to G Piercy $110 inc. GST (invoice 105).

## Solution

The appropriate journals for Theresa Green after the transactions for May have been entered:

**Theresa Green**
**General Journal**

| Date | Particulars | Fol | Debit | Credit |
|---|---|---|---|---|
| 2019 | | | $ | $ |
| 2 May | Motor vehicle | | 6 000 | |
| |    Capital – T Green | | | 6 000 |
| | *Motor vehicle contributed by owner* | | | |

| Date | Particulars | Fol | Debit | Credit |
|------|-------------|-----|-------|--------|
| 2019 | | | $ | $ |
| 10 | Tip fees expense | | 10 | |
| | GST paid | | 1 | |
| |     Capital – T Green | | | 11 |
| | *Tip fees paid by owner* | | | |
| 11 | Drawings – T Green | | 22 | |
| |     Purchases – petrol and oil | | | 20 |
| |     GST paid | | | 2 |
| | *Withdrawal of petrol by owner for personal use (memo 1)* | | | |
| 16 | Service fees – lawnmowing | | 10 | |
| | GST collected | | 1 | |
| |     Accounts receivable control | | | 11 |
| | *Allowance to A Phillip (adjustment note 001)* | | | |
| 23 | Accounts payable control | | 22 | |
| |     Purchases – petrol and oil | | | 20 |
| |     GST paid | | | 2 |
| | *Return of oil to Acme Oil Co (adjustment note 149)* | | | |

## Cash Receipts Journal

| Date | Particulars | Fol | Ref | Discount expense – Accounts receivable control | Discount expense – GST collected | Discount expense – Discount expense | Accounts receivable control | Cash services – Lawns | Cash services – Odd jobs | Sundries – Amount | Sundries – Account | GST collected | Bank |
|------|-------------|-----|-----|------|------|------|------|------|------|------|------|------|------|
| 2019 | | | | $ | $ | $ | $ | $ | $ | $ | | $ | $ |
| 1 May | T Green | | EFT | | | | | | | 5 000 | Capital – T Green | | 5 000 |
| 6 | T Perry | | 001 | | | | | 200 | | | | 20 | 220 |
| 11 | T Railer | | 002 | | | | | | 60 | | | 6 | 66 |
| 12 | J Brumby | | EFT | | | | | 200 | | | | 20 | 220 |
| 20 | J Lenders | | 003 | | | | | 60 | | | | 6 | 66 |
| 21 | J Cook | | 004 | 11 | 1 | 10 | 69 | | | | | | |
| | A Bennett | | 005 | | | | | | 40 | | | 4 | 113 |
| 23 | W Bass | | EFT | 11 | 1 | 10 | 33 | | | | | | 33 |
| | | | | $22 | $2 | $20 | $102 | $460 | $100 | $5 000 | | $56 | $5 718 |

## Cash Payments Journal

| Date | Particulars | Fol | Ref | Discount income Accounts payable control $ | GST paid $ | Discount income $ | Accounts payable control $ | Advertising $ | Wages $ | Tip fees expense $ | Sundries Amount $ | Account | GST paid $ | Bank $ |
|---|---|---|---|---|---|---|---|---|---|---|---|---|---|---|
| 2019 | | | | | | | | | | | | | | |
| 3 May | Lawn Pro | | 500 | | | | | | | | 800 | Lawn mowers | 80 | 880 |
| 4 | Tool Co | | 501 | | | | | | | | 140 | Tools | 14 | 154 |
| | Ace News | | 502 | | | | | 50 | | | | | 5 | 55 |
| 6 | Wages | | EFT | | | | | | 50 | | | | | 50 |
| 12 | Wages | | EFT | | | | | | 60 | | | | | 60 |
| 13 | Environmental Services | | 503 | | | | | | | 10 | | | 1 | 11 |
| | Ace News | | EFT | | | | | 50 | | | | | 5 | 55 |
| 14 | M Ellis | | 504 | | | | | | | | 70 | Motor vehicle repairs | 7 | 77 |
| | Lawn Pro | | 505 | | | | | | | | 30 | Mower repairs | 3 | 33 |
| 23 | Good Oil Co | | 506 | | | | 110 | | | | | | | 110 |
| | Ace News | | 507 | | | | | 50 | | | | | 5 | 55 |
| 28 | Wages | | EFT | | | | | | 20 | | | | | 20 |
| 30 | Environmental Services | | 508 | | | | | | | 10 | | | 1 | 11 |
| | | | | | | | $110 | $150 | $130 | $20 | $1 040 | | $121 | $1 571 |

## Sales and Services Journal

| Date | Debtor | Fol | Ref | Services Lawns $ | Odd jobs $ | Sundries Amount $ | Account | GST collected $ | Accounts receivable control $ |
|---|---|---|---|---|---|---|---|---|---|
| 2019 | | | | | | | | | |
| 10 May | J Cook | | 101 | 80 | | | | 8 | 88 |
| 15 | A Phillip | | 102 | 30 | | | | 3 | 33 |
| 21 | W Bass | | 103 | 40 | | | | 4 | 44 |
| 30 | AMEX | | 104 | | 140 | | | 14 | 154 |
| 31 | G Piercy | | 105 | | | 100 | Sale of asset | 10 | 110 |
| | | | | $150 | $140 | $100 | | $39 | $429 |

| | | | | Purchases and Supplies Journal | | | | | |
|---|---|---|---|---|---|---|---|---|---|
| | | | | | | Sundries | | | Accounts payable control |
| Date | Creditor | Fol | Ref | Petrol and oil | Amount | Account | GST paid | |
| 2019 | | | | $ | $ | | $ | $ |
| 3 May | Excel Trailers | | 213 | | 820 | Trailer | 82 | 902 |
| 4 | Mastercard | | 964 | 100 | | | 10 | 110 |
| 8 | Moto Reg | | 7865 | | 400 | Registration and insurance | 40 | 440 |
| 22 | Visa | | 46 | 100 | | | 10 | 110 |
| | | | | $200 | $1 220 | | $142 | $1 562 |

## EXERCISES

2.69 The following transactions relate to the business of I Drill, metal fabricator. You are required to:

a  design appropriate journals for her business

b  enter the transactions for May and total the journals at the end of the month.

*2016*

10 May  Commenced trading activities by depositing $50 000 in a business bank account (EFT).

13      Made lease payment on premises to FDY Finances, $1045 inc. GST (cheque 701).

14      Purchased equipment from B Dazzler, $25 300 inc. GST (cheque 702).

15      Purchased supplies from A B Supplies, $4840 inc. GST (cheque 703).

16      Purchased furniture on credit, $1540 inc. GST, from Mal's Furniture (invoice 8624).

17      Paid wages of assistant, $150 (EFT).

18      Cash services for F Reid, $880 inc. GST (POS).

19      Completed work on account: J Bartley, $66 inc. GST (invoice 1); and W Conn, $440 inc. GST (invoice 2).

20      Cash services for L Callinan, $990 inc. GST (POS).

21      Received invoice from Trade Insurance for insurance, $660 inc. GST (invoice T1741).
        Received $66 from debtor J Bartley (receipt 001).

22      Purchased supplies, $220 inc. GST using business AMEX card (invoice 387).
        Cash services for J Esnouf, $880 inc. GST (POS).
        Paid AG Industries for repairs to drill, $66 inc. GST (cheque 704).

25      Paid wages of assistant, $150 (EFT).

26      The owner gave supplies worth $110 inc. GST to a friend, M Allen (memo 1).
        Completed work on account: C Stubbs, $77 inc. GST (invoice 3); and on Diners Club card $55 inc. GST (POS).

27  Received part payment of account from debtor W Conn, $100 (EFT).

   Cash services for P Edwards, $660 inc. GST (POS).

31  Paid wages of assistant, $150 (EFT).

   Paid AG Industries for repairs to drill, $55 inc. GST (cheque 705).

2.70 This question is available on the CD that accompanies this text.

2.71* The following transactions relate to the nappy-cleaning business of S Craper. You are required to:

a design appropriate journals for his business

b enter the transactions for November and total the journals at the end of November.

*2017*

1 Nov Commenced trading activities by depositing $10 000 in a business bank account styled 'Happy Nappies' (EFT).

3  Paid A Robbins for rent of premises, $220 inc. GST (EFT).

6  Purchased four heavy-duty washing machines on credit from Dandy Machines, $3520 inc. GST (invoice 8946).

   Received invoice from Chem Co for purchase of chemicals, $2200 inc. GST (invoice CC1017).

7  Paid creditor AB Insurance, $440 (cheque 801).

9  S Craper contributed his personal delivery van into the business valued at $8000 (memo 1).

11  Purchased chemicals on credit from AA Chemicals, $110 inc. GST (invoice 428).

13  Paid Bell Agencies for advertising, $99 inc. GST (cheque 802).

   Washed nappies on credit for H Cha, $88 inc. GST (invoice 001).

14  Washed nappies for G Lewis and received $55 inc. GST (receipt 001).

15  Paid wages, $90 (EFT).

   Paid Max Motors for motor vehicle repairs, $385 inc. GST (cheque 803).

17  Washed nappies on credit for: L Rose, $66 inc. GST (invoice 002); F Ansen, $99 inc. GST (invoice 003).

21  Paid Andy's News for stationery, $88 inc. GST (cheque 804).

   S Craper gave chemicals costing $110 (inc. GST) to a friend (memo 2).

   S Craper paid business advertising, $99 inc. GST using his personal credit card (invoice 844).

   Washed nappies on credit for the Royal Baby Hospital, $4620 inc. GST. The amount charged included $220 inc. GST for delivery (invoice 004).

23  Paid $110 to creditor AA Chemicals (cheque 805).

   Paid wages, $90 (EFT).

   Washed nappies for T Fraser and received $88 inc. GST (EFT).

26  Washed nappies for J Bloom and received $99 inc. GST (receipt 002).

   H Cha paid her account (receipt 003).

29  Gave an allowance of $22 (inc. GST) to L Rose for delivering stained nappies (adjustment note 001).

   Purchased chemicals on credit from Nifty Chemicals, $660 inc. GST (invoice 80).

30  Washed nappies for G Georgiou, $55 inc. GST. Georgiou used her Diners Club credit card to pay for this service (invoice 005).

   Received invoice from Fix It Co for repairs to washing machine, $440 inc. GST (invoice F094).

   Returned chemicals $110 (inc. GST) to Nifty Chemicals and received an allowance (adjustment note 1946).

**SOLUTION**

2.71    a

**HAPPY NAPPIES**
**General Journal**

| Date | Particulars | Fol | Debit | Credit |
|------|-------------|-----|-------|--------|
| 2017 | | | $ | $ |
| 9 Nov | Delivery vehicle | | 8 000 | |
| |     Capital – S Craper | | | 8 000 |
| | *Delivery vehicle contributed by owner* | | | |
| 21 | Drawings – S Craper | | 110 | |
| |     Purchases – chemicals | | | 100 |
| |     GST paid | | | 10 |
| | *Gave chemicals to a friend* | | | |
| | Advertising | | 90 | |
| | GST paid | | 9 | |
| |     Capital – S Craper | | | 99 |
| | *Payment of business expense by owner* | | | |
| 29 | Services | | 20 | |
| | GST collected | | 2 | |
| |     Accounts receivable control | | | 22 |
| | *Allowance to L Rose for stained nappies (adjustment note 001)* | | | |
| 30 | Accounts payable control | | 110 | |
| |     Purchases – chemicals | | | 100 |
| |     GST paid | | | 10 |
| | *Return of chemicals to Nifty Chemicals (adjustment note 1946)* | | | |

b

**Sales and Services Journal**

| Date | Debtor | Fol | Ref | Nappy cleaning income | Sundries Amount | Sundries Account | GST collected | Accounts receivable control |
|------|--------|-----|-----|------------------------|-----------------|------------------|---------------|------------------------------|
| 2017 | | | | $ | $ | | $ | $ |
| 13 Nov | H Cha | | 001 | 80 | | | 8 | 88 |
| 17 | L Rose | | 002 | 60 | | | 6 | 66 |
| | F Ansen | | 003 | 90 | | | 9 | 99 |
| 21 | Royal Baby Hospital | | 004 | 4 000 | 200 | Delivery income | 420 | 4 620 |
| 30 | Diners Club | | 005 | 50 | | | 5 | 55 |
| | | | | $4 280 | $200 | | $448 | $4 928 |

## Purchases and Supplies Journal

| Date | Creditor | Fol | Ref | Purchases – chemicals | Sundries Amount | Sundries Account | GST paid | Accounts payable control |
|------|----------|-----|-----|----------------------|-----------------|------------------|----------|--------------------------|
| 2017 | | | | $ | $ | | $ | $ |
| 6 Nov | Dandy Machines | | 8946 | | 3 200 | Washing machines | 320 | 3 520 |
| | Chem Co | | CC1017 | 2 000 | | | 200 | 2 200 |
| 11 | AA Chemicals | | 428 | 100 | | | 10 | 110 |
| 29 | Nifty Chemicals | | 80 | 600 | | | 60 | 660 |
| 30 | Fix It Co | | F094 | | 400 | Washing machine repairs | 40 | 440 |
| | | | | $2 700 | $3 600 | | $630 | $6 930 |

## Cash Receipts Journal

| Date | Particulars | Fol | Ref | Discount expense — Accounts receivable control | Discount expense — GST collected | Discount expense — Discount expense | Accounts receivable control | Nappy cleaning income | Sundries Amount | Sundries Account | GST collected | Bank |
|------|-------------|-----|-----|------------|------------|------------|------------|------------|--------|---------|------------|------|
| 2017 | | | | $ | $ | $ | $ | $ | $ | | $ | $ |
| 1 Nov | S Craper | | EFT | | | | | | 10 000 | Capital – S Craper | | 10 000 |
| 14 | G Lewis | | 001 | | | | | 50 | | | 5 | 55 |
| 23 | T Fraser | | EFT | | | | | 80 | | | 8 | 88 |
| 26 | J Bloom | | 002 | | | | | 90 | | | 9 | |
| | H Cha | | 003 | | | | 88 | | | | | 187 |
| | | | | | | | $88 | $220 | $10 000 | | $22 | $10 330 |

**Cash Payments Journal**

| Date | Particulars | Fol | Ref | Discount income | | | Accounts payable control | Purchases chemicals | Wages | Sundries | | GST paid | Bank |
| | | | | Accounts payable control | GST paid | Discount income | | | | Amount | Account | | |
|------|-------------|-----|-----|-----|-----|-----|-----|-----|-----|-----|-----|-----|-----|
| 2017 | | | | $ | $ | $ | $ | $ | $ | $ | | $ | $ |
| 3 Nov | A Robbins | | EFT | | | | | | | 200 | Rent expense | 20 | 220 |
| 7 | AB Insurance | | 801 | | | | 440 | | | | | | 440 |
| 13 | Bell Agencies | | 802 | | | | | | | 90 | Advertising | 9 | 99 |
| 15 | Wages | | EFT | | | | | | 90 | | | | 90 |
| | Max Motors | | 803 | | | | | | | 350 | Motor vehicle repairs | 35 | 385 |
| 21 | Andy's News | | 804 | | | | | | | 80 | Stationery | 8 | 88 |
| 23 | AA Chemicals | | 805 | | | | 110 | | | | | | 110 |
| | Wages | | EFT | | | | | | 90 | | | | 90 |
| | | | | | | | $550 | $180 | $720 | | | $72 | $1 522 |

# Summary

What have you covered in this chapter?

◆ The basic features of the GST

◆ Identification and completion of source documents
- delivery docket
- receipt
- tax invoice
- adjustment note
- cheque
- point-of-sale daily summary
- purchase order
- bank deposit slip
- remittance advice
- statement of account

◆ Entering receipts and cash sales details into a columnar Cash Receipts Journal for a wholesale/retail business

◆ Entering payment details into a columnar Cash Payments Journal for a wholesale/retail business

◆ Entering tax invoices and credit card sales into a columnar Sales Journal for a wholesale/retail business

◆ Entering adjustment notes into a columnar Sales Returns and Allowances Journal for a wholesale/retail business

◆ Entering tax invoices into a columnar Purchases Journal for a wholesale/retail business

◆ Entering adjustment notes into a columnar Purchases Returns and Allowances Journal for a wholesale/retail business

◆ Preparation of General Journal entries
- correction of posting errors
- opening entries
- bad debts written off
- late payment accounting fees expense
- late payment accounting fees receivable
- withdrawal of stock by proprietor

◆ Entering source documents into journals for a service business

◆ Recording EFT, EFTPOS and credit card transactions

# 3

# LEDGER ACCOUNTS AND THE TRIAL BALANCE

## Learning objectives

Upon satisfactory completion of this chapter you should be able to:
- post entries from the following journals to the General Ledger for a wholesale/retail business, maintaining the accounting equation:
  - Cash Receipts Journal
  - Cash Payments Journal
  - Sales Journal
  - Sales Returns and Allowances Journal
  - Purchases Journal
  - Purchases Returns and Allowances Journal
  - General Journal
- extract an accurate trial balance of the General Ledger
- post entries from the journals of a service business to the General Ledger.

Chapter 2 examined the nature and purpose of business documents (source documents) and the preparation of journals of various types. The purpose of journals is simply to summarise transactions (as recorded on business documents) before they are entered into the ledger. This removes excessive and superfluous detail from the ledger, as transaction information can be entered into the ledger in summary form rather than on an individual transaction basis. Figure 3.1 illustrates this recording sequence.

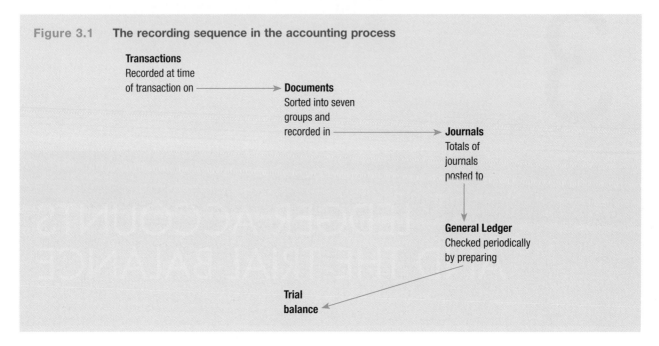

**Figure 3.1     The recording sequence in the accounting process**

**Transactions**
Recorded at time of transaction on ⟶ **Documents**
Sorted into seven groups and recorded in ⟶ **Journals**
Totals of journals posted to

**General Ledger**
Checked periodically by preparing

**Trial balance**

We will now examine the procedure involved in posting the totals of the various journals to the General Ledger. In accounting terminology, the phrase 'posting journals to the ledger' simply means entering the totals of the journals into the appropriate ledger accounts.

The posting of journal totals to the ledger is a 'mechanical' process. It is quite simple for those who have a good, working knowledge of the rules of *debit* and *credit*, which were introduced in Chapter 1 of this text.

| Rules of debit and credit | | |
|---|---|---|
| **Type of account** | **Entry required to increase the account** | **Entry required to decrease the account** |
| Asset<br>Expense | Debit | Credit |
| Liability<br>Owner's equity<br>Income | Credit | Debit |

This chapter will firstly examine the posting procedure for each journal separately. This will be illustrated with a comprehensive example covering the procedures for posting all journals together at the end of a one-week period. (**Note** For illustration purposes, it will be assumed that businesses post the totals of their journals to the General Ledger at the end of each week; this is normally done at the end of the month.)

# Posting procedure – wholesale/ retail businesses

To illustrate the procedure for posting for a wholesale/retail business, the journals of Cleo's Wine Shop (owner, Cleo Garfoot) will be used. Cleo's chart of accounts is shown below.

**CLEO'S WINE SHOP**
**Chart of accounts**

| Assets | | Income | |
|---|---|---|---|
| A1 | Cash at bank | I1 | Sales |
| A2 | Accounts receivable control | I2 | Sales returns and allowances |
| A3 | Loan to Britt Smith | I3 | Discount income |
| A4 | GST paid | I4 | Interest income |
| A5 | Motor vehicles | I5 | Commission income |
| A6 | Furniture and fittings | I6 | Sale of non-current assets* |
| A7 | Office equipment | I7 | Miscellaneous income |
| A8 | Land and buildings | | |
| | | **Expenses** | |
| **Liabilities** | | E1 | Purchases |
| L1 | Accounts payable control | E2 | Purchases returns and allowances |
| L2 | GST collected | E3 | Discount expense |
| L3 | Mortgage loan on buildings | E4 | Wages |
| | | E5 | Advertising |
| **Owner's equity** | | E6 | Electricity |
| OE1 | Capital – C Garfoot | E7 | Cleaning |
| OE2 | Drawings – C Garfoot | E8 | Repairs |
| | | E9 | Delivery expenses |
| | | E10 | Consultant's fees |

\* **Note** The chart of accounts above includes an account called 'Sale of non-current assets'. From time to time, businesses will either sell immediately or hold for future sale certain non-current assets (such as items of property, plant and equipment) that are no longer required for active use in the business. If these assets are sold for more than book value, the business will make a profit, or as more commonly termed, a *gain on sale of non-current assets*. Conversely, the business will make a loss on the sale if the asset is sold for less than book value. In order to calculate the gain or loss on items of non-current assets sold during the year, a temporary account called 'Sale of non-current assets' is used. Normally, the calculation requires recording the proceeds from the sale of the asset in the *Sale of non-current assets* account and matching these proceeds with the book value of the asset. We have included this account in the chart of accounts as a temporary account (under the income heading) for illustrative purposes; however we note that a more detailed discussion on the calculation of gain or loss from the sale of non-current assets is beyond the scope of this book.

# General Journal

Before considering the posting of General Journal entries for Cleo's Wine Shop, it is important to consider the processing cycle as it relates to the General Journal (see Figure 3.2).

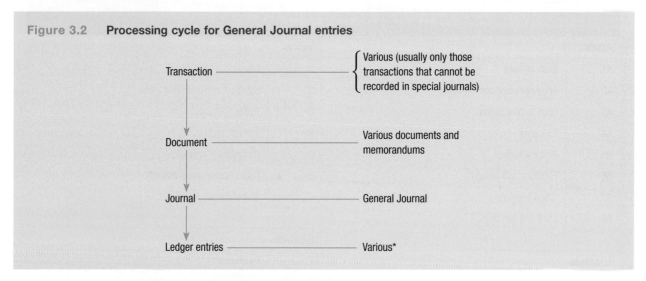

**Figure 3.2    Processing cycle for General Journal entries**

Transaction —— { Various (usually only those transactions that cannot be recorded in special journals)

Document —— Various documents and memorandums

Journal —— General Journal

Ledger entries —— Various*

* As the General Journal is used for recording a variety of types of transactions, journal totals are not used for posting and various accounts may be debited or credited.

Consider the following General Journal entry for Cleo's Wine Shop. It records the assets and liabilities introduced by Cleo at the commencement of business, which was 1 March 2017.

General Journal

| Date | Particulars | Fol | Debit | Credit |
|---|---|---|---|---|
| 2017 | | | $ | $ |
| 1 Mar | Cash at bank | A1 | Ⓐ 3 000 | |
| | Loan to Britt Smith | A3 | Ⓑ 5 000 | |
| | Land and buildings | A8 | Ⓒ 61 000 | |
| | Motor vehicle | A5 | Ⓓ 9 000 | |
| | Furniture and fittings | A6 | Ⓔ 12 000 | |
| | Mortgage loan on buildings | L3 | | Ⓕ 40 000 |
| | Capital – C Garfoot | OE1 | | Ⓖ 50 000 |
| | *Assets and liabilities introduced by proprietor to commence business* | | | |

**Journal explanations**

1 The letters Ⓐ to Ⓖ have been included to illustrate the posting of amounts to individual accounts as shown in the following General Ledger.

2 When posting the General Journal to the ledger, the number of each account (as per the chart of accounts) is recorded in the Folio column as a cross-reference to the ledger.

The General Journal is arguably the easiest of all the journals to post to the ledger, as it shows which specific accounts are to receive a debit entry and which are to receive a credit entry, and also indicates the amount of each entry. Thus to post the journal to the ledger, simply follow the instructions given in the journal. For example, the first line of the journal entry shows the Cash at Bank account in the Particulars column with a corresponding amount of $3000 in the debit column. In a practical sense this is giving the bookkeeper instructions to debit the Cash at Bank account (account no. A1) by $3000. Hence, the journal entry would be posted to the ledger as follows:

| | CLEO'S WINE SHOP | | | | |
|---|---|---|---|---|---|
| | **General Ledger** | | | | |
| Date | Particulars | Fol | Debit | Credit | Balance |
| | **A1 – Cash at Bank Account** | | | | |
| 2017 | | | $ | $ | $ |
| 1 Mar | Capital – C Garfoot | GJ | Ⓐ 3 000 | | 3 000 Dr |
| | **A3 – Loan to Britt Smith Account** | | | | |
| 2017 | | | | | |
| 1 Mar | Capital – C Garfoot | GJ | Ⓑ 5 000 | | 5 000 Dr |
| | **A8 – Land and Buildings Account** | | | | |
| 2017 | | | | | |
| 1 Mar | Capital – C Garfoot | GJ | Ⓒ 61 000 | | 61 000 Dr |

| General Ledger | | | | | |
|---|---|---|---|---|---|
| Date | Particulars | Fol | Debit | Credit | Balance |
| **A5 – Motor Vehicle Account** | | | | | |
| 2017 | | | $ | $ | $ |
| 1 Mar | Capital – C Garfoot | GJ | (D) 9 000 | | 9 000 Dr |
| **A6 – Furniture and Fittings Account** | | | | | |
| 2017 | | | | | |
| 1 Mar | Capital – C Garfoot | GJ | (E) 12 000 | | 12 000 Dr |
| **L3 – Mortgage Loan on Buildings Account** | | | | | |
| 2017 | | | | | |
| 1 Mar | Capital – C Garfoot | GJ | | (F) 40 000 | 40 000 Cr |
| **OE1 – Capital – C Garfoot Account** | | | | | |
| 2017 | | | | | |
| 1 Mar | Sundries | GJ | | (G) 50 000 | 50 000 Cr |

**Ledger explanations**

1   The letters (A) to (G) indicate the source (in the journal) and the destination (in the ledger) of each entry.

2   Specific dates must be used for all postings.

3   The Particulars column records the name of the opposite account/s involved in the transaction (the 'cross-reference'). In the first six accounts, *Capital* is the cross-reference, because these items were all introduced by Cleo as part of her capital at the commencement of business. In the Capital account, the cross-reference *Sundries* refers to the various (sundry) assets and liabilities that comprise Cleo's capital.

4   The Folio column of the ledger account contains a cross-reference (GJ) to the journal from which each entry has been posted.

The following General Journal entry for Cleo's Wine Shop shows the recording of the contribution of an office copier to the business by the owner.

| General Journal | | | | |
|---|---|---|---|---|
| Date | Particulars | Fol | Debit | Credit |
| 2017 | | | $ | $ |
| 5 Jun | Office equipment | A7 | (A) 1 200 | |
| | Capital – C Garfoot | OE1 | | (B) 1 200 |
| | *Contribution of office copier by owner* | | | |

This entry would be posted to the ledger as follows:

| Date | Particulars | Fol | Debit | Credit | Balance |
|------|-------------|-----|-------|--------|---------|
| | **General Ledger** | | | | |
| | **A7 – Office Equipment Account** | | | | |
| 2017 | | | $ | $ | $ |
| 5 Jun | Capital – C Garfoot | GJ | (A) 1 200 | | 1 200 Dr |
| | **OE1 – Capital – C Garfoot** | | | | |
| 2017 | | | | | |
| 1 Jun | Balance | GJ | | | 50 000 Cr |
| 5 | Office equipment | GJ | | (B) 1 200 | 51 200 Cr |

**Ledger explanations**

1 The letters (A) and (B) indicate the source (in the journal) and the destination (in the ledger) of each entry.

2 The entry in the Office Equipment account is cross-referenced to the Capital – C Garfoot account, as the latter is the account to which the opposite side of the entry is posted. Similarly, the entry in Capital – C Garfoot account is cross-referenced to the Office Equipment account.

# Cash Receipts Journal

As previously mentioned in Chapter 2, the Cash Receipts Journal records all cash, cheque, EFT and EFTPOS amounts received. Transactions recorded in the Cash Receipts Journal include cash sales (including EFTPOS sales), amounts received from debtors, commission received and interest received (see Figure 3.3).

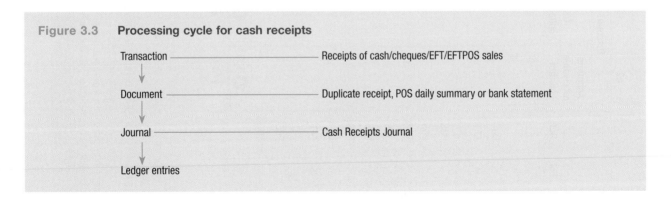

**Figure 3.3    Processing cycle for cash receipts**

Transaction ———————————————— Receipts of cash/cheques/EFT/EFTPOS sales

Document ———————————————— Duplicate receipt, POS daily summary or bank statement

Journal ———————————————— Cash Receipts Journal

Ledger entries

Consider the following Cash Receipts Journal for Cleo's Wine Shop, which records all cash receipt transactions for the first week of June 2017.

**CLEO'S WINE SHOP**
Cash Receipts Journal

| Date | Particulars | Fol | Ref | Discount expense — Accounts receivable control (A2) Cr $ | Discount expense — GST collected (L2) Dr $ | Discount expense (E3) Dr $ | Accounts receivable control (A2) Cr $ | Cash sales (I1) Cr $ | Sundries Amount Cr $ | Sundries Account | GST collected (L2) Cr $ | Bank (A1) Dr $ |
|---|---|---|---|---|---|---|---|---|---|---|---|---|
| **2017** | | | | | | | | | | | | |
| 1 June | Cash sales | | POS | | | | | 340 | | | 34 | 374 |
| | M Wilson | I4 | EFT | | | | | | 50 **(F)** | Interest income | | 50 |
| 2 | Sales – EFTPOS | | POS | | | | | 100 | | | 10 | 110 |
| | Cash sales | | POS | | | | | 180 | | | 18 | 198 |
| 3 | I Foster | | R533 | 11 | 1 | 10 | 689 | | | | | 887 |
| | Sales – EFTPOS | | POS | | | | | 110 | | | 11 | 121 |
| 4 | Cash sales | | POS | | | | | 290 | | | 29 | 319 |
| | E Glover | | R534 | 22 | 2 | 20 | 393 | | | | | 778 |
| 5 | Wineries Ltd – | I5 | EFT | | | | | | 100 **(G)** | Commission income | 10 | 110 |
| | Sales – EFTPOS | | POS | | | | | 190 | | | 19 | 209 |
| | Cash sales | | POS | | | | | 170 | | | 17 | 187 |
| | | | | **(A)** $33 | **(B)** $3 | **(C)** $30 | **(D)** $1 082 | **(E)** $1 730 | $150 | | **(H)** $183 | **(I)** $3 145 |
| | | | | ↑ Asset | ↑ Liab | ↑ Exp | ↑ Asset | ↑ Inc | ↑ Inc | | ↑ Liab | ↑ Asset |

## Journal explanations

1 When posting special journals to the ledger, it is important to remember that the heading of each column usually names the ledger account to be posted, and that it is the total of each column that is posted. An exception to this rule is in the case of the Sundries column of the special journals. As the Sundries column contains receipts of various types, each individual item in this column must be posted to the appropriate account.

2 The ledger account number applicable to each column should be written above each column heading. In the case of the Sundries column, which can contain items relating to various accounts, the account numbers are written in the Folio column opposite each entry.

3 Before posting any special journal to the ledger, it is a good idea (for learning purposes) to write the posting rules (Dr/Cr) under each column heading. When trying to determine the posting rules for a particular journal you need to consider the purpose of that particular journal and to refer to the rules of debit and credit covered in Chapter 2 and restated earlier in this chapter. For example, the purpose of the Cash Receipts Journal is to record all monies received; therefore, in the case of the above Cash Receipts Journal, the following debit and credit entries will be made in the ledger:

| Column | Ledger account | Type of account | Increase or decrease | Debit | Credit |
|---|---|---|---|---|---|
| | | | | $ | $ |
| *Discount expense section* | | | | | |
| Accounts receivable control | A2 – Accounts receivable control | Asset | Decrease | | 33 |
| GST collected | L2 – GST collected | Liability | Decrease | 3 | |
| Discount expense | E3 – Discount expense | Expense | Increase | 30 | |
| | | | | 33 | 33 |
| *Other columns* | | | | | |
| Accounts receivable control | A2 – Accounts receivable control | Asset | Decrease | | 1 082 |
| Cash sales | I1 – Sales | Income | Increase | | 1 730 |
| Sundries | I4 – Interest income | Income | Increase | | 50 |
| | and | | | | |
| | I5 – Commission income | Income | Increase | | 100 |
| GST collected | L2 – GST collected | Liability | Increase | | 183 |
| Bank | A1 – Cash at bank | Asset | Increase | 3 145 | |
| | | | | 3 145 | 3 145 |

**Note**

Discount expense section

- The total debits in this section of the journal equal the total credits.
- Discount expense represents prompt payment discount given to debtors and so is debited to the Discount Expense account.
- For GST purposes, discount given to debtors effectively reduces the price of the goods sold, and so results in the reduction of the original GST collected. This represents a reduction in the business's GST liability and consequently a debit entry is made to the GST Collected account.
- The amount owed by the debtor is reduced by the total of the discount amount and the GST adjustment. Thus the total amount is credited to the Accounts Receivable Control account.

Other columns

- The total debits in this section of the journal equal the total credits.
- The total of the Bank column represents the total receipts for the period. Receipts increase the Cash at Bank account balance, so this amount is debited to that account.
- The other columns represent the source of the receipts (Debtors, Cash Sales, Sundries and GST Collected) and so are credited to their respective accounts.

4   When posting journal column totals to the ledger at the end of a week, the date used in the ledger entry will be the last date in that week (or the last date in the month where journals are posted monthly). For transactions posted from the Sundries column, the date used is the actual date of the transaction.

With all of the above points in mind, the following shows the posting of Cleo's Cash Receipts Journal to the General Ledger. (In some accounts, existing balances have been assumed.)

| Date | Particulars | Fol | Debit | Credit | Balance |
|------|-------------|-----|-------|--------|---------|
| | | **General Ledger** | | | |
| | | | | | |
| **A2 – Accounts Receivable Control Account** | | | | | |
| 2017 | | | $ | $ | $ |
| 1 Jun | Balance | | | | 1 515 Dr |
| 5 | Discount expense and GST collected | CRJ | | A 33 | 1 482 Dr |
| | Cash at bank | CRJ | | D 1 082 | 400 Dr |
| **L2 – GST Collected Account** | | | | | |
| 2017 | | | | | |
| 1 Jun | Balance | | | | 600 Cr |
| 5 | Accounts receivable control | CRJ | B 3 | | 597 Cr |
| | Cash at bank | CRJ | | H 183 | 780 Cr |
| **E3 – Discount Expense Account** | | | | | |
| 2017 | | | | | |
| 5 Jun | Accounts receivable control | CRJ | C 30 | | 30 Dr |
| **I1 – Sales Account** | | | | | |
| 2017 | | | | | |
| 1 Jun | Balance | | | | 5 580 Cr |
| 5 | Cash at bank | CRJ | | E 1 730 | 7 310 Cr |
| **I4 – Interest Income Account** | | | | | |
| 2017 | | | | | |
| 1 Jun | Cash at bank | CRJ | | F 50 | 50 Cr |
| **I5 – Commission Income Account** | | | | | |
| 2017 | | | | | |
| 4 Jun | Cash at bank | CRJ | | G 100 | 100 Cr |
| **A1 – Cash at Bank Account** | | | | | |
| 2017 | | | | | |
| 1 Jun | Balance | | | | 6 500 Dr |
| 5 | Sundry receipts | CRJ | I 3 145 | | 9 645 Dr |

▶▶

**Ledger explanations**

1 The letters **A** to **I** indicate the source (in the journal) and the destination (in the ledger) of each entry.

2 The letters **A** to **I** also indicate a suggested sequence of posting the Cash Receipts Journal to the ledger – posting one column at a time, commencing with the first column. This procedure should be followed with all of the special journals, thereby ensuring that no column is missed in the posting process.

3 When posting the Cash Receipts Journal to the ledger, the cross-referencing of account titles is a simple process:

- In relation to the discount, the Discount Expense account and the GST Collected account are cross-referenced to the Accounts Receivable Control account, as this account receives the credit entry corresponding to the debits made in the other two accounts. In the Accounts Receivable Control account, the cross-reference is to both the Discount Expense account and the GST Collected account.

- The remaining accounts posted from the journal contain the cross-reference *cash at bank*, as these are the credits corresponding to the debit in the Cash at Bank account. In the Cash at Bank account, the debit entry is cross-referenced *sundry receipts*, meaning *various accounts* (an alternative cross-reference for this entry is 'receipts').

4 The Folio column of the ledger contains a cross-reference (CRJ) to the journal from which each entry has been posted.

5 In the above example and those that follow in this chapter, ledger accounts are arranged in order of posting, and not in chart of accounts order. Although this is not strictly correct procedure, it is a much simpler method to use when first learning to post journals to the ledger. In a business situation, accounts are often kept in loose-leaf form, so it is easy to keep them in chart of accounts sequence.

# Cash Payments Journal

As previously mentioned in Chapter 2, the Cash Payments Journal records all payments. Some examples of transactions recorded in the Cash Payments Journal include payment of various expenses (wages, rates, repairs), cash purchases and payment of creditors' accounts (see Figure 3.4).

**Figure 3.4    Processing cycle for cash payments**

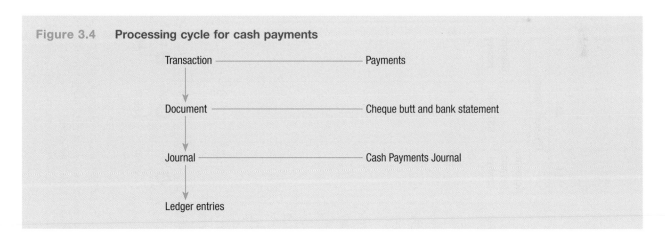

The following Cash Payments Journal for Cleo's Wine Shop shows the recording of all cash (cheque) payment transactions for the first week of June 2017.

**CLEO'S WINE SHOP**
**Cash Payments Journal**

| | | | | Discount income | | | | | | Sundries | | | |
| | | | | L1 | A4 | I3 | L1 | E1 | E4 | | | L2 | A1 |
| Date | Particulars | Fol | Ref | Accounts payable control Dr $ | GST paid Cr $ | Discount income Cr $ | Accounts payable control Dr $ | Cash purchases Dr $ | Wages Dr $ | Amount Dr $ | Account | GST paid Dr $ | Bank Cr $ |
|---|---|---|---|---|---|---|---|---|---|---|---|---|---|
| 2017 | | | | | | | | | | | | | |
| 1 Jun | Hocks Ltd | | 705 | | | | | | | | | | 506 |
| | Wages | | EFT | | | | | | 650 | | | | 650 |
| 2 | State Power Supply | | EFT | | | | 176 | | | | | | 176 |
| | Jasonwine Ltd | | 706 | | | | | 350 | | | | 35 | 385 |
| 3 | Golfer's Digest | | 707 | | | | 209 | | | | | | 209 |
| | Acme Co | E7 | 708 | | | | | | | (G) 90 | Cleaning | 9 | 165 |
| | | E8 | | | | | | | | (H) 60 | Repairs | 6 | |
| | Leiseur Winery | E9 | 709 | | | | | 470 | | | | 47 | 517 |
| 4 | AC Taxi Trucks | | 710 | | | | | | | (I) 70 | Delivery expenses | 7 | 77 |
| | R Dixon | | 711 | 33 | 3 | 30 | 467 | | | | | | 467 |
| | Hocks Ltd | | 712 | | | | | 330 | | | | 33 | 363 |
| 5 | B Muller | | EFT | 11 | 1 | 10 | 209 | | | | | | 209 |
| | | | | (A) $44 | (B) $4 | (C) $40 | (D) $1 061 | (E) $1 610 | (F) $650 | $220 | | (J) $183 | (K) $3 724 |
| | | | | ↑Liab | ↑Asset | ↑Inc | ↑Liab | ↑Exp | ↑Exp | ↑Exp | | ↑Liab | ↑Asset |

Note: Hocks Ltd (705) — Cash purchases 460, GST paid 46, Bank 506.

**Journal explanations**

1 Most of the points made in relation to the Cash Receipts Journal apply equally to the Cash Payments Journal and to all of the other special journals.

2 When trying to determine the posting rules for the Cash Payments Journal, remember that the purpose of the journal is to record all cash payments. In the case of the above Cash Payments Journal, the following debit and credit entries will be made in the ledger:

| Column | Ledger account | Type of account | Increase or decrease | Debit | Credit |
|---|---|---|---|---|---|
| | | | | $ | $ |
| *Discount income section* | | | | | |
| Accounts payable control | L1 – Accounts payable control | Liability | Decrease | 44 | |
| GST paid | A4 – GST paid | Asset | Decrease | | 4 |
| Discount revenue | I3 – Discount income | Income | Increase | | 40 |
| | | | | 44 | 44 |
| *Other columns* | | | | | |
| Accounts payable control | L1 – Accounts payable control | Liability | Decrease | 1 061 | |
| Cash purchases | E1 – Purchases | Expense | Increase | 1 610 | |
| Wages | E4 – Wages | Expense | Increase | 650 | |
| Sundries | E7 – Cleaning and | Expense | Increase | 90 | |
| | E8 – Repairs and | Expense | Increase | 60 | |
| | E9 – Delivery expenses | Expense | Increase | 70 | |
| GST paid | A4 – GST paid | Asset | Increase | 183 | |
| Bank | A1 – Cash at bank | Asset | Decrease | | 3 724 |
| | | | | 3 724 | 3 724 |

**Note**

Discount income section

- The total debits in this section of the journal equal the total credits.
- Discount income represents prompt payment discount given to the business by creditors and so is credited to the Discount Income account.
- For GST purposes, discount received from creditors effectively reduces the price of the goods purchased, and so results in the reduction of the original GST paid. Consequently a credit entry is made to the GST Paid account.
- The amount owed to the creditor is reduced by the total of the discount amount and the GST adjustment. Thus the total amount is debited to the Accounts Payable Control account.

Other columns

- The total debits in this section of the journal equal the total credits.
- The total of the Bank column represents the total payments for the period. Payments decrease the Cash at Bank account balance, so this amount is credited to that account.
- The other columns represent the source of the payments (Creditors, Cash Purchases, Wages, Cleaning, Repairs and Delivery) and so are debited to their respective accounts.

Cleo's Cash Payments Journal would be posted to the General Ledger as follows (in some accounts, existing balances have been assumed):

| Date | Particulars | Fol | Debit | Credit | Balance |
|------|-------------|-----|-------|--------|---------|
| | | **General Ledger** | | | |
| | **L1 – Accounts Payable Control Account** | | | | |
| 2017 | | | $ | $ | $ |
| 1 Jun | Balance | | | | 1 120 Cr |
| 5 | Discount income and GST paid | CPJ | (A) 44 | | 1 076 Cr |
| | Cash at bank | CPJ | (D) 1 061 | | 15 Cr |
| | **A4 – GST Paid Account** | | | | |
| 2017 | | | | | |
| 1 Jun | Balance | | | | 300 Dr |
| 5 | Accounts payable control | CPJ | | (B) 4 | 296 Dr |
| | Cash at bank | CPJ | (J) 183 | | 479 Dr |
| | **I3 – Discount Income Account** | | | | |
| 2017 | | | | | |
| 5 Jun | Accounts payable control | CPJ | | (C) 40 | 40 Cr |
| | **E1 – Purchases Account** | | | | |
| 2017 | | | | | |
| 1 Jun | Balance | | | | 4 350 Dr |
| 5 | Cash at bank | CPJ | (E) 1 610 | | 5 960 Dr |
| | **E4 – Wages Account** | | | | |
| 2017 | | | | | |
| 5 Jun | Cash at bank | CPJ | (F) 650 | | 650 Dr |
| | **E7 – Cleaning Account** | | | | |
| 2017 | | | | | |
| 3 Jun | Cash at bank | CPJ | (G) 90 | | 90 Dr |
| | **E8 – Repairs Account** | | | | |
| 2017 | | | | | |
| 3 Jun | Cash at bank | CPJ | (H) 60 | | 60 Dr |
| | **E9 – Delivery Expenses Account** | | | | |
| 2017 | | | | | |
| 4 Jun | Cash at bank | CPJ | (I) 70 | | 70 Dr |

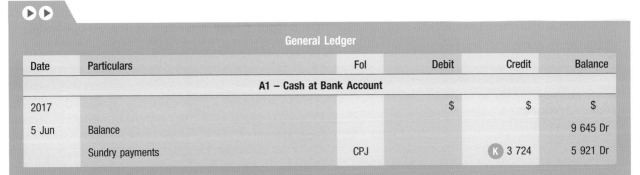

### Ledger explanations

1 The letters **A** to **K** indicate the source (in the journal) and the destination (in the ledger) of each entry.

2 As with the Cash Receipts Journal,

- columns are posted in sequence (from left to right)
- the end of the week date is used for posting totals, and specific dates are used for posting individual amounts from the Sundries column.

3 Cross-referencing of account titles also follows a similar pattern to the Cash Receipts Journal.

- In relation to the discount, the Discount Income account and the GST Paid account are cross-referenced to the Accounts Payable Control account, as this account receives the debit entry corresponding to the credits made in the other two accounts. In the Accounts Payable Control account the cross-reference is to both the Discount Income account and GST Paid account.
- The remaining accounts posted from the journal contain the cross-reference *cash at bank*, as these are the debits corresponding to the credit in the Cash at Bank account. In the Cash at Bank account, the credit entry is cross-referenced *sundry payments*, meaning *various accounts*. (An alternative cross-reference for this entry is *payments*.)

4 The Folio column in the ledger contains a cross-reference (CPJ) to the journal from which each entry has been posted.

# Posting of GST payment/refund

As mentioned previously in Chapter 2, a business that is registered for GST must, at the end of each tax period, submit a Business Activity Statement (BAS). At this time the business will either be required to remit GST to the ATO, or the business may be entitled to a refund of GST monies already paid.

Below is an extract of the Cash Payments Journal for Tommy's Clothing Company showing the payment on 28 April of the business's GST liability for the quarter ended 31 March 2016.

| | | | | 201 | 104 | 403 | 201 | 501 | 503 | | | 104 | 101 |
|---|---|---|---|---|---|---|---|---|---|---|---|---|---|
| | | | | **Discount income** | | | | | | **Sundries** | | | |
| Date | Particulars | Fol | Ref | Accounts payable control | GST paid | Discount income | Accounts payable control | Cash purchases | Wages | Amount | Account | GST paid | Bank |
| | | | | Dr | Cr | Cr | Dr | Dr | Dr | Dr | | Dr | Cr |
| 2016 | | | | $ | $ | $ | $ | $ | $ | $ | | $ | $ |
| 28 Apr | ATO | 202 | EFT | | | | | | | **A** 4 000 | GST collected | | |
| | | 104 | | | | | | | | **B** (2 500) | GST paid | | **C** 1 500 |

*Cash Payments Journal (extract)*

Assuming that there were no other payments for the month of April, the effect on the General Ledger of the above entry is shown below.

| Date | Particulars | Fol | Debit | Credit | Balance |
|---|---|---|---|---|---|
| | | | | **General Ledger** | |
| | | | | | |
| **202 – GST Collected Account** | | | | | |
| 2016 | | | $ | $ | $ |
| 1 Apr | Balance | | | | 4 000 Cr |
| 28 | Cash at bank | CPJ | Ⓐ 4 000 | | Nil |
| **104 – GST Paid Account** | | | | | |
| 2016 | | | | | |
| 1 Apr | Balance | | | | 2 500 Dr |
| 28 | Cash at bank | CPJ | | Ⓑ 2 500 | Nil |
| **101 – Cash at Bank Account** | | | | | |
| 2016 | | | | | |
| 1 Apr | Balance (assumed) | | | | 4 800 Dr |
| 30 | Sundry payments | CPJ | | Ⓒ 1 500 | 3 300 Dr |

**Ledger explanations**

1   The letters Ⓐ to Ⓒ indicate the source (in the journal) and the destination (in the ledger) of each entry.
2   As mentioned earlier in this chapter, cash payments result in a credit entry to the Cash at Bank account and debit entries to all the other accounts affected. Consequently, amounts listed in the Sundries column are debited to the relevant accounts. As GST paid is shown as a negative amount, it is posted as a credit to the GST Paid account.

Below is an extract of the Cash Receipts Journal for Willy's Video Sales showing the receipt on 14 April of a GST refund for the quarter ended 31 March 2016.

| | | | | 1-005 | 1-006 | 5-050 | 1-005 | 4-001 | | | 1-006 | 1-001 |
|---|---|---|---|---|---|---|---|---|---|---|---|---|
| **Cash Receipts Journal (extract)** | | | | | | | | | | | | |
| | | | | Discount expense | | | | | Sundries | | | |
| Date | Particulars | Fol | Ref | Accounts receivable control | GST collected | Discount expense | Accounts receivable control | Cash sales | Amount | Account | GST collected | Bank |
| | | | | Cr | Dr | Cr | Cr | Cr | Cr | | Cr | Dr |
| 2016 | | | | $ | $ | $ | $ | $ | $ | | $ | $ |
| 14 April | ATO | 1-006 | EFT | | | | | | Ⓐ 4 000 | GST paid | | |
| | | 2-010 | | | | | | | Ⓑ (3 000) | | | Ⓒ 1 000 |

Assuming that there were no other payments for the month of April, the effect on the General Ledger of the above entry is shown below.

| | General Ledger | | | | | |
|---|---|---|---|---|---|---|
| Date | Particulars | Fol | Debit | Credit | Balance |
| | **1-006 – GST Paid Account** | | | | |
| 2016 | | | $ | $ | $ |
| 1 Apr | Balance | | | | 4 000 Dr |
| 14 | Cash at bank | CRJ | | (A) 4 000 | Nil |
| | **2-010 – GST Collected Account** | | | | |
| 2016 | | | | | |
| 1 Apr | Balance | | | | 3 000 Dr |
| 14 | Cash at bank | CRJ | (B) 3 000 | | Nil |
| | **1-001 – Cash at Bank Account** | | | | |
| 2016 | | | | | |
| 1 Apr | Balance (assumed) | | | | 6 000 Dr |
| 30 | Sundry receipts | CRJ | (C) 1 000 | | 7 000 Dr |

**Ledger explanations**

1   The letters (A) to (C) indicate the source (in the journal) and the destination (in the ledger) of each entry.

2   As mentioned earlier in this chapter, cash receipts result in a debit entry to the Cash at Bank account and credit entries to all the other accounts affected. Consequently, amounts listed in the Sundries column are credited to the relevant accounts. As GST collected is shown as a negative amount, it is posted as a debit to the GST Collected account.

# Sales Journal

The Sales Journal records all credit sales of goods and services. Figure 3.5 illustrates the basic processing cycle for sales on credit.

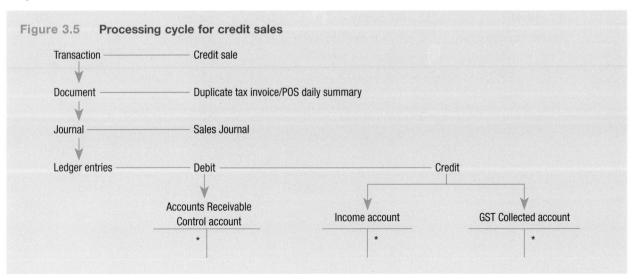

**Figure 3.5     Processing cycle for credit sales**

Consider the following Sales Journal for Cleo's Wine Shop, which records all credit sales for the first week of June 2017.

### Sales Journal

| Date | Debtor | Fol | Ref | I1 Sales | Sundries Amount | Sundries Account | L2 GST collected | A2 Accounts receivable control |
|------|--------|-----|-----|----------|--------|---------|--------------|---------------------|
| | | | | Cr | Cr | | Cr | Dr |
| 2017 | | | | $ | $ | | $ | $ |
| 1 Jun | W Bates | | S71 | 210 | | | 21 | 231 |
| | B Balmer | | S72 | 300 | | | 30 | 330 |
| 2 | Diners Club | | POS | 460 | | | 46 | 506 |
| 3 | A Roberts | I6 | S73 | | **B** 2 800 | Sale of non-current assets | 280 | 3 080 |
| 4 | American Express | | POS | 110 | | | 11 | 121 |
| | I Reid | | S74 | 90 | | | 9 | 99 |
| 5 | E Glover | I7 | S75 | | **C** 370 | Misc income | 37 | 407 |
| | | | | **A** $1 170 | $3 170 | | **D** $434 | **E** $4 774 |
| | | | | ↑ Inc | ↑ Inc | | ↑ Liab | ↑ Asset |

### Journal explanation

- When trying to memorise the posting rules for the Sales Journal, a handy hint to remember is that the purpose of the Sales Journal is to record all credit sales. In the case of the above Sales Journal, the following debit and credit entries will be made in the ledger.

| Column | Ledger account | Type of account | Increase or decrease | Debit | Credit |
|--------|----------------|-----------------|----------------------|-------|--------|
| | | | | $ | $ |
| Sales | I1 – Sales | Income | Increase | | 1 170 |
| Sundries | I6 – Sale of (non-current) assets | Income | Increase | | 2 800 |
| | I7 – Misc Income | Income | Increase | | 370 |
| GST collected | L2 – GST collected | Liability | Increase | | 434 |
| Accounts receivable control | A2 – Accounts receivable control | Asset | Increase | 4 774 | |
| | | | | 4 774 | 4 774 |

Cleo's Sales Journal would be posted to the General Ledger as follows (note that there are pre-existing balances in some accounts):

| Date | Particulars | Fol | Debit | Credit | Balance |
|------|-------------|-----|-------|--------|---------|
| \multicolumn{6}{c}{**General Ledger**} |
| \multicolumn{6}{c}{**I1 – Sales Account**} |
| 2017 | | | $ | $ | $ |
| 5 Jun | Balance | | | | 7 310 Cr |
| | Accounts receivable control | SJ | | (A) 1 170 | 8 480 Cr |
| \multicolumn{6}{c}{**I6 – Sale of Non-Current Assets Account**} |
| 2017 | | | | | |
| 3 Jun | Accounts receivable control | SJ | | (B) 2 800 | 2 800 Cr |
| \multicolumn{6}{c}{**I7 – Miscellaneous Income Account**} |
| 2017 | | | | | |
| 5 Jun | Accounts receivable control | SJ | | (C) 370 | 370 Cr |
| \multicolumn{6}{c}{**L2 – GST Collected Account**} |
| 2017 | | | | | |
| 5 Jun | Balance | | | | 780 Cr |
| | Accounts receivable control | SJ | | (D) 434 | 1 214 Cr |
| \multicolumn{6}{c}{**A2 – Accounts Receivable Control Account**} |
| 2017 | | | | | |
| 5 Jun | Balance | | | | 400 Dr |
| | Sales and GST collected | SJ | (E) 4 774 | | 5 174 Dr |

**Ledger explanations**

1    The letters (A) to (E) indicate the source (in the journal) and the destination (in the ledger) of each entry.

2    As with the cash journals,

   •    columns are posted in sequence (from left to right)
   •    the end-of-week date is used for posting totals, and specific dates are used for posting individual amounts from the Sundries column.

3    Cross-referencing of account titles follows a similar pattern to the cash journals. For example, in an account receiving a debit entry, the cross-reference is to the account(s) receiving the corresponding credit entry(ies).

4    The Folio column in the ledger contains a cross-reference (SJ) to the journal from which each entry has been posted.

# Purchases Journal

The Purchases Journal records all credit purchases of goods and services. Figure 3.6 illustrates the basic processing cycle for purchases on credit.

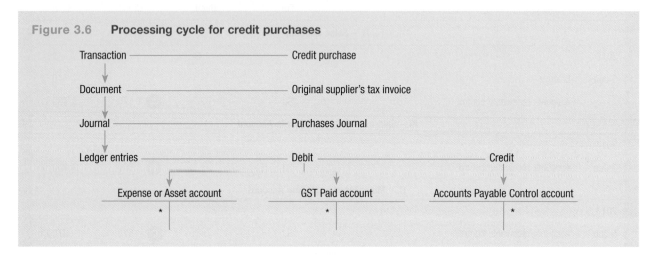

**Figure 3.6    Processing cycle for credit purchases**

The following Purchases Journal for Cleo's Wine Shop records all credit purchases for the first week of June 2017.

**CLEO'S WINE SHOP**
**Purchases Journal**

| | | | | E1 | Sundries | | A4 | L1 |
|---|---|---|---|---|---|---|---|---|
| Date | Creditor | Fol | Ref | Purchases | Amount | Account | GST paid | Accounts payable control |
| | | | | Dr | Dr | | Dr | Cr |
| 2017 | | | | $ | $ | | $ | $ |
| 1 Jun | R Dixon | | SC45 | 430 | | | 43 | 473 |
| 2 | B Muller | | 502 | 260 | | | 26 | 286 |
| | J Davis | E10 | 151 | | Ⓑ 2 000 | Consultant's fees | 200 | 2 200 |
| 3 | R Dixon | | SD105 | 280 | | | 28 | 308 |
| 4 | S Turner | | 1664 | 580 | | | 58 | 638 |
| 5 | American Express | A7 | SD264 | | Ⓒ 800 | Office equipment | 80 | 880 |
| | B Muller | | 913 | 370 | | | 37 | 407 |
| | | | | Ⓐ $1 920 | $2 800 | | Ⓓ $472 | Ⓔ $5 192 |
| | | | | ↑ Exp | ↑ Exp/Asset | | ↑ Asset | ↑ Liab |

230

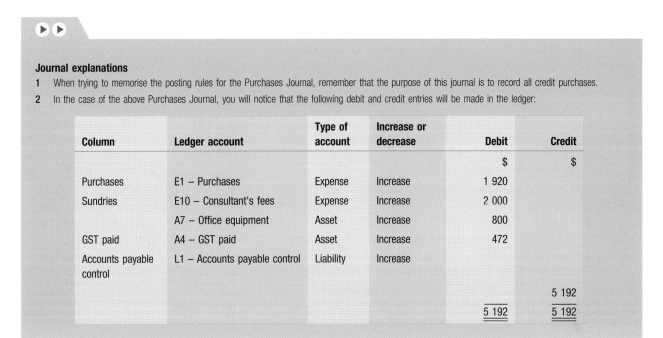

### Journal explanations

1   When trying to memorise the posting rules for the Purchases Journal, remember that the purpose of this journal is to record all credit purchases.

2   In the case of the above Purchases Journal, you will notice that the following debit and credit entries will be made in the ledger:

| Column | Ledger account | Type of account | Increase or decrease | Debit | Credit |
|---|---|---|---|---|---|
| | | | | $ | $ |
| Purchases | E1 – Purchases | Expense | Increase | 1 920 | |
| Sundries | E10 – Consultant's fees | Expense | Increase | 2 000 | |
| | A7 – Office equipment | Asset | Increase | 800 | |
| GST paid | A4 – GST paid | Asset | Increase | 472 | |
| Accounts payable control | L1 – Accounts payable control | Liability | Increase | | |
| | | | | | 5 192 |
| | | | | 5 192 | 5 192 |

Cleo's Purchases Journal would be posted to the General Ledger as follows (note some accounts have existing balances):

| | General Ledger | | | | | |
|---|---|---|---|---|---|---|
| Date | Particulars | Fol | Debit | Credit | Balance | |
| **E1 – Purchases Account** | | | | | | |
| 2017 | | | $ | $ | $ | |
| 5 Jun | Balance | | | | 5 960 Dr | |
| | Accounts payable control | PJ | 1 920 | | 7 880 Dr | |
| **E10 – Consultant's Fees Account** | | | | | | |
| 2017 | | | | | | |
| 2 Jun | Accounts payable control | PJ | 2 000 | | 2 000 Dr | |
| **A7 – Office Equipment Account** | | | | | | |
| 2017 | | | | | | |
| 5 Jun | Balance | | | | 1 200 Dr | |
| | Accounts payable control | PJ | 800 | | 2 000 Dr | |
| **L4 – GST Paid Account** | | | | | | |
| 2017 | | | | | | |
| 5 Jun | Balance | | | | 479 Dr | |
| | Accounts payable control | PJ | 472 | | 951 Dr | |

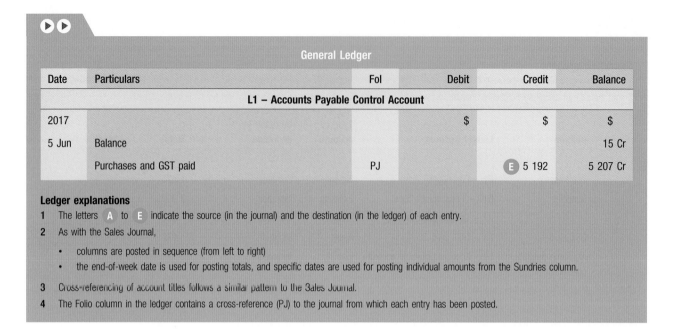

**General Ledger**

| Date | Particulars | Fol | Debit | Credit | Balance |
|---|---|---|---|---|---|
| | | **L1 – Accounts Payable Control Account** | | | |
| 2017 | | | $ | $ | $ |
| 5 Jun | Balance | | | | 15 Cr |
| | Purchases and GST paid | PJ | | E 5 192 | 5 207 Cr |

**Ledger explanations**

1 The letters A to E indicate the source (in the journal) and the destination (in the ledger) of each entry.

2 As with the Sales Journal,

  • columns are posted in sequence (from left to right)

  • the end-of-week date is used for posting totals, and specific dates are used for posting individual amounts from the Sundries column.

3 Cross-referencing of account titles follows a similar pattern to the Sales Journal.

4 The Folio column in the ledger contains a cross-reference (PJ) to the journal from which each entry has been posted.

# Sales Returns and Allowances Journal

The Sales Returns and Allowances Journal records credit given to customers for returns of goods or other allowances for overcharges etc. (Figure 3.7 illustrates the basic processing cycle for sales returns and allowances.)

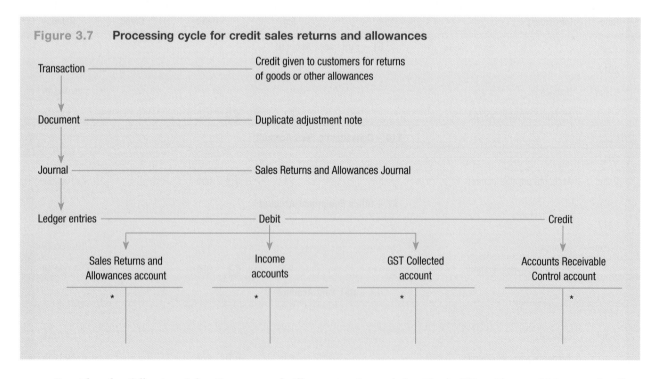

**Figure 3.7    Processing cycle for credit sales returns and allowances**

Consider the following Sales Returns and Allowances Journal for Cleo's Wine Shop, which records all credit sales returns and allowances transactions for the first week of June 2017.

## Sales Returns and Allowances Journal

| | | | | I2 | Sundries | | L2 | A2 |
|---|---|---|---|---|---|---|---|---|
| | | | | Sales returns and allowances | Amount | Account | GST collected | Accounts receivable control |
| Date | Debtor | Fol | Ref | Dr | Dr | | Dr | Cr |
| 2017 | | | | $ | $ | | $ | $ |
| 3 Jun | W Bates | | C55 | 70 | | | 7 | 77 |
| 4 | A Roberts | | C56 | 40 | | | 4 | 44 |
| | | | | **A** $110 | | | **B** $11 | **C** $121 |
| | | | | ↓ Inc | | | ↓ Liab | ↓ Asset |

**Journal explanations**

1  When trying to memorise the posting rules for the Sales Returns and Allowances Journal, remember that the purpose of this journal is to record all credits given to customers for returns of goods and other allowances.

2  In the case of the above Sales Returns and Allowances Journal, it should be noted that the following debit and credit entries will be made in the ledger:

| Column | Ledger account | Type of account | Increase or decrease | Debit | Credit |
|---|---|---|---|---|---|
| | | | | $ | $ |
| Sales returns and allowances | I2 – Sales returns and allowances | Income offset | Income decrease | 110 | |
| GST collected | L2 – GST collected | Liability | Decrease | 11 | |
| Accounts receivable control | A2 – Accounts receivable control | Asset | Decrease | | 121 |
| | | | | 121 | 121 |

Cleo's Sales Returns and Allowances Journal would be posted to the General Ledger as follows:

| | General Ledger | | | | | |
|---|---|---|---|---|---|---|
| Date | Particulars | | Fol | Debit | Credit | Balance |
| | **I2 – Sales Returns and Allowances Account** | | | | | |
| 2017 | | | | $ | $ | $ |
| 5 Jun | Accounts receivable control | | SRJ | **A** 110 | | 110 Dr |
| | **L2 – GST Collected Account** | | | | | |
| 2017 | | | | | | |
| 5 Jun | Balance | | | | | 1 214 Cr |
| | Accounts receivable control | | SRJ | **B** 11 | | 1 203 Cr |

| General Ledger | | | | | |
|---|---|---|---|---|---|
| Date | Particulars | Fol | Debit | Credit | Balance |
| **A2 – Accounts Receivable Control Account** | | | | | |
| 2017 | | | $ | $ | $ |
| 5 Jun | Balance | | | | 5 174 Dr |
| | Sales returns and GST collected | SRJ | | Ⓒ 121 | 5 053 Dr |

**Ledger explanations**

1  The letters Ⓐ to Ⓒ indicate the source (in the journal) and the destination (in the ledger) of each entry.

2  The procedure used for ledger posting and cross-referencing is similar to that illustrated earlier for other special journals.

3  For transactions in the Sundries column a debit entry is made to the appropriate income account affected by the transaction. The treatment of these transactions will be illustrated in the comprehensive example commencing on page 236.

# Purchases Returns and Allowances Journal

The Purchases Returns and Allowances Journal records credits received from suppliers for returns of goods or other allowances. Figure 3.8 illustrates the basic processing cycle for purchases returns and allowances.

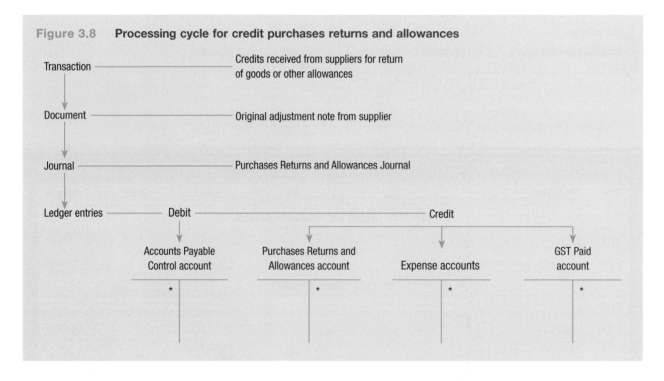

**Figure 3.8  Processing cycle for credit purchases returns and allowances**

Transaction ——— Credits received from suppliers for return of goods or other allowances

Document ——— Original adjustment note from supplier

Journal ——— Purchases Returns and Allowances Journal

Ledger entries ——— Debit ——— Credit

Accounts Payable Control account | Purchases Returns and Allowances account | Expense accounts | GST Paid account

Consider the following Purchases Returns and Allowances Journal for Cleo's Wine Shop, which records all credit purchases returns and allowances transactions for the first week of June 2017.

| | | | | E2 | | | A4 | L1 |
|---|---|---|---|---|---|---|---|---|
| | | | | **Purchases Returns and Allowances Journal** | | | | |
| | | | | Purchases returns and allowances | Sundries | | Accounts payable control | |
| Date | Creditor | Fol | Ref | | Amount | Account | GST paid | |
| | | | | Cr | Cr | | Cr | Dr |
| 2017 | | | | $ | $ | | $ | $ |
| 2 Jun | R Dixon | | RC87 | 90 | | | 9 | 99 |
| 5 | S Turner | | 65 | 30 | | | 3 | 33 |
| | | | | Ⓐ $120 | | | Ⓑ $12 | Ⓒ $132 |
| | | | | ↓ Exp | | | ↓ Asset | ↓ Liab |

**Journal explanations**

1   When learning the posting rules for the Purchases Returns and Allowances Journal, remember that the purpose of this journal is to record all credits allowed by suppliers for returns of goods and other allowances.

2   In the case of the above Purchases Returns and Allowances Journal, the following debit and credit entries will be made in the ledger.

| Column | Ledger account | Type of account | Increase or decrease | Debit | Credit |
|---|---|---|---|---|---|
| | | | | $ | $ |
| Purchases returns and allowances | E2 – Purchases returns and allowances | Expense offset | Expense decrease | | 120 |
| GST paid | A4 – GST paid | Asset | Decrease | | 12 |
| Accounts payable control | L1 – Accounts payable control | Liability | Decrease | 132 | |
| | | | | 132 | 132 |

Cleo's Purchases Returns and Allowances Journal would be posted to the General Ledger as follows:

| Date | Particulars | Fol | Debit | Credit | Balance |
|---|---|---|---|---|---|
| | | **General Ledger** | | | |
| **E2 – Purchases Returns and Allowances Account** | | | | | |
| 2017 | | | $ | $ | $ |
| 5 Jun | Accounts payable control | PRJ | | Ⓐ 120 | 120 Dr |
| **L3 – GST Paid Account** | | | | | |
| 2017 | | | | | |
| 5 Jun | Balance | | | | 951 Dr |
| | Accounts payable control | PRJ | | Ⓑ 12 | 939 Dr |
| **A2 – Accounts Payable Control Account** | | | | | |
| 2017 | | | | | |
| 5 Jun | Balance | | | | 5 207 Cr |
| | Purchases returns and GST paid | PRJ | Ⓒ 132 | | 5 075 Cr |

# Posting all journals to the ledger

This chapter has thus far examined the procedures for posting *individual* journals to the General Ledger at the end of a period; for example, posting on a weekly and monthly basis has been shown. In practice, the posting process is normally undertaken at the end of the appropriate period for *all* of the journals at the same time.

In comprehensive journal/ledger exercises, students will be expected to post all journals to the General Ledger. This should generally not present any difficulties providing a logical procedure is consistently followed. For example, the following procedure could be adopted:

1   Before posting the journals to the General Ledger, record the following information at the top of each column in each journal:
   • the number of the ledger account to which the column is to be posted (as per the chart of accounts)
   • the posting rule (Dr or Cr) applicable to that column.

2   Record any opening balances (as per the opening trial balance) in the ledger accounts.

3   Post one journal at a time, commencing with the General Journal as this journal may contain 'opening' entries.

4   When posting each journal, use the procedure outlined earlier in this chapter (sequence etc.).

5   As you are posting to *one* General Ledger, when you commence a new account (for example, the Accounts Receivable Control account), leave sufficient space in that account for subsequent entries from other journals.

# Departmental businesses

Where a business is divided into more than one sales department, the format of the journals would be expected to vary slightly from those given in the foregoing example for Cleo's Wine Shop. This different journal format, of course, means that ledger posting procedures also differ slightly. In the following example, the procedures for posting all of the journals for a departmental business are illustrated.

## Comprehensive example

Wendy Moore is the owner of *Sports Distributors*, a wholesale supplier of sporting equipment. The business is divided into two departments, indoors (indoor sports equipment) and outdoors (outdoor sports equipment). The following information is supplied in relation to the business:

1   chart of accounts

2   trial balance as at 1 November 2017

3   all journals, recording the transactions for the week ending 5 November 2017.

Commencing with the balances in the trial balance on 1 November, post the journals to the General Ledger for Sports Distributors and prepare a trial balance as at 5 November 2017.

**Note**

- The letters Ⓐ to ⓋⓋ indicate the source (in the journals) and the destination (in the ledger) of each entry. These references also indicate the sequence in which posting is completed.
- Ledger accounts are not arranged in chart of accounts sequence. It is easier to see how the posting process works when the ledger accounts are arranged in the order in which they were opened in the exercise. Ideally, you should aim to eventually complete all ledgers in chart of accounts sequence (where a chart of accounts is provided).

## 1   The chart of accounts

| SPORTS DISTRIBUTORS — Chart of accounts | | | |
|---|---|---|---|
| **Assets** | | **Income** | |
| A1 | Cash at bank | I1 | Sales – Indoors |
| A2 | Accounts receivable control | I2 | Sales – Outdoors |
| A3 | Motor vehicles | I3 | Sales returns and allowances – Indoors |
| A4 | Land and buildings | I4 | Sales returns and allowances – Outdoors |
| A5 | Furniture and fittings | I5 | Discount income |
| A6 | Stock – Indoors | I6 | Interest income |
| A7 | Stock – Outdoors | I7 | Equipment hire income |
| A8 | GST paid | | |
| | | **Expenses** | |
| **Liabilities** | | E1 | Purchases – Indoors |
| L1 | Accounts payable control | E2 | Purchases – Outdoors |
| L2 | Mortgage loan on land and buildings | E3 | Purchases returns and allowances – Indoors |
| L3 | GST collected | E4 | Purchases returns and allowances – Outdoors |
| | | E5 | Discount expense |
| **Owner's equity** | | E6 | Wages |
| OE1 | Capital – Wendy Moore | E7 | Stationery |
| OE2 | Drawings – Wendy Moore | E8 | Advertising |
| | | E9 | Bad debts |
| | | E10 | Merchant fees expense |
| | | E11 | Subscriptions expense |

## 2   The trial balance

| Sports Distributors Trial balance as at 1 November 2017 | | |
|---|---|---|
| **Account** | **Debit** | **Credit** |
| | $ | $ |
| Advertising | 1 050 | |
| Capital – Wendy Moore | | 35 000 |
| Cash at bank | 3 550 | |
| Interest income | | 680 |
| Accounts payable control | | 4 170 |
| Accounts receivable control | 4 100 | |
| Discount expense | 400 | |
| Discount income | | 300 |
| Furniture and fittings | 6 500 | |
| Land and buildings | 52 000 | |
| Mortgage loan on land and buildings | | 40 000 |
| Motor vehicles | 8 000 | |
| Purchases – Indoors | 10 100 | |
| Purchases – Outdoors | 7 200 | |
| Purchases returns and allowances – Indoors | | 200 |
| Purchases returns and allowances – Outdoors | | 110 |
| Sales – Indoors | | 15 800 |
| Sales – Outdoors | | 10 400 |
| Sales returns and allowances – Indoors | 340 | |
| Sales returns and allowances – Outdoors | 170 | |
| Stationery | 690 | |
| Stock – Indoors | 3 460 | |
| Stock – Outdoors | 2 400 | |
| Wages | 7 100 | |
| GST collected | | 1 000 |
| GST paid | 600 | |
| | $107 660 | $107 660 |

Ⓐ

Note that all the opening balances above will be referenced in the ledger by the letter Ⓐ.

## 3 Journals for the week ended 5 November 2017

### General Journal

| Date | Particulars | Fol | Debit | Credit |
|------|-------------|-----|-------|--------|
| 2017 | | | $ | $ |
| 2 Nov | Furniture and fittings | A5 | **B** 1 500 | |
| | Capital – Wendy Moore | OE1 | | **C** 1 500 |
| | *Office desk contributed by owner* | | | |
| 5 | Bad debts | E9 | **D** 600 | |
| | GST collected | L3 | **E** 60 | |
| | Accounts receivable control | A2 | | **F** 660 |
| | *Bad debt – T Turk* | | | |

### Cash Receipts Journal

| | | | | A2 | L3 | E5 | A2 | I1 | I2 | | | L3 | A1 |
|---|---|---|---|---|---|---|---|---|---|---|---|---|---|
| | | | | Discount expense | | | | Cash sales | | Sundries | | | |
| Date | Particulars | Fol | Ref | Accounts receivable control | GST collected | Discount expense | Accounts receivable control | Indoors | Outdoors | Amount | Account | GST collected | Bank |
| | | | | Cr | Dr | Dr | Cr | Cr | Cr | Cr | | Cr | Dr |
| 2017 | | | | $ | $ | $ | $ | $ | $ | $ | | $ | $ |
| 1 Nov | Cash sales | | POS | | | | | 230 | 260 | | | 49 | |
| | D Costello | | 401 | 11 | 1 | 10 | 389 | | | | | | 928 |
| 2 | Sales – EFTPOS | | POS | | | | | 80 | 50 | | | 13 | 143 |
| | Cash sales | | POS | | | | | 230 | 290 | | | 52 | 572 |
| 3 | Sales – EFTPOS | | POS | | | | | 100 | 70 | | | 17 | 187 |
| | Cash sales | | POS | | | | | 190 | 270 | | | 46 | 506 |
| | Sportco Ltd | I6 | EFT | | | | | | | **M** 70 | Interest income | | 70 |
| 4 | Cash sales | | POS | | | | | 760 | 860 | | | 162 | |
| | T Wilson | | 402 | 22 | 2 | 20 | 358 | | | | | | 2 140 |
| 5 | Diners Club | | EFT | | | | | | | | | | |
| | – Gross | | | | | | 325 | | | | | | |
| | – Merchant fee | E10 | | | | | | | | **N** (30) | Merchant fees expense | | |
| | – GST paid | A8 | | | | | | | | **O** (3) | GST paid | | 292 |
| | | | | **G** $33 | **H** $3 | **I** $30 | **J** $1 072 | **K** $1 590 | **L** $1 800 | $37 | | **P** $339 | **Q** $4 838 |

239

## Cash Payments Journal

| Date | Particulars | Fol | Ref | Discount expense — L1 Accounts payable control Dr $ | A8 GST paid Cr $ | I5 Discount income Cr $ | L1 Accounts payable control Dr $ | Cash purchases — E1 Indoors Dr $ | E2 Outdoors Dr $ | E6 Wages Dr $ | Sundries — Amount Dr $ | Sundries — Account | A8 GST paid Dr $ | A1 Bank Cr $ |
|---|---|---|---|---|---|---|---|---|---|---|---|---|---|---|
| 2017 1 Nov | Wages | | EFT | | | | | | | 350 | | | | 350 |
| | Wheato Ltd | | 016 | | | | | 270 | | | | | 27 | 297 |
| 2 | I Castles | E7 | EFT | 22 | 2 | 20 | 480 | | | | | | | 480 |
| | Phil's Newsagency | | 017 | | | | | | | | (Y) 80 | Stationery | 8 | 231 |
| | | | | | | | | | | | (Z) 130 | Advertising | 13 | |
| | Motti's | E8 | 018 | | | | | 280 | 150 | | | | 43 | 473 |
| 3 | Macca Ltd | | 019 | | | | | | 100 | | | | 10 | 110 |
| 4 | Ace Sports | | 020 | 11 | 1 | 10 | 143 | | | | | | | 143 |
| | Phone Co | E9 | EFT | | | | 220 | | | | | | | 220 |
| 5 | Wheato Ltd | | 021 | | | | | 320 | | | | | 32 | 352 |
| | | | | (R) $33 | (S) $3 | (T) $30 | (U) $843 | (V) $870 | (W) $250 | (X) $350 | $210 | | (A) $133 | (B) $2 656 |

## Sales Journal

| Date | Debtor | Fol | Ref | I1 Sales Indoors | I2 Sales Outdoors | Sundries Amount | Sundries Account | L3 GST collected | A2 Accounts receivable control |
|------|--------|-----|-----|--------|---------|--------|---------|---------------|-------------------|
| | | | | Cr | Cr | Cr | | Cr | Dr |
| 2017 | | | | $ | $ | $ | | $ | $ |
| 1 Nov | T Wilson | | 896 | 190 | 180 | | | 37 | 407 |
| 2 | American Express | | POS | | 140 | | | 14 | 154 |
| | P Gordon | | 897 | 60 | 70 | | | 13 | 143 |
| 3 | A Clayton | | 898 | 170 | 120 | | | 29 | 319 |
| 4 | W Skinner | | 899 | 100 | 40 | | | 14 | 154 |
| | D Rivers | | 900 | 90 | 120 | | | 21 | 231 |
| 5 | A Clayton | | 901 | 80 | 190 | | | 27 | 297 |
| | G Piercy | I7 | 902 | | | (E)(E) 100 | Equipment hire income | 10 | 110 |
| | | | | (C)(C) $690 | (D)(D) $860 | $100 | | (F)(F) $165 | (G)(G) $1 815 |

## Purchases Journal

| Date | Creditor | Fol | Ref | E1 Purchases Indoors | E2 Purchases Outdoors | Sundries Amount | Sundries Account | A8 GST paid | L1 Accounts payable control |
|------|----------|-----|-----|--------|---------|--------|---------|---------|-------------------|
| | | | | Dr | Dr | Dr | | Dr | Cr |
| 2017 | | | | $ | $ | $ | | $ | $ |
| 1 Nov | Sportsrite | | T442 | 350 | 260 | | | 61 | 671 |
| 2 | Ace Sports | | 395 | | 140 | | | 14 | 154 |
| 3 | AD Industries | | 521 | 290 | 90 | | | 38 | 418 |
| | Golfer's Digest | E11 | GC1014 | | – | (J)(J) 320 | Subscriptions expense | 32 | 352 |
| 4 | Sportsrite | | T609 | 200 | 60 | | | 26 | 286 |
| 5 | S Tayer | | 961 | 180 | | | | 18 | 198 |
| | | | | (H)(H) $1 020 | (I)(I) $550 | $320 | | (K)(K) $189 | (L)(L) $2 079 |

## Sales Returns and Allowances Journal

| | | | | I3 | I4 | | | L3 | A2 |
|---|---|---|---|---|---|---|---|---|---|
| | | | | Sales returns | | Sundries | | | Accounts receivable control |
| Date | Debtor | Fol | Ref | Indoors | Outdoors | Amount | Account | GST collected | |
| | | | | Dr | Dr | Dr | | Dr | Cr |
| 2017 | | | | $ | $ | $ | | $ | $ |
| 3 Nov | P Swann | | 274 | 5 | 15 | | | 2 | 22 |
| 5 | A Clayton | | 275 | 60 | | | | 6 | 66 |
| | G Piercy | I7 | 276 | | | O O 10 | Equipment hire income | 1 | 11 |
| | | | | M M $65 | N N $15 | $10 | | P P $9 | Q Q $99 |

## Purchases Returns and Allowances Journal

| | | | | E3 | E4 | | | A8 | L1 |
|---|---|---|---|---|---|---|---|---|---|
| | | | | Purchases Returns | | Sundries | | | Accounts payable control |
| Date | Creditor | Fol | Ref | Indoors | Outdoors | Amount | Account | GST paid | |
| | | | | Cr | Cr | Cr | | Cr | Dr |
| 2017 | | | | $ | $ | $ | | $ | $ |
| 2 Nov | Sports Rite | | TR22 | 25 | 15 | | | 4 | 44 |
| 4 | AD Industries | | 78 | | 10 | | | 1 | 11 |
| 5 | Golfer's Digest | E11 | 781 | | | T T 20 | Subscriptions expense | 2 | 22 |
| | | | | R R $25 | S S $25 | $20 | | U U $7 | V V $77 |

## Solution

| Sports Distributors | | | | | | |
|---|---|---|---|---|---|---|
| **General Ledger** | | | | | | |
| Date | Particulars | | Fol | Debit | Credit | Balance |
| **E8 – Advertising Account** | | | | | | |
| 2017 | | | | $ | $ | $ |
| 1 Nov | Balance | | | | | A 1 050 Dr |
| 2 | Cash at bank | | CPJ | Z 130 | | 1 180 Dr |
| **OE1 – Capital – Wendy Moore Account** | | | | | | |
| 2017 | | | | | | |
| 1 Nov | Balance | | | | | A 35 000 Cr |
| 2 | Furniture and fittings | | GJ | | C 1 500 | 36 500 Cr |

| General Ledger | | | | | |
|---|---|---|---|---|---|
| Date | Particulars | Fol | Debit | Credit | Balance |
| **A1 – Cash at Bank Account** | | | | | |
| 2017 | | | $ | $ | $ |
| 1 Nov | Balance | | | | (A) 3 550 Dr |
| 5 | Sundry receipts | CRJ | (Q) 4 838 | | 8 388 Dr |
| | Sundry payments | CPJ | | (B)(B) 2 656 | 5 732 Dr |
| **I6 – Interest Income Account** | | | | | |
| 2017 | | | | | |
| 1 Nov | Balance | | | | (A) 680 Cr |
| 3 | Cash at bank | CRJ | | (M) 70 | 750 Cr |
| **L1 – Accounts Payable Control Account** | | | | | |
| 2017 | | | | | |
| 1 Nov | Balance | | | | (A) 4 170 Cr |
| 5 | Discount income and GST paid | CPJ | (R) 33 | | 4 137 Cr |
| | Cash at bank | CPJ | (U) 843 | | 3 294 Cr |
| | Purchases and GST paid | PJ | | (L)(L) 2 079 | 5 373 Cr |
| | Purchases returns and allowances and GST paid | PRJ | (V)(V) 77 | | 5 296 Cr |
| **A2 – Accounts Receivable Control Account** | | | | | |
| 2017 | | | | | |
| 1 Nov | Balance | | | | (A) 4 100 Dr |
| 5 | Bad debts and GST collected | GJ | | (F) 660 | 3 440 Dr |
| | Discount expense and GST collected | CRJ | | (G) 33 | 3 407 Dr |
| | Cash at bank | CRJ | | (J) 1 072 | 2 335 Dr |
| | Sales and GST collected | SJ | (G)(G) 1 815 | | 4 150 Dr |
| | Sales returns and allowances and GST collected | SRJ | | (Q)(Q) 99 | 4 051 Dr |
| **E5 – Discount Expense Account** | | | | | |
| 2017 | | | | | |
| 1 Nov | Balance | | | | (A) 400 Dr |
| 5 | Accounts receivable control | CRJ | (I) 30 | | 430 Dr |
| **I5 – Discount Income Account** | | | | | |
| 2017 | | | | | |
| 1 Nov | Balance | | | | (A) 300 Cr |
| 5 | Accounts payable control | CPJ | | (T) 30 | 330 Cr |

| General Ledger | | | | | |
|---|---|---|---|---|---|
| Date | Particulars | Fol | Debit | Credit | Balance |
| **A5 – Furniture and Fittings Account** | | | | | |
| 2017 | | | $ | $ | $ |
| 1 Nov | Balance | | | | (A) 6 500 Dr |
| 2 | Capital – Wendy Moore | GJ | (B) 1 500 | | 8 000 Dr |
| **A4 – Land and Buildings Account** | | | | | |
| 2017 | | | | | |
| 1 Nov | Balance | | | | (A) 52 000 Dr |
| **L2 – Mortgage Loan on Land and Buildings Account** | | | | | |
| 2017 | | | | | |
| 1 Nov | Balance | | | | (A) 40 000 Cr |
| **A3 – Motor Vehicles Account** | | | | | |
| 2017 | | | | | |
| 1 Nov | Balance | | | | (A) 8 000 Dr |
| **E1 – Purchases – Indoors Account** | | | | | |
| 2017 | | | | | |
| 1 Nov | Balance | | | | (A) 10 100 Dr |
| 5 | Cash at bank | CPJ | (V) 870 | | 10 970 Dr |
| | Accounts payable control | PJ | (H)(H) 1 020 | | 11 990 Dr |
| **E2 – Purchases – Outdoors Account** | | | | | |
| 2017 | | | | | |
| 1 Nov | Balance | | | | (A) 7 200 Dr |
| 5 | Cash at bank | CPJ | (W) 250 | | 7 450 Dr |
| | Accounts payable control | PJ | (I)(I) 550 | | 8 000 Dr |
| **E3 – Purchases Returns and Allowances – Indoors Account** | | | | | |
| 2017 | | | | | |
| 1 Nov | Balance | | | | (A) 200 Cr |
| 5 | Accounts payable control | PRJ | | (R)(R) 25 | 225 Cr |
| **E4 – Purchases Returns and Allowances – Outdoors Account** | | | | | |
| 2017 | | | | | |
| 1 Nov | Balance | | | | (A) 110 Cr |
| 5 | Accounts payable control | PRJ | | (S)(S) 25 | 135 Cr |

| General Ledger | | | | | |
|---|---|---|---|---|---|
| Date | Particulars | Fol | Debit | Credit | Balance |
| **I1 – Sales – Indoors Account** | | | | | |
| 2017 | | | $ | $ | $ |
| 1 Nov | Balance | | | | Ⓐ 15 800 Cr |
| 5 | Cash at bank | CRJ | | Ⓚ 1 590 | 17 390 Cr |
| | Accounts receivable control | SJ | | ⒸⒸ 690 | 18 080 Cr |
| **I2 – Sales – Outdoors Account** | | | | | |
| 2017 | | | | | |
| 1 Nov | Balance | | | | Ⓐ 10 400 Cr |
| 5 | Cash at bank | CRJ | | Ⓛ 1 800 | 12 200 Cr |
| | Accounts receivable control | SJ | | ⒹⒹ 860 | 13 060 Cr |
| **I3 – Sales Returns and Allowances – Indoors Account** | | | | | |
| 2017 | | | | | |
| 1 Nov | Balance | | | | Ⓐ 340 Dr |
| 5 | Accounts receivable control | SRJ | ⓂⓂ 65 | | 405 Dr |
| **I4 – Sales Returns and Allowances – Outdoors Account** | | | | | |
| 2017 | | | | | |
| 1 Nov | Balance | | | | Ⓐ 170 Dr |
| 5 | Accounts receivable control | SRJ | ⓃⓃ 15 | | 185 Dr |
| **E7 – Stationery Account** | | | | | |
| 2017 | | | | | |
| 1 Nov | Balance | | | | Ⓐ 690 Dr |
| 2 | Cash at bank | CPJ | Ⓨ 80 | | 770 Dr |
| **A6 – Stock – Indoors Account** | | | | | |
| 2017 | | | | | |
| 1 Nov | Balance | | | | Ⓐ 3 460 Dr |
| **A7 – Stock – Outdoors Account** | | | | | |
| 2017 | | | | | |
| 1 Nov | Balance | | | | Ⓐ 2 400 Dr |
| **E6 – Wages Account** | | | | | |
| 2017 | | | | | |
| 1 Nov | Balance | | | | Ⓐ 7 100 Dr |
| 5 | Cash at bank | CPJ | Ⓧ 350 | | 7 450 Dr |

# Accounting To Trial Balance

| Date | Particulars | Fol | Debit | Credit | Balance |
|---|---|---|---|---|---|
| | | | $ | $ | $ |

**General Ledger**

**L3 – GST Collected Account**

| Date | Particulars | Fol | Debit | Credit | Balance |
|---|---|---|---|---|---|
| 2017 | | | | | |
| 1 Nov | Balance | | | | 1 000 Cr |
| 5 | Accounts receivable control | GJ | 60 | | 940 Cr |
| | Accounts receivable control | CRJ | 3 | | 937 Cr |
| | Cash at bank | CRJ | | 339 | 1 276 Cr |
| 5 Nov | Accounts receivable control | SJ | | 165 | 1 441 Cr |
| | Accounts receivable control | SRJ | 9 | | 1 432 Cr |

**A8 – GST Paid Account**

| Date | Particulars | Fol | Debit | Credit | Balance |
|---|---|---|---|---|---|
| 2017 | | | | | |
| 1 Nov | Balance | | | | 600 Dr |
| | Accounts payable control | CPJ | | 3 | 597 Dr |
| 5 | Cash at bank | CRJ | 3 | | 600 Dr |
| | Cash at bank | CPJ | 133 | | 733 Dr |
| | Accounts payable control | PJ | 189 | | 922 Dr |
| | Accounts payable control | PRJ | | 7 | 915 Dr |

**E9 – Bad Debts Account**

| Date | Particulars | Fol | Debit | Credit | Balance |
|---|---|---|---|---|---|
| 2017 | | | | | |
| 5 Nov | Accounts receivable control | GJ | 600 | | 600 Dr |

**E10 – Merchant Fees Expense Account**

| Date | Particulars | Fol | Debit | Credit | Balance |
|---|---|---|---|---|---|
| 2017 | | | | | |
| 5 Nov | Cash at bank | CRJ | 30 | | 30 Dr |

**I7 – Equipment Hire Income Account**

| Date | Particulars | Fol | Debit | Credit | Balance |
|---|---|---|---|---|---|
| 2017 | | | | | |
| 5 Nov | Accounts receivable control | SJ | | 100 | 100 Cr |
| | Accounts receivable control | SRJ | 10 | | 90 Cr |

**E11 – Subscriptions Expense Account**

| Date | Particulars | Fol | Debit | Credit | Balance |
|---|---|---|---|---|---|
| 2017 | | | | | |
| 3 Nov | Accounts payable control | PJ | 320 | | 320 Dr |
| 5 | Accounts payable control | PRJ | | 20 | 300 Dr |

246

| Trial balance as at 5 November 2017 | | |
|---|---|---|
| **Account** | **Debit** | **Credit** |
| | $ | $ |
| Advertising | 1 180 | |
| Capital – Wendy Moore | | 36 500 |
| Cash at bank | 5 732 | |
| Interest income | | 750 |
| Accounts payable control | | 5 296 |
| Accounts receivable control | 4 051 | |
| Discount expense | 430 | |
| Discount income | | 330 |
| Furniture and fittings | 8 000 | |
| Land and buildings | 52 000 | |
| Mortgage loan on land and buildings | | 40 000 |
| Motor vehicles | 8 000 | |
| Purchases – Indoors | 11 990 | |
| Purchases – Outdoors | 8 000 | |
| Purchases returns and allowances – Indoors | | 225 |
| Purchases returns and allowances – Outdoors | | 135 |
| Sales – Indoors | | 18 080 |
| Sales – Outdoors | | 13 060 |
| Sales returns and allowances – Indoors | 405 | |
| Sales returns and allowances – Outdoors | 185 | |
| Stationery | 770 | |
| Stock – Indoors | 3 460 | |
| Stock – Outdoors | 2 400 | |
| Wages | 7 450 | |
| GST collected | | 1 432 |
| GST paid | 915 | |
| Bad debts | 600 | |
| Merchant fees expense | 30 | |
| Equipment hire income | | 90 |
| Subscriptions expense | 300 | |
| | $115 898 | $115 898 |

# Analysis of errors in the trial balance

By now, students progressing through this book will have no doubt already discovered that a trial balance does not always balance the first time it is prepared. Chapter 1 provided a simple outline of ways to determine the reason for an imbalance. Now that we have examined the accounting process in more detail, it is appropriate to review the analysis of errors in the trial balance.

If a trial balance does not balance (both sides are not equal in amount), the following checking procedure is suggested.

1 Check the addition of the trial balance itself.
2 Check that all the account balances appear on the trial balance.
3 Ensure that the balance of each account is recorded in its correct debit or credit column on the trial balance.
4 Look for amounts that may be transcribed incorrectly.
5 Check the additions in the ledger accounts.
6 Check that the journals have been correctly posted to the ledger.
7 Check the additions in the journals.

There are, of course, errors that occur during the processing of information in journals and ledgers that a trial balance will not reveal. These were outlined in Chapter 1, under the heading 'Limitations of the trial balance' (page 61).

# Purpose of the trial balance

As outlined in Chapter 1, the trial balance has two main purposes.

1 It proves the arithmetic accuracy of the ledger.
2 It is used as the basis for preparing a statement of comprehensive income and a statement of financial position. This topic is further developed in the companion text *Accounting: Basic Reports*.

 **EXERCISES**

UWATCH 3.1

3.1 Post the following opening General Journal entry to the General Ledger for M Thompson at 1 January 2016.
A UWatch demonstration is available on the CD that accompanies this text for parts of this activity.

**M Thompson**
**General Journal**

| Date | Particulars | Fol | Debit | Credit |
|------|-------------|-----|-------|--------|
| 2016 | | | $ | $ |
| 1 Jan | Stock | | 50 000 | |
| | Land and buildings | | 160 000 | |
| | Motor vehicle | | 12 000 | |
| | Furniture and fittings | | 8 000 | |
| | Mortgage loan on land and buildings | | | 37 000 |
| | Bank overdraft | | | 5 000 |
| | Capital – M Thompson | | | 188 000 |
| | *Assets and liabilities at commencement of business* | | | |

**3.2**  Post the following General Journal entries to the General Ledger for K Hinkley. (Assume the following balances in the ledger at 1 July: Accounts Payable Control, $3700; Capital – K Hinkley, $40 000; Accounts Receivable Control, $4100.)

**K Hinkley**
**General Journal**

| Date | Particulars | Fol | Debit | Credit |
|------|-------------|-----|-------|--------|
| 2019 | | | $ | $ |
| 1 July | Late fees expense | | 25 | |
| | Accounts payable control | | | 25 |
| | *Late fee charged on overdue account by B Simmons* | | | |
| 3 | Motor vehicle | | 25 000 | |
| | Capital – K Hinkley | | | 25 000 |
| | *Motor vehicle introduced by owner* | | | |
| 5 | Drawings – K Hinkley | | 1 650 | |
| | GST paid | | | 150 |
| | Purchases | | | 1 500 |
| | *Withdrawal of stock by owner* | | | |
| 12 | Bad debts | | 180 | |
| | GST collected | | 18 | |
| | Accounts receivable control | | | 198 |
| | *Bad debt written off – A Bartlett* | | | |
| 17 | Accounts receivable control | | 2 695 | |
| | Sales | | | 2 450 |
| | GST collected | | | 245 |
| | *Sales invoice (no. 874 to D Mavric) overlooked in May* | | | |
| 28 | Accounts receivable control | | 50 | |
| | Late fees income | | | 50 |
| | *Late fee charged to B Carlson on overdue account* | | | |

**3.3**  This question is available on the CD that accompanies this text.

ADDITIONAL
EXERCISES

**3.4\*** Post the following Cash Receipts Journal to the General Ledger for J Bartel, sporting-goods distributor, at 31 August 2019. (Assume the following ledger account balances at 1 August: Discount Expense, $50; Accounts Receivable Control, $11 300; Sales, $76 000; Motor Vehicles, $11 000; Capital – J Bartel, $90 000; GST collected, $7600; Cash at Bank, $2300 Dr.)

A UWatch demonstration is available on the CD that accompanies this text for parts of this activity.

**UWATCH 3.2**

### J Bartel
### Cash Receipts Journal

| | | | | Discount expense | | | | | Sundries | | | |
| --- | --- | --- | --- | --- | --- | --- | --- | --- | --- | --- | --- | --- |
| Date | Particulars | Fol | Ref | Accounts receivable control | GST collected | Discount expense | Accounts receivable control | Cash sales | Amount | Account | GST collected | Bank |
| 2019 | | | | $ | $ | $ | 0 | $ | $ | | $ | $ |
| 1 Aug | EFTPOS | | POS | | | | | 380 | | | 38 | 418 |
| 8 | EFTPOS | | POS | | | | | 500 | | | 50 | 550 |
| | Sales | | POS | | | | | 400 | | | 40 | 440 |
| 10 | F Ball | | 85 | | | | 1 400 | | | | | 1 400 |
| | Zero Sports | | POS | | | | | | 100 | Commission income | 10 | 110 |
| 14 | Sales | | POS | | | | | 650 | | | 65 | 715 |
| 15 | A Barnes | | EFT | | | | | | 4 600 | Sale of non-current assets | 460 | 5 060 |
| 21 | EFTPOS | | POS | | | | | 950 | | | 95 | 1 045 |
| | Cash sales | | POS | | | | | 1 400 | | | 140 | 1 540 |
| | J Bartel | | EFT | | | | | | 2 000 | Capital – J Bartel | | 2 000 |
| 25 | G Club | | EFT | 44 | 4 | 40 | 1 596 | | | | | 1 596 |
| 30 | Sales | | POS | | | | | 1 100 | | | 110 | 1 210 |
| | | | | $44 | $4 | $40 | $2 996 | $5 380 | $6 700 | | $1 008 | $16 084 |

**3.5** This question is available on the CD that accompanies this text.

**ADDITIONAL EXERCISES**

**3.6** Post the following Cash Payments Journal to the General Ledger for P Shaw, wholesaler, at 30 April 2016. (Assume the following ledger account balances at 1 April: Discount Income, $110; Accounts Payable Control, $1700; Purchases, $14 300; Wages, $11 400; Advertising, $400; Drawings – P Shaw, $4000; Office Expenses, $1100; Cleaning, $600; GST Collected, $880; GST Paid, $250; Cash at Bank, $9600 Dr.)

A UWatch demonstration is available on the CD that accompanies this text for parts of this activity.

**UWATCH 3.3**

**P Shaw**
**Cash Payments Journal**

| Date | Particulars | Fol | Ref | Discount income Accounts payable control | GST paid | Discount income | Accounts payable control | Cash purchases | Wages | Sundries Amount | Account | GST paid | Bank |
|------|-------------|-----|-----|-------|---------|---------|---------|---------|-------|--------|---------|---------|------|
| 2016 | | | | $ | $ | $ | $ | $ | $ | $ | | $ | $ |
| 1 Apr | Purchases | | 101 | | | | | 300 | | | | 30 | 330 |
| 4 | Wages | | EFT | | | | | | 550 | | | | 550 |
| 5 | StoreWorks | | 102 | | | | | | | 110 | Advertising | 11 | 121 |
| 8 | Belmont Council | | EFT | | | | 450 | | | | | | 450 |
| 9 | J Hill | | 103 | 22 | 2 | 20 | 378 | | | | | | 378 |
| 10 | Purchases | | 104 | | | | | 450 | | | | 45 | 495 |
| 15 | Wages | | EFT | | | | | | 550 | | | | 550 |
| | LEG Insurance | | EFT | | | | 262 | | | | | | 262 |
| 25 | S Eton | | 105 | 33 | 3 | 30 | 330 | | | | | | 330 |
| | P Shaw | | EFT | | | | | | | 250 | Drawings – P Shaw | | 250 |
| 26 | N Beggs | | 106 | | | | | | | 130 | Office expenses | 13 | |
| | | | | | | | | | | 20 | Cleaning | 2 | 165 |
| 28 | ATO | | EFT | | | | | | | 880 | GST collected | | |
| | | | | | | | | | | (250) | GST paid | | 630 |
| | | | | $55 | $5 | $50 | $1 420 | $750 | $1 100 | $1 140 | | $101 | $4 511 |

3.7 This question is available on the CD that accompanies this text.

3.8 Post the following Sales Journal to the General Ledger for E Betts, used car dealer, at 31 July 2019. (Assume that the Accounts Receivable Control account had a balance of $21 300 at 1 July.)

ADDITIONAL
EXERCISES

**E Betts**
**Sales Journal**

| Date | Debtor | Fol | Ref | Sales | Sundries Amount | Account | GST collected | Accounts receivable control |
|------|--------|-----|-----|-------|--------|---------|---------------|------------------------------|
| 2019 | | | | $ | $ | | $ | $ |
| 3 Jul | J Harris | | 64 | 4 500 | | | 450 | 4 950 |
| 4 | H Alt | | 65 | 3 400 | | | 340 | 3 740 |
| 6 | AMEX | | 66 | 2 600 | | | 260 | 2 860 |
| 12 | S Dekleva | | 67 | 1 800 | | | 180 | 1 980 |
| 31 | S Motlop | | 68 | | 1 300 | Repairs income | 130 | 1 430 |
| | | | | $12 300 | $1 300 | | $1 360 | $14 960 |

ADDITIONAL
EXERCISES

UWATCH 3.4

3.9    This question is available on the CD that accompanies this text.

3.10   Post the following Sales Journal to the General Ledger for Ace Parts, motor vehicle spare parts distributor, at 31 December 2016. (Assume the following ledger account balances at 1 December: Sales – Car Parts, $6100; Sales – Truck Parts, $3400; Delivery Fees Income, $1200; GST Collected, $400; Accounts Receivable Control, $12 000.)

A UWatch demonstration is available on the CD that accompanies this text for parts of this activity.

### Ace Parts Sales Journal

| Date | Debtor | Fol | Ref | Sales Car parts | Truck parts | Sundries Amount | Account | GST collected | Accounts receivable control |
|------|--------|-----|-----|-----------|-------------|--------|---------|---------------|-----------------------------|
| 2016 | | | | $ | $ | $ | | $ | $ |
| 2 Dec | P Taylor | | 400 | 120 | 220 | | | 34 | 374 |
| 7 | P McEchnie | | 401 | 150 | 280 | | | 43 | 473 |
| 12 | A Tran | | 402 | 70 | 250 | | | 32 | 352 |
| 19 | D Dimasi | | 403 | | 750 | 70 | Delivery fees income | 82 | 902 |
| 24 | K Hamilton | | 404 | 50 | 550 | | | 60 | 660 |
| | | | | $390 | $2 050 | $70 | | $251 | $2 761 |

UWATCH 3.5

3.11   Post the following Purchases Journal to the General Ledger for P Shaw, wholesaler, at 30 April 2016. (Assume the following ledger account balances at 1 April: Purchases, $14 300; Insurance $710; Shop Fittings $6300; Accounts Payable Control, $1700.)

A UWatch demonstration is available on the CD that accompanies this text for parts of this activity.

### P Shaw Purchases Journal

| Date | Creditor | Fol | Ref | Purchases | Sundries Amount | Account | GST Paid | Accounts payable control |
|------|----------|-----|-----|-----------|--------|---------|----------|--------------------------|
| 2016 | | | | $ | $ | | $ | $ |
| 2 Apr | J Dowdle | | D45 | 320 | | | 32 | 352 |
| 6 | F Coylo | | 622 | | 360 | Shop fittings | 36 | 396 |
| 11 | A Wheeler | | 901 | 180 | | | 18 | 198 |
| 16 | Kentish Agencies | | K22 | | 410 | Insurance | 41 | 451 |
| 24 | D Jeffrey | | 442 | 240 | | | 24 | 264 |
| 30 | F Coyle | | 709 | 330 | | | 33 | 363 |
| | | | | $1 070 | $770 | | $184 | $2 024 |

3.12 This question is available on the CD that accompanies this text.

3.13 Post the following Sales Returns and Allowances Journal to the General Ledger for E Betts, used car dealer, at 31 July 2019. (Assume that the Accounts Receivable Control account had a balance of $21 300 at 1 July.)

A UWatch demonstration is available on the CD that accompanies this text for parts of this activity.

**E Betts**
**Sales Returns and Allowances Journal**

| Date | Debtor | Fol | Ref | Sales returns | Sundries Amount | Sundries Account | GST collected | Accounts receivable control |
|------|--------|-----|-----|---------------|--------|---------|---------------|-----------------------------|
| 2019 | | | | $ | $ | | $ | $ |
| 9 Jul | H Nolan | | 49 | 660 | | | 66 | 726 |
| 21 | S Pent | | 50 | 150 | | | 15 | 165 |
| | | | | $810 | | | $81 | $891 |

3.14 This question is available on the CD that accompanies this text.

3.15 Post the following Sales Returns and Allowances Journal to the General Ledger for Chapman's Wines and Spirits, liquor retailer, at 31 March 2016. (Assume the following ledger account balances at 1 March: Sales Returns and Allowances (Wines), $450; Sales Returns and Allowances (Spirits), $440; GST Collected, $1400; Accounts Receivable Control, $6900.)

**CHAPMAN'S WINES AND SPIRITS**
**Sales Returns and Allowances Journal**

| Date | Debtor | Fol | Ref | Wines | Spirits | Amount | Account | GST collected | Accounts receivable control |
|------|--------|-----|-----|-------|---------|--------|---------|---------------|-----------------------------|
| 2016 | | | | $ | $ | $ | | $ | $ |
| 7 Mar | P Galvin | | CR18 | 30 | 40 | | | 7 | 77 |
| 24 | B Horton | | CR19 | | 50 | | | 5 | 55 |
| | | | | $30 | $90 | | | $12 | $132 |

3.16 This question is available on the CD that accompanies this text.

3.17 Post the following Purchases Returns and Allowances Journal to the General Ledger for Billie's Pastry Shop at 31 July 2017 (Assume the following ledger account balances at 1 July: Accounts Payable Control $1100; Office Furniture $3500.)

A UWatch demonstration is available on the CD that accompanies this text for parts of this activity.

**BILLIE'S PASTRY SHOP**
**Purchases Returns and Allowances Journal**

| Date | Creditor | Fol | Ref | Purchases returns | | Sundries | | GST paid | Accounts payable control |
| | | | | Pies | Cakes | Amount | Account | | |
|---|---|---|---|---|---|---|---|---|---|
| 2017 | | | | $ | $ | $ | | $ | $ |
| 7 Jul | N Bourke | | 312 | | 20 | | | 2 | 22 |
| 20 | Betty's Patisserie | | 500 | 30 | | | | 3 | 33 |
| 25 | D Astbury | | CN21 | | | 150 | Office furniture | 15 | 165 |
| | | | | $30 | $20 | 150 | | $20 | $220 |

3.18 Describe (in point form) the procedure used when posting all journals to the General Ledger at the end of the month.

3.19* Bright Spark commenced business as a retailer of electrical goods on 1 July 2017. His journals for the first month's operations follow. You are required to post the journals to the General Ledger and to prepare a trial balance as at 31 July 2017. (Use of folios is optional.)

**Bright Spark**
**General Journal**

| Date | Particulars | Fol | Debit | Credit |
|---|---|---|---|---|
| 2017 | | | $ | $ |
| 1 Jul | Stock | | 3 000 | |
| | Cash at bank | | 100 000 | |
| | Premises | | 50 000 | |
| | Mortgage loan on premises | | | 40 000 |
| | Loan from B Burns | | | 20 000 |
| | Capital – B Spark | | | 93 000 |
| | *Assets and liabilities introduced by owner to commence business* | | | |
| 18 | Drawings – B Spark | | 440 | |
| | Purchases | | | 400 |
| | GST paid | | | 40 |
| | *Withdrawal of stock by the owner* | | | |

## Bright Spark
## Cash Receipts Journal

| Date | Particulars | Fol | Ref | Accounts receivable control | GST collected | Discount expense | Accounts receivable control | Cash sales | Amount | Account | GST collected | Bank |
|---|---|---|---|---|---|---|---|---|---|---|---|---|
| | | | | | Discount expense | | | | Sundries | | | |
| 2017 | | | | $ | $ | $ | $ | $ | $ | | $ | $ |
| 16 Jul | Sales | | POS | | | | | 2 200 | | | 220 | 2 420 |
| 26 | F Farrer | | 401 | 33 | 3 | 30 | 567 | | | | | 567 |
| 31 | Top Electrics | | EFT | | | | | | 200 | Commission income | 20 | 220 |
| | Sales | | POS | | | | | 4 400 | | | 440 | 4 840 |
| | | | | $33 | $3 | $30 | $567 | $6 600 | $200 | | $680 | $8 047 |

## Cash Payments Journal

| Date | Particulars | Fol | Ref | Accounts payable control | GST paid | Discount income | Accounts payable control | Cash purchases | Wages | Amount | Account | GST paid | Bank |
|---|---|---|---|---|---|---|---|---|---|---|---|---|---|
| | | | | | Discount income | | | | | Sundries | | | |
| 2017 | | | | $ | $ | $ | $ | $ | $ | $ | | $ | $ |
| 14 Jul | NBA | | EFT | | | | | | | 10 000 | Mortgage loan | | 10 000 |
| 17 | Tab Electrics | | 001 | | | | | 3 700 | | | | 370 | 4 070 |
| 24 | Wages | | EFT | | | | | | 800 | | | | 800 |
| 30 | Young & Co | | 002 | 110 | 10 | 100 | 3 900 | | | | | | 3 900 |
| | B Spark | | 003 | | | | | | | 100 | Drawings – B Spark | | 100 |
| 31 | S Tumpy | | 004 | | | | | | | 1 100 | Sales returns | | |
| | | | | | | | | | | 110 | GST collected | | 1 210 |
| | | | | $110 | $10 | $100 | $3 900 | $3 700 | $800 | $11 310 | | $370 | $20 080 |

### Sales Journal

| Date | Debtor | Fol | Ref | Sales | Sundries Amount | Sundries Account | GST collected | Accounts receivable control |
|---|---|---|---|---|---|---|---|---|
| 2017 | | | | $ | $ | | $ | $ |
| 16 Jul | F Farrer | | 301 | 1 100 | | | 110 | 1 210 |
| 19 | G Neale | | 302 | 650 | | | 65 | 715 |
| | H Brown | | 303 | 1 100 | | | 110 | 1 210 |
| 22 | S Walls | | 304 | | 450 | Sale of non-current assets | 45 | 495 |
| | | | | $2 850 | $450 | | $330 | $3 630 |

### Purchases Journal

| Date | Creditor | Fol | Ref | Purchases | Sundries Amount | Sundries Account | GST paid | Accounts payable control |
|---|---|---|---|---|---|---|---|---|
| 2017 | | | | $ | $ | | $ | $ |
| 15 Jul | Young & Co | | 15214 | 5 500 | | | 550 | 6 050 |
| | Hoon Ltd | | 600 | | 2 800 | Office equipment | 280 | 3 080 |
| 19 | Top Electrics | | P0516 | 4 500 | | | 450 | 4 950 |
| 20 | Bendigo Daily | | BD7051 | | 300 | Advertising | 30 | 330 |
| | | | | $10 000 | $3 100 | | $1 310 | $14 410 |

### Sales Returns and Allowances Journal

| Date | Debtor | Fol | Ref | Sales returns and allowances | Sundries Amount | Sundries Account | GST collected | Accounts receivable control |
|---|---|---|---|---|---|---|---|---|
| 2017 | | | | $ | $ | | $ | $ |
| 20 Jul | F Farrer | | 101 | 550 | | | 55 | 605 |
| | | | | $550 | | | $55 | $605 |

### Purchases Returns and Allowances Journal

| Date | Debtor | Fol | Ref | Purchases returns and allowances | Sundries Amount | Account | GST paid | Accounts payable control |
|------|--------|-----|-----|-----------|--------|---------|----------|----------|
| 2017 | | | | $ | $ | | $ | $ |
| 22 Jul | Young & Co | | 599 | 1 800 | | | 180 | 1 980 |
| | | | | $1 800 | | | $180 | $1 980 |

3.20 C Mackintosh is the owner of Mac's Cameras, a photographic equipment wholesaling business. The chart of accounts for the business is shown below, with a trial balance as at 1 January 2019, and all journals for the month of January 2019. You are required to:

a enter the balances from the trial balance in the General Ledger at 1 January

b post the journals to the ledger

c prepare a trial balance as at 31 January 2019.

### MAC'S CAMERAS
### Chart of accounts

| Assets | | Income | |
|--------|--------|--------|--------|
| A1 | Cash at bank | I1 | Sales |
| A2 | Accounts receivable control | I1A | Sales returns and allowances |
| A3 | Land and buildings | I2 | Interest income |
| A4 | Motor vehicles | I3 | Discount income |
| A5 | Stock | I4 | Late fees income |
| A6 | GST paid | I5 | Delivery income |

| Liabilities | | Expenses | |
|-------------|--------|----------|--------|
| L1 | Accounts payable control | E1 | Purchases |
| L2 | Mortgage loan | E1A | Purchases returns and allowances |
| L3 | GST collected | E2 | Discount expense |
| | | E3 | Wages |
| Owner's equity | | E4 | Insurance |
| OE1 | Capital – C Mackintosh | E5 | Bad debts |
| OE2 | Drawings – C Mackintosh | E6 | Repairs |
| | | E7 | Merchant fees expense |

Mac's Cameras
Trial balance as at 1 January 2019

| Account | | Debit | Credit |
|---|---|---:|---:|
| | | $ | $ |
| A1 | Cash at bank | 6 000 | |
| A2 | Accounts receivable control | 5 400 | |
| A3 | Land and buildings | 50 000 | |
| A4 | Motor vehicles | 14 500 | |
| A5 | Stock | 7 100 | |
| A6 | GST paid | 550 | |
| L1 | Accounts payable control | | 2 200 |
| L2 | Mortgage loan | | 45 000 |
| L3 | GST collected | | 1 200 |
| OE1 | Capital – C Mackintosh | | 36 350 |
| OE2 | Drawings – C Mackintosh | 2 400 | |
| I1 | Sales | | 21 000 |
| I1A | Sales returns and allowances | 900 | |
| I2 | Interest income | | 1 000 |
| I3 | Discount income | | 100 |
| E1 | Purchases | 12 700 | |
| E1A | Purchases returns and allowances | | 700 |
| E2 | Discount expense | 200 | |
| E3 | Wages | 6 000 | |
| E4 | Insurance | 150 | |
| E5 | Bad debts | 500 | |
| E6 | Repairs | 750 | |
| E7 | Merchant fees expense | 400 | |
| | | $107 550 | $107 550 |

## Journals for January

**Mac's Cameras**
**General Journal**

| Date | Particulars | Fol | Debit | Credit |
|------|-------------|-----|-------|--------|
| 2019 | | | $ | $ |
| 1 Jan | Accounts receivable control | | 20 | |
| |     Late fees income | | | 20 |
| | *Late payment accounting fee charged to D Rongo on overdue account* | | | |
| 10 | Drawings – C Mackintosh | | 330 | |
| |     Purchases | | | 300 |
| |     GST paid | | | 30 |
| | *Withdrawal of stock by owner* | | | |
| 31 | Bad debts | | 600 | |
| | GST collected | | 60 | |
| |     Accounts receivable control | | | 660 |
| | *Bad debt written off – D Rongo* | | | |

**Cash Receipts Journal**

| Date | Particulars | Fol | Ref | Discount expense — Accounts receivable control | GST collected | Discount expense | Accounts receivable control | Cash sales | Sundries — Amount | Account | GST collected | Bank |
|------|-------------|-----|-----|--------|--------|--------|--------|--------|--------|--------|--------|--------|
| 2019 | | | | $ | $ | $ | $ | $ | $ | | $ | $ |
| 4 Jan | EFTPOS sales | | POS | | | | | 400 | | | 40 | 440 |
| | Cash sales | | POS | | | | | 1 400 | | | 140 | 1 540 |
| 15 | American Express | | EFT | | | | | | | | | |
| | – Gross | | | | | | 515 | | | | | |
| | – Merchant fee | | | | | | | | (20) | Merchant fees expense | | |
| | – GST paid | | | | | | | | (2) | GST paid | | 493 |
| 16 | EFTPOS sales | | POS | | | | | 700 | | | 70 | 770 |
| | Cash sales | | POS | | | | | 1 700 | | | 170 | 1 870 |
| 26 | Cash sales | | POD | | | | | 1 800 | | | 180 | |
| | ABC Finance | | A36 | | | | | | 60 | Interest income | | 2 040 |
| | | | | | | | $515 | $6 000 | $38 | | $600 | $7 153 |

## Cash Payments Journal

| Date | Particulars | Fol | Ref | Discount income — Accounts payable control | GST paid | Discount income | Accounts payable control | Cash purchases | Wages | Sundries — Amount | Account | GST paid | Bank |
|---|---|---|---|---|---|---|---|---|---|---|---|---|---|
| 2019 | | | | $ | $ | $ | $ | $ | $ | $ | | $ | $ |
| 7 Jan | R Lamm | | 5125 | | | | | 520 | | | | 52 | 572 |
| 12 | Wages | | EFT | | | | | | 460 | | | | 460 |
| 19 | C Mackintosh | | 5126 | | | | | | | 100 | Drawings – C Mackintosh | | 100 |
| 21 | Fristo Manufacturing | | 5127 | 33 | 3 | 30 | 1 097 | | | | | | 1 097 |
| 28 | Insurers Ltd | | 5128 | | | | 165 | | | | | | 165 |
| | | | | $33 | $3 | $30 | $1 262 | $520 | $460 | $100 | | $52 | $2 394 |

## Sales Journal

| Date | Debtor | Fol | Ref | Sales | Sundries — Amount | Account | GST collected | Accounts receivable control |
|---|---|---|---|---|---|---|---|---|
| 2019 | | | | $ | $ | | $ | $ |
| 6 Jan | A Sainsbury | | M37 | 700 | | | 70 | 770 |
| 14 | M Robins | | M38 | 130 | | | 13 | 143 |
| 22 | M Hunter | | M39 | 190 | 30 | Delivery income | 22 | 242 |
| 26 | American Express | | POS | 300 | | | 30 | 330 |
| | | | | $1 320 | $30 | | $135 | $1 485 |

## Purchases Journal

| Date | Creditor | Fol | Ref | Purchases | Sundries — Amount | Account | GST paid | Accounts payable control |
|---|---|---|---|---|---|---|---|---|
| 2019 | | | | $ | $ | | $ | $ |
| 1 Jan | Photographics Ltd | | 97 | 370 | | | 37 | 407 |
| 28 | G Mannering | | 344 | 130 | | | 13 | 143 |
| | | | | $500 | | | $50 | $550 |

**Sales Returns and Allowances Journal**

| Date | Debtor | Fol | Ref | Sales returns and allowances | Sundries Amount | Sundries Account | GST collected | Accounts receivable control |
|------|--------|-----|-----|------------------------------|-----------------|------------------|---------------|------------------------------|
| 2019 | | | | $ | $ | | $ | $ |
| 17 Jan | M Robins | | MC83 | 60 | | | 6 | 66 |
| | | | | $60 | | | $6 | $66 |

**Purchases Returns and Allowances Journal**

| Date | Creditor | Fol | Ref | Purchases returns and allowances | Sundries Amount | Sundries Account | GST paid | Accounts payable control |
|------|----------|-----|-----|----------------------------------|-----------------|------------------|----------|--------------------------|
| 2019 | | | | $ | $ | | $ | $ |
| 2 Jan | Fristo Manufacturing | | C13F | 100 | | | 10 | 110 |
| 4 | Photographics Ltd | | C740 | 60 | | | 6 | 66 |
| | | | | $160 | | | $16 | $176 |

**3.21** Norm Schmidt is the owner of Schmidt's Electrical, an electrical goods wholesaling business. He provides you with the following information: the chart of accounts for the business, a trial balance as at 1 July 2017 and all journals for the month of July 2017. You are required to:

a  enter the balances from the trial balance in the General Ledger at 1 July

b  post the journals for July to the ledger

c  prepare a trial balance as at 31 July 2017.

| Schmidt's Electrical Chart of accounts | | | |
|------|------|------|------|
| **Assets** | | **Income** | |
| 001 | Cash at bank | 301 | Sales |
| 002 | Accounts receivable control | 302 | Sales returns and allowances |
| 003 | Stock | 303 | Commission income |
| 004 | Motor vehicles | 304 | Discount income |

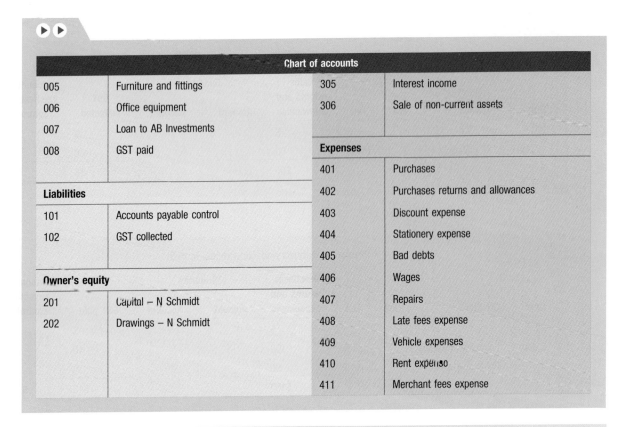

| Chart of accounts | | | |
|---|---|---|---|
| 005 | Furniture and fittings | 305 | Interest income |
| 006 | Office equipment | 306 | Sale of non-current assets |
| 007 | Loan to AB Investments | | |
| 008 | GST paid | **Expenses** | |
| | | 401 | Purchases |
| **Liabilities** | | 402 | Purchases returns and allowances |
| 101 | Accounts payable control | 403 | Discount expense |
| 102 | GST collected | 404 | Stationery expense |
| | | 405 | Bad debts |
| **Owner's equity** | | 406 | Wages |
| 201 | Capital – N Schmidt | 407 | Repairs |
| 202 | Drawings – N Schmidt | 408 | Late fees expense |
| | | 409 | Vehicle expenses |
| | | 410 | Rent expense |
| | | 411 | Merchant fees expense |

**Schmidt's Electrical**
**Trial balance as at 1 July 2017**

| Account | | Debit | Credit |
|---|---|---|---|
| | | $ | $ |
| 001 | Cash at bank | 11 300 | |
| 002 | Accounts receivable control | 3 000 | |
| 003 | Stock | 6 200 | |
| 004 | Motor vehicles | 12 500 | |
| 005 | Furniture and fittings | 2 800 | |
| 006 | Office equipment | 1 900 | |
| 007 | Loan to AB Investments | 6 000 | |
| 008 | GST paid | 600 | |
| 101 | Accounts payable control | | 2 700 |
| 102 | GST collected | | 2 000 |
| 201 | Capital – N Schmidt | | 39 600 |
| | | $44 300 | $44 300 |

## General Journal

| Date | Particulars | Fol | Debit | Credit |
|------|-------------|-----|-------|--------|
| 2017 | | | $ | $ |
| 8 July | Drawings – N Schmidt | | 110 | |
| |   Stationery expense | | | 100 |
| |   GST paid | | | 10 |
| | *Withdrawal of stationery by owner* | | | |
| | Drawings – N Schmidt | | 110 | |
| |   Purchases | | | 100 |
| |   GST paid | | | 10 |
| | *Withdrawal of stock by owner* | | | |
| 9 | Bad debts | | 1 300 | |
| | GST collected | | 130 | |
| |   Accounts receivable control | | | 1 430 |
| | *Bad debt written off – S Simpson* | | | |
| 30 | Stationery expense | | 90 | |
| |   Wages | | | 90 |
| | *Correction of error (June)* | | | |
| 31 | Late fees expense | | 10 | |
| |   Accounts payable control | | | 10 |
| | *Late fee charged by Electro Manufacturing* | | | |

## Cash Receipts Journal

| Date | Particulars | Fol | Ref | Discount expense: Accounts receivable control | GST collected | Discount expense | Accounts receivable control | Cash sales | Sundries: Amount | Account | GST collected | Bank |
|------|-------------|-----|-----|------|------|------|------|------|------|------|------|------|
| 2017 | | | | $ | $ | $ | $ | $ | $ | | $ | $ |
| 1 Jul | Sales | | POS | | | | | 600 | | | 60 | 660 |
| 4 | Sales | | POS | | | | | 700 | | | 70 | 770 |
| 9 | Sales | | POS | | | | | 800 | | | 80 | 880 |
| 14 | Diners Club | | EFT | | | | | | | | | |
| |   – Gross | | | | | | 682 | | | | | |
| |   – Merchant fees | | | | | | | | (20) | Merchant fees expense | | |
| |   – GST paid | | | | | | | | (2) | GST paid | | 660 |
| | Sales | | POS | | | | | 530 | | | 53 | 583 |
| 17 | AB Investments | | EFT | | | | | | 50 | Interest income | | 50 |
| 18 | Sales | | POS | | | | | 600 | | | 60 | 660 |
| 23 | Sales | | POS | | | | | 700 | | | 70 | |
| | Philllp Electrical | | R55 | 11 | 1 | 10 | 470 | | | | | 1 240 |
| | | | | $11 | $1 | $10 | $1 152 | $3 930 | $28 | | $393 | $5 503 |

## Schmidt's Electrical
## Cash Payments Journal

| Date | Particulars | Fol | Ref | Accounts payable control | GST paid | Discount income | Accounts payable control | Cash purchases | Wages | Amount | Account | GST paid | Bank |
|---|---|---|---|---|---|---|---|---|---|---|---|---|---|
| | | | | Discount income | | | | | | Sundries | | | |
| 2017 | | | | $ | $ | $ | $ | $ | $ | $ | | $ | $ |
| 2 Jul | Manulec Ltd | | 116 | | | | | 400 | | | | 40 | 440 |
| 7 | Jack's News | | 117 | | | | | | | 300 | Stationery expense | 30 | 330 |
| | Argo Ltd | | EFT | 22 | 2 | 20 | 453 | | | | | | 453 |
| 14 | Wages | | EFT | | | | | | 310 | | | | 310 |
| 28 | ATO | | EFT | | | | | | | 2 000 | GST paid | | |
| | | | | | | | | | | (600) | GST collected | | 1 400 |
| | | | | $22 | $2 | $20 | $453 | $400 | $310 | $1 700 | | $70 | $2 933 |

## Sales Journal

| Date | Debtor | Fol | Ref | Sales | Amount | Account | GST collected | Accounts receivable control |
|---|---|---|---|---|---|---|---|---|
| | | | | | Sundries | | | |
| 2017 | | | | $ | $ | | $ | $ |
| 4 Jul | Diners Club | | CRS | 430 | | | 43 | 473 |
| 17 | Phillip Electrical | | S107 | 700 | | | 70 | 770 |
| 22 | A Dargo | | S108 | | 300 | Sale of non-current assets | 30 | 330 |
| 28 | Watt Electrics | | S109 | 760 | | | 76 | 836 |
| | | | | $1 890 | $300 | | $219 | $2 409 |

### Purchases Journal

| Date | Creditor | Fol | Ref | Purchases | Sundries Amount | Sundries Account | GST paid | Accounts payable control |
|---|---|---|---|---|---|---|---|---|
| 2017 | | | | $ | $ | | $ | $ |
| 2 Jul | Fitto Co | | 08 | | 900 | Furniture and fittings | 90 | 990 |
| 17 | Argo Ltd | | TS300 | 400 | | | 40 | 440 |
| 19 | Electro Manufacturing | | 1411 | 650 | | | 65 | 715 |
| 23 | H Andyman | | HA107 | | 60 | Repairs | 6 | 66 |
| | | | | $1 050 | $960 | | $201 | $2 211 |

### Sales Returns and Allowances Journal

| Date | Debtor | Fol | Ref | Sales returns and allowances | Sundries Amount | Sundries Account | GST collected | Accounts receivable control |
|---|---|---|---|---|---|---|---|---|
| 2017 | | | | $ | $ | | $ | $ |
| 19 Jul | Phillip Electrical | | 403 | 150 | | | 15 | 165 |
| | | | | $150 | | | $15 | $165 |

### Purchases Returns and Allowances Journal

| Date | Creditor | Fol | Ref | Purchases returns and allowances | Sundries Amount | Sundries Account | GST paid | Accounts payable control |
|---|---|---|---|---|---|---|---|---|
| 2017 | | | | $ | $ | | $ | $ |
| 25 Jul | Electro Manufacturing | | 010 | 200 | | | 20 | 220 |
| | | | | $200 | | | $20 | $220 |

3.22 This question is available on the CD that accompanies this text.

ADDITIONAL EXERCISES

3.23 Laura Bangle commenced a wholesale dress distribution business on 1 May 2019. The information below relates to her first month's operations. You are required to:

a record the transactions for May 2019 in appropriately designed journals

b post the journals to the General Ledger

c prepare a trial balance as at 31 May 2019.

*Transactions for May 2019*

| | | |
|---|---|---|
| 1 May | Commenced business with the following assets and liabilities: cash, $8000; stock, $10 000; vehicle, $13 000; Loan from Witch Bank, $15 000. |
| | Purchased goods on credit from Dress Makers, $990 inc. GST (invoice T80). |
| 2 | Cash sales, $1650 inc. GST (POS). |
| 3 | Cash purchases from Smedts, $770 inc. GST (cheque 701). |
| 4 | Credit sales to J Garfoot, $880 inc. GST (invoice 001). |
| | Paid rent to Future Realty, $550 inc. GST (EFT). |
| 5 | Purchased furniture on credit from JK Co, $1320 inc. GST (invoice Z40). |
| | Returned goods to Dress Makers, $110 inc. GST (adjustment note 76). |
| 6 | Paid wages, $380 (EFT). |
| 9 | Received invoice no. 740 from TV Ads Co for goods, $660 inc. GST. |
| 10 | Owner withdrew $150 for her own use (EFT). |
| | Sent invoice no. 002 to T Westoff – Dress repairs, $440 inc. GST. |
| 13 | Returns from T Westoff – Goods, $55 inc. GST (adjustment note 101). |
| 16 | Cash sales, $1320 inc. GST (POS). |
| | Received $66 inc. GST commission from Kirsten Agents (EFT). |
| 17 | Paid creditor Dress Makers, $700. Discount received, $22 (cheque 702). |
| 19 | Owner withdrew stock costing $275 inc. GST for personal use. |
| 22 | Made repayment of $2000 on loan from Witch Bank (EFT). |
| 25 | Credit sales to F Rose, $1430 inc. GST (invoice 003). |
| 29 | Credit purchases from Skirt Ltd, $1100 inc. GST (invoice A432). |
| | Cash sales, $1980 inc. GST (POS). |
| 30 | Received $726 on account from J Garfoot. Discount allowed $33 (receipt 201). |
| 31 | Received invoice J61 from Free2Air for advertising, $275 inc. GST. |

# SOLUTIONS

3.4

| J Bartel | | | | | |
|---|---|---|---|---|---|
| **General Ledger** | | | | | |
| Date | Particulars | Fol | Debit | Credit | Balance |
| **Discount Expense Account** | | | | | |
| 2019 | | | $ | $ | $ |
| 1 Aug | Balance | | | | 50 Dr |
| 31 | Accounts receivable control | CRJ | 40 | | 90 Dr |

| General Ledger | | | | | |
|---|---|---|---|---|---|
| Date | Particulars | Fol | Debit | Credit | Balance |
| **Accounts Receivable Control Account** | | | | | |
| 2019 | | | $ | $ | $ |
| 1 Aug | Balance | | | | 11 300 Dr |
| 31 | Discount expense and GST collected | CRJ | | 44 | 11 256 Dr |
| | Cash at bank | CRJ | | 2 996 | 8 260 Dr |
| **Sales Account** | | | | | |
| 2019 | | | | | |
| 1 Aug | Balance | | | | 76 000 Cr |
| 31 | Cash at bank | CRJ | | 5 380 | 81 380 Cr |
| **Motor Vehicles Account** | | | | | |
| 2019 | | | | | |
| 1 Aug | Balance | | | | 11 000 Dr |
| **GST Collected Account** | | | | | |
| 2019 | | | | | |
| 1 Aug | Balance | | | | 7 600 Cr |
| 31 | Accounts receivable control | CRJ | 4 | | 7 596 Cr |
| | Accounts receivable control | CRJ | | 1 008 | 8 604 Cr |
| **Capital – J Bartel Account** | | | | | |
| 2019 | | | | | |
| 1 Aug | Balance | | | | 90 000 Cr |
| 21 | Cash at bank | CRJ | | 2 000 | 92 000 Cr |
| **Cash at Bank Account** | | | | | |
| 2019 | | | | | |
| 1 Aug | Balance | | | | 2 300 Dr |
| 31 | Sundry receipts | CRJ | 16 084 | | 18 384 Dr |
| **Commission Income Account** | | | | | |
| 2019 | | | | | |
| 10 Aug | Cash at bank | CRJ | | 100 | 100 Cr |
| **Sale of Non-Current Assets Account** | | | | | |
| 2019 | | | | | |
| 15 Aug | Cash at bank | CRJ | | 4 600 | 4 600 Cr |

3.19

| Bright Spark | | | | | |
|---|---|---|---|---|---|
| **General Ledger** | | | | | |
| Date | Particulars | Fol | Debit | Credit | Balance |
| **Stock Account** | | | | | |
| 2017 | | | $ | $ | $ |
| 1 Jul | Capital – B Spark | GJ | 3 000 | | 3 000 Dr |
| **Cash at Bank Account** | | | | | |
| 2017 | | | | | |
| 1 Jul | Capital – B Spark | GJ | 100 000 | | 100 000 Dr |
| 31 | Sundry receipts | CRJ | 8 047 | | 108 047 Dr |
| | Sundry payments | CPJ | | 20 080 | 87 967 Dr |
| **Premises Account** | | | | | |
| 2017 | | | | | |
| 1 Jul | Capital – B Spark | GJ | | | 50 000 Dr |
| **Mortgage Loan on Premises Account** | | | | | |
| 2017 | | | | | |
| 1 Jul | Capital – B Spark | GJ | | 40 000 | 40 000 Cr |
| 14 | Cash at bank | CPJ | 10 000 | | 30 000 Cr |
| **Loan from B Burns Account** | | | | | |
| 2017 | | | | | |
| 1 Jul | Capital – B Spark | GJ | | 20 000 | 20 000 Cr |
| **Capital – B Spark Account** | | | | | |
| 2017 | | | | | |
| 1 Jul | Sundries | GJ | | | 93 000 Cr |
| **Drawings – B Spark Account** | | | | | |
| 2017 | | | | | |
| 18 Jul | Purchases and GST paid | GJ | 440 | | 440 Dr |
| 30 | Cash at bank | CPJ | 100 | | 540 Dr |
| **Purchases Account** | | | | | |
| 2017 | | | | | |
| 18 Jul | Drawings – B Spark | GJ | | 400 | 400 Cr |
| 31 | Cash at bank | CPJ | 3 700 | | 3 300 Dr |
| | Accounts payable control | PJ | 10 000 | | 13 300 Dr |

| | General Ledger | | | | |
|---|---|---|---|---|---|
| Date | Particulars | Fol | Debit | Credit | Balance |
| | **GST Paid Account** | | | | |
| 2017 | | | $ | $ | $ |
| 18 | Drawings – B Spark | GJ | | 40 | 40 Cr |
| 31 | Accounts payable control | CPJ | | 10 | 50 Cr |
| | Cash at bank | CPJ | 370 | | 320 Dr |
| | Accounts payable control | PJ | 1 310 | | 1 630 Dr |
| | Accounts payable control | PRJ | | 180 | 1 450 Dr |
| | **Accounts Receivable Control Account** | | | | |
| 2017 | | | | | |
| 31 Jul | Discount expense and GST collected | CRJ | | 33 | 33 Cr |
| | Cash at bank | CRJ | | 567 | 600 Cr |
| | Sales and GST collected | SJ | 3 630 | | 3 030 Dr |
| | Sales returns and GST collected | SRJ | | 605 | 2 425 Dr |
| | **GST Collected Account** | | | | |
| 2017 | | | | | |
| 31 Jul | Accounts receivable control | CRJ | 3 | | 3 Dr |
| | Cash at bank | CRJ | | 680 | 677 Cr |
| | Cash at bank | CPJ | 110 | | 567 Cr |
| | Accounts receivable control | SJ | | 330 | 897 Cr |
| | Accounts receivable control | SRJ | 55 | | 842 Cr |
| | **Discount Expense Account** | | | | |
| 2017 | | | | | |
| 31 Jul | Accounts receivable control | CRJ | 30 | | 30 Dr |
| | **Sales Account** | | | | |
| 2017 | | | | | |
| 31 Jul | Cash at bank | CRJ | | 6 600 | 6 600 Cr |
| | Accounts receivable control | SJ | | 2 850 | 9 450 Cr |
| | **Commission Income Account** | | | | |
| 2017 | | | | | |
| 31 Jul | Cash at bank | CRJ | | 200 | 200 Cr |

| General Ledger | | | | | |
|---|---|---|---|---|---|
| Date | Particulars | Fol | Debit | Credit | Balance |
| **Accounts Payable Control Account** | | | | | |
| 2017 | | | $ | $ | $ |
| 31 Jul | Discount income and GST paid | CPJ | 110 | | 110 Dr |
| | Cash at bank | CPJ | 3 900 | | 4 010 Dr |
| | Purchases and GST paid | PJ | | 14 410 | 10 400 Cr |
| | Purchases returns and GST paid | PRJ | 1 980 | | 8 420 Cr |
| **Discount Income Account** | | | | | |
| 2017 | | | | | |
| 31 Jul | Accounts payable control | CPJ | | 100 | 100 Cr |
| **Wages Account** | | | | | |
| 2017 | | | | | |
| 31 Jul | Cash at bank | CPJ | 800 | | 800 Dr |
| **Sales Returns and Allowances Account** | | | | | |
| 2017 | | | | | |
| 31 Jul | Cash at bank | CPJ | 1 100 | | 1 100 Dr |
| | Accounts receivable control | SRJ | 550 | | 1 650 Dr |
| **Sale of Non-Current Assets Account** | | | | | |
| 2017 | | | | | |
| 22 Jul | Cash at bank | SJ | | 450 | 450 Cr |
| **Office Equipment Account** | | | | | |
| 2017 | | | | | |
| 15 Jul | Accounts payable control | PJ | 2 800 | | 2 800 Dr |
| **Advertising Account** | | | | | |
| 2017 | | | | | |
| 20 Jul | Accounts payable control | PJ | 300 | | 300 Dr |
| **Purchases Returns and Allowances Account** | | | | | |
| 2017 | | | | | |
| 31 Jul | Accounts payable control | PRJ | | 1 800 | 1 800 Cr |

**Bright Spark**
**Trial balance as at 31 July 2017**

| Account | Debit | Credit |
|---|---|---|
| | $ | $ |
| Stock | 3 000 | |
| Cash at bank | 87 967 | |
| Premises | 50 000 | |
| Mortgage on premises | | 30 000 |
| Loan from B Burns | | 20 000 |
| Capital – B Spark | | 93 000 |
| Drawings – B Spark | 540 | |
| Purchases | 13 300 | |
| GST paid | 1 450 | |
| Accounts receivable control | 2 425 | |
| GST collected | | 842 |
| Discount expense | 30 | |
| Sales | | 9 450 |
| Commission income | | 200 |
| Accounts payable control | | 8 420 |
| Discount income | | 100 |
| Wages | 800 | |
| Sales returns and allowances | 1 650 | |
| Sale of non-current assets | | 450 |
| Office equipment | 2 800 | |
| Advertising | 300 | |
| Purchases returns and allowances | | 1 800 |
| | 164 262 | 164 262 |

# Posting procedure – service businesses

The procedure for posting the journals of a service business is basically the same as for a wholesale/retail business. Service businesses use a different range of journals, with different headings to those of wholesale/retail businesses, but this does not alter the posting process significantly.

To illustrate the posting process for a service business, we will continue with the example for Theresa Green, gardener and odd-job person, as shown in Chapter 2 (page 200).

## Example

The following are the completed journals of Theresa Green, gardener and odd-job person, for the month of May 2019. You are required to:

1 post the journals to the General Ledger at 31 May

2 prepare a trial balance as at 31 May.

Ledger posting rules have been included in journal headings for illustration purposes and, for simplicity, ledger account numbers (folios) have been omitted.

**Theresa Green**
**General Journal**

| Date | Particulars | Fol | Debit | Credit |
|------|-------------|-----|-------|--------|
| 2019 | | | $ | $ |
| 2 May | Motor vehicle | | 6 000 | |
| |     Capital – T Green | | | 6 000 |
| | *Motor vehicle contributed by owner* | | | |
| 10 | Tip fees expense | | 10 | |
| | GST paid | | 1 | |
| |     Capital – T Green | | | 11 |
| | *Tip fees paid by owner* | | | |
| 11 | Drawings – T Green | | 22 | |
| |     Purchases – petrol and oil | | | 20 |
| |     GST paid | | | 2 |
| | *Withdrawal of petrol by owner for personal use (memo 1)* | | | |
| 16 | Service fees – lawnmowing | | 10 | |
| | GST collected | | 1 | |
| |     Accounts receivable control | | | 11 |
| | *Allowance to A Phillip (credit note 001)* | | | |
| 23 | Accounts payable control | | 22 | |
| |     Purchases – petrol and oil | | | 20 |
| |     GST paid | | | 2 |
| | *Return of oil to Acme Co (credit note 149)* | | | |

**Theresa Green**
**Cash Receipts Journal**

| Date | Particulars | Fol | Ref | Discount expense — Accounts receivable control Cr $ | Discount expense — GST collected Dr $ | Discount expense Dr $ | Accounts receivable control Cr $ | Cash services — Lawns Cr $ | Cash services — Odd jobs Cr $ | Sundries — Amount Cr $ | Sundries — Account | GST collected Cr $ | Bank Dr $ |
|---|---|---|---|---|---|---|---|---|---|---|---|---|---|
| 2019 | | | | | | | | | | | | | |
| 1 May | T Green | | EFT | | | | | | | 5 000 | Capital – T Green | | 5 000 |
| 6 | T Perry | | 001 | | | | | 200 | | | | 20 | 220 |
| 11 | T Railer | | 002 | | | | | | 60 | | | 6 | 66 |
| 12 | J Brumby | | EFT | | | | | 200 | | | | 20 | 220 |
| 20 | J Lenders | | 003 | | | | | 60 | | | | 6 | 66 |
| 21 | J Cook | | 004 | 11 | 1 | 10 | 69 | | | | | | 69 |
| | A Bennett | | 005 | | | | | | 40 | | | 4 | 44 |
| 23 | W Bass | | EFT | | | | 33 | | | | | | 33 |
| | | | | $11 | $1 | $10 | $102 | $460 | $100 | $5 000 | | $56 | $5 718 |

**Theresa Green**
**Cash Payments Journal**

| Date | Particulars | Fol | Ref | Discount income Accounts payable control Dr $ | GST paid Cr $ | Discount income Cr $ | Accounts payable control Dr $ | Advertising Dr $ | Wages Dr $ | Tip fees expense Dr $ | Sundries Amount Dr $ | Sundries Account | GST paid Dr $ | Bank Cr $ |
|---|---|---|---|---|---|---|---|---|---|---|---|---|---|---|
| 2019 3 May | Lawn Pro | | 500 | | | | | | | | 800 | Lawn mowers | 80 | 880 |
| 4 | Tool Co | | 501 | | | | | | | | 140 | Tools | 14 | 154 |
| 6 | Ace News | | 502 | | | | | 50 | | | | | 5 | 55 |
| | Wages | | EFT | | | | | | 50 | | | | | 50 |
| 12 | Wages | | EFT | | | | | | 60 | | | | | 60 |
| 13 | Environmental Services | | 503 | | | | | | | 10 | | | 1 | 11 |
| | Ace News | | EFT | | | | | 50 | | | | | 5 | 55 |
| 14 | M Ellis | | 504 | | | | | | | | 70 | Motor vehicle repairs | 7 | 77 |
| | Lawn Pro | | 505 | | | | | | | | 30 | Mower repairs | 3 | 33 |
| 23 | Good Oil Co | | 506 | | | | 110 | | | | | | | 110 |
| | Ace News | | 507 | | | | | 50 | | | | | 5 | 55 |
| 28 | Wages | | EFT | | | | | | 20 | | | | | 20 |
| 30 | Environmental Services | | 508 | | | | | | | 10 | | | 1 | 11 |
| | | | | | | | $110 | $150 | $130 | $20 | $1 040 | | $121 | $1 571 |

### Sales and Services Journal

| Date | Debtor | Fol | Ref | Services Lawns | Services Odd jobs | Sundries Amount | Sundries Account | GST collected | Accounts receivable control |
|------|--------|-----|-----|-------|----------|--------|---------|----------------|-----------------------------|
| | | | | Cr | Cr | Cr | | Cr | Dr |
| 2019 | | | | $ | $ | $ | | $ | $ |
| 10 May | J Cook | | 101 | 80 | | | | 8 | 88 |
| 15 | A Phillip | | 102 | 30 | | | | 3 | 33 |
| 21 | W Bass | | 103 | 40 | | | | 4 | 44 |
| 30 | AMEX | | 104 | | 140 | | | 14 | 154 |
| 31 | G Piercy | | 105 | | | 100 | Sale of asset | 10 | 110 |
| | | | | $150 | $140 | $100 | | $39 | $429 |

### Purchases and Supplies Journal

| Date | Creditor | Fol | Ref | Petrol and oil | Sundries Amount | Sundries Account | GST paid | Accounts payable control |
|------|----------|-----|-----|----------------|--------|---------|----------|--------------------------|
| | | | | Dr | Dr | | Dr | Cr |
| 2019 | | | | $ | $ | | $ | $ |
| 3 May | Excel Trailers | | 213 | | 820 | Trailer | 82 | 902 |
| 4 | Mastercard | | 964 | 100 | | | 10 | 110 |
| 8 | Motor Reg | | 7865 | | 400 | Registration and insurance | 40 | 440 |
| 22 | Visa | | 46 | 100 | | | 10 | 110 |
| | | | | $200 | $1 220 | | $142 | $1 562 |

## Solution

1   The General Ledger for Theresa Green at 31 May after the journals have been posted is shown below.

### Theresa Green
### General Ledger

| Date | Particulars | Fol | Debit | Credit | Balance |
|------|-------------|-----|-------|--------|---------|
| **Motor Vehicle Account** | | | | | |
| 2019 | | | $ | $ | $ |
| 2 May | Capital – T Green | GJ | 6 000 | | 6 000 Dr |

| General Ledger | | | | | |
|---|---|---|---|---|---|
| Date | Particulars | Fol | Debit | Credit | Balance |
| **Capital – T Green Account** | | | | | |
| 2019 | | | $ | $ | $ |
| 1 May | Cash at bank | CRJ | | 5 000 | 5 000 Cr |
| 2 | Motor vehicle | GJ | | 6 000 | 11 000 Cr |
| 10 | Tip fees expense and GST paid | GJ | | 11 | 11 011 Cr |
| **Tip Fees Expense Account** | | | | | |
| 2019 | | | | | |
| 10 May | Capital – T Green | GJ | 10 | | 10 Dr |
| 31 | Cash at bank | CPJ | 20 | | 30 Dr |
| **GST Paid Account** | | | | | |
| 2019 | | | | | |
| 10 May | Capital – T Green | GJ | 1 | | 1 Dr |
| 11 | Drawings – T Green | GJ | | 2 | 1 Cr |
| 23 | Accounts payable control | GJ | | 2 | 3 Cr |
| 31 | Cash at bank | CPJ | 121 | | 118 Dr |
| | Accounts payable control | PSJ | 142 | | 260 Dr |
| **Drawings – T Green Account** | | | | | |
| 2019 | | | | | |
| 11 May | Purchases – petrol and oil and GST paid | GJ | 22 | | 22 Dr |
| **Purchases – Petrol and Oil Account** | | | | | |
| 2019 | | | | | |
| 11 May | Drawings – T Green | GJ | | 20 | 20 Cr |
| 23 | Accounts payable control | GJ | | 20 | 40 Cr |
| 31 | Accounts payable control | PSJ | 200 | | 160 Dr |
| **Service Fees – Lawn Mowing Account** | | | | | |
| 2019 | | | | | |
| 16 May | Accounts receivable control | GJ | 10 | | 10 Dr |
| 31 | Cash at bank | CRJ | | 460 | 450 Cr |
| | Accounts receivable control | SSJ | | 150 | 600 Cr |

| General Ledger | | | | | |
|---|---|---|---|---|---|
| Date | Particulars | Fol | Debit | Credit | Balance |
| **GST Collected Account** | | | | | |
| 2019 | | | $ | $ | $ |
| 16 May | Accounts receivable control | GJ | 1 | | 1 Dr |
| 31 | Accounts receivable control | CRJ | 2 | | 3 Dr |
| | Cash at bank | CRJ | | 56 | 53 Cr |
| | Accounts receivable control | SSJ | | 39 | 92 Cr |
| **Accounts Receivable Control Account** | | | | | |
| 2019 | | | | | |
| 16 May | Sales and GST collected | GJ | | 11 | 11 Cr |
| 31 | Discount expense and GST collected | CRJ | | 22 | 33 Cr |
| | Cash at bank | CRJ | | 102 | 135 Cr |
| | Sales, services and GST collected | SSJ | 429 | | 294 Dr |
| **Accounts Payable Control Account** | | | | | |
| 2019 | | | | | |
| 23 May | Purchases and GST paid | GJ | 22 | | 22 Dr |
| 31 | Cash at bank | CPJ | 110 | | 132 Dr |
| | Purchases, supplies and GST paid | PSJ | | 1 562 | 1 430 Cr |
| **Discount Expense Account** | | | | | |
| 2019 | | | | | |
| 31 May | Accounts receivable control | CRJ | 20 | | 20 Dr |
| **Service Fees – Odd Jobs Account** | | | | | |
| 2019 | | | | | |
| 31 May | Cash at bank | CRJ | | 100 | 100 Cr |
| | Accounts receivable control | SSJ | | 140 | 240 Cr |
| **Cash at Bank Account** | | | | | |
| 2019 | | | | | |
| 31 May | Sundry receipts | CRJ | 5 718 | | 5 718 Dr |
| | Sundry payments | CPJ | | 1 571 | 4 147 Dr |

| Date | Particulars | Fol | Debit | Credit | Balance |
|------|-------------|-----|-------|--------|---------|
| | | | | | |
| | | **General Ledger** | | | |
| | | **Advertising Account** | | | |
| 2019 | | | $ | $ | $ |
| 31 May | Cash at bank | CPJ | 150 | | 150 Dr |
| | | **Wages Account** | | | |
| 2019 | | | | | |
| 31 May | Cash at bank | CPJ | 130 | | 130 Dr |
| | | **Lawnmowers Account** | | | |
| 2019 | | | | | |
| 3 May | Cash at bank | CPJ | 800 | | 800 Dr |
| | | **Tools Account** | | | |
| 2019 | | | | | |
| 4 May | Cash at bank | CPJ | 140 | | 140 Dr |
| | | **Motor Vehicle Repairs Account** | | | |
| 2019 | | | | | |
| 14 May | Cash at bank | CPJ | 70 | | 70 Dr |
| | | **Mower Repairs Account** | | | |
| 2019 | | | | | |
| 14 May | Cash at bank | CPJ | 30 | | 30 Dr |
| | | **Sale of Non-current Assets Account** | | | |
| 2019 | | | | | |
| 31 May | Accounts receivable control | SSJ | | 100 | 100 Cr |
| | | **Trailer Account** | | | |
| 2019 | | | | | |
| 3 May | Accounts payable control | PSJ | 820 | | 820 Dr |
| | | **Registration and Insurance Account** | | | |
| 2019 | | | | | |
| 8 May | Accounts payable control | PSJ | 400 | | 400 Dr |

2 The trial balance for Theresa Green:

| Theresa Green Trial balance as at 31 July 2019 | | |
|---|---|---|
| **Account** | **Debit** | **Credit** |
| | $ | $ |
| Motor vehicle | 6 000 | |
| Capital – T Green | | 11 011 |
| Tip fees expense | 30 | |
| GST paid | 260 | |
| Drawings – T Green | 22 | |
| Purchases – petrol and oil | 160 | |
| Service fees – lawnmowing | | 600 |
| GST collected | | 92 |
| Accounts receivable control | 294 | |
| Accounts payable control | | 1 430 |
| Discount expense | 20 | |
| Service fees – odd jobs | | 240 |
| Cash at bank | 4 147 | |
| Advertising | 150 | |
| Wages | 130 | |
| Lawnmowers | 800 | |
| Tools | 140 | |
| Motor vehicle repairs | 70 | |
| Mower repairs | 30 | |
| Sale of asset | | 100 |
| Trailer | 820 | |
| Registration and insurance | 400 | |
| | 13 473 | 13 473 |

 **EXERCISES**

**3.24** The following are the completed journals for May 2016 for the business of I Drill, metal fabricator. You are required to:

a post the journals to the General Ledger at 31 May

b prepare a trial balance as at 31 May.

**I Drill**
**General Journal**

| Date | Particulars | Fol | Debit | Credit |
|---|---|---|---|---|
| 2016 | | | $ | $ |
| 26 May | Drawings – I Drill | | 110 | |
| | Supplies | | | 100 |
| | GST paid | | | 10 |
| | Gave supplies to a friend (memo 10) | | | |

**I Drill**
**Cash Receipts Journal**

| Date | Particulars | Fol | Ref | Accounts receivable control | Cash services | Sundries Amount | Account | GST collected | Bank |
|---|---|---|---|---|---|---|---|---|---|
| 2016 | | | | $ | $ | $ | | $ | $ |
| 10 May | I Drill | | EFT | | | 50 000 | Capital – I Drill | | 50 000 |
| 18 | F Reid | | POS | | 800 | | | 80 | 880 |
| 20 | L Callinan | | POS | | 900 | | | 90 | 990 |
| 21 | J Bartley | | 001 | 66 | | | | | 66 |
| 22 | J Esnouf | | POS | | 800 | | | 80 | 880 |
| 27 | W Conn | | EFT | 100 | | | | | 100 |
| | P Edwards | | POS | | 600 | | | 60 | 660 |
| | | | | $166 | $3 100 | $50 000 | | $310 | $53 576 |

**I Drill**
**Cash Payments Journal**

| Date | Particulars | Fol | Ref | Supplies | Wages | Repairs | Sundries Amount | Account | GST paid | Bank |
|---|---|---|---|---|---|---|---|---|---|---|
| 2016 | | | | $ | $ | $ | $ | | $ | $ |
| 13 May | ABC Finance | | 701 | | | | 950 | Lease – premises | 95 | 1 045 |
| 14 | Equip Co | | 702 | | | | 23 000 | Equipment | 2 300 | 25 300 |
| 15 | Damian Ltd | | 703 | 4 400 | | | | | 440 | 4 840 |

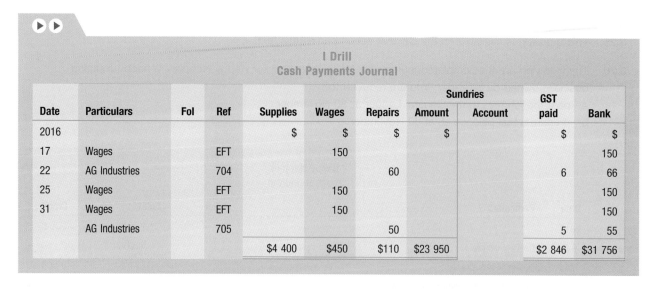

**I Drill**
**Cash Payments Journal**

| Date | Particulars | Fol | Ref | Supplies | Wages | Repairs | Sundries Amount | Sundries Account | GST paid | Bank |
|------|------------|-----|-----|----------|-------|---------|--------|---------|----------|------|
| 2016 | | | | $ | $ | $ | $ | | $ | $ |
| 17 | Wages | | EFT | | 150 | | | | | 150 |
| 22 | AG Industries | | 704 | | | 60 | | | 6 | 66 |
| 25 | Wages | | EFT | | 150 | | | | | 150 |
| 31 | Wages | | EFT | | 150 | | | | | 150 |
| | AG Industries | | 705 | | | 50 | | | 5 | 55 |
| | | | | $4 400 | $450 | $110 | $23 950 | | $2 846 | $31 756 |

**Sales and Services Journal**

| Date | Debtor | Fol | Ref | Services | Sundries Amount | Sundries Account | GST collected | Accounts receivable control |
|------|--------|-----|-----|----------|--------|---------|-----|---------|
| 2016 | | | | $ | | | $ | $ |
| 19 May | J Bartley | | 1 | 60 | | | 6 | 66 |
| | W Conn | | 2 | 400 | | | 40 | 440 |
| 26 | C Stubbs | | 3 | 70 | | | 7 | 77 |
| | Diners Club | | POS | 50 | | | 5 | 55 |
| | | | | $580 | | | $58 | $638 |

**Purchases and Supplies Journal**

| Date | Creditor | Fol | Ref | Supplies | Sundries Amount | Sundries Account | GST paid | Accounts payable control |
|------|----------|-----|-----|----------|--------|---------|----------|---------|
| 2016 | | | | $ | $ | | $ | $ |
| 16 May | Mal's Furniture | | 8624 | | 1 400 | Furniture | 140 | 1 540 |
| 21 | Trade Insurance | | T1741 | | 600 | Insurance | 60 | 660 |
| 22 | AMEX | | 387 | 200 | | | 20 | 220 |
| | | | | $200 | $2 000 | | $220 | $2 420 |

ADDITIONAL EXERCISES

**3.25**  This question is available on the CD that accompanies this text.

**3.26**  The following are the completed journals for November 2017 for Happy Nappies, a nappy cleaning business owned by S Craper. You are required to:

a  post the journals to the General Ledger at 30 November

b  prepare a trial balance as at 30 November.

**Happy Nappies**
**General Journal**

| Date | Particulars | Fol | Debit | Credit |
|---|---|---|---|---|
| 2017 | | | $ | $ |
| 9 Nov | Delivery vehicle | | 8 000 | |
| | Capital – S Craper | | | 8 000 |
| | *Delivery vehicle contributed by owner* | | | |
| 21 | Drawings – S Craper | | 110 | |
| | Purchases – chemicals | | | 100 |
| | GST paid | | | 10 |
| | *Gave chemicals to a friend* | | | |
| | Advertising | | 90 | |
| | GST paid | | 9 | |
| | Capital – S Craper | | | 99 |
| | *Payment of business expense by owner* | | | |
| 29 | Nappy cleaning income | | 20 | |
| | GST collected | | 2 | |
| | Accounts receivable control | | | 22 |
| | *Allowance to L Rose for stained nappies (adjustment note 001)* | | | |
| 30 | Accounts payable control | | 110 | |
| | Purchases – chemicals | | | 100 |
| | GST paid | | | 10 |
| | *Return of chemicals to Nifty Chemicals (adjustment note 1946)* | | | |

**Sales and Services Journal**

| Date | Debtor | Fol | Ref | Nappy cleaning income | Sundries Amount | Sundries Account | GST collected | Accounts receivable control |
|---|---|---|---|---|---|---|---|---|
| 2017 | | | | $ | $ | | $ | $ |
| 13 Nov | H Cha | | 001 | 80 | | | 8 | 88 |
| 17 | L Rose | | 002 | 60 | | | 6 | 66 |
| | F Ansen | | 003 | 90 | | | 9 | 99 |

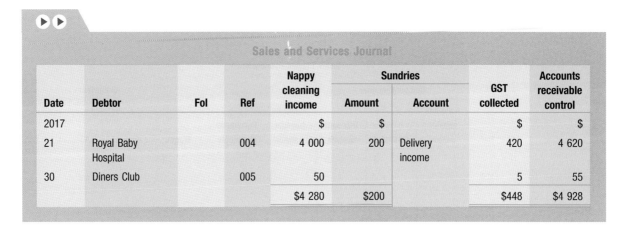

### Sales and Services Journal

| Date | Debtor | Fol | Ref | Nappy cleaning income | Sundries Amount | Sundries Account | GST collected | Accounts receivable control |
|------|--------|-----|-----|------|--------|---------|--------|--------|
| 2017 | | | | $ | $ | | $ | $ |
| 21 | Royal Baby Hospital | | 004 | 4 000 | 200 | Delivery income | 420 | 4 620 |
| 30 | Diners Club | | 005 | 50 | | | 5 | 55 |
| | | | | $4 280 | $200 | | $448 | $4 928 |

### Purchases and Supplies Journal

| Date | Creditor | Fol | Ref | Purchases–chemicals | Sundries Amount | Sundries Account | GST paid | Accounts payable control |
|------|----------|-----|-----|------|--------|---------|--------|--------|
| 2017 | | | | $ | $ | | $ | $ |
| 6 Nov | Dandy Machines | | 8946 | | 3 200 | Washing machines | 320 | 3 520 |
| | Chem Co | | CC1017 | 2 000 | | | 200 | 2 200 |
| 11 | AA Chemicals | | 428 | 100 | | | 10 | 110 |
| 29 | Nifty Chemicals | | 80 | 600 | | | 60 | 660 |
| 30 | Fix It Co | | F094 | | 400 | Washing machine repairs | 40 | 440 |
| | | | | $2 700 | $3 600 | | $630 | $ 6 930 |

### Cash Receipts Journal

| Date | Particulars | Fol | Ref | Discount expense — Accounts receivable control | Discount expense — GST collected | Discount expense | Accounts receivable control | Nappy cleaning income | Sundries Amount | Sundries Account | GST collected | Bank |
|------|-------------|-----|-----|------|------|------|------|------|------|------|------|------|
| 2017 | | | | $ | $ | $ | $ | $ | $ | | $ | $ |
| 1 Nov | S Craper | | EFT | | | | | | 10 000 | S Craper | | 10 000 |
| 14 | G Lewis | | 001 | | | | | 50 | | | 5 | 55 |
| 23 | T Fraser | | EFT | | | | | 80 | | | 8 | 88 |
| 26 | J Bloom | | 002 | | | | | 90 | | | 9 | 99 |
| | H Cha | | 003 | | | | 88 | | | | | 187 |
| | | | | | | | $88 | $220 | $10 000 | | $22 | $10 330 |

**Happy Nappies**
**Cash Payments Journal**

| Date | Particulars | Fol | Ref | Discount income | | | Accounts payable control | Purchases chemicals | Wages | Sundries | | | Bank |
|---|---|---|---|---|---|---|---|---|---|---|---|---|---|
| | | | | Accounts payable control | GST paid | Discount income | | | | Amount | Account | GST paid | |
| 2017 | | | | $ | $ | $ | $ | $ | $ | $ | | $ | $ |
| 3 Nov | A Robbins | | EFT | | | | | | | 200 | Rent expense | 20 | 220 |
| 7 | AB Insurance | | 801 | | | | 440 | | | | | | 440 |
| 13 | Bell Agencies | | 802 | | | | | | | 90 | Advertising | 9 | 99 |
| 15 | Wages | | EFT | | | | | | 90 | | | | 90 |
| | Max Motors | | 803 | | | | | | | 350 | Motor vehicle repairs | 35 | 385 |
| 21 | Andy's News | | 804 | | | | | | | 80 | Stationery | 8 | 88 |
| 23 | AA Chemicals | | 805 | | | | 110 | | | | | | 110 |
| | Wages | | EFT | | | | | | 90 | | | | 90 |
| | | | | | | | $550 | | $180 | $720 | | $72 | $1 522 |

# Cash basis versus accruals basis of accounting for GST

GST may be accounted for on either a cash or an accruals basis, depending on the annual turnover (or sales) of the business.

Under the *cash basis*, GST collected is attributable to the tax period in which the money is received from the customer. For example, suppose goods are sold in September 2018 and the customer settles the account on 7 October 2018. The GST component of the sale would be treated as relating to the quarter ending 31 December 2018 (assuming quarterly tax periods). Similarly, input tax credits (GST paid) are claimed in the tax period in which the payment is made to the supplier.

Under the *accruals basis*, GST collected is attributable to the tax period in which the earlier of the following occurs.

- Any of the proceeds of the sale (other than a deposit or a lay-by instalment) are received from the customer
- An invoice is issued to the customer

In the example in the previous paragraph, the GST component of the sale would be attributed to the quarter ending 30 September 2018.

Input tax credits (GST paid) are claimed in the tax period in which the earlier of the following occurs.

- Any payment (other than a deposit or a lay-by instalment) is paid to the supplier
- An invoice is issued by the supplier

A business with an annual turnover (sales) of $2 million or less may account for GST on either a cash or an accruals basis. Businesses with turnover exceeding the $2 million threshold must account for GST on an accruals basis unless permission is obtained from the ATO to adopt the cash basis.

The method of accounting for GST adopted in this book is the accruals method. If the cash basis of accounting for GST was adopted, a number of changes would be necessary to the way in which transactions involving GST are recorded in the journals of the business. These are summarised in Figure 3.9.

**Figure 3.9    Methods of accounting for GST**

| Journal | Changes in method of recording under cash basis of accounting for GST |
| --- | --- |
| Sales (or Sales and Services) Journal | No GST recorded at the time of sale. |
| Sales Returns and Allowances Journal | No GST adjustment recorded at the time the goods are returned or the allowance is granted. |
| Cash Receipts Journal | GST recorded when the account is settled by the debtor. GST continues to be charged on cash sales. |
| Purchases and Supplies Journal | Input tax credit not recorded at the time of purchase. |
| Purchases Returns and Allowances Journal | Input tax credit adjustment not recorded at the time the goods are returned or the allowance is given. |
| Cash Payments Journal | Input tax credit recorded when payment is made to the creditor. Input tax credits continue to be recorded on cash purchases and payments of expenses. |

It should be noted that, apart from the brief explanations provided above, a detailed discussion covering the cash basis of accounting for GST purposes is beyond the scope of this text.

# Summary

What have you covered in this chapter?

◆ Posting a variety of entries that are made from the following journals to the General Ledger for a wholesale/retail business
  - Cash Receipts Journal
  - Cash Payments Journal
  - Sales Journal
  - Sales Returns and Allowances Journal
  - Purchases Journal
  - Purchases Returns and Allowances Journal
  - General Journal

◆ Extracting an accurate trial balance of the General Ledger after the entries have been posted

◆ Posting entries from the journals of a service business to the General Ledger

# 4

# CONTROL OVER ACCOUNTS RECEIVABLE AND ACCOUNTS PAYABLE

## Learning objectives

Upon satisfactory completion of this chapter you should be able to:

- explain the purpose of subsidiary ledgers
- post the entries from the following journals to the Accounts Receivable and Accounts Payable ledgers as applicable, maintaining the accounting equation:
  - Cash Receipts Journal
  - Cash Payments Journal
  - Sales Journal
  - Sales Returns and Allowances Journal
  - Purchases Journal
  - Purchases Returns and Allowances Journal
  - General Journal
- prepare a list of debtors' balances and reconcile with the General Ledger control account
- prepare a list of creditors' balances and reconcile with the General Ledger control account
- explain internal controls that should exist over accounts receivable and accounts payable.

# Internal control over accounts receivable and accounts payable

As debtors represent money due to the business from its credit customers, it essential that a business maintains strict control over its accounts receivable in order to ensure that it collects all amounts owing on a timely basis.

Conversely, creditors represent amounts owed to suppliers of goods and services. Implementing internal control measures ensures that all amounts owing to suppliers are paid as they become due. Otherwise, the business faces the risk of suppliers refusing to grant further credit, thus jeopardising the conduct of the day-to-day operations of the business. Prompt supplier payment is also important in enabling a business to take advantage of prompt payment discounts offered by suppliers.

Internal controls in relation to accounts receivable and accounts payable can be classified into two main types:

1  separate control accounts in the General Ledger for accounts receivable and accounts payable, each supported by a subsidiary ledger containing individual debtor or creditor accounts, and
2  other processes and procedures to maintain control over accounts receivable and accounts payable.

The following sections of this chapter deal with control accounts and subsidiary ledgers. Other internal controls over accounts receivable and accounts payable are dealt with later in this chapter.

# Purpose of control accounts

In Chapter 3, when the posting of journals to the General Ledger was illustrated, it was assumed that only control accounts were kept in the General Ledger to record amounts owing by debtors (Accounts Receivable Control Account, also called Debtors' Control Account) and amounts owing to creditors (Accounts Payable Control Account, also called Creditors' Control Account). This procedure was followed to remove unnecessary detail from the General Ledger to simplify the preparation of the trial balance and subsequent reports.

# Purpose of subsidiary ledgers

To prepare debtors' statements and to monitor the amount owing by each debtor, separate accounts are kept for each trade debtor; that is, regular customers who buy goods and services from the business on credit. This does not always apply; small or infrequent customers can be grouped together and referred to as 'sundry debtors', whereas a trade debtor is likely to make repeated or large purchases. The individual accounts are kept in the Accounts Receivable Subsidiary Ledger, which is not part of the General Ledger. The total of individual debtors' balances in the Accounts Receivable Subsidiary Ledger must agree with the Accounts Receivable Control Account balance in the General Ledger.

To keep control over payments made to individual creditors, individual accounts are kept that show the amount owed to each trade creditor; that is, regular suppliers from which the business buys goods and services on credit. As with debtors, creditors from whom the business makes only infrequent, minor purchases can be grouped together and referred to as 'sundry creditors'. The accounts are kept in the Accounts Payable

Subsidiary Ledger, which – like the Accounts Receivable Subsidiary Ledger – is not part of the General Ledger. The total of individual creditors' balances in the Accounts Payable Subsidiary Ledger must agree with the balance of the Accounts Payable Control Account in the General Ledger. Figure 4.1 illustrates the relationship between the balances in subsidiary ledgers and the control accounts for debtors and creditors in the General Ledger.

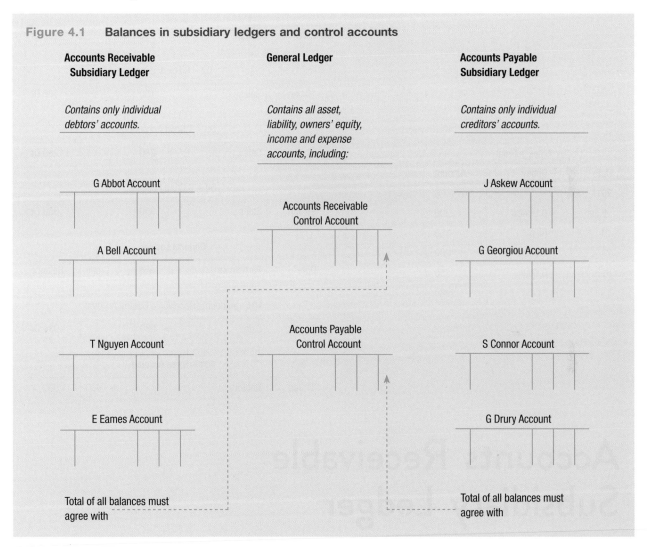

**Figure 4.1    Balances in subsidiary ledgers and control accounts**

# Posting journals to the ledgers

At the end of each month, when posting the various journals to the three ledgers (General Ledger, Accounts Receivable Subsidiary Ledger and Accounts Payable Subsidiary Ledger), the totals are posted to the control accounts in the General Ledger, while the individual transactions are posted to the individual debtors' and creditors' accounts in the subsidiary ledgers. Figure 4.2 shows the link between the sales account in the General Ledger and the individual balances of accounts in the Accounts Receivable Subsidiary Ledger.

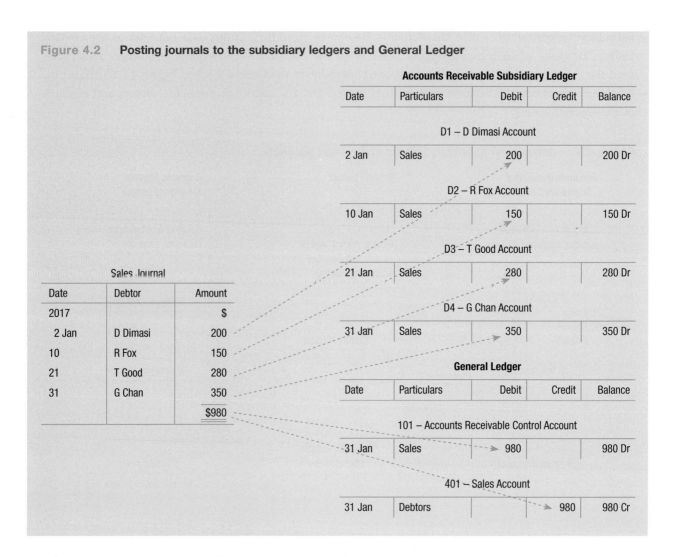

Figure 4.2    Posting journals to the subsidiary ledgers and General Ledger

# Accounts Receivable Subsidiary Ledger

## Example

The following information relates to Rodney Brown, retailer. You are required to:

a   complete the Accounts Receivable Control Account in the General Ledger for the period 1 September 2017 to 30 September 2017

b   complete all entries in the Accounts Receivable Subsidiary Ledger for the period 1 September 2017 to 30 September 2017

c   reconcile the balance of debtors' accounts in the Accounts Receivable Subsidiary Ledger with the Accounts Receivable Control Account balance in the General Ledger at 30 September 2017.

## List of debtors at 1 September 2017

| Account no. | Name | Balance | |
|---|---|---|---|
| | | $ | |
| D1 | T Hocking | 55 | |
| D2 | M Norrowon | 110 | Total $440 = balance of Accounts |
| D3 | J Every | 22 | Receivable Control Account at |
| D4 | American Express | 143 | 1 September 2017 |
| D5 | H Packer | 11 | |
| D6 | A Oakley | 99 | |

## Relevant journals for September 2017

### Sales Journal

| Date | Debtor | Fol | Ref | Sales | Sundries Amount | Sundries Account | GST collected | Accounts receivable control |
|---|---|---|---|---|---|---|---|---|
| 2017 | | | | $ | $ | | $ | $ |
| 5 Sep | T Hocking | | 368 | 110 | | | 11 | 121 |
| 14 | M Norrowon | | 369 | 50 | | | 5 | 55 |
| 15 | J Every | | 370 | 10 | | | 1 | 11 |
| 22 | American Express | | POS | 10 | | | 1 | 11 |
| 27 | H Packer | | 371 | | 20 | Repair income | 2 | 22 |
| | | | | $180 | $20 | | $20 | $220 |

### Sales Returns and Allowances Journal

| Date | Debtor | Fol | Ref | Sales returns and allowances | Sundries Amount | Sundries Account | GST collected | Accounts receivable control |
|---|---|---|---|---|---|---|---|---|
| 2017 | | | | $ | $ | | $ | $ |
| 16 Sep | M Norrowon | | 51 | 20 | | | 2 | 22 |
| 29 | H Packer | | 52 | | 10 | Repair income | 1 | 11 |
| | | | | $20 | $10 | | $3 | $33 |

## Cash Receipts Journal

| Date | Particulars | Fol | Ref | Discount expense — Accounts receivable control | Discount expense — GST collected | Discount expense | Accounts receivable control | Cash sales | Sundries — Amount | Sundries — Account | Sundries — GST collected | Bank |
|------|-------------|-----|-----|------|------|------|------|------|------|------|------|------|
| 2017 | | | | $ | $ | $ | $ | $ | $ | | $ | $ |
| 7 Sep | T Hocking | | 01 | 11 | 1 | 10 | 44 | | | | | 44 |
| 15 | J Every | | 02 | | | | 33 | | | | | 33 |
| 16 | American Exp — Gross | | EFT | | | | 143 | | | | | |
| | — Merchant fee | | | | | | | | (10) | Merchant fees expense | | |
| | — GST paid | | | | | | | | (1) | GST paid | | 132 |
| 27 | H Packer | | 03 | | | | 11 | | | | | 11 |
| | | | | $11 | $1 | $10 | $231 | | ($11) | | | $220 |

## Solution

a  The Accounts Receivable Control Account in the General Ledger:

| Date | Particulars | Fol | Debit | Credit | Balance |
|------|-------------|-----|-------|--------|---------|
| **General Ledger** | | | | | |
| **102 – Accounts Receivable Control Account** | | | | | |
| 2017 | | | $ | $ | $ |
| 1 Sep | Balance | | | | 440 Dr |
| 30 | Sales and GST collected | SJ | 220 | | 660 Dr |
| | Sales returns and GST collected | SRJ | | 33 | 627 Dr |
| | Discount expense and GST collected | CRJ | | 11 | 616 Dr |
| | Cash at bank | CRJ | | 231 | 385 Dr |

**Explanations**

1   The balance of the Accounts Receivable Control Account at 1 September 2017 agrees with the total of the list of debtors balances extracted from the Accounts Receivable Subsidiary Ledger at this date.

2   The total of credit sales and GST collected for September ($220) has been posted to the debit column of the Accounts Receivable Control Account from the Sales Journal.

3   The total of credit sales returns and GST collected for September ($33) has been posted to the credit column of the Accounts Receivable Control Account from the Sales Returns and Allowances Journal.

4   The totals of discount expense and GST collected ($11) and accounts receivable ($231) columns have been posted to the credit column of the Accounts Receivable Control Account from the Cash Receipts Journal.

5   The Accounts Receivable Control Account is a summary account only, and it shows that $385 is owed by debtors at 30 September 2017.

6   When postings are made from the Sales Journal, Sales Returns and Allowances Journal and the Cash Receipts Journal (and also the General Journal in some cases) to the Accounts Receivable Control Account in the General Ledger, postings for each particular transaction affecting debtors must also be made in the relevant debtors' accounts in the Accounts Receivable Subsidiary Ledger.

b   The Accounts Receivable Subsidiary Ledger:

| Accounts Receivable Subsidiary Ledger | | | | | |
|---|---|---|---|---|---|
| Date | Particulars | Fol | Debit | Credit | Balance |
| **D1 – T Hocking Account** | | | | | |
| 2017 | | | $ | $ | $ |
| 1 Sep | Balance | | | | 55 Dr |
| 5 | Sales and GST collected | SJ | 121 | | 176 Dr |
| 7 | Discount expense and GST collected | CRJ | | 11 | 165 Dr |
| | Cash at bank | CRJ | | 44 | 121 Dr |
| **D2 – M Norrowon Account** | | | | | |
| 2017 | | | | | |
| 1 Sep | Balance | | | | 110 Dr |
| 14 | Sales and GST collected | SJ | 55 | | 165 Dr |
| 16 | Sales returns and GST collected | SRJ | | 22 | 143 Dr |
| **D3 – J Every Account** | | | | | |
| 2017 | | | | | |
| 1 Sep | Balance | | | | 22 Dr |
| 15 | Sales and GST collected | SJ | 11 | | 33 Dr |
| | Cash at bank | CRJ | | 33 | Nil |
| **D4 – American Express Account** | | | | | |
| 2017 | | | | | |
| 1 Sep | Balance | | | | 143 Dr |
| 16 | Cash at bank, merchant fee and GST paid | CRJ | | 143 | Nil |
| 22 | Sales and GST collected | SJ | 11 | | 11 Dr |

### Accounts Receivable Subsidiary Ledger

| Date | Particulars | Fol | Debit | Credit | Balance |
|------|-------------|-----|-------|--------|---------|
| **D5 – H Packer Account** | | | | | |
| 2017 | | | $ | $ | $ |
| 1 Sep | Balance | | | | 11 Dr |
| 27 | Cash at bank | CRJ | | 11 | Nil |
| | Sales and GST collected | SJ | 22 | | 22 Dr |
| 29 | Sales returns and GST collected | SRJ | | 11 | 11 Dr |
| **D6 – A Oakley Account** | | | | | |
| 2017 | | | | | |
| 1 Sep | Balance | | | | 99 Dr |

### Explanations

1  The total of all individual debtors' account balances at 1 September agrees with the Accounts Receivable Control Account balance at that date.

2  Each individual credit sale, including GST collected, has been posted (debit entry) from the Sales Journal to the relevant debtor's account, using transaction dates.

3  Each individual credit sales return, including allowance for GST collected, has been posted (credit entry) from the Sales Returns and Allowances Journal to the relevant debtor's account, using transaction dates.

4  Each receipt of cash from debtors, together with the discount allowed (if any), including allowance for GST collected, has been posted (credit entry) from the Cash Receipts Journal to the relevant debtor's account, using transaction dates.

5  Transactions in debtors' accounts should be entered in chronological sequence.

6  The cross-reference (name of other account involved in transaction) used for each type of entry in the Accounts Receivable Subsidiary Ledger is the same as that used in the Accounts Receivable Control Account in the General Ledger.

7  The Folio column in the subsidiary ledger records the source of each posting; that is, from which journal the transaction was posted. As transactions are posted to individual accounts in the Accounts Receivable Subsidiary Ledger, debtors' account numbers should be recorded in the Folio (account number) column of each journal as follows (the Sales Journal is used as an example).

### Sales Journal (example with Folio references)

| Date | Debtor | Fol | Ref | Sales | Sundries Amount | Sundries Account | GST collected | Debtors control |
|------|--------|-----|-----|-------|--------|---------|---------------|-----------------|
| 2017 | | | | $ | $ | | $ | $ |
| 5 Sep | T Hocking | D1 | 368 | 110 | | | 11 | 121 |
| 14 | M Norrowon | D2 | 369 | 50 | | | 5 | 55 |
| 15 | J Every | D3 | 370 | 10 | | | 1 | 11 |
| 22 | American Express | D4 | POS | 10 | | | 1 | 11 |
| 27 | H Packer | D5 | 371 | | 20 | Repairs income | 2 | 22 |
| | | | | $180 | $20 | | $20 | $220 |

c

| Accounts receivable reconciliation as at 30 September 2017 | | |
|---|---|---|
| **Account no.** | **Name** | **Balance** |
| | | $ |
| D1 | T Hocking | 121 |
| D2 | M Norrowon | 143 |
| D4 | American Express | 11 |
| D5 | H Packer | 11 |
| D6 | A Oakley | 99 |
| Total as per Accounts Receivable Control Account | | $385 |

**Explanations**

1   The total of debtors' balances extracted from the Accounts Receivable Subsidiary Ledger at 30 September 2017 agrees with the balance of the Accounts Receivable Control Account in the General Ledger ($385). A debtors' reconciliation is prepared each month as a means of checking the accuracy of the Accounts Receivable Subsidiary Ledger.

2   Where a debtor's account has a nil balance (as in the case of Debtor – J Every) it is not necessary to include this debtor in the reconciliation.

# Accounts Payable Subsidiary Ledger

## Example

The following information relates to Rodney Brown, retailer. You are required to:

a   complete the Accounts Payable Control Account in the General Ledger for the period 1 September 2017 to 30 September 2017

b   complete all entries in the Accounts Payable Subsidiary Ledger for the period 1 September 2017 to 30 September 2017

c   reconcile the balance of creditors' accounts in the Accounts Payable Subsidiary Ledger with the Accounts Payable Control Account balance in the General Ledger at 30 September 2017.

### List of creditors at 1 September 2017

| Account no. | Name | Balance | |
|---|---|---|---|
| | | $ | |
| C1 | B Miokovic | 220 | Total $825 = balance of Accounts Payable Control Account at 1 September 2017 |
| C2 | K Senn | 440 | |
| C3 | J Moroney | 110 | |
| C4 | H Temple | 55 | |

*Relevant journals for September 2017*

### Purchases Journal

| Date | Creditor | Fol | Ref | Purchases | Sundries Amount | Sundries Account | GST paid | Accounts payable control |
|------|----------|-----|-----|-----------|--------|---------|----------|--------------------------|
| 2017 | | | | $ | $ | | $ | $ |
| 1 Sep | H Temple | | 6134 | 50 | | | 5 | 55 |
| 6 | J Moroney | | X1265 | | 20 | Office stationery | 2 | 22 |
| 8 | T Hocking | | 229 | 150 | | | 15 | 165 |
| 10 | B Miokovic | | 1468 | 100 | | | 10 | 110 |
| 12 | K Senn | | 995 | 500 | | | 50 | 550 |
| 20 | J Moroney | | X1496 | | 70 | Advertising | 7 | 77 |
| 28 | H Temple | | C995 | 150 | | | 15 | 165 |
| | | | | $950 | $90 | | $104 | $1 144 |

### Purchases Returns and Allowances Journal

| Date | Creditor | Fol | Ref | Purchases returns and allowances | Sundries Amount | Sundries Account | GST paid | Accounts payable control |
|------|----------|-----|-----|----------------------------------|--------|---------|----------|--------------------------|
| 2017 | | | | $ | $ | | $ | $ |
| 1 Sep | H Temple | | 14213 | 40 | | | 4 | 44 |
| 2 | J Moroney | | C189 | | 50 | Office stationery | 5 | 55 |
| 13 | K Senn | | Z612 | 20 | | | 2 | 22 |
| 29 | H Temple | | 14670 | 10 | | | 1 | 11 |
| | | | | $70 | $50 | | $12 | $132 |

### Cash Payments Journal

| Date | Particulars | Fol | Ref | Discount income Accounts payable control | Discount income GST paid | Discount income Discount income | Accounts payable control | Cash purchases | Wages | Sundries Account | Sundries Amount | GST paid | Bank |
|------|-------------|-----|-----|---------|-----|----------|----------|--------|-------|---------|--------|-----|------|
| 2017 | | | | $ | $ | $ | $ | $ | $ | $ | | $ | $ |
| 2 Sep | B Miokovic | | 1623 | 22 | 2 | 20 | 198 | | | | | | 198 |
| 4 | Wages | | 1624 | | | | | | 100 | | | | 100 |
| 30 | K Senn | | 1625 | 44 | 4 | 40 | 396 | | | | | | 396 |
| | | | | $66 | $6 | $60 | $594 | | $100 | | | | $694 |

# Solution

a The Accounts Payable Control Account in the General Ledger:

| Date | Particulars | Fol | Debit | Credit | Balance |
|------|-------------|-----|-------|--------|---------|
| | | General Ledger | | | |
| | | **202 – Accounts Payable Control Account** | | | |
| 2017 | | | $ | $ | $ |
| 1 Sep | Balance | | | | 825 Cr |
| 30 | Purchases and GST paid | PJ | | 1 144 | 1 969 Cr |
| | Purchases returns and GST paid | PRJ | 132 | | 1 837 Cr |
| | Discount income and GST paid | CPJ | 66 | | 1 771 Cr |
| | Cash at bank | CPJ | 594 | | 1 177 Cr |

**Explanations**

1   The balance of the Accounts Payable Control Account at 1 September 2017 agrees with the total of the list of debtors' balances extracted from the Accounts Receivable Subsidiary Ledger at this date.

2   The total of credit purchases and GST paid for September ($1144) has been posted to the credit column of the Accounts Payable Control Account from the Purchases Journal.

3   The total of credit purchases returns and GST paid for September ($132) has been posted to the debit column of the Creditors' Control Account from the Purchases Returns and Allowances Journal.

4   The totals of discount income and GST collected ($66) and accounts payable ($594) columns have been posted to the debit column of the Accounts Payable Control Account from the Cash Receipts Journal.

5   The Accounts Payable Control Account is a summary account only, and it shows that $1177 is owed to creditors at 30 September 2017.

6   When postings are made from the Purchases Journal, Purchases Returns and Allowances Journal and the Cash Payments Journal (and also the General Journal in some cases) to the Accounts Payable Control Account in the General Ledger, postings for each particular transaction affecting creditors also must be made in the relevant creditors' accounts in the Accounts Payable Subsidiary Ledger.

b The Accounts Payable Subsidiary Ledger:

| Date | Particulars | Fol | Debit | Credit | Balance |
|------|-------------|-----|-------|--------|---------|
| | | Creditors Subsidiary Ledger | | | |
| | | **C1 – B Miokovic Account** | | | |
| 2017 | | | $ | $ | $ |
| 1 Sep | Balance | | | | 220 Cr |
| 2 | Discount income and GST paid | CPJ | 22 | | 198 Cr |
| | Cash at bank | CPJ | 198 | | Nil |
| 10 | Purchases and GST paid | PJ | | 110 | 110 Cr |

| Creditors Subsidiary Ledger | | | | | |
|---|---|---|---|---|---|
| Date | Particulars | Fol | Debit | Credit | Balance |
| **C2 – K Senn Account** | | | | | |
| 2017 | | | $ | $ | $ |
| 1 Sep | Balance | | | | 440 Cr |
| 12 | Purchases and GST paid | PJ | | 550 | 990 Cr |
| 13 | Purchases returns and GST paid | PRJ | 22 | | 968 Cr |
| 30 | Discount income and GST paid | CPJ | 44 | | 924 Cr |
| | Cash at bank | CPJ | 396 | | 528 Cr |
| **C3 – J Moroney Account** | | | | | |
| 2017 | | | | | |
| 1 Sep | Balance | | | | 110 Cr |
| 2 | Purchases returns and GST paid | PRJ | 55 | | 55 Cr |
| 6 | Purchases and GST paid | PJ | | 22 | 77 Cr |
| 20 | Purchases and GST paid | PJ | | 77 | 154 Cr |
| **C4 – H Temple Account** | | | | | |
| 2017 | | | | | |
| 1 Sep | Balance | | | | 55 Cr |
| | Purchases and GST paid | PJ | | 55 | 110 Cr |
| | Purchases returns and GST paid | PRJ | 44 | | 66 Cr |
| 28 | Purchases and GST paid | PJ | | 165 | 231 Cr |
| 29 | Purchases returns and GST paid | PRJ | 11 | | 220 Cr |
| **C5 – T Hocking Account** | | | | | |
| 2017 | | | | | |
| 8 Sep | Purchases and GST paid | PJ | | 165 | 165 Cr |

**Explanations**

1  The total of all individual creditors' account balances at 1 September agrees with the Accounts Payable Control Account balance at that date.

2  Each individual credit purchase including GST paid has been posted (credit entry) from the Purchases Journal to the relevant creditor's account, using transaction dates.

3  Each individual credit purchases return including allowance for GST paid has been posted (debit entry) from the Purchases Returns and Allowances Journal using transaction dates.

4  Each payment of cash to creditors, together with the discount received (if any) including allowance for GST paid has been posted (debit entry) from the Cash Payments Journal using transaction dates.

5  Transactions in creditors' accounts should be entered in chronological sequence.

6  The cross-reference (name of other account involved in transaction) for each type of entry in the Accounts Payable Subsidiary Ledger is the same as that used in the Accounts Payable Control Account in the General Ledger.

7  The Folio column in the subsidiary ledger records the source of each posting; that is, from which journal the transaction was posted. As transactions are posted to individual accounts in the Accounts Payable Ledger, creditors' account numbers should be recorded in the Folio (account number) column of each journal as follows (the Purchases Journal is used as an example):

| | | | | | Sundries | | | |
|---|---|---|---|---|---|---|---|---|
| Date | Creditor | Fol | Ref | Purchases | Amount | Account | GST paid | Accounts payable control |
| 2017 | | | | $ | $ | | $ | $ |
| 1 Sep | H Temple | C4 | 6134 | 50 | | | 5 | 55 |
| 6 | J Moroney | C3 | X1265 | | 20 | Office stationery | 2 | 22 |
| 8 | T Hocking | C5 | 229 | 150 | | | 15 | 165 |
| 10 | B Miokovic | C1 | 1468 | 100 | | | 10 | 110 |
| 12 | K Senn | C2 | 995 | 500 | | | 50 | 550 |
| 20 | J Moroney | C3 | X1496 | | 70 | Advertising | 7 | 77 |
| 28 | H Temple | C4 | 6995 | 150 | | | 15 | 165 |
| | | | | $950 | $90 | | $104 | $1 144 |

Purchases Journal (example with Folio references)

c

| Accounts payable reconciliation as at 30 September 2017 | | |
|---|---|---|
| Account no. | Name | Balance |
| | | $ |
| C1 | B Miokovic | 110 |
| C2 | K Senn | 528 |
| C3 | J Moroney | 154 |
| C4 | H Temple | 220 |
| C5 | T Hocking | 165 |
| Total as per Accounts Payable Control Account | | $1 177 |

**Explanation**

The total of creditors' balances extracted from the Accounts Payable Subsidiary Ledger at 30 September 2017 agrees with the balance of the Accounts Payable Control Account in the General Ledger ($1177). A creditors' reconciliation is prepared each month as a means of checking the accuracy of the Accounts Payable Subsidiary Ledger.

# General Journal and subsidiary ledgers

Whenever a General Journal posting is made to the Accounts Receivable Control Account in the General Ledger, a posting must also be made to the relevant account in the Accounts Receivable Subsidiary Ledger, otherwise the subsidiary ledger reconciliation schedule will not balance with the control account. This principle must also be followed in the Accounts Payable Subsidiary Ledger when General Journal entries are posted to the Accounts Payable Control Account.

## Example

After Rodney Brown (see examples earlier in this chapter) had posted his special journals to the General Ledger and subsidiary ledgers at 30 September 2017, he made the following entries in his General Journal. You are required to:

a  show the Accounts Receivable Control Account as it would appear in the General Ledger after posting the entries from the General Journal

b  post the General Journal entries to the Accounts Receivable Subsidiary Ledger

c  prepare a revised accounts receivable reconciliation schedule at 30 September 2017

d  show the Accounts Payable Control Account as it would appear in the General Ledger after posting the entries from the General Journal

e  post the General Journal entries to the Accounts Payable Subsidiary Ledger

f  prepare a revised accounts payable reconciliation schedule at 30 September 2017.

### Balances at 30 September 2017 (prior to posting of General Journal entries)

| | Debtors | | | Creditors | |
|---|---|---|---|---|---|
| | | $ | | | $ |
| D1 | T Hocking | 121 | C1 | B Miokovic | 110 |
| D2 | M Norrowon | 143 | C2 | K Senn | 528 |
| D4 | American Express | 11 | C3 | J Moroney | 154 |
| D5 | H Packer | 11 | C4 | H Temple | 220 |
| D6 | A Oakley | 99 | C5 | T Hocking | 165 |
| | | $385 | | | $1 177 |

### General Journal

| Date | Particulars | Fol | Debit | Credit |
|---|---|---|---|---|
| 2017 | | | $ | $ |
| 30 Sep | Bad debts | | 90 | |
| | GST collected | | 9 | |
| |     Accounts receivable control – A Oakley, account D6 | 102 | | (A) 99 |
| | *Bad debt written off following solicitor's memo received 16.9.17* | | | |
| | Accounts receivable control – M Norrowon, account D2 | 102 | (B) 22 | |
| |     Late fees income | | | 22 |
| | *Late fee charged to M Norrowon on overdue account* | | | |
| | Accounts receivable control – J Every, account D3 | 102 | (C) 11 | |
| |     Accounts receivable control – H Packer, account D5 | 102 | | (D) 11 |
| | *Correction of error – invoice 977 dated 14.8.17 posted to incorrect debtor's account* | | | |
| | Late fees expense | | 11 | |
| |     Creditors control – J Moroney, account C3 | 202 | | (E) 11 |
| | *Late fee charged on overdue account by J Moroney* | | | |
| | Accounts payable control – T Hocking, account C5 | 202 | (F) 121 | |
| |     Accounts receivable control – T Hocking, account D1 | 102 | | (G) 121 |
| | *Contra entry\* as per memo 49* | | | |

**\*Contra entry** Circumstances can often arise where a person or an organisation is both a debtor *and* a creditor to a business (such as T Hocking in this example). In this case, instead of the debtor writing out a cheque to pay the business and, in turn, the business writing out a cheque to pay the creditor, the amounts owing by the respective parties can be offset against each other. This offset process is known as a *contra entry*. The effect of a contra entry is to reduce the Accounts Receivable Control Account (and the account of the particular debtor in the Accounts Receivable Subsidiary Ledger) and also to reduce the Accounts Payable Control Account (and the account of the particular creditor in the Accounts Payable Subsidiary Ledger).

**Note** Postings to the General Ledger, and to the Accounts Receivable and Accounts Payable Subsidiary Ledgers, are shown by (A), (B) etc. Whenever a posting is made to a control account in the General Ledger, a posting must also be made to the relevant debtor's or creditor's account in the subsidiary ledger.

In the General Journal, folios (account numbers) are shown as follows:

- The control account numbers appear in the Folio column.
- The subsidiary ledger account numbers appear in brackets in the Particulars column, after the name of the relevant debtor or creditor.

# Solution

a  The Accounts Receivable Control Account in the General Ledger:

| General Ledger | | | | | |
|---|---|---|---|---|---|
| Date | Particulars | Fol | Debit | Credit | Balance |
| **102 – Accounts Receivable Control Account** | | | | | |
| 2017 | | | $ | $ | $ |
| 30 Sep | Balance | | | | 385 Dr |
| | Bad debts and GST collected | GJ | | A 99 | 286 Dr |
| | Late fee income | GJ | B 22 | | 308 Dr |
| | Accounts receivable control | GJ | C 11 | | 319 Dr |
| | Accounts receivable control | GJ | | D 11 | 308 Dr |
| | Accounts payable control | GJ | | G 121 | 187 Dr |

b  The Accounts Receivable Subsidiary Ledger:

| Accounts Receivable Subsidiary Ledger | | | | | |
|---|---|---|---|---|---|
| Date | Particulars | Fol | Debit | Credit | Balance |
| **D1 – T Hocking Account** | | | | | |
| 2017 | | | $ | $ | $ |
| 30 Sep | Balance | | | | 121 Dr |
| | Contra entry | GJ | | G 121 | Nil |
| **D2 – M Norrowon Account** | | | | | |
| 2017 | | | | | |
| 30 Sep | Balance | | | | 143 Dr |
| | Late fees income | GJ | B 22 | | 165 Dr |
| **D3 – J Every Account** | | | | | |
| 2017 | | | | | |
| 30 Sep | Accounts receivable control – H Packer | GJ | C 11 | | 11 Dr |
| **D4 – American Express Account** | | | | | |
| 2017 | | | | | |
| 30 Sep | Balance | | | | 11 Dr |

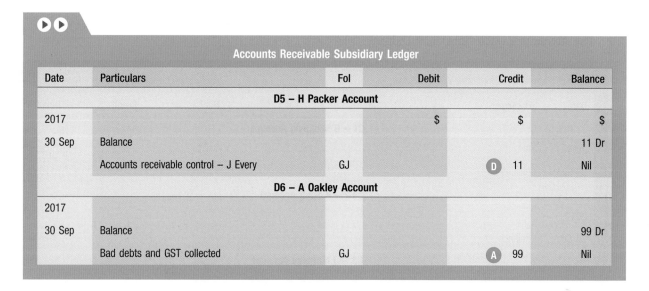

**Accounts Receivable Subsidiary Ledger**

| Date | Particulars | Fol | Debit | Credit | Balance |
|---|---|---|---|---|---|
| | **D5 – H Packer Account** | | | | |
| 2017 | | | $ | $ | $ |
| 30 Sep | Balance | | | | 11 Dr |
| | Accounts receivable control – J Every | GJ | | 11 | Nil |
| | **D6 – A Oakley Account** | | | | |
| 2017 | | | | | |
| 30 Sep | Balance | | | | 99 Dr |
| | Bad debts and GST collected | GJ | | 99 | Nil |

c   The revised accounts receivable reconciliation schedule:

**Accounts receivable reconciliation as at 30 September 2017**

| Account no. | Name | Balance |
|---|---|---|
| | | $ |
| D2 | M Norrowon | 165 |
| D3 | J Every | 11 |
| D4 | American Express | 11 |
| Total as per Accounts Receivable Control Account | | $187 |

d   The Accounts Payable Control Account in the General Ledger:

**General Ledger**

| Date | Particulars | Fol | Debit | Credit | Balance |
|---|---|---|---|---|---|
| | **202 – Accounts Payable Control Account** | | | | |
| 2017 | | | $ | $ | $ |
| 30 Sep | Balance | | | | 1 177 Cr |
| | Late fees | GJ | | 11 | 1 188 Cr |
| | Accounts receivable control | GJ | 121 | | 1 067 Cr |

e The Accounts Payable Subsidiary Ledger:

| Accounts Payable Subsidiary Ledger | | | | | |
|---|---|---|---|---|---|
| Date | Particulars | Fol | Debit | Credit | Balance |
| **C1 – B Miokovic Account** | | | | | |
| 2017 | | | $ | $ | $ |
| 30 Sep | Balance | | | | 110 Cr |
| **C2 – K Senn Account** | | | | | |
| 2017 | | | | | |
| 30 Sep | Balance | | | | 528 Cr |
| **C3 – J Moroney Account** | | | | | |
| 2017 | | | | | |
| 30 Sep | Balance | | | | 154 Cr |
| | Late fees expense | GJ | | E 11 | 165 Cr |
| **C4 – H Temple Account** | | | | | |
| 2017 | | | | | |
| 30 Sep | Balance | | | | 220 Cr |
| **C5 – T Hocking Account** | | | | | |
| 2017 | | | | | |
| 30 Sep | Balance | | | | 165 Cr |
| | Contra entry | GJ | F 121 | | 44 Cr |

f The revised accounts payable reconciliation schedule:

| Accounts payable reconciliation as at 30 September 2017 | | |
|---|---|---|
| Account no. | Name | Balance |
| | | $ |
| C1 | B Miokovic | 110 |
| C2 | K Senn | 528 |
| C3 | J Moroney | 165 |
| C4 | H Temple | 220 |
| C5 | T Hocking | 44 |
| Total as per Accounts Payable Control Account | | $1 067 |

# Comprehensive example

The following information relates to the business of Levi Laurie, wholesaler, for the month of October 2019.

## 1  The trial balance

| Trial balance as at 1 October 2019 | | | |
|---|---|---|---|
| Account no. | Account name | Debit | Credit |
| | | $ | $ |
| 101 | Cash at bank | 4 004 | |
| 102 | Accounts receivable control | 608 | |
| 103 | Furniture and equipment | 1 230 | |
| 104 | Stock | 1 869 | |
| 105 | Motor vehicles | 8 600 | |
| 106 | Land and buildings | 42 000 | |
| 107 | GST paid | 215 | |
| 201 | Accounts payable control | | 957 |
| 202 | Loan from Raymond Finance | | 32 200 |
| 203 | GST collected | | 390 |
| 301 | Capital – L Laurie | | 25 000 |
| 302 | Drawings – L Laurie | 900 | |
| 401 | Sales | | 3 900 |
| 402 | Sales returns and allowances | 300 | |
| 403 | Rent income | | 300 |
| 404 | Interest income | | 490 |
| 405 | Discount income | | 150 |
| 501 | Purchases | 2 410 | |
| 502 | Purchases returns and allowances | | 260 |
| 503 | Rent expense | 480 | |
| 504 | Wages | 300 | |
| 505 | Discount expense | 110 | |
| 506 | Bad debts | 40 | |
| 507 | Interest expense | 5 | |
| 508 | Motor vehicle expenses | 450 | |
| 509 | Merchant fees expense | 126 | |
| | | $63 647 | $63 647 |

## 2  The debtors' and creditors' balances

| Debtors' and creditors' balances as at 1 October 2019 | | | | | |
|---|---|---|---|---|---|
| **Debtors** | | | **Creditors** | | |
| **Account no.** | **Name** | **Balance** | **Account no.** | **Name** | **Balance** |
| | | $ | | | $ |
| D1 | B Border | Nil | C1 | S Harley | 88 |
| D2 | A Warne | 220 | C2 | A Hughes | 550 |
| D3 | B Cook | 33 | C3 | B O'Keefe | 165 |
| D4 | Diners Club | 155 | C4 | J Pleban | 110 |
| D5 | T Chaplin | Nil | C5 | B Border | 44 |
| D6 | A Agar | 200 | | | |
| | | $608 | | | $957 |

## 3  The journals for October 2019

| | General Journal | | | |
|---|---|---|---|---|
| **Date** | **Particulars** | **Fol** | **Debit** | **Credit** |
| 2019 | | | $ | $ |
| 17 Oct | Bad debts | 506 | 50 | |
| | GST collected | 203 | 5 | |
| | Accounts receivable control – A Warne, account D2 | 102 | | 55 |
| | *Bad debt written off – A Warne* | | | |
| 25 | Drawings – L Laurie | 302 | 220 | |
| | GST paid | 107 | | 20 |
| | Purchases | 501 | | 200 |
| | *Withdrawal of stock by owner* | | | |
| 31 | Accounts payable control – B Border, account C5 | 201 | 121 | |
| | Accounts receivable control – B Border, account D1 | 102 | | 121 |
| | *Contra entry* | | | |
| | Accounts receivable control – T Chaplin, account D5 | 102 | 200 | |
| | Accounts receivable control – A Agar, account D6 | 102 | | 200 |
| | *Correction of error – receipt from A Agar in September incorrectly credited to T Chaplin* | | | |

## Sales Journal

| Date | Debtor | Fol | Ref | 401 Sales | Sundries Amount | Sundries Account | 203 GST collected | 102 Accounts receivable control |
|------|--------|-----|-----|-----------|--------|---------|---------------|-----------------------|
| 2019 | | | | $ | $ | | $ | $ |
| 6 Oct | A Agar | D6 | 101 | 270 | | | 27 | 297 |
| 11 | B Border | D1/406 | 102 | | 160 | Sale of non-current assets | 16 | 176 |
| 13 | Diners Club | D4 | POS | 40 | | | 4 | 44 |
| 19 | B Cook | D3 | 103 | 120 | | | 12 | 132 |
| 28 | T Chaplin | D5 | 104 | 30 | | | 3 | 33 |
| | | | | $460 | $160 | | $62 | $682 |

## Purchases Journal

| Date | Creditor | Fol | Ref | 501 Purchases | Sundries Amount | Sundries Account | 107 GST paid | 201 Accounts payable control |
|------|----------|-----|-----|---------------|--------|---------|-----------|----------------------|
| 2019 | | | | $ | $ | | $ | $ |
| 2 Oct | B Border | C5 | 280 | 70 | | | 7 | 77 |
| 5 | S Harley | C1/508 | 1577 | | 120 | Motor vehicle expenses | 12 | 132 |
| 11 | J Pleban | C4 | 6410 | 30 | | | 3 | 33 |
| | B O'Keefe | C3 | X1710 | 70 | | | 7 | 77 |
| 18 | S Harley | C1 | 1606 | 100 | | | 10 | 110 |
| 27 | A Roberts | C6 | H66 | 340 | | | 34 | 374 |
| | | | | $610 | $120 | | $73 | $803 |

## Purchases Returns and Allowances Journal

| Date | Creditor | Fol | Ref | 502 Purchases returns and allowances | Sundries Amount | Sundries Account | 107 GST paid | 201 Accounts payable control |
|------|----------|-----|-----|--------------------------------------|--------|---------|-----------|----------------------|
| 2019 | | | | $ | $ | | $ | $ |
| 6 Oct | S Harley | C1/508 | 98 | | 20 | Motor vehicle expenses | 2 | 22 |
| 13 | B O'Keefe | C3 | C201 | 10 | | | 1 | 11 |
| | | | | $10 | $20 | | $3 | $33 |

## Sales Returns and Allowances Journal

| | | | | | 402 | | | 203 | 102 |
|---|---|---|---|---|---|---|---|---|---|
| | | | | | Sales returns and allowances | Sundries | | GST collected | Accounts receivable control |
| Date | Debtor | Fol | Ref | | | Amount | Account | | |
| 2019 | | | | | $ | $ | | $ | $ |
| 26 Oct | B Cook | D3 | 74 | | 20 | | | 2 | 22 |
| | | | | | $20 | | | $2 | $22 |

## Cash Receipts Journal

| | | | | 102 | 203 | 505 | 102 | 101 | | | 203 | 101 |
|---|---|---|---|---|---|---|---|---|---|---|---|---|
| | | | | Discount expense | | | | | Sundries | | | |
| | | | | Accounts receivable control | GST collected | Discount expense | Accounts receivable control | Cash sales | Amount | Account | GST collected | Bank |
| Date | Particulars | Fol | Ref | | | | | | | | | |
| 2019 | | | | $ | $ | $ | $ | $ | $ | | $ | $ |
| 6 Oct | Diners Club | | EFT | | | | | | | | | |
| | – Gross | D4 | | | | | 155 | | | | | |
| | – Merchant fee | 509 | | | | | | | (10) | Merchant fees | | |
| | – GST paid | 107 | | | | | | | (1) | GST paid | | 144 |
| 7 | B Cook | D3 | 52 | 11 | 1 | 10 | 22 | | | | | 22 |
| 11 | ZNA Bank | 404 | 53 | | | | | | 40 | Interest income | | 40 |
| 14 | D McCol | | POS | | | | | 610 | | | 61 | 671 |
| 17 | A Warne | D2 | 54 | | | | 165 | | | | | 165 |
| 28 | Cash sales | | POS | | | | | 410 | | | 41 | 451 |
| 31 | A Tenant | 403 | 55 | | | | | | 100 | Rent income | 10 | 110 |
| | | | | $11 | $1 | $10 | $342 | $1 020 | $129 | | $112 | $1 603 |

## Cash Payments Journal

| | | | | 201 | 107 | 405 | 201 | 501 | 504 | | | 107 | 101 |
|---|---|---|---|---|---|---|---|---|---|---|---|---|---|
| | | | | Discount income | | | | | | Sundries | | | |
| | | | | Accounts payable control | GST paid | Discount income | Accounts payable control | Cash purchases | Wages | Amount | Account | GST paid | Bank |
| Date | Particulars | Fol | Ref | | | | | | | | | | |
| 2019 | | | | $ | $ | $ | $ | $ | $ | $ | | $ | $ |
| 5 Oct | S Harley | C1 | 627 | | | | 88 | | | | | | 88 |
| | A Hughes | C2 | 628 | 33 | 3 | 30 | 517 | | | | | | 517 |

## Cash Payments Journal

| | | | | 201 | 107 | 405 | 201 | 501 | 504 | | | 107 | 101 |
|---|---|---|---|---|---|---|---|---|---|---|---|---|---|
| | | | | Discount income | | | | | | Sundries | | | |
| Date | Particulars | Fol | Ref | Accounts payable control | GST paid | Discount income | Accounts payable control | Cash purchases | Wages | Amount | Account | GST paid | Bank |
| 2019 | | | | $ | $ | $ | $ | $ | $ | $ | | $ | $ |
| 5 Oct | B O'Keefe | C3 | 629 | 11 | 1 | 10 | 139 | | | | | | 139 |
| 6 | Wages | | EFT | | | | | | 100 | | | | 100 |
| 11 | J Pleban | C4 | 630 | | | | 110 | | | | | | 110 |
| 19 | C Clive | 503 | 631 | | | | | | | 610 | Rent expense | 61 | 671 |
| 20 | D McCol | | EFT | | | | | | | | | | |
| | – Sales returns | 402 | | | | | | | | 300 | Sales returns | | |
| | – GST collected | 203 | | | | | | | | 30 | GST collected | | 330 |
| 30 | G Olly | | 632 | | | | | 70 | | | | 7 | 77 |
| 31 | ATO | 203 | EFT | | | | | | | 390 | GST collected | | |
| | | 107 | | | | | | | | (215) | GST paid | | 175 |
| | | | | $44 | $4 | $40 | $854 | $70 | $100 | $1 115 | | $68 | $2 207 |

## Solution

The preceding information was used to prepare Levi Laurie's ledgers for October 2019, as follows:

## General Ledger

| Date | Particulars | Fol | Debit | Credit | Balance |
|---|---|---|---|---|---|
| **101 – Cash at Bank Account** | | | | | |
| 2019 | | | $ | $ | $ |
| 1 Oct | Balance | | | | 4 004 Dr |
| 31 | Sundry receipts | CRJ | 1 603 | | 5 607 Dr |
| | Sundry payments | CPJ | | 2 207 | 3 400 Dr |
| **102 – Accounts Receivable Control Account** | | | | | |
| 2019 | | | | | |
| 1 Oct | Balance | | | | 608 Dr |
| 17 | Bad debts and GST collected | GJ | | 55 | 553 Dr |
| 31 | Accounts payable control – B Border | GJ | | 121 | 432 Dr |
| | Accounts receivable control – T Chaplin | GJ | 200 | | 632 Dr |
| | Accounts receivable control – A Agar | GJ | | 200 | 432 Dr |
| | Sales and GST collected | SJ | 682 | | 1 114 Dr |

| Date | Particulars | Fol | Debit | Credit | Balance |
|------|-------------|-----|-------|--------|---------|
| | | | | **General Ledger** | |
| | | | $ | $ | $ |

| Date | Particulars | Fol | Debit | Credit | Balance |
|------|-------------|-----|-------|--------|---------|
| **102 – Accounts Receivable Control Account (continued)** | | | | | |
| **2019** | | | $ | $ | $ |
| 31 | Sales returns and GST collected | SRJ | | 22 | 1 092 Dr |
| | Discount expense and GST collected | CRJ | | 11 | 1 081 Dr |
| | Cash at bank | CRJ | | 342 | 739 Dr |
| **103 – Furniture and Equipment Account** | | | | | |
| **2019** | | | | | |
| 1 Oct | Balance | | | | 1 230 Dr |
| **104 – Stock Account** | | | | | |
| **2019** | | | | | |
| 1 Oct | Balance | | | | 1 869 Dr |
| **105 – Motor Vehicles Account** | | | | | |
| **2019** | | | | | |
| 1 Oct | Balance | | | | 8 600 Dr |
| **106 – Land and Buildings Account** | | | | | |
| **2019** | | | | | |
| 1 Oct | Balance | | | | 42 000 Dr |
| **107 – GST Paid Account** | | | | | |
| **2019** | | | | | |
| 1 Oct | Balance | | | | 215 Dr |
| 6 | Cash at bank | CRJ | 1 | | 216 Dr |
| 25 | Drawings – L Laurie | GJ | | 20 | 196 Dr |
| 31 | Accounts payable control | PJ | 73 | | 269 Dr |
| 31 | Accounts payable control | PRJ | | 3 | 266 Dr |
| | Accounts payable control | CPJ | | 4 | 262 Dr |
| | Cash at bank | CPJ | 68 | | 330 Dr |
| | Cash at bank | CPJ | | 215 | 115 Dr |
| **201 – Accounts Payable Control Account** | | | | | |
| **2019** | | | | | |
| 1 Oct | Balance | | | | 957 Cr |
| 31 | Accounts receivable control – B Border | GJ | 121 | | 836 Cr |
| | Purchases and GST paid | PJ | | 803 | 1 639 Cr |
| | Purchases returns and GST paid | PRJ | 33 | | 1 606 Cr |

| Date | Particulars | Fol | Debit | Credit | Balance |
|------|-------------|-----|-------|--------|---------|
| **General Ledger** | | | | | |
| | | | | | |
| | **201 – Accounts Payable Control Account (continued)** | | | | |
| 2019 | | | $ | $ | $ |
| 31 | Discount income and GST paid | CPJ | 44 | | 1 562 Cr |
| | Cash at bank | CPJ | 854 | | 708 Cr |
| | **202 – Loan from Raymond Finance Account** | | | | |
| 2019 | | | | | |
| 1 Oct | Balance | | | | 32 200 Cr |
| | **203 – GST Collected Account** | | | | |
| 2019 | | | | | |
| 1 Oct | Balance | | | | 390 Cr |
| 17 | Accounts receivable control | GJ | 5 | | 385 Cr |
| 20 | Cash at bank | CPJ | 30 | | 355 Cr |
| 31 | Accounts receivable control | SJ | | 62 | 417 Cr |
| 31 Oct | Accounts receivable control | SRJ | 2 | | 415 Cr |
| | Accounts receivable control | CRJ | 1 | | 414 Cr |
| | Cash at bank | CRJ | | 112 | 526 Cr |
| | Cash at bank | CPJ | 390 | | 136 Cr |
| | **301 – Capital – L Laurie Account** | | | | |
| 2019 | | | | | |
| 1 Oct | Balance | | | | 25 000 Cr |
| | **302 – Drawings – L Laurie Account** | | | | |
| 2019 | | | | | |
| 1 Oct | Balance | | | | 900 Dr |
| 25 | Purchases and GST paid | GJ | 220 | | 1 120 Dr |
| | **401 – Sales Account** | | | | |
| 2019 | | | | | |
| 1 Oct | Balance | | | | 3 900 Cr |
| 31 | Accounts receivable control | SJ | | 460 | 4 360 Cr |
| | Cash at bank | CRJ | | 1 020 | 5 380 Cr |
| | **402 – Sales Returns and Allowances Account** | | | | |
| 2019 | | | | | |
| 1 Oct | Balance | | | | 300 Dr |
| 20 | Cash at bank | CPJ | 300 | | 600 Dr |
| 31 | Accounts receivable control | SRJ | 20 | | 620 Dr |

| General Ledger | | | | | |
|---|---|---|---|---|---|
| Date | Particulars | Fol | Debit | Credit | Balance |
| **403 – Rent Income Account** | | | | | |
| 2019 | | | $ | $ | $ |
| 1 Oct | Balance | | | | 300 Cr |
| 31 | Cash at bank | CRJ | | 100 | 400 Cr |
| **404 – Interest Income Account** | | | | | |
| 2019 | | | | | |
| 1 Oct | Balance | | | | 490 Cr |
| 11 | Cash at bank | CRJ | | 40 | 530 Cr |
| **405 – Discount Income Account** | | | | | |
| 2019 | | | | | |
| 1 Oct | Balance | | | | 150 Cr |
| 31 | Accounts payable control | CPJ | | 40 | 190 Cr |
| **406 – Sale of Non-Current Assets Account** | | | | | |
| 2019 | | | | | |
| 11 Oct | Accounts receivable control | SJ | | 160 | 160 Cr |
| **501 – Purchases Account** | | | | | |
| 2019 | | | | | |
| 1 Oct | Balance | | | | 2 410 Dr |
| 25 | Drawings – L Laurie | GJ | | 200 | 2 210 Dr |
| 31 | Accounts payable control | PJ | 610 | | 2 820 Dr |
| | Cash at bank | CPJ | 70 | | 2 890 Dr |
| **502 – Purchases Returns and Allowances Account** | | | | | |
| 2019 | | | | | |
| 1 Oct | Balance | | | | 260 Cr |
| 31 | Accounts payable control | PRJ | | 10 | 270 Cr |
| **503 – Rent Expense Account** | | | | | |
| 2019 | | | | | |
| 1 Oct | Balance | | | | 480 Dr |
| 19 | Cash at bank | CPJ | 610 | | 1 090 Dr |
| **504 – Wages Account** | | | | | |
| 2019 | | | | | |
| 1 Oct | Balance | | | | 300 Dr |
| 31 | Cash at bank | CPJ | 100 | | 400 Dr |

| General Ledger | | | | | |
|---|---|---|---|---|---|
| Date | Particulars | Fol | Debit | Credit | Balance |
| **505 – Discount Expense Account** | | | | | |
| 2019 | | | $ | $ | $ |
| 1 Oct | Balance | | | | 110 Dr |
| 31 | Accounts receivable control | CRJ | 10 | | 120 Dr |
| **506 – Bad Debts Account** | | | | | |
| 2019 | | | | | |
| 1 Oct | Balance | | | | 40 Dr |
| 17 | Accounts receivable control | GJ | 50 | | 90 Dr |
| **507 – Interest Expense Account** | | | | | |
| 2019 | | | | | |
| 1 Oct | Balance | | | | 5 Dr |
| **508 – Motor Vehicle Expenses Account** | | | | | |
| 2019 | | | | | |
| 1 Oct | Balance | | | | 450 Dr |
| 5 | Accounts payable control | PJ | 120 | | 570 Dr |
| 6 | Accounts payable control | PRJ | | 20 | 550 Dr |
| **509 – Merchant Fees Expense Account** | | | | | |
| 2019 | | | | | |
| 1 Oct | Balance | | | | 126 Dr |
| 6 | Accounts receivable control | CRJ | 10 | | 136 Dr |

| Trial balance as at 31 October 2019 | | | |
|---|---|---|---|
| Account no. | Account name | Debit | Credit |
| | | $ | $ |
| 101 | Cash at bank | 3 400 | |
| 102 | Accounts receivable control | 739 | |
| 103 | Furniture and equipment | 1 230 | |
| 104 | Stock | 1 869 | |
| 105 | Motor vehicles | 8 600 | |
| 106 | Land and buildings | 42 000 | |
| 107 | GST paid | 115 | |

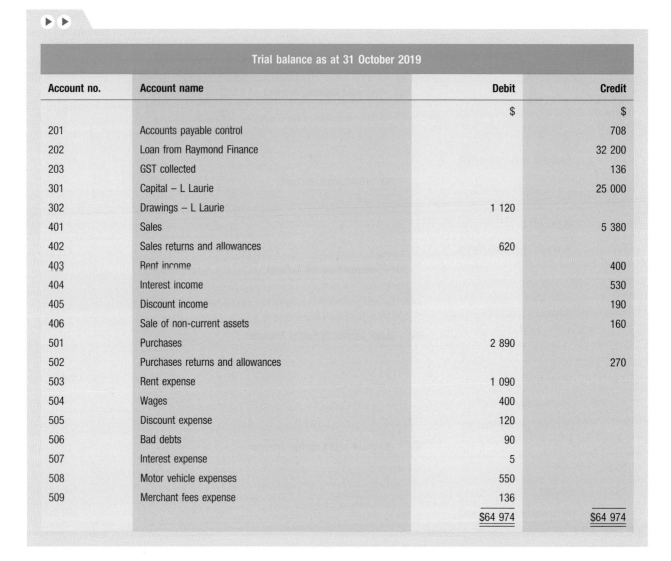

| Trial balance as at 31 October 2019 | | | |
|---|---|---|---|
| Account no. | Account name | Debit | Credit |
| | | $ | $ |
| 201 | Accounts payable control | | 708 |
| 202 | Loan from Raymond Finance | | 32 200 |
| 203 | GST collected | | 136 |
| 301 | Capital – L Laurie | | 25 000 |
| 302 | Drawings – L Laurie | 1 120 | |
| 401 | Sales | | 5 380 |
| 402 | Sales returns and allowances | 620 | |
| 403 | Rent income | | 400 |
| 404 | Interest income | | 530 |
| 405 | Discount income | | 190 |
| 406 | Sale of non-current assets | | 160 |
| 501 | Purchases | 2 890 | |
| 502 | Purchases returns and allowances | | 270 |
| 503 | Rent expense | 1 090 | |
| 504 | Wages | 400 | |
| 505 | Discount expense | 120 | |
| 506 | Bad debts | 90 | |
| 507 | Interest expense | 5 | |
| 508 | Motor vehicle expenses | 550 | |
| 509 | Merchant fees expense | 136 | |
| | | $64 974 | $64 974 |

| Accounts Receivable Subsidiary Ledger | | | | | |
|---|---|---|---|---|---|
| Date | Particulars | Fol | Debit | Credit | Balance |
| **D1 – B Border Account** | | | | | |
| 2019 | | | $ | $ | $ |
| 11 Oct | Sales and GST collected | SJ | 176 | | 176 Dr |
| 31 | Contra entry | GJ | | 121 | 55 Dr |
| **D2 – A Warne Account** | | | | | |
| 2019 | | | | | |
| 1 Oct | Balance | | | | 220 Dr |
| 17 | Bad debts and GST collected | GJ | | 55 | 165 Dr |
| | Cash at bank | CRJ | | 165 | Nil |

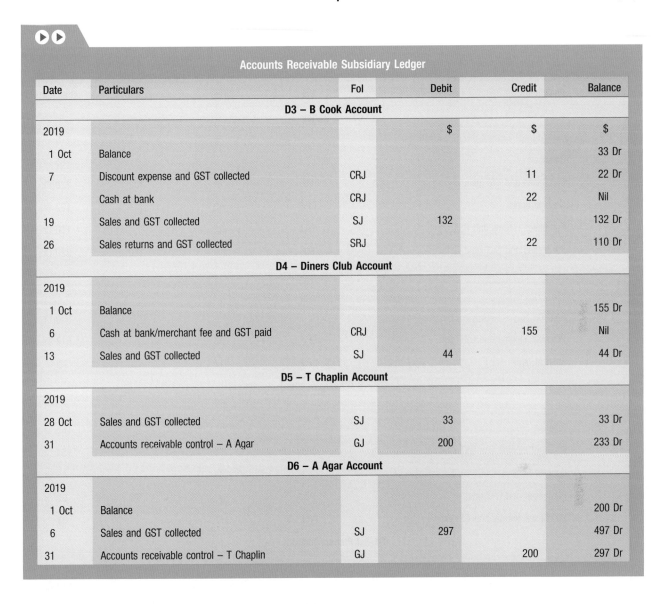

| Date | Particulars | Fol | Debit | Credit | Balance |
|------|-------------|-----|-------|--------|---------|
| | **Accounts Receivable Subsidiary Ledger** | | | | |
| | **D3 – B Cook Account** | | | | |
| 2019 | | | $ | $ | $ |
| 1 Oct | Balance | | | | 33 Dr |
| 7 | Discount expense and GST collected | CRJ | | 11 | 22 Dr |
| | Cash at bank | CRJ | | 22 | Nil |
| 19 | Sales and GST collected | SJ | 132 | | 132 Dr |
| 26 | Sales returns and GST collected | SRJ | | 22 | 110 Dr |
| | **D4 – Diners Club Account** | | | | |
| 2019 | | | | | |
| 1 Oct | Balance | | | | 155 Dr |
| 6 | Cash at bank/merchant fee and GST paid | CRJ | | 155 | Nil |
| 13 | Sales and GST collected | SJ | 44 | | 44 Dr |
| | **D5 – T Chaplin Account** | | | | |
| 2019 | | | | | |
| 28 Oct | Sales and GST collected | SJ | 33 | | 33 Dr |
| 31 | Accounts receivable control – A Agar | GJ | 200 | | 233 Dr |
| | **D6 – A Agar Account** | | | | |
| 2019 | | | | | |
| 1 Oct | Balance | | | | 200 Dr |
| 6 | Sales and GST collected | SJ | 297 | | 497 Dr |
| 31 | Accounts receivable control – T Chaplin | GJ | | 200 | 297 Dr |

| Accounts receivable reconciliation as at 31 October 2019 | | |
|-------------|------|---------|
| **Account no.** | **Name** | **Balance** |
| | | $ |
| D1 | B Border | 55 |
| D3 | B Cook | 110 |
| D4 | Diners Club | 44 |
| D5 | T Chaplin | 233 |
| D6 | A Agar | 297 |
| Total as per Accounts Receivable Control Account | | $739 |

| Accounts Payable Subsidiary Ledger | | | | | |
|---|---|---|---|---|---|
| Date | Particulars | Fol | Debit | Credit | Balance |
| **C1 – S Harley** | | | | | |
| 2019 | | | $ | $ | $ |
| 1 Oct | Balance | | | | 88 Cr |
| 5 | Purchases and GST paid | PJ | | 132 | 220 Cr |
| | Cash at bank | CPJ | 88 | | 132 Cr |
| 6 | Purchases returns and GST paid | PRJ | 22 | | 110 Cr |
| 18 | Purchases and GST paid | PJ | | 110 | 220 Cr |
| **C2 – A Hughes Account** | | | | | |
| 2019 | | | | | |
| 1 Oct | Balance | | | | 550 Cr |
| 5 | Discount income and GST paid | CPJ | 33 | | 517 Cr |
| | Cash at bank | CPJ | 517 | | Nil |
| **C3 – B O'Keefe Account** | | | | | |
| 2019 | | | | | |
| 1 Oct | Balance | | | | 165 Cr |
| 5 | Discount income and GST paid | CPJ | 11 | | 154 Cr |
| | Cash at bank | CPJ | 139 | | 15 Cr |
| 11 | Purchases and GST paid | PJ | | 77 | 92 Cr |
| 13 | Purchases returns and GST paid | PRJ | 11 | | 81 Cr |
| **C4 – J Pleban Account** | | | | | |
| 2019 | | | | | |
| 1 Oct | Balance | | | | 110 Cr |
| 11 | Purchases and GST paid | PJ | | 33 | 143 Cr |
| | Cash at bank | CPJ | 110 | | 33 Cr |
| **C5 – B Border Account** | | | | | |
| 2019 | | | | | |
| 1 Oct | Balance | | | | 44 Cr |
| 2 | Purchases and GST paid | PJ | | 77 | 121 Cr |
| 31 | Contra entry | GJ | 121 | | Nil |
| **C6 – A Roberts Account** | | | | | |
| 2019 | | | | | |
| 27 Oct | Purchases and GST paid | PJ | | 374 | 374 Cr |

| Accounts payable reconciliation as at 31 October 2019 | | |
|---|---|---|
| **Account no.** | **Name** | **Balance** |
| | | $ |
| C1 | S Harley | 220 |
| C3 | B O'Keefe | 81 |
| C4 | J Pleban | 33 |
| C6 | A Roberts | 374 |
| Total as per Accounts Payable Control Account | | $708 |

# Suggested overall procedure

When posting the journals each month to the three primary ledgers (i.e. the General Ledger and the two subsidiary ledgers), it is advisable to follow the sequential procedure outlined below.

1   Post all journals to the General Ledger.
2   Prepare a trial balance.
3   Post the following journals to the Accounts Receivable Subsidiary Ledger:
    a   General Journal (only those entries affecting debtors)
    b   Sales Journal (post the sales charged and GST collected to each debtor's account)
    c   Sales Returns and Allowances Journal (post the amount of the allowance and adjustment for GST collected to each debtor's account)
    d   Cash Receipts Journal (post the two accounts receivable columns only).
    For each debtor, sort individual transactions (from all journals) into chronological sequence and post them to the debtor's account in this sequence.
4   Prepare an accounts receivable reconciliation schedule at the end of the month.
5   Post the following journals to the Accounts Payable Subsidiary Ledger:
    a   General Journal (only those entries affecting creditors)
    b   Purchases Journal (post the purchases and GST paid to each creditor's account)
    c   Purchases Returns and Allowances Journal (post the amount of allowance and adjustment for GST paid)
    d   Cash Payments Journal (post the two accounts payable columns only).
    For each creditor, sort individual transactions (from all journals) into chronological sequence and post them to the creditor's account in this sequence.
6   Prepare an accounts payable reconciliation schedule at the end of the month.

## EXERCISES

ADDITIONAL
EXERCISES

UWATCH 4.1

4.1 This exercise is also available in a MYOB format on the CD that accompanies the workbook.

A UWatch demonstration is available on the CD that accompanies this text for parts of this activity.

The following information relates to B Jackson, retailer. You are required to:

a complete the Accounts Receivable Control Account in the General Ledger for the period 1 July 2017 to 31 July 2017

b complete entries in the Accounts Receivable Subsidiary Ledger for the period 1 July 2017 to 31 July 2017

c prepare an accounts receivable reconciliation schedule at 31 July 2017.

| List of debtors at 1 July 2017 | | |
|---|---|---|
| **Account no.** | **Name** | **Balance** |
| | | $ |
| 1 | B Bartlett | 200 |
| 2 | C Joseph | 500 |
| 3 | C Hardwood | 350 |
| 4 | L Paterson | 140 |
| Total (as per Accounts Receivable Control Account) | | $1 190 |

**B Jackson**
**Sales Journal**

| Date | Debtor | Fol | Ref | Sales | Sundries Amount | Sundries Account | GST collected | Accounts receivable control |
|---|---|---|---|---|---|---|---|---|
| 2017 | | | | $ | $ | | $ | $ |
| 2 Jul | B Bartlett | | 426 | 80 | 10 | Freight income | 9 | 99 |
| 4 | C Hardwood | | 427 | 60 | | | 6 | 66 |
| 10 | L Paterson | | 428 | 70 | | | 7 | 77 |
| 12 | C Joseph | | 429 | 180 | 20 | Freight income | 20 | 220 |
| 18 | C Hardwood | | 430 | 250 | | | 25 | 275 |
| | | | | $640 | $30 | | $67 | $737 |

### Sales Returns and Allowances Journal

| Date | Debtor | Fol | Ref | Sales returns and allowances | Sundries Amount | Sundries Account | GST collected | Accounts receivable control |
|------|--------|-----|-----|------|------|------|------|------|
| 2017 | | | | $ | $ | | $ | $ |
| 6 Jul | C Hardwood | | 51 | 20 | | | 2 | 22 |
| | | | | $20 | | | $2 | $22 |

### Cash Receipts Journal

| Date | Particulars | Fol | Ref | Discount expense: Accounts receivable control | Discount expense: GST collected | Discount expense: Discount expense | Accounts receivable control | Cash sales | Sundries: Amount | Sundries: Account | GST collected | Bank |
|------|-------------|-----|-----|------|------|------|------|------|------|------|------|------|
| 2017 | | | | $ | $ | $ | $ | $ | $ | | $ | $ |
| 2 Jul | C Joseph | | 826 | 33 | 3 | 30 | 467 | | | | | 467 |
| 8 | L Paterson | | 827 | 11 | 1 | 10 | 129 | | | | | 129 |
| 12 | Cash sales | | POS | | | | | 300 | | | 30 | 330 |
| 15 | Glen's Real Estate | | EFT | | | | | | 50 | Rent income | 5 | 55 |
| 20 | Cash sales | | POS | | | | | 400 | | | 40 | 440 |
| | B Jackson | | EFT | | | | | | 1 000 | Capital – B Jackson | | 1 000 |
| 31 | EFTPOS | | POS | | | | | 100 | | | 10 | 110 |
| | | | | $44 | $4 | $40 | $596 | $800 | $1 050 | | $85 | $2 531 |

4.2     The following information relates to I Drill, dentist. You are required to:

     a    complete the Accounts Receivable Control Account in the General Ledger for the period 1 March 2019 to 31 March 2019

     b    complete entries in the Accounts Receivable Subsidiary Ledger for the period 1 March 2019 to 31 March 2019

     c    prepare an accounts receivable reconciliation schedule at 31 March 2019.

**Note** Dental services are not subject to GST.

| List of debtors at 1 March 2019 | | |
|------|------|------|
| **Account no.** | **Name** | **$** |
| D1 | D Graham | 250 |
| D2 | G Greblo | 140 |
| D3 | J Reddrop | 30 |
| D4 | American Express | 10 |
| Total (as per Accounts Receivable Control Account) | | $430 |

## I Drill
## Services Journal

| Date | Debtor | Fol | Ref | Amount |
|------|--------|-----|-----|--------|
| 2019 | | | | $ |
| 3 Mar | J Reddrop | | 057 | 150 |
| 10 | American Express | | POS | 220 |
| 12 | G Greblo | | 058 | 80 |
| 15 | J De Araugo | | 059 | 440 |
| 23 | American Express | | POS | 120 |
| 26 | J De Araugo | | 060 | 50 |
| 29 | G Grcblo | | 061 | 70 |
| 31 | J Reddrop | | 062 | 120 |
| | | | | $1 250 |

## Cash Receipts Journal

| Date | Particulars | Fol | Ref | Discount expense — Accounts receivable control | Discount expense | Accounts receivable control | Cash services | Sundries — Amount | Sundries — Account | Bank |
|------|-------------|-----|-----|------|------|------|------|------|------|------|
| 2019 | | | | $ | $ | $ | $ | $ | | $ |
| 1 Mar | Service fees | | 194 | | | | 100 | | | 100 |
| 2 | G Greblo | | 195 | 4 | 4 | 136 | | | | 136 |
| 15 | American Express | | 196 | | | | | | | |
| | – Gross | | | | | 230 | | | | |
| | – Merchant fees | | | | | | | (10) | Merchant fees expense | |
| | – GST paid | | | | | | | (1) | GST paid | 219 |
| 20 | Service fees | | 197 | | | | 200 | | | |
| | AB Finance | | EFT | | | | | 50 | Interest income | 250 |
| 31 | D Graham | | 198 | | | 50 | | | | 50 |
| | | | | $4 | $4 | $416 | $300 | $39 | | $755 |

**4.3** This exercise is also available in a MYOB format on the CD that accompanies the workbook.

A UWatch demonstration is available on the CD that accompanies this text for parts of this activity.

The following information relates to B Jackson, retailer. You are required to:

a complete the Accounts Payable Control Account in the General Ledger for the period 1 July 2017 to 31 July 2017

b complete entries in the Accounts Payable Subsidiary Ledger for the period 1 July 2017 to 31 July 2017

c prepare an accounts payable reconciliation schedule at 31 July 2017.

ADDITIONAL
EXERCISES

UWATCH 4.2

| List of creditors at 1 July 2017 | | |
|---|---|---|
| **Account no.** | **Name** | **$** |
| 1 | M Holden | 77 |
| 2 | A Graham | 220 |
| 3 | D Senn | 44 |
| 4 | R Gilchrist | 286 |
| 5 | T Norrow | 253 |
| Total (as per Accounts Payable Control Account) | | $880 |

**Purchases Journal**

| Date | Creditor | Fol | Ref | Purchases | Sundries Amount | Sundries Account | GST paid | Accounts payable control |
|---|---|---|---|---|---|---|---|---|
| 2017 | | | | $ | $ | | $ | $ |
| 3 Jul | A Graham | | V86 | 220 | | | 22 | 242 |
| 5 | D Senn | | 1289 | | 60 | Stationery | 6 | 66 |
| 12 | T Norrow | | V8421 | 80 | | | 8 | 88 |
| 30 | R Gilchrist | | A627 | 40 | | | 4 | 44 |
| | | | | $340 | $60 | | $40 | $440 |

**Purchases Returns and Allowances Journal**

| Date | Creditor | Fol | Ref | Purchases returns and allowances | Sundries Amount | Sundries Account | GST paid | Accounts payable control |
|---|---|---|---|---|---|---|---|---|
| 2017 | | | | $ | $ | | $ | $ |
| 6 Jul | D Senn | | C14 | | 60 | Stationery | 6 | 66 |
| | | | | | $60 | | $6 | $66 |

## Cash Payments Journal

| Date | Particulars | Fol | Ref | Discount income — Accounts payable control | GST paid | Discount income | Accounts payable control | Cash purchases | Wages | Sundries — Amount | Sundries — Account | GST paid | Bank |
|------|-------------|-----|-----|------|------|------|------|------|------|------|------|------|------|
| 2017 | | | | $ | $ | $ | $ | $ | $ | $ | | $ | $ |
| 1 Jul | Purchases | | 901 | | | | | 200 | | | | 20 | 220 |
| 8 | M Holden | | 902 | | | | 77 | | | | | | 77 |
| 12 | Rent | | EFT | | | | | | 330 | | | | 330 |
| | A Graham | | 903 | 22 | 2 | 20 | 218 | | | | | | 218 |
| 31 | B Jackson | | EFT | | | | | | | 40 | Drawings – B Jackson | | 40 |
| | | | | $22 | $2 | $20 | $295 | $200 | $330 | $40 | | $20 | $885 |

**4.4** This question is available on the CD that accompanies this text.

**4.5** The following information relates to Choo Tran, retailer. You are required to:

    a complete the Accounts Receivable Control Account and Accounts Payable Control Account in the General Ledger for the period 1 October 2017 to 31 October 2017

    b complete all entries in the Accounts Receivable Subsidiary Ledger for the period 1 October 2017 to 31 October 2017

    c prepare an accounts receivable reconciliation schedule at 31 October 2017

    d complete all entries in the Accounts Payable Subsidiary Ledger for the period 1 October 2017 to 31 October 2017

    e prepare an accounts payable reconciliation schedule at 31 October 2017.

| Balances at 1 October 2017 | | | | | |
|---|---|---|---|---|---|
| **Debtors** | | | **Creditors** | | |
| **Account no.** | **Name** | **Balance** | **Account no.** | **Name** | **Balance** |
| | | $ | | | $ |
| D01 | T Larwood | 198 | C01 | R McCol | 220 |
| D02 | H Pondsford | 132 | C02 | L Hayden | 88 |
| D03 | A Haig | 88 | C03 | B Hocling | 66 |
| D04 | C Wilson | 66 | C04 | D Brand | 121 |
| D05 | S Reyne | 143 | C05 | F Morris | 253 |
| Total (as per Accounts Receivable Control Account) | | $627 | Total (as per Accounts Payable Control Account) | | $748 |

## Sales Journal

| Date | Debtor | Fol | Ref | Sales | Sundries Amount | Sundries Account | GST collected | Accounts receivable control |
|---|---|---|---|---|---|---|---|---|
| 2017 | | | | $ | $ | | $ | $ |
| 2 Oct | H Pondsford | | 132 | 180 | | | 18 | 198 |
| 7 | C Wilson | | 133 | 280 | 20 | Freight income | 30 | 330 |
| 10 | A Haig | | 134 | 80 | | | 8 | 88 |
| 14 | C Wilson | | 135 | 50 | | | 5 | 55 |
| 23 | T Larwood | | 136 | 90 | | | 9 | 99 |
| 31 | Diners Club | | POS | 120 | | | 12 | 132 |
| | | | | $800 | $20 | | $82 | $902 |

## Purchases Journal

| Date | Creditor | Fol | Ref | Purchases | Sundries Amount | Sundries Account | GST paid | Accounts payable control |
|---|---|---|---|---|---|---|---|---|
| 2017 | | | | $ | $ | | $ | $ |
| 5 Oct | D Brand | | 536 | 90 | | | 9 | 99 |
| 8 | F Morris | | M55 | 50 | | | 5 | 55 |
| 16 | R McCol | | 771 | 60 | | | 6 | 66 |
| 20 | L Hayden | | 44HA | | 160 | Insurance | 16 | 176 |
| 24 | D Brand | | 601 | 70 | | | 7 | 77 |
| | | | | $270 | $160 | | $43 | $473 |

## Sales Returns and Allowances Journal

| Date | Debtor | Fol | Ref | Sales returns and allowances | Sundries Amount | Sundries Account | GST collected | Accounts receivable control |
|---|---|---|---|---|---|---|---|---|
| 2017 | | | | $ | $ | | $ | $ |
| 3 Oct | H Pondsford | | 32 | 10 | | | 1 | 11 |
| 16 | C Wilson | | 33 | 27 | 3 | Freight income | 3 | 33 |
| | | | | $37 | $3 | | $4 | $44 |

## Purchases Returns and Allowances Journal

| Date | Creditor | Fol | Ref | Purchases returns and allowances | Sundries Amount | Sundries Account | GST paid | Accounts payable control |
|---|---|---|---|---|---|---|---|---|
| 2017 | | | | $ | $ | | $ | $ |
| 10 Oct | F Morris | | 43C | 10 | | | 1 | 11 |
| | | | | $10 | | | $1 | $11 |

## Cash Receipts Journal

| Date | Particulars | Fol | Ref | Discount expense — Accounts receivable control | Discount expense — GST collected | Discount expense — Discount expense | Accounts receivable control | Cash sales | Sundries — Amount | Sundries — Account | GST collected | Bank |
|---|---|---|---|---|---|---|---|---|---|---|---|---|
| 2017 | | | | $ | $ | $ | $ | $ | $ | | $ | $ |
| 6 Oct | EFTPOS | | POS | | | | | 400 | | | 40 | 440 |
| 11 | C O'Donoghue | | 807 | | | | | | 70 | Commission income | 7 | 77 |
| 16 | C Wilson | | 808 | | | | 66 | | | | | 66 |
| 19 | H Pondsford | | 809 | | | | 88 | | | | | 88 |
| 22 | T Larwood | | 810 | 11 | 1 | 10 | 187 | | | | | 187 |
| 25 | A Haig | | 811 | | | | 88 | | | | | 88 |
| | Sales | | POS | | | | | 500 | | | 50 | 638 |
| 31 | S Reyne | | EFT | 11 | 1 | 10 | 132 | | | | | 132 |
| | | | | $22 | $2 | $20 | $561 | $900 | $70 | | $97 | $1 628 |

## Cash Payments Journal

| Date | Particulars | Fol | Chq no. | Discount income — Accounts payable control | Discount income — GST paid | Discount income — Discount income | Accounts payable control | Cash purchases supplies | Wages | Sundries — Amount | Sundries — Account | GST paid | Bank |
|---|---|---|---|---|---|---|---|---|---|---|---|---|---|
| 2017 | | | | $ | $ | $ | $ | $ | $ | $ | | $ | $ |
| 8 Oct | D Brand | | 332 | 11 | 1 | 10 | 110 | | | | | | 110 |
| 13 | Z Holmes | | 333 | | | | | | | 240 | Rent | 24 | 264 |
| 15 | F Morris | | 334 | 22 | 2 | 20 | 231 | | | | | | 231 |
| | L Hayden | | 335 | | | | 88 | | | | | | 88 |

▶▶

## Cash Payments Journal

| Date | Particulars | Fol | Chq no. | Accounts payable control $ | GST paid $ | Discount income $ | Accounts payable control $ | Cash purchases supplies $ | Wages $ | Amount $ | Account | GST paid $ | Bank $ |
|---|---|---|---|---|---|---|---|---|---|---|---|---|---|
| 2017 | | | | | | | | | | | | | |
| 24 | Purchases | | EFT | | | | | 260 | | | | 26 | 286 |
| 31 | R McCol | | 336 | 22 | 2 | 20 | 198 | | | | | | 198 |
| | | | | $55 | $5 | $50 | $627 | $260 | | $240 | | $50 | $1 177 |

4.6\* The following information relates to the business of J Maxwell, wholesaler. You are required to:

a complete the Accounts Receivable Control Account and Accounts Payable Control Account in the General Ledger for the period 1 June 2019 to 30 June 2019

b complete all entries in the Accounts Receivable Subsidiary Ledger for the period 1 June 2019 to 30 June 2019

c prepare an accounts receivable reconciliation schedule at 30 June 2019

d complete all entries in the Accounts Payable Subsidiary Ledger for the period 1 June 2019 to 30 June 2019

e prepare an accounts payable reconciliation schedule at 30 June 2019.

### Balances as at 1 June 2019

| Debtors Account no. | Name | Balance $ | Creditors Account no. | Name | Balance $ |
|---|---|---|---|---|---|
| D1 | J Graham | 500 | C1 | N Jackson | 836 |
| D2 | American Express | 260 | C2 | P Marsh | 4 180 |
| D3 | A Howard | 420 | C3 | R Moore | 198 |
| D4 | L McDermott | 986 | C4 | A Blight | 500 |
| D5 | J Enright | 1 390 | C5 | A Howard | 600 |
| Total as per Accounts Receivable Control Account | | $3 556 | Total as per Accounts Payable Control Account | | $6 314 |

### Sales Journal

| Date | Debtor | Fol | Ref | Sales $ | Sundries Amount $ | Account | GST collected $ | Accounts receivable control $ |
|---|---|---|---|---|---|---|---|---|
| 2019 | | | | | | | | |
| 3 Jun | American Express | | POS | 300 | | | 30 | 330 |
| 8 | L McDermott | | 453 | 490 | | | 49 | 539 |

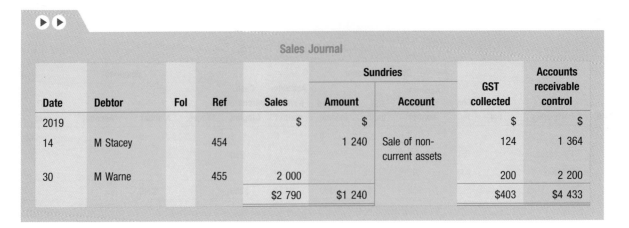

### Sales Journal

| Date | Debtor | Fol | Ref | Sales | Sundries Amount | Sundries Account | GST collected | Accounts receivable control |
|------|--------|-----|-----|-------|--------|---------|---------------|------------------|
| 2019 | | | | $ | $ | | $ | $ |
| 14 | M Stacey | | 454 | | 1 240 | Sale of non-current assets | 124 | 1 364 |
| 30 | M Warne | | 455 | 2 000 | | | 200 | 2 200 |
| | | | | $2 790 | $1 240 | | $403 | $4 433 |

### Sales Returns and Allowances Journal

| Date | Debtor | Fol | Ref | Sales returns and allowances | Sundries Amount | Sundries Account | GST collected | Accounts receivable control |
|------|--------|-----|-----|------------------------------|--------|---------|---------------|------------------|
| 2019 | | | | $ | $ | | $ | $ |
| 12 Jun | A Howard | | 65 | 120 | | | 12 | 132 |
| 16 | M Stacey | | 66 | | 600 | Sale of non-current assets | 60 | 660 |
| | | | | $120 | $600 | | $72 | $792 |

### Purchases Journal

| Date | Creditor | Fol | Ref | Purchases | Sundries Amount | Sundries Account | GST paid | Accounts payable control |
|------|----------|-----|-----|-----------|--------|---------|----------|------------------|
| 2019 | | | | $ | $ | | $ | $ |
| 3 Jun | T Murphy | | M44 | | 250 | Insurance | 25 | 275 |
| 8 | P Marsh | | 52 | 500 | | | 50 | 550 |
| 14 | A Blight | | 218 | 700 | | | 70 | 770 |
| 20 | R Moore | | 33N | 400 | | | 40 | 440 |
| | | | | $1 600 | $250 | | $185 | $2 035 |

### Purchases Returns and Allowances Journal

| Date | Creditor | Fol | Ref | Purchases returns and allowances | Sundries Amount | Sundries Account | GST paid | Accounts payable control |
|------|----------|-----|-----|------|------|------|------|------|
| 2019 | | | | $ | $ | | $ | $ |
| 9 Jun | N Jackson | | 755 | 100 | | | 10 | 110 |
| | | | | $100 | | | $10 | $110 |

### Cash Receipts Journal

| Date | Particulars | Fol | Ref | Discount expense Accounts receivable control | Discount expense GST collected | Discount expense Discount expense | Accounts receivable control | Cash sales | Sundries Amount | Sundries Account | GST collected | Bank |
|------|-------------|-----|-----|------|------|------|------|------|------|------|------|------|
| 2019 | | | | $ | $ | $ | $ | $ | $ | | $ | $ |
| 1 Jun | Sales | | POS | | | | | 1 000 | | | 100 | 1 100 |
| 2 | L McCrae | | 510 | 22 | 2 | 20 | 854 | | | | | 854 |
| | EFTPOS | | POS | | | | | 2 000 | | | 200 | 2 200 |
| 5 | American Express | | EFT | | | | | | | | | |
| | – Gross | | | | | | 260 | | | | | |
| | – Merchant fees | | | | | – | | | (10) | Merchant fee expense | | |
| | – GST paid | | | | | | | | (1) | GST paid | | 249 |
| 30 | J Graham | | 511 | | | | 104 | | | | | 104 |
| | | | | $22 | $2 | $20 | $1 218 | $3 000 | $(11) | | $300 | $4 507 |

### Cash Payments Journal

| Date | Particulars | Fol | Ref | Discount income Accounts payable control | Discount income GST paid | Discount income Discount income | Accounts payable control | Cash purchases | Wages | Sundries Amount | Sundries Account | GST paid | Bank |
|------|-------------|-----|-----|------|------|------|------|------|------|------|------|------|------|
| 2019 | | | | $ | $ | $ | $ | $ | $ | $ | | $ | $ |
| 3 Jun | Purchases | | 071 | | | | | 350 | | | | 35 | 385 |
| 12 | A Blight | | 072 | 11 | 1 | 10 | 489 | | | | | | 489 |
| 15 | R Moore | | 073 | 22 | 2 | 20 | 176 | | | | | | 176 |
| 30 | A Howard | | EFT | | | | 300 | | | | | | 300 |
| | | | | $33 | $3 | $30 | $965 | $350 | | | | $35 | $1 350 |

## General Journal

| Date | Particulars | Fol | Debit | Credit |
|---|---|---|---|---|
| 2019 | | | $ | $ |
| 30 Jun | Bad debts | | 360 | |
| | GST collected | | 36 | |
| |     Accounts receivable control – J Graham, D1 | | | 396 |
| | *Bad debt written off – J Graham* | | | |
| | Accounts receivable control – J Enright, D5 | | 33 | |
| |     Late fees income | | | 33 |
| | *Late fee charged to J Enright on overdue account* | | | |
| | Accounts payable control – A Howard, C5 | | 288 | |
| |     Accounts receivable control – A Howard, D3 | | | 288 |
| | *Contra entry* | | | |
| | Late fees expenses | | 55 | |
| |     Accounts payable control – P Marsh, C2 | | | 55 |
| | *Late fee charge on overdue account – P Marsh* | | | |
| | Accounts receivable control – L McCrae, D6 | | 876 | |
| |     Accounts receivable control – L McDermott, D4 | | | 876 |
| | *Correction of error – goods sold on credit to McCrae in May 2019 were incorrectly recorded as being sold to McDermott* | | | |
| | Sales | | 100 | |
| | GST collected | | 10 | |
| |     Accounts receivable – L McDermott, D4 | | | 110 |
| | *Sales invoice 448 to L McDermott overstated in Sales Journal in May by $110* | | | |

**4.7** The following information relates to Redpath Retailers. You are required to prepare:

a the General Ledger for June 2019

b the Accounts Receivable and Accounts Payable Subsidiary Ledgers for June 2019

c a trial balance of the General Ledger at 30 June 2019

d an accounts receivable reconciliation schedule at 30 June 2019

e an accounts payable reconciliation schedule at 30 June 2019.

| Redpath Retailers Trial balance as at 1 June 2019 | | |
|---|---|---|
| Account | Debit | Credit |
| | $ | $ |
| Accounts receivable control | 8 000 | |
| Accounts payable control | | 7 440 |
| Cash at bank | 8 750 | |
| Stock | 3 400 | |
| Furniture and equipment | 24 500 | |
| Motor vehicles | 18 000 | |
| Capital – J Redpath | | 22 560 |
| Sales | | 121 000 |
| Sales returns and allowances | 5 500 | |
| Freight income | | 2 000 |
| Purchases | 66 000 | |
| Purchases returns and allowances | | 1 650 |
| Advertising | 2 200 | |
| Wages | 13 200 | |
| Rent | 5 500 | |
| GST collected | | 1 050 |
| GST paid | 650 | |
| | $155 700 | $155 700 |

| Subsidiary ledger balances at 1 June 2019 | | | |
|---|---|---|---|
| Accounts receivable | | Accounts payable | |
| | $ | | $ |
| H Milburn | 1 400 | R Hutton | 1 800 |
| P Walters | 1 200 | B Clarke | 2 700 |
| D Chaplin | 4 800 | L Haig | 2 340 |
| J Chapman | 600 | S Lin | 600 |
| | $8 000 | | $7 440 |

## General Journal

| Date | Particulars | Fol | Debit | Credit |
|------|-------------|-----|-------|--------|
| 2019 | | | $ | $ |
| 24 Jun | Land and buildings | | 50 000 | |
| | GST paid | | 5 000 | |
| |     Mortgage loan on land and buildings | | | 55 000 |
| | *Purchase of new building* | | | |
| 30 | Bad debts | | 600 | |
| | GST collected | | 60 | |
| |     Accounts receivable control – P Walters | | | 660 |
| | *P Walters bankrupt; write off as bad debt* | | | |

## Cash Receipts Journal

| Date | Particulars | Fol | Ref | Discount expense — Accounts receivable control | Discount expense — GST collected | Discount expense | Accounts receivable control | Cash sales | Sundries — Amount | Sundries — Account | GST collected | Bank |
|------|-------------|-----|-----|----|----|----|----|----|----|----|----|----|
| 2019 | | | | $ | $ | $ | $ | $ | $ | | $ | $ |
| 2 Jun | J Chapman | | F61 | 66 | 6 | 60 | 534 | | | | | |
| | Sales | | POS | | | | | 1 300 | | | 130 | 1 964 |
| 5 | Sales | | POS | | | | | 480 | | | 48 | 528 |
| 8 | D Chaplin | | F62 | 220 | 20 | 200 | 4 580 | | | | | 4 580 |
| 12 | Sales | | POS | | | | | 1 100 | | | 110 | 1 210 |
| 14 | H Milburn | | F63 | 77 | 7 | 70 | 1 323 | | | | | 1 323 |
| 19 | Sales | | POS | | | | | 750 | | | 75 | 825 |
| 21 | J Chapman | | EFT | 22 | 2 | 20 | 506 | | | | | 506 |
| 24 | Sales | | POS | | | | | 360 | | | 36 | 396 |
| 26 | Sales | | POS | | | | | 1 800 | | | 180 | |
| | D Chaplin | | F64 | 44 | 4 | 40 | 1 408 | | | | | 3 388 |
| 30 | P Walters | | F65 | | | | 540 | | | | | 540 |
| | | | | $429 | $39 | $390 | $8 891 | $5 790 | | | $579 | $15 260 |

## Cash Payments Journal

| Date | Particulars | Fol | Ref | Accounts payable control (Discount income) | GST paid | Discount income | Accounts payable control | Cash purchases | Wages | Amount (Sundries) | Account (Sundries) | GST paid | Bank |
|------|-------------|-----|-----|------|------|------|------|------|------|------|------|------|------|
| 2019 | | | | $ | $ | $ | $ | $ | $ | $ | | $ | $ |
| 3 Jun | Wages | | EFT | | | | | | 600 | | | | 600 |
| 4 | Purchases | | D91 | | | | | 500 | | | | 50 | 550 |
| | B Clarke | | D92 | 132 | 12 | 120 | 2 568 | | | | | | 2 568 |
| 6 | Jay's Garage | | D93 | | | | | | | 500 | Motor vehicle expenses | 50 | 550 |
| 9 | Purchases | | D94 | | | | | 800 | | | | 80 | 880 |
| 11 | L Haig | | D95 | 110 | 10 | 100 | 2 230 | | | | | | 2 230 |
| 15 | J Peschi | | D96 | | | | | | | 200 | Rent | 20 | 220 |
| 17 | Wages | | EFT | | | | | | 600 | | | | 600 |
| 20 | R Hutton | | D97 | 88 | 8 | 80 | 1 712 | | | | | | 1 712 |
| 23 | Purchases | | D98 | | | | | 400 | | | | 40 | 440 |
| 24 | Elite Construction | | D99 | | | | | | | 5 000 | Land and buildings | 500 | 5 500 |
| 30 | ATO | | EFT | | | | | | | 1 050 | GST collected | | |
| | | | | | | | | | | (650) | GST paid | | 400 |
| | | | | $330 | $30 | $300 | $6 510 | $1 700 | $1 200 | $6 100 | | $740 | $16 250 |

## Sales Journal

| Date | Debtor | Fol | Ref | Sales | Account (Sundries) | Amount (Sundries) | GST collected | Accounts receivable control |
|------|--------|-----|-----|-------|------|------|------|------|
| 2019 | | | | $ | $ | | $ | $ |
| 5 Jun | J Chapman | | E106 | 600 | | | 60 | 660 |
| 9 | D Chaplin | | E107 | 1 400 | 40 | Freight income | 144 | 1 584 |
| 14 | H Milburn | | E108 | 1 800 | | | 180 | 1 980 |
| 20 | J Chapman | | E109 | 1 200 | | | 120 | 1 320 |
| 25 | D Chaplin | | E110 | 700 | 20 | Freight income | 72 | 792 |
| | | | | $5 700 | $60 | | $576 | $6 336 |

## Purchases Journal

| Date | Creditor | Fol | Ref | Purchases | Sundries Amount | Sundries Account | GST paid | Accounts payable control |
|------|----------|-----|-----|-----------|--------|---------|----------|------------------|
| 2019 | | | | $ | $ | | $ | $ |
| 3 Jun | B Clarke | | SA80 | 700 | | | 70 | 770 |
| 9 | S Lin | | LA903 | 1 000 | | | 100 | 1 100 |
| 15 | L Haig | | WM88 | | 500 | Advertising | 50 | 550 |
| 22 | R Hutton | | RC605 | 1 200 | | | 120 | 1 320 |
| 27 | B Clarke | | SA103 | 500 | | | 50 | 550 |
| | | | | $3 400 | $500 | | $390 | $4 290 |

## Sales Returns and Allowances Journal

| Date | Debtor | Fol | Ref | Sales returns and allowances | Sundries Amount | Sundries Account | GST collected | Accounts receivable control |
|------|--------|-----|-----|------------------------------|--------|---------|---------------|-------------------|
| 2019 | | | | $ | $ | | $ | $ |
| 9 Jun | J Chapman | | W17 | 120 | | | 12 | 132 |
| 16 | H Milburn | | W18 | 240 | | | 24 | 264 |
| 27 | D Chaplin | | W19 | 100 | 20 | Freight income | 12 | 132 |
| | | | | $460 | $20 | | $48 | $528 |

## Purchases Returns and Allowances Journal

| Date | Creditor | Fol | Ref | Purchases returns and allowances | Sundries Amount | Sundries Account | GST paid | Accounts payable control |
|------|----------|-----|-----|----------------------------------|--------|---------|----------|------------------|
| 2019 | | | | $ | $ | | $ | $ |
| 11 Jun | S Lin | | CN60 | 100 | | | 10 | 110 |
| 19 | L Haig | | MC108 | 50 | | | 5 | 55 |
| | | | | $150 | | | $15 | $165 |

4.8 The following information relates to Eaglehawk Enterprises (proprietor, G Uderzo). You are required to prepare:

a the General Ledger for June 2019

b the Accounts Receivable and Accounts Payable Subsidiary Ledgers for June 2019

c a trial balance of the General Ledger at 30 June 2019

d an accounts receivable reconciliation schedule at 30 June 2019

e an accounts payable reconciliation schedule at 30 June 2019.

| Eaglehawk Enterprises Trial balance as at 1 June 2019 | | |
| --- | --- | --- |
| Account | Debit | Credit |
| | $ | $ |
| Stock | 3 000 | |
| Cash at bank | 17 530 | |
| Premises | 87 800 | |
| Furniture and fittings | 20 000 | |
| Motor vehicle | 25 000 | |
| Motor vehicle expenses | 12 000 | |
| Mortgage on premises | | 30 000 |
| Loan from R Goscinny | | 20 000 |
| Capital – G Uderzo | | 95 300 |
| Office equipment | 3 000 | |
| GST paid | 1 980 | |
| Drawings – G Uderzo | 2 540 | |
| Purchases | 346 500 | |
| Accounts receivable control | 11 000 | |
| GST collected | | 4 500 |
| Discount expense | 430 | |
| Sales | | 500 720 |
| Commission income | | 6 600 |
| Accounts payable control | | 9 400 |
| Discount income | | 260 |
| Wages | 132 000 | |
| Merchant fees | 1 200 | |
| Stationery | 500 | |
| Advertising | 11 000 | |
| Insurance | 1 200 | |
| Sales returns and allowances | 8 470 | |
| Purchases returns and allowances | | 18 370 |
| | $685 150 | $685 150 |

| Subsidiary ledger balances at 1 June 2019 | | | |
|---|---|---|---|
| **Accounts receivable** | | **Accounts payable** | |
| | $ | | $ |
| M Murphy | 4 000 | B Mitchell | 3 000 |
| B Green | 1 500 | L Grant | 2 500 |
| E Carson | 2 500 | P Corelli | 1 500 |
| Diners Club | 3 000 | G Selton | 2 400 |
| | $11 000 | | $9 400 |

| | General Journal | | | | |
|---|---|---|---|---|---|
| **Date** | **Particulars** | **Fol** | **Debit** | **Credit** |
| 2019 | | | $ | $ |
| 15 Jun | Drawings – G Uderzo | | 3 300 | |
| | GST paid | | | 300 |
| | Purchases | | | 3 000 |
| | *Withdrew goods for own use* | | | |
| 28 | Bad debts | | 2 245 | |
| | GST collected | | 225 | |
| | Accounts receivable control – E Carson | | | 2 470 |
| | *Bad debt written off – E Carson* | | | |

| | | | | Sales Journal | | | | |
|---|---|---|---|---|---|---|---|---|
| | | | | | | **Sundries** | | |
| **Date** | **Debtor** | **Fol** | **Ref** | **Sales** | **Amount** | **Account** | **GST collected** | **Accounts receivable control** |
| 2019 | | | | $ | $ | | $ | $ |
| 1 Jun | M Murphy | | K101 | 2 420 | | | 242 | 2 662 |
| 3 | B Green | | K102 | 5 000 | | | 500 | 5 500 |
| 7 | R Rosen | | K103 | | 2 300 | Commission income | 230 | 2 530 |
| 14 | Diners Club | | POS | 7 300 | | | 730 | 8 030 |
| 23 | M Murphy | | K104 | 9 000 | | | 900 | 9 900 |
| | | | | $23 720 | $2 300 | | $2 602 | $28 622 |

## Sales Returns and Allowances Journal

| Date | Debtor | Fol | Ref | Sales returns and allowances | Sundries Amount | Account | GST collected | Accounts receivable control |
|------|--------|-----|-----|------|------|------|------|------|
| 2019 | | | | $ | $ | | $ | $ |
| 5 Jun | M Murphy | | Z691 | 440 | | | 44 | 484 |
| 11 | R Rosen | | Z692 | 300 | | | 30 | 330 |
| | | | | $740 | | | $74 | $814 |

## Purchases Journal

| Date | Creditor | Fol | Ref | Purchases | Sundries Amount | Account | GST paid | Accounts payable control |
|------|--------|-----|-----|------|------|------|------|------|
| 2019 | | | | $ | $ | | $ | $ |
| 5 Jun | B Mitchell | | ZK103 | 6 100 | | | 610 | 6 710 |
| 9 | L Grant | | T1917 | 4 000 | | | 400 | 4 400 |
| 20 | P Corelli | | J1763 | | 3 330 | Stationery | 333 | 3 663 |
| 27 | G Selton | | I9764 | 7 000 | | | 700 | 7 700 |
| | | | | $17 100 | $3 330 | | $2 043 | $22 473 |

## Purchases Returns and Allowances Journal

| Date | Creditor | Fol | Ref | Purchases returns and allowances | Sundries Amount | Account | GST paid | Accounts payable control |
|------|--------|-----|-----|------|------|------|------|------|
| 2019 | | | | $ | $ | | $ | $ |
| 17 Jun | L Grant | | CT106 | 770 | | | 77 | 847 |
| 24 | P Corelli | | KN938 | | 900 | Stationery | 90 | 990 |
| | | | | $770 | $900 | | $167 | $1 837 |

## Cash Receipts Journal

| Date | Particulars | Fol | Ref | Discount expense | | | Accounts receivable control | Cash sales | Sundries | | GST collected | Bank |
|------|-------------|-----|-----|-----------------|---|---|------|------|------|------|------|------|
| | | | | Accounts receivable control | GST collected | Discount expense | Accounts receivable control | Cash sales | Amount | Account | GST collected | Bank |
| 2019 | | | | $ | $ | $ | $ | $ | $ | | $ | $ |
| 1 Jun | Sales | | POS | | | | | 5 000 | | | 500 | 5 500 |
| 9 | M Murphy | | EFT | 99 | 9 | 90 | 900 | | | | | 900 |
| 13 | B Green | | 119 | | | | 2 000 | | | | | 2 000 |
| 15 | Sales | | POS | | | | | 4 000 | | | 400 | 4 400 |
| 17 | R Rosen | | 120 | 88 | 8 | 80 | 2 112 | | | | | 2 112 |
| 24 | Sales | | POS | | | | | 11 100 | | | 1 110 | 12 210 |
| 26 | Diners Club | | 121 | | | | | | | | | |
| | – Gross | | | | | | 8 000 | | | | | |
| | – Merchant fees | | | | | | | | (180) | Merchant fees expense | | |
| | – GST paid | | | | | | | | (18) | GST paid | | 7 802 |
| 28 | E Carson | | 121 | | | | 30 | | | | | 30 |
| | | | | $187 | $17 | $170 | $13 042 | $20 100 | ($198) | | $2 010 | $34 954 |

## Cash Payments Journal

| Date | Particulars | Fol | Ref | Discount income | | | Accounts payable control | Cash purchases | Wages | Sundries | | GST paid | Bank |
|---|---|---|---|---|---|---|---|---|---|---|---|---|---|
| | | | | Accounts payable control | GST paid | Discount income | | | | Amount | Account | | |
| | | | | $ | $ | $ | $ | $ | $ | $ | | $ | $ |
| 2019 | | | | | | | | | | | | | |
| 3 Jun | Wages | | EFT | | | | | | 6 000 | | | | 6 000 |
| 7 | B Mitchell | | 1002 | 220 | 20 | 200 | 4 780 | | | | | | 4 780 |
| 10 | C Lisner | | 1003 | | | | | 4 000 | | | | 400 | 4 400 |
| 11 | A Abel | | EFT | | | | | 1 900 | | | | 190 | 2 090 |
| 15 | A Abel | | EFT | | | | | | | 50 | Stationery | 5 | 55 |
| 16 | L Grant | | 1004 | | | | 3 230 | | | | | | 3 230 |
| 19 | Wages | | EFT | | | | | | 6 000 | | | | 6 000 |
| 20 | G Uderzo | | 1005 | | | | | | | 1 800 | Drawings – G Uderzo | | 1 800 |
| 23 | P Corelli | | 1006 | 110 | 10 | 100 | 1 880 | | | | | | 1 880 |
| 27 | G Selton | | 1007 | | | | 7 000 | | | | | | 7 000 |
| 29 | G Melville | | EFT | | | | | 7 070 | | | | 707 | 7 777 |
| 30 | ATO | | EFT | | | | | | | 4 500 | GST collected | | 2 520 |
| | | | | | | | | | | (1 980) | GST paid | | |
| | | | | $330 | $30 | $300 | $16 890 | $12 970 | $12 000 | $4 370 | | $1 302 | $47 532 |

4.9 The following information relates to Ye Olde Antiques (proprietor, J Morton). You are required to prepare:

a   the General Ledger for November 2019

b   the Accounts Receivable and Accounts Payable Subsidiary Ledgers for November 2019

c   a trial balance of the General Ledger at 30 November 2019

d   an accounts receivable reconciliation schedule at 30 November 2019

e   an accounts payable reconciliation schedule at 30 November 2019.

After completing the exercise, design an appropriate chart of accounts for the business.

| Ye Olde Antiques Trial balance as at 1 November 2019 | | |
|---|---|---|
| **Account** | **Debit** | **Credit** |
| | $ | $ |
| Advertising | 7 000 | |
| Capital – J Morton | | 70 000 |
| Cash at bank | 4 295 | |
| Interest income | | 750 |
| Commission expense | 30 | |
| Accounts payable control | | 15 200 |
| Accounts receivable control | 12 300 | |
| Discount expense | 430 | |
| Discount income | | 330 |
| Furniture and fittings | 8 000 | |
| Land and buildings | 130 000 | |
| Mortgage loan on land and buildings | | 100 000 |
| Motor vehicles | 88 000 | |
| Purchases | 132 280 | |
| Purchases returns and allowances | | 25 880 |
| Commission income | | 400 |
| Loan from J Morton | | 25 640 |
| Sales | | 186 960 |
| Motor vehicle expenses | 4 200 | |
| Sales returns and allowances | 19 500 | |
| Cartage inwards | 770 | |
| Stock | 3 460 | |
| Rent | 7 400 | |
| Wages | 7 450 | |
| Repair income | | 1 650 |
| Bad debts | 600 | |
| Telephone | 1 200 | |
| GST collected | | 4 170 |
| GST paid | 4 065 | |
| | $430 980 | $430 980 |

| Subsidiary ledger balances at 1 November 2019 | | | |
|---|---|---|---|
| **Accounts receivable** | | **Accounts payable** | |
| | $ | | $ |
| Sandberg Services Co | 4 500 | Fine Furnishings Pty Ltd | 4 700 |
| Jon's Distributors | 3 800 | Marti & Co | 6 300 |
| Millie's Imports | 2 300 | Geneva Fittings Ltd | 1 800 |
| Heritage Warehouse | 1 700 | Villikins & Sons | 2 400 |
| | $12 300 | | $15 200 |

| General Journal | | | | |
|---|---|---|---|---|
| **Date** | **Particulars** | **Fol** | **Debit** | **Credit** |
| 2019 | | | $ | $ |
| 5 Nov | Drawings – J Morton | | 4 400 | |
| | GST paid | | | 400 |
| | Purchases | | | 4 000 |
| | *The owner withdrew stock for personal use* | | | |
| 13 | Accounts receivable control – Sandberg Services Co | | 165 | |
| | Late fees income | | | 165 |
| | *Charged Sandberg Services Co late fee on overdue account* | | | |
| 30 | Bad debts | | 500 | |
| | GST collected | | 50 | |
| | Accounts receivable control – Millie's Imports | | | 550 |
| | *Bad debt written off – Millie's Imports* | | | |
| | Accounts payable control – Marti & Co | | 300 | |
| | Accounts payable control – Geneva Fittings Ltd | | | 300 |
| | *Correction of error – goods purchased on credit (invoice 247D) from Geneva Fittings in Oct incorrectly recorded as being purchased from Marti & Co* | | | |

## Sales Journal

| Date | Debtor | Fol | Ref | Sales | Sundries Amount | Account | GST collected | Accounts receivable control |
|------|--------|-----|-----|-------|--------|---------|---------------|------------------|
| 2019 | | | | $ | $ | | $ | $ |
| 3 Nov | Sandberg Services Co | | Z256 | 4 200 | | | 420 | 4 620 |
| 7 | Jon's Distributors | | Z257 | 8 400 | | | 840 | 9 240 |
| 18 | Heritage Warehouse | | Z258 | 9 000 | 2 400 | Repair income | 1 140 | 12 540 |
| 23 | Sandberg Services Co | | Z259 | 5 760 | | | 576 | 6 336 |
| 29 | Heritage Warehouse | | Z260 | 6 540 | | | 654 | 7 194 |
| | | | | $33 900 | $2 400 | | $3 630 | $39 930 |

## Sales Returns and Allowances Journal

| Date | Debtor | Fol | Ref | Sales returns and allowances | Sundries Amount | Account | GST collected | Accounts receivable control |
|------|--------|-----|-----|------------------------------|--------|---------|---------------|------------------|
| 2019 | | | | $ | $ | | $ | $ |
| 13 Nov | Millie's Imports | | CR100 | 1 500 | | | 150 | 1 650 |
| 19 | Heritage Warehouse | | CR101 | | 910 | Repair income | 91 | 1 001 |
| 24 | Jon's Distributors | | CR102 | 2 400 | | | 240 | 2 640 |
| | | | | $3 900 | $910 | | $481 | $5 291 |

## Purchases Journal

| Date | Creditor | Fol | Ref | Purchases | Sundries Amount | Account | GST paid | Accounts payable control |
|------|----------|-----|-----|-----------|--------|---------|----------|------------------|
| 2019 | | | | $ | $ | | $ | $ |
| 5 Nov | Villikins & Sons | | H171Z | | 8 000 | Furniture and fittings | 800 | 8 800 |
| 11 | Fine Furnishings | | 46781 | 9 750 | | | 975 | 10 725 |
| 13 | Marti & Co | | 0731T | 12 000 | | | 1 200 | 13 200 |
| 21 | Geneva Fittings Ltd | | M7309 | 17 780 | 200 | Cartage inwards | 1 798 | 19 778 |
| 28 | Fine Furnishings | | 46802 | 10 240 | 100 | Cartage inwards | 1 034 | 11 374 |
| | | | | $49 770 | $8 300 | | $5 807 | $63 877 |

## Purchases Returns and Allowances Journal

| Date | Creditor | Fol | Ref | Purchases returns and allowances | Sundries Amount | Sundries Account | GST paid | Accounts payable control |
|---|---|---|---|---|---|---|---|---|
| 2019 | | | | $ | $ | | $ | $ |
| 7 Nov | Villikins & Sons | | HC109 | 2 820 | | | 282 | 3 102 |
| 15 | Fine Furnishings | | TC736 | 1 900 | | | 190 | 2 090 |
| 26 | Geneva Fittings Ltd | | 1730T | 1 700 | 50 | Cartage inwards | 175 | 1 925 |
| | | | | $6 420 | $50 | | $647 | $7 117 |

## Cash Receipts Journal

| Date | Particulars | Fol | Ref | Discount expense — Accounts receivable control | Discount expense — GST collected | Discount expense | Accounts receivable control | Cash sales | Sundries Amount | Sundries Account | GST collected | Bank |
|---|---|---|---|---|---|---|---|---|---|---|---|---|
| 2019 | | | | $ | $ | $ | $ | $ | $ | | $ | $ |
| 1 Nov | J Duff | | 172 | | | | | | 100 | Commission income | 10 | 110 |
| | Which Bank | | EFT | | | | | | 150 | Interest income | | 150 |
| 3 | Heritage Warehouse | | 173 | 110 | 10 | 100 | 1 590 | | | | | 1 590 |
| 6 | Cash Sales | | POS | | | | | 3 360 | | | 336 | 3 696 |
| 13 | Jon's Distributors | | 174 | 88 | 8 | 80 | 1 900 | | | | | 1 900 |
| 15 | Cash sales | | POS | | | | | 4 080 | | | 408 | 4 488 |
| 23 | Sandberg Services Co | | 175 | 132 | 12 | 120 | 2 800 | | | | | 2 800 |
| 24 | Cash sales | | POS | | | | | 3 000 | | | 300 | 3 300 |
| 29 | Sandberg Services Co | | 176 | | | | 1 600 | | | | | 1 600 |
| 30 | Millie's Imports | | 177 | | | | 100 | | | | | 100 |
| | | | | $330 | $30 | $300 | $7 990 | $10 440 | $250 | | $1 054 | $19 734 |

### Cash Payments Journal

| Date | Particulars | Fol | Ref | Discount income — Accounts payable control | GST paid | Discount income | Accounts payable control | Cash purchases | Wages | Sundries — Amount | Account | GST paid | Bank |
|---|---|---|---|---|---|---|---|---|---|---|---|---|---|
| 2019 | | | | $ | $ | $ | $ | $ | $ | $ | | $ | $ |
| 1 Nov | Cash/wages | | EFT | | | | | | 1 050 | | | | 1 050 |
| 3 | J Watts | | 011 | | | | | 700 | | | | 70 | 770 |
| 6 | Honest Real Estate | | 012 | | | | | | | 1 050 | Rent | 105 | 1 155 |
| 10 | Fine Furnishings | | 013 | 110 | 10 | 100 | 2 600 | | | | | | 2 600 |
| 15 | Marti & Co | | 014 | | | | 4 000 | | | | | | 4 000 |
| 18 | Geneva Fittings Ltd | | 015 | 88 | 8 | 80 | 1 000 | | | | | | 1 000 |
| 21 | J Morton | | EFT | | | | | | | 3 850 | Loan from J Morton | | 3 850 |
| 23 | Jed Motors | | EFT | | | | | | | 450 | Motor vehicle expenses | 45 | 495 |
| 26 | Villikins & Sons | | 016 | 99 | 9 | 90 | 1 800 | | | | | | 1 800 |
| 29 | Fine Furnishings | | 017 | 198 | 18 | 180 | 3 000 | | | | | | 3 000 |
| 30 | ATO | | EFT | | | | | | | 4 170 | GST collected | | |
| | | | | | | | | | | (4 065) | GST paid | | 105 |
| | | | | $495 | $45 | $450 | $12 400 | $700 | $1 050 | $5 455 | | $220 | $19 825 |

## SOLUTIONS

4.6    a

| Date | Particulars | Fol | Debit | Credit | Balance |
|---|---|---|---|---|---|
| | | | | | |
| J Maxwell General Ledger | | | | | |

**J Maxwell**
**General Ledger**

| Date | Particulars | Fol | Debit | Credit | Balance |
|---|---|---|---|---|---|
| **Accounts Receivable Control Account** | | | | | |
| 2019 | | | $ | $ | $ |
| 1 Jun | Balance | | | | 3 556 Dr |
| 30 | Sales and GST collected | SJ | 4 433 | | 7 989 Dr |
| | Sales returns and GST collected | SRJ | | 792 | 7 197 Dr |
| | Discount expense and GST collected | CRJ | | 22 | 7 175 Dr |
| | Cash at bank | CRJ | | 1 218 | 5 957 Dr |
| | Bad debts and GST collected | GJ | | 396 | 5 561 Dr |
| | Late fees income | GJ | 33 | | 5 594 Dr |
| | Accounts payable control – A Howard | GJ | | 288 | 5 306 Dr |
| | Accounts receivable control – L McCrae | GJ | 876 | | 6 182 Dr |
| | Accounts receivable control – L McDermott | GJ | | 876 | 5 306 Dr |
| | Sales and GST collected | GJ | | 110 | 5 196 Dr |
| **Accounts Payable Control Account** | | | | | |
| 2019 | | | | | |
| 1 Jun | Balance | | | | 6 314 Cr |
| 30 | Purchases and GST paid | PJ | | 2 035 | 8 349 Cr |
| | Purchases returns and GST paid | PRJ | 110 | | 8 239 Cr |
| | Discount income and GST paid | CPJ | 33 | | 8 206 Cr |
| | Cash at bank | CPJ | 965 | | 7 241 Cr |
| | Accounts receivable control – A Howard | GJ | 288 | | 6 953 Cr |
| | Late fee expense | GJ | | 55 | 7 008 Cr |

b

| | | | J Maxwell | | |
|---|---|---|---|---|---|
| | | | **Accounts Receivable Subsidiary Ledger** | | |
| Date | Particulars | Fol | Debit | Credit | Balance |
| | | **D1 – J Graham Account** | | | |
| 2019 | | | $ | $ | $ |
| 1 Jun | Balance | | | | 500 Dr |
| 30 | Cash at bank | CRJ | | 104 | 396 Dr |
| | Bad debts and GST collected | GJ | | 396 | Nil |
| | | **D2 – American Express Account** | | | |
| 2019 | | | | | |
| 1 Jun | Balance | | | | 260 Dr |
| 3 | Sales and GST collected | SJ | 330 | | 590 Dr |
| 5 | Cash at bank/merchant fees and GST paid | CRJ | | 260 | 330 Dr |
| | | **D3 – A Howard Account** | | | |
| 2019 | | | | | |
| 1 Jun | Balance | | | | 420 Dr |
| 12 | Sales returns and GST collected | SRJ | | 132 | 288 Dr |
| 30 | Contra entry | GJ | | 288 | Nil |
| | | **D4 – L McDermott Account** | | | |
| 2019 | | | | | |
| 1 Jun | Balance | | | | 986 Dr |
| 8 | Sales and GST collected | SJ | 539 | | 1 525 Dr |
| 30 | L McCrae | GJ | | 876 | 649 Dr |
| | Sales and GST collected | GJ | | 110 | 539 Dr |
| | | **D5 – J Enright Account** | | | |
| 2019 | | | | | |
| 1 Jun | Balance | | | | 1 390 Dr |
| 30 | Late fees income | GJ | 33 | | 1 423 Dr |
| | | **D6 – L McCrae Account** | | | |
| 2019 | | | | | |
| 2 Jun | Discount expense and GST collected | CRJ | | 22 | 22 Cr |
| | Cash at bank | CRJ | | 854 | 876 Cr |
| 30 | L McDermott | GJ | 876 | | Nil |

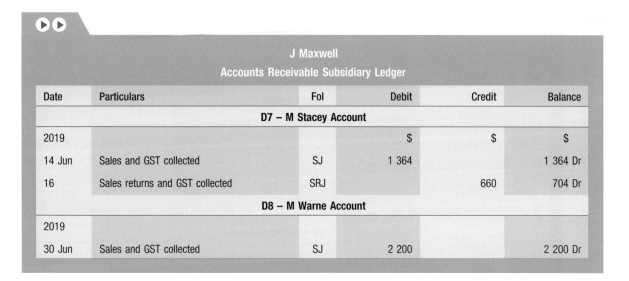

**J Maxwell**
**Accounts Receivable Subsidiary Ledger**

| Date | Particulars | Fol | Debit | Credit | Balance |
|------|-------------|-----|-------|--------|---------|
| **D7 – M Stacey Account** | | | | | |
| 2019 | | | $ | $ | $ |
| 14 Jun | Sales and GST collected | SJ | 1 364 | | 1 364 Dr |
| 16 | Sales returns and GST collected | SRJ | | 660 | 704 Dr |
| **D8 – M Warne Account** | | | | | |
| 2019 | | | | | |
| 30 Jun | Sales and GST collected | SJ | 2 200 | | 2 200 Dr |

c

| Accounts receivable reconciliation schedule as at 30 June 2019 | | |
|------|------|---------|
| **Account no.** | **Name** | **Balance** |
| D2 | American Express | 330 |
| D4 | L McDermott | 539 |
| D5 | J Enright | 1 423 |
| D7 | M Stacey | 704 |
| D8 | M Warne | 2 200 |
| Total as per Accounts Receivable Control Account | | $5 196 |

d

| Accounts Payable Subsidiary Ledger | | | | | |
|------|-------------|-----|-------|--------|---------|
| Date | Particulars | Fol | Debit | Credit | Balance |
| **C1 – N Jackson Account** | | | | | |
| 2019 | | | $ | $ | $ |
| 1 Jun | Balance | | | | 836 Cr |
| 9 | Purchases returns and GST paid | PRJ | 110 | | 726 Cr |
| **C2 – P Marsh Account** | | | | | |
| 2019 | | | | | |
| 1 Jun | Balance | | | | 4 180 Cr |
| 8 | Purchases and GST paid | PJ | | 550 | 4 730 Cr |
| 30 | Late fees expense | GJ | | 55 | 4 785 Cr |

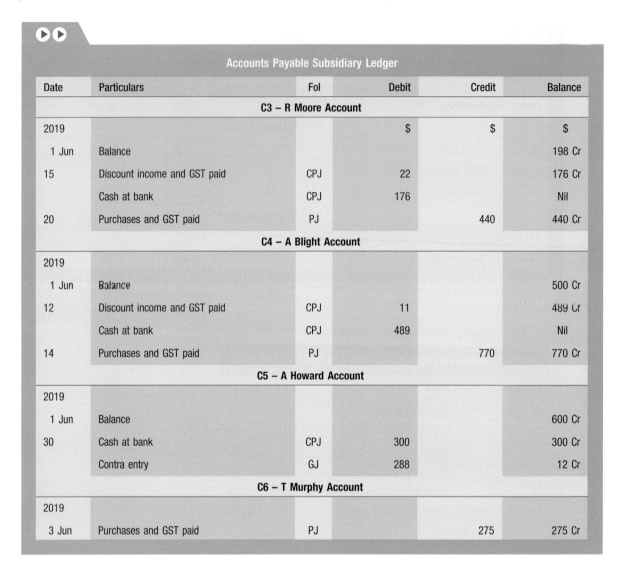

| Date | Particulars | Fol | Debit | Credit | Balance |
|---|---|---|---|---|---|
| | **C3 – R Moore Account** | | | | |
| 2019 | | | $ | $ | $ |
| 1 Jun | Balance | | | | 198 Cr |
| 15 | Discount income and GST paid | CPJ | 22 | | 176 Cr |
| | Cash at bank | CPJ | 176 | | Nil |
| 20 | Purchases and GST paid | PJ | | 440 | 440 Cr |
| | **C4 – A Blight Account** | | | | |
| 2019 | | | | | |
| 1 Jun | Balance | | | | 500 Cr |
| 12 | Discount income and GST paid | CPJ | 11 | | 489 Cr |
| | Cash at bank | CPJ | 489 | | Nil |
| 14 | Purchases and GST paid | PJ | | 770 | 770 Cr |
| | **C5 – A Howard Account** | | | | |
| 2019 | | | | | |
| 1 Jun | Balance | | | | 600 Cr |
| 30 | Cash at bank | CPJ | 300 | | 300 Cr |
| | Contra entry | GJ | 288 | | 12 Cr |
| | **C6 – T Murphy Account** | | | | |
| 2019 | | | | | |
| 3 Jun | Purchases and GST paid | PJ | | 275 | 275 Cr |

e

| Accounts payable reconciliation schedule as at 30 June 2019 | | |
|---|---|---|
| **Account no.** | **Name** | **Balance** |
| C1 | N Jackson | 726 |
| C2 | P Marsh | 4 785 |
| C3 | R Moore | 440 |
| C4 | A Blight | 770 |
| C5 | A Howard | 12 |
| C6 | T Murphy | 275 |
| Total as per Accounts Payable Control Account | | $7 008 |

# Administration of and control over accounts receivable

The accounts receivable function of a business involves all facets of a business's financial dealings with its debtors and involves the following functions:

- development of a credit policy
- credit terms
- credit approval
- recording and processing of accounts receivable transactions
- statements of account
- monitoring of accounts receivable
- identification of bad and doubtful debts
- writing off bad debts
- reasonableness checks
- answering customer enquiries.

## Development of a credit policy

Many businesses that sell goods or provide services to customers provide credit facilities either via an external credit card provider (such as Visa, Mastercard, AMEX, Diners Club etc.) and/or their own credit facilities. Where a business provides its own credit facilities to customers it is essential to establish an effective credit policy. A credit policy covers areas such as credit approval, credit terms, credit limits, procedures for recording accounts receivable transactions, monitoring of accounts receivable and debt collection procedures. In larger organisations, these duties would normally be the responsibility of a separate credit department that would have clearly defined levels of responsibility, authority and reporting. The manager of the credit department (or credit manager) would normally be responsible to the chief financial officer of the organisation.

Once established, it is important that credit policies and procedures are regularly reviewed so that they remain effective tools in recovering monies owed to the organisation and thus optimising the organisation's cash flow management.

## Credit terms

An important aspect of an organisation's credit policy is the terms upon which it offers credit to customers. Credit terms include considerations such as standard length of credit period (such as 7 days, 14 days or 30 days from invoice date), discounts for prompt payment (such as 2% if paid within 7 days), credit limits (the limit that a customer can owe the business at any time which will vary between customers and will mainly depend on their ability to pay outstanding amounts on time) and policies regarding late payment.

# Credit approval

Before a business agrees to supply goods or services to a customer on credit terms, it is wise for the business to investigate the creditworthiness of the customer. This can be achieved in two ways:

1 Credit application

Prior to any goods or services being supplied to the customer on credit terms the customer is requested to complete a credit application form. This document normally asks the customer for details of credit history and details of referees who can vouch for the customer's creditworthiness.

2 Credit check approved by the prospective customer

A number of private agencies can, for a fee, provide information on the credit history (and other details) of an individual or business. Further information can be obtained from the Institute of Mercantile Agents Limited (IMA) website at www.imal.com.au. The IMA:

> represents collectors, investigators, process servers and repossession agents throughout Australia. Elected members networked across Australia work on matters of licensing, privacy, training and ethics affecting members. Members generally work as agents for principals such as banks, financiers, lawyers, insurers and the business community. Depending upon State regulations, most members hold a commercial agent/private inquiry agent licence* or equivalent. The IMA demands high standards from its members. IMA membership requires an applicant to abide to the IMA's Code of Conduct and Code of Ethics which encourage recognised professional and ethical standards.
>
> http://www.imal.com.au

It is important to note that before any credit check is undertaken, the business must receive written consent from the prospective customer, authorising the business to allow such procedures to be undertaken. This is a legislative requirement; in particular, it is specified in the provisions of the *Information Privacy Act 2000* (Vic.).

Whatever method is used to determine the creditworthiness of customers, the usual practice – once a customer's application for credit is approved – is to grant the customer an initial *credit limit*. A credit limit is the maximum amount that the business will allow the customer to have owing at any one time.

# Recording and processing of accounts receivable transactions

An accounts receivable system involves the preparation and recording of sales invoices and adjustment notes, and the processing and recording of remittances from debtors.

Because debtors are an important source of cash flow to a business it is vitally important that accurate records are maintained of amounts owed to the business by its debtors. This is usually achieved by maintaining an Accounts Receivable Subsidiary Ledger linked to an Accounts Receivable Control Account in the General Ledger.

In processing accounts receivable transactions, internal control measures may include the following.

## Sales invoices

- When a customer order is received it is important to ascertain that the customer has been approved for credit and, if so, whether the proposed sale will cause the customer's credit limit to be exceeded.
- Before the sales invoice and a delivery docket are prepared, it is necessary to check stock availability.
- A sales invoice and a delivery docket are prepared. Where the price to be charged differs from the standard price list, it must be approved by a person in authority (such as the sales manager).
- A copy of the invoice or a delivery docket should be forwarded to the despatch department as authority to ship the goods to the customer. Another copy of the sales invoice should be sent to accounts receivable staff for recording.
- Sales invoices should be serially pre-numbered to ensure that all invoices issued are accounted for.
- In order to maximise cash flow, customers should be invoiced promptly, preferably at the time of sale.

## Adjustment notes

- Customer requests for credit allowances should be carefully scrutinised and an adjustment note should not be issued without approval by the appropriate person.
- Sales adjustment notes should be serially pre-numbered to ensure that all adjustment notes issued are accounted for.

## Remittances from customers

- Each customer remittance must be matched against the invoices and adjustment notes to which the payment relates.
- Where a receipt from a customer has insufficient documentation to enable this matching, it is normal practice to assume that the remittance relates to the earliest invoices/adjustment notes relating to that customer. Alternatively, the customer may be contacted to ascertain the details relating to the remittance. In any case, the action taken should be in accordance with the organisation's established credit policy and procedures.
- In some cases, customers may make a part payment, underpayment or overpayment of an amount owing. Such instances must be identified, investigated and recorded according to the organisation's credit policy and procedures.
- Internal control over remittances from customers should conform to the principles of cash control. These principles are outlined in Chapter 5.

In all processing and recording of transactions, it is of course important that errors are kept to a minimum. Documents should be checked for accuracy and completeness before they are recorded in the accounts receivable system. Errors will inevitably be discovered after processing, often following customer enquiries relating to discrepancies in their statement of account. Such errors should be rectified without delay.

Accounts receivable records should be stored in a secure place, with only authorised persons having access. Where accounts receivable records are computerised, access can be restricted by appropriate user identification and passwords. Proper storage and filing of records is important for statutory and audit purposes as well as for accounts receivable enquiries.

# Statements of account

The issue of regular statements of account to customers is an important internal control measure. Account irregularities are often brought to the attention of the business by customers who have discovered discrepancies between the statement and their records. Depending on the needs of customers, statements can be issued in either hard-copy or electronic form.

# Monitoring of accounts receivable

As part of the cash flow management of a business, it is important that the account of each debtor is monitored to ensure that they are complying with the business's trading terms; that is, that debtors have not exceeded their agreed credit limits and are paying their accounts on time.

# Credit limits

Where a customer exceeds his or her credit limit it is customary for some businesses to refuse to supply any further goods or services on credit until the customer has paid for previous purchases. If a customer's payment history proves to be satisfactory, the business may be prepared, if requested by the customer, to review the customer's credit limit with a view to increasing it.

# Monitoring overdue accounts

The *Accounts Receivable Age Analysis* report is an invaluable tool in monitoring accounts receivable. This report, which is normally prepared monthly, shows the amount owing by each debtor by age (that is, how long the debt has been outstanding). A simple age analysis report is shown below.

| | | | Age analysis | | | |
|---|---|---|---|---|---|---|
| **Acc. no.** | **Name** | **Balance** | **Current** | **30 days** | **60 days** | **90 days** |
| | | $ | $ | $ | $ | $ |
| DI98 | Emma Diss | 178.50 | 155.00 | 23.50 | | |
| FL43 | Kristyn Floyd | 345.45 | 167.45 | 148.00 | 30.00 | |
| PI78 | Kristie Pickering | 260.00 | | | 80.00 | 180.00 |
| Total | | $783.95 | $322.45 | $171.50 | $110.00 | $180.00 |

**Dwayne Pipe, Plumber**
**Accounts Receivable Age Analysis as at 31 May 2017**

This report allows a business to easily identify customer accounts that are overdue, and serves as a trigger for follow-up action. The organisation's credit policy and procedures should specify actions to be taken when a customer's account is overdue. These actions may include:

- enquiries to credit department staff to ascertain whether contact has been made with customers whose accounts are overdue and whether all recovery avenues have been exhausted

- direct contact with the customer in the form of telephone calls, emails or letters of demand, overdue stickers on reminder notices, and suspension of further credit until outstanding amounts have been paid
- charging a late payment fee to the customer's account
- meeting with the customer and setting out a debt recovery plan
- placing the debt in the hand of a debt collection agency, and/or
- taking legal action to recover the debt.

# Communication with customers

The credit controller of the business should contact customers as soon as their accounts become overdue. Initially contact can be in the form of a phone call or email. Non-payments by customers are not always intentional as invoices might be misplaced or overlooked. Customers should be asked if they have any valid reason for not making payments. Businesses may be willing to temporarily extend credit terms, or suspend customer's account if payments are not made. Any communication with customers (especially telephone conversations) should be documented and recorded on the customer file so that it can be referred to later if necessary.

Examples of emails that can be sent as a friendly reminder or overdue account notice, suggested by Business Victoria, are shown below.

## Friendly reminder email

**To:** *<insert recipient email (generally accounts payable)>*
**CC:** *<insert other relevant emails (e.g. Business Director or owner)>*
Subject: Invoice Payment Reminder - IMPORTANT

**Dear** *<insert accounts payable name>*

*Note: it is best if you use their name as it makes it more personal.*

This is a friendly reminder that the following invoice is now 7 days overdue

Invoice Date: *<insert date of original invoice>*
Invoice No: *<insert invoice number>*
Invoice Amount: *<insert invoice amount>*

We understand that oversights happen but would appreciate prompt payment of this amount. Could you please let me know when I can expect payment?

If payment has already been made please disregard this email.

Thanks in advance for your cooperation.

Best regards,
*<Insert Name>*
*<insert position title>*

Business Victoria. http://www.business.vic.gov.au > Money, profit and accounting > Getting paid on time > Debt collection guidelines and recovery

## Overdue reminder email

**To:** *<Insert recipient email (generally accounts payable)>*
**CC:** *<insert other relevant emails (e.g. Business Director or owner)>*
Subject: Overdue Invoice Reminder – URGENT ACTION REQUIRED

**Dear** *<insert accounts payable name>*

*Note: it is best if you use their name as it makes it more personal.*

We regret to advise that the following invoice is now 14 days overdue:

**Invoice Date:** *<insert date of original invoice>*
**Invoice No:** *<insert invoice number>*
**Invoice Amount:** *<insert invoice amount>*

We require immediate payment of this amount to avoid further action. Could you please let me know when we can expect payment?

If payment has already been made please disregard this email.

Thanks in advance for your understanding and cooperation.

Best regards
*<Insert Name>*
*<insert position title>*

Business Victoria. http://www.business.vic.gov.au > Money, profit and accounting > Getting paid on time > Debt collection guidelines and recovery

Late payment fees or interest charges have a twofold purpose. Firstly, they are used to encourage the customer to pay and secondly they cover part of the cost of monitoring and administering the outstanding amount.

# Debt recovery plans

Debt recovery plans generally include specific details relating to the recovery of the outstanding amount, including specific dates when amounts will be received and other terms and conditions, such as interest charges and other recovery costs. The plan should also outline the consequences if the payments are not made.

# Letters of demand

A letter of demand should outline the relevant details relating to the outstanding debt(s); for example, dates, agreements, amounts due, and days overdue. Letters of demand should also be accompanied by copies of applicable quotes or invoices.

A final and important component of a letter of demand is the *statement of demand* itself, that is, a demand that payment be made by a certain date along with a warning that debt recovery options will be pursued if payment is not received by the nominated date. An example of a letter of demand, suggested by Business Victoria, is shown below.

## Letter of demand

*<Insert Name>*
*<Insert address line 1>*
*<Insert address line 2>*

Dear *< insert payers name>*,

Re: Letter of Demand for unpaid invoice
Invoice Date: *<insert date of original invoice>*
Invoice No: *<insert invoice number>*
Invoice Amount: *<insert invoice amount>*

As you are aware the above invoice remains unpaid by you. Despite numerous reminder emails and telephone calls requesting payment of this account, the debt remains owing.

Accordingly we advise that if payment in the sum of *<insert invoice amount>* is not received by this office within seven days of the date of this letter, we will instruct our solicitor to issue proceedings against you, to recover the unpaid debt together with our legal costs.

Yours sincerely
*<Insert Name>*
*<insert position title>*

Business Victoria. http://www.business.vic.gov.au > Money, profit and accounting > Getting paid on time > Debt collection guidelines and recovery

# Debt collection agency

A debt collection agency recovers payment on behalf of the business. Demands for payment can be made in writing, verbally over the telephone, or in person. Debt collection agencies charge a fee or percentage of the total amount collected.

When evaluating debt recovery options, the business should consider the following issues: the probability of debt recovery, the time consumed by the business in pursuing the debt, the debt collection costs, the possible legal and court costs, and whether these costs would be recoverable from the debtor.

The normal sequence of collection procedures is listed below.

- 0–30 days overdue Invoice sent with goods, discounts offered for early payment, monthly statement with overdue sticker at end of month
- 31–60 days overdue Phone call and final notice sticker on statement, customer informed of late payment fee being added to their account
- 61–90 days overdue Phone call and suspension of further credit until overdue amounts are paid
- 90+ days overdue Letter of demand threatening legal action if payment not made with 14 days or a letter informing the customer that their account is now being administered by a collection agency.

From a management perspective it is important that the activities of the credit department are regularly monitored. The department should account for its actions through regular reporting to management, providing details of customer payment frequency, debt collection, bad debt write-offs and other debt recovery issues. Management reporting requirements should be specified in the organisation's credit policies and procedures.

# Disputed accounts

In offering credit facilities to customers it is inevitable that disputes will arise over customer account balances. Disputes can result from such circumstances as:

- errors in invoicing such as incorrect prices or extensions or missing invoices
- short deliveries
- inadequate record keeping
- disputed returns and discounts
- damaged or faulty merchandise.

An organisation's credit policies and procedures should contain guidelines relating to resolution of disputes with credit customers. Disputes should be handled in a prompt and efficient manner with the aim of preserving customer relations and minimising costs and disruptions to business routines.

# Identification of bad and doubtful debts

Bad debts are an inevitable outcome of providing credit facilities to customers. Debts are written off for a number of reasons, including a customer's insolvency (a customer being declared bankrupt), the inability of the accounts department to trace the customer's whereabouts, or in circumstances where the outstanding amount is not of a material (significant) nature and thus not worth pursuing. A sound system of internal control over accounts receivable including effective credit management procedures will assist in minimising bad debt write-offs.

A key component in a bad debt minimisation strategy is the early identification of doubtful debts. Doubtful debts are amounts owed by customers where there are reasonable doubts as to the collectability of the amount owed. The most effective method of identifying doubtful debts is the preparation of an Accounts Receivable Age Analysis, coupled with a detailed analysis of problem accounts. Communication with the customer during this process would assist in further clarifying the collection status of the debt. The identification of doubtful debts has important implications for:

- bad debt minimisation; early identification of problem accounts may lead to more positive collection outcomes
- the preparation of end-of-period financial reports (covered in the companion text, *Accounting: Basic Reports*)
- the continuous improvement of an organisation's credit policies and procedures.

A business should take all reasonable steps to identify doubtful debts and collect amounts owing by its customers. Where a debt proves to be uncollectable, any decision to write it off as a bad debt should be approved by the appropriate person. In most organisations, the level of authority required to approve a bad debt write-off will depend on the amount of the debt. Senior management should periodically review the extent of bad debt write-offs and take appropriate policy action where necessary.

# Reasonableness checks

Periodically, a senior member of the accounting staff should peruse the accounts receivable records – in particular the Accounts Receivable Age Analysis report – for reasonableness. Checking for reasonableness involves a scrutiny of accounting records with an emphasis on investigating amounts, accounts or transactions that appear unusual. Any items identified should be further analysed and investigated.

Reasonableness checks can act as a deterrent to fraudulent practices by staff.

# Answering customer enquiries

Accounts receivable staff also have the responsibility of dealing with customer account enquiries. Enquiries could relate to such things as transaction amounts, late deliveries, prices, requests for credit adjustments and account balances.

# Administration of and control over accounts payable

The accounts payable function of a business involves all facets of a business's financial dealings with its creditors and involves the following functions:

- development of accounts payable policies and procedures
- issue of purchase orders
- receipt of goods or services from suppliers
- recording and processing of accounts payable transactions
- reconciliation of supplier statements of account
- monitoring of accounts payable
- reasonableness checks
- answering supplier enquiries
- issue of and control over business credit cards.

Internal control over accounts payable transactions is important so as to ensure that the business only accepts liability for goods and services that it has requested and which have been supplied to it.

Some of the internal control implications of each of the above-mentioned accounts payable functions are discussed below.

# Development of accounts payable policies and procedures

In order for an organisation to effectively monitor and record its credit dealings with suppliers of goods and services, it must have properly documented accounts payable policies and procedures. An accounts payable policy will cover areas such as approved suppliers, obtaining quotes, purchase order approval, acceptance of goods and services, procedures for recording accounts payable transactions, requests for credit for returns and allowances, monitoring of accounts payable and accounts payable payment procedures. In large organisations the above functions may be spread over several departments, such as purchasing, receiving, accounts payable and accounting. Lines of authority will vary between organisations, with the final responsibility generally resting with the chief financial officer.

Once established, it is important that accounts payable policies and procedures are regularly reviewed so that they remain effective tools for ensuring that accounts payable transactions are properly authorised, monitored and recorded. Clear accounts payable policies and well-documented procedures provide the framework for the development of effective internal control measures.

# Issue of purchase orders

As outlined in Chapter 2, a *purchase order* is a request by a business to a supplier to supply goods and/or services. The following internal controls should exist over purchase orders.

- A purchase order should be raised for each purchase of goods or services.
- Purchase orders should be in writing. This provides written evidence that goods and/or services have been ordered.
- Purchase orders should be sequentially pre-numbered and all numbers accounted for.
- Purchase orders should be authorised by a designated person. This helps to ensure that only goods and services required for the efficient running of the business are purchased.
- Blank purchase order forms should be stored securely and controlled by a register held by a nominated person, who only issues them to authorised persons.
- Persons authorising purchase orders should not be involved in recording goods received or in processing supplier invoices.

Even where a business places an order with a supplier over the telephone or over the Internet, some sort of purchase authority should exist. For example, a written purchase order may be completed and filed by the business even though the goods are ordered verbally or electronically. In this way there is written evidence that the purchase has been properly authorised.

# Receipt of goods or services

The following internal controls should exist over the receipt of goods.

- Goods received should be counted and, where possible, examined to ensure that they are in good order and condition. Any damaged goods should be noted and set aside for return to the supplier.
- The goods delivered should be reconciled with a copy of the purchase order and any short deliveries noted.
- A *receiving report* should be prepared as evidence that the goods have been received.
- As already mentioned, persons receiving goods should not be able to authorise purchase orders or be involved in the processing of supplier invoices.

# Recording and processing of accounts payable transactions

The following internal controls should exist over the processing of accounts payable transactions.

## Supplier invoices

- As already mentioned, the person processing supplier invoices should not be able to authorise purchase orders or be involved in recording the receipt of goods.
- All supplier invoices should be sent to the accounts payable department for processing.
- Where the invoice is for the supply of goods the accounts department should match the details contained in the invoice with their copy of the purchase order and the receiving report. The three documents should be stapled together.
- Where the invoice is for the supply of services, the accounts department should match the details with their copy of the purchase order and staple the two documents together. As there would be no receiving report, the invoice may be presented to an appropriate person (such as the head of the department that requested the service) to indicate on the invoice that the service has been supplied.
- All calculations on the invoice should be checked by the accounts department. Any discrepancies identified should be investigated and rectified without delay.
- The accounts department should record the correct General Ledger account number(s) on each invoice with reference to the General Ledger Chart of Accounts and the nature of the goods or services supplied.

## Supplier adjustment notes

- As outlined in Chapter 2, when goods or services have been supplied it is sometimes necessary for a business to seek an adjustment to the amount charged by the supplier. In such circumstances, a *request for credit* should be completed and forwarded to the supplier. A copy of this document should also be retained by the business.
- When the adjustment note is received from the supplier it should be matched against the appropriate request for credit and the relevant invoice from the supplier.

## Payments to suppliers

- A remittance advice, providing details of all relevant transactions, should be prepared for each supplier payment.
- Supporting documentation (remittance advices, purchase orders, invoices, receiving reports and adjustment notes) should be forwarded to the person responsible for initiating payments to suppliers.
- Internal control over payments to suppliers should conform to the principles of cash control. These principles are outlined in Chapter 5.

As with accounts receivable records, accounts payable records should be stored in a secure place with access limited to authorised personnel.

# Reconciliation of supplier statements of account

In some cases where a business deals with a supplier on a regular basis, the business may wait until it receives a monthly *statement of account* from the supplier and then make a payment for the full amount owing, rather than processing a payment for each invoice as it is received from the supplier. As outlined in Chapter 2, a statement of account is a document that summarises the transactions with the supplier for the month and indicates the total amount owing.

An important internal control measure is to *reconcile* the supplier's statement of account with the business's records prior to making any payment. The aim of this reconciliation is to:

- ensure that the business does not pay invoices that it has not received
- ensure that it does not pay for goods that have been returned or for which an allowance has been requested
- ensure that all payments made to the supplier have been taken into account.

## Example

The following statement of account was received by Wally Industries from Hi-Tech Supplies:

| To:<br>Wally Industries<br>256 Pope Rd<br>Black Stump 8759 | **HI-TECH SUPPLIES**<br>24 McCol St<br>Woop Woop 9845<br>Ph 09 2364 7195 | | | Statement for month of _August 2015_ | |

| Date | Particulars | Ref | Debit | Credit | Balance |
|---|---|---|---|---|---|
| 2015 | | | $ | $ | $ |
| 1 Aug | Balance | | | | 900 Dr |
| 5 | Invoice | 729 | 800 | | 1 700 Dr |
| 12 | Invoice | 781 | 500 | | 2 200 Dr |
| 13 | Adjustment note | 23 | | 100 | 2 100 Dr |
| 26 | Invoice | 799 | 400 | | 2 500 Dr |
| 31 | Invoice | 834 | 600 | | 3 100 Dr |

The accounts payable clerk at Wally Industries, Emma Lloyd, found the following discrepancies when comparing the statement of account from Hi-Tech Supplies with her records for the month of August 2015:

- Invoice no. 834 had not been received from Hi-Tech Supplies.
- The goods on invoice no. 799 had been returned to Hi-Tech Supplies because they were damaged, but no adjustment note has been received from Hi-Tech Supplies.
- A payment of $900 made by Wally Industries to Hi-Tech Supplies on 31 August did not appear on the statement.

To determine the amount payable to Hi-Tech Supplies, Emma performed the following reconciliation:

| | $ |
|---|---|
| Balance as per supplier's statement of account | 3 100 |
| *less* Invoice 834 not received | (600) |
| Goods on invoice 799 returned | (400) |
| Payment not recorded | (900) |
| Amount payable | $1 200 |

Therefore, Wally Industries would process a payment (with a remittance advice) for $1200 to Hi-Tech Supplies to settle their August account.

# Monitoring of accounts payable

As part of a business's cash flow management, it is important that the account of each creditor is monitored to ensure that the business is complying with the supplier's trading terms; that is, that the business is paying its accounts on time. The *Accounts Payable Age Analysis* report is an invaluable tool in monitoring accounts payable. This report, which is normally prepared monthly, shows the amount owing to each creditor by age (that is, how long the debt has been outstanding). A simple age analysis report is shown below.

| Wally Industries Accounts Payable Age Analysis as at 31 May 2017 | | | | | | |
|---|---|---|---|---|---|---|
| | | | | Age Analysis | | |
| Acc. No. | Name | Balance | Current | 30 days | 60 days | 90 days |
| | | $ | $ | $ | $ | $ |
| C101 | Hi-Tech Supplies | 3 450 | 3 250 | 200 | | |
| C107 | Ace Distributors | 950 | 950 | | | |
| C115 | Daffy Industries | 2 310 | | 2 000 | 310 | |
| Total | | $6 710 | $4 200 | $2 200 | $310 | |

This report allows a business to easily identify supplier accounts that are overdue and serves as a trigger for further action. Each overdue balance should be carefully investigated and payment made without undue delay. Late payment to suppliers could result in:

- loss of prompt payment discounts
- damage to the business's credit rating
- possible refusal of further credit from suppliers.

# Reasonableness checks

Periodically, a senior member of the accounting staff should peruse the accounts payable records, in particular the Accounts Payable Age Analysis report, for reasonableness. Checking for reasonableness involves a scrutiny of accounting records with an emphasis on investigating amounts, accounts or transactions that appear unusual. Any items identified should be further analysed and investigated.

Reasonableness checks can act as a deterrent to fraudulent practices by staff.

# Answering supplier enquiries

Accounts payable staff also have the responsibility of dealing with supplier account enquiries. Enquiries could relate to such things as transaction amounts, late deliveries, prices, requests for credit adjustments, account balances and overdue accounts.

# Issue of and control over business credit cards

As mentioned in earlier chapters, some businesses find it convenient to issue business credit cards to designated staff for use in purchasing goods and services on behalf of the business. The issue of such cards should be strictly controlled and subject to the organisation's accounts payable policies and procedures. Such policies and procedures would, for example, govern:

- personnel entitled to a business credit card
- the types of approved expenditure
- appropriate credit limits
- staff expenditure reporting
- management review of business credit card use and expenditure.

 **EXERCISES**

4.10   a   Briefly explain the importance of the development of credit policies and procedures.
      b   Briefly outline the areas that may be covered by an organisation's credit policy.

4.11   Briefly outline the importance of customer credit approval in the accounts receivable process.

4.12   List five internal control measures that should exist in the processing of sales invoices.

4.13   Outline the internal control benefits of issuing statements of account to customers.

4.14   a   Briefly explain the nature and content of the report that businesses prepare to determine debtors with overdue amounts.
      b   Once overdue debtors' balances have been determined, what action should the business take to facilitate prompt collection of the amounts overdue?

4.15    Briefly comment on the following statement:

'A key component of a bad debt minimisation strategy is the early identification of doubtful debts.'

4.16    The following statement of account was received from XYZ Wholesalers:

| | | | | | |
|---|---|---|---|---|---|
| To:<br>*Doofus Enterprises*<br>*247 Mayfield Ave*<br>*Bendigo 3550* | **XYZ WHOLESALERS**<br>158 View St<br>Bendigo 3550<br>Ph 5442 3698 | | | Statement of account<br>for month of July 2017 | |
| Date | Particulars | Ref | Debit | Credit | Balance |
| *2017* | | | *$* | *$* | *$* |
| *1 Jul* | *Balance* | | | | *600 Dr* |
| *3* | *Invoice* | *1245* | *485* | | *1 085 Dr* |
| *9* | *Invoice* | *1299* | *1 100* | | *2 185 Dr* |
| *12* | *Adjustment note* | *C456* | | *100* | *2 085 Dr* |
| *22* | *Invoice* | *1369* | *410* | | *2 495 Dr* |
| *30* | *Invoice* | *1421* | *500* | | *2 995 Dr* |
| *Terms: 2% discount if paid within 7 days*<br>*Otherwise net cash 30 days* | | | | | |

On comparing the above statement with the accounting records, the accounts payable clerk at Doofus Enterprises discovered the following discrepancies:

- A payment of $600 made by Doofus Enterprises to XYZ Wholesalers on 31 July 2017 does not appear on the statement.
- Invoice 1421 from XYZ Wholesalers (shown on the statement above) has not yet been received by Doofus Enterprises.

You are required to calculate the amount that Doofus Enterprises should pay to XYZ Wholesalers to settle their account. Assume that the amount is paid within seven days. Show workings.

4.17    Briefly outline the internal controls that should exist over:

a    receipt of goods from suppliers

b    processing of supplier invoices.

4.18    Briefly explain why it is important for a business to monitor its accounts payable.

4.19    Briefly comment on the following statement:

'The issue of business credit cards to staff should be strictly controlled and subject to the organisation's accounts payable policies and procedures.'

4.20    Briefly explain the concept of reasonableness checks in relation to accounts receivable and accounts payable.

# Summary

What have you covered in this chapter?

◆ The purpose of subsidiary ledgers

◆ How to post a variety of entries from the following journals to the Accounts Receivable and Accounts Payable ledgers

  - Cash Receipts Journal
  - Cash Payments Journal
  - Sales Journal
  - Sales Returns and Allowances Journal
  - Purchases Journal
  - Purchases Returns and Allowances Journal
  - General Journal

◆ The preparation of a list of debtors' balances and reconciliation of the list with the General Ledger control account

◆ The preparation of a list of creditors' balances and reconciliation of the list with the General Ledger control account

◆ The various internal control measures that exist relating to accounts receivable and accounts payable

# 5

# CASH CONTROL AND BANK RECONCILIATION

## Learning objectives

Upon satisfactory completion of this chapter you should be able to:

- compare cash records with bank statements
- adjust cash journals for dishonoured cheques, bank fees, direct bank debits and direct bank credits; total cash journals and post to the General Ledger
- prepare a bank reconciliation statement incorporating unpresented cheques and deposits not yet credited
- explain other internal controls over cash.

# Internal control over cash

Cash is perhaps the most vulnerable of all of the assets in any business and, as such, requires a sound system of internal control to protect it from fraud, misappropriation and misuse. For the purposes of this text we have classified internal controls over cash as follows:

- the preparation of a bank reconciliation, which is covered in detail in this chapter
- the imprest system of petty cash (covered in Chapter 6), and
- other internal controls over cash, which are also dealt with in this chapter.

# Bank reconciliation

The *bank reconciliation statement* is, in simple terms, a statement (or document) that reconciles the cash records of the business itself with the records of the business that are maintained by the bank. This includes the bank statement, which banks send to their customers (either in hard copy or electronically).

## The relationship between the bank and the business

Previous chapters have mentioned that all payments by the business are normally recorded in the Cash Payments Journal; also, that receipts (monies received by the business) are recorded in the Cash Receipts Journal. The totals of the Bank columns in both of these journals are posted to the Cash at Bank Account in the General Ledger, and in this way the bank balance in the business's record-keeping system is updated continually.

Figure 5.1 summarises the cash-recording process.

## How the bank records the transactions of the business

The way in which the bank records transactions on behalf of the business will now be examined. Most businesses maintain a bank account with a bank and this account would normally operate on the following basis.

- The business is able to deposit cash and cheques into the bank account.
- EFTPOS sales are automatically deposited into the bank account.
- The business is able to write cheques, drawing on the funds in the bank account.
- EFT payments are automatically deducted from the bank account.
- EFT receipts are automatically added to the bank account.
- The bank deducts EFTPOS merchant fees from the bank account. These are charges to the business for the provision of EFTPOS facilities by the bank.

Figure 5.1    **The cash-recording process**

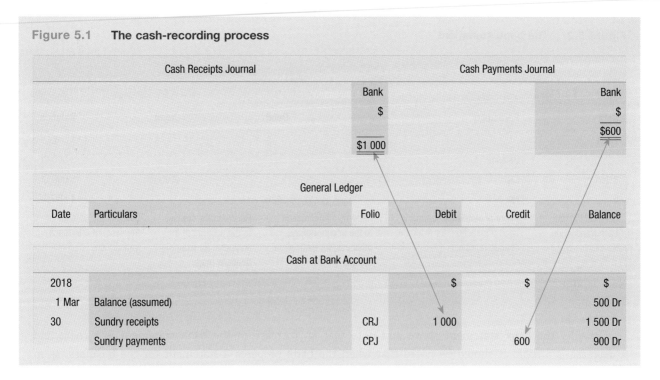

- Where there is a positive balance (as we will soon explain, this means a credit balance) in the bank account of the business, the bank will periodically deposit interest directly into the account (assuming that interest applies to that account). Conversely, the business is normally charged interest if payments exceed the balance in the account.
- The bank periodically deducts other bank fees and charges directly from the account.
- The business has the option of authorising the bank to make deductions directly from the account. For example, if the business is repaying a loan, it can authorise the bank to draw directly on its account to pay the monthly instalments. Similar arrangements can be made to pay for insurance, rent and other regular payments. This is referred to as a *direct debit*.
- The business has the option to authorise direct deposits into the account. For example, a business may receive regular payments from a customer, which could be directly deposited in the business's bank account. Rent received is a common example of a direct deposit. These transactions are generally referred to as *direct credits*.
- As outlined in Chapter 2, the bank prepares a formal account statement (referred to as a *bank statement*) on a regular basis outlining the transactions of the business for a certain period. A bank statement is effectively a copy of the business's account as shown in the bank's ledger. Businesses can also access their bank account via the electronic banking software provided by the bank, and may therefore choose not to receive bank statements in hard copy form.

An examination of a bank statement shows the way in which the bank records the *transactions* of the business (see Figure 5.2).

**Figure 5.2    The bank statement**

| Bank statement for month of June 2018 | | Account name J Jorgason | | | Account number 316-42497 |
|---|---|---|---|---|---|
| **Date** | **Particulars** | | **Debit** | **Credit** | **Balance** |
| 2018 | | | $ | $ | $ |
| | Balance | | | | 3 000 Cr |
| 3 Jun | C/C | | | 2 000 | 5 000 Cr |
| 5 | No. 317 | | 420 | | 4 580 Cr |
| Records the date of each transaction. | Records details (in summary) of each transaction; for example, cheque number. | | Records all decreases to the account of the business; for example a cheque drawn | Records all increases to the account of the business; for example, deposits made. | Records the balance of the account after each transaction. |

**Note**  The letters 'C/C' in the Particulars column above is an abbreviation for cash and cheques deposited by the business.

Consider the bank statement above and note that an increase in the bank statement is a *credit* and a decrease is a *debit*. It should be noted that when the bank prepares a statement for the business, as in Figure 5.2, the statement is prepared from the bank's point of view.

**Figure 5.3    Explanation of debits and credits shown in the bank statement**

| Type of transaction | Entry in bank's records |
|---|---|
| Deposits (cash, cheques, EFT receipts, EFTPOS, direct credits, interest) | Credit |
| Money is deposited in the business bank account by the business or by others via EFT. | The bank records this as a *credit* because it is now money that *is owed* to the business. (Remember, in normal accounting rules, money that is owed is credited as a liability.) |
| Withdrawals (cheques drawn, EFT payments, direct debits and bank charges) | Debit |
| The business draws a cheque, which is presented to the bank (by the person receiving the cheque) for payment. EFT payments made are deducted from the account. Payments are made by the bank on behalf of the business (direct debits) from the business bank account and bank charges are deducted from the account. | The bank records this as a *debit* because it is money that has been withdrawn from the account. Thus, the amount owed by the bank to the business (credit) has been decreased (debit). |

The following example illustrates the principle of *debit* and *credit* (shown in Figure 5.3) from the bank's point of view. J Jorgason, builder and supplier, operates a bank account with the Commonwealth Bank of Australia. The opening balance of the account was $500 Dr and the cash transactions for the month of June 2018 are shown in these Cash Receipts and Cash Payments Journals.

### J Jorgason
### Cash Receipts Journal

| Date | Particulars | Fol | Ref | Accounts receivable control (Discount expense) | GST collected | Discount expense | Accounts receivable control | Cash services | Amount (Sundries) | Account | GST collected | Bank |
|---|---|---|---|---|---|---|---|---|---|---|---|---|
| 2018 | | | | $ | $ | $ | $ | $ | $ | | $ | $ |
| 1 Jun | R Watson | | 307 | 55 | 5 | 50 | 950 | | | | | 950 |
| 3 | J Lovett | | 308 | | | | 2 000 | | | | | 2 000 |
| 11 | P Smith | | 309 | | | | 150 | | | | | 150 |
| 21 | J Lovett | | 310 | | | | | 3 420 | | | 342 | |
| | R Argo | | 311 | | | | | 180 | | | 18 | 3 960 |
| 26 | ABC Sales | | EFT | | | | | | 200 | Commission income | 20 | 220 |
| 28 | EFTPOS sales | | POS | | | | | 1 950 | | | 195 | 2 145 |
| 29 | L Simmonds | | 312 | 165 | 15 | 150 | 1 450 | | | | | 1 450 |
| | | | | $220 | $20 | $200 | $4 550 | $5 550 | $200 | | $575 | $10 875 |

### Cash Payments Journal

| Date | Particulars | Fol | Ref | Accounts payable control (Discount income) | GST paid | Discount income | Accounts payable control | Cash purchases | Wages | Amount (Sundries) | Account | GST paid | Bank |
|---|---|---|---|---|---|---|---|---|---|---|---|---|---|
| 2018 | | | | $ | $ | $ | $ | $ | $ | $ | | $ | $ |
| 3 Jun | Amaroo Timber | | 214 | 66 | 6 | 60 | 640 | | | | | | 640 |
| 5 | John's Hardware | | 215 | | | | | 300 | | | | 30 | 330 |
| 7 | John's Hardware | | 216 | | | | | 1 500 | | | | 150 | 1 650 |
| | Ray's Pines | | 217 | 22 | 2 | 20 | 180 | | | | | | 180 |
| 21 | John Subby | | 218 | | | | | | 275 | | | | 275 |
| 22 | Chris Mortem | | 219 | | | | | | 275 | | | | 275 |
| 24 | XYZ Insurance Ltd | | EFT | | | | | | | 140 | Insurance | 14 | 154 |
| | | | | $88 | $8 | $80 | $820 | $1 800 | $550 | $140 | | $194 | $3 504 |

J Jorgason's Cash at Bank Account in the General Ledger as at 30 June 2018 appears as follows:

| | General Ledger | | | | |
|---|---|---|---|---|---|
| Date | Particulars | Fol | Debit | Credit | Balance |
| | **Cash at Bank Account** | | | | |
| 2018 | | | $ | $ | $ |
| 1 Jun | Balance | | | | 500 Dr |
| 30 | Sundry receipts | CRJ | 10 875 | | 11 375 Dr |
| | Sundry payments | CPJ | | 3 504 | 7 871 Dr |

Assuming that the bank has recorded all of the above transactions, the bank statement would appear as follows:

| | Statement of Account | | | | |
|---|---|---|---|---|---|
| Bank statement for the month of June | Account name J Jorgason | | | Account number 316-42497 | |
| Date | Details | | Debit | Credit | Balance |
| 2018 | | | $ | $ | $ |
| 1 Jun | Balance b/f | | | | 500 Cr |
| | C/C | Cash and cheques deposited by J Jorgason | | 950 | 1 450 Cr |
| 4 | No. 214 | | 640 | | 810 Cr |
| 3 | C/C | | | 2 000 | 2 810 Cr |
| 6 | No. 215 | | 330 | | 2 480 Cr |
| 8 | No. 216 | Cheque no. 216 issued/drawn by J Jorgason | 1 650 | | 830 Cr |
| 9 | No. 217 | | 180 | | 650 Cr |
| 11 | C/C | | | 150 | 800 Cr |
| 21 | C/C | | | 3 960 | 4 760 Cr |
| 22 | No. 218 | | 275 | | 4 485 Cr |
| 24 | No. 219 | | 275 | | 4 210 Cr |
| 25 | XYZ Insurance Ltd | EFT payment to XYZ Insurance Ltd | 154 | | 4 056 Cr |
| 26 | ABC Sales (commission) | EFT receipt from ABC Sales | | 220 | 4 276 Cr |
| 28 | EFTPOS | EFTPOS sales | | 2 145 | 6 421 Cr |
| 29 | C/C | | | 1 450 | 7 871 Cr |
| Closing balance 30 June 2018 | | | | | $7 871 Cr |

**Explanations**

1    In this example, the transactions are recorded by the bank in the same sequence as in the cash journals of the business. This is not always the case, particularly with cheques that have been written (more commonly referred to as drawn cheques); these can be presented and recorded by the bank in a sequence different from that of the business.

2    The balance of the Cash at Bank Account in J Jorgason's General Ledger at 30 June 2018 is the same as the balance of the bank statement. That is, the Cash at Bank Account in J Jorgason's General Ledger has a balance of $7871 Dr, indicating that, according to Jorgason's records, the business has $7871 in the bank. The bank statement prepared by the bank shows a balance of $7871 Cr, indicating that the bank owes J Jorgason $7871.

Thus, the cash records of the business and the bank are *reconciled*, as both totals agree. In practice, however, the balance of the Cash at Bank Account in the General Ledger at a given point in time seldom agrees with the balance in the bank statement at that same time. There may be many reasons why the two balances do not agree, but the main reason is that the bank will often record entries that the business has not yet recorded and, conversely, the business will record entries that the bank has not yet recorded. These differences will be examined in more detail after the following exercises.

 **EXERCISES**

5.1    Explain the following:
    a    bank reconciliation statement
    b    bank overdraft
    c    bank fees
    d    bank statement.

5.2    Explain how a bank account is operated.

5.3    Give three examples each of deposits to and withdrawals from a business's bank account.

5.4    Why does the bank treat an account balance as a credit when there is money in the account, while in the cash records of the business, this balance is treated as a debit? Explain.

# Reconciling transactions recorded by the bank

The bank may be authorised by the business to deposit money directly into the business account or to draw money from, or charge, the account. There are various transactions that may be authorised by the business.

## Deposits (direct credits to the account)

Any of the following may be received by the bank on behalf of the business and deposited directly in the account of the business.

- EFTPOS sales (including bank-issued credit cards)
- Direct deposits or electronic transfers (EFT) for:
  - American Express and Diners Club sales
  - dividends (from shares held in companies)
  - commissions from various traders
  - interest from various sources such as banks
  - rent
  - receipts from debtors
  - other income and transfers from other accounts

# Payments/charges (direct debits to the account)

Any of the following may be charged to the business by the bank.

- Bank fees and charges
- Interest on overdrafts
- EFTPOS merchant fees charged by the bank
- Direct debits or electronic transfers:
  - transfers to other accounts
  - direct payments (for example, loan repayments and annual insurance premiums)
  - EFT payments made by the business (for example, wages and payments to creditors)

All of the above transactions will be recorded by the bank in its own records and then used to prepare the bank statement, which will be sent to the business. The treatment of these transactions is considered in more detail in the following bank statement. Some items have been highlighted by an (A), (B) etc. and these items are explained in more detail at the foot of the statement shown.

| Commonwealth Bank Statement of Account | | | | | |
|---|---|---|---|---|---|
| **Bank statement for month of December 2018** | | **Account name J Jorgason** | | **Account number 316-42497** | |
| Date | Details | | Debit | Credit | Balance |
| 2018 | | | $ | $ | $ |
| 1 Dec | Balance b/f | | | | 1 000.00 Cr |
| | BHT Ltd (dividends) | (A) | | 100.00 | 1 100.00 Cr |
| 2 | No. 327 | | 110.00 | | 990.00 Cr |
| | No. 328 | | 220.00 | | 770.00 Cr |
| 4 | C/C | | | 400.00 | 1 170.00 Cr |
| 5 | J Smith (commission) | (B) | | 110.00 | 1 280.00 Cr |
| | Interest (JNZ Bank deposit) | (C) | | 15.00 | 1 295.00 Cr |
| 6 | No. 329 | | 500.00 | | 795.00 Cr |
| 9 | No. 330 | | 660.00 | | 135.00 Cr |

▶ ▶

| | | Commonwealth Bank Statement of Account | | | | |
|---|---|---|---|---|---|---|
| **Bank statement**<br>**for month of December 2018** | | | **Account name**<br>**J Jorgason** | | | **Account number**<br>**316-42497** |
| Date | Details | | | Debit | Credit | Balance |
| 2018 | | | | $ | $ | $ |
| 10 | No. 331 | | | 410.00 | | 275.00 Dr |
| 11 | Wages – L Smith |  D | | 150.00 | | 425.00 Dr |
| | Int O/D | E | | 10.00 | | 435.00 Dr |
| 12 | EFTPOS | F | | | 110.00 | 325.00 Dr |
| 13 | Transfer A/c 36072 | G | | | 1 200.00 | 875.00 Cr |
| 15 | No. 332 | | | 165.00 | | 710.00 Cr |
| 16 | Deposit – F Adams (Rent) | H | | | 150.00 | 860.00 Cr |
| 17 | No. 333 | | | 55.00 | | 805.00 Cr |
| 21 | No. 334 | | | 110.00 | | 695.00 Cr |
| 24 | Bank fee | I | | 30.00 | | 665.00 Cr |
| 29 | C/C | | | | 1 100.00 | 1 765.00 Cr |
| 30 | EFTPOS | | | | 550.00 | 2 315.00 Cr |
| | Loan no. X1879 – Commonwealth Bank (direct debit) | J | | 980.00 | | 1 335.00 Cr |
| 31 | T Watts (creditor) | K | | 1 040.00 | | 295.00 Cr |
| | EFTPOS merchant fee | L | | 22.00 | | 273.00 Cr |
| | Closing balance 31 December 2018 | | | | | 273.00 Cr |

**Explanations**

While this type of bank statement is not uncommon in practice, the number of additional items included ('bank statement transactions') can make the statement look a little complicated, so we will explain further.

**A** **BHT Ltd (dividends)** This represents an EFT dividend payment from BHT Ltd. The amount of $100 was deposited in the account of the business and thus appears in the bank statement as a credit entry.

**B** **J Smith (commission)** This represents a deposit or EFT receipt of commission from J Smith. The amount of $110 was deposited in the account of the business and thus appears in the bank statement as a credit entry.

**C** **Interest (JNZ Bank deposit)** This represents an amount of interest earned by the business from a deposit with another bank (JNZ). The interest from the JNZ Bank was transferred by EFT and the amount of $15 was deposited in the business account. This appears in the bank statement as a credit entry.

**D** **Wages – L Smith** This represents wages paid by EFT to employee L Smith. This is a payment from the business bank account and therefore appears as a debit entry in the bank statement.

**E** **Interest O/D** On 10 December 2018, the account went into overdraft (that is, payments exceeded the balance of money in the account). When this happens, the bank charges interest directly to the account for the period that the account is in overdraft. The amount of $10 represents interest on the overdraft amount for 10 and 11 December. This appears in the bank statement as a debit entry.

**F** **EFTPOS** This represents EFTPOS sales; that is, sales to customers who paid with a debit card or bank-issued credit card (such as MasterCard or Visa). This is a deposit to the business's bank account and therefore appears as a credit entry on the bank statement.

**G** **Transfer A/c 36072** This represents an amount that has been transferred from another account maintained by the business. In addition to having an operating account, it is usual for businesses to have other accounts, such as investment accounts. In this situation, the business has a fixed deposit (account no. 36072), which is added to or drawn on from time to time. On 13 December the owner transferred $1200 by EFT from the fixed deposit account to the operating account, thereby remedying the overdraft situation. This is a deposit in the operating account and appears in the bank statement as a credit entry.

H  **Deposit – F Adams (Rent)** This represents an amount of rent earned by the business from F Adams. The amount of $150 represents an amount deposited directly into the business's bank account by F Adams (that is, a direct credit). This appears in the bank statement as a credit entry.

I  **Bank fee** This represents a fee that the bank has charged the business for maintaining the account. The fee of $30 was charged directly to the account and thus appears in the bank statement as a debit entry.

J  **Loan X1879 – Commonwealth Bank (direct debit)** This represents an amount deducted by the bank directly from the business bank account as a regular repayment on loan no. X1879.

K  **T Watts (creditor)** This represents an EFT payment to a creditor of the business and is therefore recorded as a debit entry in the bank statement.

L  **EFTPOS merchant fee** This represents a charge by the bank to the business for the provision of EFTPOS facilities, recorded as a debit by the bank.

# Adjustments to the cash journals

As outlined in Chapter 2, a business that uses electronic banking software is able to identify and record all *bank statement transactions* on a continuous basis. To simplify the learning process in this chapter, only EFT receipts, EFT payments, direct credits and direct debits have thus far been identified and recorded on a continuous basis during the accounting period. All other bank statement transactions will be identified and adjusted as part of the bank reconciliation process covered later in this chapter.

In the past, businesses received printed bank statements in the mail on a regular basis, often monthly. This triggered a process in which entries on the bank statement were checked off against entries in the cash journals. Invariably, there would be entries such as bank fees and charges, unpresented cheques, direct debits, direct credits and EFTPOS merchant fees recorded on the bank statement that did not appear in the cash journals. Entries would then be made in the cash journals to account for the missing items.

However, where a business has electronic banking facilities, bank reconciliation procedures can be either an ongoing process during the accounting period or completed in the traditional manner. In the examples and exercises in this chapter, it has been assumed that EFT transactions are identified and recorded continuously during the accounting period and all other bank statement transactions are recorded as adjustments in the traditional manner at the time of reconciliation. This text has adopted this method in the belief that it best illustrates the process of bank reconciliation at a basic level.

## Bank reconciliation process

In the example for J Jorgason on pages 371–2 there were numerous bank statement transactions that had not been accounted for by the business. Therefore, in order to reconcile the cash records of J Jorgason with those of the bank, it is necessary to record each transaction in the appropriate journals of the business. Figure 5.4 illustrates this process.

On receipt of the bank statement, it is necessary for the business to update the cash journals and reconcile these records with the bank statement. We will now examine how this is done. (Assume that the Cash at Bank Account balance in the General Ledger of J Jorgason at 30 November 2018 was $1000 Dr.)

Figure 5.4    **Processing the bank statement**

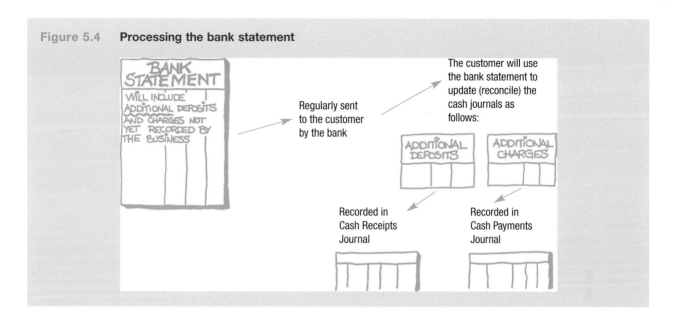

## Example

A UWatch demonstration is available on the CD that accompanies this text for this example.

The following are the cash journals of J Jorgason for the month of December 2018 (before receiving a statement from the bank for that month).

*Cash Receipts Journal*

UWATCH 5.1

| | | | | Discount expense | | | | | Sundries | | | |
| Date | Particulars | Fol | Ref | Accounts receivable control | GST collected | Discount expense | Accounts receivable control | Sales | Amount | Account | GST collected | Bank |
| 2018 | | | | $ | $ | $ | $ | $ | $ | | $ | $ |
| 1 Dec | BHT Ltd | | EFT | | | | | | 100 | Dividends income | | 100 |
| 4 | C Ecil | | 417 | 22 | 2 | 20 | 400 | | | | | 400 |
| 5 | J Smith | | EFT | | | | | | 100 | Commission income | 10 | 110 |
| 12 | EFTPOS | | POS | | | | | 100 | | | 10 | 110 |
| 13 | Transfer a/c 36072 | | EFT | | | | | | 1 200 | Fixed deposit | | 1 200 |
| 16 | F Adams | | DC | | | | | | 150 | Rent income | | 150 |
| 29 | Cash sales | | POS | | | | | 1 000 | | | 100 | 1 100 |
| 30 | EFTPOS | | POS | | | | | 500 | | | 50 | 550 |

## Cash Payments Journal

| | | | | Discount income | | | | | | Sundries | | | |
|---|---|---|---|---|---|---|---|---|---|---|---|---|---|
| Date | Particulars | Fol | Ref | Accounts payable control | GST paid | Discount income | Accounts payable control | Purchases | Wages | Amount | Account | GST paid | Bank |
| 2018 | | | | $ | $ | $ | $ | $ | $ | $ | | $ | $ |
| 1 Dec | J Frederick | | 327 | | | | | 100 | | | | 10 | 110 |
| | S Tirrer | | 328 | | | | | 200 | | | | 20 | 220 |
| 5 | T Watts | | 329 | 22 | 2 | 20 | 500 | | | | | | 500 |
| 7 | A Lie | | 330 | | | | | 600 | | | | 60 | 660 |
| 9 | J Uroon | | 331 | 11 | 1 | 10 | 110 | | | | | | 410 |
| 11 | L Smith | | EFT | | | | | | 150 | | | | 150 |
| 13 | Bendigo Daily | | 332 | | | | | | | 150 | Advertising | 15 | 165 |
| 15 | M Johnson | | 333 | | | | | 50 | | | | 5 | 55 |
| 20 | B King | | 334 | | | | | 100 | | | | 10 | 110 |
| 30 | Commonwealth Bank – Loan X1879 | | DD | | | | | | | 980 | Loan – Commonwealth Bank | | 980 |
| 31 | T Watts | | EFT | 66 | 6 | 60 | 1 040 | | | | | | 1 040 |

## Solution

*After* receiving the bank statement, J Jorgason would adjust his cash journals as follows:

## Cash Receipts Journal

| | | | | Discount expense | | | | | | Sundries | | | |
|---|---|---|---|---|---|---|---|---|---|---|---|---|---|
| Date | Particulars | Fol | Ref | Accounts receivable control | GST collected | Discount expense | Accounts receivable control | Sales | Amount | Account | | GST collected | Bank |
| 2018 | | | | $ | $ | $ | $ | $ | $ | | | $ | $ |
| 1 Dec | BHT Ltd Ⓐ | | EFT | | | | | | 100 | Dividends income | | | 100 |
| 4 | C Ecil | | 417 | 22 | 2 | 20 | 400 | | | | | | 400 |
| 5 | J Smith Ⓑ | | EFT | | | | | | 100 | Commission income | | 10 | 110 |

### Cash Receipts Journal

| Date | Particulars | Fol | Ref | Discount expense — Accounts receivable control | Discount expense — GST collected | Discount expense — Discount expense | Accounts receivable control | Sales | Sundries — Amount | Sundries — Account | GST collected | Bank |
|---|---|---|---|---|---|---|---|---|---|---|---|---|
| 2018 | | | | $ | $ | $ | $ | $ | $ | | $ | $ |
| 12 | EFTPOS F | | POS | | | | | 100 | | | 10 | 110 |
| 13 | Transfer a/c 36072 G | | EFT | | | | | | 1200 | Fixed deposit | | 1 200 |
| 16 | F Adams H | | DC | | | | | | 150 | Rent income | | 150 |
| 29 | Cash sales | | POS | | | | | 1 000 | | | 100 | 1 100 |
| 30 | EFTPOS | | POS | | | | | 500 | | | 50 | 550 |
| | *Bank statement adjustments:* | | | | | | | | | | | |
| 31 | JNZ Bank C | | BS | | | | | | 15 | Interest income | | 15 |
| | | | | $22 | $2 | $20 | $400 | $1 600 | $1 565 | | $170 | $3 735 |

### Explanations

1  As most of the bank statement receipt transactions had already been recorded by the business, the only bank statement adjustment required at the end of the month is to record the interest on the JNZ bank deposit. This was a credit entry in the bank statement not accounted for in the Cash Receipts Journal. It must therefore be recorded as a bank statement adjustment in the Cash Receipts Journal.

2  The date of the entry of any bank statement adjustments is usually the last day of the month, at which time the bank reconciliation is also undertaken. Where bank statement adjustments are recorded on a continuous basis throughout the month, the actual date of the transaction can be shown in the Cash Receipts Journal. This practice also applies to updating the Cash Payments Journal (see later in this chapter).

3  As this bank statement adjustment is for interest income, no GST applies to the transaction.

4  When all the above adjustments are recorded in the Cash Receipts Journal, the journal is totalled and then posted to the General Ledger. To continue the example, the Bank column of the Cash Receipts Journal is posted to the Cash at Bank Account in the General Ledger as follows:

### Cash Receipts Journal

| | Bank |
|---|---|
| | $ |
| | 3 735 |

### General Ledger

| Date | Particulars | Fol | Debit | Credit | Balance |
|---|---|---|---|---|---|
| **Cash at Bank Account** | | | | | |
| 2018 | | | $ | $ | $ |
| 30 Nov | Balance | | | | 1 000 Dr |
| | Sundry receipts | CRJ | 3 735 | | 4 735 Dr |

## Cash Payments Journal

| | | | | Discount income | | | | | | Sundries | | | |
|---|---|---|---|---|---|---|---|---|---|---|---|---|---|
| Date | Particulars | Fol | Ref | Accounts payable control | GST paid | Discount income | Accounts payable control | Purchases | Wages | Amount | Account | GST paid | Bank |
| 2018 | | | | $ | $ | $ | $ | $ | $ | $ | | $ | |
| 1 Dec | J Frederick | | 327 | | | | | 100 | | | | 10 | 110 |
| | S Tirrer | | 328 | | | | | 200 | | | | 20 | 220 |
| 5 | T Watts | | 329 | 22 | 2 | 20 | 500 | | | | | | 500 |
| 7 | A Lie | | 330 | | | | | 600 | | | | 60 | 660 |
| 9 | J Uroon | | 331 | 11 | 1 | 10 | 410 | | | | | | 410 |
| 11 | L Smith  | | EFT | | | | | | 150 | | | | 150 |
| 13 | Bendigo Daily | | 332 | | | | | | | 150 | Advertising | 15 | 165 |
| 15 | M Johnson | | 333 | | | | | 50 | | | | 5 | 55 |
| 20 | B King | | 334 | | | | | 100 | | | | 10 | 110 |
| 30 | Commonwealth Bank – Loan X1879 | | DD | | | | | | | 980 | Loan – Common-wealth Bank | | 980 |
| 31 | T Watts | | EFT | 66 | 6 | 60 | 1 040 | | | | | | 1 040 |
| | *Bank statement adjustments:* | | | | | | | | | | | | |
| | Interest on overdraft | | BS | | | | | | | 10 | Interest expense | | 10 |
| | Bank fee | | BS | | | | | | | 30 | Bank fees and charges | | 30 |
| | EFTPOS merchant fee | | BS | | | | | | | 20 | Merchant fees | 2 | 22 |
| | | | | $99 | $9 | $90 | $1 950 | $1 050 | $150 | $1 190 | | $122 | $4 462 |

**Explanations**

1 The bank statement adjustments were debit entries to the account of J Jorgason. When the statement is received, these transactions are identified and recorded by the business in the Cash Payments Journal.

2 The EFTPOS merchant fee is subject to GST as it is a payment for the supply of a service (EFTPOS facilities). None of the other bank statement adjustments are subject to GST.

3 When all the above adjustments are recorded in the Cash Payments Journal, the journal is totalled and then posted to the General Ledger. To continue the example, the Bank column of the Cash Payments Journal is posted to the Cash at Bank Account in the General Ledger as follows:

| | | Bank | Date | Particulars | Fol | Debit | Credit | Balance |
|---|---|---|---|---|---|---|---|---|
| Cash Payments Journal | | | General Ledger | | | | | |
| | | $ | | **Cash at Bank Account** | | | | |
| | | $4 462 | 2018 | | | $ | $ | $ |
| | | | 30 Nov | Balance | | | | 1 000 Dr |
| | | | 31 Dec | Sundry receipts | CRJ | 3 735 | | 4 735 Dr |
| | | | | Sundry payments | CPJ | | 4 462 | 273 Dr |

**Note** The balance of the Cash at Bank Account in the ledger ($273 Dr) is now reconciled with the balance in the bank statement ($273 Cr).

# Other cash journal adjustments (required when reconciling the cash records)

## Errors in recording transactions in the journals

It is not uncommon for transcription errors to occur when transactions are recorded in the cash journals. These errors are often detected when comparing the bank statement to the cash records of the business. For example, a cheque received or drawn could be overstated or understated in the journals. Errors of this nature can be simply corrected by crossing out the incorrect amount and writing in the correct amount as shown below.

| | | | | Discount expense | | | | | Sundries | | | | |
|---|---|---|---|---|---|---|---|---|---|---|---|---|---|
| Date | Particulars | Fol | Ref | Accounts receivable control | GST collected | Discount expense | Accounts receivable control | Sales | Amount | Account | GST collected | Bank |
| 2018 | | | | $ | $ | $ | $ | $ | $ | | $ | $ |
| | | | | | | | 400 | | | | | 400 |
| 4 Dec | C Ecil | | 417 | 22 | 2 | 20 | ~~4 000~~ | | | | | ~~4 000~~ |

Cash Receipts Journal

For control purposes, it is important not to obliterate the original error completely. The original details must be known, as they are evidence of the need for making an adjustment.

*Alternatively*, an adjusting entry can be made at the end of the journal as shown below.

| | | | | Discount expense | | | Sundries | | | | | |
| | | | | Accounts receivable control | GST collected | Discount expense | Accounts receivable control | Sales | Amount | Account | GST collected | Bank |
| **Cash Receipts Journal** | | | | | | | | | | | | |
| Date | Particulars | Fol | Ref | | | | | | | | | |
| 2018 | | | | $ | $ | $ | $ | $ | $ | | $ | $ |
| 4 Dec | C Ecil | | 417 | 22 | 2 | 20 | ~~4 000~~ | | | | | ~~4 000~~ |
| | Adjustments: | | | | | | | | | | | |
| 31 | Adjustment C Ecil (see rec. 417 above) | | BS | | | | (3 600) | | | | | (3 600) |

In this example, negative or subtracted amounts are denoted by ( ). Red ink can also be used to denote a negative entry.

# Dishonoured cheques

This is a situation that becomes apparent after a cheque has been received by the business and deposited in the bank. The bank will credit the account of the business but if at some later stage the cheque is dishonoured – that is, there are insufficient funds available in the drawer's (sender's) bank account to honour the cheque – the bank will reverse its original entry. Consider the following bank statement for J Jorgason for February 2019.

| Statement of account | | | | |
|---|---|---|---|---|
| **Bank statement** for month of February | *Account name* J Jorgason | | *Account number* 316-42497 | |
| Date | Details | Debit | Credit | Balance |
| 2019 | | $ | $ | $ |
| 1 Feb | Balance | | | 2 040 Cr |
| 3 | C/C | | 1 740 | 3 780 Cr |
| 4 | 342 | 40 | | 3 740 Cr |
| 5 | 343 | 100 | | 3 640 Cr |
| 7 | Dishonoured cheque (J Roberts) Ⓐ | 200 | | 3 440 Cr |

1 The transaction represented by Ⓐ is an amount of $200 that the business had received from J Roberts and deposited in the bank. The bank credited the amount of $200 to the account of the business as part of the deposit on 3 February 2019 ($1740). When the bank became aware that the drawer (J Roberts) had insufficient funds to honour the cheque, however, a reversal entry (debit) was entered into the account of the business.

2 When this situation arises, an adjustment is required in the Cash Receipts Journal before it is totalled for posting. This can be processed using either of the following methods:

- **Cross out** the original entry and enter adjusted amounts (where appropriate). The discount allowed when the cheque was received is also crossed out. The discount is no longer applicable as Roberts's debt is still outstanding.

### Cash Receipts Journal

| Date | Particulars | Fol | Ref | Discount expense Accounts receivable control | GST collected | Discount expense | Accounts receivable control | Sales | Sundries Amount | Account | GST collected | Bank |
|---|---|---|---|---|---|---|---|---|---|---|---|---|
| 2019 | | | | $ | $ | $ | $ | $ | $ | | $ | $ |
| 3 Feb | J Roberts | | 530 | ~~22~~ | ~~2~~ | ~~20~~ | ~~200~~ | | | | | ~~200~~ |
| 3 | Cash sales | | POS | | | | | 1 400 | | | 140 | 1 540 |
| 8 | Cash sales | | POS | | | | | 600 | | | 60 | 660 |
| 9 | Cash sales | | POS | | | | | 100 | | | 10 | 110 |
| 10 | J Boan | | 531 | 44 | 4 | 40 | 900 | | | | | 900 |
| 11 | R Watson | | EFT | 66 | 6 | 60 | 1 090 | | | | | 1 090 |
| 20 | Cash sales | | POS | | | | | 100 | | | 10 | 110 |
| 28 | Cash sales | | POS | | | | | 1 000 | | | 100 | 1 100 |
| | | | | $110 | $10 | $100 | $1 990 | $3 200 | | | $320 | $5 510 |

- *Alternatively* (and perhaps most commonly), enter a reversal entry at the end of the month.

### Cash Receipts Journal

| Date | Particulars | Fol | Ref | Discount expense Accounts receivable control | GST collected | Discount expense | Accounts receivable control | Sales | Sundries Amount | Account | GST collected | Bank |
|---|---|---|---|---|---|---|---|---|---|---|---|---|
| 2019 | | | | $ | $ | $ | $ | $ | $ | | $ | $ |
| 3 Feb | J Roberts | | 530 | 22 | 2 | 20 | 200 | | | | | |
| 3 | Cash sales | | POS | | | | | 1 400 | | | 140 | 1 740 |
| 8 | Cash sales | | POS | | | | | 600 | | | 60 | 660 |
| 9 | Cash sales | | POS | | | | | 100 | | | 10 | 110 |
| 10 | J Boan | | 531 | 44 | 4 | 40 | 900 | | | | | 900 |
| 11 | R Watson | | EFT | 66 | 6 | 60 | 1 090 | | | | | 1 090 |
| 20 | Cash sales | | POS | | | | | 100 | | | 10 | 110 |
| 28 | Cash sales | | POS | | | | | 1 000 | | | 100 | 1 100 |
| | Adjustments: | | | | | | | | | | | |
| | Dis. chq – J Roberts | | BS | (22) | (2) | (20) | (200) | | | | | (200) |
| | | | | $110 | $10 | $100 | $1 990 | $3 200 | | | $320 | $5 510 |

5.5    The information below relates to the business of P Parker. You are required to:

a    examine the statement of account from the Commonwealth Bank

b    complete the cash journals by adding any necessary bank statement adjustments at 30 June 2017

c    total the cash journals at 30 June 2017

d    post the cash journals to the Cash at Bank Account in the General Ledger at 30 June 2017.
       (**Note** The final balance should then agree with that shown on the bank statement.)

### Commonwealth Bank
### Statement of account

P Parker
10 Moorabool St
Albany 5607

*Account number*
836214

| Date | Details | Debit | Credit | Balance |
|------|---------|-------|--------|---------|
| 2017 | Brought forward | | | 1 000 Cr |
| 2 Jun | C/C | | 1 320 | 2 320 Cr |
| | No. 741 | 77 | | 2 243 Cr |
| 3 | No. 742 | 198 | | 2 045 Cr |
| 5 | No. 743 | 99 | | 1 946 Cr |
| 7 | C/C | | 1 749 | 3 695 Cr |
| | Bank fee | 10 | | 3 685 Cr |
| 8 | P Alt (wages) | 300 | | 3 385 Cr |
| | No. 744 | 44 | | 3 341 Cr |
| 10 | Interest | | 50 | 3 391 Cr |
| 13 | C/C | | 880 | 4 271 Cr |
| | No. 745 | 110 | | 4 161 Cr |
| 15 | GN Electrics (dividend) | | 400 | 4 561 Cr |
| 18 | No. 746 | 11 | | 4 550 Cr |
| 24 | No. 747 | 80 | | 4 470 Cr |
| | Annual service fee | 20 | | 4 450 Cr |
| 29 | C/C | | 200 | 4 650 Cr |
| 30 | No. 748 | 300 | | 4 350 Cr |

Date of issue 30 June 2017

### Cash Receipts Journal

| Date | Particulars | Fol | Ref | Discount expense | | | Accounts receivable control | Cash sales | Sundries | | | Bank |
|---|---|---|---|---|---|---|---|---|---|---|---|---|
| | | | | Accounts receivable control | GST collected | Discount expense | | | Amount | Account | GST collected | |
| 2017 | | | | $ | $ | $ | $ | $ | $ | | $ | $ |
| 2 Jun | Sales | | 304 | | | | | 1 200 | | | 120 | 1 320 |
| 6 | Sales | | 305 | | | | | 1 500 | | | 150 | |
| | D Avid | | 306 | 11 | 1 | 10 | 99 | | | | | 1 749 |
| 12 | Sales | | 307 | | | | | 800 | | | 80 | 880 |
| 14 | GN Corp | | EFT | | | | | | 400 | Dividends income | | 400 |
| 28 | N Naylor | | 308 | | | | 200 | | | | | 200 |

### Cash Payments Journal

| Date | Particulars | Fol | Ref | Discount income | | | Accounts payable control | Cash purchases | Wages | Sundries | | | Bank |
|---|---|---|---|---|---|---|---|---|---|---|---|---|---|
| | | | | Accounts payable control | GST paid | Discount income | | | | Amount | Account | GST paid | |
| 2017 | | | | $ | $ | $ | $ | $ | $ | $ | | $ | $ |
| 1 Jun | Blond Co | | 741 | | | | | | | 70 | Advertising | 7 | 77 |
| 2 | R Grace | | 742 | 22 | 2 | 20 | 198 | | | | | | 198 |
| 3 | P McDonald | | 743 | 11 | 1 | 10 | 99 | | | | | | 99 |
| 8 | P Melon | | EFT | | | | | | 300 | | | | 300 |
| | J Taylor | | 744 | | | | | 40 | | | | 4 | 44 |
| 10 | G Judd | | 745 | | | | | 100 | | | | 10 | 110 |
| 16 | Aust Post | | 746 | | | | | | | 10 | Postage | 1 | 11 |
| 22 | B Artel | | 747 | | | | 80 | | | | | | 80 |
| 27 | P Chapman | | 748 | | | | | | | 300 | Drawings | | 300 |

### General Ledger

| Date | Particulars | Fol | Debit | Credit | Balance |
|---|---|---|---|---|---|
| | | Cash at Bank Account | | | |
| 2017 | | | $ | $ | $ |
| 1 Jun | Balance | | | | 1 000 Dr |

5.6*   The information below relates to the business of Con Constable, of Con's Menswear, retailer of trendy clothing. You are required to:

a   examine the statement of account from the Commonwealth Bank

b   complete Con's cash journals by adding any necessary bank statement adjustments at 30 November 2019

c   total the cash journals at 30 November 2019

d   post the cash journals to the Cash at Bank Account in the General Ledger at 30 November 2019. (The final balance should then agree with that shown on the bank statement.)

**Note** Any differences between the bank statement amounts and Con Constable records are to be regarded as errors in his recording.

| | **Commonwealth Bank**<br>**Statement of account** | | | |
|---|---|---|---|---|
| **Con Constable** | | | | **Account No. 704 11T** |
| Date | Details | Debit | Credit | Balance |
| 2019 | | $ | $ | $ |
| 1 Nov | Balance brought forward | | | 2 000.00 Cr |
| 3 | C/C | | 154.00 | 2 154.00 Cr |
| | F Nerk (wages) | 150.00 | | 2 004.00 Cr |
| 5 | No. 95 | 50.00 | | 1 954.00 Cr |
| 7 | C/C | | 190.00 | 2 144.00 Cr |
| 8 | No. 96 | 90.00 | | 2 054.00 Cr |
| | Bank fee | 25.00 | | 2 029.00 Cr |
| 11 | C/C | | 550.00 | 2 579.00 Cr |
| 12 | Dishonoured cheque – R Lewis | 190.00 | | 2 389.00 Cr |
| 14 | No. 97 | 110.00 | | 2 279.00 Cr |
| | AGR Ltd (interest on loan) | | 100.00 | 2 379.00 Cr |
| 18 | C/C | | 385.00 | 2 764.00 Cr |
| | No. 98 | 110.00 | | 2 654.00 Cr |
| | Transfer – loan 10048 | 200.00 | | 2 454.00 Cr |
| 21 | No. 99 | 150.00 | | 2 304.00 Cr |
| 25 | No. 100 | 105.00 | | 2 199.00 Cr |
| | C/C | | 220.00 | 2 419.00 Cr |
| | G Topp (debtor) | | 80.00 | 2 499.00 Cr |
| 30 | C/C | | 220.00 | 2 719.00 Cr |
| | C Parker (purchases) | 220.00 | | 2 499.00 Cr |

Date of issue 30 November 2019

## Con Constable
## Cash Receipts Journal

| Date | Particulars | Fol | Ref | Discount expense — Accounts receivable control | Discount expense — GST collected | Discount expense — Discount expense | Accounts receivable control | Cash sales | Sundries — Amount | Sundries — Account | Sundries — GST collected | Bank |
|---|---|---|---|---|---|---|---|---|---|---|---|---|
| 2019 | | | | $ | $ | $ | $ | $ | $ | | $ | $ |
| 2 Nov | Sales | | POS | | | | | 140 | | | 14 | 154 |
| 6 | R Lewis | | POS | 11 | 1 | 10 | 190 | | | | | 190 |
| 10 | Sales | | POS | | | | | 400 | | | 40 | |
| | T Ennant | | 715 | | | | | | 100 | Rent income | 10 | 550 |
| 14 | AGR Ltd | | EFT | | | | | | 100 | Interest income | | 100 |
| 17 | Sales | | POS | | | | | 350 | | | 35 | 385 |
| 24 | Sales | | POS | | | | | 200 | | | 20 | 220 |
| 25 | G Topp | | EFT | 22 | 2 | 20 | 80 | | | | | 80 |
| 29 | Sales | | POS | | | | | 200 | | | 20 | 220 |

**Note** The rent received on 10 November relates to a shop leased by Con Constable to the owner of another business. The rent is therefore subject to GST.

## Cash Payments Journal

| Date | Particulars | Fol | Ref | Discount income — Accounts payable control | Discount income — GST paid | Discount income — Discount income | Accounts payable control | Cash purchases | Wages | Sundries — Amount | Sundries — Account | Sundries — GST paid | Bank |
|---|---|---|---|---|---|---|---|---|---|---|---|---|---|
| 2019 | | | | $ | $ | $ | $ | $ | $ | $ | | $ | $ |
| 3 Nov | F Nerk | | EFT | | | | | | 150 | | | | 150 |
| 4 | Petty cash | | 95 | | | | | | | 50 | Petty cash advance | | 50 |
| 7 | G Wilson | | 96 | 11 | 1 | 10 | 90 | | | | | | 90 |
| 11 | J Parsons | | 97 | | | | 100 | | | | | 10 | 110 |
| 14 | J Edwards | | 98 | | | | | | | 100 | Repairs | 10 | 110 |
| 15 | Cash | | 99 | | | | | 150 | | | | | 150 |
| 18 | Transfer loan 10048 | | DD | | | | | | | 200 | Loan from Comm Bank | | 200 |
| 23 | M Hesse | | 100 | 11 | 1 | 10 | 85 | | | | | | 85 |
| 30 | C Parker | | EFT | | | | | 200 | | | | 20 | 220 |

| General Ledger | | | | | | |
|---|---|---|---|---|---|---|
| Date | Particulars | Fol | Debit | Credit | Balance | |
| | | Cash at Bank Account | | | | |
| 2019 | | | $ | $ | $ | |
| 1 Nov | Balance | | | | 2 000 Dr | |

**SOLUTION**

5.6   b, c

**Con Constable**
**Cash Receipts Journal**

| Date | Particulars | Fol | Ref | Discount expense | | | Accounts receivable control | Cash sales | Sundries | | | Bank |
|---|---|---|---|---|---|---|---|---|---|---|---|---|
| | | | | Accounts receivable control | GST collected | Discount expense | | | Amount | Account | GST collected | |
| 2019 | | | | $ | $ | $ | $ | $ | $ | | $ | $ |
| 30 Nov | Subtotals to date | | | 33 | 3 | 30 | 270 | 1 290 | 200 | | 139 | 1 899 |
| | Adjustments: | | | | | | | | | | | |
| | Dis. Cheque – R Lewis | | BS | (11) | (1) | (10) | (190) | | | | | (190) |
| | | | | $22 | $2 | $20 | $80 | $1 290 | $200 | | $139 | $1 709 |

**Cash Payments Journal**

| Date | Particulars | Fol | Ref | Discount income | | | Accounts payable control | Cash purchases | Wages | Sundries | | | Bank |
|---|---|---|---|---|---|---|---|---|---|---|---|---|---|
| | | | | Accounts payable control | GST paid | Discount income | | | | Amount | Account | GST paid | |
| 2019 | | | | $ | $ | $ | $ | $ | $ | $ | | $ | $ |
| 30 Nov | Subtotal to date | | | 22 | 2 | 20 | 175 | 300 | 300 | 350 | | 40 | 1 165 |
| | Adjustments: | | | | | | | | | | | | |
| | Bank fee | | BS | | | | | | | 25 | Bank fees | | 25 |
| | Adjustment chq. 100 – M Hesse | | BS | | | | 20 | | | | | | 20 |
| | | | | $22 | $2 | $20 | $195 | $300 | $300 | $375 | | $40 | $1 210 |

d

| | | General Ledger | | | | |
|---|---|---|---|---|---|---|
| Date | Particulars | | Fol | Debit | Credit | Balance |
| | | Cash at Bank Account | | | | |
| 2019 | | | | $ | $ | $ |
| 1 Nov | Balance | | | | | 2 000 Dr |
| 30 | Sundry receipts | | CRJ | 1 709 | | 3 709 Dr |
| | Sundry payments | | CPJ | | 1 210 | 2 499 Dr |

# Reconciling transactions not recorded by the bank

Some transactions recorded by the business during a period may not appear on the bank statement. These transactions fall into two categories.

1   Unpresented cheques These are cheques drawn by the business that have not been presented for payment by the recipients by the time of preparation of the bank statement. Such cheques are said to be *unpresented* and will not appear as a debit in the current bank statement prepared for the business.

2   Deposits not credited These are amounts deposited in the bank by the business but not recorded by the bank until after the time of preparing the bank statement. These deposits will therefore not appear as a credit on the current bank statement prepared for the business. This is a common occurrence where deposits are made by the business near the end of a month.

Consider the following example, which illustrates the treatment of unpresented cheques and deposits not credited.

*Cash journals of J Jorgason for the month of March 2019*

| | | | | Cash Receipts Journal | | | | | | | | | |
|---|---|---|---|---|---|---|---|---|---|---|---|---|---|
| | | | | Discount expense | | | | | Sundries | | | | |
| Date | Particulars | Fol | Ref | Accounts receivable control | GST collected | Discount expense | Accounts receivable control | Cash sales | Amount | Account | GST collected | Bank |
| 2019 | | | | $ | $ | $ | $ | $ | $ | | $ | $ |
| 3 Mar | J Knobben | | EFT | 44 | 4 | 40 | 960 | | | | | 960 |
| 18 | Cash sales | | POS | | | | | 1 000 | | | 100 | 1 100 |
| 21 | Cash sales | | POS | | | | | 2 000 | | | 200 | 2 200 |

## Cash Receipts Journal

| Date | Particulars | Fol | Ref | Accounts receivable control | GST collected | Discount expense | Accounts receivable control | Cash sales | Amount | Account | GST collected | Bank |
|------|-------------|-----|-----|------------------------------|---------------|------------------|------------------------------|------------|--------|---------|---------------|------|
| | | | | *Discount expense* | | | | | *Sundries* | | | |
| 2019 | | | | $ | $ | $ | $ | $ | $ | | $ | $ |
| 30 | N Crunch | | 424 | 55 | 5 | 50 | 1 050 | | | | | |
| | Cash sales | | POS | | | | | 2 500 | | | 250 | 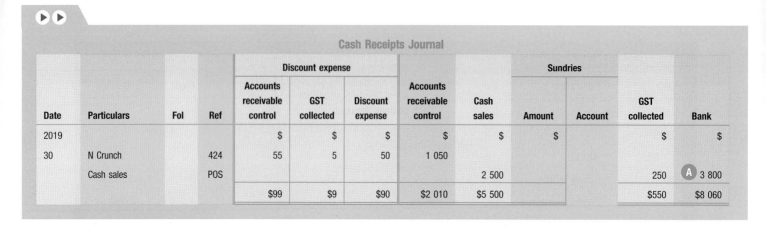 3 800 |
| | | | | $99 | $9 | $90 | $2 010 | $5 500 | | | $550 | $8 060 |

## Cash Payments Journal

| Date | Particulars | Fol | Ref | Accounts payable control | GST paid | Discount income | Accounts payable control | Cash purchases | Wages | Amount | Account | GST paid | Bank |
|------|-------------|-----|-----|---------------------------|----------|-----------------|---------------------------|----------------|-------|--------|---------|----------|------|
| | | | | *Discount income* | | | | | | *Sundries* | | | |
| 2019 | | | | $ | $ | $ | $ | $ | $ | $ | | $ | $ |
| 4 Mar | T Wanton | | 367 | 33 | 3 | 30 | 600 | | | | | | 600 |
| 5 | L Spear | | EFT | | | | 200 | | | | | | 200 |
| 20 | J Twomey | | 368 | | | | | 1 000 | | | | 100 | B 1 100 |
| 25 | B Banker | | EFT | | | | | 2 500 | | | | 250 | 2 750 |
| 29 | A Hood | | 369 | | | | | 100 | | | | 10 | C 110 |
| 30 | J Alloy | | 370 | 11 | 1 | 10 | 290 | | | | | | D 290 |
| | | | | $44 | $4 | $40 | $1 090 | $3 600 | | | | $360 | $5 050 |

## General Ledger

| Date | Particulars | Fol | Debit | Credit | Balance |
|------|-------------|-----|-------|--------|---------|
| | **Cash at Bank Account** | | | | |
| 2019 | | | $ | $ | $ |
| 1 Mar | Balance | | | | 2 400 Dr |

## Statement from the bank for the month of March 2019

| Bank statement for month of March | Account name J Jorgason | | | Account number 316-42497 |
|---|---|---|---|---|
| Date | Details | Debit | Credit | Balance |
| 2019 | | $ | $ | $ |
| 1 Mar | Balance | | | 2 400 Cr |
| 3 | J Knobben (debtor) | | 960 | 3 360 Cr |
| 5 | 367 | 600 | | 2 760 Cr |
| | L Spear (creditor) | 200 | | 2 560 Cr |
| 20 | C/C | | 1 100 | 3 660 Cr |
| 21 | C/C | | 2 200 | 5 860 Cr |
| 25 | B Banker (purchases) | 2 750 | | 3 110 Cr |
| 31 | Balance | | | 3 110 Cr |

All transactions that have been recorded by the bank have also been recorded by the business, so there is no need to update the cash journals any further. The totals of the journals (for the purposes of the example, the Bank column totals) can be posted to the General Ledger as shown below.

| General Ledger | | | | | |
|---|---|---|---|---|---|
| Date | Particulars | Fol | Debit | Credit | Balance |
| **Cash at Bank Account** | | | | | |
| 2019 | | | $ | $ | $ |
| 1 Mar | Balance | | | | 2 400 Dr |
| 31 | Sundry receipts | CRJ | 8 060 | | 10 460 Dr |
| | Sundry payments | CPJ | | 5 050 | 5 410 Dr |

It is obvious from the above that the balance of the bank statement at 31 March 2019 ($3110) does not agree with the balance in the Cash at Bank ledger account ($5410). There are two main reasons, as represented by **A** to **D** shown next to some of the journal entries on page 386.

1 Deposits not credited The amount of $3800 shown at item **A** (in CRJ) represents a deposit recorded in the Cash Receipts Journal of the business but not by the bank in its records for that particular month. As this deposit was made late in the month, it had not been recorded by the bank when the bank statement was prepared for the business.

2 Unpresented cheques The amounts shown in the Cash Payments Journal at items Ⓑ, Ⓒ and Ⓓ ($1100, $110 and $290) represent cheques that have been drawn by the business (and thus recorded in the Cash Payments Journal) but not presented to the bank for payment (and thus not recorded by the bank).

# The bank reconciliation statement

How then are the cash records of the business reconciled with those of the bank? As the bank statement received from the bank cannot be altered, a separate statement (or worksheet) is prepared which accounts for (reconciles) the differences. This statement is called a *bank reconciliation statement*.

For the example above, a bank reconciliation statement would be prepared as shown below.

| | J Jorgason<br>Bank reconciliation statement as at 31 March 2019 | | |
|---|---|---|---|
| | | $ | $ |
| *Credit* | Balance as per bank statement (at 31 March 2019) | | 3 110 |
| *add* | Deposits not credited | | 3 800 |
| | | | 6 910 |
| *less* | Unpresented cheques | | |
| | No. 368 | 1 100 | |
| | 369 | 110 | |
| | 370 | 290 | 1 500 |
| *Debit* | Balance as per Cash at Bank ledger account (at 31 March 2019) | | $5 410 |

Both records are now reconciled. To summarise: where there are transactions recorded by the business that for some reason are not recorded by the bank, the bank statement is not altered to include those items that the bank did not record. Instead, a reconciliation statement is prepared using the following simple rules:

1 Start with the closing balance of the bank statement (in this case, $3110 Cr – in bank terms).
2 Add the deposits not recorded by the bank, since this is what the bank would have done if the entries had been recorded. In this case, $3800 was added, as the opening balance was a credit (meaning that the business had money in its account).

   Of course, if the opening balance had been a debit (that is, account overdrawn), deposits not credited would be subtracted since this would have the effect of reducing the overdrawn balance.
3 Deduct unpresented cheques, as this is what the bank would have done if the cheques had been presented for payment. In this case, the amounts of $1100, $110 and $290 were deducted. These items were deducted from the credit balance as they had the effect of decreasing the amount held in the account.

If the opening balance had been a debit, unpresented cheques would be added, as they have the effect of increasing the overdrawn balance.

**Note** While the above can generally be used as a basic guide, it is wiser to try to understand the *principles of debit and credit* when preparing an actual bank reconciliation statement.

The reconciliation statement above started with the closing balance amount as reported by the bank. Items were then added and subtracted in order to reconcile the closing balance as reported by the business. It can be said, therefore, that the bank records are being reconciled back to those of the business. For this reason, it is customary to use the following words on the last line of the reconciliation statement 'balance (Dr or Cr, as applicable) as per Cash at Bank ledger account at . . .'

 **EXERCISES**

5.7   a  Briefly explain the terms 'deposits not credited' and 'unpresented cheques'.
      b  Explain the reasons for the treatment of the deposit not credited and the unpresented cheques in DU Werk's bank reconciliation statement.

| DU Werk<br>Bank reconciliation statement as at 30 June 2019 | | $ | $ |
|---|---|---|---|
| *Credit* | Balance as per bank statement | | 2 010.00 |
| *add* | Outstanding deposit | | 500.00 |
| | | | 2 510.00 |
| *less* | Unpresented cheques | | |
| | No. 146589 | 1 000.00 | |
| | 146596 | 50.00 | 1 050.00 |
| *Debit* | Balance as per Cash at Bank ledger account | | $1 460.00 |

5.8   The information below relates to the business of B Wallace. You are required to:
      a  total the simplified Cash Receipts Journal and Cash Payments Journal
      b  complete the Cash at Bank Account in the General Ledger at 31 July 2019
      c  prepare a bank reconciliation statement as at 31 July 2019.

| Statement of account | | | | | |
|---|---|---|---|---|---|
| B Wallace<br>12 Clene Road<br>Broomehill 6318 | | | | | Account No. 24289 |
| Date | Details | | Debit | Credit | Balance |
| 2019 | | | $ | $ | $ |
| | Brought forward | | | | 5 000.00 Cr |
| 3 Jul | DEP | | | 1 760.00 | 6 760.00 Cr |
| 4 | DEP | | | 143.00 | 6 903.00 Cr |
| 8 | 808 | | 40.00 | | 6 863.00 Cr |
| 14 | R Spry (wages) | | 250.00 | | 6 613.00 Cr |
| 17 | DEP | | | 77.00 | 6 690.00 Cr |
| 18 | A Large (rent) | | | 132.00 | 6 822.00 Cr |
| | DEP | | | 660.00 | 7 482.00 Cr |
| 21 | 811 | | 20.00 | | 7 462.00 Cr |
| 29 | R Spry (wages) | | 200.00 | | 7 262.00 Cr |
| 31 | 810 | | 44.00 | | 7 218.00 Cr |

| Cash Receipts Journal (simplified) | | | | | |
|---|---|---|---|---|---|
| Date | Particulars | Ref | Amount | GST<br>collected | Bank |
| 2019 | | | $ | $ | $ |
| 1 July | Cash sales | POS | 1 600 | 160 | 1 760 |
| 3 | PC Sales – Commission | 65 | 30 | 3 | |
| | Cash sales | POS | 100 | 10 | 143 |
| 15 | Cash sales | POS | 70 | 7 | 77 |
| 18 | A Large – Rent | EFT | 120 | 12 | 132 |
| | Cash sales | POS | 600 | 60 | 660 |
| 31 | Cash sales | 66 | 800 | 80 | 880 |

### Cash Payments Journal (simplified)

| Date | Particulars | Ref | Amount | GST paid | Bank |
|------|-------------|-----|--------|----------|------|
| 2019 | | | $ | $ | $ |
| 5 July | Creditor – G Sprinsteen | 808 | 40 | | 40 |
| 10 | B Lond – Advertising | 809 | 50 | 5 | 55 |
| 11 | C Chaplin – Purchases | 810 | 40 | 4 | 44 |
| 14 | R Spry – Wages | EFT | 250 | | 250 |
| 18 | Creditor – L Miokovic | 811 | 20 | | 20 |
| 20 | R Abbott – Purchases | 812 | 10 | 1 | 11 |
| 29 | R Spry – Wages | EFT | 200 | | 200 |

### General Ledger

| Date | Particulars | Fol | Debit | Credit | Balance |
|------|-------------|-----|-------|--------|---------|
| | **Cash at Bank Account** | | | | |
| 2019 | | | $ | $ | $ |
| 1 July | Balance | | | | 5 000 Dr |

5.9 This question is available on the CD that accompanies this text.

5.10* The information below relates to the business of A Mark. You are required to:
  a  total the simplified cash journals for August 2019
  b  complete the Cash at Bank Account in the General Ledger at 31 August 2019
  c  prepare a bank reconciliation statement as at 31 August 2019.

ADDITIONAL EXERCISES

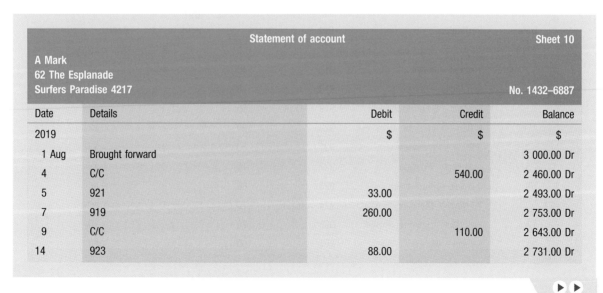

### Statement of account — Sheet 10

**A Mark**
**62 The Esplanade**
**Surfers Paradise 4217**

No. 1432–6887

| Date | Details | Debit | Credit | Balance |
|------|---------|-------|--------|---------|
| 2019 | | $ | $ | $ |
| 1 Aug | Brought forward | | | 3 000.00 Dr |
| 4 | C/C | | 540.00 | 2 460.00 Dr |
| 5 | 921 | 33.00 | | 2 493.00 Dr |
| 7 | 919 | 260.00 | | 2 753.00 Dr |
| 9 | C/C | | 110.00 | 2 643.00 Dr |
| 14 | 923 | 88.00 | | 2 731.00 Dr |

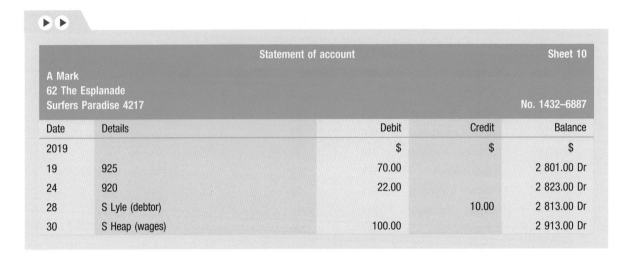

| Date | Details | Debit | Credit | Balance |
|------|---------|-------|--------|---------|
| 2019 | | $ | $ | $ |
| 19 | 925 | 70.00 | | 2 801.00 Dr |
| 24 | 920 | 22.00 | | 2 823.00 Dr |
| 28 | S Lyle (debtor) | | 10.00 | 2 813.00 Dr |
| 30 | S Heap (wages) | 100.00 | | 2 913.00 Dr |

## Cash Receipts Journal (simplified)

| Date | Particulars | Ref | Amount | GST collected | Bank |
|------|-------------|-----|--------|---------------|------|
| 2019 | | | $ | $ | $ |
| 3 Aug | Cash sales | POS | 400 | 40 | |
| | Debtor – S Baird | 016 | 100 | | 540 |
| 9 | Cash sales | POS | 100 | 10 | 110 |
| 28 | Debtor – S Lyle | EFT | 10 | | 10 |
| 30 | Cash sales | POS | 100 | 10 | |
| | Debtor – J Gallagher | 017 | 150 | | 260 |

## Cash Payments Journal (simplified)

| Date | Particulars | Ref | Amount | GST paid | Bank |
|------|-------------|-----|--------|----------|------|
| 2019 | | | $ | $ | $ |
| 2 Aug | J Bloom – Rent | 917 | 40 | 4 | 44 |
| 3 | Red Cross – Donation | 918 | 10 | | 10 |
| | Creditor – S Fernando | 919 | 260 | | 260 |
| | N Barr – Purchases | 920 | 20 | 2 | 22 |
| | J Flynn – Purchases | 921 | 30 | 3 | 33 |
| 5 | Aust Post – Postage | 922 | 15 | | 15 |
| 8 | J Wilkes – Purchases | 923 | 80 | 8 | 88 |
| | TR News – Stationery | 924 | 10 | 1 | 11 |
| 12 | BNP Bank – Loan repayment | 925 | 70 | | 70 |
| 30 | S Heap – Wages | EFT | 100 | | 100 |

| General Ledger | | | | | | |
|---|---|---|---|---|---|---|
| Date | Particulars | Fol | Debit | Credit | Balance | |
| | | Cash at Bank Account | | | **101** | |
| 2019 | | | $ | $ | $ | |
| 1 Aug | Balance | | | | 3 000 Cr | |

**SOLUTION**

5.10    a

**A Mark**
**Cash Receipts Journal (simplified)**

| Date | Particulars | Ref | Amount | GST collected | Bank |
|---|---|---|---|---|---|
| 2019 | | | $ | $ | $ |
| 3 Aug | Cash sales | POS | 400 | 40 | |
| | Debtor – S Baird | 016 | 100 | | 540 |
| 9 | Cash sales | POS | 100 | 10 | 110 |
| 28 | Debtor – S Lyle | EFT | 10 | | 10 |
| 30 | Cash sales | POS | 100 | 10 | |
| | Debtor – J Gallagher | 017 | 150 | | 260 |
| | | | $860 | $60 | $920 |

**Cash Payments Journal (simplified)**

| Date | Particulars | Ref | Amount | GST paid | Bank |
|---|---|---|---|---|---|
| 2019 | | | $ | $ | $ |
| 2 Aug | J Bloom – Rent | 917 | 40 | 4 | 44 |
| 3 | Red Cross – Donation | 918 | 10 | | 10 |
| | Creditor – S Fernando | 919 | 260 | | 260 |
| | N Barr – purchases | 920 | 20 | 2 | 22 |
| | J Flynn – Purchases | 921 | 30 | 3 | 33 |
| 5 | Aust Post – Postage | 922 | 15 | | 15 |
| 8 | J Wilkes – Purchases | 923 | 80 | 8 | 88 |
| | TR News – Stationery | 924 | 10 | 1 | 11 |
| 12 | BNP Bank – Loan repayment | 925 | 70 | | 70 |
| 30 | S Heap – Wages | EFT | 100 | | 100 |
| | | | $635 | $18 | $653 |

b

| | | | General Ledger | | | |
|---|---|---|---|---|---|---|
| Date | Particulars | Fol | Debit | Credit | Balance | |
| | | **Cash at Bank Account** | | | **101** | |
| 2019 | | | $ | $ | $ | |
| 1 Aug | Balance | | | | 3 000.00 Cr | |
| 31 | Sundries | CPJ | | 653.00 | 3 653.00 Cr | |
| | Sundries | CRJ | 920.00 | | 2 733.00 Cr | |

| | Bank reconciliation statement as at 31 August 2019 | | |
|---|---|---|---|
| | | $ | $ |
| *Debit* | Balance as per bank statement (at 31 August 2019) | | 2 913.00 |
| *add* | Unpresented cheques | | |
| | No. 917 | 44.00 | |
| | 918 | 10.00 | |
| | 922 | 15.00 | |
| | 924 | 11.00 | 80.00 |
| | | | 2 993.00 |
| *less* | Outstanding deposit 30 August 2019 | | 260.00 |
| *Credit* | Balance as per Cash at Bank ledger account (at 31 August 2019) | | $2 733.00 |

# Other entries requiring adjustments on the bank reconciliation statement

From time to time, it may be necessary to include other items in the reconciliation statement in order to balance the cash records. One uncommon item that should be mentioned is an error made by the bank. While this seldom happens, the possibility should not be overlooked. (This topic will be considered in more detail later in the chapter.)

# A systematic approach

Having considered all of the above points, the task of preparing a bank reconciliation statement may seem rather complicated, as many rules need to be remembered. Thus, a system of cross-checking and ticking items is recommended to help remember the rules and procedures, and to ensure that items are not missed. In the exercises at the end of this chapter, cash journals (usually requiring adjustment and totalling), a bank statement, an extract of the Cash at Bank Account in the General Ledger and sometimes a previous bank reconciliation statement (the purpose of which will be discussed later) are provided. Given this information, the following systematic procedures are commonly used:

Step 1    Examine outstanding deposits and unpresented cheques on the previous month's bank reconciliation statement to see whether they appear on the current bank statement.

If they appear, tick (✓) the appropriate entry in both the bank reconciliation statement and the bank statement. Any unticked items must be recorded on the bank reconciliation statement for the current month (see Step 5).

Step 2    Examine each entry in the Bank column of the Cash Receipts Journal to see whether it appears in the bank statement.

If receipts *do appear on the bank statement*, tick (✓) the appropriate entry in both the journal and the bank statement. If any amounts remain unticked, they must be processed as follows:

- *Items not ticked in the journal* (usually deposits not credited) will be used for preparing the bank reconciliation statement as previously discussed. It is useful to circle these items on the journal as a reminder to include them when preparing the bank reconciliation statement.
- *Items not ticked in the bank statement* will be used to update the Cash Receipts Journal (bank statement adjustments such as bank interest).
- Errors can be corrected by updating the Cash Receipts Journal (errors by the business) or by making a provision for the error on the bank reconciliation statement (errors by the bank).

Step 3    Examine each entry in the Bank column of the Cash Payments Journal to see whether it appears in the bank statement.

If payments *do appear on the bank statement*, tick (✓) the appropriate entry in both the journal and the bank statement. If any amounts remain unticked, they must be processed as follows:

- *Items not ticked in the journal* (usually unpresented cheques) will be used for preparing the bank reconciliation statement. It is useful to circle these items on the journal as a reminder to include them when preparing the bank reconciliation statement.
- *Items not ticked in the bank statement* will be used to update the Cash Payments Journal (bank statement adjustments; for example, bank charges).
- Errors can be corrected by updating the Cash Payments Journal (errors by the business) or by making a provision for the error on the bank reconciliation statement (errors by the bank).

Step 4    Total the cash journals and post the totals of the Bank columns to the Cash at Bank ledger account.

Step 5    Prepare a bank reconciliation statement, commencing with the final balance on the bank statement.

**Note** Where a business utilises electronic banking facilities, its cash journals may be updated for bank statement transactions progressively during the period. This would simplify the bank reconciliation process, as most bank statement transactions will already have been recorded in the business's cash journals prior to the reconciliation date.

## Comprehensive examples:

## Example 1

From the following information for Michelle Tran you are required to:

a complete the cash journals for October and post the relevant information to the Cash at Bank ledger account

b prepare a bank reconciliation statement as at 31 October 2018.

**Note** Step 1 is not appropriate in this example as there is no bank reconciliation statement for the previous month.

*Bank statement received at the end of October 2018*

| Bank statement for month of October 2018 | Account name M Tran | | | Account number 376249 |
|---|---|---|---|---|
| Date | Details | Debit | Credit | Balance |
| 2018 | | $ | $ | $ |
| 1 Oct | Balance b/f | | | 8 160.00 Cr |
| 10 | C Nguyen (debtor) | | 1 000 | 9 160.00 Cr |
| | C/C | | 1 028.40 | 10 188.40 Cr |
| 12 | C/C | | 1 340.80 | 11 529.20 Cr |
| 13 | 1624 | 520.00 | | 11 009.20 Cr |
| | Quarterly fee | 19.60 | | 10 989.60 Cr |
| 14 | 1627 | 200.00 | | 10 789.60 Cr |
| 15 | 1628 | 300.00 | | 10 489.60 Cr |
| 16 | Wages | 1 822.00 | | 8 667.60 Cr |
| 31 | 1630 | 57.20 | | 8 610.40 Cr |
| | 2964 | 100.00 | | 8 510.40 Cr |
| | Int C/wealth bonds (direct credit) | | 80.00 | 8 590.40 Cr |
| | Dis. chq. (R Johnson) | 820.00 | | 7 770.40 Cr |
| | Closing balance 31 October 2018 | | | $7 770.40 Cr |

## Cash journals of M Tran for October 2018

### Cash Receipts Journal

| Date | Particulars | Fol | Ref | Discount expense — Accounts receivable control | GST collected | Discount expense | Accounts receivable control | Cash sales | Sundries — Amount | Account | GST collected | Bank |
|------|-------------|-----|-----|------|------|------|------|------|------|------|------|------|
| 2018 | | | | $ | $ | $ | $ | $ | $ | | $ | $ |
| 10 Oct | C Nguyen | | EFT | | | | 1 000.00 | | | | | 1 000.00 |
| | J Watson | | 146 | | | | 400.00 | | | | | |
| | Cash sales | | POS | | | | | 571.27 | | | 57.13 | 1 028.40 |
| 12 | R Johnson | | 147 | 8.20 | 0.75 | 7.45 | 820.00 | | | | | |
| | P Harrod | | 148 | | | | 300.00 | | | | | |
| | Cash sales | | POS | | | | | 200.73 | | | 20.07 | 1 340.80 |
| 31 | L Tarantule | | 149 | 4.40 | 0.40 | 4.00 | 150.00 | | | | | |
| | Cash sales | | POS | | | | | 266.18 | | | 26.62 | 442.80 |
| | Interest on bonds | | EFT | | | | | | 80 | Interest income | | 80 |

### Cash Payments Journal

| Date | Particulars | Fol | Ref | Discount income — Accounts payable control | GST paid | Discount income | Accounts payable control | Cash purchases | Wages | Sundries — Amount | Account | GST paid | Bank |
|------|-------------|-----|-----|------|------|------|------|------|------|------|------|------|------|
| 2018 | | | | $ | $ | $ | $ | $ | $ | $ | | $ | $ |
| 1 Oct | M Sintell | | 1624 | 10.40 | 0.95 | 9.45 | 520.00 | | | | | | 520.00 |
| 12 | K Andrews | | 1625 | | | | | | | 1 072.73 | Office equipment | 107.27 | 1 180.00 |
| | P Small | | 1626 | | | | 48.00 | | | | | | 48.00 |
| | R Sludge | | 1627 | 8.80 | 0.80 | 8.00 | 200.00 | | | | | | 200.00 |
| 13 | M Tran | | 1628 | | | | | | | 260.00 | Drawings – M Tran | | 260.00 |
| 16 | Wages | | EFT | | | | | | 1 822.00 | | | | 1 822.00 |
| | Purchases | | 1629 | | | | | 790.91 | | | | 79.09 | 870.00 |
| 31 | T Abbott | | 1630 | | | | | | | 52.00 | Rent | 5.20 | 57.20 |

The journals above have not yet been totalled, as there may be additional entries required in the journals following the examination of the bank statement.

| General Ledger (extract) | | | | | | |
|---|---|---|---|---|---|---|
| Date | Particulars | Fol | Debit | Credit | Balance |
| **Cash at Bank Account** | | | | | | |
| 2018 | | | $ | $ | $ |
| 1 Oct | Balance | | | | 8 160.00 Dr |

## Solution

a

| Bank statement for month of October 2018 | | Account name M Tran | | Account number 376249 |
|---|---|---|---|---|
| Date | Details | Debit | Credit | Balance |
| 2018 | | $ | $ | $ |
| 1 Oct | Balance b/f | | | 8 160.00 Cr |
| 10 | C Nguyen (debtor) | | 1 000✓ | 9 160.00 Cr |
| | C/C | | 1 028.40✓ | 10 188.40 Cr |
| 12 | C/C | | 1 340.80✓ | 11 529.20 Cr |
| 13 | 1624 | 520.00✓ | | 11 009.20 Cr |
| | Quarterly fee | (A) 19.60 | | 10 989.60 Cr |
| 14 | 1627 | 200.00✓ | | 10 789.60 Cr |
| 15 | 1628 | (B) 300.00✓ | | 10 489.60 Cr |
| 16 | Wages | 1 822.00✓ | | 8 667.60 Cr |
| 31 | 1630 | 57.20✓ | | 8 610.40 Cr |
| | 2964 | (C) 100.00 | | 8 510.40 Cr |
| | Int C/wealth bonds (direct credit) | | 80.00✓ | 8 590.40 Cr |
| | Dis. chq. (R Johnson) | (D) 820.00 | | 7 770.40 Cr |
| | Closing balance 31 October 2018 | | | $7 770.40 Cr |

(A) Bank charge (must be recorded in Cash Payments Journal)
(B) Amount understated in Cash Payments Journal, corrected in same journal
(C) Cheque erroneously recorded in account by bank (appears on bank reconciliation)
(D) Dishonoured cheque, R Johnson (must be deducted from the Cash Receipts Journal)

**M Tran**
**Cash Receipts Journal for October 2018**

| Date | Particulars | Fol | Ref | Accounts receivable control | GST collected | Discount expense | Accounts receivable control | Cash sales | Amount | Account | GST collected | Bank |
|---|---|---|---|---|---|---|---|---|---|---|---|---|
| | | | | | | Discount expense | | | | Sundries | | |
| 2018 | | | | $ | $ | $ | $ | $ | $ | | $ | $ |
| 10 Oct | C Nguyen | | EFT | | | | 1 000.00 | | | | | 1 000.00✓ |
| | J Watson | | 146 | | | | 400.00 | | | | | |
| | Cash sales | | POS | | | | | 571.27 | | | 57.13 | 1 028.40✓ |
| 12 | R Johnson | | 147 | 8.20 | 0.75 | 7.45 | 820.00 | | | | | |
| | P Harrod | | 148 | | | | 300.00 | | | | | |
| | Cash sales | | POS | | | | | 200.73 | | | 20.07 | 1 340.80✓ |
| 31 | L Tarantule | | 149 | 4.40 | 0.40 | 4.00 | 150.00 | | | | | |
| | Cash sales | | POS | | | | | 266.18 | | | 26.62 | Ⓔ 442.80 |
| | Interest on bonds | | EFT | | | | | | 80.00 | Interest income | | 80.00✓ |
| | *Adjustments:* | | | | | | | | | | | |
| | Dis. chq. – R Johnson | | BS | (8.20) | (0.75) | (7.45) | (820.00) | | | | | (820.00) |
| | | | | $4.40 | $0.40 | $4.00 | $1 850.00 | $1 038.18 | $80.00 | | $103.82 | $3 072.00 |

Ⓔ Deposit not credited. This will appear on the bank reconciliation statement.

**M Tran**
**Cash Payments Journal for October 2018**

| Date | Particulars | Fol | Ref | Accounts payable control | GST paid | Discount income | Accounts payable control | Cash purchases | Wages | Amount | Account | GST paid | Bank |
|---|---|---|---|---|---|---|---|---|---|---|---|---|---|
| | | | | | | Discount income | | | | | Sundries | | |
| 2018 | | | | $ | $ | $ | $ | $ | $ | $ | | $ | $ |
| 1 Oct | M Sintell | | 1624 | 10.40 | 0.95 | 9.45 | 520.00 | | | | | | 520.00✓ |
| 12 | K Andews | | 1625 | | | | | | | 1 072.73 | Office equipment | 107.27 | Ⓕ 1 180.00 |
| | P Small | | 1626 | | | | 48.00 | | | | | | Ⓖ 48.00 |
| | R Sludge | | 1627 | 8.80 | 0.80 | 8.00 | 200.00 | | | | | | 200.00✓ |
| 13 | M Tran | | 1628 | | | | | | | 260.00 | Drawings – M Tran | | 260.00✓ |
| 16 | Wages | | EFT | | | | | | 1 822.00 | | | | 1 822.00✓ |
| | Purchases | | 1629 | | | | | 790.91 | | | | 79.09 | Ⓗ 870.00 |

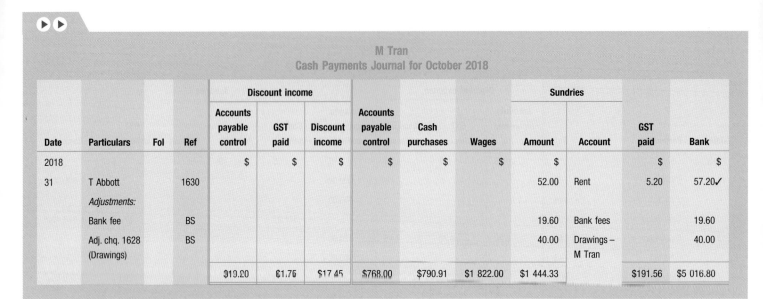

**M Tran**
**Cash Payments Journal for October 2018**

| Date | Particulars | Fol | Ref | Discount income | | | Accounts payable control | Cash purchases | Wages | Sundries | | GST paid | Bank |
|------|-------------|-----|-----|-----------------|--|--|--------------------------|----------------|-------|----------|--|----------|------|
| | | | | Accounts payable control | GST paid | Discount income | | | | Amount | Account | | |
| 2018 | | | | $ | $ | $ | $ | $ | $ | $ | | $ | $ |
| 31 | T Abbott | | 1630 | | | | | | | 52.00 | Rent | 5.20 | 57.20✓ |
| | Adjustments: | | | | | | | | | | | | |
| | Bank fee | | BS | | | | | | | 19.60 | Bank fees | | 19.60 |
| | Adj. chq. 1628 (Drawings) | | BS | | | | | | | 40.00 | Drawings – M Tran | | 40.00 |
| | | | | $19.20 | $1.76 | $17.45 | $768.00 | $790.91 | $1 822.00 | $1 444.33 | | $191.56 | $5 016.80 |

**F**, **G** and **H** Unpresented cheques. These will appear on the bank reconciliation statement.

**M Tran**
**General Ledger (extract)**

| Date | Particulars | Fol | Debit | Credit | Balance |
|------|-------------|-----|-------|--------|---------|
| | | **Cash at Bank Account** | | | |
| 2018 | | | $ | $ | $ |
| 1 Oct | Balance | | | | 8 160.00 Dr |
| 31 | Sundry receipts | CRJ | 3 072.00 | | 11 232.00 Dr |
| | Sundry payments | CPJ | | 5 016.80 | 6 215.20 Dr |

b

**M Tran**
**Bank reconciliation statement as at 31 October 2018**

| | | $ | $ | $ |
|--|--|---|---|---|
| *Credit* | Balance as per bank statement (at 31 October 2018) | | | 7 770.40 |
| *add* | Deposits not credited | | | |
| | Deposit 31 October 2018 | 442.80 | | |
| *add* | Bank error (cheque erroneously recorded) | 100.00 | | 542.80 |
| | | | | 8 313.20 |
| *less* | Unpresented cheques | | | |
| | No. 1625 | | 1 180.00 | |
| | 1626 | | 48.00 | |
| | 1629 | | 870.00 | 2 098.00 |
| *Debit* | Balance as per Cash at Bank ledger account (at 31 October 2018) | | | $6 215.20 |

When Michelle Tran prepares the bank reconciliation statement for November 2018, she may find that some cheques or deposits shown on the bank statement will not appear in the current cash journals. For example, an unpresented cheque drawn in October may be presented for payment in November. Because it will not appear in the current Cash Payments Journal, Michelle Tran will use the October bank reconciliation statement to tick (✓) the appropriate entry, as illustrated below.

| Bank reconciliation statement October | | | Bank statement November | | | | |
|---|---|---|---|---|---|---|---|
| Unpresented cheques: | $ | | Date | Particulars | Debit | Credit | Balance |
| | | | | | $ | $ | $ |
| No. 1625 | 1 180.00 | | 4 Nov | No. 1626 | 48.00✓ | | |
| 1626 | 48.00✓ | | | | | | |
| 1629 | 870.00 | | | | | | |

Items remaining unticked on the October bank reconciliation statement will be carried forward to the November bank reconciliation statement; for example, cheques 1625 and 1629 above.

## Example 2 (overdraft situation, when the bank statement is in debit)

A UWatch demonstration is available on the CD that accompanies this text for this example.

The following information relates to the business of E Bedi. You are required to:

a   complete the cash journals of E Bedi for November 2016
b   post the cash journals to the Cash at Bank Account in the General Ledger at 30 November 2016
c   prepare a bank reconciliation statement as at 30 November 2016.

(Any differences between the bank statement amounts and E Bedi's records are to be regarded as errors in his recording.)

The previous month's bank reconciliation statement showed the following:

| E Bedi Bank reconciliation statement as at 31 October 2016 | | | |
|---|---|---|---|
| | | $ | $ |
| *Credit* | Balance as per bank statement (at 31 October 2016) | | 320.00 |
| *add* | Deposits not credited | | 300.00 |
| | | | 620.00 |
| *less* | Unpresented cheques | | |
| | No. 60 | 175.00 | |
| | 61 | 220.00 | |
| | 64 | 45.00 | |
| | 67 | 100.00 | 540.00 |
| *Debit* | Balance as per Cash at Bank ledger account (at 31 October 2016) | | $80.00 |

The bank statement for the month of November 2016 showed the following:

| Bank statement for month of November 2016 | Account name E Bedi | Debit | Credit | Account number 3672 Balance |
|---|---|---|---|---|
| Date | Details | Debit | Credit | Balance |
| 2016 | | $ | $ | $ |
| 1 Nov | Balance | | | 320.00 Cr |
| | C/C | | 300.00 | 620.00 Cr |
| 2 | No. 67 | 100.00 | | 520.00 Cr |
| | M Abbott (debtor) | | 290.00 | 810.00 Cr |
| 3 | C/C | | 300.00 | 1 110.00 Cr |
| 5 | No. 60 | 175.00 | | 935.00 Cr |
| 6 | EFTPOS | | 850.00 | 1 705.00 Cr |
| 7 | D Spencer (debtor) | | 320.00 | 2 105.00 Cr |
| 8 | No. 69 | 720.00 | | 1 385.00 Cr |
| | C/C | | 150.00 | 1 535.00 Cr |
| 10 | Wages | 1 200.00 | | 335.00 Cr |
| 15 | C/C | | 390.00 | 725.00 Cr |
| | Bank fee | 20.00 | | 705.00 Cr |
| 19 | No. 72 | 850.00 | | 145.00 Dr |
| 21 | C/C | | 990.00 | 845.00 Cr |
| | BNP Ltd (dividend) | | 200.00 | 1 045.00 Cr |
| 22 | Overdrawn a/c fee | 12.00 | | 1 033.00 Cr |
| 23 | E Bedi – Drawings | 660.00 | | 373.00 Cr |
| 24 | EFTPOS | | 690.00 | 1 063.00 Cr |
| 28 | No. 73 | 290.00 | | 773.00 Cr |
| 30 | C/C | | 350.00 | 1 123.00 Cr |
| | Wages | 1 300.00 | | 177.00 Dr |
| | Deposit – P Trueman (rent) | | 250.00 | 73.00 Cr |
| | No. 70 | 250.00 | | 177.00 Dr |
| | No. 71 | 480.00 | | 657.00 Dr |
| | Dis. chq. – F Frogger | 190.00 | | 847.00 Dr |
| | EFTPOS merchant fee | 33.00 | | 880.00 Dr |
| | Closing balance at 30 November 2016 | | | $880.00 Dr |

It should be noted that a *debit bank statement balance* as above means that the bank views E Bedi as a *debtor*. That is, the account is in overdraft and therefore E Bedi owes the bank money.

The cash journals for the month of November 2016 showed the following:

### Cash Receipts Journal

| Date | Particulars | Fol | Ref | Discount expense | | | Accounts receivable control | Fees and sales | Sundries | | | Bank |
| | | | | Accounts receivable control | GST collected | Discount expense | | | Amount | Account | GST collected | |
|---|---|---|---|---|---|---|---|---|---|---|---|---|
| 2016 | | | | $ | $ | $ | $ | $ | $ | | $ | $ |
| 2 Nov | M Abbott | | EFT | 10.00 | 0.91 | 9.09 | 290.00 | | | | | 290.00 |
| | Sales | | POS | | | | | 272.73 | | | 27.27 | 300.00 |
| 4 | EFTPOS sales | | POS | | | | | 772.73 | | | 77.27 | 850.00 |
| 7 | D Spencer | | EFT | 15.00 | 1.36 | 13.64 | 320.00 | | | | | 320.00 |
| | Sales | | POS | | | | | 136.36 | | | 13.64 | 150.00 |
| 14 | Sales | | POS | | | | | 354.55 | | | 35.45 | 390.00 |
| 20 | F Frogger | | 177 | 10.00 | 0.91 | 9.09 | 190.00 | | | | | |
| | Sales | | POS | | | | | 727.27 | | | 72.73 | 990.00 |
| 21 | BNP Ltd | | EFT | | | | | | 200.00 | Dividends income | | 200.00 |
| 23 | EFTPOS sales | | POS | | | | | 627.27 | | | 62.73 | 690.00 |
| 29 | Sales | | POS | | | | | 318.18 | | | 31.82 | 350.00 |
| 30 | B Bishop | | 178 | | | | | | 95.00 | Commission income | | 95.00 |
| | P Trueman | | DC | | | | | | 227.27 | Rent income | 22.73 | 250.00 |

### Cash Payments Journal

| Date | Particulars | Fol | Ref | Discount income | | | Accounts payable control | Materials | Wages | Sundries | | | Bank |
| | | | | Accounts payable control | GST paid | Discount income | | | | Amount | Account | GST paid | |
|---|---|---|---|---|---|---|---|---|---|---|---|---|---|
| 2016 | | | | $ | $ | $ | $ | $ | $ | $ | | $ | $ |
| 3 Nov | Purchases | | 69 | | | | | 654.55 | | | | 65.45 | 720.00 |
| 4 | M Turnbull | | 70 | | | | | | | 227.27 | Rent income | 22.73 | 250.00 |
| | K Boronia | | 71 | 20.00 | 1.82 | 18.18 | 480.00 | | | | | | 480.00 |
| 10 | Wages | | EFT | | | | | | 1 200.00 | | | | 1 200.00 |
| 14 | Purchases | | 72 | | | | | 772.73 | | | | 77.27 | 850.00 |
| 19 | J Chelsea | | 73 | 10.00 | 0.91 | 9.09 | 290.00 | | | | | | 290.00 |
| 22 | AB News | | 74 | | | | | | | 272.73 | Advertising | 27.27 | 300.00 |

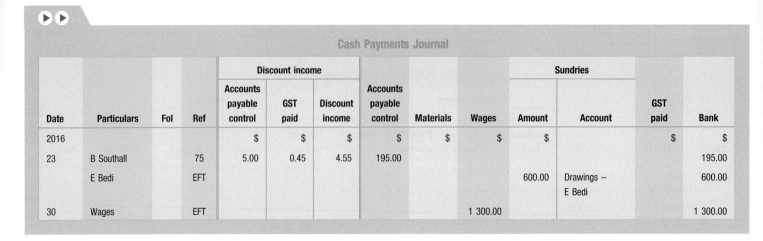

| | | | | Discount income | | | | | | Sundries | | | |
|---|---|---|---|---|---|---|---|---|---|---|---|---|---|
| Date | Particulars | Fol | Ref | Accounts payable control | GST paid | Discount income | Accounts payable control | Materials | Wages | Amount | Account | GST paid | Bank |
| 2016 | | | | $ | $ | $ | $ | $ | $ | $ | | $ | $ |
| 23 | B Southall | | 75 | 5.00 | 0.45 | 4.55 | 195.00 | | | | | | 195.00 |
| | E Bedi | | EFT | | | | | | | 600.00 | Drawings – E Bedi | | 600.00 |
| 30 | Wages | | EFT | | | | | | 1 300.00 | | | | 1 300.00 |

An extract of the General Ledger of E Bedi showed the following:

**E Bedi**
**General Ledger (extract)**

| Date | Particulars | Fol | Debit | Credit | Balance |
|---|---|---|---|---|---|
| | | **Cash at Bank Account** | | | |
| 2016 | | | $ | $ | $ |
| 1 Nov | Balance | | | | 80.00 Dr |

## Solution

a  The previous month's bank reconciliation statement showed the following:

**E Bedi**
**Bank reconciliation statement as at 31 October 2016**

| | | | $ | $ |
|---|---|---|---|---|
| *Credit* | Balance as per bank statement (at 31 October 2016) | | | 320.00 |
| *add* | Deposits not credited | | | 300.00✓ |
| | | | | 620.00 |
| *less* | Unpresented cheques | | | |
| | No. 60 | | 175.00✓ | |
| | 61 | | Ⓐ 220.00 | |
| | 64 | | Ⓑ 45.00 | |
| | 67 | | 100.00✓ | 540.00 |
| *Debit* | Balance as per Cash at Bank ledger account (at 31 October 2016) | | | $80.00 |

Ⓐ and Ⓑ are cheques that still remain unpresented. (These will appear on the next bank reconciliation statement.)

The bank statement for the month of November 2016 showed the following:

| Bank statement for month of November 2016 | Account name E Bedi | Debit | Credit | Account number 3672 Balance |
|---|---|---|---|---|
| Date | Details | Debit | Credit | Balance |
| 2016 | | $ | $ | $ |
| 1 Nov | Balance | | | 320.00 Cr |
| | C/C | | 300.00✓ | 620.00 Cr |
| 2 | No. 67 | 100.00✓ | | 520.00 Cr |
| | M Abbott | | 290.00✓ | 810.00 Cr |
| 3 | C/C | | 300.00✓ | 1 110.00 Cr |
| 5 | No. 60 | 175.00✓ | | 935.00 Cr |
| 6 | EFTPOS | | 850.00✓ | 1 785.00 Cr |
| 7 | D Spencer (debtor) | | 320.00✓ | 2 105.00 Cr |
| 8 | No. 69 | 720.00✓ | | 1 385.00 Cr |
| | C/C | | 150.00✓ | 1 535.00 Cr |
| 10 | Wages | 1 200.00✓ | | 335.00 Cr |
| 15 | C/C | | 390.00✓ | 725.00 Cr |
| | Bank fee | **C** 20.00 | | 705.00 Cr |
| 19 | No. 72 | 850.00✓ | | 145.00 Dr |
| 21 | C/C | | 990.00✓ | 845.00 Cr |
| | BNP Ltd (dividend) | | 200.00✓ | 1 045.00 Cr |
| 22 | Overdrawn a/c fee | **D** 12.00 | | 1 033.00 Cr |
| 23 | E Bedi – Drawings | **E** 660.00✓ | | 373.00 Cr |
| 24 | EFTPOS | | 690.00✓ | 1 063.00 Cr |
| 28 | No. 73 | 290.00✓ | | 773.00 Cr |
| 30 | C/C | | 350.00✓ | 1 123.00 Cr |
| | Wages | 1 300.00✓ | | 177.00 Dr |
| | Deposit – P Trueman (rent) | | 250.00✓ | 73.00 Cr |
| | No. 70 | 250.00✓ | | 177.00 Dr |
| | No. 71 | 480.00✓ | | 657.00 Dr |
| | Dis. chq. – F Frogger | **F** 190.00 | | 847.00 Dr |
| | EFTPOS merchant fee | **G** 33.00 | | 880.00 Dr |
| | Closing balance at 30 November 2016 | | | $880.00 Dr |

**C** Bank fee (must be recorded in the Cash Payments Journal)
**D** Overdrawn account fee (must be recorded in Cash Payments Journal)
**E** Amount understated in Cash Payments Journal, corrected in same journal
**F** Dishonoured cheque – F Frogger (must be deducted from the Cash Receipts Journal)
**G** EFTPOS merchant fee (must be recorded in the Cash Payments Journal)

It should also be noted that the EFT payment in the bank statement on 23 November 2106 appears as $660 here and only $600 in the Cash Payments Journal. This is an error in recording by E Bedi and must be corrected in the Cash Payments Journal.

| | | | | Discount expense | | | | | Sundries | | | | |
|---|---|---|---|---|---|---|---|---|---|---|---|---|---|
| Date | Particulars | Fol | Ref | Accounts receivable control | GST collected | Discount expense | Accounts receivable control | Fees and sales | Amount | Account | GST collected | Bank |
| 2016 | | | | $ | $ | $ | $ | $ | $ | | $ | $ |
| 2 Nov | M Abbott | | EFT | 10.00 | 0.91 | 9.09 | 290.00 | | | | | 290.00✓ |
| | Sales | | POS | | | | | 272.73 | | | 27.27 | 300.00✓ |
| 4 | EFTPOS sales | | POS | | | | | 772.73 | | | 77.27 | 850.00✓ |
| 7 | D Spencer | | EFT | 15.00 | 1.36 | 13.64 | 320.00 | | | | | 320.00✓ |
| | Sales | | POS | | | | | 136.36 | | | 13.64 | 150.00✓ |
| 14 | Sales | | POS | | | | | 354.55 | | | 35.45 | 390.00✓ |
| 20 | F Frogger | | 177 | 10.00 | 0.91 | 9.09 | 190.00 | | | | | |
| | Sales | | POS | | | | | 727.27 | | | 72.73 | 990.00✓ |
| 21 | BNP Ltd | | EFT | | | | | | 200.00 | Dividend income | | 200.00✓ |
| 23 | EFTPOS sales | | POS | | | | | 627.27 | | | 62.73 | 690.00✓ |
| 29 | Sales | | POS | | | | | 318.18 | | | 31.82 | 350.00✓ |
| 30 | B Bishop | | 178 | | | | | | 95.00 | Commission income | | 95.00 |
| | P Trueman | | DC | | | | | | 227.27 | Rent income | 22.73 | 250.00✓ |
| | Bank statement adjustments: | | | | | | | | | | | |
| | Dis. chq. – F Frogger | | BS | (10.00) | (0.91) | (9.09) | (190.00) | | | | | (190.00) |
| | | | | $25.00 | $2.27 | $22.73 | $610.00 | $3 209.09 | $522.27 | | $343.64 | $4 685.00 |

Deposit not credited. This will appear on the bank reconciliation statement.

## Cash Payments Journal

| Date | Particulars | Fol | Ref | Discount income | | | Accounts payable control | Materials | Wages | Sundries | | GST paid | Bank |
|------|-------------|-----|-----|----------------------------|----------|-----------------|--------------------------|-----------|-------|----------|---------|----------|------|
| | | | | Accounts payable control | GST paid | Discount income | | | | Amount | Account | | |
| 2016 | | | | $ | $ | $ | $ | $ | $ | $ | | $ | $ |
| 3 Nov | Purchases | | 69 | | | | | 654.55 | | | | 65.45 | 720.00✓ |
| 4 | M Turnbull | | 70 | | | | | | | 227.27 | Rent income | 22.73 | 250.00✓ |
| | K Boronia | | 71 | 20.00 | 1.82 | 18.18 | 480.00 | | | | | | 480.00✓ |
| 10 | Wages | | EFT | | | | | | 1 200.00 | | | | 1 200.00✓ |
| 14 | Purchases | | 72 | | | | | 772.73 | | | | 77.27 | 850.00✓ |
| 19 | J Chelsea | | 73 | 10.00 | 0.91 | 9.09 | 290.00 | | | | | | 290.00✓ |
| 22 | AB News | | 74 | | | | | | | 272.73 | Advertising | 27.27 | (I) 300.00 |
| 23 | B Southall | | 75 | 5.00 | 0.45 | 4.55 | 195.00 | | | | | | (J) 195.00 |
| | E Bedi | | EFT | | | | | | | 600.00 | Drawings – E Bedi | | 600.00✓ |
| 30 | Wages | | EFT | | | | | | 1 300.00 | | | | 1 300.00✓ |
| | *Bank statement adjustments:* | | | | | | | | | | | | |
| | Bank fee | | BS | | | | | | | 20.00 | Bank fees | | 20.00 |
| | Overdrawn a/c fee | | BS | | | | | | | 12.00 | Bank fees | | 12.00 |
| | Adj. EFT payment 23 Nov (Drawings) | | BS | | | | | | | 60.00 | Drawings – E Bedi | | 60.00 |
| | Merchant fees | | BS | | | | | | | 30.00 | Merchant fees expense | 3.00 | 33.00 |
| | | | | $35.00 | $3.18 | $31.82 | $965.00 | $1 427.28 | $2 500.00 | $1 222.00 | | $195.72 | $6 310.00 |

(I) and (J) are unpresented cheques. These will appear on the bank reconciliation statement.

b An extract of the General Ledger of E Bedi showed the following:

| | E Bedi General Ledger (extract) | | | | |
|---|---|---|---|---|---|
| Date | Particulars | Fol | Debit | Credit | Balance |
| | **Cash at Bank Account** | | | | |
| 2016 | | | $ | $ | $ |
| 1 Nov | Balance | | | | 80.00 Dr |
| 30 | Sundry receipts | CRJ | 4 685.00 | | 4 765.00 Dr |
| | Sundry payments | CPJ | | 6 310.00 | 1 545.00 Cr |

c A bank reconciliation statement as at 30 November 2016 showed the following:

| | E Bedi Bank reconciliation statement as at 30 November 2016 | | |
|---|---|---|---|
| | | $ | $ |
| Debit | Balance as per bank statement (at 30 November 2016) | | 880.00 |
| add | Unpresented cheques | | |
| | No. 61 (from previous bank reconciliation statement) | 220.00 | |
| | 64 (from previous bank reconciliation statement) | 45.00 | |
| | 74 | 300.00 | |
| | 75 | 195.00 | 760.00 |
| | | | 1 640.00 |
| less | Deposits not credited | | |
| | Deposit 30 November 2016 | | 95.00 |
| Credit | Balance as per Cash at Bank ledger account (at 30 November 2016) | | $1 545.00 |

**Explanations**

1   After reconciling the bank statement, the total of the reconciliation statement ($1545.00) must agree with the overdrawn balance in the Cash at Bank Account ($1545.00).

2   In order to reconcile E Bedi's debit bank statement balance (that is, where cheques drawn exceed bank deposits) with his credit ledger account balance, unpresented cheques *must be added* to the bank statement balance and the deposit not yet recorded on the bank statement *must be subtracted*.

Unpresented cheques are added because these cheques have yet to be added to E Bedi's overdraft balance at the bank. The outstanding deposit is subtracted, as this deposit has yet to appear on his bank statement.

 **EXERCISES**

**5.11** The information below relates to the business of D Dimasi. You are required to:

a complete and total the simplified cash journals for June 2018

b complete the Cash at Bank Account in the General Ledger at 30 June 2018

c prepare a bank reconciliation statement as at 30 June 2018.

| Account: | D Dimasi 10 Main Street Grassy 7256 | | | | Statement number 326–589 |
|---|---|---|---|---|---|
| Date | Details | Debit | Credit | | Balance |
| 2018 | | $ | $ | | $ |
| 1 Jun | Brought forward | | | | 5 000.00 Dr |
| 5 | 814 | 10.00 | | | 5 010.00 Dr |
| 6 | 811 | 50.00 | | | 5 060.00 Dr |
| 8 | C/C | | 100.00 | | 4 960.00 Dr |
| 12 | Overdraft establishment fee | 60.00 | | | 5 020.00 Dr |
| 15 | C/C | | 200.00 | | 4 820.00 Dr |
| 18 | C/C | | 300.00 | | 4 520.00 Dr |
| 20 | 816 | 140.00 | | | 4 660.00 Dr |
| 25 | Interest on fixed deposit | | 150.00 | | 4 510.00 Dr |
| 30 | 812 | 80.00 | | | 4 590.00 Dr |
| | C Muttonbird (debtor) | | 200.00 | | 4 390.00 Dr |

| | Cash Receipts Journal (simplified) | | | | |
|---|---|---|---|---|---|
| Date | Particulars | Ref | Amount | GST collected | Bank |
| 2018 | | | $ | $ | $ |
| 7 Jun | Cash sales | POS | 45.45 | 4.55 | |
| | Debtor – A Fish | 121 | 50.00 | | 100.00 |
| 14 | Cash sales | POS | 181.82 | 18.18 | 200.00 |
| 17 | Debtor – B Bullock | 122 | 190.00 | | |
| | Cash sales | POS | 100.00 | 10.00 | 300.00 |
| 30 | Debtor – C Muttonbird | EFT | 200.00 | | 200.00 |
| | Cash sales | POS | 100.00 | 10.00 | |
| | Debtor – D Kelp | 123 | 140.00 | | 250.00 |

### Cash Payments Journal (simplified)

| Date | Particulars | Ref | Amount | GST paid | Bank |
|------|-------------|-----|--------|----------|------|
| 2018 | | | $ | $ | $ |
| 1 Jun | Wages | 810 | 35.00 | | 35.00 |
| | Cleaning | 811 | 45.45 | 4.55 | 50.00 |
| | Cash purchases | 812 | 72.73 | 7.27 | 80.00 |
| | Creditor – General | | | | |
| | Industries | 813 | 25.00 | | 25.00 |
| | Stationery | 814 | 9.09 | 0.91 | 10.00 |
| 10 | Cash purchases | 815 | 54.55 | 5.45 | 60.00 |
| 15 | Cash purchases | 816 | 127.27 | 12.73 | 140.00 |
| 30 | Wagoc | 817 | 80.00 | | 80.00 |

### General Ledger

| Date | Particulars | Fol | Debit | Credit | Balance |
|------|-------------|-----|-------|--------|---------|
| | **Cash at Bank Account** | | | | |
| 2018 | | | $ | $ | $ |
| 31 May | Balance | | | | 5 000.00 Cr |

5.12 The information below relates to the business of B Panchez. You are required to:
 a   update and total the simplified cash journals for May 2019
 b   complete the Cash at Bank Account in the General Ledger at 31 May 2019
 c   prepare a bank reconciliation statement as at 31 May 2019.

| Account: | B Panchez 2036 Forest Street Mount Druitt 2770 | | | | Statement number 1623–49 |
|----------|------------------------------------------------|---|---|---|---------------------------|
| Date | Details | | Debit | Credit | Balance |
| 2019 | | | $ | $ | $ |
| 1 May | Brought forward | | | | 1 000.00 Dr |
| 6 | Fee | | 10.00 | | 1 010.00 Dr |
| 7 | C/C | | | 500.00 | 510.00 Dr |
| | 126 | | 90.00 | | 600.00 Dr |
| 10 | C/C | | | 150.00 | 450.00 Dr |

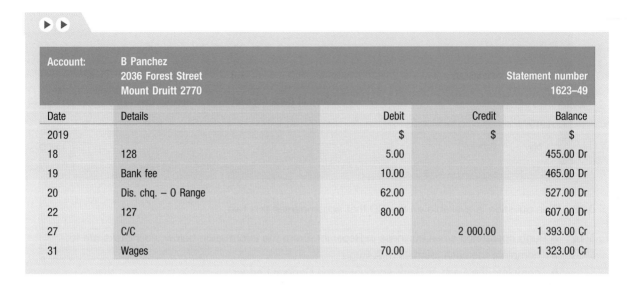

| Account: | B Panchez<br>2036 Forest Street<br>Mount Druitt 2770 | | | Statement number<br>1623–49 |
|---|---|---|---|---|
| Date | Details | Debit | Credit | Balance |
| 2019 | | $ | $ | $ |
| 18 | 128 | 5.00 | | 455.00 Dr |
| 19 | Bank fee | 10.00 | | 465.00 Dr |
| 20 | Dis. chq. – O Range | 62.00 | | 527.00 Dr |
| 22 | 127 | 80.00 | | 607.00 Dr |
| 27 | C/C | | 2 000.00 | 1 393.00 Cr |
| 31 | Wages | 70.00 | | 1 323.00 Cr |

### Cash Receipts Journal (simplified)

| Date | Particulars | Rec. no. | Amount | GST collected | Bank |
|---|---|---|---|---|---|
| 2019 | | | $ | $ | $ |
| 6 May | Cash sales | POS | 100.00 | 10.00 | |
| | Debtor – B Boyd | 85 | 390.00 | | 500.00 |
| 10 | Cash sales | POS | 80.00 | 8.00 | |
| | Debtor – O Range | 86 | 62.00 | | 150.00 |
| 26 | Cash sales | POS | 1 818.18 | 181.82 | 2 000.00 |
| | Debtor – E Hunter | 87 | 1 000.00 | | 1 000.00 |

### Cash Payments Journal (simplified)

| Date | Particulars | Chq. no. | Amount | GST paid | Bank |
|---|---|---|---|---|---|
| 2019 | | | $ | $ | $ |
| 5 | Rent | 126 | 81.82 | 8.18 | 90.00 |
| 10 | Advertising | 127 | 72.73 | 7.27 | 80.00 |
| 15 | Stationery | 128 | 4.55 | 0.45 | 5.00 |
| 30 | Cash purchases | 129 | 90.91 | 9.09 | 100.00 |
| | Cash purchases | 130 | 181.82 | 18.18 | 200.00 |
| | Wages | EFT | 70.00 | | 70.00 |

| General Ledger | | | | | | |
|---|---|---|---|---|---|---|
| Date | Particulars | Fol | Debit | Credit | | Balance |
| | **Cash at Bank Account** | | | | | **101** |
| 2019 | | | $ | $ | | $ |
| 1 May | Balance | | | | | 1 000.00 Cr |

5.13    This question is available on the CD that accompanies this text.

5.14*   A Bugg operates a small business in Repalant. From the information below, your tasks are to:

    a  complete the cash journals of A Bugg

    b  complete the Cash at Bank Account in the General Ledger

    c  prepare a bank reconciliation statement as at 31 August 2019.

| A Bugg Bank reconciliation statement as at 31 July 2019 | | | |
|---|---|---|---|
| | | $ | $ |
| *Credit* | Balance as per bank statement | | 5 000.00 |
| *add* | Deposits not credited | | 400.00 |
| | | | 5 400.00 |
| *less* | Unpresented cheques | | |
| | No. 951 | 180.00 | |
| | 133 | 241.50 | |
| | 134 | 412.50 | 834.00 |
| *Debit* | Balance as per Cash at Bank ledger account | | $4 566.00 |

| Cash Receipts Journal | | | | | | | | | | | | |
|---|---|---|---|---|---|---|---|---|---|---|---|---|
| | | | | Discount expense | | | | | | Sundries | | |
| Date | Particulars | Fol | Ref | Accounts receivable control | GST collected | Discount expense | Accounts receivable control | Cash sales | Amount | Account | GST collected | Bank |
| 2019 | | | | $ | $ | $ | $ | $ | $ | | $ | $ |
| 3 Aug | C Butter | | 25 | 10.00 | 0.91 | 9.09 | 100.00 | | | | | 100.00 |
| 8 | A Fly | | 26 | 40.00 | 3.64 | 36.36 | 360.00 | | | | | 360.00 |
| | Cash sales | | POS | | | | | 405.45 | | | 40.55 | 446.00 |

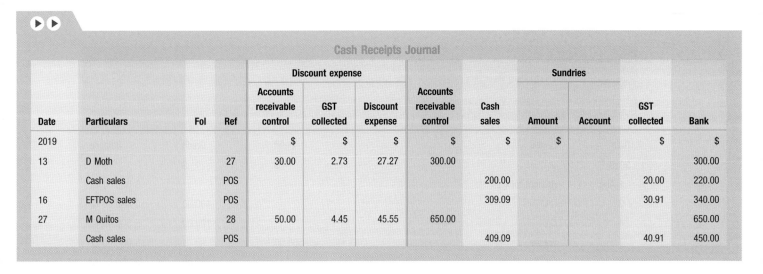

### Cash Receipts Journal

| Date | Particulars | Fol | Ref | Accounts receivable control (Discount expense) | GST collected (Discount expense) | Discount expense | Accounts receivable control | Cash sales | Amount (Sundries) | Account (Sundries) | GST collected (Sundries) | Bank |
|------|-------------|-----|-----|----|----|----|----|----|----|----|----|----|
| 2019 | | | | $ | $ | $ | $ | $ | $ | | $ | $ |
| 13 | D Moth | | 27 | 30.00 | 2.73 | 27.27 | 300.00 | | | | | 300.00 |
| | Cash sales | | POS | | | | | 200.00 | | | 20.00 | 220.00 |
| 16 | EFTPOS sales | | POS | | | | | 309.09 | | | 30.91 | 340.00 |
| 27 | M Quitos | | 28 | 50.00 | 4.45 | 45.55 | 650.00 | | | | | 650.00 |
| | Cash sales | | POS | | | | | 409.09 | | | 40.91 | 450.00 |

### Cash Payments Journal

| Date | Particulars | Fol | Ref | Accounts payable control (Discount income) | GST paid (Discount income) | Discount income | Accounts payable control | Cash purchases | Wages | Amount (Sundries) | Account (Sundries) | GST paid (Sundries) | Bank |
|------|-------------|-----|-----|----|----|----|----|----|----|----|----|----|----|
| 2019 | | | | $ | $ | $ | $ | $ | $ | $ | | $ | $ |
| 7 Aug | Wages | | EFT | | | | | | 500.00 | | | | 500.00 |
| 9 | G Austin | | 146 | | | | | 18.09 | | | | 1.81 | 19.90 |
| | M Middlin | | 147 | 3.10 | 0.28 | 2.82 | 120.90 | | | | | | 120.90 |
| | S Williams | | 148 | 7.50 | 0.68 | 6.82 | 292.50 | | | | | | 292.50 |
| | A Parsons | | EFT | | | | | | | 909.09 | Rent | 90.91 | 1 000.00 |
| 15 | Wages | | EFT | | | | | | 530.00 | | | | 530.00 |
| | T Over | | 149 | 6.00 | 0.55 | 5.45 | 234.00 | | | | | | 234.00 |
| 21 | Wages | | EFT | | | | | | 560.00 | | | | 560.00 |
| | B Downe | | 150 | | | | | 69.47 | | | | 6.95 | 76.42 |
| 28 | Wages | | EFT | | | | | | 530.00 | | | | 530.00 |
| | G Course | | 151 | 16.00 | 1.45 | 14.55 | 624.00 | | | | | | 624.00 |
| | Stationery Suppliers | | 152 | | | | | | | 46.22 | Stationery | 4.62 | 50.84 |

413

| Statement of account | | | | |
|---|---|---|---|---|

A Bugg
28 Hopper Grove
Repalant 2194

Account number
169–6994

| Date | Details | Debit | Credit | Balance |
|---|---|---|---|---|
| 2019 | | $ | $ | $ |
| 1 Aug | Brought forward | | | 5 000.00 Cr |
| 2 | C/C | | 400.00 | 5 400.00 Cr |
| 4 | C/C | | 100.00 | 5 500.00 Cr |
| 7 | Wages | 500.00 | | 5 000.00 Cr |
| 9 | C/C | | 360.00 | 5 360.00 Cr |
| | EFTPOS | | 446.00 | 5 806.00 Cr |
| | 133 | 241.50 | | 5 564.50 Cr |
| | Bank fee | 4.50 | | 5 560.00 Cr |
| | Deposit – A Parsons (rent)* | 1 000.00 | | 4 560.00 Cr |
| 10 | 148 | 292.50 | | 4 267.50 Cr |
| 13 | 147 | 120.90 | | 4 146.60 Cr |
| | EFTPOS | | 220.00 | 4 366.60 Cr |
| 15 | 149 | 234.00 | | 4 132.60 Cr |
| | 146 | 19.90 | | 4 112.70 Cr |
| | Wages | 530.00 | | 3 582.70 Cr |
| | C/C | | 300.00 | 3 882.70 Cr |
| 16 | Account service fee | 8.60 | | 3 874.10 Cr |
| | 951 | 180.00 | | 3 694.10 Cr |
| 17 | EFTPOS | | 340.00 | 4 034.10 Cr |
| 21 | Wages | 560.00 | | 3 474.10 Cr |
| 22 | 150 | 76.42 | | 3 397.68 Cr |
| 27 | EFTPOS | | 450.00 | 3 847.68 Cr |
| 28 | C/C | | 650.00 | 4 497.68 Cr |
| | Wages | 530.00 | | 3 967.68 Cr |
| 29 | Interest | | 100.00 | 4 067.68 Cr |
| | Dis. chq. – A Fly | 360.00 | | 3 707.68 Cr |
| | EFTPOS merchant fee | 5.00 | | 3 702.68 Cr |
| Date of issue 31 August 2019 | | Final balance | | $3 702.68 Cr |

*Rent relates to a commercial property and is therefore subject to GST.

ADDITIONAL
EXERCISES

5.15    This question is available on the CD that accompanies this text.

5.16   The following information is extracted from the records of D Kickett. You are required to:

a   complete and total the cash journals for March 2019

b   post the cash journals to the General Ledger Cash at Bank Account and balance this account at
31 March 2019

c   prepare a bank reconciliation statement at 31 March 2019.

(Any differences between the bank statement amounts and D Kickett's records are to be regarded as
errors in his recording.)

| D Kickett Bank reconciliation statement as at 28 February 2019 | | $ | $ |
|---|---|---|---|
| Debit | Balance as per bank statement | | 840.00 |
| less | Deposits not credited | | 300.00 |
| | | | 540.00 |
| add | Unpresented cheques | | |
| | No. 64 | 60.00 | |
| | 69 | 110.00 | 170.00 |
| Credit | Balance as per Cash at Bank ledger account | | $710.00 |

| D Kickett Statement of account | | | | Account number 221–345 |
|---|---|---|---|---|
| Date | Details | Debit | Credit | Balance |
| 2019 | | $ | $ | $ |
| 1 Mar | Brought forward | | | 840.00 Dr |
| | C/C | | 300.00 | 540.00 Dr |
| 4 | No. 64 | 60.00 | | 600.00 Dr |
| 5 | C/C | | 280.00 | 320.00 Dr |
| 9 | Interest | | 100.00 | 220.00 Dr |
| 16 | C/C | | 200.00 | 20.00 Dr |
| | No. 71 | 140.00 | | 160.00 Dr |
| 18 | G Brook – dishonoured cheque | 200.00 | | 360.00 Dr |
| 19 | D Creek (rent) | | 100.00 | 260.00 Dr |
| 20 | C Ribbon (creditor) | 88.00 | | 348.00 Dr |
| | C/C | | 200.00 | 148.00 Dr |
| 31 | Fee | 10.00 | | 158.00 Dr |

### Cash Receipts Journal

| Date | Particulars | Fol | Ref | Discount expense | | | Accounts receivable control | Cash sales | Sundries | | | Bank |
| | | | | Accounts receivable control | GST collected | Discount expense | | | Amount | Account | GST collected | |
|---|---|---|---|---|---|---|---|---|---|---|---|---|
| 2019 | | | | $ | $ | $ | $ | $ | $ | | $ | $ |
| 4 Mar | R River | | 860 | 20.00 | 1.82 | 18.18 | 280.00 | | | | | 280.00 |
| 15 | G Brook | | 861 | 10.00 | 0.91 | 9.09 | 200.00 | | | | | 200.00 |
| 19 | Cash sales | | POS | | | | | 181.82 | | | 18.18 | 200.00 |
| | D Creek | | EFT | | | | | | 90.91 | Rent income | 9.09 | 100.00 |
| 29 | G Brook | | 862 | 20.00 | 1.82 | 18.18 | 240.00 | | | | | 240.00 |
| 31 | B Stream | | 863 | | | | 680.00 | | | | | 680.00 |

### Cash Payments Journal

| Date | Particulars | Fol | Ref | Discount income | | | Acounts payable control | Cash purchases | Wages | Sundries | | | Bank |
| | | | | Accounts payable control | GST paid | Discount income | | | | Amount | Account | GST paid | |
|---|---|---|---|---|---|---|---|---|---|---|---|---|---|
| 2019 | | | | $ | $ | $ | $ | $ | $ | $ | | $ | $ |
| 4 Mar | A Gift | | 70 | 10.00 | 0.91 | 9.09 | 200.00 | | | | | | 200.00 |
| 9 | B Wrapper | | 71 | | | | 140.00 | | | | | | 140.00 |
| 20 | C Ribbon | | EFT | | | | 80.00 | | | | | | 80.00 |
| 27 | Cash purchases | | 72 | | | | | 272.73 | | | | 27.27 | 300.00 |

5.17* The following information is extracted from the records of B Purchest, antique dealer of Armidale. You are required to:

a complete and total the cash journals for April 2019

b post the cash journals to the General Ledger Cash at Bank Account in columnar form, and balance this account at 30 April 2019

c prepare a bank reconciliation statement as at 30 April 2019.

**Notes**

· Any differences between the bank statement amounts and B Purchest's records are to be regarded as errors in her recording.

· B Purchest does not utilise electronic banking facilities and therefore only accounts for all 'bank statement' transactions at month end.

| | | $ | $ |
|---|---|---|---|
| | **B Purchest**<br>**Bank reconciliation statement as at 31 March 2019** | | |
| *Debit* | Balance as per bank statement | | 1 200.00 |
| *less* | Deposits not yet credited | | 800.00 |
| | | | 400.00 |
| *add* | Unpresented cheques | | |
| | No. 126 | 120.00 | |
| | 128 | 40.00 | |
| | 110 | 250.00 | 410.00 |
| *Credit* | Balance as per Cash at Bank ledger account | | $810.00 |

**Statement of account**

B Purchest
12 Cedar Avenue
Armidale 2350

Account number

4216

April 2019

| Date | Details | Debit | Credit | Balance |
|---|---|---|---|---|
| 2019 | | $ | $ | $ |
| 1 Apr | Balance | | | 1 200.00 Dr |
| | C/C | | 800.00 | 400.00 Dr |
| | 126 | 120.00 | | 520.00 Dr |
| 6 | 120 | 69.00 | | 589.00 Dr |
| 9 | Fee | 15.00 | | 604.00 Dr |
| 12 | C/C | | 550.00 | 54.00 Dr |
| 15 | C/C | | 360.00 | 306.00 Cr |
| 24 | Dis. chq. – C Bowler | 100.00 | | 206.00 Cr |
| | 131 | 85.00 | | 121.00 Cr |
| | 134 | 125.00 | | 4.00 Dr |
| | Loan repayment | 200.00 | | 204.00 Dr |
| | 132 | 30.00 | | 234.00 Dr |
| 29 | EFTPOS | | 2 000.00 | 1 766.00 Cr |
| 30 | EFTPOS merchant fee | 22.00 | | 1 744.00 Cr |

### Cash Receipts Journal

| | | | | Discount expense | | | | | Sundries | | | |
| | | | | Accounts receivable control | GST coll. | Discount expense | Accounts receivable control | Cash sales | Amount | Account | GST coll. | Bank |
| Date | Particulars | Fol | Ref | | | | | | | | | |
|---|---|---|---|---|---|---|---|---|---|---|---|---|
| 2019 | | | | $ | $ | $ | $ | $ | $ | | $ | $ |
| 11 Apr | E Site | | 74 | 10.00 | 0.91 | 9.09 | 100.00 | | | | | |
| | Cash sales | | POS | | | | | 409.09 | | | 40.91 | 550.00 |
| 14 | B Tabal | | 75 | | | | 260.00 | | | | | |
| | C Bowler | | 76 | | | | 100.00 | | | | | 360.00 |
| 28 | EFTPOS sales | | POS | | | | | 1 818.18 | | | 181.82 | 2 000.00 |
| 30 | Cash sales | | POS | | | | | 1 363.64 | | | 136.36 | 1 500.00 |

### Cash Payments Journal

| | | | | Discount income | | | | | | Sundries | | | |
| | | | | Accounts payable control | GST paid | Discount income | Accounts payable control | Cash purchases | Wages | Amount | Account | GST paid | Bank |
| Date | Particulars | Fol | Ref | | | | | | | | | | |
|---|---|---|---|---|---|---|---|---|---|---|---|---|---|
| 2019 | | | | $ | $ | $ | $ | $ | $ | $ | | $ | $ |
| 1 Apr | Bendigo Daily | | 129 | | | | | | | 87.27 | Advertising | 8.73 | 96.00 |
| 9 | Laden Supplies | | 130 | 10.00 | 0.91 | 9.09 | 290.00 | | | | | | 290.00 |
| 18 | Wages | | 131 | | | | | | 85.00 | | | | 85.00 |
| 19 | D Course Supplies | | 132 | | | | | 27.27 | | | | 2.73 | 30.00 |
| | Shelac Ltd | | 133 | | | | | 136.36 | | | | 13.64 | 150.00 |
| | B Wax Suppliers | | 134 | | | | | 113.64 | | | | 11.36 | 125.00 |
| 30 | Lead Light Co | | 135 | 4.00 | 0.36 | 3.64 | 196.00 | | | | | | 196.00 |

## SOLUTIONS

5.14 a

### A Bugg
### Cash Receipts Journal

| Date | Particulars | Fol | Ref | Discount expense | | | Accounts receivable control | Cash sales | Sundries | | | | Bank |
|------|-------------|-----|-----|------------------|--|--|------------------|-----------|----------|--|--|--|------|
| | | | | Accounts receivable control | GST collected | Discount expense | | | Amount | Account | GST collected | |
| 2019 | | | | $ | $ | $ | $ | $ | $ | | $ | $ |
| 31 Aug | Subtotal to date | | | 130.00 | 11.73 | 118.27 | 1 410.00 | 1 323.63 | | | 132.37 | 2 866.00 |
| | *Adjustments:* | | | | | | | | | | | |
| | Interest | | BS | | | | | | 100.00 | Interest income | | 100.00 |
| | Dis. chq. (A Fly) | | BS | (40.00) | (3.64) | (36.36) | (360.00) | | | | | (360.00) |
| | | | | $90.00 | $8.09 | $81.91 | $1 050.00 | $1 323.63 | $100.00 | | $132.37 | $2 606.00 |

### Cash Payments Journal

| Date | Particulars | Fol | Ref | Discount income | | | Accounts payable control | Cash purchases | Wages | Sundries | | | Bank |
|------|-------------|-----|-----|-----------------|--|--|------------------|---------------|-------|----------|--|--|------|
| | | | | Accounts payable control | GST paid | Discount income | | | | Amount | Account | GST paid | |
| 2019 | | | | $ | $ | $ | $ | $ | $ | $ | | | $ |
| 31 Aug | Subtotal to date | | | 32.60 | 2.96 | 29.64 | 1 271.40 | 87.56 | 2 120.00 | 955.31 | | 104.29 | 4 538.56 |
| | *Adjustments:* | | | | | | | | | | | | |
| | Bank fee | | BS | | | | | | | 4.50 | Bank fees and charges | | 4.50 |
| | Account service fee | | BS | | | | | | | 8.60 | Bank fees and charges | | 8.60 |
| | Merchant fees | | BS | | | | | | | 4.55 | Merchant fees | 0.45 | 5.00 |
| | | | | $32.60 | $2.96 | $29.64 | $1 271.40 | $87.56 | $2 120.00 | $972.96 | | $104.74 | $4 556.66 |

b

| | | | General Ledger | | | |
|---|---|---|---|---|---|---|
| Date | Particulars | Fol | | Debit | Credit | Balance |
| | | | **Cash at Bank Account** | | | |
| 2019 | | | | $ | $ | $ |
| 1 Aug | Balance | | | | | 4 566.00 Dr |
| 31 | Sundry receipts | CRJ | | 2 606.00 | | 7 172.00 Dr |
| | Sundry payments | CPJ | | | 4 556.66 | 2 615.34 Dr |

o

| | Bank reconciliation statement as at 31 August 2019 | | |
|---|---|---|---|
| | | $ | $ |
| Credit | Balance as per bank statement (at 31 August 2019) | | 3 702.68 |
| less | Unpresented cheques | | |
| | No. 134 | 412.50 | |
| | 151 | 624.00 | |
| | 152 | 50.84 | 1 087.34 |
| Debit | Balance as per Cash at Bank ledger account at 31 August 2019) | | $2 615.34 |

5.17 a

| | | | | B Purchest Cash Receipts Journal | | | | | | | | |
|---|---|---|---|---|---|---|---|---|---|---|---|---|
| | | | | Discount expense | | | | | Sundries | | | |
| Date | Particulars | Fol | Ref | Accounts receivable control | GST collected | Discount expense | Accounts receivable control | Cash sales | Amount | Account | GST collected | Bank |
| 2019 | | | | $ | $ | $ | $ | $ | $ | | $ | $ |
| 30 Apr | Subtotal to date | | | 10.00 | 0.91 | 9.09 | 460.00 | 3 590.91 | | | 359.09 | 4 410.00 |
| | Adjustments: | | | | | | | | | | | |
| | Dis. chq. – C Bowler | | BS | | | | (100.00) | | | | | (100.00) |
| | | | | $10.00 | $0.91 | $9.09 | $360.00 | $3 590.91 | | | $359.09 | $4 310.00 |

### Cash Payments Journal

| Date | Particulars | Fol | Ref | Discount income — Accounts payable control | GST paid | Discount income | Accounts payable control | Cash purchases | Wages | Sundries — Amount | Account | GST paid | Bank |
|------|-------------|-----|-----|-------------------|----------|-----------------|---------------------------|----------------|-------|--------|---------|----------|------|
| 2019 | | | | $ | $ | $ | $ | $ | $ | $ | | $ | $ |
| 30 Apr | Subtotal to date | | | 14.00 | 1.27 | 12.73 | 486.00 | 277.27 | 85.00 | 87.27 | | 36.46 | 972.00 |
| | *Adjustments:* | | | | | | | | | | | | |
| | Adj. chq. 129 | | BS | | | | | | | (24.55) | Advertising | (2.45) | (27.00) |
| | Bank fees | | BS | | | | | | | 15.00 | Bank fees and charges | | 15.00 |
| | Loan repayment | | BS | | | | | | | 200.00 | Loan | | 200.00 |
| | Merchant fees | | BS | | | | | | | 20.00 | Merchant fees expense | 2.00 | 22.00 |
| | | | | $14.00 | $1.27 | $12.73 | $486.00 | $277.27 | $85.00 | $297.72 | | $36.01 | $1 182.00 |

**b**

### General Ledger

| Date | Particulars | Fol | Debit | Credit | Balance |
|------|-------------|-----|-------|--------|---------|
| | | **Cash at Bank Account** | | | |
| 2019 | | | $ | $ | $ |
| 1 Aug | Balance | | | | 810.00 Cr |
| 30 | Sundry receipts | CRJ | 4 310.00 | | 3 500.00 Dr |
| | Sundry payments | CPJ | | 1 182.00 | 2 318.00 Dr |

### B Purchest
#### Bank reconciliation statement as at 30 April 2019

| | | $ | $ |
|---|---|---|---|
| *Credit* | Balance as per bank statement (at 30 April 2019) | | 1 744.00 |
| *add* | Deposit not credited | | 1 500.00 |
| | | | 3 244.00 |

| | | | $ | $ |
|---|---|---|---:|---:|
| | | **B Purchest** | | |
| | | **Bank reconciliation statement as at 30 April 2019** | | |
| *less* | Unpresented cheques | | | |
| | No. 128 | | 40.00 | |
| | 110 | | 250.00 | |
| | 130 | | 290.00 | |
| | 133 | | 150.00 | |
| | 135 | | 196.00 | 926.00 |
| *Debit* | Balance as per Cash at Bank ledger account (at 30 April 2019) | | | $2 318.00 |

# Other internal controls over cash

Because cash is susceptible to fraud and misappropriation, a business needs to implement a system of sound internal control over cash. Thus far, this chapter has examined one important internal control over cash; that is, the bank reconciliation process. The next chapter examines specific internal controls over petty cash.

In addition to bank reconciliation and petty cash, some other suggested internal controls over cash are detailed below.

## Control over cash receipts

### Importance of internal control over cash receipts

Control over cash receipts is important because cash is easily misappropriated by persons with dishonest intentions. It is therefore important that strict controls are implemented to help ensure that all cash receipts are properly recorded and banked and that any misappropriation will be detected.

### Internal control principles and cash receipts

A sound system of internal control over cash receipts should include the features listed below.

- All cash received should be recorded at the time it is received. Moreover, cheques and other negotiable instruments received in the mail should be processed as soon as possible, and where practical, mail should be opened soon after it has been received (further controls relating to cheques are discussed below).
- Only authorised persons should have access to and be able to handle cash receipts.

- Cash receipts awaiting banking should be securely stored in a safe place.
- All cash receipts should be banked intact daily. Small cash payments should be made from a separate petty cash fund (see Chapter 6).
- Proper security measures should be employed in the transfer of cash receipts from the business premises to the bank. For large amounts, this may involve the use of security companies and guards.
- Employees who receive or handle cash should not be involved with the recording of these transactions in the accounting records. This *segregation of duties* is designed to prevent an employee misappropriating cash receipts and disguising the fact by making false entries in the business's accounting records.
- Regular rotation of staff involved in cash collection and recording duties is a measure designed to act as a deterrent to fraudulent behaviour because it will increase the chances of irregularities being detected. Where employees take annual holidays and other staff are required to perform their duties in their absence, this also acts as a deterrent to misappropriation.
- As part of its regular bank reconciliation process, the business's records of cash receipts should be reconciled with an independent record provided by the bank (the bank statement). The bank reconciliation should be performed by a person who is independent of the handling or recording of cash receipts. This is another example of segregation of duties.

Implementation of the internal controls outlined will make it difficult for an individual employee to misappropriate cash receipts without being detected.

# Specific internal controls over cash receipts

## Cash (over-the-counter) sales

The overriding consideration with cash sales is to ensure that any amounts received are correctly recorded *at the time of sale*.

The most common form of internal control dealing with over-the-counter sales is the *cash register* or *point-of-sale* (POS) device. This assists in internal control over cash receipts in the following ways.

- The cash register or POS device ensures that the transaction is recorded at the time the transaction occurs. The sale must be recorded immediately in order to produce a cash register receipt for the customer and also to provide the customer with change if required.
- In many businesses, such as supermarkets and department stores, each item of merchandise is electronically scanned at the register, which means that the sale is recorded immediately and at the correct price.
- Cash registers are generally positioned so that the customer can see each item recorded. This is a desirable practice as it allows a customer to detect discrepancies between the sale price of each item and the amount keyed in or scanned by the cash register operator. This provides a strong deterrent to misappropriation by the operator.
- The use of bar codes that are automatically scanned eliminates keying (input) errors by cash register operators.
- A cash register or POS device provides a daily summary of sales recorded. At the end of the day, once the *float* from the start of the day is removed, the daily summary is reconciled with the cash in the register.

Another method of accounting for over-the-counter sales is the writing of a pre-numbered *cash sales docket* at the time of sale. Generally, two copies are prepared; the original is given to the customer and the duplicate is retained by the business for recording purposes. At the end of the day the total of the duplicate sales dockets should equal the amount of cash in the till (after removing the float). Pre-numbered cash sales dockets prevent an employee taking the money from the customer, issuing the customer with the original copy and then destroying the duplicate copy. A numerical sequence check on the duplicate cash sales dockets would uncover such a fraud.

## EFTPOS and credit card sales

In terms of internal control over EFTPOS and credit card transactions, the following procedures should be adopted.

- Most businesses process credit card transactions on-line, and stolen or defaulting cards are automatically identified. However, those businesses that still use a paper based system should check that the card is not on the list of cards that have been reported lost or stolen. Businesses with EFTPOS and credit card facilities are regularly provided with this information.
- Since 1 August 2014, signatures have been disallowed when using a credit or EFTPOS card, and personal identification numbers (PINs) have become the primary form of identification. However, where a customer's signature is required, the operator must ensure that the signature on the transaction summary matches the signature on the card.
- The total daily amount shown on the bank statement for EFTPOS and credit card sales must be reconciled with the total daily EFTPOS and credit card sales as determined from the business's cash register or POS daily summaries.

# Other cash received (not received through a cash register or POS device)

For all other money received, a pre-numbered receipt form should be completed with the original given to the customer, if appropriate, and the duplicate retained for recording purposes. Blank receipt books should be locked away and controlled by a register of receipts, which should be held by a nominated person. Receipt books are issued only to authorised persons, who are required to sign for each receipt book taken. In addition, where a receipt form is cancelled for any reason, both copies should be marked 'Cancelled' and left in the book.

Where money is received by mail (normally in the form of cheques or money orders) control measures need to be implemented to ensure that all amounts received are correctly recorded and banked. The following internal control measures should be implemented.

- At least two people should be present when the mail is opened and a record, often in the form of a *mail register*, kept of all money received. The presence of two people guards against misappropriation of money by the person who opens the mail but does not record it in the mail register.
- The employees opening the mail should not be involved in the recording process or have access to other cash receipts.

- Any cheques received in the mail should be carefully examined to ensure that they are dated, signed and crossed 'not negotiable'. If not crossed 'not negotiable', they should be so crossed by one of the employees opening the mail. If not dated or signed, they should be referred to a supervisor who would then contact the payer with a view to having the cheque properly completed.
- Once all the mail is opened, any money received should be taken to the cashier and the appropriate receipts written.

Often, money is paid electronically, directly into the business bank account. This is referred to as *electronic funds transfer* (EFT). In these situations the business needs to regularly examine its bank account for these items and ensure that they are properly recorded in the accounting records of the business. Bank account details can be accessed from the bank statement, which is either provided regularly by the bank or accessed using electronic banking facilities.

# Banking of cash receipts

Where the business has to deposit notes, coins, cheques and money orders in its bank account it is important that proper security measures are taken to ensure that the money is safely deposited at the bank. Many businesses, particularly those with large amounts of money to deposit, engage the services of specialist security firms such as Armaguard or Chubb. For a fee, these companies will collect the business's takings in an armoured van and transport them under armed guard to the premises of the security firm, where the money is counted, processed and banked on behalf of the client business.

If a business chooses to do its own banking, there are other security measures that can be taken.

- Avoid banking at the same time each day.
- Vary the route taken to the bank.
- Rotate the duties of banking among several employees.
- Choose a bank with adequate car parking facilities to minimise the distance that the money has to be transported on foot.
- Ensure that the copy of the deposit slip stamped by the bank is retained and filed.

# Control over cash payments
## Payments to suppliers of goods and services

In Chapter 4 it was stated that the following internal controls should exist over payments to suppliers.

- A remittance advice, providing details of all relevant transactions, should be prepared for each supplier payment.
- Supporting documentation (i.e. remittance advices, purchase orders, invoices, receiving reports and adjustment notes) should be forwarded to the person responsible for initiating payments to suppliers.

It was also stated that payments to suppliers should conform to the principles of internal control over cash payments. Some suggested internal controls over cash payments are listed below.

## Cheque payments

- Where payments are made by cheque, the cheques and remittance advices, together with the supporting documentation (orders, receiving reports, invoices and adjustment notes) should be forwarded to the cheque signatories. The cheque signatories should check the supporting documentation prior to signing the cheques.
- Some organisations utilise an additional document known as a *cheque requisition* when making payments by cheque. In this case, the accounts payable staff would prepare the cheque requisitions to accompany supporting documentation (orders, receiving reports, invoices and adjustment notes). A cheque requisition is a request to the cashier to prepare a cheque, which is then sent with all the supporting documentation to the cheque signatories.
- All cheques should be signed by two cheque signatories. The business should ordinarily have more than two people authorised to sign cheques in the event that one or more of the cheque signatories is absent or not available.
- The cheque signatories should be persons in authority who are not involved in the processing of accounts payable.
- One of the cheque signatories should *cancel* the supporting documentation to indicate, for example, that the invoices have been paid. This is usually achieved by stamping the documents as PAID and writing the cheque number and date of the cheque. This prevents a dishonest employee presenting an invoice that has already been paid and then misappropriating the cheque.
- The cancelled supporting documentation should be filed for audit purposes, usually in cheque number order.
- Once the cheques have been signed they should not be returned to the employee who processed the invoices. This prevents that employee submitting a bogus invoice and then misappropriating the cheque. The cheques should be mailed by someone independent of the processing of supplier invoices.

## EFT payments

Where payments to suppliers are made by EFT the following additional internal controls are suggested.

- The responsibility for making EFT payments should be restricted to a limited number of individuals.
- Individuals authorised to make EFT payments should be persons in authority who are not involved in the processing of accounts payable.
- Access codes and passwords required for the initiation of EFT payments should be kept in a secure place and only made available to those authorised to make such payments.
- Prior to the processing of each EFT payment, the supporting documentation (orders, receiving reports, invoices and adjustment notes) should be reviewed by someone in authority, who should authorise the payment in writing.

## Credit card payments

Internal controls over payments by credit card were discussed in Chapter 4.

# Other payments

Other payments such as wages and salaries, remittance of GST and PAYG withholding (tax withheld from employees' earnings) to the ATO, remittance of payroll deductions such as superannuation and payment of payroll tax should all be reviewed and approved in a similar manner to payments to suppliers of goods and services.

 **EXERCISES**

5.18    Briefly explain how the use of a cash register or POS device provides internal control over cash receipts.

5.19    Briefly explain how a business verifies that its EFTPOS and credit card sales have been correctly credited by the bank to the business's bank account.

5.20    In relation to the banking of cash receipts, briefly explain one security measure that a business can employ.

5.21    Briefly explain the internal control measures that should exist for EFT payments.

## Summary

What have you covered in this chapter?

◆ Comparison of the cash records with the bank statements

◆ Adjustment of the cash journals for dishonoured cheques, bank fees, direct bank debits and direct bank credits; totalling of cash journals and posting to the General Ledger

◆ Preparation of a bank reconciliation statement, incorporating unpresented cheques and deposits not yet credited

◆ An explanation of other internal controls over cash

# 6

# PETTY CASH

## Learning objectives

Upon satisfactory completion of this chapter you should be able to:
- check petty cash claims for accuracy and authenticity before processing
- record and balance petty cash transactions
- present records of transactions to the relevant authority for checking within relevant timelines
- prepare the reimbursement cheque
- discuss internal controls over petty cash.

# The need for a petty cash system

In earlier chapters it was noted that it is good business practice to make all business payments by cheque or EFT. It is not always convenient, however, and in some cases it may be quite expensive to make many small payments in this manner. Where minor payments need to be made for such things as bus fares, newspapers, coffee, postage and dry-cleaning, it is more convenient to make such payments out of a small supply of cash on hand which is regularly maintained. This reserve of cash is referred to as *petty cash* and is specifically set aside by the business in order to meet payments of a petty (minor) nature. For security purposes, and to comply with auditing and tax requirements, it is important that a receipt or docket is used for every petty cash withdrawal made. Petty cash is normally stored in a cash box and used when the need to make small payments arises.

# The petty cash imprest system

Most firms that operate a petty cash fund use the imprest system. *Imprest* means to borrow. Thus, the basis of the petty cash imprest system is to advance a *set amount* of money to the *petty cashier*, a responsible person who will make payments of a petty nature from time to time using that money. When the money is fully expended or is at a low level, the petty cashier produces receipted vouchers which verify all the payments made. On receipt of this documentation, the general cashier reimburses the petty cashier for the total amount spent during the period. In this way, petty cash is replenished ready for the next round of petty cash payments.

# Establishing the fund

There are three main procedures to follow in establishing a petty cash fund. These can be stated simply as follows:

1   Determine the amount of money required in the petty cash fund. To do this, it is necessary to make an accurate estimate of the number of small payments made during a period of, say, one month. It is also necessary to determine the total amount of those payments and whether GST will be paid. From this information, the amount of petty cash required for that period can be calculated. Consider the example of Adam's Pie Shop, which makes the following payments of a minor nature each week.

| | $ |
|---|---|
| Milk, coffee, sugar | 6.00 |
| Postage (inc. GST) | 8.80 |
| Newspapers (inc. GST) | 8.50 |
| Bus fares (inc. GST) | 6.60 |
| Freight charges (inc. GST) | 4.40 |
| Total for the week | $34.30 |

From the above, it can be seen that Adam's Pie Shop would need approximately $150 per month ($34.30 × 4 weeks) for payments of a minor nature. Thus, a petty cash fund of $100–$150 should suffice.

Most businesses have petty cash funds ranging between $20 and $1000, depending on the size of the business and the need to make payments of a minor nature.

2 Nominate a petty cashier to become custodian of the fund. Perhaps more than any other asset, cash is most susceptible to fraud, so it is important to choose a person who is trustworthy and responsible. The duties of the petty cashier normally include:
   - the safe keeping of petty cash money
   - distributing the cash as required
   - completing the necessary documentation for distributing the money
   - maintaining the Petty Cash Book
   - claiming reimbursement of the petty cash fund.

   These duties will be examined later in this chapter.

3 Prepare a cheque for the amount of money required for the petty cash fund. When the amount of the fund has been determined as in 1 above, a cheque is written in favour of the petty cashier or, more commonly, for cash. This is called a petty cash advance. On receiving the cheque, the petty cashier will cash it and deposit the money in a locked cash box for safekeeping.

# Petty cash vouchers

To obtain money from petty cash, members of staff may need to sign a *petty cash voucher* and, where possible, provide receipts that support the expenditure. Here is an example of a petty cash voucher.

| | |
|---|---|
| Date ................................................ | No. ................................ |
| **PETTY CASH VOUCHER** | |
| Paid to ...................................................................................................... | |
| For ............................................................................................................ | |
| ................................................................................................................ | |
| Amount $ ............................... GST Paid $ ........................... Account No. ................... | |
| Signatures ........................... Cashier ...................................... | |
| Recipient ................................... | |

Petty cash vouchers have three important functions.

1 They provide a record of expenditure and thus serve to control the money disbursed from the petty cash fund. Note that the voucher is normally signed by the (petty) cashier and, in some cases, the recipient of the money.

2 They are used to record entries in the Petty Cash Book, which will be discussed in the next section of this chapter.

3 They are used as the basis for replenishing the fund, consistent with the imprest system. This, too, will be examined later in the chapter.

Before processing claims for petty cash, the petty cashier must check all petty cash vouchers and accompanying receipts for accuracy and authenticity.

# The Petty Cash Book

The Petty Cash Book is used periodically to record details of all vouchers prepared by the cashier. A simple Petty Cash Book is shown below. We have assumed that a fund of $150 has been established for Frank's Pie Shop.

This question can also be completed in a spreadsheet that is available on the CD accompanying this text.

A UWatch demonstration is available on the CD that accompanies this text for this example.

**Frank's Pie Shop**
**Petty Cash Book**

| | | | | | 3070/A | 3071/A | 3073/A | Sundries | | |
| Date | Particulars (name) | Voucher no. | Amount received | Petty cash amount | Postage | Travel | News-papers | Amount | Account no. | GST paid |
|---|---|---|---|---|---|---|---|---|---|---|
| 2019 | | | $ | $ | $ | $ | $ | $ | | $ |
| 1 July | Advance | Chq. 107 | 150.00 | | | | | | | |
| 2 | T Cotton | 1 | | 6.00 | 5.45 | | | | | 0.55 |
| 5 | G Miokovic | 2 | | 26.40 | | 24.00 | | | | 2.40 |
| 21 | R Frank | 3 | | 4.40 | | 4.00 | | | | 0.40 |
| 30 | R Frank | 4 | | 15.40 | | 14.00 | | | | 1.40 |
| 31 | T Cotton | 5 | | 30.80 | | | 28.00 | | | 2.80 |
| | J Smith | 6 | | 22.00 | | | | 20.00 | Freight 3072/A | 2.00 |
| | | | | 105.00 | $5.45 | $42.00 | $28.00 | $20.00 | | $9.55 |
| | Balance | | | 45.00 | | | | | | |

The Petty Cash Book above was prepared from the following documents:

*Butt of original cheque drawn to establish fund (cheque no. 107):*

| | |
|---|---|
| Date | *1. 7. 2019* |
| To | *Cash* |
| For | *Petty cash advance* |
| | |
| | |
| | |
| Amount | *$105.00* |
| Balance | |
| **000107** | |

SA0162731A

*Petty cash vouchers 1–6:*

| Date: 2.7.19 | No. 1 |
|---|---|

**PETTY CASH VOUCHER**

Paid to *T Cotton*

For *Postage*

| Amount (inc. GST) | GST | Acc No. |
|---|---|---|
| $ *6.00* | $ *0.55* | *3070/A* |

Signatures  Cashier *G Adson*

Recipient

---

| Date: 5.7.19 | No. 2 |
|---|---|

**PETTY CASH VOUCHER**

Paid to *G Miokovic*

For *Travel to Melton*

| Amount (inc. GST) | GST | Acc No. |
|---|---|---|
| $ *26.40* | $ *2.40* | *3071/A* |

Signatures  Cashier *G Adson*

Recipient

---

| Date: 21.7.19 | No. 3 |
|---|---|

**PETTY CASH VOUCHER**

Paid to *R Frank*

For *Travel Exp*

| Amount (inc. GST) | GST | Acc No. |
|---|---|---|
| $ *4.40* | $ *0.40* | *3071/A* |

Signatures  Cashier *G Adson*

Recipient

---

| Date: 30.7.19 | No. 4 |
|---|---|

**PETTY CASH VOUCHER**

Paid to *R Frank*

For *Travel Exp*

| Amount (inc. GST) | GST | Acc No. |
|---|---|---|
| $ *15.40* | $ *1.40* | *3071/A* |

Signatures  Cashier *G Adson*

Recipient

---

| Date: 31.7.19 | No. 5 |
|---|---|

**PETTY CASH VOUCHER**

Paid to *T Cotton*

For *Newspapers*

| Amount (inc. GST) | GST | Acc No. |
|---|---|---|
| $ *30.80* | $ *2.80* | *3073/A* |

Signatures  Cashier *G Adson*

Recipient

---

| Date: 31.7.19 | No. 6 |
|---|---|

**PETTY CASH VOUCHER**

Paid to *J Smith*

For *Freight to Melton*

| Amount (inc. GST) | GST | Acc No. |
|---|---|---|
| $ *22.00* | $ *2.00* | *3072/A* |

Signatures  Cashier *G Adson*

Recipient

---

**Note** Account numbers relate to the relevant General Ledger accounts, as per the chart of accounts of the business. Note also that GST paid will appear as a standard column in the Cash Payments Journal, and therefore a separate account number for GST paid is not usually required in the petty cash voucher.

# Replenishing the petty cash fund

The totals of the Petty Cash Book are used as the basis for replenishing the petty cash fund. In the previous example for Frank's Pie Shop, the Petty Cash Book showed that six vouchers were used to pay out a total of $105.00 cash. On 31 July 2019, there is a balance of $45.00 remaining in the fund, so it is necessary to reimburse the fund on 31 July 2019 to restore it to the original imprest amount of $150. This is called petty cash reimbursement. The reimbursement of the fund is made on the following basis:

|  | $ |
|---|---|
| Original advance deposited in the fund | 150.00 |
| *less* Total of vouchers 1–6 | 105.00 |
| Balance remaining | 45.00 |
| Reimbursement required | 105.00 |
| Original balance restored | $150.00 |

When the reimbursement amount is determined, a cheque is drawn to the favour of the petty cashier, or to cash (in this case, for $105.00). When the cheque is cashed, the money is deposited in the cash box. The petty cash fund is restored to its original amount (in this case, $150). Assume cheque no. 132 was drawn to reimburse petty cash.

## The completed Petty Cash Book

Frank's Pie Shop
Petty Cash Book

| Date | Particulars (name) | Voucher no. | Amount received | Petty cash amount | 3070/A Postage | 3071/A Travel | 3073/A News-papers | Sundries Amount | Sundries Account no. | GST paid |
|---|---|---|---|---|---|---|---|---|---|---|
| 2019 | | | $ | $ | $ | $ | $ | $ | | $ |
| 1 Jul | Advance | Chq. 107 | 150.00 | | | | | | | |
| 2 | T Cotton | 1 | | 6.00 | 5.45 | | | | | 0.55 |
| 5 | G Miokovic | 2 | | 26.40 | | 24.00 | | | | 2.40 |
| 21 | R Frank | 3 | | 4.40 | | 4.00 | | | | 0.40 |
| 30 | R Frank | 4 | | 15.40 | | 14.00 | | | | 1.40 |
| 31 | T Cotton | 5 | | 30.80 | | | 28.00 | | | 2.80 |
| | J Smith | 6 | | 22.00 | | | | 20.00 | Freight 3072/A | 2.00 |
| | | | | 105.00 | $5.45 | $42.00 | $28.00 | $20.00 | | $9.55 |
| | Balance | | | 45.00 | | | | | | |
| | | | $150.00 | $150.00 | | | | | | |
| | Balance | | 45.00 | | | | | | | |
| | Reimbursement | Chq. 132 | 105.00 | | | | | | | |

### The cheque drawn for reimbursing the fund

| | | | |
|---|---|---|---|
| Date | 31. 7. 2019 | | |
| To | Cash | | |
| For | Petty cash | | |
| | reimbursement | | |

**Commonwealth** Bank
Commonwealth Bank of Australia

Date   31. 7. 2019

WENDOURIE

Pay   Cash

The sum of   One hundred five dollars oo

$   105.00

| Amount | $105.00 |
| Balance | |

SA0162731A

G  ADAM

G. Adam

000132    ⑈000132⑈ 068⑈888⑈ 1003⑈1234⑈

It is not uncommon for a cash discrepancy to be discovered when the petty cash fund is balanced prior to reimbursement. In this case the amount of the discrepancy must be recorded in the Petty Cash Book. This will also require the establishment of an account in the General Ledger titled *Cash under/over*. The procedure for recording petty cash discrepancies is illustrated in the comprehensive example commencing on page 439 of this chapter.

# Journal entries

Normally, there are only two types of journal entries required for petty cash. They are:

1   The journal entry to record the cheque drawn for the establishment of the petty cash fund. In the example of Frank's Pie Shop, cheque no. 107 was drawn for petty cash. This transaction would be recorded in the Cash Payments Journal as follows:

**Cash Payments Journal**

| | | | | Discount income | | | | | | Sundries | | | |
|---|---|---|---|---|---|---|---|---|---|---|---|---|---|
| Date | Particulars | Fol | Ref | Accounts payable control | GST paid | Discount income | Accounts payable control | Cash purchases | Wages | Amount | Account | GST paid | Bank |
| 2019 | | | | $ | $ | $ | $ | $ | $ | $ | | $ | $ |
| 1 Jul | Petty cash advance | | 107 | | | | | | | 150.00 | Petty cash advance | | 150.00 |

Using columnar accounts, the General Ledger entries that would result from the above entry are shown below.

| General Ledger | | | | | |
|---|---|---|---|---|---|
| Date | Particulars | Fol | Debit | Credit | Balance |
| **Petty Cash Advance Account (asset)** | | | | | |
| 2019 | | | $ | $ | $ |
| 1 Jul | Cash at bank | CPJ | 150.00 | | 150.00 Dr |
| **Cash at Bank Account (asset)** | | | | | |
| 2019 | | | | | |
| 1 Jul | Petty cash advance | CPJ | | 150.00 | 150.00 Cr |

The petty cash advance is treated as an asset rather than an expense. Because petty cash works on an imprest system – that is, the amount of the original petty cash advance is replenished continually – it represents a relatively stable asset to the business. For example, in the case of Frank's Pie Shop, $150 was used to establish the petty cash fund on 1 July 2019. Even after payments are made from the fund, the asset account, Petty Cash, will *remain intact* (see Figure 6.1). This point will be further illustrated when the journal entry for petty cash reimbursement is examined.

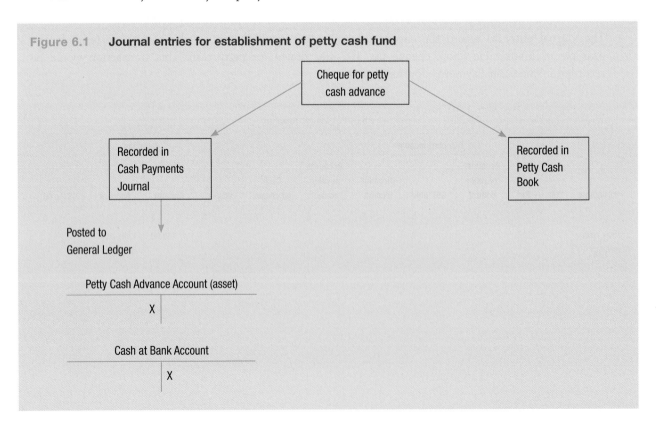

**Figure 6.1    Journal entries for establishment of petty cash fund**

2 The journal entry to record the cheque drawn to reimburse the petty cash fund. Unlike the previous journal entry, which is usually required only once (to establish the petty cash fund), the entry to reimburse the petty cash fund is required regularly to replenish petty cash funds used. In the example, cheque no. 132 was drawn to reimburse the fund. This transaction would be recorded in the Cash Payments Journal as follows:

**Frank's Pie Shop**
**Cash Payments Journal**

| | | | | Discount income | | | | | | Sundries | | | |
|---|---|---|---|---|---|---|---|---|---|---|---|---|---|
| Date | Particulars | Fol | Ref | Accounts payable control | GST paid | Discount income | Accounts payable control | Cash purchases | Wages | Amount | Account | GST paid | Bank |
| 2019 | | | | $ | $ | $ | $ | $ | $ | $ | | $ | $ |
| 31 Jul | Petty cash reimbursement | | 132 | | | | | | | | | | |
| | – Postage | | | | | | | | | 5.45 | Postage | | |
| | – Travel | | | | | | | | | 42.00 | Travel | | |
| | – Newspapers | | | | | | | | | 28.00 | Newspapers | | |
| | – Freight | | | | | | | | | 20.00 | Freight | 9.55 | 105.00 |

**Note** The individual items recorded in the Sundries column are, in fact, the totals of the individual analysis columns of the Petty Cash Book, representing the various expenses paid from petty cash.

Note also that GST paid has been shown as a total in the Cash Payments Journal, thus reflecting the amount of GST paid on all expenses subject to GST (rather than showing GST individually on each item). However, should the need arise, details of GST paid on individual transactions can be sourced from the Petty Cash Book, and of course the original tax invoice. This would be a typical procedure, for instance, if goods were returned and GST paid had to be reduced.

The General Ledger entries resulting from the Cash Payments Journal entry above are as follows:

| | General Ledger | | | | | |
|---|---|---|---|---|---|---|
| Date | Particulars | Fol | Debit | Credit | Balance | |
| | **Cash at Bank Account** | | | | | |
| 2019 | | | $ | $ | $ | |
| 31 Jul | Sundry payments | CPJ | | 105.00 | 105.00 Cr | |
| | **Postage Account** | | | | | |
| 2019 | | | | | | |
| 31 Jul | Cash at bank | CPJ | 5.45 | | 5.45 Dr | |
| | **Travel Account** | | | | | |
| 2019 | | | | | | |
| 31 Jul | Cash at bank | CPJ | 42.00 | | 42.00 Dr | |

▶▶▶

| | | | | | |
|---|---|---|---|---|---|
| | | | **General Ledger** | | |

| Date | Particulars | Fol | Debit | Credit | Balance |
|---|---|---|---|---|---|
| | | **Newspapers Account** | | | |
| 2019 | | | $ | $ | $ |
| 31 Jul | Cash at bank | CPJ | 28.00 | | 28.00 Dr |
| | | **Freight Account** | | | |
| 2019 | | | | | |
| 31 Jul | Cash at bank | CPJ | 20.00 | | 20.00 Dr |
| | | **GST Paid Account** | | | |
| 2019 | | | | | |
| 31 Jul | Cach at bank | CPJ | 9.55 | | 9.55 Dr |

The asset account, Petty Cash Advance, is not affected by this entry. Instead, the totals of the Petty Cash Book (that is, postage, $5.45; travel, $42; newspapers, $28; freight, $20; GST paid, $9.55) are debited to the relevant expense accounts and the GST Paid Account (see Figure 6.2).

Figure 6.2 **Journal entries for reimbursement of petty cash fund**

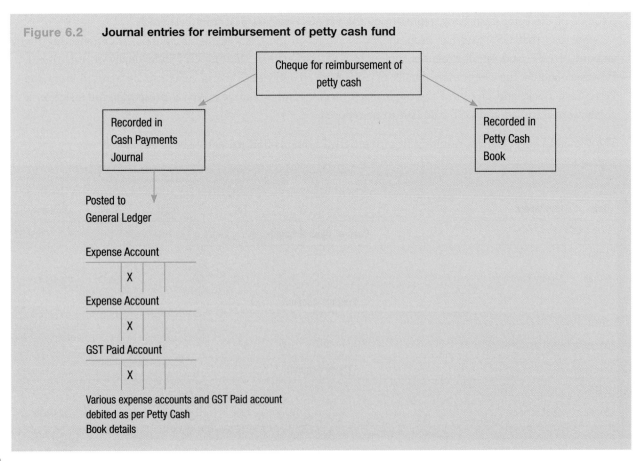

# Comprehensive example

From the following financial information of G Gomez, you are required to:

a  draw up a cash cheque (including the cheque butt) to set up a petty cash fund

b  record the cheque in the Cash Payments Journal of G Gomez

c  i  complete the Petty Cash Book by recording the advance received and the petty cash vouchers for the month of July

ii  balance the Petty Cash Book

d  draw up a cash cheque (including the cheque butt) to reimburse the petty cash fund

e  record the reimbursement cheque in the Petty Cash Book and the Cash Payments Journal of G Gomez

f  post the Cash Payments Journal entries to the General Ledger of G Gomez.

## Background information

Petty cashier – Chris Parkin (junior clerical assistant)

Fund – $200 set up by cheque (no. 0248) on 1 July 2019

(Make up your own account numbers where necessary.)

## Journal headings required

| | | | | Cash Payments Journal | | | | | | | | | | |
|---|---|---|---|---|---|---|---|---|---|---|---|---|---|---|
| | | | | Discount income | | | | | | | Sundries | | | |
| Date | Particulars | Fol | Ref | Accounts payable control | GST paid | Discount income | Accounts payable control | Cash purchases | Wages | Amount | Account | GST paid | Bank |
| | | | | $ | $ | $ | $ | $ | $ | $ | | $ | $ |

## Petty Cash Book headings required

| | | | | Petty Cash Book | | | | | | | |
|---|---|---|---|---|---|---|---|---|---|---|---|
| | | | | Petty cash | | | News- | Sundries | | GST |
| Date | Particulars (name) | Voucher no. | Amount received | amount | Postage | Travel | papers | Amount | Account no. | paid |
| | | | $ | $ | $ | $ | $ | $ | | $ |

## Petty cash vouchers for July 2019

| Date: 3.7.19 | | No. 1 |
|---|---|---|
| **PETTY CASH VOUCHER** | | |
| Paid to A Tournier | | |
| For Postage | | |
| | | |
| Amount (inc. GST) | GST | Acc No. |
| $ 4.40 | $ 0.40 | 327 |
| Signatures | Cashier C Parkin | |
| | Recipient | |

| Date: 7.7.19 | | No. 2 |
|---|---|---|
| **PETTY CASH VOUCHER** | | |
| Paid to A Tournier | | |
| For Travel | | |
| | | |
| Amount (inc. GST) | GST | Acc No. |
| $ 19.80 | $ 1.80 | 328 |
| Signatures | Cashier C Parkin | |
| | Recipient | |

| Date: 9.7.19 | | No. 3 |
|---|---|---|
| **PETTY CASH VOUCHER** | | |
| Paid to A Tournier | | |
| For Stamps | | |
| | | |
| Amount (inc. GST) | GST | Acc No. |
| $ 5.50 | $ 0.50 | 327 |
| Signatures | Cashier C Parkin | |
| | Recipient | |

| Date: 21.7.19 | | No. 4 |
|---|---|---|
| **PETTY CASH VOUCHER** | | |
| Paid to J Watson | | |
| For Coffee/tea supplies | | |
| | | |
| Amount (inc. GST) | GST | Acc No. |
| $ 50.00 | $ | 307 |
| Signatures | Cashier C Parkin | |
| | Recipient | |

| Date: 28.7.19 | | No. 5 |
|---|---|---|
| **PETTY CASH VOUCHER** | | |
| Paid to A Lu | | |
| For Postage | | |
| | | |
| Amount (inc. GST) | GST | Acc No. |
| $ 3.30 | $ 0.30 | 327 |
| Signatures | Cashier C Parkin | |
| | Recipient | |

| Date: 31.7.19 | | No. 6 |
|---|---|---|
| **PETTY CASH VOUCHER** | | |
| Paid to D Roberts | | |
| For Newspapers | | |
| | | |
| Amount (inc. GST) | GST | Acc No. |
| $ 13.20 | $ 1.20 | 316 |
| Signatures | Cashier C Parkin | |
| | Recipient | |

**Note** Cash remaining in the petty cash fund at 31 July was $101.80.

## Solution

a   The cash cheque and butt to set up a petty cash fund:

b   The entry in the Cash Payments Journal:

| | | | | Discount income | | | | | | Sundries | | | |
|---|---|---|---|---|---|---|---|---|---|---|---|---|---|
| Date | Particulars | Fol | Ref | Accounts payable control | GST paid | Discount income | Accounts payable control | Cash purchases | Wages | Amount | Account | GST paid | Bank |
| 2019 | | | | $ | $ | $ | $ | $ | $ | $ | | $ | $ |
| 1 Jul | Petty cash advance | 106 | 0248 | | | | | | | 200 | Petty cash advance | | 200 |

c   i, ii   The Petty Cash Book completed for July 2019 and balanced:

### Petty Cash Book

| Date | Particulars (name) | Voucher no. | Amount received | Petty cash amount | Postage | Travel | Coffee/ Tea | Misc. selling | Sundries Amount | Account no. | GST paid |
|---|---|---|---|---|---|---|---|---|---|---|---|
| 2019 | | | $ | $ | $ | $ | $ | $ | $ | | $ |
| 1 Jul | Advance | Chq. 0248 | 200 | | | | | | | | |
| 3 | A Tournier | 1 | | 4.40 | 4.00 | | | | | | 0.40 |
| 7 | A Tournier | 2 | | 19.80 | | 18.00 | | | | | 1.80 |
| 9 | A Tournier | 3 | | 5.50 | 5.00 | | | | | | 0.50 |
| 21 | J Watson | 4 | | 50.00 | | | 50.00 | | | | |
| 28 | A Lu | 5 | | 3.30 | 3.00 | | | | | | 0.30 |
| 31 | D Roberts | 6 | | 13.20 | | | | | 12.00 | 316 N/ papers | 1.20 |
| | | | | 96.20 | 12.00 | 18.00 | 50.00 | | 12.00 | | 4.20 |

▶▶

### Petty Cash Book

| Date | Particulars (name) | Voucher no. | Amount received | Petty cash amount | Postage | Travel | Coffee/ Tea | Misc. selling | Sundries Amount | Sundries Account no. | GST paid |
|---|---|---|---|---|---|---|---|---|---|---|---|
| 2019 | | | $ | $ | $ | $ | $ | $ | $ | | $ |
| | Balance in till | | | 101.80 | | | | | | | |
| | Cash under | | | 2.00 | | | | | | | |
| | | | $200.00 | $200.00 | | | | | | | |
| | Balance in till | | | 101.80 | | | | | | | |
| | Reimbursement | Chq. 0249 | 98.20 | | | | | | | | |

**Note** When balancing the above Petty Cash Book it was necessary to record a *cash under* adjustment in the Petty cash amount column in order to balance that column with the Amount received column. When reimbursing the fund, an additional $2 must be included in the reimbursement cheque amount to allow for the cash under adjustment. The amount of the reimbursement cheque ($98.20) is equal to the total petty cash payments for the period ($96.20) plus the cash under adjustment ($2.00).

d   The reimbursement cheque and butt:

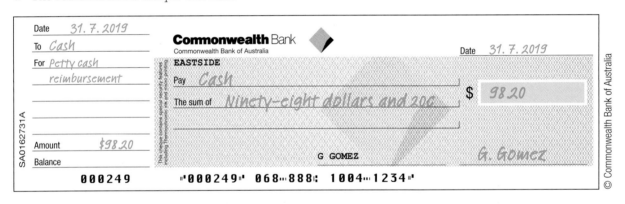

e   The recording of the reimbursement in the Cash Payments Journal:

### Cash Payments Journal

| Date | Particulars | Fol | Ref | Discount income — Accounts payable control | Discount income — GST paid | Discount income — Discount income | Accounts payable control | Cash purchases | Wages | Sundries Amount | Sundries Account | GST paid | Bank |
|---|---|---|---|---|---|---|---|---|---|---|---|---|---|
| 2019 | | | | $ | $ | $ | $ | $ | $ | $ | | $ | $ |
| 31 Jul | Petty cash reimbursement | | 0249 | | | | | | | | | | |
| | – Postage | 327 | | | | | | | | 12.00 | Postage | | |

▶▶

### Cash Payments Journal

| Date | Particulars | Fol | Ref | Discount income — Accounts payable control | GST paid | Discount income | Accounts payable control | Cash purchases | Wages | Sundries — Amount | Sundries — Account | GST paid | Bank |
|------|-------------|-----|-----|----|----|----|----|----|----|----|----|----|----|
| 2019 | | | | $ | $ | $ | $ | $ | $ | $ | | $ | $ |
| | – Travel | 328 | | | | | | | | 18.00 | Travel | | |
| | – Coffee | 307 | | | | | | | | 50.00 | Coffee | | |
| | – Newspapers | 316 | | | | | | | | 12.00 | Newspapers | | |
| | – Cash under/ over | 399 | | | | | | | | 2.00 | Cash under/ over | 4.20 | 98.20 |

**Note** The cash under adjustment recorded in the Petty Cash Book is posted via the Cash Payments Journal to the *Cash Under/Over* account in the General Ledger. This account is classified as an expense account.

f The General Ledger, using columnar accounts, after the information in the Cash Payments Journal has been posted (assuming that no other cash payment transactions occurred during July). First, the Cash Payments Journal:

### Cash Payments Journal

| Date | Particulars | Fol | Ref | Discount income — Accounts payable control | GST paid | Discount income | Accounts payable control | Cash purchases | Wages | Sundries — Amount | Sundries — Account | GST paid | Bank |
|------|-------------|-----|-----|----|----|----|----|----|----|----|----|----|----|
| 2019 | | | | $ | $ | $ | $ | $ | $ | $ | | $ | $ |
| 1 Jul | Petty cash advance | 106 | 0248 | | | | | | | 200.00 | Petty cash advance | | 200.00 |
| 31 | Petty cash reimbursement | | | | | | | | | | | | |
| | – Postage | 327 | | | | | | | | 12.00 | Postage | | |
| | – Travel | 328 | | | | | | | | 18.00 | Travel | | |
| | – Coffee | 307 | | | | | | | | 50.00 | Coffee | | |
| | – Newspapers | 316 | 0249 | | | | | | | 12.00 | Newspapers | | |
| | – Cash under/ over | 399 | | | | | | | | 2.00 | Cash under/ over | 4.20 | 98.20 |
| | | | | | | | | | | $294.00 | | $4.20 | $298.20 |

| | General Ledger | | | | | |
|---|---|---|---|---|---|---|
| Date | Particulars | | Fol | Debit | Credit | Balance |
| **106 – Petty Cash Advance Account** | | | | | | |
| 2019 | | | | $ | $ | $ |
| 1 Jul | Cash at bank | | CPJ | 200.00 | | 200.00 Dr |
| **327 – Postage Account** | | | | | | |
| 2019 | | | | | | |
| 31 Jul | Cash at bank | | CPJ | 12.00 | | 12.00 Dr |
| **328 – Travel Account** | | | | | | |
| 2019 | | | | | | |
| 31 Jul | Cash at bank | | CPJ | 18.00 | | 18.00 Dr |
| **307 – Coffee/Tea Account** | | | | | | |
| 2019 | | | | | | |
| 31 Jul | Cash at bank | | CPJ | 50.00 | | 50.00 Dr |
| **316 – Newspapers Account** | | | | | | |
| 2019 | | | | | | |
| 31 Jul | Cash at bank | | CPJ | 12.00 | | 12.00 Dr |
| **399 – Cash Under/Over Account** | | | | | | |
| 2019 | | | | | | |
| 31 Jul | Cash at bank | | CPJ | 2.00 | | 2.00 Dr |
| **101 – GST Paid Account** | | | | | | |
| 2019 | | | | | | |
| 31 Jul | Cash at bank | | CPJ | 4.20 | | 4.20 Dr |
| **100 – Cash at Bank Account** | | | | | | |
| 2019 | | | | | | |
| 31 Jul | Balance (assumed) | | | | | 6 100.00 Dr |
| | Sundry payments | | CPJ | | 298.20 | 5 801.80 Dr |

**Note** In this comprehensive example, a cash under adjustment was necessary due to a discrepancy between the Petty Cash Book and the balance of petty cash funds on hand at the end of the period. It is, of course, equally possible that the balance of petty cash funds on hand at the end of the period could exceed the balance indicated by the petty cash transactions for the period. In this case, a cash over adjustment is required. Where this occurs a negative entry for the amount of the cash over adjustment is required in both the Petty Cash Book and the Cash Payments Journal, resulting in a credit entry to the Cash Under/ Over account in the General Ledger. A cash over adjustment is illustrated in the solutions to exercises 6.9 and 6.11 later in this chapter.

# Petty cash controls

Internal controls over cash were discussed in the previous chapter. In addition to these controls, there are a number of internal controls that apply specifically to petty cash. Some important internal control principles in relation to petty cash are listed below.

- The petty cash fund should be kept in a locked safe or drawer.
- The petty cashier should be a reliable and trustworthy employee who is regularly in the office, for example a receptionist, accounts clerk or a personal assistant.
- The task of petty cashier should occasionally be rotated between different employees.
- The petty cashier should only dispense cash from the petty cash fund on the production of a properly authorised petty cash voucher. Where required, the receipts/tax invoices for amounts spent should be attached to the relevant petty cash vouchers.
- The Petty Cash Book should be updated regularly.
- The petty cashier should ensure that the petty cash fund is reimbursed when required or when funds reach a low level.
- When the cheque is prepared to reimburse the petty cash fund, the cheque signatories should review the petty cash vouchers for the money expended from the fund. Any discrepancies should be followed up.
- Occasional random surprise audits of the petty cash fund should be conducted.
- The accountant or office manager should periodically peruse the Petty Cash Book. Any irregularities, such as cash under or over, should be followed up.

The use of an imprest system to record petty cash transactions is an important aspect of control over cash in that it:

- identifies discrepancies in petty cash, and
- ensures that the fund is only reimbursed for amounts actually spent.

 **EXERCISES**

6.1    What is petty cash? Explain.

6.2    Why is it important for many businesses to have a petty cash fund? Explain.

6.3    What is the petty cash imprest system? Explain.

6.4    Why is 'petty cash advance' an asset? Explain.

6.5    When the petty cash fund is replenished by drawing a reimbursement cheque, explain why the Petty Cash Advance account is not debited.

6.6    What factors should an employer consider when appointing a petty cashier? Explain briefly.

6.7    From the following information, you are required to write the petty cash vouchers for E Macquire, used car dealer, for June 2017. The petty cashier is K Everitt.

*Voucher details*

| Date | Voucher no. | Paid to | For | Account no. | GST paid | Amount (inc. GST) |
|------|-------------|---------|-----|-------------|----------|-------------------|
| 2017 | | | | | $ | $ |
| 2 Jun | 1 | J Stewart | Travel | 426 | 1.50 | 16.50 |
| 5 | 2 | B Oddie | Travel | 426 | 0.80 | 8.80 |
| | 3 | D Bartlett | Tea/coffee | 394 | | 3.30 |
| 12 | 4 | L Askew | Newspapers | 395 | 0.70 | 7.70 |
| 17 | 5 | F Clark | Milk | 394 | | 2.50 |
| 18 | 6 | J McDonald | Taxi truck | 427 | 2.20 | 24.20 |
| 26 | 7 | G Black | Stamps | 421 | 0.30 | 3.30 |
| 27 | 8 | B Allitt | Bulk mail | 421 | 2.75 | 30.25 |
| 30 | 9 | T Van der Geest | Printing (cards) | 440 | 0.50 | 5.50 |
| | 10 | S Lane | Stamps | 421 | 0.25 | 2.75 |

6.8    From the information provided, you are required to complete the Petty Cash Book for C Constable for the month of July 2019. (Make up your own account numbers where applicable.) In your answer, use the following Petty Cash Book headings.

This question can also be completed in a spreadsheet that is available on the CD accompanying this text.

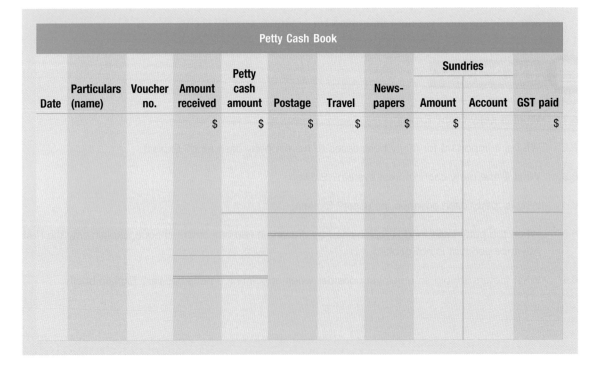

| | | | | | Petty Cash Book | | | | Sundries | | |
|---|---|---|---|---|---|---|---|---|---|---|---|
| Date | Particulars (name) | Voucher no. | Amount received | Petty cash amount | Postage | Travel | News-papers | Amount | Account | GST paid |
| | | | $ | $ | $ | $ | $ | $ | | $ |

a  Petty cash advance cheque

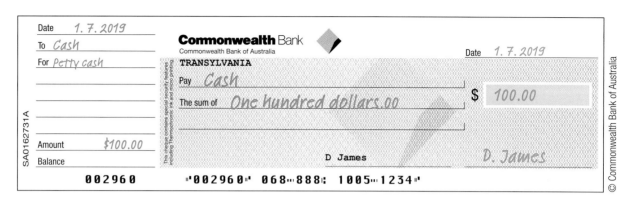

| Date | 1. 7. 2019 | | | | | | |
|---|---|---|---|---|---|---|---|
| To | Cash | | | | | | |
| For | Petty cash | | | | | | |

Amount  $100.00
Balance

002960

**Commonwealth** Bank
Commonwealth Bank of Australia

TRANSYLVANIA

Pay  Cash                                    Date  1. 7. 2019

The sum of  One hundred dollars.00        $  100.00

D James                          D. James

"002960"  068···888:  1005···1234"

This cheque contains special security features including Thermochromic ink and micro printing.

SA0162731A

© Commonwealth Bank of Australia

b  Petty cash vouchers for July

| Date: 2.7.19 | | No. 1 |
|---|---|---|
| **PETTY CASH VOUCHER** | | |
| Paid to R Bartlett | | |
| For Travel | | |
| Amount (inc. GST) | GST | Acc No. |
| $ 12.65 | $ 1.15 | 374 |
| Signed DJ | | |

| Date: 5.7.19 | | No. 2 |
|---|---|---|
| **PETTY CASH VOUCHER** | | |
| Paid to R Bartlett | | |
| For Travel | | |
| Amount (inc. GST) | GST | Acc No. |
| $ 6.60 | $ 0.60 | 374 |
| Signed DJ | | |

| Date: 10.7.19 | | No. 3 |
|---|---|---|
| **PETTY CASH VOUCHER** | | |
| Paid to J Smith | | |
| For Stamps | | |
| Amount (inc. GST) | GST | Acc No. |
| $ 14.30 | $ 1.30 | 375 |
| Signed DJ | | |

| Date: 16.7.19 | | No. 4 |
|---|---|---|
| **PETTY CASH VOUCHER** | | |
| Paid to A O'Neil | | |
| For Tea bags | | |
| Amount (inc. GST) | GST | Acc No. |
| $ 10.50 | $ | 370 |
| Signed DJ | | |

| Date: 21.7.19 | | No. 5 |
|---|---|---|
| **PETTY CASH VOUCHER** | | |
| Paid to B Cook | | |
| For Taxi truck | | |
| Amount (inc. GST) | GST | Acc No. |
| $ 17.60 | $ 1.60 | 373 |
| Signed DJ | | |

| Date: 28.7.19 | | No. 6 |
|---|---|---|
| **PETTY CASH VOUCHER** | | |
| Paid to S Joseph | | |
| For Newspaper | | |
| Amount (inc. GST) | GST | Acc No. |
| $ 5.50 | $ 0.50 | 379 |
| Signed DJ | | |

| Date: 29.7.19 | | No. 7 |
|---|---|---|
| **PETTY CASH VOUCHER** | | |
| Paid to A O'Neil | | |
| For Milk | | |
| Amount (inc. GST) | GST | Acc No. |
| $ 4.50 | $ | 370 |
| Signed DJ | | |

c   Reimbursement cheque

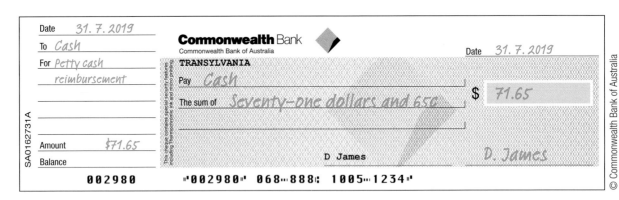

6.9*   Using the Petty Cash Book headings shown in exercise 6.8 and the information provided below, you are required to complete the Petty Cash Book for G Wanganeen for the month of August 2019. The petty cashier for the business is Rosemary Button. (Make up your own account numbers where applicable.)
This question can also be completed in a spreadsheet that is available on the CD accompanying this text.

a    Petty cash establishment cheque

Date _1. 8. 2019_

To _R Button_

For _Petty cash_

SA0162731A

Amount _$600.00_

Balance

000360

**Commonwealth** Bank
Commonwealth Bank of Australia

EDISON

Date _1. 8. 2019_

Pay    _R Button_

The sum of    _Six hundred dollars.00_    $ _600.00_

D SMITHFIELD    _D. Smithfield_

This cheque contains special security features including Thermochromic ink and micro printing

⑈000360⑈ 068⑈888⑆ 1006⑈1234⑈

© Commonwealth Bank of Australia

b    Petty cash vouchers for August

Date: _1.8.19_    No. _1_

**PETTY CASH VOUCHER**

Paid to _J Keats_

For _Taxi fare_

| Amount (inc. GST) | GST | Acc No. |
|---|---|---|
| $ _14.30_ | $ _1.30_ | _720_ |

Signed _R Button_


Date: _3.8.19_    No. _2_

**PETTY CASH VOUCHER**

Paid to _J Donne_

For _Stamps_

| Amount (inc. GST) | GST | Acc No. |
|---|---|---|
| $ _4.60_ | $ _0.42_ | _712_ |

Signed _R Button_


Date: _5.8.19_    No. _3_

**PETTY CASH VOUCHER**

Paid to _T Eliot_

For _Stamps_

| Amount (inc. GST) | GST | Acc No. |
|---|---|---|
| $ _7.25_ | $ _0.66_ | _712_ |

Signed _R Button_


Date: _6.8.19_    No. _4_

**PETTY CASH VOUCHER**

Paid to _C Dickens_

For _Freight_

| Amount (inc. GST) | GST | Acc No. |
|---|---|---|
| $ _15.95_ | $ _1.45_ | _722_ |

Signed _R Button_

| Date: 13.8.19 | | No. 5 |
|---|---|---|
| **PETTY CASH VOUCHER** | | |

Paid to J Eyre

For Milk

| Amount (inc. GST) | GST | Acc No. |
|---|---|---|
| $ 4.80 | $ | 729 |

Signed R Button

| Date: 15.8.19 | | No. 6 |
|---|---|---|
| **PETTY CASH VOUCHER** | | |

Paid to J Eyre

For Taxi

| Amount (inc. GST) | GST | Acc No. |
|---|---|---|
| $ 9.90 | $ 0.90 | 720 |

Signed R Button

| Date: 18.8.18 | | No. 7 |
|---|---|---|
| **PETTY CASH VOUCHER** | | |

Paid to T Hardy

For Biscuits

| Amount (inc. GST) | GST | Acc No. |
|---|---|---|
| $ 5.90 | $ 0.54 | 729 |

Signed R Button

| Date: 20.8.19 | | No. 8 |
|---|---|---|
| **PETTY CASH VOUCHER** | | |

Paid to C Dickens

For Milk

| Amount (inc. GST) | GST | Acc No. |
|---|---|---|
| $ 2.40 | $ | 729 |

Signed R Button

| Date: 21.8.19 | | No. 9 |
|---|---|---|
| **PETTY CASH VOUCHER** | | |

Paid to J Eyre

For Stamps

| Amount (inc. GST) | GST | Acc No. |
|---|---|---|
| $ 7.25 | $ 0.65 | 712 |

Signed R Button

| Date: 23.8.19 | | No. 10 |
|---|---|---|
| **PETTY CASH VOUCHER** | | |

Paid to C Bronte

For City parking
(travel)

| Amount (inc. GST) | GST | Acc No. |
|---|---|---|
| $ 13.20 | $ 1.20 | 720 |

Signed R Button

| Date: 29.8.19 | | No. 11 |
|---|---|---|
| **PETTY CASH VOUCHER** | | |

Paid to _S Clemens_

For _Taxi_

| Amount (inc. GST) | GST | Acc No. |
|---|---|---|
| $ 22.00 | $ 2.00 | 720 |

Signed _R Button_

| Date: 31.8.19 | | No. 12 |
|---|---|---|
| **PETTY CASH VOUCHER** | | |

Paid to _C Byron_

For _Tea and coffee_

| Amount (inc. GST) | GST | Acc No. |
|---|---|---|
| $ 29.20 | $ | 729 |

Signed _R Button_

| Date: 31.8.19 | | No. 13 |
|---|---|---|
| **PETTY CASH VOUCHER** | | |

Paid to _G Orwell_

For _Newspapers_

    _(3 weeks)_

| Amount (inc. GST) | GST | Acc No. |
|---|---|---|
| $ 40.00 | $ 3.64 | 715 |

Signed _R Button_

| Date: 31.8.19 | | No. 14 |
|---|---|---|
| **PETTY CASH VOUCHER** | | |

Paid to _J Conrad_

For _Stationery_

| Amount (inc. GST) | GST | Acc No. |
|---|---|---|
| $ 7.50 | $ 0.68 | 705 |

Signed _R Button_

**Note** Cash remaining in the petty cash fund at 31 Aug was $418.75.

c   Reimbursement cheque

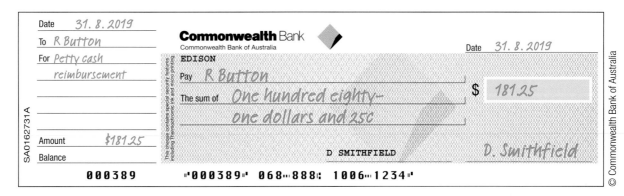

6.10   This question is available on the CD that accompanies this text.

6.11*   Enter the following transactions in the Petty Cash Book of B Minotta, balance the Petty Cash Book, make the necessary entries in the Cash Payments Journal and post the Cash Payments Journal to the General Ledger at 12 June 2019. (Make up your own account numbers where necessary.)

This question can also be completed in a spreadsheet that is available on the CD accompanying this text.

| Date | *1. 6. 2019* |
|---|---|
| To | *Cash* |
| For | *Petty cash* |
| | *advance (Acct 102)* |
| | |
| | |
| Amount | *$80.00* |
| Balance | |
| | **AAA132** |

SA0162731A

---

No. *1*

**PETTY CASH VOUCHER**

*2 June* 2019

Paid to *Travel–Acc 418*

Particulars *S Sinvet*

*(Taxi fare)*

Signed *L Abbott*

Petty Cashier

$ *10.50 (inc. GST $0.95)*

---

No. *2*

**PETTY CASH VOUCHER**

*2 June* 2019

Paid to *Postage–Acc 416*

Particulars *R McHenry*

Signed *L Abbott*

Petty Cashier

$ *8.00 (inc. GST $0.73)*

---

No. *3*

**PETTY CASH VOUCHER**

*4 June* 2019

Paid to *Stationery–Acc 419*

Particulars *S Featherston*

*Note pads*

Signed *L Abbott*

Petty Cashier

$ *2.00 (inc. GST $0.18)*

---

No. *4*

**PETTY CASH VOUCHER**

*5 June* 2019

Paid to *Coffee/Tea–Acc 403*

Particulars *R McHenry*

*Tea bags*

Signed *L Abbott*

Petty Cashier

$ *2.70*

---

No. *5*

**PETTY CASH VOUCHER**

*10 June* 2019

Paid to *Travel–Acc 418*

Particulars *S Williams*

*Taxi fare*

Signed *L Abbott*

Petty Cashier

$ *9.00 (inc. GST $0.82)*

<table>
<tr><td>

No. 6

**PETTY CASH VOUCHER**

11 June 2019

Paid to Newspaper–Acc 422

Particulars J Arandale

(Newspaper for one week)

Signed L Abbott

Petty Cashier

$ 7.30 (inc. GST $0.66)

</td><td>

No. 7

**PETTY CASH VOUCHER**

12 June 2019

Paid to Donations–Acc 410

Particulars G Loney – Red Cross

Donation

Signed L Abbott

Petty Cashier

$ 13.30

</td></tr>
</table>

**Note** Cash remaining in the petty cash fund at 30 June was $28.20.

Date 12. 6. 2019
To Cash
For Petty cash
reimbursement

Amount $51.80
Balance

000138

SA0162731A

6.12 The petty cash transactions below relate to the business of T Bright. You are required to:

a write up the Petty Cash Book, using the following headings for group expenses: postage (account no. 416), travel (account no. 418), stationery (account no. 402), sundry expenses (account no. 422), GST paid (account no. 207)

b prepare the reimbursement cheque and butt (format shown on next page)

c balance the Petty Cash Book and record the reimbursement cheque

d write up the Cash Payments Journal

e post the Cash Payments Journal to the General Ledger at 30 June 2019.

(Assume that no other cheques have been written during the month.)

This question can also be completed in a spreadsheet that is available on the CD accompanying this text.

ADDITIONAL
EXERCISES

453

*Petty cash details*

| Voucher/cheque no. | Date | Amount (inc. GST) | GST paid | Details |
|---|---|---|---|---|
| | 2019 | $ | $ | |
| 000633 | 1 Jun | 100.00 | | Imprest cheque |
| 001 | 6 | 11.55 | 1.05 | Taxi fares |
| 002 | 9 | 22.00 | 2.00 | Stamps |
| 003 | 12 | 3.50 | | Tea and milk |
| 004 | 15 | 13.20 | 1.20 | Copy paper |
| 005 | 20 | 19.80 | 1.80 | Taxi fares |
| 006 | 25 | 4.95 | 0.45 | Pens |
| 007 | 30 | 13.75 | 1.25 | Stamps |
| 000634 | 30 | ? | | Reimbursement |

**Note** Cash remaining in the petty cash fund at 30 June was $11.25.

*Reimbursement cheque*

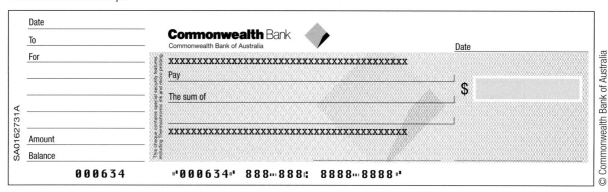

6.13 The petty cash transactions below relate to the business of J Peart. You are required to:

a write up the Petty Cash Book using the headings shown below:

b balance the Petty Cash Book and record the reimbursement cheque

c make any necessary entries in the Cash Payments Journal

d post the Cash Payments Journal to the General Ledger at 30 June 2019, assuming that no other cheques have been written during the month.

This question can also be completed in a spreadsheet that is available on the CD accompanying this text.

| | | | | Petty Cash Book | | | | | | |
|---|---|---|---|---|---|---|---|---|---|---|
| Date | Particulars (name) | Voucher no. | Amount received | Petty cash amount | Postage | Travel | News-papers | Sundries | | GST paid |
| | | | | | | | | Amount | Account no. | |

*Petty cash vouchers and cheque butts*

| Date | 1. 6. 2019 |
|------|-----------|
| To | Cash |
| For | Petty cash advance |

SA0162731A

| Amount | $120.00 |
|--------|---------|
| Balance | |

**000640**

---

Date: 2.6.19                                No. 1

### PETTY CASH VOUCHER

Paid to *T Spasmos*

For *Postage stamps*

Amount $ *22.00 (inc. GST $2.00)*

Signed *G Rees*

---

Date: 5.6.19                                No. 2

### PETTY CASH VOUCHER

Paid to *R Waterman*

For *Taxi fare*

Amount $ *13.00 (inc. GST $1.18)*

Signed *G Rees*

---

Date: 10.6.19                              No. 3

### PETTY CASH VOUCHER

Paid to *P Canetto*

For        *Pens and correction*
           *fluid*

Amount $ *13.00 (inc. GST $1.18)*

Signed *G Rees*

---

Date: 10.6.19                              No. 4

### PETTY CASH VOUCHER

Paid to *S Keystone*

For *Copy paper*

Amount $ *6.50 (inc. GST $0.59)*

Signed *G Rees*

---

Date: 14.6.19                              No. 5

### PETTY CASH VOUCHER

Paid to *S Aloysius*

For        *Tea and Coffee*
           *(Misc)*

Amount $ *9.60*

Signed *G Rees*

---

Date: 26.6.19                              No. 6

### PETTY CASH VOUCHER

Paid to *T Spasmos*

For *Stamps*

Amount $ *31.50 (inc. GST $2.86)*

Signed *G Rees*

---

Date: 30.6.19                              No. 7

### PETTY CASH VOUCHER

Paid to *A Plasmoderm*

For *Red Cross donation*
           *(Misc)*

Amount $ *13.30*

Signed *G Rees*

---

**Note** Cash remaining in the petty cash fund at 30 June was $10.10.

```
Date        30. 6. 2019
To    Cash
For   Petty cash
      reimbursement
_____
_____
_____
Amount        $109.90
Balance
          0 0 0 6 9 0
```

SA0162731A

6.14    This question is available on the CD that accompanies this text.

**ADDITIONAL EXERCISES**

6.15    Briefly outline the control procedures that should be present when recording petty cash transactions.

6.16    How does the imprest system assist in internal control over petty cash?

 **SOLUTIONS**

6.9

G Wanganeen
Petty Cash Book

| Date | Particulars (name) | Voucher no. | Amount received | Petty cash amount | Postage | Travel | News-papers | Sundries Amount | Sundries Account no. | GST paid |
|---|---|---|---|---|---|---|---|---|---|---|
| 2019 | | | $ | $ | $ | $ | $ | $ | | $ |
| 1 Aug | Advance | Chq. 0360 | 600.00 | | | | | | | |
| | J Keats | 1 | | 14.30 | | 13.00 | | | | 1.30 |
| 3 | J Donne | 2 | | 4.60 | 4.18 | | | | | 0.42 |
| 5 | T Eliot | 3 | | 7.25 | 6.59 | | | | | 0.66 |
| 6 | A Jones | 4 | | 15.95 | | | | 14.50 | 722 – Freight | 1.45 |
| 13 | J Eyre | 5 | | 4.80 | | | | 4.80 | 729 – Coffee/Tea | |
| 15 | J Eyre | 6 | | 9.90 | | 9.00 | | | | 0.90 |
| 19 | T Hardy | 7 | | 5.90 | | | | 5.36 | 729 – Coffee/Tea | 0.54 |
| 20 | C Dickens | 8 | | 2.40 | | | | 2.40 | 729 – Coffee/Tea | |
| 21 | J Eyre | 9 | | 7.25 | 6.60 | | | | | 0.65 |
| 23 | C Bronte | 10 | | 13.20 | | 12.00 | | | | 1.20 |
| 29 | S Clemens | 11 | | 22.00 | | 20.00 | | | | 2.00 |
| 31 | C Byron | 12 | | 29.20 | | | | 29.20 | 729 – Coffee/Tea | |

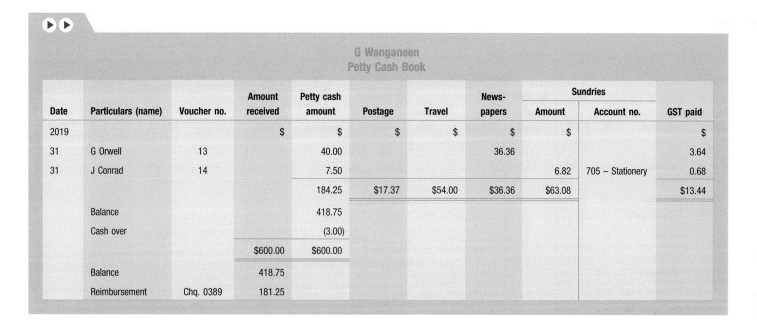

**G Wanganeen**
**Petty Cash Book**

| Date | Particulars (name) | Voucher no. | Amount received | Petty cash amount | Postage | Travel | News-papers | Sundries Amount | Sundries Account no. | GST paid |
|---|---|---|---|---|---|---|---|---|---|---|
| 2019 | | | $ | $ | $ | $ | $ | $ | | $ |
| 31 | G Orwell | 13 | | 40.00 | | | 36.36 | | | 3.64 |
| 31 | J Conrad | 14 | | 7.50 | | | | 6.82 | 705 – Stationery | 0.68 |
| | | | | 184.25 | $17.37 | $54.00 | $36.36 | $63.08 | | $13.44 |
| | Balance | | | 418.75 | | | | | | |
| | Cash over | | | (3.00) | | | | | | |
| | | | $600.00 | $600.00 | | | | | | |
| | Balance | | | 418.75 | | | | | | |
| | Reimbursement | Chq. 0389 | | 181.25 | | | | | | |

6.11

**B Minotta**
**Petty Cash Book**

| Date | Particulars (name) | Voucher no. | Amount received | Petty cash amount | Postage | Travel | News-papers | Sundries Amount | Sundries Account no. | GST paid |
|---|---|---|---|---|---|---|---|---|---|---|
| 2019 | | | $ | $ | $ | $ | $ | $ | | $ |
| 1 Jun | Advance | Chq. 0132 | 80.00 | | | | | | | |
| 2 | S Sinvet | 1 | | 10.50 | | 9.55 | | | | 0.95 |
| | R McHenry | 2 | | 8.00 | 7.27 | | | | | 0.73 |
| 4 | S Featherston | 3 | | 2.00 | | | | 1.82 | 419 – Stationery | 0.18 |
| 5 | R McHenry | 4 | | 2.70 | | | | 2.70 | 403 – Coffee/Tea | |
| 10 | S Williams | 5 | | 9.00 | | 8.18 | | | | 0.82 |
| 11 | J Arandale | 6 | | 7.30 | | | 6.64 | | | 0.66 |
| 12 | G Loney | 7 | | 13.30 | | | | 13.30 | 410 – Donations | |
| | | | | 52.80 | $7.27 | $17.73 | $6.64 | $17.82 | | $3.34 |
| | Balance | | | 28.20 | | | | | | |
| | Cash over | | | (1.00) | | | | | | |
| | | | $80.00 | $80.00 | | | | | | |
| | Balance | | | 28.20 | | | | | | |
| | Reimbursement | Chq. 0138 | | 51.80 | | | | | | |

## Cash Payments Journal

| Date | Particulars | Fol | Ref | Discount income | | | Accounts payable control | Cash purchases | Wages | Sundries | | GST paid | Bank |
|------|-------------|-----|-----|-----------------|---|---|--------------------------|----------------|-------|----------|---|----------|------|
| | | | | Accounts payable control | GST paid | Discount income | | | | Amount | Account | | |
| 2019 | | | | $ | $ | $ | $ | $ | $ | $ | | $ | $ |
| 1 Jun | Petty cash advance | 102 | 0132 | | | | | | | 80.00 | Petty cash advance | | 80.00 |
| 12 | Petty cash reimbursement | | 0138 | | | | | | | | | | |
| | Postage | 416 | | | | | | | | 7.27 | Postage | | |
| | Travel | 418 | | | | | | | | 17.73 | Travel | | |
| | Coffee/tea | 403 | | | | | | | | 2.70 | Coffee/tea | | |
| | Donations | 410 | | | | | | | | 13.30 | Donations | | |
| | Stationery | 419 | | | | | | | | 1.82 | Stationery | | |
| | Newspapers | 422 | | | | | | | | 6.64 | Newspapers | | |
| | Cash under/over | 499 | | | | | | | | (1.00) | Cash under/over | 3.34 | 51.80 |
| | | | | | | | | | | $128.46 | | $3.34 | $131.80 |

## General Ledger

| Date | Particulars | Fol | Debit | Credit | Balance |
|------|-------------|-----|-------|--------|---------|
| **102 – Petty Cash Advance Account** | | | | | |
| 2019 | | | $ | $ | $ |
| 1 Jun | Cash at bank | CPJ | 80.00 | | 80.00 Dr |
| **416 – Postage Account** | | | | | |
| 2019 | | | | | |
| 12 Jun | Cash at bank | CPJ | 7.27 | | 7.27 Dr |
| **418 – Travel Account** | | | | | |
| 2019 | | | | | |
| 12 Jun | Cash at bank | CPJ | 17.73 | | 17.73 Dr |
| **403 – Coffee/Tea Account** | | | | | |
| 2019 | | | | | |
| 12 Jun | Cash at bank | CPJ | 2.70 | | 2.70 Dr |

| Date | Particulars | Fol | Debit | Credit | Balance |
|---|---|---|---|---|---|
| | | | General Ledger | | |
| | **410 – Donations Account** | | | | |
| 2019 | | | $ | $ | $ |
| 12 Jun | Cash at bank | CPJ | 13.30 | | 13.30 Dr |
| | **419 – Stationery Account** | | | | |
| 2019 | | | | | |
| 12 Jun | Cash at bank | CPJ | 1.82 | | 1.82 Dr |
| | **422 – Newspapers Account** | | | | |
| 2019 | | | | | |
| 12 Jun | Cash at bank | CPJ | 6.64 | | 6.64 Dr |
| | **499 – Cash Under/Over Account** | | | | |
| 2019 | | | | | |
| 12 Jun | Cash at bank | CPJ | | 1.00 | 1.00 Cr |
| | **101 – Cash at Bank Account** | | | | |
| 2019 | | | | | |
| 12 Jun | Sundry payments | CPJ | | 131.80 | 131.80 Cr |
| | **103 – GST Paid Account** | | | | |
| 2019 | | | | | |
| 12 Jun | Cash at bank | CPJ | 3.34 | | 3.34 Dr |

## Summary

What have you covered in this chapter?

◆ Checking petty cash claims for accuracy and authenticity before processing
◆ Recording and balancing petty cash transactions
◆ Presentation of records of transactions to the relevant authority for checking within relevant timelines
◆ The steps involved in preparing the reimbursement cheque
◆ Review of the internal controls procedures for petty cash

# PAYROLL

## Learning objectives

Upon satisfactory completion of this chapter you should be able to:

- outline the employee records and controls necessary in a typical payroll system
- calculate the weekly net pay of a minimum of three employees taking into account starting and finishing time each day, overtime, paid leave, unpaid leave, employee deductions (union fees, medical benefits, superannuation) and PAYG withholding
- prepare entries for the weekly payroll in relevant employee and other records
- prepare entries for the payment of balances of PAYG withholding and employee deduction liability accounts created from the payroll
- complete all journal and General Ledger entries arising from payroll transactions
- outline an employer's responsibilities in relation to PAYG withholding, payroll tax, workers' compensation and superannuation guarantee
- discuss internal controls over payroll.

*Salaries* and *wages* are expenses normally incurred by most business entities for work undertaken by employees. Before we can define these terms it is perhaps worth noting the relationship that exists between an employer and an employee.

An *employer* is a person or an entity that hires the employment services (labour) of another person, referred to as an *employee*. An employee is thus the person who actually undertakes the work on behalf of the employer. Consider Figure 7.1.

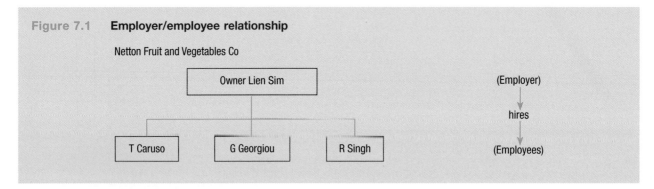

Figure 7.1   **Employer/employee relationship**

When an employee is appointed, a *contract* is established which requires the employer to pay (remunerate) the employee for all duties performed. This payment is referred to as *salaries* or *wages*.

Traditionally, a distinction is drawn between the terms 'salaries' and 'wages'. 'Wages' usually relates to payments made to employees who work a fixed number of hours per week. Hours worked by a wage earner in addition to the fixed hours are normally considered as *overtime* hours and are paid at special rates. Wages are paid on an hourly basis; thus, having some means of recording and accounting for each hour worked is essential. Clock cards or timesheets are maintained for this purpose and these key source documents form the basis for the payment and recording of wages.

'Salaries' is a term that usually relates to payments made to employees for the performance of specific duties. Extra time taken by salary earners in performing the specified duties does not normally attract overtime payments. Salary payments are based on annual figures that can be converted by formula to a weekly amount (or whatever the pay period might be; for example, fortnightly or monthly). While a timesheet may be maintained for some salary earners, it does not normally form the basis for payment of the set salary calculated.

# Internal control over payroll

As wages and salaries represent a major cost to most businesses, it is important that rigorous internal controls are developed to monitor and control payroll and thus minimise the possibility of losses attributable to fraud. Some basic internal controls over payroll are discussed below.

## Separation of duties

One of the most effective controls is to separate the human resources (HR) or *personnel* function from the *payroll* function. The HR section or department of a business has the responsibility for the hiring of staff, maintenance of employee records etc., whereas Payroll has the responsibility for the preparation, recording and payment of wages and salaries. This is necessary to prevent fraud by ensuring that:

- payments of wages and salaries are not made to fictitious employees
- employees do not receive more than their correct entitlement.

# Authorisation of hours worked

It is important that employees are only paid for hours actually worked. This requires the maintenance of attendance records such as clock cards, time sheets, attendance books or similar records. Attendance records are discussed in more detail later in this chapter. Each employee's attendance record should be authorised by the responsible manager or supervisor prior to the preparation of the payroll.

# Adequate documentation and procedures

Proper payroll records and procedures are vital for a number of reasons.

- An employer has a legal obligation to pay employees their correct entitlements.
- An employer is required to withhold tax from employees' earnings and remit it to the ATO on a regular basis. Additionally, at the end of the financial year, the employer is required to provide each employee with a *payment summary*, with details of earnings and tax withheld during the year.
- Other amounts withheld from employees' earnings, such as superannuation, union dues and private health insurance premiums, must be recorded and remitted to the relevant authorities on a timely basis.
- Under superannuation guarantee legislation (the *Superannuation Guarantee (Administration) Act 1992* (Cth), the *Superannuation Guarantee Charge Act 1992* (Cth) and amendments) an employer is required to contribute to superannuation on behalf of each employee. It is essential that such payments are made and recorded on a timely basis.
- Employees are entitled to various types of leave, including annual leave, sick leave and long service leave. It is essential that leave accrued and leave taken is accurately recorded.
- Management require payroll information for budgeting, costing and financial reporting purposes.

# Legal issues affecting employees

A business must have appropriate policies and procedures in place to ensure that it complies with the requirements of the relevant codes of practice and legislation, including:

- anti-discrimination legislation An employer is prohibited from discriminating against existing or prospective employees on grounds such as race, gender, religion or disability.
- occupational health and safety (OH&S) legislation A business has a moral and legal obligation to provide a safe working environment.
- environmental protection legislation Employees must be made aware of their obligation to be environmentally responsible in all aspects of their work.

It is important that employers and employees share the responsibility for issues such as those listed above.

# Privacy and security of employee and payroll records

Employee and payroll records contain information that is personal and confidential. Employers must take adequate steps to protect the confidentiality of this information. Such records and information should be stored in a secure environment with access limited to authorised personnel.

In a computerised environment, access to employee and payroll records can be controlled through the use of user identification names and passwords.

# Reconciliation/review of payroll

Periodically, certain reconciliations/reviews relating to payroll should be performed, including those listed below.

- Each pay period, prior to the payment of the payroll, the accountant or some other senior person in the organisation should review the payroll records, such as payroll registers and journals, which are discussed below. Any unusual items or major variations between pay periods should be investigated. Hard copies of these records should then be signed off by the accountant or other person as the appropriate authorisation for the payroll department to pay employees.
- As discussed earlier, amounts deducted from employee earnings must be remitted (sent) to the relevant authorities in a timely manner. The accountant should review the relevant liability accounts in the General Ledger to ensure that the liabilities are being correctly recorded each pay period and are being remitted to the relevant organisations by the due date.
- To ensure that no unauthorised payments are being made to employees, the accountant should ensure that the total amount paid to employees each pay period reconciles with the total net pay for the period as recorded on the payroll register, which summarises the payroll details for all employees for a particular week, fortnight or month.

# Backup and disaster recovery

In a computerised payroll environment it is vital that policies and procedures exist regarding payroll data backup and recovery. These should provide for regular backup of payroll data (for instance, each pay period). Backup media should be stored in a secure environment, and procedures for recovery of payroll data in the event of a system malfunction should be specified.

# Responsibility for payroll preparation and recording

In a medium-to-large enterprise, the processing and recording of the payroll would be the responsibility of the *payroll department* or some similarly named unit, section or department of the organisation. This department would typically consist of a manager and one or more assistants, depending upon the size of the organisation. The manager's role would be to oversee the entire payroll process and be responsible to higher-level management for operation of the department. The assistants would perform the detailed processing and recording tasks, such as:

- ensuring that hours worked have been correctly calculated
- ensuring that hours worked have been authorised by the appropriate person
- calculation of payroll amounts for each employee
- accurate recording of payroll information
- preparation of reports for management and accounting purposes
- answering payroll enquiries from individual employees.

In a small organisation, one or two people may be responsible for the entire accounting function, including payroll.

# Payroll enquiries

On occasions, individual employees may make enquiries regarding their pay. Such enquiries need to be handled in a timely manner by the appropriate person. An organisation may have specific policies and procedures relating to the provision of payroll and other information to employees.

Typically, an employee with a payroll enquiry would approach the payroll department directly; in many cases, this can effectively resolve any typical enquiry. In other cases, staff in the payroll department may need to seek advice from or refer the enquiry to some other authorised person or department. For example, enquiries relating to rates of pay and leave entitlements may need to be referred to the HR department, or enquiries relating to calculation of tax may need to be referred to the payroll manager or accountant.

# Employee records
## Employee history cards

When an employee is first appointed, an *employee history card* is completed and forwarded to the payroll clerk. The card is also referred to as the *personnel card*, since it is a record normally kept and maintained by the Personnel (or HR) department of the business. The employee history card records details of a personal nature, including the employee's name, address, date of birth, home telephone number, deductions, date started, rate of pay and other personal information (see Figure 7.2). It should be noted also that while employee history cards were traditionally in hardcopy form – that is, literally a 'card' – it is now more common for employee history information to be stored electronically in computer files.

**Figure 7.2**    **Employee history card**

EMPLOYEE HISTORY CARD

Name........................................................................................    Employee no.........................................

Address.....................................................................................    Position................................................

Telephone no. (home)........................... (mobile)..........................    Date of birth........................................

Email.........................................................................................    Date appointed....................................

TFN Dec. lodged:            Yes [   ]            No [   ]            Pay rate..............................................

Withholding Dec. lodged:  Yes [   ]            No [   ]            Awards................................................

Offsets $.....................................................

Deductions from pay                                                    Weekly [   ]                    Monthly [   ]

Union                  ..........................................................$                          $

Superannuation        ..........................................................$                          ℃

Other                 ..........................................................$                          $

                      ..........................................................$                          $

| Date | Classification | Rate | Auth | | Date | Classification | Rate | Auth |
|------|----------------|------|------|--|------|----------------|------|------|
| ......... | ......... | ......... | ......... | | ......... | ......... | ......... | ......... |

Date terminated ................................................................ Reasons ..........................................................

**Reverse side**

| Sick leave | | | | Annual leave | | | |
|------------|----|------|---------|------|----|------|---------|
| From | To | Days | Remarks | From | To | Days | Remarks |
| | | | | | | | |
| | | | | **Other leave** | | | |
| | | | | | | | |

From time to time an employee's history card will need to be updated to reflect changes, such as:

- salary review
- reclassification
- promotion/demotion
- change of address
- change of PAYG withholding status
- change to payment arrangements
- change to regular payroll deductions.

Such changes should be authorised in accordance with organisation policies and procedures.

# Employee earnings records

An *employee earnings record* normally records all pay details of each individual employee, both on a pay period basis and on a cumulative basis (see Figure 7.3).

Figure 7.3  **Employee earnings record**

| Week ending | Gross pay | Deductions | | | | | | Net pay | Accumulated figures | | | | |
|---|---|---|---|---|---|---|---|---|---|---|---|---|---|
| | | Tax | Union | Super | Ins. | Other | Total | | Gross | Tax | Super | Union | Ins. |
| | $ | $ | $ | $ | $ | $ | $ | $ | $ | $ | $ | $ | $ |
| | | | | | | | | | | | | | |

**Employee earnings record**

Name .................... Employee no. ....................

Address ....................

An employee earnings record is often referred to as a *cumulative earnings record*, since it records accumulated figures for gross pay and all deductions. These figures are essential at the end of the financial period for preparing PAYG payment summaries and general payroll reconciliation.

PAYG payment summary preparation and related year-end procedures will be discussed later in this chapter.

In a computerised payroll system, the employee earnings record is automatically updated each pay period. At the end of the financial year, the PAYG payment summaries can be printed and distributed to employees.

# Employee time records

As previously mentioned, wages are normally paid on an hourly basis and thus some method of accounting for the amount of time worked by each employee is necessary. This information can be collected by a variety of means, including time clocks and time books.

## Time clocks

Time clock methods are used widely in industry, most typically at work sites such as factories where it is necessary to keep track of hours worked for a large number of employees. Employees insert a *clock card* into a time clock, which records the time of arrival at work and time of departure when the card is re-inserted at various times during the day (see Figure 7.4). At the end of the pay period the total number of hours worked for the pay period is computed.

**Figure 7.4    Completed clock card**

| Name | Tony Gonsalvis Di Paolo | | | | Employee no. | 670 | |
|------|-------------------------|--|--|--|--------------|-----|--|
| Week ending | 15.7.16 | | | | | | |
| Days | Normal hours worked | | | | Overtime | | Total hours |
| | In | Out | In | Out | In | Out | |
| Mon | 8.48 | 12.00 | 12.30 | 5.30 | | | 8 |
| Tue | 8.50 | 12.05 | 12.30 | 5.30 | | | 8 |
| Wed | 8.55 | 12.10 | 12.35 | 5.30 | | | 8 |
| Thu | 8.45 | 12.05 | 12.30 | 5.35 | | | 8 |
| Fri | 8.50 | 12.00 | 12.35 | 5.30 | 6.00 | 9.00 | 11 |
| Sat | | | | | | | |
| Sun | | | | | | | |
| Total normal hours | | | | | | | 40 |
| Total overtime hours | | | | | | | 3 |
| Sick/annual leave | | | | | | | — |
| Total hours | | | | | | | 43 |

## Time books

Time books (or timesheets, as they are commonly termed) are typically used by salaried employees who need to account for their time in a specific manner. For example, an employee working in a service business, such as a public accounting firm, will record the time spent on jobs for each individual client, on a daily basis. Some time books, however, merely require a signature verifying total hours of attendance by the employee.

In some situations, such as with particular salaried employees, no formal attendance records are maintained. In these circumstances, the total number of normal hours worked is assumed and any variation would need to be authorised by the use of a special form (such as an *overtime authority form* or *leave application form*).

# Awards, individual contracts and enterprise agreements

For payroll purposes it is necessary to be aware of individual employees' terms and conditions of employment, such as hours of work, pay rates, allowances, leave and other entitlements. These can be determined by reference to industrial awards, individual employment agreements and enterprise agreements.

## Awards

Employees in many industries are covered by industrial awards, which are either federal or state awards. An *award* is a determination, handed down by the relevant state or federal body, which stipulates the terms and conditions of employment, including work hours, rates of pay, annual leave, long service leave and so on. An award covers employees in a particular industry (such as the metal industry or building industry) or occupational group (for example, shop assistants or teachers), and is legally binding on both the employer and the employee.

## Individual agreements

Alternatively, an employee's terms and conditions of employment may be determined by an *individual employment contract* or agreement. In this situation the employment terms and conditions are determined by the parties (employer and individual employee) and set out in a written contract. Such agreements are legally binding and override any applicable award, although where the agreement is silent on a particular matter the relevant award provision, if any, continues to apply. Further, if the employer wishes to include provisions in the employment contract not covered by an award, the contract may need to be submitted to the Fair Work Commission for review and approval.

## Enterprise agreements

Employment terms and conditions may also be determined by enterprise bargaining. *Enterprise bargaining* involves negotiations between employer and employees, culminating in a *certified agreement* covering all employees, or a group of employees, within an enterprise or workplace.

 **EXERCISES**

7.1     Malcolm Soprano, an employee of Protection Services Ltd, is concerned about details on his latest pay advice slip; in particular, his hourly rate of pay and the amount of tax withheld.
    a   To whom should Malcolm direct an enquiry in relation to his concerns?
    b   Which sections or departments of the business are likely to be involved in providing an answer to Malcolm's enquiry?

7.2     What are the objectives of a system of control over payroll? Discuss.

7.3  Briefly summarise the typical internal control measures that should be present in a payroll system.

7.4  In a payroll system, what records need to be kept for each employee? Discuss.

7.5  What is an award? How does it differ from an individual or enterprise agreement? Discuss.

# Wages schemes

Depending on the particular industrial award or agreement, there may be a number of methods used in calculating employee entitlements. We will briefly consider the main methods of calculating pay entitlements.

## Salary

As previously mentioned, a salary is normally an annual figure, which is converted by formula to a *pay period* basis. In the following examples for instance, annual salaries are converted to a weekly and fortnightly basis:

### Example 1

R McDonald is entitled to a salary of $75 946 per annum and is paid weekly. To calculate the entitlement on a weekly basis, simply divide the annual salary by 52 (number of whole weeks in the year).

$$
\begin{aligned}
\text{Salary} &= \$75\,946 \text{ p.a.} \\
\text{Weekly salary} &= \frac{\$75\,946}{52} \\
&= \$1\,460.50
\end{aligned}
$$

### Example 2

J Stewart is entitled to a salary of $124 800 per annum and is paid fortnightly. To calculate the entitlement on a fortnightly basis divide the annual salary by 26 (number of whole fortnights in the year).

$$
\begin{aligned}
\text{Salary} &= \$124\,800 \text{ p.a.} \\
\text{Fortnightly salary} &= \frac{\$124\,800}{26} \\
&= \$4\,800.00
\end{aligned}
$$

## Hourly rates

An employee paid on this basis receives wage entitlements calculated by multiplying the number of hours worked by the basic rate of pay per hour. For example:

In the case of M Nickos, 35 hours were worked for the pay period ending 8 July 2019. The hourly rate of pay is $24.50.

$$
\begin{aligned}
\text{Wage entitlement} &= 35 \text{ hours} \times \$24.50 \\
&= \$857.50
\end{aligned}
$$

For hours worked beyond the normal weekly agreement, an *overtime rate* of pay is applied. Overtime rates are stipulated in the appropriate award or agreement applicable to the employee. We will consider the following rates of overtime.

1 Overtime at normal rates   In this situation, additional hours worked are paid at the normal rates. For example:

M Nickos works an additional hour (8.00–9.00 a.m.) at the commencement of the working week, which, according to the award applicable to M Nickos, is payable at normal rates. The overtime payment for the week is calculated by multiplying the extra hour by the hourly rate: $1 \times \$24.50 = \$24.50$.

2 Overtime at penalty rates   In this situation, additional hours worked are paid at a penalty rate which is achieved by adding a 'premium' to each overtime hour worked. For example:

- Time and a half (one-and-a-half times the standard rate)   Thus, in the previous case of M Nickos, if four additional hours were worked (at time-and-a-half), the overtime payment would be calculated as shown below.

$$\text{Penalty rate} = 1\tfrac{1}{2} \times 4 = 6 \text{ hours}$$
$$\text{Overtime} \quad = 6 \text{ hours} \times \$24.50$$
$$= \$147.00$$

In this case, a premium of 50% has been added to each overtime hour worked.

- Double time (two times the standard rate)   Thus, in the previous example of M Nickos, if four additional hours were worked (at double time), the overtime pay would be calculated as follows:

$$\text{Penalty rate} = 2 \times 4 = 8 \text{ hours}$$
$$\text{Overtime} \quad = 8 \text{ hours} \times \$24.50$$
$$= \$196.00$$

In this case, a premium has been added by doubling each overtime hour worked.

- Triple time (three times the standard rate)   For certain awards and agreements, employees may be entitled to receive triple time for working on public holidays.

# Commission

In this situation, an employee's entitlement is a percentage of sales made or fees earned during the period.

For example, O Olsten is employed by a real estate agent and receives a 1% commission on monthly sales. Sales for the month of July were $600 000. Commission payment for July is calculated as follows.

$$\text{Sales} = \$600\,000 \times 1\%$$
$$= \$6\,000.00$$

# Retainer/commission

In this situation, the pay entitlement for an employee is a fixed retainer (salary) plus a fixed percentage of sales (commission).

Using the previous example of O Olsten, let us assume that an annual retainer of $12 000 is also paid. Payment to the employee for July would be calculated as follows.

| | |
|---|---|
| Annual salary | $12 000 |
| ÷ No. of months (12) | |
| = Monthly salary | $1 000 |
| *plus* Commission | |
| (as calculated above) | $6 000 |
| Total payment to employee | $7 000 |

## Piece rate

An employee is paid at a set rate for each item produced. For example:

| | |
|---|---|
| Items produced | 1200 |
| Rate per item | 80 cents |
| Gross wage | $= 1200 \times 80$ cents |
| | $= \$960$ |

## Other schemes

Some businesses use a variety of incentive payment schemes to maintain and increase production. These range from bonuses, safety achievements and efficiency awards to profit-sharing arrangements for employees.

# Special employee benefits

## Employee entitlements

Industrial awards and employment agreements provide for a range of entitlements, including some or all of those listed below.

- Sick leave Paid leave while an employee is ill. Normally an employee is entitled to between 10 and 15 days per year as sick leave.
- Carer's leave Paid leave to care for a family member who is ill. Carer's leave taken is normally deducted from sick leave entitlements.
- Annual leave pay Normally four weeks per annum
- Annual leave loading Normally 17.5% of four weeks' annual leave pay
- Long service leave Normally three months' leave after 10 or 15 years' service
- Bereavement leave Normally granted on the death of a family member
- Study leave Paid leave enabling employees to attend school, college or university
- Parental leave Paid or unpaid leave for a woman or her partner to care for a newborn or adopted child
- Jury service Paid leave while on jury service.

## Fringe benefits

Employers will often provide employees with certain fringe benefits in lieu of salary. These benefits can take many forms, including the use of a company car, access to low-interest loans, subsidised accommodation, payment of club memberships and subscriptions.

## EXERCISES

**7.6** If a supervisor earns a salary of $52 000 per year, what is her fortnightly salary?

**7.7*** A mechanic is paid at the rate of $22.50 per hour plus time and a half for the first four hours' overtime and double time thereafter. If the normal working week is 38 hours, what will be his weekly earnings if he worked 46 hours for the week?

**7.8** A sales representative is paid $1000 per month plus 5% commission on monthly sales. What would the month's earnings be if sales for the month were $100 000?

**7.9*** A manufacturing company pays its employees a base salary of $300 per week plus $0.50 per unit for each unit over the minimum production of 5000 units per week. If an employee produces 7200 units in a week, what will be her gross earnings?

## SOLUTIONS

| 7.7 | Ordinary earnings | $ |
|---|---|---|
| | 38 hours @ $22.50 | 855.00 |
| | Overtime earnings | |
| | (1.5 × 4 hours) @ $22.50 | 135.00 |
| | (2 × 4 hours) @ $22.50 | 180.00 |
| | | $1 170.00 |
| | | |
| 7.9 | Base salary | 300.00 |
| | Piece rate | |
| | (7200 − 5000) @ $0.50 | 1 100.00 |
| | | $1 400.00 |

# Tax withheld from wages and salaries

The *Pay As You Go* (PAYG) system of tax collection requires all employers to withhold income tax from employees' wages and salaries at the appropriate rate.

The amount to be withheld is set out in a table entitled *NAT 1005 Weekly tax table*. Schedules are also available with fortnightly and monthly rates. Figure 7.5 shows the weekly table dated 1 July 2012 (current at the time of writing). Note that tax rates change regularly, so it is important to obtain the most recent version of tax rates. We further note that solutions to exercises in this chapter are based on 1 July 2012 rates.

473

# Tax File Number Declaration and Withholding Declaration

The amount of tax to be withheld depends on the employee's income and whether or not the employee has lodged a *Tax File Number Declaration* form with the employer. This form is reproduced as Figure 7.6. Where tax offsets are to be claimed, the employee must also complete a *Withholding Declaration* form and lodge it with the employer. This form is reproduced as Figure 7.7.

A Tax File Number Declaration should be lodged with each separate employer. The information provided in this form affects tax instalments in the following ways.

1  Tax file number  If an employee does not provide a tax file number on the Tax File Number Declaration form, tax will be withheld at a higher rate of tax. Refer to item 1 on the Tax File Number Declaration form.

2  Tax-free threshold  The employee can choose whether to claim the tax-free threshold or not. If the employee elects not to claim the threshold, tax will be withheld at a higher rate. If an employee has more than one employer, only one tax-free threshold can be claimed. The tax-free threshold will also not apply if the employee has not lodged a Tax File Number Declaration form or has not quoted a tax file number on that form. Refer to item 8 on the Tax File Number Declaration form.

3  HELP  Where the employee has an outstanding debt under the Higher Education Loan Program (HELP), extra tax is withheld. Refer to item 11 on the Tax File Number Declaration form.

4  Tax offsets (rebates)  Some employees may be entitled to a tax offset (rebate of tax). Tax offsets reduce the amount of tax withheld. An employee wanting to claim tax offsets must also complete a withholding declaration form. Refer to item 10 on the Tax File Number Declaration form and items 9 and 10 on the Withholding Declaration form.

# Higher education loan program

As already mentioned, additional tax is withheld where the employee has a HELP debt. The additional amounts to be withheld are set out in the table *Pay as you go NAT 2173 Higher Education Loan Program (HELP) weekly tax table*. The rates applicable from 1 July 2012, which were current at the time of writing, are reproduced in Figure 7.8.

# Tax offsets

(The following information may be found on the ATO website http://www.ato.gov.au.)

As part of the 2012–13 Budget, the federal government announced a new tax offset: the Dependant (invalid and carer) tax offset. This new offset consolidated eight dependency tax offsets into a single, streamlined and non-refundable tax offset from 1 July 2012. As this consolidated offset is based on the highest rate of the previous offsets that have been replaced, eligible taxpayers may benefit from an increased entitlement. Those who were eligible to claim more than one offset amount for multiple dependants under the old system can still do so.

The tax offsets that have been consolidated are:

- invalid spouse tax offset
- carer spouse tax offset
- housekeeper tax offset
- housekeeper (with child) tax offset
- child-housekeeper tax offset
- child-housekeeper (with child) tax offset
- invalid relative tax offset
- parent/parent-in-law tax offsets.

The Dependant (invalid and carer) tax offset is available to those taxpayers who maintain a dependant who is genuinely unable to work due to invalidity or carer obligations. Tax offsets are no longer available for a child-housekeeper, child-housekeeper (with child), housekeeper or housekeeper (with child), as those dependants do not meet the requirement of being genuinely unable to work.

If a dependent spouse was born on or after 1 July 1952, it may no longer be possible to claim the dependent spouse tax offset, which is being phased out as the population ages.

Taxpayers may still be eligible to claim more than one tax offset amount for multiple dependants. For example, a taxpayer who maintains an invalid spouse and an invalid parent-in-law may receive both the invalid spouse and the invalid parent-in-law tax offsets.

The Dependant (invalid and carer) tax offset is equal to the highest value existing dependency tax offset, which was $2423 in 2012–13, and will be indexed annually in line with CPI.

A detailed examination of the eligibility criteria for each of the tax offsets is beyond the scope of this book.

An employee's entitlement to an offset is affected by the income of the dependant(s) concerned. The calculation of the actual offset entitlement is also beyond the scope of this book.

Other tax offsets exist for a range of situations, including a zone tax offset for persons living in remote areas of Australia, an overseas defence forces tax offset for defence personnel involved in overseas service and an overseas civilian tax offset An examination of these tax offsets is beyond the scope of this book.

# Medicare levy variation

The Weekly tax table (see Figure 7.5) includes the Medicare levy. The Medicare levy, at the time of writing, was levied at the rate of 1.5% of taxable income. The tax tables upon which examples in this text are based apply for the 2013–14 tax year and include the levy at 1.5%. However, from 1 July 2014 this rate increases to 2.0%.

Some employees, such as low-income earners, are entitled to an exemption or reduction in the Medicare levy. An employee seeking a variation in the Medicare levy must complete a *Medicare levy variation declaration form* (see Figure 7.9) and lodge it with the employer. To calculate the amount to be withheld from salaries and wages, the employer must then subtract the amount of the Medicare levy adjustment (determined from the *Medicare levy adjustment weekly tax table*) from the weekly PAYG amount otherwise applicable.

In all examples and exercises in this chapter, it is assumed that the full Medicare levy is payable.

# Calculation of PAYG income tax to be withheld from salaries and wages

The amount of PAYG income tax to be withheld from an employee's wages or salary is determined by reference to:

- *Weekly tax table*
- *Higher Education Loan Program (HELP) weekly tax table*, and
- the employee's Tax File Number Declaration and Withholding Declaration, if any.

To calculate the amount to be withheld from an employee's salary or wages:

1 from the employee's Tax File Number Declaration (if lodged), ascertain whether the employee has:
   - provided a Tax File Number
   - claimed the tax-free threshold
   - a HELP debt
   - claimed any tax offsets
2 determine the amount to be withheld from the *Weekly tax table*
3 if the employee has a HELP debt, work out the HELP component from the *Higher Education Loan Program (HELP) weekly tax table* and add this amount to the amount to be withheld
4 where the employee has claimed tax offsets, determine the total amount of these from the employee's Withholding Declaration
5 determine the weekly value of the tax offsets from the *Ready reckoner for tax offsets* (contained in the *Weekly tax table*) and deduct this amount from the amount to be withheld.

In summary, the amount to be withheld is calculated as follows:

$$\begin{aligned} \text{PAYG withholding} = {} & \text{amount to be withheld} \\ & + \text{HELP component (if any)} \\ & - \text{tax offsets (if any)} \end{aligned}$$

Figure 7.10 further illustrates the procedure for calculating the PAYG amount to be withheld from wages and salaries.

UWATCH 7.1

## Examples of calculation of PAYG withholding amounts

A UWatch demonstration is available on the CD that accompanies this text for parts of this activity.

### Example 1

J Sauvig earned $720 gross for the week. She has lodged a tax file number declaration with her employer, giving her tax file number and claiming the tax-free threshold. Tax withheld would be $82.00.

| Weekly earnings | With tax-free threshold | No tax-free threshold |
|---|---|---|
| 1 | 2 | 3 |
| $ | $ | $ |
| 716 | 80.00 | 201.00 |
| 717 | 81.00 | 201.00 |
| 718 | 81.00 | 201.00 |
| 719 | 81.00 | 202.00 |
| 720 | (82.00) | 202.00 |

## Example 2

T Frontig earned $840 gross for the week. He did not provide a tax file number declaration (and so no tax file number has been quoted). The tax to be withheld is $390.00. This is calculated as 46.5% of $840 and includes a Medicare levy of 1.5%. However, from 1 July 2014 the levy increases to 2.0%.

$840 × 46.5% = $390 (ignoring cents)

## Example 3

A Fields earned $568 for the week. She has lodged a tax file number declaration but has not claimed the tax-free threshold. Tax withheld would be $150.00.

| | | |
|---|---|---|
| 566 | 49.00 | 149.00 |
| 567 | 49.00 | 149.00 |
| 568 | 49.00 | (150.00) |
| 569 | 49.00 | 150.00 |
| 570 | 50.00 | 150.00 |

## Example 4

S Freud earned $1461.70 for the week. He has lodged a tax file number declaration, providing his tax file number and claiming the tax-free threshold. He has a HELP debt. He has also lodged a withholding declaration, claiming tax offsets of $2500. Tax withheld would be calculated as follows:

| | | |
|---|---|---|
| 1461 | (335.00) | 467.00 |
| 1462 | 335.00 | 467.00 |
| 1463 | 336.00 | 467.00 |
| 1464 | 336.00 | 468.00 |
| 1465 | 336.00 | 468.00 |

| | | |
|---|---|---|
| Amount withheld | $335.00 | |
| *add* HELP component | 88.00 | see Figure 7.8 (HELP weekly tax table) |
| | $423.00 | |
| *less* Tax offsets weekly value | 48.00 | see Figure 7.10 (Ready reckoner) |
| Total amount withheld | $375.00 | |

Note that the HELP component is not added and the tax offsets are not deducted if the employee has not provided his or her tax file number.

## Example 5

S Hussein earned $700 gross for the week. He has lodged a tax file number declaration, claiming the tax-free threshold, but has not provided his tax file number. He has also lodged a withholding declaration, claiming tax offsets of $1400. The tax to be withheld is $325.00 (46.5% of $700).

In this example, because the employee has not provided his tax file number, he is not entitled to an adjustment for tax offsets. The same applies if he has not claimed the tax-free threshold.

$700 × 46.5% = $325 (ignoring cents)

# PAYG withholding – special situations

## Annual leave

The calculation of PAYG withholding tax for an employee taking annual leave or long service leave will depend on the method by which the employee is paid while on leave. Some businesses pay employees in advance for the period of the leave. Others pay the employee each week while the employee is on leave; that is, the employee continues to receive a weekly pay during the leave period.

## Employee paid each week while on leave

Where the employee is paid each week while on leave, PAYG withholding is calculated in the normal manner.

## Employee paid in advance

Where the employee is paid in advance for the full period of the leave, it is necessary to calculate tax on one week's leave and multiply the weekly result by the number of weeks leave taken.

For example, Ho Won Cha is taking four weeks' annual leave, with payment made in advance prior to his going on leave. He has lodged a tax file number declaration with his employer, giving his tax file number and claiming the tax-free threshold. The amount of tax to be withheld from his annual leave pay would be calculated as follows:

| | |
|---|---|
| Tax on one week's pay (i.e. tax on $800) | $109.00 |
| Total amount withheld ($109.00 × 4) | $436.00 |

## Annual leave loading

## Leave loading changes

There is no longer a separate withholding scale for employees who are entitled to leave loading and they will no longer have higher withholding from every pay. These payees will now be taxed more accurately when the leave loading is paid.

Previously, the leave loading scale provided for extra withholding throughout the year to allow $320 of leave loading to be tax-free when paid.

If leave loading is paid as a lump sum, it is now necessary to use the relevant *Tax tables for back payments, commissions, bonuses and similar payments* (NAT 3348) to calculate withholding amounts of tax.

If leave loading is paid on a pro-rata basis, then it is necessary to add the leave loading payment to earnings for the period to calculate the withholding amount. That is, instead of the one lump sum payment, multiple payments are made during the year when leave is being taken.

For example, M Sheen's gross pay for the week ending 28 October 2018 is $1280. In addition she is taking annual leave for the next two weeks and is to be paid, in advance, two weeks' annual leave pay plus 17.5% annual leave loading. She has lodged a tax file number declaration with her employer, giving her tax file number and claiming the tax-free threshold.

Her total gross earnings for the week are calculated as follows:

| | |
|---|---:|
| Gross pay w/e 28 October 2018 | $1 280.00 |
| Annual leave pay $1280 × 2 weeks | 2 560.00 |
| Annual leave loading 17.5% × $2560 | 448.00 |
| Total gross earnings | $4 288.00 |

Sheen is taking two weeks' annual leave, so her leave loading must be apportioned over two weeks. Therefore $224.00 ($448.00 × ÷ 2) must be added to each week's annual leave pay for the purposes of determining the amount of tax to be withheld.

The amount of tax to be withheld is calculated as follows:

| | | |
|---|---:|---:|
| Tax on gross pay w/e 28 October 2018: | | |
| ($1280.00 column 2) | | $274.00 |
| Tax on annual leave and annual leave loading | | |
| Annual leave pay per week | $1 280.00 | |
| *add* Excess leave loading per week ($448 ÷ 2) | 224.00 | |
| | $1 504.00 | |
| Tax on $1504.00, column 2 | 350.00 | |
| Multiplied by 2 | | 700.00 |
| Total tax to be withheld | | $974.00 |

# Long service leave

The taxation of long service leave payments is treated in a similar manner to annual leave except that no loading applies to long service leave payments.

# Lump sum annual leave and long service leave

Upon termination of employment, an employee is paid (in a lump sum) any annual leave, annual leave loading and long service leave entitlements unused at the date of termination.

The calculation of PAYG withholding from these amounts is complex and beyond the scope of this text. Advice should be sought from the Australian Taxation Office prior to processing such payments.

# Eligible termination payments

In simple terms, an eligible termination payment (ETP) is any payment made on termination of employment other than wages and salaries, lump sum annual leave and lump sum long service leave.

The calculation of PAYG withholding from eligible termination payments is complex and beyond the scope of this text. Advice should be sought from the Australian Taxation Office prior to processing such payments.

 **EXERCISES**

In each of the following exercises, determine the PAYG withholding amount for the week. Assume, unless otherwise stated, that each employee has lodged a tax file number declaration, giving his or her tax file number, and has claimed the tax-free threshold.

7.10    V Barbarino earned $550.

7.11    L Sim earned $980. She has not provided her tax file number.

7.12    I Burnett earned $1250. He has not claimed the tax-free threshold.

7.13    J Garfoot earned $956. She has a HELP debt.

7.14    A Alt earned $764. He has claimed tax offsets totalling $1320.

7.15    P Daley earned $1240. He has not provided his tax file number and has claimed tax offsets totalling $2250.

7.16*   G Flowers earned $1520. He has claimed tax offsets totalling $2325. He also has a HELP debt.

7.17    L Watts earned $2120.

7.18    J Andrews earned $1200. He has a HELP debt.

7.19    B Hall had gross earnings for the week of $520, including $30 overtime. She is also to be paid, in advance, two weeks' annual leave plus 17.5% annual leave loading. This is the first time she has taken annual leave in the current financial year.

7.20    L Rose had gross earnings for the week of $1226, including $300 overtime. She is also to be paid, in advance, three weeks' annual leave plus 17.5% annual leave loading.

7.21*   A Raeburn had gross earnings for the week of $1300, including $100 overtime. He is also to be paid, in advance, two weeks' annual leave plus 17.5% annual leave loading. He has claimed tax offsets totalling $1606.

**SOLUTIONS**

| 7.16 | | $ | $ |
|---|---|---|---|
| | Tax on $1520.00 | 355.00 | |
| | *add* HELP component | 99.00 | |
| | | 454.00 | |
| | *less* Tax offsets weekly value | 44.00 | |
| | Total amount to be withheld | $410.00 | |

| 7.21 | | | $ |
|---|---|---|---|
| | Gross earnings for week | | 1 300.00 |
| | Annual leave pay | | 2 400.00 |
| | (excludes overtime of $100)    2 weeks × $1200.00 | | |
| | Annual leave loading        17.5% × $2400.00 | | 420.00 |
| | Total gross earnings | | 4 120.00 |
| | Tax on gross earnings for the week | | |
| | $1300.00, column 2 | 280.00 | |
| | *less* Tax offsets weekly value | 30.00 | 250.00 |
| | Tax on annual leave | | |
| | Annual leave pay per week | 1 200.00 | |
| | *add* Leave loading per week ($420 ÷ 2) | 210.00 | |
| | | 1 410.00 | |
| | Tax on $1410.00, column 2 | 318.00 | |
| | *less* Tax offsets weekly value | 30.00 | |
| | | 288.00 | |
| | Multiplied by 2 | | 576.00 |
| | Total tax to be withheld | | $826.00 |

# Other deductions

An employer may be authorised by an employee to make other deductions from the employee's pay; for example, union dues, superannuation, health insurance premiums, savings and social club dues.

Generally, apart from income tax, no other deductions should be made from an employee's pay unless the employee has provided the employer with a signed authority for each deduction.

# Payroll preparation

The preparation of the payroll will normally require access to the following information:

- clock cards, timesheets etc.
- employee history cards
- weekly tax tables, HELP weekly table
- Medicare levy variation declaration form.

Gross pay is calculated by multiplying the hours worked by the pay rate per hour, as shown in the employee history card. Tax is calculated by reference to the employee history card (which shows whether the employee has claimed the tax-free threshold, provided a tax file number and claimed tax offsets) and the tax tables listed above. Other deductions are also shown in the employee history card.

Net pay is determined by subtracting all deductions, including tax, from gross pay.

## Example

A Poustie worked 42 hours for the week. His pay rate is $24 per hour. The normal working week is 38 hours and overtime is paid at time-and-a-half. He has claimed the tax-free threshold and provided a tax file number. He has authorised the following weekly deductions: union dues $10 and superannuation $40.

| | | $ | $ |
|---|---|---:|---:|
| Gross pay | | | |
| Ordinary | 38 hours @ $24 | 912.00 | |
| Overtime | (1.5 × 4 hours) @ $24 | 144.00 | |
| | | | 1 056.00 |
| Deductions | | | |
| Tax | | 197.00 | |
| Union | | 10.00 | |
| Superannuation | | 40.00 | 247.00 |
| Net pay | | | $809.00 |

## Pay slip

A pay slip is prepared for each employee giving details of his or her gross pay, deductions and net pay for the pay period. This is provided to the employee each pay period after the payroll has been processed, either in hardcopy form or electronic form.

## Payroll register

The payroll register is a summary of the payroll for the period. It is also referred to as the payroll summary, payroll sheet or a similar name.

| | Gross earnings | | | Deductions | | | | Net pay |
|---|---|---|---|---|---|---|---|---|
| | Ord | O'time | Total | Tax | Med | Union | Total | |
| **Employee** | $ | $ | $ | $ | $ | $ | $ | $ |
| R Scott | 800.00 | 80.00 | 880.00 | 136.00 | 60.00 | 10.00 | 206.00 | 674.00 |
| D Jones | 640.00 | | 640.00 | 64.00 | | 10.00 | 74.00 | 566.00 |
| M Lower | 1 030.00 | 188.00 | 1 218.00 | 252.00 | 40.00 | | 292.00 | 926.00 |
| | 2 470.00 | 268.00 | 2 738.00 | 452.00 | 100.00 | 20.00 | 572.00 | 2 166.00 |

**Star Enterprises**
**Payroll register for week ending 14 July 2019**

The payroll register forms the basis for the accounting entries to record the payroll. Payroll accounting entries are dealt with later in this chapter.

# Employee earnings records

Once the payroll has been completed the employee earnings records are updated with the payroll details for the period. The details of each employee's pay, as shown in the payroll register, are updated to the relevant employee earnings record.

Using the payroll register above, the employee earnings record for R Scott would appear as shown below. (Note that the payroll figures for the week ending 7 July have been assumed.)

**Employee earnings record**

Name: Robert Scott

Employee no: 456

Address: 2 Railway Pde, Geelong 3220

| Week ending | Gross pay | Deductions | | | | Net pay | Accumulated figures | | | |
|---|---|---|---|---|---|---|---|---|---|---|
| | | Tax | Med | Union | Total | | Gross | Tax | Med | Union |
| 2019 | $ | $ | $ | $ | $ | $ | $ | $ | $ | $ |
| 7 Jul | 800.00 | 109.00 | 60.00 | 10.00 | 179.00 | 621.00 | 800.00 | 109.00 | 60.00 | 10.00 |
| 14 Jul | 880.00 | 136.00 | 60.00 | 10.00 | 206.00 | 674.00 | 1 680.00 | 245.00 | 120.00 | 20.00 |

# Payroll payment

Employees can receive their wages and salaries in a number of ways, as discussed below.

## Cash

Since the emergence of electronic banking, the payment of wages and salaries in cash is rare. However, where employees are actually paid in cash, a cheque is generally drawn for the total amount of the wages. The cheque is cashed and the proceeds are used to make up pay envelopes.

Prior to cashing the payroll cheque it is necessary to prepare a coinage analysis to determine the exact number of each denomination of notes and coins required.

The coinage analysis for Star Enterprises for the week ending 14 July 2019 is as follows:

| | | Notes | | | | | Coins | | | | | |
|---|---|---|---|---|---|---|---|---|---|---|---|---|
| Employee | Net pay | $100 | $50 | $20 | $10 | $5 | $2 | $1 | 50c | 20c | 10c | 5c |
| R Scott | 674.00 | 6 | 1 | 1 | | | 2 | | | | | |
| D Jones | 566.00 | 5 | 1 | | 1 | 1 | | 1 | | | | |
| M Lower | 926.00 | 9 | | 1 | | 1 | | 1 | | | | |
| No. of units | | 20 | 2 | 2 | 1 | 2 | 2 | 2 | | | | |
| Value $ | | 2 000 | 100 | 40 | 10 | 10 | 4 | 2 | | | | |
| Total $ | 2 166.00 | | | 2 160.00 | | | | | 6.00 | | | |

## Cheque

Where employees are paid by cheque it is necessary to prepare a cheque payable to each employee. However, as with the payment of wages in cash, the payment of wages and salaries by cheque has also become relatively uncommon.

## Credit to employee's bank account

Most employers pay their employees' wages and salaries directly into each employee's personal bank account. A prerequisite for this type of arrangement is for the employee to provide the employer with written authority, specifying the bank and the branch where the employee's account is held, together with the employee's account number.

Where a business pays wages and salaries by direct credit it must submit details of its employees' earnings and bank account details to its bank each pay period. It would normally transmit this information electronically via its Internet banking software. On receipt of this information the bank will debit the business's bank account with the total earnings and then disburse the appropriate amounts to employees' bank accounts by electronic funds transfer (EFT). Once the bank has processed an employee's pay the employee is free to draw upon it.

## Comprehensive example

Tuft's Building Supplies processes its payroll weekly.

a  Complete the payroll register for the week ending 14 March 2019.
b  Update the individual earnings record for Jay Bernstein.

*Employee history cards*

| | No. 1 |
|---|---|
| Jay Bernstein | |
| 14 High St | |
| MOOROOPNA | |
| | |
| Tax file no. | |
| Tax-free threshold | Yes |
| HELP debt | Yes |
| Salary | $78 000 p.a. |
| Deductions (per week) | |
| Union | $12.00 |
| Superannuation | $75.00 |

| | No. 2 |
|---|---|
| Alice Lu | |
| 153 Low St | |
| SHEPPARTON | |
| | |
| Tax file no. | 444 444 444 |
| Tax offsets | $1340 |
| Tax-free threshold | Yes |
| Rate | $22.00 per hour |
| Deductions (per week) | |
| Union | $12.00 |
| Superannuation | $50.00 |

| | No. 3 |
|---|---|
| Rachel Harding | |
| 2 McKenzie St | |
| KYABRAM | |
| | |
| Tax file no. | 777 777 777 |
| Tax offsets | $3603 |
| Tax-free threshold | Yes |
| Rate | $28.00 per hour |
| Deductions (per week) | |
| Union | $12.00 |
| Superannuation | $50.00 |

*Additional information*

Employees normally work a 40-hour week. Hours worked in excess of 40 per week are paid at time and a half. Jay Bernstein is the supervisor and is not entitled to overtime.

Hours worked for the week ending 14 March 2019 were:

| | | | |
|---|---|---|---|
| Jay Bernstein | 42 | | |
| Alice Lu | 36 | plus | 8 hours' sick leave |
| Rachel Harding | 45 | plus | 2 hours' unauthorised leave to attend a funeral |

Alice Lu is taking annual leave and is to be paid two weeks' annual leave plus 17.5% annual leave loading in addition to her normal pay for the week ending 14 March 2019. She has not previously taken any annual leave in the current financial year.

All employees are entitled to annual leave loading.

The business pays its wages and salaries by direct credit to employees' bank accounts

# Solution

a

| Payroll register for week ending 14 March 2019 | | | | |
|---|---|---|---|---|
| | **Employee** | | | |
| | **J Bernstein** | **A Lu** | **R Harding** | **Total** |
| | $ | $ | $ | $ |
| Ordinary | 1 500.00 | 880.00 | 1 120.00 | 3 500.00 |
| Overtime | | 132.00 | 210.00 | 342.00 |
| Annual leave | | 1 760.00 | | 1 760.00 |
| Leave loading | | 308.00 | | 308.00 |
| GROSS PAY | 1 500.00 | 3 080.00 | 1 330.00 | 5 910.00 |
| Tax | 697.00 | 482.00 | 223.00 | 1 402.00 |
| Superannuation | 75.00 | 150.00 | 50.00 | 275.00 |
| Union | 12.00 | 36.00 | 12.00 | 60.00 |
| Total deductions | 784.00 | 668.00 | 285.00 | 1 737.00 |
| NET PAY | 716.00 | 2 412.00 | 1 045.00 | 4 173.00 |

*Calculation of tax*

| | $ | $ | $ |
|---|---|---|---|
| J Bernstein | | | |
| Tax on $1500 (No TFN 46.5% × $1500) | | | 697.50 |
| *add* HELP component (no HELP where TFN not quoted) | | | NIL |
| | | | $697.50 |
| | | | |
| A Lu | | | |
| Tax on ($880 + $132 = $1012) | | 182.00 | |
| *less* Tax offsets weekly value | | 26.00 | 156.00 |
| Tax on annual leave and annual leave loading | | | |
| Annual leave pay per week | 880.00 | | |
| *add* Leave loading per week ($308 ÷ 2) | 154.00 | | |
| | 1 034.00 | | |
| | | | |
| Tax on $1034 | | 189.00 | |
| *less* Tax offsets weekly value . | | 26.00 | |
| | | 163.00 | |
| Multiply by 2 | | | 326.00 |
| | | | $482.00 |
| | | | |
| R Harding | | | |
| Tax on ($1120 + $210 = $1330) | | | 291.00 |
| *less* Tax offsets weekly value | | | 68.00 |
| | | | $223.00 |

## Explanations

- Three weeks' superannuation and union dues have been deducted from A Lu's pay to cover the period she is on leave.
- A Lu has been paid for eight hours' sick leave. This has been included in her ordinary gross pay. This assumes that she has sufficient accumulated sick leave available.
- R Harding has not been paid for the two hours taken to attend a funeral, as this was not authorised leave.

b

| | | | | | | | | | | |
|---|---|---|---|---|---|---|---|---|---|---|
| **Employee earnings record** | | | | | | | | | | |

**Name:** Jay Bernstein  **Employee No: 456**

**Address:** 14 High Street, Mooroopna

| | Gross | Deductions | | | | | Accumulated figures | | | |
|---|---|---|---|---|---|---|---|---|---|---|
| **Week** | **pay** | **Tax** | **Super** | **Union** | **Total** | **Net pay** | **Gross** | **Tax** | **Super** | **Union** |
| 2019 | $ | $ | $ | $ | $ | $ | $ | $ | $ | $ |
| 7 Mar* | | | | | | | 53 500.00 | 24 877.00 | 2 625.00 | 420.00 |
| 14 Mar | 1 500.00 | 697.00 | 75.00 | 12.00 | 784.00 | 716.00 | 55 000.00 | 25 574.00 | 2 700.00 | 432.00 |

*Accumulated balances assumed

## EXERCISES

**Note** In all exercises, unless otherwise specified, all employees are entitled to annual leave loading.

**ADDITIONAL
EXERCISES**

7.22 The following information relates to Outback Caravan Sales. You are required to:

  a  prepare the payroll registers for the weeks ending 6, 13, 20 and 27 September 2017

  b  complete the individual earnings record for Paulene Piper.

  This exercise is also available in a MYOB format on the CD that accompanies the workbook.

*Information extracted from time cards*

| Employee | 7 Sep | 14 Sep | 21 Sep | 28 Sep |
|---|---|---|---|---|
| P Piper | | | | |
|     Ord hrs | 40 | 40 | 40 | 40 |
|     O'time hrs | 3 | – | – | 3 |
| B Peep | | | | |
|     Ord hrs | 40 | 40 | 40 | 40 |
|     O'time hrs | 6 | 5 | – | 5 |
| B Blue | | | | |
|     Ord hrs | 40 | 40 | 40 | 40 |
|     O'time hrs | – | 2 | – | 4 |

*Employee history cards*

|  | No. 1 |
|---|---|
| Paulene Piper | |
| 23 Brash St | |
| MILL PARK | |
| | |
| | |
| Tax file no. | 333 333 333 |
| Tax-free threshold | No |
| Rate | $24.00 per hour |
| Deductions (per week) | |
|   Union | $10.00 |
|   Superannuation | 5% of ordinary gross earnings |

|  | No. 2 |
|---|---|
| Brian Peep | |
| 14 High St | |
| RESERVOIR | |
| | |
| Tax offsets | $1606 |
| Tax file no. | 444 444 444 |
| Tax-free threshold | Yes |
| Rate | $30.00 per hour |
| Deductions (per week) | |
|   Union | $10.00 |

|  | No. 3 |
|---|---|
| Brendan Blue | |
| 235 Myop St | |
| YARRA GLEN | |
| | |
| Tax offsets | $2840 |
| Tax file no. | 555 555 555 |
| Tax-free threshold | Yes |
| HELP debt | Yes |
| Rate | $30.00 per hour |
| Deductions (per week) | |
|   Union | $10.00 |
|   Superannuation | 5% of ordinary gross earnings |

*Additional information*

- The business pays its wages and salaries by direct credit to employees' bank accounts. Normal hours are 40 per week.
- Overtime is paid at time and a half.
- The individual earnings record for Paulene Piper at 31 August 2017 is shown below.

| Employee earnings record | | | | | | | | | | |
|---|---|---|---|---|---|---|---|---|---|---|
| **Name:** Paulene Piper | | | | | | **Employee No: 1** | | | | |
| **Address:** 23 Brash Street, Mill Park | | | | | | | | | | |
| **Week** | **Gross** | **Deductions** | | | | | **Accumulated figures** | | | |
| **ending** | **pay** | **Tax** | **Super** | **Union** | **Total** | **Net pay** | **Gross** | **Tax** | **Super** | **Union** |
| 2017 | $ | $ | $ | $ | $ | $ | $ | $ | $ | $ |
| 31 Aug | | | | | | | 7 680.00 | 2 272* | 384.00 | 80.00 |

*$960 per week tax (col 3) = $284 × 8 weeks

7.23    This question is available on the CD that accompanies this text.

7.24*   Bright Spark Electrical Services processes its payroll weekly. You are required to complete the payroll register for the week ending 30 June 2018.

ADDITIONAL
EXERCISES

*Employee history cards*

| Employee name | Employee name | Employee name |
|---|---|---|
| Britt Eckland | Ryan Redgrave | Kanit Wanachote |
| Hourly rate $30.00 | Hourly rate $24.00 | Hourly rate $36.00 |
| Tax offsets $2800 | | HELP debt Yes |
| Tax-free threshold Yes | Tax-free threshold Yes | Tax-free threshold Yes |
| Weekly deductions | Weekly deductions | Weekly deductions |
| Superannuation $60.00 | Superannuation $50.00 | Superannuation Nil |
| Medical $70.00 | Medical $48.00 | Medical Nil |
| Union $10.00 | Union Nil | Union $10.00 |

*Additional information*

- Overtime is paid at time and a half on all hours in excess of 35 per week.
- Details of hours worked for week ended 30 June 2018 are as shown.

| | |
|---|---|
| Eckland | 42 hours |
| Redgrave | 40 hours |
| Wanachote | { 30 hours |
| | 8 hours' sick leave |

- Eckland will be taking three weeks' annual leave, so her pay will include annual leave pay (plus a 17.5% annual leave loading).
- All employees receive a travelling allowance of $100 per week. This allowance is not taxed and is not paid while an employee is on leave.
- All employees have provided a tax file number.

 **SOLUTION**

7.24

| | | | | | | | | | | | | |
|---|---|---|---|---|---|---|---|---|---|---|---|---|
| **BRIGHT SPARK ELECTRICAL SERVICES** | | | | | | | | | | | | |
| **Payroll register for week ending 30 June 2018** | | | | | | | | | | | | |
| | Gross earnings | | | | | | Deductions | | | | | |
| **Employee** | **Ord** | **O/T** | **Annual leave** | **A/L load'g** | **Other** | **Total** | **Tax** | **Med** | **Union** | **Super** | **Total** | **Net pay** |
| | $ | $ | $ | $ | $ | $ | $ | $ | $ | $ | $ | $ |
| B Eckland | 1 050.00 | 315.00 | 3 150.00 | 551.00 | 100.00 | 5 166.00 | 857.00 | 280.00 | 40.00 | 240.00 | 1 417.00 | 3 749.00 |
| R Redgrave | 840.00 | 180.00 | | | 100.00 | 1 120.00 | 184.00 | 48.00 | | 50.00 | 282.00 | 838.00 |
| K Wanachote | 1 260.00 | 162.00 | | | 100.00 | 1 522.00 | 407.00 | | 10.00 | | 417.00 | 1 105.00 |
| Total | 3 150.00 | 657.00 | 3 150.00 | 551.00 | 300.00 | 7 808.00 | 1 448.00 | 328.00 | 50.00 | 290.00 | 2 116.00 | 5 692.00 |

*Calculation of tax*

| B Eckland | $ | $ | $ |
|---|---|---|---|
| Tax on earnings for week ended 30 June 2018 | | | |
| $1365.00, column 2 | | 302.00 | |
| *less* Tax offsets weekly value | | 54.00 | 248.00 |
| Tax on annual leave and leave loading | | | |
| Annual leave pay per week | 1 050.00 | | |
| *add* Leave loading per week ($551 ÷ 3) | 183.00 | | |
| | 1 233.00 | | |
| Tax on $1233.00, column 2 | | 257.00 | |
| *less* Tax offsets weekly value | | 54.00 | |
| | | 203.00 | |
| Multiplied by 3 | | | 609.00 |
| Total tax to be withheld | | | $857.00 |
| | | | |
| R Redgrave | | | |
| Tax on $1020.00, column 2 | | | $184.00 |
| | | | |
| K Wanachote | | | |
| Tax on $1422.00, column 2 | | | 322.00 |
| *add* HELP component | | | 85.00 |
| Total amount withheld | | | $407.00 |

# Payroll accounting entries

From an accounting point of view there are two aspects to payroll.

1   The cost of wages and salaries is an *expense* to the business. The expense is the gross amount of the payroll, as this represents the total cost to the business of wages and salaries.
2   Payroll creates several *liabilities*. The deductions from employees' wages and salaries are payable to the relevant authorities. For example, PAYG withholding is payable to the Australian Taxation Office, union dues are payable to the relevant union and superannuation is payable to the appropriate superannuation fund. The net wages are payable to the employees of the business.

The accounting entries relating to payroll consist of:

- General Journal entries to record the payroll and associated liabilities for the period
- Cash Payments Journal entries to record the payment of the wages
- Cash Payments Journal entries to record the payment of the associated liabilities at regular intervals.

## Comprehensive example

The payroll registers for Tuft's Building Supplies for the month of March 2017 are provided below. Complete the General Journal, Cash Payments Journal and General Ledger entries relating to payroll for this period.

| Payroll register for week ending 7 March 2017 | | | |
|---|---|---|---|
| | Employee | | |
| | J Bernstein | A Lu | R Harding | Total |
| | $ | $ | $ | $ |
| Ordinary | 1 500.00 | 880.00 | 1 120.00 | 3 500.00 |
| Overtime | | 66.00 | | 66.00 |
| Annual leave | | | | |
| Leave loading | | | | |
| Long service leave | | | | |
| GROSS PAY | 1 500.00 | 946.00 | 1 120.00 | 3 566.00 |
| Tax | 697.00 | 133.00 | 151.00 | 981.00 |
| Superannuation | 75.00 | 50.00 | 50.00 | 175.00 |
| Union | 12.00 | 12.00 | 12.00 | 36.00 |
| Total deductions | 784.00 | 195.00 | 213.00 | 1 192.00 |
| NET PAY | 716.00 | 751.00 | 907.00 | 2 374.00 |

| Payroll register for week ending 14 March 2017 | | | |
|---|---|---|---|
| | Employee | | |
| | J Bernstein | A Lu | R Harding | Total |
| | $ | $ | $ | $ |
| Ordinary | 1 500.00 | 880.00 | 1 120.00 | 3 500.00 |
| Overtime | | 132.00 | 210.00 | 342.00 |
| Annual leave | | 1 760.00 | | 1 760.00 |
| Leave loading | | 308.00 | | 308.00 |
| Long service leave | | | | |
| GROSS PAY | 1 500.00 | 3 080.00 | 1 330.00 | 5 910.00 |
| Tax | 697.00 | 482.00 | 223.00 | 1 402.00 |
| Superannuation | 75.00 | 150.00 | 50.00 | 275.00 |
| Union | 12.00 | 36.00 | 12.00 | 60.00 |
| Total deductions | 784.00 | 668.00 | 285.00 | 1 737.00 |
| NET PAY | 716.00 | 2 412.00 | 1 045.00 | 4 173.00 |

| Payroll register for week ending 21 March 2017 | | | |
| --- | --- | --- | --- |
| | Employee | | |
| | J Bernstein | A Lu | R Harding | Total |
| | $ | $ | $ | $ |
| Ordinary | 1 500.00 | | 1 120.00 | 2 620.00 |
| Overtime | | | | |
| Annual leave | | | | |
| Leave loading | | | | |
| Long service leave | | | | |
| GROSS PAY | 1 500.00 | | 1 120.00 | 2 620.00 |
| Tax | 697.00 | | 151.00 | 848.00 |
| Superannuation | 75.00 | | 50.00 | 125.00 |
| Union | 12.00 | | 12.00 | 24.00 |
| Total deductions | 784.00 | | 213.00 | 997.00 |
| NET PAY | 716.00 | | 907.00 | 1 623.00 |

| Payroll register for week ending 28 March 2017 | | | |
| --- | --- | --- | --- |
| | Employee | | |
| | J Bernstein | A Lu | R Harding | Total |
| | $ | $ | $ | $ |
| Ordinary | 1 500.00 | | 1 120.00 | 2 620.00 |
| Overtime | | | | |
| Annual leave | | | | |
| Leave loading | | | | |
| Long service leave | | | 4 480.00 | 4 480.00 |
| GROSS PAY | 1 500.00 | | 5 600.00 | 7 100.00 |
| Tax | 697.00 | | 755.00 | 1 452.00 |
| Superannuation | 75.00 | | 250.00 | 325.00 |
| Union | 12.00 | | 60.00 | 72.00 |
| Total deductions | 784.00 | | 1 065.00 | 1 849.00 |
| NET PAY | 716.00 | | 4 535.00 | 5 251.00 |

*Additional information*
- Cheques for PAYG withholding, superannuation and union dues deducted from employees' wages and salaries are forwarded to the relevant body on the last day of the month.
- Employees are paid by direct credit to their bank accounts each week.

# Solution

| | General Journal | | | |
|---|---|---|---|---|
| **Date** | **Particulars** | **Fol** | **Debit** | **Credit** |
| 2017 | | | $ | $ |
| 7 Mar | Wages expense | | 3 566 | |
| | PAYG withholding payable | | | 981 |
| | Superannuation payable | | | 175 |
| | Union dues payable | | | 36 |
| | Wages payable | | | 2 374 |
| | *Payroll and associated liabilities for week ending 7 March 2017* | | | |
| 14 | Wages expense | | 3 842 | |
| | Provision for annual leave | | 2 068 | |
| | PAYG withholding payable | | | 1 402 |
| | Superannuation payable | | | 275 |
| | Union dues payable | | | 60 |
| | Wages payable | | | 4 173 |
| | *Payroll and associated liabilities for week ending 14 March 2017* | | | |
| 21 | Wages expense | | 2 620 | |
| | PAYG withholding payable | | | 848 |
| | Superannuation payable | | | 125 |
| | Union dues payable | | | 24 |
| | Wages payable | | | 1 623 |
| | *Payroll and associated liabilities for week ending 21 March 2017* | | | |
| 28 | Wages expense | | 2 620 | |
| | Provision for long service leave | | 4 480 | |
| | PAYG withholding payable | | | 1 452 |
| | Superannuation payable | | | 325 |
| | Union dues payable | | | 72 |
| | Wages payable | | | 5 251 |
| | *Payroll and associated liabilities for week ending 28 March 2017* | | | |

## Cash Payments Journal

| Date | Particulars | Fol | Ref | Discount income: Accounts payable control | Discount income: GST paid | Discount income: Discount income | Accounts payable control | Cash purchases | Wages | Sundries: Amount | Sundries: Account | GST paid | Bank |
|------|-------------|-----|-----|------|------|------|------|------|------|------|------|------|------|
| 2017 | | | | $ | $ | $ | $ | $ | $ | $ | | $ | $ |
| 7 Mar | Wages payable | | EFT | | | | | | 2 374 | | | | 2 374 |
| 14 | Wages payable | | EFT | | | | | | 4 173 | | | | 4 173 |
| 21 | Wages payable | | EFT | | | | | | 1 623 | | | | 1 623 |
| 28 | Wages payable | | EFT | | | | | | 5 251 | | | | 5 251 |
| 31 | PAYG withholding payable | | 101 | | | | | | | 4 683 | PAYG withholding payable | | 4 683 |
| | Super-annuation payable | | 102 | | | | | | | 900 | Super-annuation payable | | 900 |
| | Union dues payable | | 103 | | | | | | | 192 | Union dues payable | | 192 |
| | | | | | | | | | $13 421 | $5 775 | | | $19 196 |

## General Ledger

| Date | Particulars | Fol | Debit | Credit | Balance |
|------|-------------|-----|-------|--------|---------|
| **Wages Expense Account** | | | | | |
| 2017 | | | $ | $ | $ |
| 1 Mar | Balance (assumed) | | | | 90 000 Dr |
| 7 | Sundries | GJ | 3 566 | | 93 566 Dr |
| 14 | Sundries | GJ | 3 842 | | 97 408 Dr |
| 21 | Sundries | GJ | 2 620 | | 100 028 Dr |
| 28 | Sundries | GJ | 2 620 | | 102 648 Dr |
| **PAYG Withholding Payable Account** | | | | | |
| 2017 | | | | | |
| 7 Mar | Wages expense | GJ | | 981 | 981 Cr |
| 14 | Sundries | GJ | | 1 402 | 2 383 Cr |
| 21 | Wages expense | GJ | | 848 | 3 231 Cr |
| 28 | Sundries | GJ | | 1 452 | 4 683 Cr |
| 31 | Bank | CPJ | 4 683 | | Nil |

| | | | | | |
|---|---|---|---|---|---|
| | | | | **General Ledger** | |

| Date | Particulars | Fol | Debit | Credit | Balance |
|---|---|---|---|---|---|
| | | | | | |
| **Superannuation Payable Account** | | | | | |
| 2017 | | | $ | $ | $ |
| 7 Mar | Wages expense | GJ | | 175 | 175 Cr |
| 14 | Sundries | GJ | | 275 | 450 Cr |
| 21 | Wages expense | GJ | | 125 | 575 Cr |
| 28 | Sundries | GJ | | 325 | 900 Cr |
| 31 | Bank | CPJ | 900 | | Nil |
| **Union Dues Payable Account** | | | | | |
| 2017 | | | | | |
| 7 Mar | Wages expense | GJ | | 36 | 36 Cr |
| 14 | Sundries | GJ | | 60 | 96 Cr |
| 21 | Wages expense | GJ | | 24 | 120 Cr |
| 28 | Sundries | GJ | | 72 | 192 Cr |
| 31 | Bank | CPJ | 192 | | Nil |
| **Wages Payable Account** | | | | | |
| 2017 | | | | | |
| 7 Mar | Wages expense | GJ | | 2 374 | 2 374 Cr |
| 14 | Sundries | GJ | | 4 173 | 6 547 Cr |
| 21 | Wages expense | GJ | | 1 623 | 8 170 Cr |
| 28 | Sundries | GJ | | 5 251 | 13 421 Cr |
| 31 | Bank | CPJ | 13 421 | | Nil |
| **Provision for Annual Leave Account** | | | | | |
| 2017 | | | | | |
| 1 Mar | Balance (assumed) | | | | 20 000 Cr |
| 14 | Sundries | GJ | 2 068 | | 17 932 Cr |
| **Provision for Long Service Leave Account** | | | | | |
| 2017 | | | | | |
| 1 Mar | Balance (assumed) | | | | 15 000 Cr |
| 28 | Sundries | GJ | 4 480 | | 10 520 Cr |
| **Cash at Bank Account** | | | | | |
| 2017 | | | | | |
| 1 Mar | Balance (assumed) | | | | 40 000 Dr |
| 31 | Payments | CPJ | | 19 196 | 20 804 Dr |

**Explanations**

- In the General Journal, the entry on 14 March shows a debit to the Provision for Annual Leave account, and the entry on 28 March shows a debit to the Provision for Long Service Leave account. These entries represent the totals of the annual leave and long service leave payments to A Lu and R Harding for those weeks.

- The Provision for Annual Leave and Provision for Long Service Leave accounts are credited at the end of each accounting period to reflect the future liability of employers for unused leave entitlements. While outside the scope of this text, there are important accounting standards in Australia (specifically AASB119 – Employee Benefits, and AASB137 – Provisions, Contingent Liabilities and Contingent Assets) that prescribe the accounting treatment of employee entitlements. For example, AASB119 requires long service leave entitlements that are to be paid in the future should be recognised as liabilities in the current financial statements. AASB137 also requires provisions relating to employee entitlements to be recognised as liabilities.

- When an employee takes annual or long service leave, it is necessary to reduce the balance of the relevant provision account, as the business's future liability for leave payments has been reduced. Thus a debit is made to the relevant provision account to reflect this reduction in liability.

 **EXERCISES**

**7.25** Using the payroll registers prepared for Exercise 7.22, you are required to:
- a prepare the General Journal entries to record the payroll and associated liabilities for each of the four weeks
- b prepare the Cash Payments Journal entries to record the payment of the payroll for each of the four weeks and to pay the PAYG withholding tax, superannuation and union dues at the end of the month
- c post the journal entries in **a** and **b** to the General Ledger.

**7.26** Below are the payroll registers for Rex Wholesalers for the month of February 2018. You are required to:
- a prepare the General Journal and Cash Payments Journal entries to record the payroll for each of the four weeks
- b prepare the Cash Payments Journal entries to pay the payroll liabilities
- c post the journal entries in **a** and **b** to the General Ledger.

| | Payroll register for week ending 6 February 2018 | | | | | | | |
|---|---|---|---|---|---|---|---|---|
| | **Gross earnings** | | | **Deductions** | | | | |
| **Employee** | **Gross wage** | **Annual leave** | **Total** | **Tax** | **Med** | **Union** | **Total** | **Net pay** |
| | $ | $ | $ | $ | $ | $ | $ | $ |
| M Wallis | 1 240.00 | | 1 240.00 | 260.00 | 50.00 | 10.00 | 320.00 | 920.00 |
| D Peacock | 1 160.00 | | 1 160.00 | 232.00 | | 10.00 | 242.00 | 918.00 |
| P Hiscock | 920.00 | | 920.00 | 150.00 | 40.00 | 10.00 | 200.00 | 720.00 |
| | 3 320.00 | | 3 320.00 | 642.00 | 90.00 | 30.00 | 762.00 | 2 558.00 |

| Payroll register for week ending 13 February 2018 | | | | | | | |
|---|---|---|---|---|---|---|---|
| | Gross earnings | | | Deductions | | | |
| Employee | Gross wage | Annual leave | Total | Tax | Med | Union | Total | Net pay |
| | $ | $ | $ | $ | $ | $ | $ | $ |
| M Wallis | 1 240.00 | 60.00 | 1 300.00 | 260 | 50.00 | 10.00 | 320.00 | 980.00 |
| D Peacock | 1 160.00 | | 1 160.00 | 232.00 | | 10.00 | 242.00 | 918.00 |
| P Hiscock | 920.00 | | 920.00 | 150.00 | 40.00 | 10.00 | 200.00 | 720.00 |
| | 3 320.00 | 60.00 | 3 380.00 | 642.00 | 90.00 | 30.00 | 762.00 | 2 618.00 |

| Payroll register for week ending 20 February 2018 | | | | | | | |
|---|---|---|---|---|---|---|---|
| | Gross earnings | | | Deductions | | | |
| Employee | Gross wage | Annual leave | Total | Tax | Med | Union | Total | Net pay |
| | $ | $ | $ | $ | $ | $ | $ | $ |
| M Wallis | 1 240.00 | | 1 240.00 | 260.00 | 50.00 | 10.00 | 320.00 | 920.00 |
| D Peacock | 1 160.00 | | 1 160.00 | 232.00 | | 10.00 | 202.00 | 918.00 |
| P Hiscock | 920.00 | 1 081.00 | 2 001.00 | 355.00 | 80.00 | 20.00 | 455.00 | 1 546.00 |
| | 3 320.00 | 1 081.00 | 4 401.00 | 847.00 | 130.00 | 40.00 | 977.00 | 3 384.00 |

| Payroll register for week ending 27 February 2018 | | | | | | | |
|---|---|---|---|---|---|---|---|
| | Gross earnings | | | Deductions | | | |
| Employee | Gross wage | Long service leave | Total | Tax | Med | Union | Total | Net pay |
| | $ | $ | $ | $ | $ | $ | $ | $ |
| M Wallis | 1 240.00 | | 1 240.00 | 260.00 | 50.00 | 10.00 | 320.00 | 920.00 |
| D Peacock | 1 160.00 | 4 640.00 | 5 800.00 | 1 160.00 | | 50.00 | 1 210.00 | 4 590.00 |
| | 2 400.00 | 4 640.00 | 7 040.00 | 1 420.00 | 50.00 | 60.00 | 1 530.00 | 5 510.00 |

*Additional information*

- Assume the following General Ledger account balances at 1 February.

| | |
|---|---|
| Cash at Bank | $19 850 Dr |
| Provision for Annual Leave | 36 500 Cr |
| Provision for Long Service Leave | 32 200 Cr |
| Wages Expense | 90 200 Dr |

- Payroll liabilities are paid on the last day of the month.
- Employees are paid by direct credit to their bank accounts each week.

7.27*  Laidler Distributors has provided the following payroll information for the month of August 2019. You are required to:

a  prepare the General Journal and Cash Payments Journal entries to record the payroll for each of the four weeks

b  prepare the Cash Payments Journal entries to pay the payroll liabilities

c  post the journal entries in **a** and **b** to the General Ledger.

| Payroll register for week ending 6 August 2019 | | | | |
|---|---|---|---|---|
| | **Employee** | | | |
| | **F Zurcas** | **J Dooley** | **R Murphy** | **Total** |
| | $ | $ | $ | $ |
| Ordinary | 840.00 | 800.00 | 960.00 | 2 600.00 |
| Overtime | 90.00 | 60.00 | | 150.00 |
| Car allowance | 80.00 | | | 80.00 |
| GROSS PAY | 1 010.00 | 860.00 | 960.00 | 2 830.00 |
| Tax | 181.00 | 130.00 | 164.00 | 475.00 |
| Superannuation | 40.00 | | 50.00 | 90.00 |
| Social club | 10.00 | 10.00 | | 20.00 |
| Union | 10.00 | 10.00 | | 20.00 |
| Total deductions | 241.00 | 150.00 | 214.00 | 605.00 |
| NET PAY | 769.00 | 710.00 | 746.00 | 2 225.00 |

| Payroll register for week ending 13 August 2019 | | | |
|---|---|---|---|
| | **Employee** | | **Total** |
| | **F Zurcas** | **J Dooley** | **R Murphy** | |
| | $ | $ | $ | $ |
| Ordinary | 840.00 | 800.00 | 960.00 | 2 600.00 |
| Overtime | | 80.00 | 60.00 | 140.00 |
| Car allowance | 80.00 | | | 80.00 |
| GROSS PAY | 920.00 | 880.00 | 1 020.00 | 2 820.00 |
| Tax | 150.00 | 136.00 | 184.00 | 470.00 |
| Superannuation | 40.00 | | 50.00 | 90.00 |
| Social club | 10.00 | 10.00 | | 20.00 |
| Union | 10.00 | 10.00 | | 20.00 |
| Total deductions | 210.00 | 156.00 | 234.00 | 600.00 |
| NET PAY | 710.00 | 724.00 | 786.00 | 2 220.00 |

| Payroll register for week ending 20 August 2019 | | | |
|---|---|---|---|
| | **Employee** | | **Total** |
| | **F Zurcas** | **J Dooley** | **R Murphy** | |
| | $ | $ | $ | $ |
| Ordinary | 840.00 | 800.00 | 960.00 | 2 600.00 |
| Overtime | 90.00 | 60.00 | | 150.00 |
| Car allowance | 80.00 | | | 80.00 |
| GROSS PAY | 1 010.00 | 860.00 | 960.00 | 2 830.00 |
| Tax | 181.00 | 130.00 | 164.00 | 475.00 |
| Superannuation | 40.00 | | 50.00 | 90.00 |
| Social club | 10.00 | 10.00 | | 20.00 |
| Union | 10.00 | 10.00 | | 20.00 |
| Total deductions | 241.00 | 150.00 | 214.00 | 605.00 |
| NET PAY | 769.00 | 710.00 | 746.00 | 2 225.00 |

| Payroll register for week ending 27 August 2019 | | | |
|---|---|---|---|
| | Employee | | Total |
| | F Zurcas | J Dooley | R Murphy | |
| | $ | $ | $ | $ |
| Ordinary | 840.00 | 800.00 | 960.00 | 2 600.00 |
| Overtime | 90.00 | 80.00 | | 170.00 |
| Car allowance | 80.00 | | | 80.00 |
| Annual leave | | | 2 256.00 | 2 256.00 |
| Long service leave | | | 3 840.00 | 3 840.00 |
| GROSS PAY | 1 010.00 | 880.00 | 7 056.00 | 8 946.00 |
| Tax | 181.00 | 136.00 | 1 262.00 | 1 579.00 |
| Superannuation | 40.00 | | 350.00 | 390.00 |
| Social club | 10.00 | 10.00 | | 20.00 |
| Union | 10.00 | 10.00 | | 20.00 |
| Total deductions | 241.00 | 156.00 | 1 612.00 | 2 009.00 |
| NET PAY | 769.00 | 724.00 | 5 444.00 | 6 937.00 |

## Additional information

- Assume the following General Ledger account balances at 1 August.

| | |
|---|---|
| Cash at Bank | $21 500 Dr |
| Provision for Annual Leave | 32 500 Cr |
| Provision for Long Service Leave | 32 700 Cr |
| Wages Expense | 12 000 Dr |

- Payroll liabilities are paid on the last day of the month.
- Employees are paid by cheque each week.

## SOLUTION

**7.27 a**

|  |  |  |  |  |
|---|---|---|---|---|
| | **Laidler Distributors**<br>**General Journal** | | | |
| **Date** | **Particulars** | **Fol** | **Debit** | **Credit** |
| 2019 | | | $ | $ |
| 6 Aug | Wages expense | | 2 830 | |
| | PAYG withholding payable | | | 475 |
| | Superannuation payable | | | 90 |
| | Social club payable | | | 20 |
| | Union dues payable | | | 20 |
| | Wages payable | | | 2 225 |
| | *Payroll and associated liabilities for week ending 6 August 2019* | | | |
| 13 | Wages expense | | 2 820 | |
| | PAYG withholding payable | | | 470 |
| | Superannuation payable | | | 90 |
| | Social club payable | | | 20 |
| | Union dues payable | | | 20 |
| | Wages payable | | | 2 220 |
| | *Payroll and associated liabilities for week ending 13 August 2019* | | | |
| 20 Aug | Wages expense | | 2 830 | |
| | PAYG withholding payable | | | 475 |
| | Superannuation payable | | | 90 |
| | Social club payable | | | 20 |
| | Union dues payable | | | 20 |
| | Wages payable | | | 2 225 |
| | *Payroll and associated liabilities for week ending 20 August 2019* | | | |
| 27 | Wages expense | | 2 850 | |
| | Provision for annual leave | | 2 256 | |
| | Provision for long service leave | | 3 840 | |
| | PAYG withholding payable | | | 1 579 |
| | Superannuation payable | | | 390 |
| | Social club payable | | | 20 |
| | Union dues payable | | | 20 |
| | Wages payable | | | 6 937 |
| | *Payroll and associated liabilities for week ending 27 August 2019* | | | |

b

| | | | | **Cash Payments Journal (simplified)** | | | | | | | |
|---|---|---|---|---|---|---|---|---|---|---|---|
| | | | | Accounts payable control | Cash purchases | Wages | Sundries | | GST paid | Bank |
| Date | Particulars | Fol | Ref | | | | Amount | Account | | |
| 2019 | | | | $ | $ | $ | $ | | $ | $ |
| 6 Aug | F Zurcas | | 101 | | | 769 | | | | 769 |
| | J Dooley | | 102 | | | 710 | | | | 710 |
| | R Murphy | | 103 | | | 746 | | | | 746 |
| 13 | F Zurcas | | 104 | | | 710 | | | | 710 |
| | J Dooley | | 105 | | | 724 | | | | 724 |
| | R Murphy | | 106 | | | 786 | | | | 786 |
| 20 | F Zurcas | | 107 | | | 769 | | | | 769 |
| | J Dooley | | 108 | | | 710 | | | | 710 |
| | R Murphy | | 109 | | | 746 | | | | 746 |
| 27 | F Zurcas | | 110 | | | 769 | | | | 769 |
| | J Dooley | | 111 | | | 724 | | | | 724 |
| | R Murphy | | 112 | | | 5 444 | | | | 5 444 |
| 31 | PAYG withholding payable | | 113 | | | | 2 999 | PAYG withholding payable | | 2 999 |
| | Superannuation payable | | 114 | | | | 660 | Superannuation payable | | 660 |
| | Social club payable | | 115 | | | | 80 | Social club payable | | 80 |
| | Union dues payable | | 116 | | | | 80 | Union dues payable | | 80 |
| | | | | | | $13 607 | $3 819 | | | $17 426 |

c

| | | **General Ledger** | | | | |
|---|---|---|---|---|---|---|
| Date | Particulars | | Fol | Debit | Credit | Balance |
| | | **Wages Expense Account** | | | | |
| 2019 | | | | $ | $ | $ |
| 1 Aug | Balance | | | | | 12 000 Dr |
| 6 | Sundries | | GJ | 2 830 | | 14 830 Dr |
| 13 | Sundries | | GJ | 2 820 | | 17 650 Dr |
| 20 | Sundries | | GJ | 2 830 | | 20 480 Dr |
| 27 | Sundries | | GJ | 2 850 | | 23 330 Dr |

| General Ledger | | | | | |
|---|---|---|---|---|---|
| Date | Particulars | Fol | Debit | Credit | Balance |
| **PAYG Withholding Payable Account** | | | | | |
| 2019 | | | $ | $ | $ |
| 6 Aug | Wages expense | GJ | | 475 | 475 Cr |
| 13 | Wages expense | GJ | | 470 | 945 Cr |
| 20 | Wages expense | GJ | | 475 | 1 420 Cr |
| 27 | Sundries | GJ | | 1 579 | 2 999 Cr |
| 31 | Bank | CPJ | 2 999 | | Nil |
| **Superannuation Payable Account** | | | | | |
| 2019 | | | | | |
| 6 Aug | Wages expense | GJ | | 90 | 90 Cr |
| 13 | Wages expense | GJ | | 90 | 180 Cr |
| 20 | Wages expense | GJ | | 90 | 270 Cr |
| 27 | Sundries | GJ | | 390 | 660 Cr |
| 31 | Bank | CPJ | 660 | | Nil |
| **Social Club Payable Account** | | | | | |
| 2019 | | | | | |
| 6 Aug | Wages expense | GJ | | 20 | 20 Cr |
| 13 | Wages expense | GJ | | 20 | 40 Cr |
| 20 | Wages expense | GJ | | 20 | 60 Cr |
| 27 | Sundries | GJ | | 20 | 80 Cr |
| 31 | Bank | CPJ | 80 | | Nil |
| **Union Dues Payable Account** | | | | | |
| 2019 | | | | | |
| 6 Aug | Wages expense | GJ | | 20 | 20 Cr |
| 13 | Wages expense | GJ | | 20 | 40 Cr |
| 20 | Wages expense | GJ | | 20 | 60 Cr |
| 27 | Sundries | GJ | | 20 | 80 Cr |
| 31 | Bank | CPJ | 80 | | Nil |

| Date | Particulars | Fol | Debit | Credit | Balance |
|------|-------------|-----|-------|--------|---------|
| | General Ledger | | | | |
| | **Wages Payable Account** | | | | |
| 2019 | | | $ | $ | $ |
| 6 Aug | Wages expense | GJ | | 2 225 | 2 225 Cr |
| 13 | Wages expense | GJ | | 2 220 | 4 445 Cr |
| 20 | Wages expense | GJ | | 2 225 | 6 670 Cr |
| 27 | Sundries | GJ | | 6 937 | 13 607 Cr |
| 31 | Bank | CPJ | 13 607 | | Nil |
| | **Provision for Annual Leave Account** | | | | |
| 2019 | | | | | |
| 1 Aug | Balance | | | | 32 500 Cr |
| 27 | Sundries | GJ | 2 656 | | 29 844 Cr |
| | **Provision for Long Service Leave Account** | | | | |
| 2019 | | | | | |
| 1 Aug | Balance | | | | 32 700 Cr |
| 27 | Sundries | GJ | 3 840 | | 28 860 Cr |
| | **Cash at Bank Account** | | | | |
| 2019 | | | | | |
| 1 Aug | Balance | | | | 21 500 Dr |
| 13 | Payments | CPJ | | 17 426 | 4 074 Dr |

# PAYG withholding – employer registration

For PAYG withholding purposes, an employer must apply to the ATO for registration. Application must be made by the first day on which the employer is required to withhold an amount from employees' wages or salaries.

## Remittance of PAYG withholding

PAYG withheld from employees' wages and salaries must be remitted regularly to the ATO. The due date depends on whether the business is classified as a:

- small withholder
- medium withholder, or
- large withholder.

# Small withholder

A business is a small withholder if it withheld $25 000 or less in the previous financial year. A small withholder must remit PAYG withheld to the ATO quarterly, within 28 days of the end of the quarter, with an extension of one month applicable to the December quarter. The due dates are as follows:

| Quarter ended | Due date |
|---|---|
| 30 September | 28 October |
| 31 December | 28 February |
| 31 March | 28 April |
| 30 June | 28 July |

# Medium withholder

A medium withholder is a business that withheld more than $25 000 but not more than $1 million in the previous financial year. A medium withholder must remit PAYG withheld on a monthly basis within 21 days of the end of the month.

# Large withholder

A large withholder is a business that withheld more than $1 million in the previous financial year. Special rules apply to the remittance of PAYG withheld by large withholders. The rules can be summarised as follows:

| Date amount withheld | Due date |
|---|---|
| Saturday or Sunday | The second Monday after that day |
| Monday or Tuesday | The first Monday after that day |
| Wednesday | The second Thursday after that day |
| Thursday or Friday | The first Thursday after that day |

# Business Activity Statement

In addition to remitting PAYG withheld from salaries and wages, businesses must also pay various other amounts to the ATO. Some examples are:

- GST
- income tax instalments (called PAYG instalments)
- fringe benefits tax instalments
- other PAYG withholding amounts, including amounts withheld from payments to suppliers who have not quoted an Australian Business Number (ABN), amounts withheld from payments to contractors under voluntary agreements and amounts withheld under labour hire agreements.

Reporting and payment of these amounts (including PAYG withheld from wages and salaries) are included on a single form called a *Business Activity Statement* (BAS). Figure 7.11 shows a Business Activity Statement with the sections that relate to PAYG withheld from wages and salaries circled.

Special arrangements apply for the remittance of PAYG withheld by large withholders. These are not dealt with here as they are beyond the scope of this text. The ATO can provide details of these arrangements if required.

# Employer's year-end responsibilities

An employer must furnish each employee with a *PAYG payment summary – individual non-business* form by 14 July. This form details the total payments made to the employee and the total PAYG withheld, and is used by the employee to complete his or her income tax return. Businesses can choose to use the form provided by the ATO (see Figure 7.12) or can print their own in accordance with ATO specifications.

In the case of eligible termination payments (ETPs), a separate payment summary must be prepared for each such payment.

By 14 August the employer must submit a *PAYG Payment Summary Statement* to the ATO. This report includes a summary of all payments from which PAYG has been withheld and must be accompanied by copies of all payment summaries issued for the financial year.

# Other matters relating to payroll

From an accounting viewpoint there are three other matters related to payroll that require further discussion. These are payroll tax, workers' compensation (WorkCover) and the Superannuation Guarantee.

Each of these areas is legally complex and this text cannot give an in-depth coverage of the legal aspects. Rather, the nature of each is briefly explained, followed by a detailed explanation of the accounting treatment.

## Payroll tax

Each state and territory has legislation that imposes a payroll tax on employers. The amount of tax payable is based on the employer's gross annual payroll. The rate of payroll tax and the exemption levels vary between states and territories.

## Workers' compensation/WorkCover

In each of the states and territories, employers are required to pay workers' compensation premiums or levies.

When an employee is unable to work due to a work-related injury the employee is paid compensation to cover loss of earnings. The amount of compensation is usually a fixed percentage of the pre-injury earnings subject to a maximum upper limit. The compensation to injured workers is paid out of the premiums or levies paid by employers.

# Superannuation Guarantee

The *Superannuation Guarantee (Administration) Act 1992* (Cth) and the *Superannuation Guarantee Charge Act 1992* (Cth) require all employers to make superannuation contributions for each of their employees.

At the time of writing the legislation requires that the employer contribute 9.25% of each employee's normal gross earnings to a superannuation fund on behalf of the employee. The compulsory amount is changing over the next few years. By the year 2020 the amount contributed by the employer will have increased to 12% with small increases each year from now until then. The aim is to provide benefits, in the form of a pension or a lump sum, to the employee on retirement. The prescribed contribution rate is the minimum requirement. Employers may contribute at higher rates.

If an employer fails to make the required contribution for each employee, a *Superannuation Guarantee Charge* is imposed by the Australian Taxation Office. This consists of any shortfall in contributions together with an administration fee and an interest component.

Employees may also make superannuation contributions on their own behalf. These can either be paid direct by the employee or, as is generally the case, be deducted from pay each week.

# Accounting treatment

To be consistent with the *accrual concept of accounting* and the *matching process*, the expenses (and corresponding liabilities etc.) for payroll tax, workers' compensation and employer superannuation contributions should be recognised at the time they are incurred as distinct from the time at which they are paid.

The expenses are recognised in the same month as the payroll to which they relate. This will not normally be the month in which they are paid. Payments are made as shown below.

- *Payroll tax* Payment is required by the seventh day of the following month.
- *Workers' compensation* An annual premium, based on the employer's estimated total payroll, is paid annually in advance. This 'prepaid' premium is subsequently allocated as an expense monthly, based on the wages expense for each month. Businesses can choose to pay the premiums by instalment either monthly or quarterly.
- *Superannuation guarantee* Employers are required to pay the minimum contribution to a 'complying fund' within 28 days of the end of each quarter.

Therefore the accounting entries consist of:

- General Journal entries to record the expenses and associated entries in the month in which the expenses are incurred
- Cash Payments Journal entries to record the payment of the liabilities.

# Comprehensive example

Morgan Developments' gross payroll for the month of November 2018 is $62 500. This figure consists of $57 500 normal gross earnings and $5000 overtime earnings.

At the time of writing, in Victoria, payroll tax is payable at the rate of 4.9% on the excess of the gross monthly payroll over $45 833. For the purposes of this example, assume that workers' compensation (WorkCover) is payable at the rate of 5% of total gross monthly payroll. Employer superannuation contributions are made at the rate of 11.5% (this is be the rate that will be applicable in November 2018) of the normal gross earnings of each employee.

Expenses (and associated entries) for payroll tax, workers' compensation and employer superannuation contributions are recorded at the end of each month. Payroll tax is paid by the seventh day of the following month, workers' compensation is paid annually in advance and employer superannuation contributions are paid quarterly.

The expense figures for Morgan Developments for the month of November 2018 would be calculated as shown below.

Payroll tax
4.90% × ($62 500 − $45 833)                    $816.68

Workers' compensation
5% × $62 500                                   $3 125.00

Superannuation
11.5% × $57 500                                $6 612.00

The General Journal and ledger entries relating to these expenses appear below.

| Date | Particulars | Fol | Debit | Credit |
|------|-------------|-----|-------|--------|
| | General Journal | | | |
| 2018 | | | $ | $ |
| 30 Nov | Payroll tax expense | | 816.68 | |
| |     Payroll tax payable | | | 816.68 |
| | *Payroll tax for November 2018* | | | |
| | Workers' compensation expense | | 3 125.00 | |
| |     Workers' compensation prepaid | | | 3 125.00 |
| | *Workers' compensation for November 2018* | | | |
| | Superannuation expense | | 6 612.00 | |
| |     Superannuation payable | | | 6 612.00 |
| | *Employer superannuation contributions for November 2018* | | | |

### Cash Payments Journal (simplified)

| Date | Particulars | Fol | Ref | Accounts payable control | Cash purchases | Wages | Sundries | | GST paid | Bank |
|------|-------------|-----|-----|--------------------------|----------------|-------|----------|---------|----------|------|
| | | | | | | | Amount | Account | | |
| 2018 | | | | $ | $ | $ | $ | | $ | $ |
| 7 Dec | Payroll tax payable | | 225 | | | | 816.68 | Payroll tax payable | | 816.68 |
| | | | | | | | $816.68 | | | $816.68 |

### General Ledger

| Date | Particulars | Fol | Debit | Credit | Balance |
|------|-------------|-----|-------|--------|---------|
| **Payroll Tax Expense Account** | | | | | |
| 2018 | | | $ | $ | $ |
| 1 Nov | Balance (assumed) | | | | 6 000.00 Dr |
| 30 | Payroll tax payable | GJ | 816.68 | | 6 816.68 Dr |
| **Payroll Tax Payable Account** | | | | | |
| 2018 | | | | | |
| 30 Nov | Payroll tax expense | GJ | | 816.68 | 816.68 Cr |
| 7 Dec | Bank | CPJ | 816.68 | | Nil |
| **Workers' Compensation Expense Account** | | | | | |
| 2018 | | | | | |
| 1 Nov | Balance (assumed) | | | | 12 500.00 Dr |
| 30 | Workers' compensation prepaid | GJ | 3 125.00 | | 15 625.00 Dr |
| **Workers' Compensation Prepaid Account** | | | | | |
| 2018 | | | | | |
| 1 Nov | Balance (assumed) | | | | 25 000.00 Dr |
| 30 Dec | Workers' compensation expense | GJ | | 3 125.00 | 21 875.00 Dr |
| **Superannuation Expense Account** | | | | | |
| 2018 | | | | | |
| 1 Nov | Balance (assumed) | | | | 20 000.00 Dr |
| 30 | Superannuation payable | GJ | 6 612.00 | | 26 612.00 Dr |
| **Superannuation Payable Account** | | | | | |
| 2018 | | | | | |
| 1 Nov | Balance (assumed) | | | | 10 000.00 Cr |
| 30 | Superannuation expense | GJ | | 6 612.00 | 16 612.00 Cr |

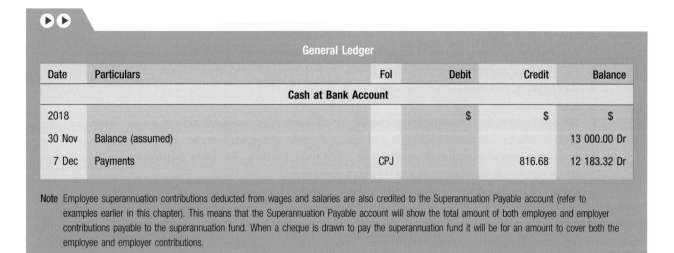

| Date | Particulars | Fol | Debit | Credit | Balance |
|------|-------------|-----|-------|--------|---------|
| | **Cash at Bank Account** | | | | |
| 2018 | | | $ | $ | $ |
| 30 Nov | Balance (assumed) | | | | 13 000.00 Dr |
| 7 Dec | Payments | CPJ | | 816.68 | 12 183.32 Dr |

**Note** Employee superannuation contributions deducted from wages and salaries are also credited to the Superannuation Payable account (refer to examples earlier in this chapter). This means that the Superannuation Payable account will show the total amount of both employee and employer contributions payable to the superannuation fund. When a cheque is drawn to pay the superannuation fund it will be for an amount to cover both the employee and employer contributions.

# EXERCISES

**Note** In all exercises unless otherwise specified, all employees are entitled to annual leave loading.

7.28 Richardson and Hafajee, Master Builders, process their business payroll manually each week. You are required to:

  a   complete the payroll registers for the month of March 2018

  b   prepare the General Journal and Cash Payments Journal entries to record the payroll and payment of the associated liabilities

  c   post the journal entries in **b** to the General Ledger

  d   briefly outline the responsibilities of an employer at the end of each financial year in relation to PAYG withheld from salaries and wages.

*Employee history cards*

| Employee no. 1 | |
|---|---|
| Name | ABDULLAH DAVIS |
| Date commenced | 14.6.2007 |
| Salary | $63 440 p.a. |
| Tax offsets | $1606 |
| Tax file no. | Yes |
| Tax-free threshold | Yes |
| Weekly deductions | |
| Medical | $40.00 |
| Insurance | $18.00 |
| Superannuation | $81.00 |

| Employee no. 2 | |
|---|---|
| Name | BARRY HALL |
| Date commenced | 10.4.2000 |
| Pay rate | $22.00 per hour |
| | |
| Tax file no. | No |
| Tax-free threshold | N/A |
| Weekly deductions | |
| Medical | $50.00 |
| Superannuation | $54.00 |

| Employee no. 3 | |
|---|---|
| Name | GORDON FLOWERS |
| Date commenced | 6.10.2004 |
| Pay rate | $20.00 per hour |
| HELP debt | Yes |
| Tax file no. | Yes |
| Tax-free threshold | Yes |
| Weekly deductions | |
| Insurance | $31.00 |
| Superannuation | $49.00 |

*Additional information*

- Assume the following General Ledger balances at 1 March: Bank, $15 500 Dr, Wages expense $88 400 Dr, Provision for annual leave $6000 Cr, Provision for long service leave $8200 Cr.
- Barry Hall is entitled to $100 per week travel allowance. The firm's policy is not to withhold tax from such allowances.
- Gordon Flowers will be taking three weeks' annual leave, so his pay will include annual leave pay (plus 17.5% annual leave loading) in addition to his pay for the week ended 18 March 2018.
- Abdullah Davis is manager of the firm and is not paid overtime. The other employees are paid at time and a half for all hours in excess of 35 hours per week.
- Details of hours worked for the month of March 2018 are shown below.

| | Week ending 4 Mar | W/e 11 Mar | W/e 18 Mar | W/e 25 Mar |
|---|---|---|---|---|
| Abdullah Davis | 45 hours | 35 | 40 | 45 |
| Barry Hall | 39 hours | 39 | 35 | 35 |
| Gordon Flowers | 37 hours | 39 | 35 | – |

- Employees are paid by EFT each week.
- Deductions from employees' wages and salaries are remitted to the relevant organisation on the last day of the month.

7.29 Lane's Plumbing uses a manual system to process its payroll. You are required to:

a complete the payroll register for the week ended 7 May 2018

b prepare the General Journal and Cash Payments Journal entries required to record the payroll for the week ended 7 May 2018.

*Employee history cards*

| Employee no. 1 | |
|---|---|
| Name Phyllis Swann | |
| Pay rate $28 per hour | |
| | |
| Tax-free threshold | No |
| Weekly deductions | |
| Medical | $50.00 |
| Superannuation | $50.00 |

| Employee no. 2 | |
|---|---|
| Name Bob Lane | |
| Pay rate $30 per hour | |
| Tax offsets | $3554 |
| Tax-free threshold | Yes |
| Weekly deductions | |
| Union | $10.00 |
| Medical | $40.00 |

| Employee no. 3 | |
|---|---|
| Name Sam Septik | |
| Pay rate $20 per hour | |
| Tax offsets | $4635 |
| Tax-free threshold | Yes |
| Weekly deductions | |
| Medical | $50.00 |
| Union | $10.00 |

| Employee no. 4 | |
|---|---|
| Name Fred Flask | |
| Pay rate $24.00 per hour | |
| HELP debt | Yes |
| Tax-free threshold | Yes |
| Weekly deductions | |
| Medical | $40.00 |
| Union | $10.00 |

*Time cards*

| Employee P Swann | | |
|---|---|---|
| Week ended 7 May 2018 | | |
| | Hrs worked | Gross pay |
| | | $ |
| Ordinary .. .. .. | 40 | 1 120 |
| Overtime .. .. .. | 5 | 210 |
| Total .. .. .. | 45 | 1 330 |

| Employee B Lane | | |
|---|---|---|
| Week ended 7 May 2018 | | |
| | Hrs worked | Gross pay |
| | | $ |
| Ordinary .. .. .. | 40 | 1 200 |
| Overtime .. .. .. | 2 | 90 |
| Total .. .. .. | 42 | 1 290 |

| Employee S Septik | | |
|---|---|---|
| Week ended 7 May 2018 | | |
| | Hrs worked | Gross pay |
| | | $ |
| Ordinary .. .. .. | 40 | 800 |
| Overtime .. .. .. | 6 | 180 |
| Total .. .. .. | 46 | 980 |

| Employee F Flask | | |
|---|---|---|
| Week ended 7 May 2018 | | |
| | Hrs worked | Gross pay |
| | | $ |
| Ordinary .. .. .. | 40 | 960 |
| Overtime .. .. .. | – | – |
| Total .. .. .. | 40 | 960 |

*Additional information*

- Sam Septik receives a car allowance of $40 per week. The firm's policy is not to withhold tax from such allowances.
- Bob Lane will be taking annual leave, so his pay will include three weeks' annual leave pay (plus 17.5% annual leave loading) in addition to his pay for the week ended 7 May 2018.
- All employees have provided a tax file number.
- Each employee is paid by direct credit to his or her personal bank account.

7.30* Zoe Products has a manual accounting system. You are required to:

a calculate the income tax payable for each employee and complete the payroll register for the selling department for the week ended 16 November 2017

b update the individual pay record for Aisha Zeta Mrosky

c complete the PAYG payment summary for Aisha Zeta Mrosky.

*Additional information*

- Income tax details:

| Employee no. | 2306 | 2318 | 2324 | 3976 | 3982 | 3983 |
|---|---|---|---|---|---|---|
| Tax-free threshold | Yes | Yes | Yes | Yes | Yes | Yes |
| Tax offsets | Nil | $1 204 | Nil | Nil | $3 406 | $1 340 |
| HELP debt | No | No | No | No | No | Yes |

- Gross earnings adjustments codes:

| 01 | Annual leave pay |
|---|---|
| 02 | Sick pay |
| 03 | Long service leave pay |

- Travel allowances paid by Zoe Products are not subject to PAYG withholding.
- Annual leave by employee 2324 is for three weeks.
- Aisha Mrosky ceased working for Zoe Products on 16 November 2017 and the firm agreed to issue a PAYG payment summary immediately.
- All employees have provided a tax file number.
- Employees are not entitled to annual leave loading.
- Zoe Products' ABN is 32 460 190 674.
- Aisha Mrosky's tax file number is 996 432 111 and her address is 15 Noles Court, Wendouree 3355.

| | | $ | ¢ | ¢ | $ | $ | $ | $ |
|---|---|---|---|---|---|---|---|---|
| **Payroll Register** | | | | | **DEPARTMENT** | **Selling** | | |
| **Period ending** *16 November 2017* | | | | | | | | |
| GROSS EARNINGS | Ord | 1 220.00 | 1 300.00 | 1 120.00 | 1 560.00 | 1 680.00 | 2 060.00 | 8 940.00 |
| | O/T | | | | | 300.00 | 160.00 | 460.00 |
| | Travel allowance | 160.00 | | 160.00 | 160.00 | 160.00 | | 640.00 |
| | Adjustments | | | (01) 3 360.00 | | | | 3 360.00 |
| | Total | 1 380.00 | 1 300.00 | 4 640.00 | 1 720.00 | 2 140.00 | 2 220.00 | 13 400.00 |
| DEDUCTIONS | Tax | | | | | | | |
| | Super | 70.00 | | 220.00 | 90.00 | 120.00 | | 500.00 |
| | Medical | 50.00 | 70.00 | | | 44.00 | | 164.00 |
| | Savings | 100.00 | | 120.00 | 80.00 | 40.00 | 200.00 | 540.00 |
| | Total | | | | | | | |
| Net pay | | | | | | | | |
| Employee no. | | 2306 | 2318 | 2324 | 3976 | 3982 | 3983 | Total |

| | Gross earnings to date | | | | | Deductions to date | | | | | Net pay to date |
|---|---|---|---|---|---|---|---|---|---|---|---|
| **Date** | **Ord** | **O/Time** | **Travel** | **Adj** | **Total** | **Tax** | **Super** | **Med** | **Sav** | **Total** | |
| 9/11/17 | 30 240.00 | 2 880.00 | 2 720.00 | (01) 720.00 | 36 560.00 | 8 100.00 | 1 840.00 | 792.00 | 720.00 | 11 452.00 | 25 108.00 |

**Individual Pay Record**
Name  Aisha Zeta Mrosky
Number  3982
Location  Selling Department
Tax file number  996 432 111

Address  15 Noles Court,
Wendouree, Vic 3355
Commenced
1 January 1985

7.31  Skidmore Car Sales has provided the following payroll information for the month of March 2019. You are required to:

a  prepare the General Journal entries to record the expenses (and associated liabilities) for payroll tax, workers' compensation and employer superannuation contributions

b  prepare the Cash Payments Journal entry to record the subsequent payment of payroll tax

c  post the journal entries in **a** and **b** to the General Ledger.

| Payroll summary – March 2019 | | | | |
|---|---|---|---|---|
| | 5/3/19 | 12/3/19 | 19/3/19 | 26/3/19 |
| | $ | $ | $ | $ |
| Ordinary | 12 317 | 14 240 | 13 500 | 13 800 |
| Overtime | 1 500 | 2 120 | 2 000 | |
| Annual leave | | | | 2 600 |
| Total gross | 13 817 | 16 360 | 15 500 | 16 400 |
| Tax | 2 760 | 3 270 | 5 100 | 3 280 |
| Union | 400 | 420 | 400 | 480 |
| | 3 160 | 3 690 | 5 500 | 3 760 |
| Net pay | 10 657 | 12 670 | 10 000 | 12 640 |

*Additional information*
- Payroll tax is payable at the rate of 4.90% on monthly payrolls over $45 833. Payroll tax is paid by the seventh day of the month following the month incurred.
- The firm's workers' compensation is calculated at 4% of gross payroll. Workers' compensation is paid yearly in advance.
- Employer superannuation contributions are made at the rate of 11.5% (this is be the rate that will be applicable in March 2019) of normal gross earnings (including annual leave). Employer superannuation contributions are paid quarterly.
- Assume the following General Ledger balances at 1 March.

| | $ |
|---|---|
| Bank | 24 000 Dr |
| Payroll tax expense | 4 200 Dr |
| Workers' compensation expense | 19 200 Dr |
| Workers' compensation prepaid | 9 600 Dr |
| Superannuation expense | 40 000 Dr |
| Superannuation payable | 10 000 Cr |

## SOLUTION

7.30  a

| Payroll Register<br>Period ending *16 November 2017* | | | | | DEPARTMENT Selling | | |
|---|---|---|---|---|---|---|---|
| | $ | $ | $ | $ | $ | $ | $ |
| **GROSS EARNINGS** Ord | 1 220.00 | 1 300.00 | 1 120.00 | 1 560.00 | 1 680.00 | 2 060.00 | 8 940.00 |
| O/Time | | | | | 300.00 | 160.00 | 460.00 |
| Travel allowance | 160.00 | | 160.00 | 160.00 | 160.00 | | 640.00 |
| Adjustments | | | (01) 3 360.00 | | | | 3 360.00 |
| Total | 1 380.00 | 1 300.00 | 4 640.00 | 1 720.00 | 2 140.00 | 2 220.00 | 13 400.00 |
| **DEDUCTIONS** Tax | 253.00 | 257.00 | 876.00 | 370.00 | 466.00 | 776.00 | 2 998.00 |
| Super | 70.00 | | 220.00 | 90.00 | 120.00 | | 500.00 |
| Medical | 50.00 | 70.00 | | | 44.00 | | 164.00 |
| Savings | 100.00 | | 120.00 | 80.00 | 40.00 | 200.00 | 540.00 |
| Total | 473.00 | 327.00 | 1 216.00 | 540.00 | 670.00 | 976.00 | 4 202.00 |
| Net pay | 907.00 | 973.00 | 3 424.00 | 1 180.00 | 1 470.00 | 1 244.00 | 9 198.00 |
| Employee no. | 2306 | 2318 | 2324 | 3976 | 3982 | 3983 | Total |

### Calculation of tax:

*Employee 2306*

| Tax on $1220 | | $253 |
|---|---|---|

*Employee 2318*

| Tax on $1300 | 280 |
|---|---|
| *less* Tax offsets weekly value | 23 |
| | $257 |

516

*Employee 2324*

| | |
|---|---:|
| Tax on $1120 | 219 |
| Tax on annual leave: | |
|    Tax on one week's annual leave $1120 (no leave loading)     219 | |
|    Multiplied by 3 | 657 |
| | $876 |

*Employee 3976*

| | |
|---|---:|
| Tax on $1560 | $370 |

*Employee 3982*

| | |
|---|---:|
| Tax on $1980 | $531 |
| *less* Tax offsets weekly value | 65 |
| | $466 |

*Employee 3983*

| | |
|---|---:|
| Tax on $2220 | $624 |
| *add* HELP debt weekly value | 178 |
| | $802 |
| *less* Tax offsets weekly value | 26 |
| | $776 |

b

| Individual Pay Record | Address | 15 Noles Court, |
|---|---|---|
| Name   Aisha Zeta Mrosky | | Wendouree, Vic 3355 |
| Number   3982 | | Commenced |
| Location   Selling Department | | 1 January 1985 |
| Tax file number   996 432 111 | | |

| | Gross earnings to date | | | | | Deductions to date | | | | | Net pay to date |
|---|---|---|---|---|---|---|---|---|---|---|---|
| | **Ord** | **O/Time** | **Travel** | **Adj** | **Total** | **Tax** | **Super** | **Med** | **Sav** | **Total** | |
| **Date** | $ | $ | $ | $ | $ | $ | $ | $ | $ | $ | $ |
| 9/11/17 | 30 240.00 | 2 880.00 | 2 720.00 | (01) 720.00 | 36 560.00 | 8 100.00 | 1 840.00 | 792.00 | 720.00 | 11 452.00 | 25 108.00 |
| 16/11/17 | 31 920.00 | 3 180.00 | 2 880.00 | (01) 720.00 | 38 700.00 | 8 566.00 | 1 960.00 | 836.00 | 760.00 | 12 122.00 | 26 578.00 |

c

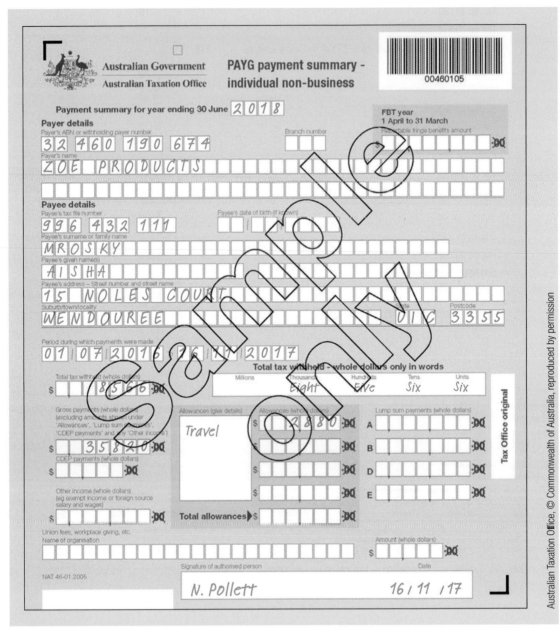

Figure 7.5    **Weekly tax table**

# Weekly tax table

Including instructions for calculating monthly and quarterly withholding

**❶ FOR PAYMENTS MADE ON OR AFTER 1 JULY 2012**

From 1 July 2012, the temporary flood and cyclone reconstruction levy (flood levy) will no longer apply.

## WHO SHOULD USE THIS TABLE?

You should use this table if you make any of the following payments on a weekly basis:

- salary, wages, allowances and leave loading to employees
- paid parental leave to an eligible worker
- director's fees
- salary and allowances to office holders (including members of parliament, statutory office holders, defence force members and police officers)
- payments to labour hire workers
- payments to religious practitioners
- government education or training payments
- compensation, sickness or accident payments that are calculated at a periodical rate and made because a person is unable to work (unless the payment is made under an insurance policy to the policy owner).

Also use this table for payments made to foreign residents.

Other tax tables may apply if you made payments to shearers, workers in the horticultural industry, performing artists and those engaged on a daily or casual basis.

**❶** This tax table includes instructions for calculating withholding for payments made on a monthly or quarterly basis. For more information, see page 4.

**❯** For a full list of tax tables, visit our website at **www.ato.gov.au/taxtables**

Alternatively, we have a calculator to help work out the correct amount of tax to withhold from payments to most payees. To access the calculator, visit our website at **www.ato.gov.au/taxwithheldcalculator**

**❶** This document is a withholding schedule made by the Commissioner of Taxation in accordance with sections 15-25 and 15-30 of schedule 1 to the *Taxation Administration Act 1953*. It applies to withholding payments covered by Subdivisions 12-B (except sections 12-50 and 12-55), and 12-D of schedule 1.

**Australian Government**
**Australian Taxation Office**

NAT 1005-05.2012

**Figure 7.5**

**Why are withholding rates changing?**
The government has changed personal income tax rates so most individuals will have less tax withheld from their pay.

> For more information, refer to *Household assistance package – tax reforms* (NAT 74144).

**Can you use a formula?**
The withholding amounts shown in this table can be expressed in a mathematical form.

If you have developed your own payroll software package, you will need to refer to *Statement of formulas for calculating amounts to be withheld* (NAT 1004) available on our website at **www.ato.gov.au/taxtables**

**TAX FILE NUMBER (TFN) DECLARATIONS**
The answers your payees provide on their *Tax file number declaration* (NAT 3092) determines the amount you need to withhold from their payments. A *Tax file number declaration* applies to any payments made after you receive the declaration. If you receive an updated declaration from a payee, it will override the previous one.

If a payee does not give you a valid *Tax file number declaration* within **14 days** of starting a payer/payee relationship, you must complete a *Tax file number declaration* with all available details of the payee and send it to us.

**What if a TFN has not been provided?**
You must withhold 46.5% from any payment you make to a resident payee and 45% from a foreign resident payee (ignoring any cents) if one of the following applies:
■ they have not quoted their TFN
■ they have not claimed an exemption from quoting their TFN
■ they have not advised you that they have applied for a TFN or have made an enquiry with us.

If a payee states at question 1 of the *Tax file number declaration* they have lodged a *Tax file number – application or enquiry for individuals* (NAT 1432) with us, they have **28 days** to provide you with their TFN.

If the payee has not given you their TFN within **28 days**, you must withhold 46.5% from any payment you make to a resident payee and 45% from a foreign resident payee (ignoring any cents) unless we tell you not to.

> ❗ Do not allow for any tax offsets or Medicare levy adjustment. Do not withhold any amount for:
> ■ Higher Education Loan Program (HELP) debts
> ■ Financial Supplement (FS) debts.

**What if your payee is under 18?**
There is no requirement for payees who are under 18 years of age to provide you with their TFN, provided that the payment you make to them does not exceed:
■ $350 per week (if you pay weekly)
■ $700 per fortnight (if you pay fortnightly)
■ $1,517 per month (if you pay monthly).

**How do changes to the tax-free threshold affect your payees?**
From 1 July 2012:
■ payees who claim the tax-free threshold will have less tax withheld from their pay
■ payees who do not claim the tax-free threshold will have more tax withheld from their pay.

A payee can claim the tax-free threshold only from one payer at a time, generally from the payee's main source of income.

> ❗ If your payee believes that for their circumstances the amount you withhold will be too much, they may apply to us for a variation to reduce the amount of withholding.
>
> For more information, refer to *PAYG withholding – varying your PAYG withholding* (NAT 70791) available on our website at **www.ato.gov.au**

**What if your payee is a foreign resident?**
If your payee has answered **no** to the question 'Are you an Australian resident for tax purposes?' on their *Tax file number declaration*, you will need to use the foreign resident tax rates.

There are two ways you can withhold from a foreign resident's earnings:
■ If they have not given you a valid TFN, you need to withhold 45% for each $1 of earnings (ignoring any cents).
■ If they have given you a valid TFN, you need to withhold the amount calculated in the foreign resident tax rates below, rounding any cents to the nearest dollar.

**Foreign resident tax rates**

| Weekly earnings $ | | Weekly rate |
|---|---|---|
| 0 to 1,538 | | 32.5 cents for each dollar of earnings |
| 1,539 to 3,462 | | $500 plus 37 cents for each $1 of earnings over $1,538 |
| 3,463 and over | | $1,212 plus 45 cents for each $1 of earnings over $3,462 |

Generally, foreign resident payees cannot claim tax offsets. In limited circumstances, they may be entitled to claim a zone or overseas forces offset. If your foreign resident payee has claimed a tax offset on the *Tax file number declaration*, you don't need to make any adjustments to the amount you withhold.

**WITHHOLDING DECLARATIONS**
A payee may use a *Withholding declaration* (NAT 3093) to advise you of a tax offset they choose to claim through reduced withholding from you. For more information, see page 3.

Payees can also use a *Withholding declaration* to advise you of any changes to their situation that may affect the amount you need to withhold from their payments.

Changes that may affect the amount you need to withhold include:
■ becoming or ceasing to be an Australian resident for tax purposes
■ claiming or discontinuing a claim for the tax-free threshold
■ advising of a HELP or FS debt, or changes to them
■ entitlement to a seniors and pensioners tax offset
■ upward variation to increase the rate or amount to be withheld.

When your payee provides you with a *Withholding declaration* it will take effect from the next payment you make. If you receive an updated declaration from a payee, it will override the previous one.

> ❗ A valid *Tax file number declaration* must be in place before your payee can provide you with a *Withholding declaration*.

**What if your payee has a HELP or FS debt?**
If your payee has an accumulated HELP or FS debt, you may need to withhold additional amounts from their payments. Your payee will need to notify you of this on their *Tax file number declaration* or *Withholding declaration*.

> To calculate additional withholding amounts for:
> ■ HELP debts, refer to *Higher Education Loan Program weekly tax table – including statement of formulas for calculating weekly and monthly withholding* (NAT 2173)
> ■ FS debts, refer to *Student Financial Supplement Scheme weekly tax table – including statement of formulas for calculating weekly and monthly withholding* (NAT 3306).

**SCHEDULE 2** WEEKLY TAX TABLE

**Figure 7.5**

❗ If your payee has not given you their TFN, do not withhold any amount for HELP or FS debts.

## ALLOWANCES

Generally, allowances are added to normal earnings and the amount to withhold is calculated on the total amount of earnings and allowances.

❯ For more information, refer to *Withholding from allowances* (NAT 5448).

## LEAVE LOADING CHANGES

There is no longer a separate withholding scale for payees who are entitled to leave loading and they will no longer have higher withholding from every pay. These payees will now be taxed more accurately when the leave loading is paid.

Previously, the leave loading scale provided for extra withholding throughout the year to allow $320 of leave loading to be tax-free when paid.

If you pay leave loading as a lump sum, you now need to use *Tax table for back payments, commissions, bonuses and similar payments* (NAT 3348) to calculate withholding.

If you pay leave loading on a pro-rata basis, then add the leave loading payment to earnings for the period to calculate withholding. That is, instead of the one lump sum payment, you make multiple payments during the year when leave is being taken.

## HOLIDAY PAY, LONG SERVICE LEAVE AND EMPLOYMENT TERMINATION PAYMENTS

### Payees who continue working for you

You must include holiday pay (including any leave loading) and long service leave payments as part of normal earnings, except when they are paid on termination of employment.

❯ For more information, refer to *PAYG withholding – calculation sheet – holiday and long service leave payments for continuing employment* (NAT 7138).

### Payees who stop working for you

This tax table does not cover any lump sum payments made to a payee who stops working for you.

If a payee has unused annual leave, leave loading or long service leave, refer to *Tax table for unused leave payments on termination of employment* (NAT 3351).

Any other lump sum payments may be employment termination payments, refer to *Tax table for employment termination payments* (NAT 70980).

❗ Do not withhold any amount for HELP or FS debts from lump sum termination payments.

## CLAIMING TAX OFFSETS

If your payee chooses to claim their entitlement to a tax offset through reduced withholding, they must provide you with a *Withholding declaration*.

To work out the payee's annual tax offset entitlement into a weekly or monthly value, use the 'Ready reckoner for tax offsets' on page 4. For weekly payments deduct the weekly amount from the amount shown in column 2 of the table on page 5. For the monthly value, deduct the monthly tax offset amount from the withholding amount calculated for monthly payments. If you pay monthly, see page 4.

❗ Do not allow for any tax offsets if any of the following apply:
- you are using column 3
- you are using foreign resident rates
- when a payee does not provide you with their TFN.

## EXAMPLE

A payee has weekly earnings of $563 and, if using column 2, the amount to be withheld is $48.

The payee claims a tax offset entitlement of $1,000 on their *Withholding declaration*.

Using the 'Ready reckoner for tax offsets' on page 4, the weekly value is $19.

The total amount to be withheld is worked out as follows:

| | |
|---|---|
| Amount to be withheld on $563 | $48.00 |
| *less* weekly offset value | $19.00 |
| **Total amount to be withheld** | **$29.00** |

## MEDICARE LEVY ADJUSTMENT

To claim the Medicare levy adjustment available to some low income earners with dependants, your payee must lodge a *Medicare levy variation declaration* (NAT 0929) with their *Tax file number declaration*.

Some payees may be liable for an increased rate of Medicare levy or the Medicare levy surcharge as a result of new income tests. They can lodge a *Medicare levy variation declaration*, requesting you to increase the amount to be withheld from their payments.

❯ For instructions on how to work out the Medicare levy adjustment, refer to *Medicare levy adjustment weekly tax table* (NAT 1010).

## HOW TO WORK OUT THE WITHHOLDING AMOUNT

To work out the amount you need to withhold, you must:
1. Add any allowances and irregular payments that are to be included in this week's pay to the normal weekly earnings, ignoring any cents.
2. Find your payee's total weekly earnings in column 1.
3. Use the appropriate column to find the correct amount to withhold. If your payee is
   - claiming the tax-free threshold, use column 2
   - not claiming the tax-free threshold, use column 3
4. If your payee has an end-of-year entitlement to a tax offset, use the 'Ready reckoner for tax offsets' shown on page 4 to convert the payee's estimate of their full-year entitlement into a weekly offset value. Then subtract this value from the withholding amount found in step 3.
5. If your payee is entitled to make an adjustment for the Medicare levy, subtract the value of the adjustment, determined from the *Medicare levy adjustment weekly tax table* (NAT 1010) from the amount found in step 4.
6. If your payee has advised you of a HELP or FS debt, add the amount determined from the *HELP weekly tax table including formulas for calculating monthly withholding* (NAT 2173) or *SFSS weekly tax table including formulas for calculating monthly withholding* (NAT 3306) to the amount you calculated in step 5.

❗ Do not allow for any tax offsets or Medicare levy adjustment if any of the following apply:
- you use column 3
- you use foreign resident tax rates
- when your payee has not provided you with their TFN.

**Figure 7.5**

**EXAMPLE**

A payee has weekly earnings of $563.60.

To work out the correct amount to withhold, ignore cents, use column 1 and find $563.

If the payee is:

- claiming the tax-free threshold, use column 2 to find the correct amount to withhold ($48).
- not claiming the tax-free threshold, use column 3 to find the correct amount to withhold ($148).

### What if there are 53 pay periods in a financial year?

In some years, you may pay your payees 53 times instead of the usual 52. As this table is based on 52 pays, the extra pay may result in insufficient amounts being withheld. You should let your payees know when this occurs so if they are concerned about a shortfall, they can ask you to withhold the additional amount in the table below.

| Weekly earnings $ | | | Additional withholding $ |
|---|---|---|---|
| 700 | to | 1,549 | 3 |
| 1,550 | to | 3,449 | 4 |
| 3,450 | and over | | 9 |

### What if you pay monthly?

To work out the amount to withhold from monthly payments:

1 Work out the monthly gross earnings. Where this amount ends in 33 cents, add one cent.
2 Multiply the monthly gross earnings by 12.
3 Divide this figure by 52 to obtain the weekly gross amount (ignore any cents).
4 Use the appropriate column to find the withholding amount.
5 Multiply this withholding amount by 52 and then divide by 12 to obtain the monthly withholding figure.

**EXAMPLE**

A payee has monthly earnings of $2,250.39.

1 Gross monthly earnings are $2,250.39
$2,250.39 × 12 = $27,004.68
2 $27,004.68 ÷ 52 = $519.32
($519 ignoring cents)
3 Amount using column 2 on $519 is $39.00
4 $39 × 52 = $2,028.00

$2,028 ÷ 12 = $169.00 withholding for the month.

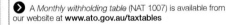 A *Monthly withholding table* (NAT 1007) is available from our website at **www.ato.gov.au/taxtables**

### What if you pay quarterly?

To work out the amount to withhold from quarterly payments:

1 Multiply the quarterly gross earnings by 4.
2 Divide this figure by 52 to obtain the weekly gross amount (ignore any cents).
3 Use the appropriate column to find the withholding amount.
4 Multiply this withholding amount by 52 and then divide by 4 to obtain the quarterly withholding figure.

**EXAMPLE**

A payee has quarterly earnings of $21,526.48.

1 Gross quarterly earnings are $21,526.48
$21,526.48 × 4 = $86,105.92
2 $86,105.92 ÷ 52 = $1,655.88
($1,655 ignoring cents)
3 Amount using column 2 on $1,655 is $406.00
4 $406 × 52 = $21,112.00

$21,112 ÷ 4 = $5,278 withholding for the quarter.

### Resident income tax rates from 1 July 2012 (not including Medicare levy)

| Taxable income range $ | | | Tax rate % |
|---|---|---|---|
| 0 | to | 18,200 | 0 |
| 18,201 | to | 37,000 | 19 |
| 37,001 | to | 80,000 | 32.5 |
| 80,001 | to | 180,000 | 37 |
| Greater than | | 180,000 | 45 |

### Ready reckoner for tax offsets

| Amount claimed $ | Weekly value $ | Monthly value $ | Amount claimed $ | Weekly value $ | Monthly value $ |
|---|---|---|---|---|---|
| 1 | — | — | 400 | 8.00 | 33.00 |
| 2 | — | — | 500 | 10.00 | 42.00 |
| 3 | — | — | 600 | 11.00 | 50.00 |
| 4 | — | — | 700 | 13.00 | 58.00 |
| 5 | — | — | 800 | 15.00 | 66.00 |
| 6 | — | — | 850 | 16.00 | 71.00 |
| 7 | — | 1.00 | 900 | 17.00 | 75.00 |
| 8 | — | 1.00 | 1000 | 19.00 | 83.00 |
| 9 | — | 1.00 | 1100 | 21.00 | 91.00 |
| 10 | — | 1.00 | 1173 | 22.00 | 97.00 |
| 20 | — | 2.00 | 1200 | 23.00 | 100.00 |
| 30 | 1.00 | 2.00 | 1300 | 25.00 | 108.00 |
| 40 | 1.00 | 3.00 | 1400 | 27.00 | 116.00 |
| 50 | 1.00 | 4.00 | 1500 | 29.00 | 125.00 |
| 57 | 1.00 | 5.00 | 1600 | 30.00 | 133.00 |
| 60 | 1.00 | 5.00 | 1700 | 32.00 | 141.00 |
| 70 | 1.00 | 6.00 | 1750 | 33.00 | 145.00 |
| 80 | 2.00 | 7.00 | 1800 | 34.00 | 149.00 |
| 90 | 2.00 | 7.00 | 1900 | 36.00 | 158.00 |
| 100 | 2.00 | 8.00 | 2000 | 38.00 | 166.00 |
| 200 | 4.00 | 17.00 | 2250 | 43.00 | 187.00 |
| 300 | 6.00 | 25.00 | 2500 | 48.00 | 208.00 |
| 338 | 6.00 | 28.00 | 3000 | 57.00 | 249.00 |

If the exact tax offset amount claimed is not shown in the ready reckoner, add the values for an appropriate combination.

**EXAMPLE**

Tax offsets of $422 claimed. For a weekly value add values of $400, $20 and $2 from the weekly value column.
= $8.00 + $0.00 + $0.00
= $8.00

Therefore, reduce the amount to be withheld from weekly payments by $8.00.

### PAYG WITHHOLDING PUBLICATIONS

You can access all PAYG withholding tax tables and other PAYG withholding publications quickly and easily from our website at **www.ato.gov.au/paygw**

Copies of weekly and fortnightly tax tables are available from most newsagents. Newsagents also hold copies of the following:

- *Tax file number declaration* (NAT 3092)
- *Withholding declaration* (NAT 3093).

4

SCHEDULE 2 WEEKLY TAX TABLE

Figure 7.5

## WEEKLY TAX TABLE – INCORPORATING MEDICARE LEVY

❗ Leave loading column has been removed from this tax table. For more information about leave loading changes, see page 3.

| Weekly earnings 1 $ | With tax-free threshold 2 $ | No tax-free threshold 3 $ | Weekly earnings 1 $ | With tax-free threshold 2 $ | No tax-free threshold 3 $ | Weekly earnings 1 $ | With tax-free threshold 2 $ | No tax-free threshold 3 $ | Weekly earnings 1 $ | With tax-free threshold 2 $ | No tax-free threshold 3 $ | Weekly earnings 1 $ | With tax-free threshold 2 $ | No tax-free threshold 3 $ |
|---|---|---|---|---|---|---|---|---|---|---|---|---|---|---|
| 1.00 | — | — | 86.00 | — | 18.00 | 171.00 | — | 37.00 | 256.00 | — | 56.00 | 341.00 | — | 74.00 |
| 2.00 | — | — | 87.00 | — | 18.00 | 172.00 | — | 37.00 | 257.00 | — | 56.00 | 342.00 | — | 75.00 |
| 3.00 | — | 1.00 | 88.00 | — | 18.00 | 173.00 | — | 37.00 | 258.00 | — | 56.00 | 343.00 | — | 75.00 |
| 4.00 | — | 1.00 | 89.00 | — | 19.00 | 174.00 | — | 37.00 | 259.00 | — | 56.00 | 344.00 | — | 75.00 |
| 5.00 | — | 1.00 | 90.00 | — | 19.00 | 175.00 | — | 38.00 | 260.00 | — | 56.00 | 345.00 | — | 75.00 |
| 6.00 | — | 1.00 | 91.00 | — | 19.00 | 176.00 | — | 38.00 | 261.00 | — | 57.00 | 346.00 | — | 75.00 |
| 7.00 | — | 1.00 | 92.00 | — | 19.00 | 177.00 | — | 38.00 | 262.00 | — | 57.00 | 347.00 | — | 76.00 |
| 8.00 | — | 2.00 | 93.00 | — | 19.00 | 178.00 | — | 38.00 | 263.00 | — | 57.00 | 348.00 | — | 76.00 |
| 9.00 | — | 2.00 | 94.00 | — | 20.00 | 179.00 | — | 39.00 | 264.00 | — | 57.00 | 349.00 | — | 76.00 |
| 10.00 | — | 2.00 | 95.00 | — | 20.00 | 180.00 | — | 39.00 | 265.00 | — | 58.00 | 350.00 | — | 76.00 |
| 11.00 | — | 2.00 | 96.00 | — | 20.00 | 181.00 | — | 39.00 | 266.00 | — | 58.00 | 351.00 | — | 77.00 |
| 12.00 | — | 2.00 | 97.00 | — | 20.00 | 182.00 | — | 39.00 | 267.00 | — | 58.00 | 352.00 | — | 77.00 |
| 13.00 | — | 2.00 | 98.00 | — | 21.00 | 183.00 | — | 39.00 | 268.00 | — | 58.00 | 353.00 | — | 77.00 |
| 14.00 | — | 3.00 | 99.00 | — | 21.00 | 184.00 | — | 40.00 | 269.00 | — | 58.00 | 354.00 | — | 77.00 |
| 15.00 | — | 3.00 | 100.00 | — | 21.00 | 185.00 | — | 40.00 | 270.00 | — | 59.00 | 355.00 | — | 77.00 |
| 16.00 | — | 3.00 | 101.00 | — | 21.00 | 186.00 | — | 40.00 | 271.00 | — | 59.00 | 356.00 | — | 78.00 |
| 17.00 | — | 3.00 | 102.00 | — | 21.00 | 187.00 | — | 40.00 | 272.00 | — | 59.00 | 357.00 | 1.00 | 78.00 |
| 18.00 | — | 3.00 | 103.00 | — | 22.00 | 188.00 | — | 40.00 | 273.00 | — | 59.00 | 358.00 | 1.00 | 78.00 |
| 19.00 | — | 4.00 | 104.00 | — | 22.00 | 189.00 | — | 41.00 | 274.00 | — | 60.00 | 359.00 | 1.00 | 78.00 |
| 20.00 | — | 4.00 | 105.00 | — | 22.00 | 190.00 | — | 41.00 | 275.00 | — | 60.00 | 360.00 | 1.00 | 79.00 |
| 21.00 | — | 4.00 | 106.00 | — | 22.00 | 191.00 | — | 41.00 | 276.00 | — | 60.00 | 361.00 | 1.00 | 79.00 |
| 22.00 | — | 4.00 | 107.00 | — | 23.00 | 192.00 | — | 41.00 | 277.00 | — | 60.00 | 362.00 | 2.00 | 79.00 |
| 23.00 | — | 4.00 | 108.00 | — | 23.00 | 193.00 | — | 42.00 | 278.00 | — | 60.00 | 363.00 | 2.00 | 80.00 |
| 24.00 | — | 5.00 | 109.00 | — | 23.00 | 194.00 | — | 42.00 | 279.00 | — | 61.00 | 364.00 | 2.00 | 80.00 |
| 25.00 | — | 5.00 | 110.00 | — | 23.00 | 195.00 | — | 42.00 | 280.00 | — | 61.00 | 365.00 | 2.00 | 80.00 |
| 26.00 | — | 5.00 | 111.00 | — | 23.00 | 196.00 | — | 42.00 | 281.00 | — | 61.00 | 366.00 | 2.00 | 81.00 |
| 27.00 | — | 5.00 | 112.00 | — | 24.00 | 197.00 | — | 42.00 | 282.00 | — | 61.00 | 367.00 | 2.00 | 81.00 |
| 28.00 | — | 5.00 | 113.00 | — | 24.00 | 198.00 | — | 43.00 | 283.00 | — | 62.00 | 368.00 | 3.00 | 81.00 |
| 29.00 | — | 6.00 | 114.00 | — | 24.00 | 199.00 | — | 43.00 | 284.00 | — | 62.00 | 369.00 | 3.00 | 82.00 |
| 30.00 | — | 6.00 | 115.00 | — | 24.00 | 200.00 | — | 43.00 | 285.00 | — | 62.00 | 370.00 | 3.00 | 82.00 |
| 31.00 | — | 6.00 | 116.00 | — | 25.00 | 201.00 | — | 43.00 | 286.00 | — | 62.00 | 371.00 | 3.00 | 82.00 |
| 32.00 | — | 6.00 | 117.00 | — | 25.00 | 202.00 | — | 44.00 | 287.00 | — | 62.00 | 372.00 | 3.00 | 83.00 |
| 33.00 | — | 6.00 | 118.00 | — | 25.00 | 203.00 | — | 44.00 | 288.00 | — | 63.00 | 373.00 | 4.00 | 83.00 |
| 34.00 | — | 6.00 | 119.00 | — | 25.00 | 204.00 | — | 44.00 | 289.00 | — | 63.00 | 374.00 | 4.00 | 83.00 |
| 35.00 | — | 7.00 | 120.00 | — | 25.00 | 205.00 | — | 44.00 | 290.00 | — | 63.00 | 375.00 | 4.00 | 84.00 |
| 36.00 | — | 7.00 | 121.00 | — | 26.00 | 206.00 | — | 44.00 | 291.00 | — | 63.00 | 376.00 | 4.00 | 84.00 |
| 37.00 | — | 7.00 | 122.00 | — | 26.00 | 207.00 | — | 45.00 | 292.00 | — | 64.00 | 377.00 | 4.00 | 84.00 |
| 38.00 | — | 7.00 | 123.00 | — | 26.00 | 208.00 | — | 45.00 | 293.00 | — | 64.00 | 378.00 | 5.00 | 85.00 |
| 39.00 | — | 7.00 | 124.00 | — | 26.00 | 209.00 | — | 45.00 | 294.00 | — | 64.00 | 379.00 | 5.00 | 85.00 |
| 40.00 | — | 8.00 | 125.00 | — | 26.00 | 210.00 | — | 45.00 | 295.00 | — | 64.00 | 380.00 | 5.00 | 85.00 |
| 41.00 | — | 8.00 | 126.00 | — | 27.00 | 211.00 | — | 46.00 | 296.00 | — | 64.00 | 381.00 | 5.00 | 86.00 |
| 42.00 | — | 8.00 | 127.00 | — | 27.00 | 212.00 | — | 46.00 | 297.00 | — | 65.00 | 382.00 | 5.00 | 86.00 |
| 43.00 | — | 8.00 | 128.00 | — | 27.00 | 213.00 | — | 46.00 | 298.00 | — | 65.00 | 383.00 | 5.00 | 86.00 |
| 44.00 | — | 8.00 | 129.00 | — | 27.00 | 214.00 | — | 46.00 | 299.00 | — | 65.00 | 384.00 | 6.00 | 87.00 |
| 45.00 | — | 9.00 | 130.00 | — | 28.00 | 215.00 | — | 46.00 | 300.00 | — | 65.00 | 385.00 | 6.00 | 87.00 |
| 46.00 | — | 9.00 | 131.00 | — | 28.00 | 216.00 | — | 47.00 | 301.00 | — | 65.00 | 386.00 | 6.00 | 87.00 |
| 47.00 | — | 9.00 | 132.00 | — | 28.00 | 217.00 | — | 47.00 | 302.00 | — | 66.00 | 387.00 | 6.00 | 88.00 |
| 48.00 | — | 9.00 | 133.00 | — | 28.00 | 218.00 | — | 47.00 | 303.00 | — | 66.00 | 388.00 | 6.00 | 88.00 |
| 49.00 | — | 10.00 | 134.00 | — | 28.00 | 219.00 | — | 47.00 | 304.00 | — | 66.00 | 389.00 | 7.00 | 88.00 |
| 50.00 | — | 10.00 | 135.00 | — | 29.00 | 220.00 | — | 48.00 | 305.00 | — | 66.00 | 390.00 | 7.00 | 89.00 |
| 51.00 | — | 10.00 | 136.00 | — | 29.00 | 221.00 | — | 48.00 | 306.00 | — | 67.00 | 391.00 | 7.00 | 89.00 |
| 52.00 | — | 10.00 | 137.00 | — | 29.00 | 222.00 | — | 48.00 | 307.00 | — | 67.00 | 392.00 | 7.00 | 89.00 |
| 53.00 | — | 11.00 | 138.00 | — | 29.00 | 223.00 | — | 48.00 | 308.00 | — | 67.00 | 393.00 | 7.00 | 90.00 |
| 54.00 | — | 11.00 | 139.00 | — | 30.00 | 224.00 | — | 48.00 | 309.00 | — | 67.00 | 394.00 | 8.00 | 90.00 |
| 55.00 | — | 11.00 | 140.00 | — | 30.00 | 225.00 | — | 49.00 | 310.00 | — | 67.00 | 395.00 | 8.00 | 91.00 |
| 56.00 | — | 11.00 | 141.00 | — | 30.00 | 226.00 | — | 49.00 | 311.00 | — | 68.00 | 396.00 | 8.00 | 91.00 |
| 57.00 | — | 11.00 | 142.00 | — | 30.00 | 227.00 | — | 49.00 | 312.00 | — | 68.00 | 397.00 | 8.00 | 91.00 |
| 58.00 | — | 12.00 | 143.00 | — | 30.00 | 228.00 | — | 49.00 | 313.00 | — | 68.00 | 398.00 | 9.00 | 92.00 |
| 59.00 | — | 12.00 | 144.00 | — | 31.00 | 229.00 | — | 50.00 | 314.00 | — | 68.00 | 399.00 | 9.00 | 92.00 |
| 60.00 | — | 12.00 | 145.00 | — | 31.00 | 230.00 | — | 50.00 | 315.00 | — | 69.00 | 400.00 | 9.00 | 92.00 |
| 61.00 | — | 12.00 | 146.00 | — | 31.00 | 231.00 | — | 50.00 | 316.00 | — | 69.00 | 401.00 | 10.00 | 93.00 |
| 62.00 | — | 13.00 | 147.00 | — | 31.00 | 232.00 | — | 50.00 | 317.00 | — | 69.00 | 402.00 | 10.00 | 93.00 |
| 63.00 | — | 13.00 | 148.00 | — | 32.00 | 233.00 | — | 50.00 | 318.00 | — | 69.00 | 403.00 | 10.00 | 93.00 |
| 64.00 | — | 13.00 | 149.00 | — | 32.00 | 234.00 | — | 51.00 | 319.00 | — | 69.00 | 404.00 | 10.00 | 94.00 |
| 65.00 | — | 13.00 | 150.00 | — | 32.00 | 235.00 | — | 51.00 | 320.00 | — | 70.00 | 405.00 | 11.00 | 94.00 |
| 66.00 | — | 13.00 | 151.00 | — | 32.00 | 236.00 | — | 51.00 | 321.00 | — | 70.00 | 406.00 | 11.00 | 94.00 |
| 67.00 | — | 14.00 | 152.00 | — | 32.00 | 237.00 | — | 51.00 | 322.00 | — | 70.00 | 407.00 | 11.00 | 95.00 |
| 68.00 | — | 14.00 | 153.00 | — | 33.00 | 238.00 | — | 52.00 | 323.00 | — | 70.00 | 408.00 | 12.00 | 95.00 |
| 69.00 | — | 14.00 | 154.00 | — | 33.00 | 239.00 | — | 52.00 | 324.00 | — | 71.00 | 409.00 | 12.00 | 95.00 |
| 70.00 | — | 14.00 | 155.00 | — | 33.00 | 240.00 | — | 52.00 | 325.00 | — | 71.00 | 410.00 | 12.00 | 96.00 |
| 71.00 | — | 15.00 | 156.00 | — | 33.00 | 241.00 | — | 52.00 | 326.00 | — | 71.00 | 411.00 | 13.00 | 96.00 |
| 72.00 | — | 15.00 | 157.00 | — | 34.00 | 242.00 | — | 52.00 | 327.00 | — | 71.00 | 412.00 | 13.00 | 96.00 |
| 73.00 | — | 15.00 | 158.00 | — | 34.00 | 243.00 | — | 53.00 | 328.00 | — | 71.00 | 413.00 | 13.00 | 97.00 |
| 74.00 | — | 15.00 | 159.00 | — | 34.00 | 244.00 | — | 53.00 | 329.00 | — | 72.00 | 414.00 | 13.00 | 97.00 |
| 75.00 | — | 15.00 | 160.00 | — | 34.00 | 245.00 | — | 53.00 | 330.00 | — | 72.00 | 415.00 | 14.00 | 97.00 |
| 76.00 | — | 16.00 | 161.00 | — | 34.00 | 246.00 | — | 53.00 | 331.00 | — | 72.00 | 416.00 | 14.00 | 98.00 |
| 77.00 | — | 16.00 | 162.00 | — | 35.00 | 247.00 | — | 54.00 | 332.00 | — | 72.00 | 417.00 | 14.00 | 98.00 |
| 78.00 | — | 16.00 | 163.00 | — | 35.00 | 248.00 | — | 54.00 | 333.00 | — | 73.00 | 418.00 | 15.00 | 98.00 |
| 79.00 | — | 16.00 | 164.00 | — | 35.00 | 249.00 | — | 54.00 | 334.00 | — | 73.00 | 419.00 | 15.00 | 99.00 |
| 80.00 | — | 17.00 | 165.00 | — | 35.00 | 250.00 | — | 54.00 | 335.00 | — | 73.00 | 420.00 | 15.00 | 99.00 |
| 81.00 | — | 17.00 | 166.00 | — | 36.00 | 251.00 | — | 54.00 | 336.00 | — | 73.00 | 421.00 | 15.00 | 99.00 |
| 82.00 | — | 17.00 | 167.00 | — | 36.00 | 252.00 | — | 55.00 | 337.00 | — | 73.00 | 422.00 | 16.00 | 100.00 |
| 83.00 | — | 17.00 | 168.00 | — | 36.00 | 253.00 | — | 55.00 | 338.00 | — | 74.00 | 423.00 | 16.00 | 100.00 |
| 84.00 | — | 17.00 | 169.00 | — | 36.00 | 254.00 | — | 55.00 | 339.00 | — | 74.00 | 424.00 | 16.00 | 100.00 |
| 85.00 | — | 18.00 | 170.00 | — | 36.00 | 255.00 | — | 55.00 | 340.00 | — | 74.00 | 425.00 | 17.00 | 101.00 |

SCHEDULE 2 WEEKLY TAX TABLE    5

Figure 7.5

## WEEKLY TAX TABLE – INCORPORATING MEDICARE LEVY

❗ Leave loading column has been removed from this tax table. For more information about leave loading changes, see page 3.

| Weekly earnings 1 $ | With tax-free threshold 2 $ | No tax-free threshold 3 $ | Weekly earnings 1 $ | With tax-free threshold 2 $ | No tax-free threshold 3 $ | Weekly earnings 1 $ | With tax-free threshold 2 $ | No tax-free threshold 3 $ | Weekly earnings 1 $ | With tax-free threshold 2 $ | No tax-free threshold 3 $ | Weekly earnings 1 $ | With tax-free threshold 2 $ | No tax-free threshold 3 $ |
|---|---|---|---|---|---|---|---|---|---|---|---|---|---|---|
| 426.00 | 17.00 | 101.00 | 511.00 | 37.00 | 130.00 | 596.00 | 55.00 | 159.00 | 681.00 | 72.00 | 189.00 | 766.00 | 97.00 | 218.00 |
| 427.00 | 17.00 | 101.00 | 512.00 | 38.00 | 131.00 | 597.00 | 55.00 | 160.00 | 682.00 | 73.00 | 189.00 | 767.00 | 98.00 | 218.00 |
| 428.00 | 17.00 | 102.00 | 513.00 | 38.00 | 131.00 | 598.00 | 55.00 | 160.00 | 683.00 | 73.00 | 189.00 | 768.00 | 98.00 | 218.00 |
| 429.00 | 18.00 | 102.00 | 514.00 | 38.00 | 131.00 | 599.00 | 56.00 | 160.00 | 684.00 | 73.00 | 190.00 | 769.00 | 98.00 | 219.00 |
| 430.00 | 18.00 | 102.00 | 515.00 | 38.00 | 132.00 | 600.00 | 56.00 | 161.00 | 685.00 | 73.00 | 190.00 | 770.00 | 99.00 | 219.00 |
| 431.00 | 18.00 | 103.00 | 516.00 | 39.00 | 132.00 | 601.00 | 56.00 | 161.00 | 686.00 | 73.00 | 190.00 | 771.00 | 99.00 | 219.00 |
| 432.00 | 19.00 | 103.00 | 517.00 | 39.00 | 132.00 | 602.00 | 56.00 | 161.00 | 687.00 | 74.00 | 191.00 | 772.00 | 99.00 | 220.00 |
| 433.00 | 19.00 | 104.00 | 518.00 | 39.00 | 133.00 | 603.00 | 56.00 | 162.00 | 688.00 | 74.00 | 191.00 | 773.00 | 100.00 | 220.00 |
| 434.00 | 19.00 | 104.00 | 519.00 | 39.00 | 133.00 | 604.00 | 57.00 | 162.00 | 689.00 | 74.00 | 191.00 | 774.00 | 100.00 | 220.00 |
| 435.00 | 19.00 | 104.00 | 520.00 | 39.00 | 133.00 | 605.00 | 57.00 | 162.00 | 690.00 | 74.00 | 192.00 | 775.00 | 100.00 | 221.00 |
| 436.00 | 20.00 | 105.00 | 521.00 | 40.00 | 134.00 | 606.00 | 57.00 | 163.00 | 691.00 | 74.00 | 192.00 | 776.00 | 101.00 | 221.00 |
| 437.00 | 20.00 | 105.00 | 522.00 | 40.00 | 134.00 | 607.00 | 57.00 | 163.00 | 692.00 | 75.00 | 192.00 | 777.00 | 101.00 | 221.00 |
| 438.00 | 20.00 | 105.00 | 523.00 | 40.00 | 134.00 | 608.00 | 57.00 | 163.00 | 693.00 | 75.00 | 193.00 | 778.00 | 102.00 | 222.00 |
| 439.00 | 21.00 | 106.00 | 524.00 | 40.00 | 135.00 | 609.00 | 58.00 | 164.00 | 694.00 | 75.00 | 193.00 | 779.00 | 102.00 | 222.00 |
| 440.00 | 21.00 | 106.00 | 525.00 | 40.00 | 135.00 | 610.00 | 58.00 | 164.00 | 695.00 | 75.00 | 193.00 | 780.00 | 102.00 | 222.00 |
| 441.00 | 21.00 | 106.00 | 526.00 | 41.00 | 135.00 | 611.00 | 58.00 | 165.00 | 696.00 | 75.00 | 194.00 | 781.00 | 103.00 | 223.00 |
| 442.00 | 21.00 | 107.00 | 527.00 | 41.00 | 136.00 | 612.00 | 58.00 | 165.00 | 697.00 | 76.00 | 194.00 | 782.00 | 103.00 | 223.00 |
| 443.00 | 22.00 | 107.00 | 528.00 | 41.00 | 136.00 | 613.00 | 58.00 | 165.00 | 698.00 | 76.00 | 194.00 | 783.00 | 103.00 | 223.00 |
| 444.00 | 22.00 | 107.00 | 529.00 | 41.00 | 136.00 | 614.00 | 59.00 | 166.00 | 699.00 | 76.00 | 195.00 | 784.00 | 104.00 | 224.00 |
| 445.00 | 22.00 | 108.00 | 530.00 | 41.00 | 137.00 | 615.00 | 59.00 | 166.00 | 700.00 | 76.00 | 195.00 | 785.00 | 104.00 | 224.00 |
| 446.00 | 23.00 | 108.00 | 531.00 | 42.00 | 137.00 | 616.00 | 59.00 | 166.00 | 701.00 | 76.00 | 195.00 | 786.00 | 104.00 | 224.00 |
| 447.00 | 23.00 | 108.00 | 532.00 | 42.00 | 137.00 | 617.00 | 59.00 | 167.00 | 702.00 | 77.00 | 196.00 | 787.00 | 105.00 | 225.00 |
| 448.00 | 23.00 | 109.00 | 533.00 | 42.00 | 138.00 | 618.00 | 59.00 | 167.00 | 703.00 | 77.00 | 196.00 | 788.00 | 105.00 | 225.00 |
| 449.00 | 24.00 | 109.00 | 534.00 | 42.00 | 138.00 | 619.00 | 60.00 | 167.00 | 704.00 | 77.00 | 196.00 | 789.00 | 105.00 | 226.00 |
| 450.00 | 24.00 | 109.00 | 535.00 | 42.00 | 138.00 | 620.00 | 60.00 | 168.00 | 705.00 | 77.00 | 197.00 | 790.00 | 106.00 | 226.00 |
| 451.00 | 24.00 | 110.00 | 536.00 | 43.00 | 139.00 | 621.00 | 60.00 | 168.00 | 706.00 | 77.00 | 197.00 | 791.00 | 106.00 | 226.00 |
| 452.00 | 24.00 | 110.00 | 537.00 | 43.00 | 139.00 | 622.00 | 60.00 | 168.00 | 707.00 | 78.00 | 197.00 | 792.00 | 106.00 | 227.00 |
| 453.00 | 25.00 | 110.00 | 538.00 | 43.00 | 140.00 | 623.00 | 60.00 | 169.00 | 708.00 | 78.00 | 198.00 | 793.00 | 107.00 | 227.00 |
| 454.00 | 25.00 | 111.00 | 539.00 | 43.00 | 140.00 | 624.00 | 61.00 | 169.00 | 709.00 | 78.00 | 198.00 | 794.00 | 107.00 | 227.00 |
| 455.00 | 25.00 | 111.00 | 540.00 | 43.00 | 140.00 | 625.00 | 61.00 | 169.00 | 710.00 | 78.00 | 198.00 | 795.00 | 107.00 | 228.00 |
| 456.00 | 26.00 | 111.00 | 541.00 | 44.00 | 141.00 | 626.00 | 61.00 | 170.00 | 711.00 | 79.00 | 199.00 | 796.00 | 108.00 | 228.00 |
| 457.00 | 26.00 | 112.00 | 542.00 | 44.00 | 141.00 | 627.00 | 61.00 | 170.00 | 712.00 | 79.00 | 199.00 | 797.00 | 108.00 | 228.00 |
| 458.00 | 26.00 | 112.00 | 543.00 | 44.00 | 141.00 | 628.00 | 61.00 | 170.00 | 713.00 | 79.00 | 199.00 | 798.00 | 108.00 | 229.00 |
| 459.00 | 26.00 | 112.00 | 544.00 | 44.00 | 142.00 | 629.00 | 62.00 | 171.00 | 714.00 | 80.00 | 200.00 | 799.00 | 109.00 | 229.00 |
| 460.00 | 27.00 | 113.00 | 545.00 | 44.00 | 142.00 | 630.00 | 62.00 | 171.00 | 715.00 | 80.00 | 200.00 | 800.00 | 109.00 | 229.00 |
| 461.00 | 27.00 | 113.00 | 546.00 | 45.00 | 142.00 | 631.00 | 62.00 | 171.00 | 716.00 | 80.00 | 201.00 | 801.00 | 109.00 | 230.00 |
| 462.00 | 27.00 | 113.00 | 547.00 | 45.00 | 143.00 | 632.00 | 62.00 | 172.00 | 717.00 | 81.00 | 201.00 | 802.00 | 110.00 | 230.00 |
| 463.00 | 28.00 | 114.00 | 548.00 | 45.00 | 143.00 | 633.00 | 63.00 | 172.00 | 718.00 | 81.00 | 201.00 | 803.00 | 110.00 | 230.00 |
| 464.00 | 28.00 | 114.00 | 549.00 | 45.00 | 143.00 | 634.00 | 63.00 | 172.00 | 719.00 | 81.00 | 202.00 | 804.00 | 110.00 | 231.00 |
| 465.00 | 28.00 | 114.00 | 550.00 | 45.00 | 144.00 | 635.00 | 63.00 | 173.00 | 720.00 | 82.00 | 202.00 | 805.00 | 111.00 | 231.00 |
| 466.00 | 28.00 | 115.00 | 551.00 | 46.00 | 144.00 | 636.00 | 63.00 | 173.00 | 721.00 | 82.00 | 202.00 | 806.00 | 111.00 | 231.00 |
| 467.00 | 28.00 | 115.00 | 552.00 | 46.00 | 144.00 | 637.00 | 63.00 | 173.00 | 722.00 | 82.00 | 203.00 | 807.00 | 111.00 | 232.00 |
| 468.00 | 29.00 | 116.00 | 553.00 | 46.00 | 145.00 | 638.00 | 64.00 | 174.00 | 723.00 | 83.00 | 203.00 | 808.00 | 112.00 | 232.00 |
| 469.00 | 29.00 | 116.00 | 554.00 | 46.00 | 145.00 | 639.00 | 64.00 | 174.00 | 724.00 | 83.00 | 203.00 | 809.00 | 112.00 | 232.00 |
| 470.00 | 29.00 | 116.00 | 555.00 | 47.00 | 145.00 | 640.00 | 64.00 | 174.00 | 725.00 | 83.00 | 204.00 | 810.00 | 112.00 | 233.00 |
| 471.00 | 29.00 | 117.00 | 556.00 | 47.00 | 146.00 | 641.00 | 64.00 | 175.00 | 726.00 | 84.00 | 204.00 | 811.00 | 113.00 | 233.00 |
| 472.00 | 29.00 | 117.00 | 557.00 | 47.00 | 146.00 | 642.00 | 64.00 | 175.00 | 727.00 | 84.00 | 204.00 | 812.00 | 113.00 | 233.00 |
| 473.00 | 30.00 | 117.00 | 558.00 | 47.00 | 146.00 | 643.00 | 65.00 | 175.00 | 728.00 | 84.00 | 205.00 | 813.00 | 114.00 | 234.00 |
| 474.00 | 30.00 | 118.00 | 559.00 | 47.00 | 147.00 | 644.00 | 65.00 | 176.00 | 729.00 | 85.00 | 205.00 | 814.00 | 114.00 | 234.00 |
| 475.00 | 30.00 | 118.00 | 560.00 | 48.00 | 147.00 | 645.00 | 65.00 | 176.00 | 730.00 | 85.00 | 205.00 | 815.00 | 114.00 | 234.00 |
| 476.00 | 30.00 | 118.00 | 561.00 | 48.00 | 147.00 | 646.00 | 65.00 | 177.00 | 731.00 | 85.00 | 206.00 | 816.00 | 115.00 | 235.00 |
| 477.00 | 31.00 | 119.00 | 562.00 | 48.00 | 148.00 | 647.00 | 66.00 | 177.00 | 732.00 | 86.00 | 206.00 | 817.00 | 115.00 | 235.00 |
| 478.00 | 31.00 | 119.00 | 563.00 | 48.00 | 148.00 | 648.00 | 66.00 | 177.00 | 733.00 | 86.00 | 206.00 | 818.00 | 115.00 | 235.00 |
| 479.00 | 31.00 | 119.00 | 564.00 | 48.00 | 148.00 | 649.00 | 66.00 | 178.00 | 734.00 | 86.00 | 207.00 | 819.00 | 116.00 | 236.00 |
| 480.00 | 31.00 | 120.00 | 565.00 | 49.00 | 149.00 | 650.00 | 66.00 | 178.00 | 735.00 | 87.00 | 207.00 | 820.00 | 116.00 | 236.00 |
| 481.00 | 31.00 | 120.00 | 566.00 | 49.00 | 149.00 | 651.00 | 66.00 | 178.00 | 736.00 | 87.00 | 207.00 | 821.00 | 116.00 | 236.00 |
| 482.00 | 32.00 | 120.00 | 567.00 | 49.00 | 149.00 | 652.00 | 66.00 | 179.00 | 737.00 | 87.00 | 208.00 | 822.00 | 117.00 | 237.00 |
| 483.00 | 32.00 | 121.00 | 568.00 | 49.00 | 150.00 | 653.00 | 67.00 | 179.00 | 738.00 | 88.00 | 208.00 | 823.00 | 117.00 | 237.00 |
| 484.00 | 32.00 | 121.00 | 569.00 | 49.00 | 150.00 | 654.00 | 67.00 | 179.00 | 739.00 | 88.00 | 208.00 | 824.00 | 117.00 | 238.00 |
| 485.00 | 32.00 | 121.00 | 570.00 | 50.00 | 150.00 | 655.00 | 67.00 | 180.00 | 740.00 | 88.00 | 209.00 | 825.00 | 118.00 | 238.00 |
| 486.00 | 32.00 | 122.00 | 571.00 | 50.00 | 151.00 | 656.00 | 67.00 | 180.00 | 741.00 | 89.00 | 209.00 | 826.00 | 118.00 | 238.00 |
| 487.00 | 33.00 | 122.00 | 572.00 | 50.00 | 151.00 | 657.00 | 67.00 | 180.00 | 742.00 | 89.00 | 209.00 | 827.00 | 118.00 | 239.00 |
| 488.00 | 33.00 | 122.00 | 573.00 | 50.00 | 152.00 | 658.00 | 68.00 | 181.00 | 743.00 | 90.00 | 210.00 | 828.00 | 119.00 | 239.00 |
| 489.00 | 33.00 | 123.00 | 574.00 | 50.00 | 152.00 | 659.00 | 68.00 | 181.00 | 744.00 | 90.00 | 210.00 | 829.00 | 119.00 | 239.00 |
| 490.00 | 33.00 | 123.00 | 575.00 | 51.00 | 152.00 | 660.00 | 68.00 | 181.00 | 745.00 | 90.00 | 210.00 | 830.00 | 119.00 | 240.00 |
| 491.00 | 33.00 | 123.00 | 576.00 | 51.00 | 153.00 | 661.00 | 68.00 | 182.00 | 746.00 | 91.00 | 211.00 | 831.00 | 120.00 | 240.00 |
| 492.00 | 34.00 | 124.00 | 577.00 | 51.00 | 153.00 | 662.00 | 68.00 | 182.00 | 747.00 | 91.00 | 211.00 | 832.00 | 120.00 | 240.00 |
| 493.00 | 34.00 | 124.00 | 578.00 | 51.00 | 153.00 | 663.00 | 69.00 | 182.00 | 748.00 | 91.00 | 211.00 | 833.00 | 120.00 | 241.00 |
| 494.00 | 34.00 | 124.00 | 579.00 | 51.00 | 154.00 | 664.00 | 69.00 | 183.00 | 749.00 | 92.00 | 212.00 | 834.00 | 121.00 | 241.00 |
| 495.00 | 34.00 | 125.00 | 580.00 | 52.00 | 154.00 | 665.00 | 69.00 | 183.00 | 750.00 | 92.00 | 212.00 | 835.00 | 121.00 | 241.00 |
| 496.00 | 34.00 | 125.00 | 581.00 | 52.00 | 154.00 | 666.00 | 69.00 | 183.00 | 751.00 | 92.00 | 213.00 | 836.00 | 121.00 | 242.00 |
| 497.00 | 35.00 | 125.00 | 582.00 | 52.00 | 155.00 | 667.00 | 69.00 | 184.00 | 752.00 | 93.00 | 213.00 | 837.00 | 122.00 | 242.00 |
| 498.00 | 35.00 | 126.00 | 583.00 | 52.00 | 155.00 | 668.00 | 70.00 | 184.00 | 753.00 | 93.00 | 213.00 | 838.00 | 122.00 | 242.00 |
| 499.00 | 35.00 | 126.00 | 584.00 | 52.00 | 155.00 | 669.00 | 70.00 | 184.00 | 754.00 | 93.00 | 214.00 | 839.00 | 122.00 | 243.00 |
| 500.00 | 35.00 | 126.00 | 585.00 | 53.00 | 156.00 | 670.00 | 70.00 | 185.00 | 755.00 | 94.00 | 214.00 | 840.00 | 123.00 | 243.00 |
| 501.00 | 35.00 | 127.00 | 586.00 | 53.00 | 156.00 | 671.00 | 70.00 | 185.00 | 756.00 | 94.00 | 214.00 | 841.00 | 123.00 | 243.00 |
| 502.00 | 36.00 | 127.00 | 587.00 | 53.00 | 156.00 | 672.00 | 70.00 | 185.00 | 757.00 | 94.00 | 215.00 | 842.00 | 123.00 | 244.00 |
| 503.00 | 36.00 | 128.00 | 588.00 | 53.00 | 157.00 | 673.00 | 71.00 | 186.00 | 758.00 | 95.00 | 215.00 | 843.00 | 124.00 | 244.00 |
| 504.00 | 36.00 | 128.00 | 589.00 | 53.00 | 157.00 | 674.00 | 71.00 | 186.00 | 759.00 | 95.00 | 215.00 | 844.00 | 124.00 | 244.00 |
| 505.00 | 36.00 | 128.00 | 590.00 | 54.00 | 157.00 | 675.00 | 71.00 | 186.00 | 760.00 | 95.00 | 216.00 | 845.00 | 124.00 | 245.00 |
| 506.00 | 36.00 | 129.00 | 591.00 | 54.00 | 158.00 | 676.00 | 71.00 | 187.00 | 761.00 | 96.00 | 216.00 | 846.00 | 125.00 | 245.00 |
| 507.00 | 37.00 | 129.00 | 592.00 | 54.00 | 158.00 | 677.00 | 72.00 | 187.00 | 762.00 | 96.00 | 216.00 | 847.00 | 125.00 | 245.00 |
| 508.00 | 37.00 | 129.00 | 593.00 | 54.00 | 158.00 | 678.00 | 72.00 | 187.00 | 763.00 | 96.00 | 217.00 | 848.00 | 126.00 | 246.00 |
| 509.00 | 37.00 | 130.00 | 594.00 | 55.00 | 159.00 | 679.00 | 72.00 | 188.00 | 764.00 | 97.00 | 217.00 | 849.00 | 126.00 | 246.00 |
| 510.00 | 37.00 | 130.00 | 595.00 | 55.00 | 159.00 | 680.00 | 72.00 | 188.00 | 765.00 | 97.00 | 217.00 | 850.00 | 126.00 | 246.00 |

6

SCHEDULE 2 WEEKLY TAX TABLE

## Figure 7.5

### WEEKLY TAX TABLE – INCORPORATING MEDICARE LEVY

❗ Leave loading column has been removed from this tax table. For more information about leave loading changes, see page 3.

| Weekly earnings 1 ($) | With tax-free threshold 2 ($) | No tax-free threshold 3 ($) | Weekly earnings 1 ($) | With tax-free threshold 2 ($) | No tax-free threshold 3 ($) | Weekly earnings 1 ($) | With tax-free threshold 2 ($) | No tax-free threshold 3 ($) | Weekly earnings 1 ($) | With tax-free threshold 2 ($) | No tax-free threshold 3 ($) | Weekly earnings 1 ($) | With tax-free threshold 2 ($) | No tax-free threshold 3 ($) |
|---|---|---|---|---|---|---|---|---|---|---|---|---|---|---|
| 851.00 | 127.00 | 247.00 | 936.00 | 156.00 | 276.00 | 1021.00 | 185.00 | 305.00 | 1106.00 | 214.00 | 334.00 | 1191.00 | 243.00 | 363.00 |
| 852.00 | 127.00 | 247.00 | 937.00 | 156.00 | 276.00 | 1022.00 | 185.00 | 305.00 | 1107.00 | 214.00 | 334.00 | 1192.00 | 243.00 | 363.00 |
| 853.00 | 127.00 | 247.00 | 938.00 | 156.00 | 277.00 | 1023.00 | 185.00 | 305.00 | 1108.00 | 215.00 | 334.00 | 1193.00 | 244.00 | 364.00 |
| 854.00 | 128.00 | 248.00 | 939.00 | 157.00 | 277.00 | 1024.00 | 186.00 | 306.00 | 1109.00 | 215.00 | 335.00 | 1194.00 | 244.00 | 364.00 |
| 855.00 | 128.00 | 248.00 | 940.00 | 157.00 | 277.00 | 1025.00 | 186.00 | 306.00 | 1110.00 | 215.00 | 335.00 | 1195.00 | 244.00 | 364.00 |
| 856.00 | 128.00 | 248.00 | 941.00 | 157.00 | 278.00 | 1026.00 | 187.00 | 306.00 | 1111.00 | 216.00 | 335.00 | 1196.00 | 245.00 | 365.00 |
| 857.00 | 129.00 | 249.00 | 942.00 | 158.00 | 278.00 | 1027.00 | 187.00 | 307.00 | 1112.00 | 216.00 | 336.00 | 1197.00 | 245.00 | 365.00 |
| 858.00 | 129.00 | 249.00 | 943.00 | 158.00 | 278.00 | 1028.00 | 187.00 | 307.00 | 1113.00 | 216.00 | 336.00 | 1198.00 | 245.00 | 365.00 |
| 859.00 | 129.00 | 250.00 | 944.00 | 158.00 | 279.00 | 1029.00 | 188.00 | 308.00 | 1114.00 | 217.00 | 336.00 | 1199.00 | 246.00 | 366.00 |
| 860.00 | 130.00 | 250.00 | 945.00 | 159.00 | 279.00 | 1030.00 | 188.00 | 308.00 | 1115.00 | 217.00 | 337.00 | 1200.00 | 246.00 | 366.00 |
| 861.00 | 130.00 | 250.00 | 946.00 | 159.00 | 279.00 | 1031.00 | 188.00 | 308.00 | 1116.00 | 217.00 | 337.00 | 1201.00 | 246.00 | 367.00 |
| 862.00 | 130.00 | 251.00 | 947.00 | 159.00 | 280.00 | 1032.00 | 189.00 | 309.00 | 1117.00 | 218.00 | 337.00 | 1202.00 | 247.00 | 367.00 |
| 863.00 | 131.00 | 251.00 | 948.00 | 160.00 | 280.00 | 1033.00 | 189.00 | 309.00 | 1118.00 | 218.00 | 338.00 | 1203.00 | 247.00 | 367.00 |
| 864.00 | 131.00 | 251.00 | 949.00 | 160.00 | 280.00 | 1034.00 | 189.00 | 309.00 | 1119.00 | 218.00 | 338.00 | 1204.00 | 248.00 | 368.00 |
| 865.00 | 131.00 | 252.00 | 950.00 | 160.00 | 281.00 | 1035.00 | 190.00 | 310.00 | 1120.00 | 219.00 | 338.00 | 1205.00 | 248.00 | 368.00 |
| 866.00 | 132.00 | 252.00 | 951.00 | 161.00 | 281.00 | 1036.00 | 190.00 | 310.00 | 1121.00 | 219.00 | 339.00 | 1206.00 | 248.00 | 369.00 |
| 867.00 | 132.00 | 252.00 | 952.00 | 161.00 | 281.00 | 1037.00 | 190.00 | 310.00 | 1122.00 | 219.00 | 339.00 | 1207.00 | 249.00 | 369.00 |
| 868.00 | 132.00 | 253.00 | 953.00 | 161.00 | 282.00 | 1038.00 | 191.00 | 311.00 | 1123.00 | 220.00 | 339.00 | 1208.00 | 249.00 | 369.00 |
| 869.00 | 133.00 | 253.00 | 954.00 | 162.00 | 282.00 | 1039.00 | 191.00 | 311.00 | 1124.00 | 220.00 | 340.00 | 1209.00 | 249.00 | 370.00 |
| 870.00 | 133.00 | 253.00 | 955.00 | 162.00 | 282.00 | 1040.00 | 191.00 | 311.00 | 1125.00 | 220.00 | 340.00 | 1210.00 | 250.00 | 370.00 |
| 871.00 | 133.00 | 254.00 | 956.00 | 163.00 | 283.00 | 1041.00 | 192.00 | 312.00 | 1126.00 | 221.00 | 340.00 | 1211.00 | 250.00 | 370.00 |
| 872.00 | 134.00 | 254.00 | 957.00 | 163.00 | 283.00 | 1042.00 | 192.00 | 312.00 | 1127.00 | 221.00 | 341.00 | 1212.00 | 250.00 | 371.00 |
| 873.00 | 134.00 | 254.00 | 958.00 | 163.00 | 283.00 | 1043.00 | 192.00 | 312.00 | 1128.00 | 221.00 | 341.00 | 1213.00 | 251.00 | 371.00 |
| 874.00 | 134.00 | 255.00 | 959.00 | 164.00 | 284.00 | 1044.00 | 193.00 | 313.00 | 1129.00 | 222.00 | 342.00 | 1214.00 | 251.00 | 372.00 |
| 875.00 | 135.00 | 255.00 | 960.00 | 164.00 | 284.00 | 1045.00 | 193.00 | 313.00 | 1130.00 | 222.00 | 342.00 | 1215.00 | 251.00 | 372.00 |
| 876.00 | 135.00 | 255.00 | 961.00 | 164.00 | 284.00 | 1046.00 | 193.00 | 313.00 | 1131.00 | 222.00 | 342.00 | 1216.00 | 252.00 | 372.00 |
| 877.00 | 135.00 | 256.00 | 962.00 | 165.00 | 285.00 | 1047.00 | 194.00 | 314.00 | 1132.00 | 223.00 | 343.00 | 1217.00 | 252.00 | 373.00 |
| 878.00 | 136.00 | 256.00 | 963.00 | 165.00 | 285.00 | 1048.00 | 194.00 | 314.00 | 1133.00 | 223.00 | 343.00 | 1218.00 | 252.00 | 373.00 |
| 879.00 | 136.00 | 256.00 | 964.00 | 165.00 | 285.00 | 1049.00 | 194.00 | 314.00 | 1134.00 | 224.00 | 343.00 | 1219.00 | 253.00 | 373.00 |
| 880.00 | 136.00 | 257.00 | 965.00 | 166.00 | 286.00 | 1050.00 | 195.00 | 315.00 | 1135.00 | 224.00 | 344.00 | 1220.00 | 253.00 | 374.00 |
| 881.00 | 137.00 | 257.00 | 966.00 | 166.00 | 286.00 | 1051.00 | 195.00 | 315.00 | 1136.00 | 224.00 | 344.00 | 1221.00 | 253.00 | 374.00 |
| 882.00 | 137.00 | 257.00 | 967.00 | 166.00 | 286.00 | 1052.00 | 195.00 | 315.00 | 1137.00 | 225.00 | 344.00 | 1222.00 | 254.00 | 375.00 |
| 883.00 | 138.00 | 258.00 | 968.00 | 167.00 | 287.00 | 1053.00 | 196.00 | 316.00 | 1138.00 | 225.00 | 345.00 | 1223.00 | 254.00 | 375.00 |
| 884.00 | 138.00 | 258.00 | 969.00 | 167.00 | 287.00 | 1054.00 | 196.00 | 316.00 | 1139.00 | 225.00 | 345.00 | 1224.00 | 254.00 | 375.00 |
| 885.00 | 138.00 | 258.00 | 970.00 | 167.00 | 287.00 | 1055.00 | 196.00 | 316.00 | 1140.00 | 226.00 | 345.00 | 1225.00 | 255.00 | 376.00 |
| 886.00 | 139.00 | 259.00 | 971.00 | 168.00 | 288.00 | 1056.00 | 197.00 | 317.00 | 1141.00 | 226.00 | 346.00 | 1226.00 | 255.00 | 376.00 |
| 887.00 | 139.00 | 259.00 | 972.00 | 168.00 | 288.00 | 1057.00 | 197.00 | 317.00 | 1142.00 | 226.00 | 346.00 | 1227.00 | 255.00 | 377.00 |
| 888.00 | 139.00 | 259.00 | 973.00 | 168.00 | 288.00 | 1058.00 | 197.00 | 317.00 | 1143.00 | 227.00 | 346.00 | 1228.00 | 256.00 | 377.00 |
| 889.00 | 140.00 | 260.00 | 974.00 | 169.00 | 289.00 | 1059.00 | 198.00 | 318.00 | 1144.00 | 227.00 | 347.00 | 1229.00 | 256.00 | 377.00 |
| 890.00 | 140.00 | 260.00 | 975.00 | 169.00 | 289.00 | 1060.00 | 198.00 | 318.00 | 1145.00 | 227.00 | 347.00 | 1230.00 | 256.00 | 378.00 |
| 891.00 | 140.00 | 260.00 | 976.00 | 169.00 | 289.00 | 1061.00 | 199.00 | 318.00 | 1146.00 | 228.00 | 347.00 | 1231.00 | 257.00 | 378.00 |
| 892.00 | 141.00 | 261.00 | 977.00 | 170.00 | 290.00 | 1062.00 | 199.00 | 319.00 | 1147.00 | 228.00 | 348.00 | 1232.00 | 257.00 | 379.00 |
| 893.00 | 141.00 | 261.00 | 978.00 | 170.00 | 290.00 | 1063.00 | 199.00 | 319.00 | 1148.00 | 228.00 | 348.00 | 1233.00 | 257.00 | 379.00 |
| 894.00 | 141.00 | 262.00 | 979.00 | 170.00 | 291.00 | 1064.00 | 200.00 | 319.00 | 1149.00 | 229.00 | 348.00 | 1234.00 | 258.00 | 379.00 |
| 895.00 | 142.00 | 262.00 | 980.00 | 171.00 | 291.00 | 1065.00 | 200.00 | 320.00 | 1150.00 | 229.00 | 349.00 | 1235.00 | 258.00 | 380.00 |
| 896.00 | 142.00 | 262.00 | 981.00 | 171.00 | 291.00 | 1066.00 | 200.00 | 320.00 | 1151.00 | 229.00 | 349.00 | 1236.00 | 258.00 | 380.00 |
| 897.00 | 142.00 | 263.00 | 982.00 | 171.00 | 292.00 | 1067.00 | 201.00 | 320.00 | 1152.00 | 230.00 | 349.00 | 1237.00 | 259.00 | 380.00 |
| 898.00 | 143.00 | 263.00 | 983.00 | 172.00 | 292.00 | 1068.00 | 201.00 | 321.00 | 1153.00 | 230.00 | 350.00 | 1238.00 | 259.00 | 381.00 |
| 899.00 | 143.00 | 263.00 | 984.00 | 172.00 | 292.00 | 1069.00 | 201.00 | 321.00 | 1154.00 | 230.00 | 350.00 | 1239.00 | 260.00 | 381.00 |
| 900.00 | 143.00 | 264.00 | 985.00 | 172.00 | 293.00 | 1070.00 | 202.00 | 321.00 | 1155.00 | 231.00 | 350.00 | 1240.00 | 260.00 | 382.00 |
| 901.00 | 144.00 | 264.00 | 986.00 | 173.00 | 293.00 | 1071.00 | 202.00 | 322.00 | 1156.00 | 231.00 | 351.00 | 1241.00 | 260.00 | 382.00 |
| 902.00 | 144.00 | 264.00 | 987.00 | 173.00 | 293.00 | 1072.00 | 202.00 | 322.00 | 1157.00 | 231.00 | 351.00 | 1242.00 | 261.00 | 382.00 |
| 903.00 | 144.00 | 265.00 | 988.00 | 173.00 | 294.00 | 1073.00 | 203.00 | 322.00 | 1158.00 | 232.00 | 351.00 | 1243.00 | 261.00 | 383.00 |
| 904.00 | 145.00 | 265.00 | 989.00 | 174.00 | 294.00 | 1074.00 | 203.00 | 323.00 | 1159.00 | 232.00 | 352.00 | 1244.00 | 261.00 | 383.00 |
| 905.00 | 145.00 | 265.00 | 990.00 | 174.00 | 294.00 | 1075.00 | 203.00 | 323.00 | 1160.00 | 232.00 | 352.00 | 1245.00 | 262.00 | 384.00 |
| 906.00 | 145.00 | 266.00 | 991.00 | 175.00 | 295.00 | 1076.00 | 204.00 | 323.00 | 1161.00 | 233.00 | 352.00 | 1246.00 | 262.00 | 384.00 |
| 907.00 | 146.00 | 266.00 | 992.00 | 175.00 | 295.00 | 1077.00 | 204.00 | 324.00 | 1162.00 | 233.00 | 353.00 | 1247.00 | 262.00 | 384.00 |
| 908.00 | 146.00 | 266.00 | 993.00 | 175.00 | 295.00 | 1078.00 | 204.00 | 324.00 | 1163.00 | 233.00 | 353.00 | 1248.00 | 263.00 | 385.00 |
| 909.00 | 146.00 | 267.00 | 994.00 | 176.00 | 296.00 | 1079.00 | 205.00 | 325.00 | 1164.00 | 234.00 | 353.00 | 1249.00 | 263.00 | 385.00 |
| 910.00 | 147.00 | 267.00 | 995.00 | 176.00 | 296.00 | 1080.00 | 205.00 | 325.00 | 1165.00 | 234.00 | 354.00 | 1250.00 | 263.00 | 385.00 |
| 911.00 | 147.00 | 267.00 | 996.00 | 176.00 | 296.00 | 1081.00 | 205.00 | 325.00 | 1166.00 | 234.00 | 354.00 | 1251.00 | 264.00 | 386.00 |
| 912.00 | 147.00 | 268.00 | 997.00 | 177.00 | 297.00 | 1082.00 | 206.00 | 326.00 | 1167.00 | 235.00 | 354.00 | 1252.00 | 264.00 | 386.00 |
| 913.00 | 148.00 | 268.00 | 998.00 | 177.00 | 297.00 | 1083.00 | 206.00 | 326.00 | 1168.00 | 235.00 | 355.00 | 1253.00 | 264.00 | 387.00 |
| 914.00 | 148.00 | 268.00 | 999.00 | 177.00 | 297.00 | 1084.00 | 206.00 | 326.00 | 1169.00 | 236.00 | 355.00 | 1254.00 | 265.00 | 387.00 |
| 915.00 | 148.00 | 269.00 | 1000.00 | 178.00 | 298.00 | 1085.00 | 207.00 | 327.00 | 1170.00 | 236.00 | 355.00 | 1255.00 | 265.00 | 387.00 |
| 916.00 | 149.00 | 269.00 | 1001.00 | 178.00 | 298.00 | 1086.00 | 207.00 | 327.00 | 1171.00 | 236.00 | 356.00 | 1256.00 | 265.00 | 388.00 |
| 917.00 | 149.00 | 269.00 | 1002.00 | 178.00 | 298.00 | 1087.00 | 207.00 | 327.00 | 1172.00 | 237.00 | 356.00 | 1257.00 | 266.00 | 388.00 |
| 918.00 | 149.00 | 270.00 | 1003.00 | 179.00 | 299.00 | 1088.00 | 208.00 | 328.00 | 1173.00 | 237.00 | 356.00 | 1258.00 | 266.00 | 389.00 |
| 919.00 | 150.00 | 270.00 | 1004.00 | 179.00 | 299.00 | 1089.00 | 208.00 | 328.00 | 1174.00 | 237.00 | 357.00 | 1259.00 | 266.00 | 389.00 |
| 920.00 | 150.00 | 270.00 | 1005.00 | 179.00 | 299.00 | 1090.00 | 208.00 | 328.00 | 1175.00 | 238.00 | 357.00 | 1260.00 | 267.00 | 389.00 |
| 921.00 | 151.00 | 271.00 | 1006.00 | 180.00 | 300.00 | 1091.00 | 209.00 | 329.00 | 1176.00 | 238.00 | 357.00 | 1261.00 | 267.00 | 390.00 |
| 922.00 | 151.00 | 271.00 | 1007.00 | 180.00 | 300.00 | 1092.00 | 209.00 | 329.00 | 1177.00 | 238.00 | 358.00 | 1262.00 | 267.00 | 390.00 |
| 923.00 | 151.00 | 271.00 | 1008.00 | 180.00 | 300.00 | 1093.00 | 209.00 | 329.00 | 1178.00 | 239.00 | 358.00 | 1263.00 | 268.00 | 390.00 |
| 924.00 | 152.00 | 272.00 | 1009.00 | 181.00 | 301.00 | 1094.00 | 210.00 | 330.00 | 1179.00 | 239.00 | 359.00 | 1264.00 | 268.00 | 391.00 |
| 925.00 | 152.00 | 272.00 | 1010.00 | 181.00 | 301.00 | 1095.00 | 210.00 | 330.00 | 1180.00 | 239.00 | 359.00 | 1265.00 | 268.00 | 391.00 |
| 926.00 | 152.00 | 272.00 | 1011.00 | 181.00 | 301.00 | 1096.00 | 210.00 | 330.00 | 1181.00 | 240.00 | 359.00 | 1266.00 | 269.00 | 392.00 |
| 927.00 | 153.00 | 273.00 | 1012.00 | 182.00 | 302.00 | 1097.00 | 211.00 | 331.00 | 1182.00 | 240.00 | 360.00 | 1267.00 | 269.00 | 392.00 |
| 928.00 | 153.00 | 273.00 | 1013.00 | 182.00 | 302.00 | 1098.00 | 211.00 | 331.00 | 1183.00 | 240.00 | 360.00 | 1268.00 | 269.00 | 392.00 |
| 929.00 | 153.00 | 274.00 | 1014.00 | 182.00 | 302.00 | 1099.00 | 212.00 | 331.00 | 1184.00 | 241.00 | 360.00 | 1269.00 | 270.00 | 393.00 |
| 930.00 | 154.00 | 274.00 | 1015.00 | 183.00 | 303.00 | 1100.00 | 212.00 | 332.00 | 1185.00 | 241.00 | 361.00 | 1270.00 | 270.00 | 393.00 |
| 931.00 | 154.00 | 274.00 | 1016.00 | 183.00 | 303.00 | 1101.00 | 212.00 | 332.00 | 1186.00 | 241.00 | 361.00 | 1271.00 | 270.00 | 394.00 |
| 932.00 | 154.00 | 275.00 | 1017.00 | 183.00 | 303.00 | 1102.00 | 213.00 | 332.00 | 1187.00 | 242.00 | 361.00 | 1272.00 | 271.00 | 394.00 |
| 933.00 | 155.00 | 275.00 | 1018.00 | 184.00 | 304.00 | 1103.00 | 213.00 | 333.00 | 1188.00 | 242.00 | 362.00 | 1273.00 | 271.00 | 394.00 |
| 934.00 | 155.00 | 275.00 | 1019.00 | 184.00 | 304.00 | 1104.00 | 213.00 | 333.00 | 1189.00 | 242.00 | 362.00 | 1274.00 | 271.00 | 395.00 |
| 935.00 | 155.00 | 276.00 | 1020.00 | 184.00 | 304.00 | 1105.00 | 214.00 | 333.00 | 1190.00 | 243.00 | 362.00 | 1275.00 | 272.00 | 395.00 |

SCHEDULE 2 WEEKLY TAX TABLE

7

Figure 7.5

## WEEKLY TAX TABLE – INCORPORATING MEDICARE LEVY

❗ Leave loading column has been removed from this tax table. For more information about leave loading changes, see page 3.

| Weekly earnings 1 $ | With tax-free threshold 2 $ | No tax-free threshold 3 $ | Weekly earnings 1 $ | With tax-free threshold 2 $ | No tax-free threshold 3 $ | Weekly earnings 1 $ | With tax-free threshold 2 $ | No tax-free threshold 3 $ | Weekly earnings 1 $ | With tax-free threshold 2 $ | No tax-free threshold 3 $ | Weekly earnings 1 $ | With tax-free threshold 2 $ | No tax-free threshold 3 $ |
|---|---|---|---|---|---|---|---|---|---|---|---|---|---|---|
| 1276.00 | 272.00 | 395.00 | 1361.00 | 301.00 | 428.00 | 1446.00 | 330.00 | 461.00 | 1531.00 | 359.00 | 494.00 | 1616.00 | 391.00 | 526.00 |
| 1277.00 | 273.00 | 396.00 | 1362.00 | 301.00 | 429.00 | 1447.00 | 330.00 | 461.00 | 1532.00 | 359.00 | 494.00 | 1617.00 | 392.00 | 527.00 |
| 1278.00 | 273.00 | 396.00 | 1363.00 | 302.00 | 429.00 | 1448.00 | 331.00 | 462.00 | 1533.00 | 360.00 | 494.00 | 1618.00 | 392.00 | 527.00 |
| 1279.00 | 273.00 | 397.00 | 1364.00 | 302.00 | 429.00 | 1449.00 | 331.00 | 462.00 | 1534.00 | 360.00 | 495.00 | 1619.00 | 392.00 | 528.00 |
| 1280.00 | 274.00 | 397.00 | 1365.00 | 302.00 | 430.00 | 1450.00 | 331.00 | 462.00 | 1535.00 | 360.00 | 495.00 | 1620.00 | 393.00 | 528.00 |
| 1281.00 | 274.00 | 397.00 | 1366.00 | 303.00 | 430.00 | 1451.00 | 332.00 | 463.00 | 1536.00 | 361.00 | 496.00 | 1621.00 | 393.00 | 528.00 |
| 1282.00 | 274.00 | 398.00 | 1367.00 | 303.00 | 431.00 | 1452.00 | 332.00 | 463.00 | 1537.00 | 361.00 | 496.00 | 1622.00 | 394.00 | 529.00 |
| 1283.00 | 275.00 | 398.00 | 1368.00 | 303.00 | 431.00 | 1453.00 | 332.00 | 464.00 | 1538.00 | 361.00 | 496.00 | 1623.00 | 394.00 | 529.00 |
| 1284.00 | 275.00 | 399.00 | 1369.00 | 304.00 | 431.00 | 1454.00 | 333.00 | 464.00 | 1539.00 | 362.00 | 497.00 | 1624.00 | 394.00 | 529.00 |
| 1285.00 | 275.00 | 399.00 | 1370.00 | 304.00 | 432.00 | 1455.00 | 333.00 | 464.00 | 1540.00 | 362.00 | 497.00 | 1625.00 | 395.00 | 530.00 |
| 1286.00 | 276.00 | 399.00 | 1371.00 | 304.00 | 432.00 | 1456.00 | 333.00 | 465.00 | 1541.00 | 362.00 | 497.00 | 1626.00 | 395.00 | 530.00 |
| 1287.00 | 276.00 | 400.00 | 1372.00 | 305.00 | 432.00 | 1457.00 | 334.00 | 465.00 | 1542.00 | 363.00 | 498.00 | 1627.00 | 396.00 | 531.00 |
| 1288.00 | 276.00 | 400.00 | 1373.00 | 305.00 | 433.00 | 1458.00 | 334.00 | 466.00 | 1543.00 | 363.00 | 498.00 | 1628.00 | 396.00 | 531.00 |
| 1289.00 | 277.00 | 400.00 | 1374.00 | 306.00 | 433.00 | 1459.00 | 334.00 | 466.00 | 1544.00 | 364.00 | 499.00 | 1629.00 | 396.00 | 531.00 |
| 1290.00 | 277.00 | 401.00 | 1375.00 | 306.00 | 434.00 | 1460.00 | 335.00 | 466.00 | 1545.00 | 364.00 | 499.00 | 1630.00 | 397.00 | 532.00 |
| 1291.00 | 277.00 | 401.00 | 1376.00 | 306.00 | 434.00 | 1461.00 | 335.00 | 467.00 | 1546.00 | 364.00 | 499.00 | 1631.00 | 397.00 | 532.00 |
| 1292.00 | 278.00 | 402.00 | 1377.00 | 307.00 | 434.00 | 1462.00 | 335.00 | 467.00 | 1547.00 | 365.00 | 500.00 | 1632.00 | 397.00 | 533.00 |
| 1293.00 | 278.00 | 402.00 | 1378.00 | 307.00 | 435.00 | 1463.00 | 336.00 | 467.00 | 1548.00 | 365.00 | 500.00 | 1633.00 | 398.00 | 533.00 |
| 1294.00 | 278.00 | 402.00 | 1379.00 | 307.00 | 435.00 | 1464.00 | 336.00 | 468.00 | 1549.00 | 366.00 | 501.00 | 1634.00 | 398.00 | 533.00 |
| 1295.00 | 279.00 | 403.00 | 1380.00 | 308.00 | 436.00 | 1465.00 | 336.00 | 468.00 | 1550.00 | 366.00 | 501.00 | 1635.00 | 399.00 | 534.00 |
| 1296.00 | 279.00 | 403.00 | 1381.00 | 308.00 | 436.00 | 1466.00 | 337.00 | 469.00 | 1551.00 | 366.00 | 501.00 | 1636.00 | 399.00 | 534.00 |
| 1297.00 | 279.00 | 404.00 | 1382.00 | 308.00 | 436.00 | 1467.00 | 337.00 | 469.00 | 1552.00 | 367.00 | 502.00 | 1637.00 | 399.00 | 534.00 |
| 1298.00 | 280.00 | 404.00 | 1383.00 | 309.00 | 437.00 | 1468.00 | 337.00 | 469.00 | 1553.00 | 367.00 | 502.00 | 1638.00 | 400.00 | 535.00 |
| 1299.00 | 280.00 | 404.00 | 1384.00 | 309.00 | 437.00 | 1469.00 | 338.00 | 470.00 | 1554.00 | 367.00 | 503.00 | 1639.00 | 400.00 | 535.00 |
| 1300.00 | 280.00 | 405.00 | 1385.00 | 309.00 | 437.00 | 1470.00 | 338.00 | 470.00 | 1555.00 | 368.00 | 503.00 | 1640.00 | 401.00 | 536.00 |
| 1301.00 | 281.00 | 405.00 | 1386.00 | 310.00 | 438.00 | 1471.00 | 338.00 | 471.00 | 1556.00 | 368.00 | 503.00 | 1641.00 | 401.00 | 536.00 |
| 1302.00 | 281.00 | 405.00 | 1387.00 | 310.00 | 438.00 | 1472.00 | 339.00 | 471.00 | 1557.00 | 369.00 | 504.00 | 1642.00 | 401.00 | 536.00 |
| 1303.00 | 281.00 | 406.00 | 1388.00 | 310.00 | 439.00 | 1473.00 | 339.00 | 471.00 | 1558.00 | 369.00 | 504.00 | 1643.00 | 402.00 | 537.00 |
| 1304.00 | 282.00 | 406.00 | 1389.00 | 311.00 | 439.00 | 1474.00 | 340.00 | 472.00 | 1559.00 | 369.00 | 504.00 | 1644.00 | 402.00 | 537.00 |
| 1305.00 | 282.00 | 407.00 | 1390.00 | 311.00 | 439.00 | 1475.00 | 340.00 | 472.00 | 1560.00 | 370.00 | 505.00 | 1645.00 | 402.00 | 538.00 |
| 1306.00 | 282.00 | 407.00 | 1391.00 | 311.00 | 440.00 | 1476.00 | 340.00 | 472.00 | 1561.00 | 370.00 | 505.00 | 1646.00 | 403.00 | 538.00 |
| 1307.00 | 283.00 | 407.00 | 1392.00 | 312.00 | 440.00 | 1477.00 | 341.00 | 473.00 | 1562.00 | 371.00 | 506.00 | 1647.00 | 403.00 | 538.00 |
| 1308.00 | 283.00 | 408.00 | 1393.00 | 312.00 | 441.00 | 1478.00 | 341.00 | 473.00 | 1563.00 | 371.00 | 506.00 | 1648.00 | 404.00 | 539.00 |
| 1309.00 | 283.00 | 408.00 | 1394.00 | 312.00 | 441.00 | 1479.00 | 341.00 | 474.00 | 1564.00 | 371.00 | 506.00 | 1649.00 | 404.00 | 539.00 |
| 1310.00 | 284.00 | 409.00 | 1395.00 | 313.00 | 441.00 | 1480.00 | 342.00 | 474.00 | 1565.00 | 372.00 | 507.00 | 1650.00 | 404.00 | 539.00 |
| 1311.00 | 284.00 | 409.00 | 1396.00 | 313.00 | 442.00 | 1481.00 | 342.00 | 474.00 | 1566.00 | 372.00 | 507.00 | 1651.00 | 405.00 | 540.00 |
| 1312.00 | 284.00 | 409.00 | 1397.00 | 313.00 | 442.00 | 1482.00 | 342.00 | 475.00 | 1567.00 | 372.00 | 508.00 | 1652.00 | 405.00 | 540.00 |
| 1313.00 | 285.00 | 410.00 | 1398.00 | 314.00 | 442.00 | 1483.00 | 343.00 | 475.00 | 1568.00 | 373.00 | 508.00 | 1653.00 | 406.00 | 541.00 |
| 1314.00 | 285.00 | 410.00 | 1399.00 | 314.00 | 443.00 | 1484.00 | 343.00 | 476.00 | 1569.00 | 373.00 | 508.00 | 1654.00 | 406.00 | 541.00 |
| 1315.00 | 285.00 | 410.00 | 1400.00 | 314.00 | 443.00 | 1485.00 | 343.00 | 476.00 | 1570.00 | 374.00 | 509.00 | 1655.00 | 406.00 | 541.00 |
| 1316.00 | 286.00 | 411.00 | 1401.00 | 315.00 | 444.00 | 1486.00 | 344.00 | 476.00 | 1571.00 | 374.00 | 509.00 | 1656.00 | 407.00 | 542.00 |
| 1317.00 | 286.00 | 411.00 | 1402.00 | 315.00 | 444.00 | 1487.00 | 344.00 | 477.00 | 1572.00 | 374.00 | 509.00 | 1657.00 | 407.00 | 542.00 |
| 1318.00 | 286.00 | 412.00 | 1403.00 | 315.00 | 444.00 | 1488.00 | 344.00 | 477.00 | 1573.00 | 375.00 | 510.00 | 1658.00 | 407.00 | 543.00 |
| 1319.00 | 287.00 | 412.00 | 1404.00 | 316.00 | 445.00 | 1489.00 | 345.00 | 477.00 | 1574.00 | 375.00 | 510.00 | 1659.00 | 408.00 | 543.00 |
| 1320.00 | 287.00 | 412.00 | 1405.00 | 316.00 | 445.00 | 1490.00 | 345.00 | 478.00 | 1575.00 | 376.00 | 511.00 | 1660.00 | 408.00 | 543.00 |
| 1321.00 | 287.00 | 413.00 | 1406.00 | 316.00 | 446.00 | 1491.00 | 345.00 | 478.00 | 1576.00 | 376.00 | 511.00 | 1661.00 | 409.00 | 544.00 |
| 1322.00 | 288.00 | 413.00 | 1407.00 | 317.00 | 446.00 | 1492.00 | 346.00 | 479.00 | 1577.00 | 376.00 | 511.00 | 1662.00 | 409.00 | 544.00 |
| 1323.00 | 288.00 | 414.00 | 1408.00 | 317.00 | 446.00 | 1493.00 | 346.00 | 479.00 | 1578.00 | 377.00 | 512.00 | 1663.00 | 409.00 | 544.00 |
| 1324.00 | 289.00 | 414.00 | 1409.00 | 317.00 | 447.00 | 1494.00 | 346.00 | 479.00 | 1579.00 | 377.00 | 512.00 | 1664.00 | 410.00 | 545.00 |
| 1325.00 | 289.00 | 414.00 | 1410.00 | 318.00 | 447.00 | 1495.00 | 347.00 | 480.00 | 1580.00 | 377.00 | 513.00 | 1665.00 | 410.00 | 545.00 |
| 1326.00 | 289.00 | 415.00 | 1411.00 | 318.00 | 447.00 | 1496.00 | 347.00 | 480.00 | 1581.00 | 378.00 | 513.00 | 1666.00 | 411.00 | 546.00 |
| 1327.00 | 290.00 | 415.00 | 1412.00 | 318.00 | 448.00 | 1497.00 | 347.00 | 481.00 | 1582.00 | 378.00 | 513.00 | 1667.00 | 411.00 | 546.00 |
| 1328.00 | 290.00 | 415.00 | 1413.00 | 319.00 | 448.00 | 1498.00 | 348.00 | 481.00 | 1583.00 | 379.00 | 514.00 | 1668.00 | 411.00 | 546.00 |
| 1329.00 | 290.00 | 416.00 | 1414.00 | 319.00 | 449.00 | 1499.00 | 348.00 | 481.00 | 1584.00 | 379.00 | 514.00 | 1669.00 | 412.00 | 547.00 |
| 1330.00 | 291.00 | 416.00 | 1415.00 | 319.00 | 449.00 | 1500.00 | 348.00 | 482.00 | 1585.00 | 379.00 | 514.00 | 1670.00 | 412.00 | 547.00 |
| 1331.00 | 291.00 | 417.00 | 1416.00 | 320.00 | 449.00 | 1501.00 | 349.00 | 482.00 | 1586.00 | 380.00 | 515.00 | 1671.00 | 413.00 | 548.00 |
| 1332.00 | 291.00 | 417.00 | 1417.00 | 320.00 | 450.00 | 1502.00 | 349.00 | 482.00 | 1587.00 | 380.00 | 515.00 | 1672.00 | 413.00 | 548.00 |
| 1333.00 | 292.00 | 417.00 | 1418.00 | 320.00 | 450.00 | 1503.00 | 349.00 | 483.00 | 1588.00 | 381.00 | 516.00 | 1673.00 | 413.00 | 548.00 |
| 1334.00 | 292.00 | 418.00 | 1419.00 | 321.00 | 451.00 | 1504.00 | 350.00 | 483.00 | 1589.00 | 381.00 | 516.00 | 1674.00 | 414.00 | 549.00 |
| 1335.00 | 292.00 | 418.00 | 1420.00 | 321.00 | 451.00 | 1505.00 | 350.00 | 484.00 | 1590.00 | 381.00 | 516.00 | 1675.00 | 414.00 | 549.00 |
| 1336.00 | 293.00 | 419.00 | 1421.00 | 321.00 | 451.00 | 1506.00 | 350.00 | 484.00 | 1591.00 | 382.00 | 517.00 | 1676.00 | 414.00 | 549.00 |
| 1337.00 | 293.00 | 419.00 | 1422.00 | 322.00 | 452.00 | 1507.00 | 351.00 | 484.00 | 1592.00 | 382.00 | 517.00 | 1677.00 | 415.00 | 550.00 |
| 1338.00 | 293.00 | 419.00 | 1423.00 | 322.00 | 452.00 | 1508.00 | 351.00 | 485.00 | 1593.00 | 382.00 | 518.00 | 1678.00 | 415.00 | 550.00 |
| 1339.00 | 294.00 | 420.00 | 1424.00 | 323.00 | 452.00 | 1509.00 | 351.00 | 485.00 | 1594.00 | 383.00 | 518.00 | 1679.00 | 416.00 | 551.00 |
| 1340.00 | 294.00 | 420.00 | 1425.00 | 323.00 | 453.00 | 1510.00 | 352.00 | 486.00 | 1595.00 | 383.00 | 518.00 | 1680.00 | 416.00 | 551.00 |
| 1341.00 | 294.00 | 420.00 | 1426.00 | 323.00 | 453.00 | 1511.00 | 352.00 | 486.00 | 1596.00 | 384.00 | 519.00 | 1681.00 | 416.00 | 551.00 |
| 1342.00 | 295.00 | 421.00 | 1427.00 | 324.00 | 454.00 | 1512.00 | 352.00 | 486.00 | 1597.00 | 384.00 | 519.00 | 1682.00 | 417.00 | 552.00 |
| 1343.00 | 295.00 | 421.00 | 1428.00 | 324.00 | 454.00 | 1513.00 | 353.00 | 487.00 | 1598.00 | 384.00 | 519.00 | 1683.00 | 417.00 | 552.00 |
| 1344.00 | 295.00 | 422.00 | 1429.00 | 324.00 | 454.00 | 1514.00 | 353.00 | 487.00 | 1599.00 | 385.00 | 520.00 | 1684.00 | 418.00 | 553.00 |
| 1345.00 | 296.00 | 422.00 | 1430.00 | 325.00 | 455.00 | 1515.00 | 353.00 | 487.00 | 1600.00 | 385.00 | 520.00 | 1685.00 | 418.00 | 553.00 |
| 1346.00 | 296.00 | 422.00 | 1431.00 | 325.00 | 455.00 | 1516.00 | 354.00 | 488.00 | 1601.00 | 386.00 | 521.00 | 1686.00 | 418.00 | 553.00 |
| 1347.00 | 296.00 | 423.00 | 1432.00 | 325.00 | 456.00 | 1517.00 | 354.00 | 488.00 | 1602.00 | 386.00 | 521.00 | 1687.00 | 419.00 | 554.00 |
| 1348.00 | 297.00 | 423.00 | 1433.00 | 326.00 | 456.00 | 1518.00 | 354.00 | 489.00 | 1603.00 | 386.00 | 521.00 | 1688.00 | 419.00 | 554.00 |
| 1349.00 | 297.00 | 424.00 | 1434.00 | 326.00 | 456.00 | 1519.00 | 355.00 | 489.00 | 1604.00 | 387.00 | 522.00 | 1689.00 | 419.00 | 554.00 |
| 1350.00 | 297.00 | 424.00 | 1435.00 | 326.00 | 457.00 | 1520.00 | 355.00 | 489.00 | 1605.00 | 387.00 | 522.00 | 1690.00 | 420.00 | 555.00 |
| 1351.00 | 298.00 | 424.00 | 1436.00 | 327.00 | 457.00 | 1521.00 | 355.00 | 490.00 | 1606.00 | 387.00 | 523.00 | 1691.00 | 420.00 | 555.00 |
| 1352.00 | 298.00 | 425.00 | 1437.00 | 327.00 | 457.00 | 1522.00 | 356.00 | 490.00 | 1607.00 | 388.00 | 523.00 | 1692.00 | 421.00 | 556.00 |
| 1353.00 | 298.00 | 425.00 | 1438.00 | 327.00 | 458.00 | 1523.00 | 356.00 | 491.00 | 1608.00 | 388.00 | 523.00 | 1693.00 | 421.00 | 556.00 |
| 1354.00 | 299.00 | 426.00 | 1439.00 | 328.00 | 458.00 | 1524.00 | 357.00 | 491.00 | 1609.00 | 389.00 | 524.00 | 1694.00 | 421.00 | 556.00 |
| 1355.00 | 299.00 | 426.00 | 1440.00 | 328.00 | 459.00 | 1525.00 | 357.00 | 491.00 | 1610.00 | 389.00 | 524.00 | 1695.00 | 422.00 | 557.00 |
| 1356.00 | 299.00 | 426.00 | 1441.00 | 328.00 | 459.00 | 1526.00 | 357.00 | 492.00 | 1611.00 | 389.00 | 524.00 | 1696.00 | 422.00 | 557.00 |
| 1357.00 | 300.00 | 427.00 | 1442.00 | 329.00 | 459.00 | 1527.00 | 358.00 | 492.00 | 1612.00 | 390.00 | 525.00 | 1697.00 | 423.00 | 558.00 |
| 1358.00 | 300.00 | 427.00 | 1443.00 | 329.00 | 460.00 | 1528.00 | 358.00 | 492.00 | 1613.00 | 390.00 | 525.00 | 1698.00 | 423.00 | 558.00 |
| 1359.00 | 300.00 | 427.00 | 1444.00 | 329.00 | 460.00 | 1529.00 | 358.00 | 493.00 | 1614.00 | 391.00 | 526.00 | 1699.00 | 423.00 | 558.00 |
| 1360.00 | 301.00 | 428.00 | 1445.00 | 330.00 | 461.00 | 1530.00 | 359.00 | 493.00 | 1615.00 | 391.00 | 526.00 | 1700.00 | 424.00 | 559.00 |

8

SCHEDULE 2 WEEKLY TAX TABLE

Figure 7.5

## WEEKLY TAX TABLE – INCORPORATING MEDICARE LEVY

❗ Leave loading column has been removed from this tax table. For more information about leave loading changes, see page 3.

| Weekly earnings 1 $ | With tax-free threshold 2 $ | No tax-free threshold 3 $ | Weekly earnings 1 $ | With tax-free threshold 2 $ | No tax-free threshold 3 $ | Weekly earnings 1 $ | With tax-free threshold 2 $ | No tax-free threshold 3 $ | Weekly earnings 1 $ | With tax-free threshold 2 $ | No tax-free threshold 3 $ | Weekly earnings 1 $ | With tax-free threshold 2 $ | No tax-free threshold 3 $ |
|---|---|---|---|---|---|---|---|---|---|---|---|---|---|---|
| 1701.00 | 424.00 | 559.00 | 1786.00 | 457.00 | 592.00 | 1871.00 | 490.00 | 625.00 | 1956.00 | 522.00 | 657.00 | 2041.00 | 555.00 | 690.00 |
| 1702.00 | 424.00 | 559.00 | 1787.00 | 457.00 | 592.00 | 1872.00 | 490.00 | 625.00 | 1957.00 | 523.00 | 658.00 | 2042.00 | 555.00 | 690.00 |
| 1703.00 | 425.00 | 560.00 | 1788.00 | 458.00 | 593.00 | 1873.00 | 490.00 | 625.00 | 1958.00 | 523.00 | 658.00 | 2043.00 | 556.00 | 691.00 |
| 1704.00 | 425.00 | 560.00 | 1789.00 | 458.00 | 593.00 | 1874.00 | 491.00 | 626.00 | 1959.00 | 523.00 | 658.00 | 2044.00 | 556.00 | 691.00 |
| 1705.00 | 426.00 | 561.00 | 1790.00 | 458.00 | 593.00 | 1875.00 | 491.00 | 626.00 | 1960.00 | 524.00 | 659.00 | 2045.00 | 556.00 | 692.00 |
| 1706.00 | 426.00 | 561.00 | 1791.00 | 459.00 | 594.00 | 1876.00 | 491.00 | 626.00 | 1961.00 | 524.00 | 659.00 | 2046.00 | 557.00 | 692.00 |
| 1707.00 | 426.00 | 561.00 | 1792.00 | 459.00 | 594.00 | 1877.00 | 492.00 | 627.00 | 1962.00 | 525.00 | 660.00 | 2047.00 | 557.00 | 692.00 |
| 1708.00 | 427.00 | 562.00 | 1793.00 | 459.00 | 595.00 | 1878.00 | 492.00 | 627.00 | 1963.00 | 525.00 | 660.00 | 2048.00 | 558.00 | 693.00 |
| 1709.00 | 427.00 | 562.00 | 1794.00 | 460.00 | 595.00 | 1879.00 | 493.00 | 628.00 | 1964.00 | 525.00 | 660.00 | 2049.00 | 558.00 | 693.00 |
| 1710.00 | 428.00 | 563.00 | 1795.00 | 460.00 | 595.00 | 1880.00 | 493.00 | 628.00 | 1965.00 | 526.00 | 661.00 | 2050.00 | 558.00 | 693.00 |
| 1711.00 | 428.00 | 563.00 | 1796.00 | 461.00 | 596.00 | 1881.00 | 493.00 | 628.00 | 1966.00 | 526.00 | 661.00 | 2051.00 | 559.00 | 694.00 |
| 1712.00 | 428.00 | 563.00 | 1797.00 | 461.00 | 596.00 | 1882.00 | 494.00 | 629.00 | 1967.00 | 526.00 | 662.00 | 2052.00 | 559.00 | 694.00 |
| 1713.00 | 429.00 | 564.00 | 1798.00 | 461.00 | 596.00 | 1883.00 | 494.00 | 629.00 | 1968.00 | 527.00 | 662.00 | 2053.00 | 560.00 | 695.00 |
| 1714.00 | 429.00 | 564.00 | 1799.00 | 462.00 | 597.00 | 1884.00 | 495.00 | 630.00 | 1969.00 | 527.00 | 662.00 | 2054.00 | 560.00 | 695.00 |
| 1715.00 | 429.00 | 564.00 | 1800.00 | 462.00 | 597.00 | 1885.00 | 495.00 | 630.00 | 1970.00 | 528.00 | 663.00 | 2055.00 | 560.00 | 695.00 |
| 1716.00 | 430.00 | 565.00 | 1801.00 | 463.00 | 598.00 | 1886.00 | 495.00 | 630.00 | 1971.00 | 528.00 | 663.00 | 2056.00 | 561.00 | 696.00 |
| 1717.00 | 430.00 | 565.00 | 1802.00 | 463.00 | 598.00 | 1887.00 | 496.00 | 631.00 | 1972.00 | 528.00 | 663.00 | 2057.00 | 561.00 | 696.00 |
| 1718.00 | 431.00 | 566.00 | 1803.00 | 463.00 | 598.00 | 1888.00 | 496.00 | 631.00 | 1973.00 | 529.00 | 664.00 | 2058.00 | 561.00 | 697.00 |
| 1719.00 | 431.00 | 566.00 | 1804.00 | 464.00 | 599.00 | 1889.00 | 496.00 | 631.00 | 1974.00 | 529.00 | 664.00 | 2059.00 | 562.00 | 697.00 |
| 1720.00 | 431.00 | 566.00 | 1805.00 | 464.00 | 599.00 | 1890.00 | 497.00 | 632.00 | 1975.00 | 530.00 | 665.00 | 2060.00 | 562.00 | 697.00 |
| 1721.00 | 432.00 | 567.00 | 1806.00 | 464.00 | 600.00 | 1891.00 | 497.00 | 632.00 | 1976.00 | 530.00 | 665.00 | 2061.00 | 563.00 | 698.00 |
| 1722.00 | 432.00 | 567.00 | 1807.00 | 465.00 | 600.00 | 1892.00 | 498.00 | 633.00 | 1977.00 | 530.00 | 665.00 | 2062.00 | 563.00 | 698.00 |
| 1723.00 | 433.00 | 568.00 | 1808.00 | 465.00 | 600.00 | 1893.00 | 498.00 | 633.00 | 1978.00 | 531.00 | 666.00 | 2063.00 | 563.00 | 698.00 |
| 1724.00 | 433.00 | 568.00 | 1809.00 | 466.00 | 601.00 | 1894.00 | 498.00 | 633.00 | 1979.00 | 531.00 | 666.00 | 2064.00 | 564.00 | 699.00 |
| 1725.00 | 433.00 | 568.00 | 1810.00 | 466.00 | 601.00 | 1895.00 | 499.00 | 634.00 | 1980.00 | 531.00 | 667.00 | 2065.00 | 564.00 | 699.00 |
| 1726.00 | 434.00 | 569.00 | 1811.00 | 466.00 | 601.00 | 1896.00 | 499.00 | 634.00 | 1981.00 | 532.00 | 667.00 | 2066.00 | 565.00 | 700.00 |
| 1727.00 | 434.00 | 569.00 | 1812.00 | 467.00 | 602.00 | 1897.00 | 500.00 | 635.00 | 1982.00 | 532.00 | 667.00 | 2067.00 | 565.00 | 700.00 |
| 1728.00 | 434.00 | 569.00 | 1813.00 | 467.00 | 602.00 | 1898.00 | 500.00 | 635.00 | 1983.00 | 533.00 | 668.00 | 2068.00 | 565.00 | 700.00 |
| 1729.00 | 435.00 | 570.00 | 1814.00 | 468.00 | 603.00 | 1899.00 | 500.00 | 635.00 | 1984.00 | 533.00 | 668.00 | 2069.00 | 566.00 | 701.00 |
| 1730.00 | 435.00 | 570.00 | 1815.00 | 468.00 | 603.00 | 1900.00 | 501.00 | 636.00 | 1985.00 | 533.00 | 668.00 | 2070.00 | 566.00 | 701.00 |
| 1731.00 | 436.00 | 571.00 | 1816.00 | 468.00 | 603.00 | 1901.00 | 501.00 | 636.00 | 1986.00 | 534.00 | 669.00 | 2071.00 | 567.00 | 702.00 |
| 1732.00 | 436.00 | 571.00 | 1817.00 | 469.00 | 604.00 | 1902.00 | 501.00 | 636.00 | 1987.00 | 534.00 | 669.00 | 2072.00 | 567.00 | 702.00 |
| 1733.00 | 436.00 | 571.00 | 1818.00 | 469.00 | 604.00 | 1903.00 | 502.00 | 637.00 | 1988.00 | 535.00 | 670.00 | 2073.00 | 567.00 | 702.00 |
| 1734.00 | 437.00 | 572.00 | 1819.00 | 469.00 | 605.00 | 1904.00 | 502.00 | 637.00 | 1989.00 | 535.00 | 670.00 | 2074.00 | 568.00 | 703.00 |
| 1735.00 | 437.00 | 572.00 | 1820.00 | 470.00 | 605.00 | 1905.00 | 503.00 | 638.00 | 1990.00 | 535.00 | 670.00 | 2075.00 | 568.00 | 703.00 |
| 1736.00 | 438.00 | 573.00 | 1821.00 | 470.00 | 605.00 | 1906.00 | 503.00 | 638.00 | 1991.00 | 536.00 | 671.00 | 2076.00 | 568.00 | 703.00 |
| 1737.00 | 438.00 | 573.00 | 1822.00 | 471.00 | 606.00 | 1907.00 | 503.00 | 638.00 | 1992.00 | 536.00 | 671.00 | 2077.00 | 569.00 | 704.00 |
| 1738.00 | 438.00 | 573.00 | 1823.00 | 471.00 | 606.00 | 1908.00 | 504.00 | 639.00 | 1993.00 | 536.00 | 672.00 | 2078.00 | 569.00 | 704.00 |
| 1739.00 | 439.00 | 574.00 | 1824.00 | 471.00 | 606.00 | 1909.00 | 504.00 | 639.00 | 1994.00 | 537.00 | 672.00 | 2079.00 | 570.00 | 705.00 |
| 1740.00 | 439.00 | 574.00 | 1825.00 | 472.00 | 607.00 | 1910.00 | 505.00 | 640.00 | 1995.00 | 537.00 | 672.00 | 2080.00 | 570.00 | 705.00 |
| 1741.00 | 439.00 | 574.00 | 1826.00 | 472.00 | 607.00 | 1911.00 | 505.00 | 640.00 | 1996.00 | 538.00 | 673.00 | 2081.00 | 570.00 | 705.00 |
| 1742.00 | 440.00 | 575.00 | 1827.00 | 473.00 | 608.00 | 1912.00 | 505.00 | 640.00 | 1997.00 | 538.00 | 673.00 | 2082.00 | 571.00 | 706.00 |
| 1743.00 | 440.00 | 575.00 | 1828.00 | 473.00 | 608.00 | 1913.00 | 506.00 | 641.00 | 1998.00 | 538.00 | 673.00 | 2083.00 | 571.00 | 706.00 |
| 1744.00 | 441.00 | 576.00 | 1829.00 | 473.00 | 608.00 | 1914.00 | 506.00 | 641.00 | 1999.00 | 539.00 | 674.00 | 2084.00 | 572.00 | 707.00 |
| 1745.00 | 441.00 | 576.00 | 1830.00 | 474.00 | 609.00 | 1915.00 | 506.00 | 641.00 | 2000.00 | 539.00 | 674.00 | 2085.00 | 572.00 | 707.00 |
| 1746.00 | 441.00 | 576.00 | 1831.00 | 474.00 | 609.00 | 1916.00 | 507.00 | 642.00 | 2001.00 | 540.00 | 675.00 | 2086.00 | 572.00 | 707.00 |
| 1747.00 | 442.00 | 577.00 | 1832.00 | 474.00 | 610.00 | 1917.00 | 507.00 | 642.00 | 2002.00 | 540.00 | 675.00 | 2087.00 | 573.00 | 708.00 |
| 1748.00 | 442.00 | 577.00 | 1833.00 | 475.00 | 610.00 | 1918.00 | 508.00 | 643.00 | 2003.00 | 540.00 | 675.00 | 2088.00 | 573.00 | 708.00 |
| 1749.00 | 443.00 | 578.00 | 1834.00 | 475.00 | 610.00 | 1919.00 | 508.00 | 643.00 | 2004.00 | 541.00 | 676.00 | 2089.00 | 573.00 | 708.00 |
| 1750.00 | 443.00 | 578.00 | 1835.00 | 476.00 | 611.00 | 1920.00 | 508.00 | 643.00 | 2005.00 | 541.00 | 676.00 | 2090.00 | 574.00 | 709.00 |
| 1751.00 | 443.00 | 578.00 | 1836.00 | 476.00 | 611.00 | 1921.00 | 509.00 | 644.00 | 2006.00 | 541.00 | 677.00 | 2091.00 | 574.00 | 709.00 |
| 1752.00 | 444.00 | 579.00 | 1837.00 | 476.00 | 611.00 | 1922.00 | 509.00 | 644.00 | 2007.00 | 542.00 | 677.00 | 2092.00 | 575.00 | 710.00 |
| 1753.00 | 444.00 | 579.00 | 1838.00 | 477.00 | 612.00 | 1923.00 | 510.00 | 645.00 | 2008.00 | 542.00 | 677.00 | 2093.00 | 575.00 | 710.00 |
| 1754.00 | 444.00 | 580.00 | 1839.00 | 477.00 | 612.00 | 1924.00 | 510.00 | 645.00 | 2009.00 | 543.00 | 678.00 | 2094.00 | 575.00 | 710.00 |
| 1755.00 | 445.00 | 580.00 | 1840.00 | 478.00 | 613.00 | 1925.00 | 510.00 | 645.00 | 2010.00 | 543.00 | 678.00 | 2095.00 | 576.00 | 711.00 |
| 1756.00 | 445.00 | 580.00 | 1841.00 | 478.00 | 613.00 | 1926.00 | 511.00 | 646.00 | 2011.00 | 543.00 | 678.00 | 2096.00 | 576.00 | 711.00 |
| 1757.00 | 446.00 | 581.00 | 1842.00 | 478.00 | 613.00 | 1927.00 | 511.00 | 646.00 | 2012.00 | 544.00 | 679.00 | 2097.00 | 577.00 | 712.00 |
| 1758.00 | 446.00 | 581.00 | 1843.00 | 479.00 | 614.00 | 1928.00 | 511.00 | 646.00 | 2013.00 | 544.00 | 679.00 | 2098.00 | 577.00 | 712.00 |
| 1759.00 | 446.00 | 581.00 | 1844.00 | 479.00 | 614.00 | 1929.00 | 512.00 | 647.00 | 2014.00 | 545.00 | 680.00 | 2099.00 | 577.00 | 712.00 |
| 1760.00 | 447.00 | 582.00 | 1845.00 | 479.00 | 615.00 | 1930.00 | 512.00 | 647.00 | 2015.00 | 545.00 | 680.00 | 2100.00 | 578.00 | 713.00 |
| 1761.00 | 447.00 | 582.00 | 1846.00 | 480.00 | 615.00 | 1931.00 | 513.00 | 648.00 | 2016.00 | 545.00 | 680.00 | 2101.00 | 578.00 | 713.00 |
| 1762.00 | 448.00 | 583.00 | 1847.00 | 480.00 | 615.00 | 1932.00 | 513.00 | 648.00 | 2017.00 | 546.00 | 681.00 | 2102.00 | 578.00 | 713.00 |
| 1763.00 | 448.00 | 583.00 | 1848.00 | 481.00 | 616.00 | 1933.00 | 513.00 | 648.00 | 2018.00 | 546.00 | 681.00 | 2103.00 | 579.00 | 714.00 |
| 1764.00 | 448.00 | 583.00 | 1849.00 | 481.00 | 616.00 | 1934.00 | 514.00 | 649.00 | 2019.00 | 546.00 | 682.00 | 2104.00 | 579.00 | 714.00 |
| 1765.00 | 449.00 | 584.00 | 1850.00 | 481.00 | 616.00 | 1935.00 | 514.00 | 649.00 | 2020.00 | 547.00 | 682.00 | 2105.00 | 580.00 | 715.00 |
| 1766.00 | 449.00 | 584.00 | 1851.00 | 482.00 | 617.00 | 1936.00 | 515.00 | 650.00 | 2021.00 | 547.00 | 682.00 | 2106.00 | 580.00 | 715.00 |
| 1767.00 | 449.00 | 585.00 | 1852.00 | 482.00 | 617.00 | 1937.00 | 515.00 | 650.00 | 2022.00 | 548.00 | 683.00 | 2107.00 | 580.00 | 715.00 |
| 1768.00 | 450.00 | 585.00 | 1853.00 | 483.00 | 618.00 | 1938.00 | 515.00 | 650.00 | 2023.00 | 548.00 | 683.00 | 2108.00 | 581.00 | 716.00 |
| 1769.00 | 450.00 | 585.00 | 1854.00 | 483.00 | 618.00 | 1939.00 | 516.00 | 651.00 | 2024.00 | 548.00 | 683.00 | 2109.00 | 581.00 | 716.00 |
| 1770.00 | 451.00 | 586.00 | 1855.00 | 483.00 | 618.00 | 1940.00 | 516.00 | 651.00 | 2025.00 | 549.00 | 684.00 | 2110.00 | 582.00 | 717.00 |
| 1771.00 | 451.00 | 586.00 | 1856.00 | 484.00 | 619.00 | 1941.00 | 516.00 | 651.00 | 2026.00 | 549.00 | 684.00 | 2111.00 | 582.00 | 717.00 |
| 1772.00 | 451.00 | 586.00 | 1857.00 | 484.00 | 619.00 | 1942.00 | 517.00 | 652.00 | 2027.00 | 550.00 | 685.00 | 2112.00 | 582.00 | 717.00 |
| 1773.00 | 452.00 | 587.00 | 1858.00 | 484.00 | 620.00 | 1943.00 | 517.00 | 652.00 | 2028.00 | 550.00 | 685.00 | 2113.00 | 583.00 | 718.00 |
| 1774.00 | 452.00 | 587.00 | 1859.00 | 485.00 | 620.00 | 1944.00 | 518.00 | 653.00 | 2029.00 | 550.00 | 685.00 | 2114.00 | 583.00 | 718.00 |
| 1775.00 | 453.00 | 588.00 | 1860.00 | 485.00 | 620.00 | 1945.00 | 518.00 | 653.00 | 2030.00 | 551.00 | 686.00 | 2115.00 | 583.00 | 718.00 |
| 1776.00 | 453.00 | 588.00 | 1861.00 | 486.00 | 621.00 | 1946.00 | 518.00 | 653.00 | 2031.00 | 551.00 | 686.00 | 2116.00 | 584.00 | 719.00 |
| 1777.00 | 453.00 | 588.00 | 1862.00 | 486.00 | 621.00 | 1947.00 | 519.00 | 654.00 | 2032.00 | 551.00 | 687.00 | 2117.00 | 584.00 | 719.00 |
| 1778.00 | 454.00 | 589.00 | 1863.00 | 486.00 | 621.00 | 1948.00 | 519.00 | 654.00 | 2033.00 | 552.00 | 687.00 | 2118.00 | 585.00 | 720.00 |
| 1779.00 | 454.00 | 589.00 | 1864.00 | 487.00 | 622.00 | 1949.00 | 520.00 | 655.00 | 2034.00 | 552.00 | 687.00 | 2119.00 | 585.00 | 720.00 |
| 1780.00 | 454.00 | 590.00 | 1865.00 | 487.00 | 622.00 | 1950.00 | 520.00 | 655.00 | 2035.00 | 553.00 | 688.00 | 2120.00 | 585.00 | 720.00 |
| 1781.00 | 455.00 | 590.00 | 1866.00 | 488.00 | 623.00 | 1951.00 | 520.00 | 655.00 | 2036.00 | 553.00 | 688.00 | 2121.00 | 586.00 | 721.00 |
| 1782.00 | 455.00 | 590.00 | 1867.00 | 488.00 | 623.00 | 1952.00 | 521.00 | 656.00 | 2037.00 | 553.00 | 688.00 | 2122.00 | 586.00 | 721.00 |
| 1783.00 | 456.00 | 591.00 | 1868.00 | 488.00 | 623.00 | 1953.00 | 521.00 | 656.00 | 2038.00 | 554.00 | 689.00 | 2123.00 | 587.00 | 722.00 |
| 1784.00 | 456.00 | 591.00 | 1869.00 | 489.00 | 624.00 | 1954.00 | 521.00 | 657.00 | 2039.00 | 554.00 | 689.00 | 2124.00 | 587.00 | 722.00 |
| 1785.00 | 456.00 | 591.00 | 1870.00 | 489.00 | 624.00 | 1955.00 | 522.00 | 657.00 | 2040.00 | 555.00 | 690.00 | 2125.00 | 587.00 | 722.00 |

**SCHEDULE 2** WEEKLY TAX TABLE

9

**Figure 7.5**

## WEEKLY TAX TABLE – INCORPORATING MEDICARE LEVY

❗ Leave loading column has been removed from this tax table. For more information about leave loading changes, see page 3.

| Weekly earnings 1 $ | Amount to be withheld — With tax-free threshold 2 $ | Amount to be withheld — No tax-free threshold 3 $ | Weekly earnings 1 $ | With tax-free threshold 2 $ | No tax-free threshold 3 $ | Weekly earnings 1 $ | With tax-free threshold 2 $ | No tax-free threshold 3 $ | Weekly earnings 1 $ | With tax-free threshold 2 $ | No tax-free threshold 3 $ | Weekly earnings 1 $ | With tax-free threshold 2 $ | No tax-free threshold 3 $ |
|---|---|---|---|---|---|---|---|---|---|---|---|---|---|---|
| 2126.00 | 588.00 | 723.00 | 2211.00 | 620.00 | 755.00 | 2296.00 | 653.00 | 788.00 | 2381.00 | 686.00 | 821.00 | 2466.00 | 719.00 | 854.00 |
| 2127.00 | 588.00 | 723.00 | 2212.00 | 621.00 | 756.00 | 2297.00 | 654.00 | 789.00 | 2382.00 | 686.00 | 821.00 | 2467.00 | 719.00 | 854.00 |
| 2128.00 | 588.00 | 723.00 | 2213.00 | 621.00 | 756.00 | 2298.00 | 654.00 | 789.00 | 2383.00 | 687.00 | 822.00 | 2468.00 | 719.00 | 854.00 |
| 2129.00 | 589.00 | 724.00 | 2214.00 | 622.00 | 757.00 | 2299.00 | 654.00 | 789.00 | 2384.00 | 687.00 | 822.00 | 2469.00 | 720.00 | 855.00 |
| 2130.00 | 589.00 | 724.00 | 2215.00 | 622.00 | 757.00 | 2300.00 | 655.00 | 790.00 | 2385.00 | 687.00 | 822.00 | 2470.00 | 720.00 | 855.00 |
| 2131.00 | 590.00 | 725.00 | 2216.00 | 622.00 | 757.00 | 2301.00 | 655.00 | 790.00 | 2386.00 | 688.00 | 823.00 | 2471.00 | 721.00 | 856.00 |
| 2132.00 | 590.00 | 725.00 | 2217.00 | 623.00 | 758.00 | 2302.00 | 655.00 | 790.00 | 2387.00 | 688.00 | 823.00 | 2472.00 | 721.00 | 856.00 |
| 2133.00 | 590.00 | 725.00 | 2218.00 | 623.00 | 758.00 | 2303.00 | 656.00 | 791.00 | 2388.00 | 689.00 | 824.00 | 2473.00 | 721.00 | 856.00 |
| 2134.00 | 591.00 | 726.00 | 2219.00 | 623.00 | 759.00 | 2304.00 | 656.00 | 791.00 | 2389.00 | 689.00 | 824.00 | 2474.00 | 722.00 | 857.00 |
| 2135.00 | 591.00 | 726.00 | 2220.00 | 624.00 | 759.00 | 2305.00 | 657.00 | 792.00 | 2390.00 | 689.00 | 824.00 | 2475.00 | 722.00 | 857.00 |
| 2136.00 | 592.00 | 727.00 | 2221.00 | 624.00 | 759.00 | 2306.00 | 657.00 | 792.00 | 2391.00 | 690.00 | 825.00 | 2476.00 | 722.00 | 857.00 |
| 2137.00 | 592.00 | 727.00 | 2222.00 | 625.00 | 760.00 | 2307.00 | 657.00 | 792.00 | 2392.00 | 690.00 | 825.00 | 2477.00 | 723.00 | 858.00 |
| 2138.00 | 592.00 | 727.00 | 2223.00 | 625.00 | 760.00 | 2308.00 | 658.00 | 793.00 | 2393.00 | 690.00 | 826.00 | 2478.00 | 723.00 | 858.00 |
| 2139.00 | 593.00 | 728.00 | 2224.00 | 625.00 | 760.00 | 2309.00 | 658.00 | 793.00 | 2394.00 | 691.00 | 826.00 | 2479.00 | 724.00 | 859.00 |
| 2140.00 | 593.00 | 728.00 | 2225.00 | 626.00 | 761.00 | 2310.00 | 659.00 | 794.00 | 2395.00 | 691.00 | 826.00 | 2480.00 | 724.00 | 859.00 |
| 2141.00 | 593.00 | 728.00 | 2226.00 | 626.00 | 761.00 | 2311.00 | 659.00 | 794.00 | 2396.00 | 692.00 | 827.00 | 2481.00 | 724.00 | 859.00 |
| 2142.00 | 594.00 | 729.00 | 2227.00 | 627.00 | 762.00 | 2312.00 | 659.00 | 794.00 | 2397.00 | 692.00 | 827.00 | 2482.00 | 725.00 | 860.00 |
| 2143.00 | 594.00 | 729.00 | 2228.00 | 627.00 | 762.00 | 2313.00 | 660.00 | 795.00 | 2398.00 | 692.00 | 827.00 | 2483.00 | 725.00 | 860.00 |
| 2144.00 | 595.00 | 730.00 | 2229.00 | 627.00 | 762.00 | 2314.00 | 660.00 | 795.00 | 2399.00 | 693.00 | 828.00 | 2484.00 | 726.00 | 861.00 |
| 2145.00 | 595.00 | 730.00 | 2230.00 | 628.00 | 763.00 | 2315.00 | 660.00 | 795.00 | 2400.00 | 693.00 | 828.00 | 2485.00 | 726.00 | 861.00 |
| 2146.00 | 595.00 | 730.00 | 2231.00 | 628.00 | 763.00 | 2316.00 | 661.00 | 796.00 | 2401.00 | 694.00 | 829.00 | 2486.00 | 726.00 | 861.00 |
| 2147.00 | 596.00 | 731.00 | 2232.00 | 628.00 | 764.00 | 2317.00 | 661.00 | 796.00 | 2402.00 | 694.00 | 829.00 | 2487.00 | 727.00 | 862.00 |
| 2148.00 | 596.00 | 731.00 | 2233.00 | 629.00 | 764.00 | 2318.00 | 662.00 | 797.00 | 2403.00 | 694.00 | 829.00 | 2488.00 | 727.00 | 862.00 |
| 2149.00 | 597.00 | 732.00 | 2234.00 | 629.00 | 764.00 | 2319.00 | 662.00 | 797.00 | 2404.00 | 695.00 | 830.00 | 2489.00 | 727.00 | 862.00 |
| 2150.00 | 597.00 | 732.00 | 2235.00 | 630.00 | 765.00 | 2320.00 | 662.00 | 797.00 | 2405.00 | 695.00 | 830.00 | 2490.00 | 728.00 | 863.00 |
| 2151.00 | 597.00 | 732.00 | 2236.00 | 630.00 | 765.00 | 2321.00 | 663.00 | 798.00 | 2406.00 | 695.00 | 831.00 | 2491.00 | 728.00 | 863.00 |
| 2152.00 | 598.00 | 733.00 | 2237.00 | 630.00 | 765.00 | 2322.00 | 663.00 | 798.00 | 2407.00 | 696.00 | 831.00 | 2492.00 | 729.00 | 864.00 |
| 2153.00 | 598.00 | 733.00 | 2238.00 | 631.00 | 766.00 | 2323.00 | 664.00 | 799.00 | 2408.00 | 696.00 | 831.00 | 2493.00 | 729.00 | 864.00 |
| 2154.00 | 598.00 | 734.00 | 2239.00 | 631.00 | 766.00 | 2324.00 | 664.00 | 799.00 | 2409.00 | 697.00 | 832.00 | 2494.00 | 729.00 | 864.00 |
| 2155.00 | 599.00 | 734.00 | 2240.00 | 632.00 | 767.00 | 2325.00 | 664.00 | 799.00 | 2410.00 | 697.00 | 832.00 | 2495.00 | 730.00 | 865.00 |
| 2156.00 | 599.00 | 734.00 | 2241.00 | 632.00 | 767.00 | 2326.00 | 665.00 | 800.00 | 2411.00 | 697.00 | 832.00 | 2496.00 | 730.00 | 865.00 |
| 2157.00 | 600.00 | 735.00 | 2242.00 | 632.00 | 767.00 | 2327.00 | 665.00 | 800.00 | 2412.00 | 698.00 | 833.00 | 2497.00 | 731.00 | 866.00 |
| 2158.00 | 600.00 | 735.00 | 2243.00 | 633.00 | 768.00 | 2328.00 | 665.00 | 800.00 | 2413.00 | 698.00 | 833.00 | 2498.00 | 731.00 | 866.00 |
| 2159.00 | 600.00 | 735.00 | 2244.00 | 633.00 | 768.00 | 2329.00 | 666.00 | 801.00 | 2414.00 | 699.00 | 834.00 | 2499.00 | 731.00 | 866.00 |
| 2160.00 | 601.00 | 736.00 | 2245.00 | 633.00 | 769.00 | 2330.00 | 666.00 | 801.00 | 2415.00 | 699.00 | 834.00 | 2500.00 | 732.00 | 867.00 |
| 2161.00 | 601.00 | 736.00 | 2246.00 | 634.00 | 769.00 | 2331.00 | 667.00 | 802.00 | 2416.00 | 699.00 | 834.00 | 2501.00 | 732.00 | 867.00 |
| 2162.00 | 602.00 | 737.00 | 2247.00 | 634.00 | 769.00 | 2332.00 | 667.00 | 802.00 | 2417.00 | 700.00 | 835.00 | 2502.00 | 732.00 | 867.00 |
| 2163.00 | 602.00 | 737.00 | 2248.00 | 635.00 | 770.00 | 2333.00 | 667.00 | 802.00 | 2418.00 | 700.00 | 835.00 | 2503.00 | 733.00 | 868.00 |
| 2164.00 | 602.00 | 737.00 | 2249.00 | 635.00 | 770.00 | 2334.00 | 668.00 | 803.00 | 2419.00 | 700.00 | 836.00 | 2504.00 | 733.00 | 868.00 |
| 2165.00 | 603.00 | 738.00 | 2250.00 | 635.00 | 770.00 | 2335.00 | 668.00 | 803.00 | 2420.00 | 701.00 | 836.00 | 2505.00 | 734.00 | 869.00 |
| 2166.00 | 603.00 | 738.00 | 2251.00 | 636.00 | 771.00 | 2336.00 | 669.00 | 804.00 | 2421.00 | 701.00 | 836.00 | 2506.00 | 734.00 | 869.00 |
| 2167.00 | 603.00 | 739.00 | 2252.00 | 636.00 | 771.00 | 2337.00 | 669.00 | 804.00 | 2422.00 | 702.00 | 837.00 | 2507.00 | 734.00 | 869.00 |
| 2168.00 | 604.00 | 739.00 | 2253.00 | 637.00 | 772.00 | 2338.00 | 669.00 | 804.00 | 2423.00 | 702.00 | 837.00 | 2508.00 | 735.00 | 870.00 |
| 2169.00 | 604.00 | 739.00 | 2254.00 | 637.00 | 772.00 | 2339.00 | 670.00 | 805.00 | 2424.00 | 702.00 | 837.00 | 2509.00 | 735.00 | 870.00 |
| 2170.00 | 605.00 | 740.00 | 2255.00 | 637.00 | 772.00 | 2340.00 | 670.00 | 805.00 | 2425.00 | 703.00 | 838.00 | 2510.00 | 736.00 | 871.00 |
| 2171.00 | 605.00 | 740.00 | 2256.00 | 638.00 | 773.00 | 2341.00 | 670.00 | 805.00 | 2426.00 | 703.00 | 838.00 | 2511.00 | 736.00 | 871.00 |
| 2172.00 | 605.00 | 740.00 | 2257.00 | 638.00 | 773.00 | 2342.00 | 671.00 | 806.00 | 2427.00 | 704.00 | 839.00 | 2512.00 | 736.00 | 871.00 |
| 2173.00 | 606.00 | 741.00 | 2258.00 | 638.00 | 774.00 | 2343.00 | 671.00 | 806.00 | 2428.00 | 704.00 | 839.00 | 2513.00 | 737.00 | 872.00 |
| 2174.00 | 606.00 | 741.00 | 2259.00 | 639.00 | 774.00 | 2344.00 | 672.00 | 807.00 | 2429.00 | 704.00 | 839.00 | 2514.00 | 737.00 | 872.00 |
| 2175.00 | 607.00 | 742.00 | 2260.00 | 639.00 | 774.00 | 2345.00 | 672.00 | 807.00 | 2430.00 | 705.00 | 840.00 | 2515.00 | 737.00 | 872.00 |
| 2176.00 | 607.00 | 742.00 | 2261.00 | 640.00 | 775.00 | 2346.00 | 672.00 | 807.00 | 2431.00 | 705.00 | 840.00 | 2516.00 | 738.00 | 873.00 |
| 2177.00 | 607.00 | 742.00 | 2262.00 | 640.00 | 775.00 | 2347.00 | 673.00 | 808.00 | 2432.00 | 705.00 | 841.00 | 2517.00 | 738.00 | 873.00 |
| 2178.00 | 608.00 | 743.00 | 2263.00 | 640.00 | 775.00 | 2348.00 | 673.00 | 808.00 | 2433.00 | 706.00 | 841.00 | 2518.00 | 739.00 | 874.00 |
| 2179.00 | 608.00 | 743.00 | 2264.00 | 641.00 | 776.00 | 2349.00 | 674.00 | 809.00 | 2434.00 | 706.00 | 841.00 | 2519.00 | 739.00 | 874.00 |
| 2180.00 | 608.00 | 744.00 | 2265.00 | 641.00 | 776.00 | 2350.00 | 674.00 | 809.00 | 2435.00 | 707.00 | 842.00 | 2520.00 | 739.00 | 874.00 |
| 2181.00 | 609.00 | 744.00 | 2266.00 | 642.00 | 777.00 | 2351.00 | 674.00 | 809.00 | 2436.00 | 707.00 | 842.00 | 2521.00 | 740.00 | 875.00 |
| 2182.00 | 609.00 | 744.00 | 2267.00 | 642.00 | 777.00 | 2352.00 | 675.00 | 810.00 | 2437.00 | 707.00 | 842.00 | 2522.00 | 740.00 | 875.00 |
| 2183.00 | 610.00 | 745.00 | 2268.00 | 642.00 | 777.00 | 2353.00 | 675.00 | 810.00 | 2438.00 | 708.00 | 843.00 | 2523.00 | 741.00 | 876.00 |
| 2184.00 | 610.00 | 745.00 | 2269.00 | 643.00 | 778.00 | 2354.00 | 675.00 | 811.00 | 2439.00 | 708.00 | 843.00 | 2524.00 | 741.00 | 876.00 |
| 2185.00 | 610.00 | 745.00 | 2270.00 | 643.00 | 778.00 | 2355.00 | 676.00 | 811.00 | 2440.00 | 709.00 | 844.00 | 2525.00 | 741.00 | 876.00 |
| 2186.00 | 611.00 | 746.00 | 2271.00 | 644.00 | 779.00 | 2356.00 | 676.00 | 811.00 | 2441.00 | 709.00 | 844.00 | 2526.00 | 742.00 | 877.00 |
| 2187.00 | 611.00 | 746.00 | 2272.00 | 644.00 | 779.00 | 2357.00 | 677.00 | 812.00 | 2442.00 | 709.00 | 844.00 | 2527.00 | 742.00 | 877.00 |
| 2188.00 | 612.00 | 747.00 | 2273.00 | 644.00 | 779.00 | 2358.00 | 677.00 | 812.00 | 2443.00 | 710.00 | 845.00 | 2528.00 | 742.00 | 877.00 |
| 2189.00 | 612.00 | 747.00 | 2274.00 | 645.00 | 780.00 | 2359.00 | 677.00 | 812.00 | 2444.00 | 710.00 | 845.00 | 2529.00 | 743.00 | 878.00 |
| 2190.00 | 612.00 | 747.00 | 2275.00 | 645.00 | 780.00 | 2360.00 | 678.00 | 813.00 | 2445.00 | 710.00 | 846.00 | 2530.00 | 743.00 | 878.00 |
| 2191.00 | 613.00 | 748.00 | 2276.00 | 645.00 | 780.00 | 2361.00 | 678.00 | 813.00 | 2446.00 | 711.00 | 846.00 | 2531.00 | 744.00 | 879.00 |
| 2192.00 | 613.00 | 748.00 | 2277.00 | 646.00 | 781.00 | 2362.00 | 679.00 | 814.00 | 2447.00 | 711.00 | 846.00 | 2532.00 | 744.00 | 879.00 |
| 2193.00 | 613.00 | 749.00 | 2278.00 | 646.00 | 781.00 | 2363.00 | 679.00 | 814.00 | 2448.00 | 712.00 | 847.00 | 2533.00 | 744.00 | 879.00 |
| 2194.00 | 614.00 | 749.00 | 2279.00 | 647.00 | 782.00 | 2364.00 | 679.00 | 814.00 | 2449.00 | 712.00 | 847.00 | 2534.00 | 745.00 | 880.00 |
| 2195.00 | 614.00 | 749.00 | 2280.00 | 647.00 | 782.00 | 2365.00 | 680.00 | 815.00 | 2450.00 | 712.00 | 847.00 | 2535.00 | 745.00 | 880.00 |
| 2196.00 | 615.00 | 750.00 | 2281.00 | 647.00 | 782.00 | 2366.00 | 680.00 | 815.00 | 2451.00 | 713.00 | 848.00 | 2536.00 | 746.00 | 881.00 |
| 2197.00 | 615.00 | 750.00 | 2282.00 | 648.00 | 783.00 | 2367.00 | 680.00 | 816.00 | 2452.00 | 713.00 | 848.00 | 2537.00 | 746.00 | 881.00 |
| 2198.00 | 615.00 | 750.00 | 2283.00 | 648.00 | 783.00 | 2368.00 | 681.00 | 816.00 | 2453.00 | 714.00 | 849.00 | 2538.00 | 746.00 | 881.00 |
| 2199.00 | 616.00 | 751.00 | 2284.00 | 649.00 | 784.00 | 2369.00 | 681.00 | 816.00 | 2454.00 | 714.00 | 849.00 | 2539.00 | 747.00 | 882.00 |
| 2200.00 | 616.00 | 751.00 | 2285.00 | 649.00 | 784.00 | 2370.00 | 682.00 | 817.00 | 2455.00 | 714.00 | 849.00 | 2540.00 | 747.00 | 882.00 |
| 2201.00 | 617.00 | 752.00 | 2286.00 | 649.00 | 784.00 | 2371.00 | 682.00 | 817.00 | 2456.00 | 715.00 | 850.00 | 2541.00 | 747.00 | 882.00 |
| 2202.00 | 617.00 | 752.00 | 2287.00 | 650.00 | 785.00 | 2372.00 | 682.00 | 817.00 | 2457.00 | 715.00 | 850.00 | 2542.00 | 748.00 | 883.00 |
| 2203.00 | 617.00 | 752.00 | 2288.00 | 650.00 | 785.00 | 2373.00 | 683.00 | 818.00 | 2458.00 | 715.00 | 851.00 | 2543.00 | 748.00 | 883.00 |
| 2204.00 | 618.00 | 753.00 | 2289.00 | 650.00 | 785.00 | 2374.00 | 683.00 | 818.00 | 2459.00 | 716.00 | 851.00 | 2544.00 | 749.00 | 884.00 |
| 2205.00 | 618.00 | 753.00 | 2290.00 | 651.00 | 786.00 | 2375.00 | 684.00 | 819.00 | 2460.00 | 716.00 | 851.00 | 2545.00 | 749.00 | 884.00 |
| 2206.00 | 618.00 | 754.00 | 2291.00 | 651.00 | 786.00 | 2376.00 | 684.00 | 819.00 | 2461.00 | 717.00 | 852.00 | 2546.00 | 749.00 | 884.00 |
| 2207.00 | 619.00 | 754.00 | 2292.00 | 652.00 | 787.00 | 2377.00 | 684.00 | 819.00 | 2462.00 | 717.00 | 852.00 | 2547.00 | 750.00 | 885.00 |
| 2208.00 | 619.00 | 754.00 | 2293.00 | 652.00 | 787.00 | 2378.00 | 685.00 | 820.00 | 2463.00 | 717.00 | 852.00 | 2548.00 | 750.00 | 885.00 |
| 2209.00 | 620.00 | 755.00 | 2294.00 | 652.00 | 787.00 | 2379.00 | 685.00 | 820.00 | 2464.00 | 718.00 | 853.00 | 2549.00 | 751.00 | 886.00 |
| 2210.00 | 620.00 | 755.00 | 2295.00 | 653.00 | 788.00 | 2380.00 | 685.00 | 821.00 | 2465.00 | 718.00 | 853.00 | 2550.00 | 751.00 | 886.00 |

## Figure 7.5

### WEEKLY TAX TABLE – INCORPORATING MEDICARE LEVY

❗ Leave loading column has been removed from this tax table. For more information about leave loading changes, see page 3.

| Weekly earnings 1 $ | With tax-free threshold 2 $ | No tax-free threshold 3 $ | Weekly earnings 1 $ | With tax-free threshold 2 $ | No tax-free threshold 3 $ | Weekly earnings 1 $ | With tax-free threshold 2 $ | No tax-free threshold 3 $ | Weekly earnings 1 $ | With tax-free threshold 2 $ | No tax-free threshold 3 $ | Weekly earnings 1 $ | With tax-free threshold 2 $ | No tax-free threshold 3 $ |
|---|---|---|---|---|---|---|---|---|---|---|---|---|---|---|
| 2551.00 | 751.00 | 886.00 | 2636.00 | 784.00 | 919.00 | 2721.00 | 817.00 | 952.00 | 2806.00 | 849.00 | 985.00 | 2891.00 | 882.00 | 1017.00 |
| 2552.00 | 752.00 | 887.00 | 2637.00 | 784.00 | 919.00 | 2722.00 | 817.00 | 952.00 | 2807.00 | 850.00 | 985.00 | 2892.00 | 883.00 | 1018.00 |
| 2553.00 | 752.00 | 887.00 | 2638.00 | 785.00 | 920.00 | 2723.00 | 818.00 | 953.00 | 2808.00 | 850.00 | 985.00 | 2893.00 | 883.00 | 1018.00 |
| 2554.00 | 752.00 | 888.00 | 2639.00 | 785.00 | 920.00 | 2724.00 | 818.00 | 953.00 | 2809.00 | 851.00 | 986.00 | 2894.00 | 883.00 | 1018.00 |
| 2555.00 | 753.00 | 888.00 | 2640.00 | 786.00 | 921.00 | 2725.00 | 818.00 | 953.00 | 2810.00 | 851.00 | 986.00 | 2895.00 | 884.00 | 1019.00 |
| 2556.00 | 753.00 | 888.00 | 2641.00 | 786.00 | 921.00 | 2726.00 | 819.00 | 954.00 | 2811.00 | 851.00 | 986.00 | 2896.00 | 884.00 | 1019.00 |
| 2557.00 | 754.00 | 889.00 | 2642.00 | 786.00 | 921.00 | 2727.00 | 819.00 | 954.00 | 2812.00 | 852.00 | 987.00 | 2897.00 | 885.00 | 1020.00 |
| 2558.00 | 754.00 | 889.00 | 2643.00 | 787.00 | 922.00 | 2728.00 | 819.00 | 954.00 | 2813.00 | 852.00 | 987.00 | 2898.00 | 885.00 | 1020.00 |
| 2559.00 | 754.00 | 889.00 | 2644.00 | 787.00 | 922.00 | 2729.00 | 820.00 | 955.00 | 2814.00 | 853.00 | 988.00 | 2899.00 | 885.00 | 1020.00 |
| 2560.00 | 755.00 | 890.00 | 2645.00 | 787.00 | 923.00 | 2730.00 | 820.00 | 955.00 | 2815.00 | 853.00 | 988.00 | 2900.00 | 886.00 | 1021.00 |
| 2561.00 | 755.00 | 890.00 | 2646.00 | 788.00 | 923.00 | 2731.00 | 821.00 | 956.00 | 2816.00 | 853.00 | 988.00 | 2901.00 | 886.00 | 1021.00 |
| 2562.00 | 756.00 | 891.00 | 2647.00 | 788.00 | 923.00 | 2732.00 | 821.00 | 956.00 | 2817.00 | 854.00 | 989.00 | 2902.00 | 886.00 | 1021.00 |
| 2563.00 | 756.00 | 891.00 | 2648.00 | 789.00 | 924.00 | 2733.00 | 821.00 | 956.00 | 2818.00 | 854.00 | 989.00 | 2903.00 | 887.00 | 1022.00 |
| 2564.00 | 756.00 | 891.00 | 2649.00 | 789.00 | 924.00 | 2734.00 | 822.00 | 957.00 | 2819.00 | 854.00 | 990.00 | 2904.00 | 887.00 | 1022.00 |
| 2565.00 | 757.00 | 892.00 | 2650.00 | 789.00 | 924.00 | 2735.00 | 822.00 | 957.00 | 2820.00 | 855.00 | 990.00 | 2905.00 | 888.00 | 1023.00 |
| 2566.00 | 757.00 | 892.00 | 2651.00 | 790.00 | 925.00 | 2736.00 | 823.00 | 958.00 | 2821.00 | 855.00 | 990.00 | 2906.00 | 888.00 | 1023.00 |
| 2567.00 | 757.00 | 893.00 | 2652.00 | 790.00 | 925.00 | 2737.00 | 823.00 | 958.00 | 2822.00 | 856.00 | 991.00 | 2907.00 | 888.00 | 1023.00 |
| 2568.00 | 758.00 | 893.00 | 2653.00 | 791.00 | 926.00 | 2738.00 | 823.00 | 958.00 | 2823.00 | 856.00 | 991.00 | 2908.00 | 889.00 | 1024.00 |
| 2569.00 | 758.00 | 893.00 | 2654.00 | 791.00 | 926.00 | 2739.00 | 824.00 | 959.00 | 2824.00 | 856.00 | 991.00 | 2909.00 | 889.00 | 1024.00 |
| 2570.00 | 759.00 | 894.00 | 2655.00 | 791.00 | 926.00 | 2740.00 | 824.00 | 959.00 | 2825.00 | 857.00 | 992.00 | 2910.00 | 890.00 | 1025.00 |
| 2571.00 | 759.00 | 894.00 | 2656.00 | 792.00 | 927.00 | 2741.00 | 824.00 | 959.00 | 2826.00 | 857.00 | 992.00 | 2911.00 | 890.00 | 1025.00 |
| 2572.00 | 759.00 | 894.00 | 2657.00 | 792.00 | 927.00 | 2742.00 | 825.00 | 960.00 | 2827.00 | 858.00 | 993.00 | 2912.00 | 890.00 | 1025.00 |
| 2573.00 | 760.00 | 895.00 | 2658.00 | 792.00 | 928.00 | 2743.00 | 825.00 | 960.00 | 2828.00 | 858.00 | 993.00 | 2913.00 | 891.00 | 1026.00 |
| 2574.00 | 760.00 | 895.00 | 2659.00 | 793.00 | 928.00 | 2744.00 | 826.00 | 961.00 | 2829.00 | 858.00 | 993.00 | 2914.00 | 891.00 | 1026.00 |
| 2575.00 | 761.00 | 896.00 | 2660.00 | 793.00 | 928.00 | 2745.00 | 826.00 | 961.00 | 2830.00 | 859.00 | 994.00 | 2915.00 | 891.00 | 1026.00 |
| 2576.00 | 761.00 | 896.00 | 2661.00 | 794.00 | 929.00 | 2746.00 | 826.00 | 961.00 | 2831.00 | 859.00 | 994.00 | 2916.00 | 892.00 | 1027.00 |
| 2577.00 | 761.00 | 896.00 | 2662.00 | 794.00 | 929.00 | 2747.00 | 827.00 | 962.00 | 2832.00 | 859.00 | 995.00 | 2917.00 | 892.00 | 1027.00 |
| 2578.00 | 762.00 | 897.00 | 2663.00 | 794.00 | 929.00 | 2748.00 | 827.00 | 962.00 | 2833.00 | 860.00 | 995.00 | 2918.00 | 893.00 | 1028.00 |
| 2579.00 | 762.00 | 897.00 | 2664.00 | 795.00 | 930.00 | 2749.00 | 828.00 | 963.00 | 2834.00 | 860.00 | 995.00 | 2919.00 | 893.00 | 1028.00 |
| 2580.00 | 762.00 | 898.00 | 2665.00 | 795.00 | 930.00 | 2750.00 | 828.00 | 963.00 | 2835.00 | 861.00 | 996.00 | 2920.00 | 893.00 | 1028.00 |
| 2581.00 | 763.00 | 898.00 | 2666.00 | 796.00 | 931.00 | 2751.00 | 828.00 | 963.00 | 2836.00 | 861.00 | 996.00 | 2921.00 | 894.00 | 1029.00 |
| 2582.00 | 763.00 | 898.00 | 2667.00 | 796.00 | 931.00 | 2752.00 | 829.00 | 964.00 | 2837.00 | 861.00 | 996.00 | 2922.00 | 894.00 | 1029.00 |
| 2583.00 | 764.00 | 899.00 | 2668.00 | 796.00 | 931.00 | 2753.00 | 829.00 | 964.00 | 2838.00 | 862.00 | 997.00 | 2923.00 | 895.00 | 1030.00 |
| 2584.00 | 764.00 | 899.00 | 2669.00 | 797.00 | 932.00 | 2754.00 | 829.00 | 965.00 | 2839.00 | 862.00 | 997.00 | 2924.00 | 895.00 | 1030.00 |
| 2585.00 | 764.00 | 899.00 | 2670.00 | 797.00 | 932.00 | 2755.00 | 830.00 | 965.00 | 2840.00 | 863.00 | 998.00 | 2925.00 | 895.00 | 1030.00 |
| 2586.00 | 765.00 | 900.00 | 2671.00 | 798.00 | 933.00 | 2756.00 | 830.00 | 965.00 | 2841.00 | 863.00 | 998.00 | 2926.00 | 896.00 | 1031.00 |
| 2587.00 | 765.00 | 900.00 | 2672.00 | 798.00 | 933.00 | 2757.00 | 831.00 | 966.00 | 2842.00 | 863.00 | 998.00 | 2927.00 | 896.00 | 1031.00 |
| 2588.00 | 766.00 | 901.00 | 2673.00 | 798.00 | 933.00 | 2758.00 | 831.00 | 966.00 | 2843.00 | 864.00 | 999.00 | 2928.00 | 896.00 | 1031.00 |
| 2589.00 | 766.00 | 901.00 | 2674.00 | 799.00 | 934.00 | 2759.00 | 831.00 | 966.00 | 2844.00 | 864.00 | 999.00 | 2929.00 | 897.00 | 1032.00 |
| 2590.00 | 766.00 | 901.00 | 2675.00 | 799.00 | 934.00 | 2760.00 | 832.00 | 967.00 | 2845.00 | 864.00 | 1000.00 | 2930.00 | 897.00 | 1032.00 |
| 2591.00 | 767.00 | 902.00 | 2676.00 | 799.00 | 934.00 | 2761.00 | 832.00 | 967.00 | 2846.00 | 865.00 | 1000.00 | 2931.00 | 898.00 | 1033.00 |
| 2592.00 | 767.00 | 902.00 | 2677.00 | 800.00 | 935.00 | 2762.00 | 833.00 | 968.00 | 2847.00 | 865.00 | 1000.00 | 2932.00 | 898.00 | 1033.00 |
| 2593.00 | 767.00 | 903.00 | 2678.00 | 800.00 | 935.00 | 2763.00 | 833.00 | 968.00 | 2848.00 | 866.00 | 1001.00 | 2933.00 | 898.00 | 1033.00 |
| 2594.00 | 768.00 | 903.00 | 2679.00 | 801.00 | 936.00 | 2764.00 | 833.00 | 968.00 | 2849.00 | 866.00 | 1001.00 | 2934.00 | 899.00 | 1034.00 |
| 2595.00 | 768.00 | 903.00 | 2680.00 | 801.00 | 936.00 | 2765.00 | 834.00 | 969.00 | 2850.00 | 866.00 | 1001.00 | 2935.00 | 899.00 | 1034.00 |
| 2596.00 | 769.00 | 904.00 | 2681.00 | 801.00 | 936.00 | 2766.00 | 834.00 | 969.00 | 2851.00 | 867.00 | 1002.00 | 2936.00 | 900.00 | 1035.00 |
| 2597.00 | 769.00 | 904.00 | 2682.00 | 802.00 | 937.00 | 2767.00 | 834.00 | 970.00 | 2852.00 | 867.00 | 1002.00 | 2937.00 | 900.00 | 1035.00 |
| 2598.00 | 769.00 | 904.00 | 2683.00 | 802.00 | 937.00 | 2768.00 | 835.00 | 970.00 | 2853.00 | 868.00 | 1003.00 | 2938.00 | 900.00 | 1035.00 |
| 2599.00 | 770.00 | 905.00 | 2684.00 | 803.00 | 938.00 | 2769.00 | 835.00 | 970.00 | 2854.00 | 868.00 | 1003.00 | 2939.00 | 901.00 | 1036.00 |
| 2600.00 | 770.00 | 905.00 | 2685.00 | 803.00 | 938.00 | 2770.00 | 836.00 | 971.00 | 2855.00 | 868.00 | 1003.00 | 2940.00 | 901.00 | 1036.00 |
| 2601.00 | 771.00 | 906.00 | 2686.00 | 803.00 | 938.00 | 2771.00 | 836.00 | 971.00 | 2856.00 | 869.00 | 1004.00 | 2941.00 | 901.00 | 1036.00 |
| 2602.00 | 771.00 | 906.00 | 2687.00 | 804.00 | 939.00 | 2772.00 | 836.00 | 971.00 | 2857.00 | 869.00 | 1004.00 | 2942.00 | 902.00 | 1037.00 |
| 2603.00 | 771.00 | 906.00 | 2688.00 | 804.00 | 939.00 | 2773.00 | 837.00 | 972.00 | 2858.00 | 869.00 | 1005.00 | 2943.00 | 902.00 | 1037.00 |
| 2604.00 | 772.00 | 907.00 | 2689.00 | 804.00 | 939.00 | 2774.00 | 837.00 | 972.00 | 2859.00 | 870.00 | 1005.00 | 2944.00 | 903.00 | 1038.00 |
| 2605.00 | 772.00 | 907.00 | 2690.00 | 805.00 | 940.00 | 2775.00 | 838.00 | 973.00 | 2860.00 | 870.00 | 1005.00 | 2945.00 | 903.00 | 1038.00 |
| 2606.00 | 772.00 | 908.00 | 2691.00 | 805.00 | 940.00 | 2776.00 | 838.00 | 973.00 | 2861.00 | 871.00 | 1006.00 | 2946.00 | 903.00 | 1038.00 |
| 2607.00 | 773.00 | 908.00 | 2692.00 | 806.00 | 941.00 | 2777.00 | 838.00 | 973.00 | 2862.00 | 871.00 | 1006.00 | 2947.00 | 904.00 | 1039.00 |
| 2608.00 | 773.00 | 908.00 | 2693.00 | 806.00 | 941.00 | 2778.00 | 839.00 | 974.00 | 2863.00 | 871.00 | 1006.00 | 2948.00 | 904.00 | 1039.00 |
| 2609.00 | 774.00 | 909.00 | 2694.00 | 806.00 | 941.00 | 2779.00 | 839.00 | 974.00 | 2864.00 | 872.00 | 1007.00 | 2949.00 | 905.00 | 1040.00 |
| 2610.00 | 774.00 | 909.00 | 2695.00 | 807.00 | 942.00 | 2780.00 | 839.00 | 975.00 | 2865.00 | 872.00 | 1007.00 | 2950.00 | 905.00 | 1040.00 |
| 2611.00 | 774.00 | 909.00 | 2696.00 | 807.00 | 942.00 | 2781.00 | 840.00 | 975.00 | 2866.00 | 873.00 | 1008.00 | 2951.00 | 905.00 | 1040.00 |
| 2612.00 | 775.00 | 910.00 | 2697.00 | 808.00 | 943.00 | 2782.00 | 840.00 | 975.00 | 2867.00 | 873.00 | 1008.00 | 2952.00 | 906.00 | 1041.00 |
| 2613.00 | 775.00 | 910.00 | 2698.00 | 808.00 | 943.00 | 2783.00 | 841.00 | 976.00 | 2868.00 | 873.00 | 1008.00 | 2953.00 | 906.00 | 1041.00 |
| 2614.00 | 776.00 | 911.00 | 2699.00 | 808.00 | 943.00 | 2784.00 | 841.00 | 976.00 | 2869.00 | 874.00 | 1009.00 | 2954.00 | 906.00 | 1042.00 |
| 2615.00 | 776.00 | 911.00 | 2700.00 | 809.00 | 944.00 | 2785.00 | 841.00 | 976.00 | 2870.00 | 874.00 | 1009.00 | 2955.00 | 907.00 | 1042.00 |
| 2616.00 | 776.00 | 911.00 | 2701.00 | 809.00 | 944.00 | 2786.00 | 842.00 | 977.00 | 2871.00 | 875.00 | 1010.00 | 2956.00 | 907.00 | 1042.00 |
| 2617.00 | 777.00 | 912.00 | 2702.00 | 809.00 | 944.00 | 2787.00 | 842.00 | 977.00 | 2872.00 | 875.00 | 1010.00 | 2957.00 | 908.00 | 1043.00 |
| 2618.00 | 777.00 | 912.00 | 2703.00 | 810.00 | 945.00 | 2788.00 | 843.00 | 978.00 | 2873.00 | 875.00 | 1010.00 | 2958.00 | 908.00 | 1043.00 |
| 2619.00 | 777.00 | 913.00 | 2704.00 | 810.00 | 945.00 | 2789.00 | 843.00 | 978.00 | 2874.00 | 876.00 | 1011.00 | 2959.00 | 908.00 | 1043.00 |
| 2620.00 | 778.00 | 913.00 | 2705.00 | 811.00 | 946.00 | 2790.00 | 843.00 | 978.00 | 2875.00 | 876.00 | 1011.00 | 2960.00 | 909.00 | 1044.00 |
| 2621.00 | 778.00 | 913.00 | 2706.00 | 811.00 | 946.00 | 2791.00 | 844.00 | 979.00 | 2876.00 | 876.00 | 1011.00 | 2961.00 | 909.00 | 1044.00 |
| 2622.00 | 779.00 | 914.00 | 2707.00 | 811.00 | 946.00 | 2792.00 | 844.00 | 979.00 | 2877.00 | 877.00 | 1012.00 | 2962.00 | 910.00 | 1045.00 |
| 2623.00 | 779.00 | 914.00 | 2708.00 | 812.00 | 947.00 | 2793.00 | 844.00 | 980.00 | 2878.00 | 877.00 | 1012.00 | 2963.00 | 910.00 | 1045.00 |
| 2624.00 | 779.00 | 914.00 | 2709.00 | 812.00 | 947.00 | 2794.00 | 845.00 | 980.00 | 2879.00 | 878.00 | 1013.00 | 2964.00 | 910.00 | 1045.00 |
| 2625.00 | 780.00 | 915.00 | 2710.00 | 813.00 | 948.00 | 2795.00 | 845.00 | 980.00 | 2880.00 | 878.00 | 1013.00 | 2965.00 | 911.00 | 1046.00 |
| 2626.00 | 780.00 | 915.00 | 2711.00 | 813.00 | 948.00 | 2796.00 | 846.00 | 981.00 | 2881.00 | 878.00 | 1013.00 | 2966.00 | 911.00 | 1046.00 |
| 2627.00 | 781.00 | 916.00 | 2712.00 | 813.00 | 948.00 | 2797.00 | 846.00 | 981.00 | 2882.00 | 879.00 | 1014.00 | 2967.00 | 911.00 | 1047.00 |
| 2628.00 | 781.00 | 916.00 | 2713.00 | 814.00 | 949.00 | 2798.00 | 846.00 | 981.00 | 2883.00 | 879.00 | 1014.00 | 2968.00 | 912.00 | 1047.00 |
| 2629.00 | 781.00 | 916.00 | 2714.00 | 814.00 | 949.00 | 2799.00 | 847.00 | 982.00 | 2884.00 | 880.00 | 1015.00 | 2969.00 | 912.00 | 1047.00 |
| 2630.00 | 782.00 | 917.00 | 2715.00 | 814.00 | 949.00 | 2800.00 | 847.00 | 982.00 | 2885.00 | 880.00 | 1015.00 | 2970.00 | 913.00 | 1048.00 |
| 2631.00 | 782.00 | 917.00 | 2716.00 | 815.00 | 950.00 | 2801.00 | 848.00 | 983.00 | 2886.00 | 880.00 | 1015.00 | 2971.00 | 913.00 | 1048.00 |
| 2632.00 | 782.00 | 918.00 | 2717.00 | 815.00 | 950.00 | 2802.00 | 848.00 | 983.00 | 2887.00 | 881.00 | 1016.00 | 2972.00 | 913.00 | 1048.00 |
| 2633.00 | 783.00 | 918.00 | 2718.00 | 816.00 | 951.00 | 2803.00 | 848.00 | 983.00 | 2888.00 | 881.00 | 1016.00 | 2973.00 | 914.00 | 1049.00 |
| 2634.00 | 783.00 | 918.00 | 2719.00 | 816.00 | 951.00 | 2804.00 | 849.00 | 984.00 | 2889.00 | 881.00 | 1016.00 | 2974.00 | 914.00 | 1049.00 |
| 2635.00 | 784.00 | 919.00 | 2720.00 | 816.00 | 951.00 | 2805.00 | 849.00 | 984.00 | 2890.00 | 882.00 | 1017.00 | 2975.00 | 915.00 | 1050.00 |

SCHEDULE 2 WEEKLY TAX TABLE    11

Figure 7.5

# WEEKLY TAX TABLE – INCORPORATING MEDICARE LEVY

! Leave loading column has been removed from this tax table. For more information about leave loading changes, see page 3.

| Weekly earnings 1 $ | With tax-free threshold 2 $ | No tax-free threshold 3 $ | Weekly earnings 1 $ | With tax-free threshold 2 $ | No tax-free threshold 3 $ | Weekly earnings 1 $ | With tax-free threshold 2 $ | No tax-free threshold 3 $ | Weekly earnings 1 $ | With tax-free threshold 2 $ | No tax-free threshold 3 $ | Weekly earnings 1 $ | With tax-free threshold 2 $ | No tax-free threshold 3 $ |
|---|---|---|---|---|---|---|---|---|---|---|---|---|---|---|
| 2976.00 | 915.00 | 1050.00 | 3036.00 | 938.00 | 1073.00 | 3096.00 | 961.00 | 1096.00 | 3156.00 | 984.00 | 1123.00 | 3216.00 | 1007.00 | 1151.00 |
| 2977.00 | 915.00 | 1050.00 | 3037.00 | 938.00 | 1073.00 | 3097.00 | 962.00 | 1097.00 | 3157.00 | 985.00 | 1123.00 | 3217.00 | 1008.00 | 1151.00 |
| 2978.00 | 916.00 | 1051.00 | 3038.00 | 939.00 | 1074.00 | 3098.00 | 962.00 | 1097.00 | 3158.00 | 985.00 | 1124.00 | 3218.00 | 1008.00 | 1152.00 |
| 2979.00 | 916.00 | 1051.00 | 3039.00 | 939.00 | 1074.00 | 3099.00 | 962.00 | 1097.00 | 3159.00 | 985.00 | 1124.00 | 3219.00 | 1008.00 | 1152.00 |
| 2980.00 | 916.00 | 1052.00 | 3040.00 | 940.00 | 1075.00 | 3100.00 | 963.00 | 1098.00 | 3160.00 | 986.00 | 1125.00 | 3220.00 | 1009.00 | 1153.00 |
| 2981.00 | 917.00 | 1052.00 | 3041.00 | 940.00 | 1075.00 | 3101.00 | 963.00 | 1098.00 | 3161.00 | 986.00 | 1125.00 | 3221.00 | 1009.00 | 1153.00 |
| 2982.00 | 917.00 | 1052.00 | 3042.00 | 940.00 | 1075.00 | 3102.00 | 963.00 | 1098.00 | 3162.00 | 987.00 | 1126.00 | 3222.00 | 1010.00 | 1154.00 |
| 2983.00 | 918.00 | 1053.00 | 3043.00 | 941.00 | 1076.00 | 3103.00 | 964.00 | 1099.00 | 3163.00 | 987.00 | 1126.00 | 3223.00 | 1010.00 | 1154.00 |
| 2984.00 | 918.00 | 1053.00 | 3044.00 | 941.00 | 1076.00 | 3104.00 | 964.00 | 1099.00 | 3164.00 | 987.00 | 1127.00 | 3224.00 | 1010.00 | 1155.00 |
| 2985.00 | 918.00 | 1053.00 | 3045.00 | 941.00 | 1077.00 | 3105.00 | 965.00 | 1100.00 | 3165.00 | 988.00 | 1127.00 | 3225.00 | 1011.00 | 1155.00 |
| 2986.00 | 919.00 | 1054.00 | 3046.00 | 942.00 | 1077.00 | 3106.00 | 965.00 | 1100.00 | 3166.00 | 988.00 | 1128.00 | 3226.00 | 1011.00 | 1155.00 |
| 2987.00 | 919.00 | 1054.00 | 3047.00 | 942.00 | 1077.00 | 3107.00 | 965.00 | 1100.00 | 3167.00 | 988.00 | 1128.00 | 3227.00 | 1012.00 | 1156.00 |
| 2988.00 | 920.00 | 1055.00 | 3048.00 | 943.00 | 1078.00 | 3108.00 | 966.00 | 1101.00 | 3168.00 | 989.00 | 1128.00 | 3228.00 | 1012.00 | 1156.00 |
| 2989.00 | 920.00 | 1055.00 | 3049.00 | 943.00 | 1078.00 | 3109.00 | 966.00 | 1101.00 | 3169.00 | 989.00 | 1129.00 | 3229.00 | 1012.00 | 1157.00 |
| 2990.00 | 920.00 | 1055.00 | 3050.00 | 943.00 | 1078.00 | 3110.00 | 967.00 | 1102.00 | 3170.00 | 990.00 | 1129.00 | 3230.00 | 1013.00 | 1157.00 |
| 2991.00 | 921.00 | 1056.00 | 3051.00 | 944.00 | 1079.00 | 3111.00 | 967.00 | 1102.00 | 3171.00 | 990.00 | 1130.00 | 3231.00 | 1013.00 | 1158.00 |
| 2992.00 | 921.00 | 1056.00 | 3052.00 | 944.00 | 1079.00 | 3112.00 | 967.00 | 1102.00 | 3172.00 | 990.00 | 1130.00 | 3232.00 | 1013.00 | 1158.00 |
| 2993.00 | 921.00 | 1057.00 | 3053.00 | 945.00 | 1080.00 | 3113.00 | 968.00 | 1103.00 | 3173.00 | 991.00 | 1131.00 | 3233.00 | 1014.00 | 1159.00 |
| 2994.00 | 922.00 | 1057.00 | 3054.00 | 945.00 | 1080.00 | 3114.00 | 968.00 | 1103.00 | 3174.00 | 991.00 | 1131.00 | 3234.00 | 1014.00 | 1159.00 |
| 2995.00 | 922.00 | 1057.00 | 3055.00 | 945.00 | 1080.00 | 3115.00 | 968.00 | 1104.00 | 3175.00 | 992.00 | 1132.00 | 3235.00 | 1015.00 | 1160.00 |
| 2996.00 | 923.00 | 1058.00 | 3056.00 | 946.00 | 1081.00 | 3116.00 | 969.00 | 1104.00 | 3176.00 | 992.00 | 1132.00 | 3236.00 | 1015.00 | 1160.00 |
| 2997.00 | 923.00 | 1058.00 | 3057.00 | 946.00 | 1081.00 | 3117.00 | 969.00 | 1105.00 | 3177.00 | 992.00 | 1133.00 | 3237.00 | 1015.00 | 1161.00 |
| 2998.00 | 923.00 | 1058.00 | 3058.00 | 946.00 | 1082.00 | 3118.00 | 970.00 | 1105.00 | 3178.00 | 993.00 | 1133.00 | 3238.00 | 1016.00 | 1161.00 |
| 2999.00 | 924.00 | 1059.00 | 3059.00 | 947.00 | 1082.00 | 3119.00 | 970.00 | 1106.00 | 3179.00 | 993.00 | 1134.00 | 3239.00 | 1016.00 | 1162.00 |
| 3000.00 | 924.00 | 1059.00 | 3060.00 | 947.00 | 1082.00 | 3120.00 | 970.00 | 1106.00 | 3180.00 | 993.00 | 1134.00 | 3240.00 | 1017.00 | 1162.00 |
| 3001.00 | 925.00 | 1060.00 | 3061.00 | 948.00 | 1083.00 | 3121.00 | 971.00 | 1107.00 | 3181.00 | 994.00 | 1135.00 | 3241.00 | 1017.00 | 1162.00 |
| 3002.00 | 925.00 | 1060.00 | 3062.00 | 948.00 | 1083.00 | 3122.00 | 971.00 | 1107.00 | 3182.00 | 994.00 | 1135.00 | 3242.00 | 1017.00 | 1163.00 |
| 3003.00 | 925.00 | 1060.00 | 3063.00 | 948.00 | 1083.00 | 3123.00 | 972.00 | 1108.00 | 3183.00 | 995.00 | 1135.00 | 3243.00 | 1018.00 | 1163.00 |
| 3004.00 | 926.00 | 1061.00 | 3064.00 | 949.00 | 1084.00 | 3124.00 | 972.00 | 1108.00 | 3184.00 | 995.00 | 1136.00 | 3244.00 | 1018.00 | 1164.00 |
| 3005.00 | 926.00 | 1061.00 | 3065.00 | 949.00 | 1084.00 | 3125.00 | 972.00 | 1108.00 | 3185.00 | 995.00 | 1136.00 | 3245.00 | 1018.00 | 1164.00 |
| 3006.00 | 926.00 | 1062.00 | 3066.00 | 950.00 | 1085.00 | 3126.00 | 973.00 | 1109.00 | 3186.00 | 996.00 | 1137.00 | 3246.00 | 1019.00 | 1165.00 |
| 3007.00 | 927.00 | 1062.00 | 3067.00 | 950.00 | 1085.00 | 3127.00 | 973.00 | 1109.00 | 3187.00 | 996.00 | 1137.00 | 3247.00 | 1019.00 | 1165.00 |
| 3008.00 | 927.00 | 1062.00 | 3068.00 | 950.00 | 1085.00 | 3128.00 | 973.00 | 1110.00 | 3188.00 | 997.00 | 1138.00 | 3248.00 | 1020.00 | 1166.00 |
| 3009.00 | 928.00 | 1063.00 | 3069.00 | 951.00 | 1086.00 | 3129.00 | 974.00 | 1110.00 | 3189.00 | 997.00 | 1138.00 | 3249.00 | 1020.00 | 1166.00 |
| 3010.00 | 928.00 | 1063.00 | 3070.00 | 951.00 | 1086.00 | 3130.00 | 974.00 | 1111.00 | 3190.00 | 997.00 | 1139.00 | 3250.00 | 1020.00 | 1167.00 |
| 3011.00 | 928.00 | 1064.00 | 3071.00 | 952.00 | 1087.00 | 3131.00 | 975.00 | 1111.00 | 3191.00 | 998.00 | 1139.00 | 3251.00 | 1021.00 | 1167.00 |
| 3012.00 | 929.00 | 1064.00 | 3072.00 | 952.00 | 1087.00 | 3132.00 | 975.00 | 1112.00 | 3192.00 | 998.00 | 1140.00 | 3252.00 | 1021.00 | 1168.00 |
| 3013.00 | 929.00 | 1064.00 | 3073.00 | 952.00 | 1087.00 | 3133.00 | 975.00 | 1112.00 | 3193.00 | 998.00 | 1140.00 | 3253.00 | 1022.00 | 1168.00 |
| 3014.00 | 930.00 | 1065.00 | 3074.00 | 953.00 | 1088.00 | 3134.00 | 976.00 | 1113.00 | 3194.00 | 999.00 | 1141.00 | 3254.00 | 1022.00 | 1168.00 |
| 3015.00 | 930.00 | 1065.00 | 3075.00 | 953.00 | 1088.00 | 3135.00 | 976.00 | 1113.00 | 3195.00 | 999.00 | 1141.00 | 3255.00 | 1022.00 | 1169.00 |
| 3016.00 | 930.00 | 1065.00 | 3076.00 | 953.00 | 1088.00 | 3136.00 | 977.00 | 1114.00 | 3196.00 | 1000.00 | 1142.00 | 3256.00 | 1023.00 | 1169.00 |
| 3017.00 | 931.00 | 1066.00 | 3077.00 | 954.00 | 1089.00 | 3137.00 | 977.00 | 1114.00 | 3197.00 | 1000.00 | 1142.00 | 3257.00 | 1023.00 | 1170.00 |
| 3018.00 | 931.00 | 1066.00 | 3078.00 | 954.00 | 1089.00 | 3138.00 | 977.00 | 1115.00 | 3198.00 | 1000.00 | 1142.00 | 3258.00 | 1023.00 | 1170.00 |
| 3019.00 | 931.00 | 1067.00 | 3079.00 | 955.00 | 1090.00 | 3139.00 | 978.00 | 1115.00 | 3199.00 | 1001.00 | 1143.00 | 3259.00 | 1024.00 | 1171.00 |
| 3020.00 | 932.00 | 1067.00 | 3080.00 | 955.00 | 1090.00 | 3140.00 | 978.00 | 1115.00 | 3200.00 | 1001.00 | 1143.00 | 3260.00 | 1024.00 | 1171.00 |
| 3021.00 | 932.00 | 1067.00 | 3081.00 | 955.00 | 1090.00 | 3141.00 | 978.00 | 1116.00 | 3201.00 | 1002.00 | 1144.00 | 3261.00 | 1025.00 | 1172.00 |
| 3022.00 | 933.00 | 1068.00 | 3082.00 | 956.00 | 1091.00 | 3142.00 | 979.00 | 1116.00 | 3202.00 | 1002.00 | 1144.00 | 3262.00 | 1025.00 | 1172.00 |
| 3023.00 | 933.00 | 1068.00 | 3083.00 | 956.00 | 1091.00 | 3143.00 | 979.00 | 1117.00 | 3203.00 | 1002.00 | 1145.00 | 3263.00 | 1025.00 | 1173.00 |
| 3024.00 | 933.00 | 1068.00 | 3084.00 | 957.00 | 1092.00 | 3144.00 | 980.00 | 1117.00 | 3204.00 | 1003.00 | 1145.00 | 3264.00 | 1026.00 | 1173.00 |
| 3025.00 | 934.00 | 1069.00 | 3085.00 | 957.00 | 1092.00 | 3145.00 | 980.00 | 1118.00 | 3205.00 | 1003.00 | 1146.00 | 3265.00 | 1026.00 | 1174.00 |
| 3026.00 | 934.00 | 1069.00 | 3086.00 | 957.00 | 1092.00 | 3146.00 | 980.00 | 1118.00 | 3206.00 | 1003.00 | 1146.00 | 3266.00 | 1027.00 | 1174.00 |
| 3027.00 | 935.00 | 1070.00 | 3087.00 | 958.00 | 1093.00 | 3147.00 | 981.00 | 1119.00 | 3207.00 | 1004.00 | 1147.00 | 3267.00 | 1027.00 | 1175.00 |
| 3028.00 | 935.00 | 1070.00 | 3088.00 | 958.00 | 1093.00 | 3148.00 | 981.00 | 1119.00 | 3208.00 | 1004.00 | 1147.00 | 3268.00 | 1027.00 | 1175.00 |
| 3029.00 | 935.00 | 1070.00 | 3089.00 | 958.00 | 1093.00 | 3149.00 | 982.00 | 1120.00 | 3209.00 | 1005.00 | 1148.00 | 3269.00 | 1028.00 | 1175.00 |
| 3030.00 | 936.00 | 1071.00 | 3090.00 | 959.00 | 1094.00 | 3150.00 | 982.00 | 1120.00 | 3210.00 | 1005.00 | 1148.00 | 3270.00 | 1028.00 | 1176.00 |
| 3031.00 | 936.00 | 1071.00 | 3091.00 | 959.00 | 1094.00 | 3151.00 | 982.00 | 1121.00 | 3211.00 | 1005.00 | 1148.00 | 3271.00 | 1029.00 | 1176.00 |
| 3032.00 | 936.00 | 1072.00 | 3092.00 | 960.00 | 1095.00 | 3152.00 | 983.00 | 1121.00 | 3212.00 | 1006.00 | 1149.00 | 3272.00 | 1029.00 | 1177.00 |
| 3033.00 | 937.00 | 1072.00 | 3093.00 | 960.00 | 1095.00 | 3153.00 | 983.00 | 1122.00 | 3213.00 | 1006.00 | 1149.00 | 3273.00 | 1029.00 | 1177.00 |
| 3034.00 | 937.00 | 1072.00 | 3094.00 | 960.00 | 1095.00 | 3154.00 | 983.00 | 1122.00 | 3214.00 | 1007.00 | 1150.00 | 3274.00 | 1030.00 | 1178.00 |
| 3035.00 | 938.00 | 1073.00 | 3095.00 | 961.00 | 1096.00 | 3155.00 | 984.00 | 1122.00 | 3215.00 | 1007.00 | 1150.00 | 3275.00 | 1030.00 | 1178.00 |

! Where the tax-free threshold is claimed and your payee earns:
- more than $3,275 but less than $3,461, withhold $1,030 plus 38.50 cents for each $1 of earnings in excess of $3,275
- more than $3,460, withhold $1,102 plus 46.50 cents for each $1 of earnings in excess of $3,460.

Where the tax-free threshold is **not** claimed and your payee earns more than $3,275, withhold $1,178 plus 46.50 cents for each $1 of earnings in excess of $3,275.

**For all withholding amounts calculated, round the result to the nearest dollar.**

**PUBLISHED BY**
Australian Taxation Office, Canberra, May 2012
JS 22918

**OUR COMMITMENT TO YOU**
We are committed to providing you with accurate, consistent and clear information to help you understand your rights and entitlements and meet your obligations. If you feel that this publication does not fully cover your circumstances, or you are unsure how it applies to you, you can seek further assistance from us.

We regularly revise our publications to take account of any changes to the law, so make sure that you have the latest information. If you are unsure, you can check for more recent information on our website at **www.ato.gov.au** or contact us.

This publication was current at **May 2012**.

**Figure 7.6    Tax file number declaration form**

**Figure 7.6**

Payer's copy

**Australian Government**
**Australian Taxation Office**

ato.gov.au

# Tax file number declaration

This declaration is NOT an application for a tax file number.
■ Use a black or blue pen and print clearly in BLOCK LETTERS.
■ Print X in the appropriate boxes.
■ Read all the instructions before you complete this declaration.

## Section A: To be completed by the PAYEE

**1 What is your tax file number (TFN)?**

➤ For more information, see question 1 on page 2 of the instructions.

**OR** I have made a separate application/enquiry to the ATO for a new or existing TFN.

**OR** I am claiming an exemption because I am under 18 years of age and do not earn enough to pay tax.

**OR** I am claiming an exemption because I am in receipt of a pension, benefit or allowance.

**2 What is your name?** Title: Mr ☐ Mrs ☐ Miss ☐ Ms ☐

Surname or family name

First given name

Other given names

**3 If you have changed your name since you last dealt with us, show your previous family name**

**4 What is your date of birth?** Day Month Year

**5 What is your home address in Australia?**

Suburb or town

State/territory    Postcode

**6 On what basis are you paid?** (Select only one.)
Full-time employment ☐    Part-time employment ☐    Labour hire ☐    Superannuation or annuity income stream ☐    Casual employment ☐

**7 Are you an Australian resident for tax purposes?**
(Visit ato.gov.au/residency to check) Yes ☐ No ☐ ➤ You must answer **no** at question 8.

**8 Do you want to claim the tax-free threshold from this payer?**

Only claim the tax-free threshold from one payer at a time, unless your total income from all sources for the financial year will be less than the tax-free threshold.

Yes ☐ No ☐ ➤ Answer **no** at questions 9 and 10 unless you are a foreign resident claiming a seniors and pensioners, zone or overseas forces tax offset.

**9 Do you want to claim the seniors and pensioners tax offset by reducing the amount withheld from payments made to you?**
Yes ☐ ➤ Complete a *Withholding declaration* (NAT 3093), but only if you are claiming the tax-free threshold from this payer. If you have more than one payer, see page 3 of the instructions. No ☐

**10 Do you want to claim a zone, overseas forces, dependent spouse or dependent (invalid and carer) tax offset by reducing the amount withheld from payments made to you?**
Yes ☐ ➤ Complete a *Withholding declaration* (NAT 3093). No ☐

**11 (a) Do you have an accumulated Higher Education Loan Program (HELP) debt?**
Yes ☐ ➤ Your payer will withhold additional amounts to cover any compulsory repayments that may be raised on your notice of assessment. No ☐

**(b) Do you have an accumulated Financial Supplement debt?**
Yes ☐ ➤ Your payer will withhold additional amounts to cover any compulsory repayments that may be raised on your notice of assessment. No ☐

**DECLARATION by payee:** *I declare that the information I have given is true and correct.*
Signature

You MUST SIGN here

Date Day Month Year

➖ There are penalties for deliberately making a false or misleading statement.

❗ Once section A is completed and signed, give it to your payer to complete section B.

## Section B: To be completed by the PAYER (if you are not lodging online)

**1 What is your Australian business number (ABN) or your withholding payer number?**    Branch number (if applicable)

**2 If you don't have an ABN or withholding payer number, have you applied for one?**
Yes ☐ No ☐

**3 What is your legal name or registered business name (or your individual name if not in business)?**

**4 What is your business address?**

Suburb or town

State/territory    Postcode

**5 Who is your contact person?**

Business phone number

**6 If you no longer make payments to this payee, print X in this box** ☐

**DECLARATION by payer:** *I declare that the information I have given is true and correct.*
Signature of payer

Date Day Month Year

➖ There are penalties for deliberately making a false or misleading statement.

➤ Return the completed original ATO copy to:
**For WA, SA, NT, VIC or TAS**
Australian Taxation Office
PO Box 795
ALBURY NSW 2640

**For NSW, QLD or ACT**
Australian Taxation Office
PO Box 9004
PENRITH NSW 2740

❗ **IMPORTANT**
See reverse side of Payer's copy for:
■ payer obligations
■ lodging online.

**TAXPAYER-SENSITIVE (when completed)**

NAT 3092-07.2013 [JS 27654]

**Figure 7.6**

# PAYER INFORMATION

The following information will help you comply with your pay as you go (PAYG) withholding obligations.

 **IS YOUR EMPLOYEE ENTITLED TO WORK IN AUSTRALIA?**

It is a criminal offence to knowingly or recklessly allow someone to work, or to refer someone for work, where that person is from overseas and is either in Australia illegally or is working in breach of their visa conditions.

People or companies convicted of these offences may face fines and/or imprisonment. To avoid penalties, ensure your prospective employee has a valid visa to work in Australia before you employ them. For more information and to check a visa holder's status online, visit the Department of Immigration and Citizenship website at **immi.gov.au**

## PAYER OBLIGATIONS

If you withhold amounts from payments, or are likely to withhold amounts, the payee may give you this form with section A completed. A TFN declaration applies to payments made after the declaration is provided to you. The information provided on this form is used to determine the amount of tax to be withheld from payments based on the PAYG withholding tax tables we publish. If the payee gives you another declaration, it overrides any previous declarations.

## HAS YOUR PAYEE ADVISED YOU THAT THEY HAVE APPLIED FOR A TFN, OR ENQUIRED ABOUT THEIR EXISTING TFN?

Where the payee indicates at question 1 on this form that they have applied for an individual TFN, or enquired about their existing TFN, they have 28 days to give you their TFN. **You must withhold tax for 28 days at the standard rate according to the PAYG withholding tax tables.** After 28 days, if the payee has not given you their TFN, you must then withhold the highest rate of tax plus the Medicare levy (or the highest rate of tax if they are not an Australian resident for tax purposes) from future payments, unless we tell you not to.

## IF YOUR PAYEE HAS NOT GIVEN YOU A COMPLETED FORM YOU MUST:

- notify us within 14 days of the start of the withholding obligation by completing as much of the payee section of the form as you can. Print 'PAYER' in the payee declaration and lodge the form – see 'Lodging the form'.
- withhold the highest rate of tax plus the Medicare levy (or the highest rate of tax if they are not an Australian resident for tax purposes) from any payment to that payee.

## LODGING THE FORM

You need to lodge TFN declarations with us within 14 days after the form is either signed by the payee or completed by you (if not provided by the payee). You need to retain the payer's copy for your records. For information about storage and disposal, see below.

You may lodge the information:

- online – lodge your TFN declaration reports using software that complies with our specifications. There is no need to complete section B of each form as the payer information is supplied by your software.
- by paper – complete section B and send the original to us within 14 days.

 For more information about lodging your TFN declaration report online, visit our website at **ato.gov.au/lodgetfndeclaration**

## PROVISION OF PAYEE'S TFN TO THE PAYEE'S SUPER FUND

If you make a super contribution for your payee, you need to give your payee's TFN to their super fund on the day of contribution, or if the payee has not yet quoted their TFN, within 14 days of receiving this form from your payee.

## STORING AND DISPOSING OF TFN DECLARATIONS

The TFN guidelines issued under the *Privacy Act 1988* require you to use secure methods when storing and disposing of TFN information. You may store electronic files of scanned forms as an alternative to storing paper forms. Scanned forms must be clear and not altered in any way.

If a payee:

- submits a new *TFN declaration* (NAT 3092), you must retain a copy of the earlier form for the current and following financial year.
- has not received payments from you for 12 months, you must retain a copy of the last completed form for the current and following financial year.

 **PENALTIES**

You may incur a penalty if you do not:

- lodge TFN declarations with us
- keep the payer copy of completed TFN declarations for your records
- provide the payee's TFN to their super fund where the payee quoted their TFN to you.

Figure 7.7    **Withholding declaration form**

**Australian Government**
**Australian Taxation Office**

PAYER'S COPY

# Withholding declaration

Complete this declaration to authorise your payer to adjust the amount withheld from payments made to you.

You must provide, or have previously provided, your payer with a completed *Tax file number declaration* (NAT 3092) (or *Employment declaration* or *Annuity and superannuation pension declaration* completed before 1 July 2000), quoting your tax file number or claiming an exemption from quoting it, before you can make a *Withholding declaration*.

❗ The information in the completed *Withholding declaration* form must be treated as sensitive.

■ Refer to the Instructions to help you complete this declaration.
■ Print neatly in BLOCK LETTERS and use a black or dark blue pen.
■ Print ☒ in the appropriate boxes.

## Section A: **Payee's declaration**

❯ To be completed by payee.

**1    What is your name?**    Title:    Mr ☐    Mrs ☐    Miss ☐    Ms ☐    Other _____

Family name
_____

Given names
_____

**2    What is your date of birth?**    Day ☐☐ / Month ☐☐ / Year ☐☐☐☐

❯ For more information, see 'Privacy' inside the front cover of the instructions.

**3    What is your tax file number (TFN)?**    _____

If you have not provided your TFN, indicate if any of the following reasons apply:

☐ I have lodged a TFN application.        ☐ I am claiming an exemption because I am a pensioner.        ☐ I am claiming an exemption because I am under 18 years of age and do not earn enough to pay tax.

**4    Are you an Australian resident for tax purposes?**    Yes ☐    No ☐    You must answer **no** at question 5.

**5    Are you claiming or do you want to claim the tax-free threshold from this payer?**    Yes ☐    No ☐    You must answer **no** at questions 7 and 8 unless you are a foreign resident claiming a seniors and pensioners, zone or overseas forces tax offset.

**6    (a) Do you have an accumulated Higher Education Loan Program debt?**    Yes ☐    No ☐

**(b) Do you have an accumulated Financial Supplement debt?**    Yes ☐    No ☐

**7    Do you want to claim or vary your tax offset by reducing the amount withheld from payments made to you?**    Yes ☐    No ☐

Insert your estimated total tax offset amount.    ❯ $ _____

**8    Do you want to claim or vary the seniors and pensioners tax offset entitlement by reducing the amount withheld from payments made to you?**    Yes ☐    No ☐

Are you:
☐ single        ☐ a member of an illness-separated couple        ☐ a member of a couple

NAT 3093-07.2013        **Sensitive** (when completed)

▶ ▶ ▶

**Figure 7.7**

9 **Do you want to increase the rate or amount withheld from payments made to you?** Yes ☐ No ☐

You need to complete the *Upwards variation agreement.*
As stated in the agreement, I elect that my payer will:

(a) withhold amounts from payments made to me at the rate of ☐☐ . ☐☐ %
OR

(b) increase the amount that would otherwise be withheld by $ ☐☐☐☐ . ☒ per payment.

This applies to payments made to me from the ☐☐ / ☐☐ / ☐☐☐☐ pay period.
(Day / Month / Year)

I understand that the varied rate or increased amount will apply only to the payments made to me starting from the date indicated above, when it results in a higher amount being withheld than would otherwise apply under the PAYG withholding tax tables or by regulation for the relevant withholding event.

**DECLARATION BY PAYEE**

*I declare that the information I have given on this form is true and correct.*

Signature of payee

⊖ The tax laws impose heavy penalties for giving false or misleading statements.

Date ☐☐ / ☐☐ / ☐☐☐☐
(Day / Month / Year)

## Section B: **Payer's declaration**

❗ The information in the completed *Withholding declaration* form must be treated as sensitive. ▶ To be completed by payer.

**YOUR DETAILS**

1 **What is your Australian business number (ABN) (or your withholding payer number if you are not in business)?** ☐☐☐☐☐☐☐☐☐☐☐☐

2 **What is your registered business name or trading name (or your individual name if you are not in business)?** ☐☐☐☐☐☐☐☐☐☐☐☐

▶ HOW MUCH SHOULD YOU WITHHOLD?

| The payee's answers to questions 4 and 5 will indicate which of the weekly, fortnightly or monthly tax tables you should use as the base rate of withholding. | A **yes** answer at question 6 will require an amount to be withheld as specified in the HELP tax tables or Student Financial Supplement Scheme tax tables. | A **yes** answer at question 7 or 8 will generally require a variation of the rate of withholding specified in the tax tables. | A **yes** answer at question 9 may require a higher rate or amount of withholding than may otherwise apply under the PAYG withholding tax tables or by regulation for the relevant withholding event. |
|---|---|---|---|

**WITHHOLDING AGREEMENT**

As elected by my payee, I agree to:

(a) withhold amounts from payments made to them at the rate of ☐☐ . ☐☐ %
OR

(b) increase the amount that would otherwise be withheld by $ ☐☐☐☐ . ☒ per payment.

This applies to payments made from the ☐☐ / ☐☐ / ☐☐☐☐ pay period.
(Day / Month / Year)

**DECLARATION BY PAYER**

*I declare that the information I have given on this form is true and correct.*
*I agree to increase the amount withheld from payments made, as indicated at either (a) or (b).*

Signature of payer

⊖ The tax laws impose heavy penalties for giving false or misleading statements.

Date ☐☐ / ☐☐ / ☐☐☐☐
(Day / Month / Year)

**WRITTEN NOTICE**

This declaration will constitute written notice under section 15-15 of schedule 1 to the *Taxation Administration Act 1953* (TAA 1953) of the Commissioner's approval to vary the amount required to be withheld where:
■ the payments specified in section B, at (a) or (b) in the form, are covered by Subdivision 12-B, 12-C or 12-D in schedule 1 to the TAA 1953
■ the payee has given a completed *Tax file number declaration* (or *Employment declaration* or *Annuity and superannuation pension declaration*) to the payer, or they have entered into a voluntary agreement with the payer
■ the payee has notified the payer of the varied rate of withholding in writing on this approved form at section A
■ the varied rate of withholding or increased amount of withholding results in a higher amount of withholding than would otherwise apply under the PAYG withholding tax tables or by regulation for the relevant withholding event.

**STORING AND DISPOSING OF WITHHOLDING DECLARATIONS**

The information in the completed *Withholding declaration* form must be treated as sensitive. Once you have completed, signed and dated the declaration, file the declaration form. If the declaration is accompanied by a completed *Upward variation agreement*, return the signed agreement to the payee for their records. **Do not send the declaration or agreement to us.**

Under the TFN guidelines in the *Privacy Act 1988*, you must use secure methods when storing and disposing of TFN information. Under tax laws, if a payee submits a new *Withholding declaration* or leaves your employment, you must still keep this declaration for the current and next financial year.

❗ Do not send this declaration form to us.

[ Print form ] [ Save form ]

[ Reset form ]

**Sensitive** (when completed)

**Figure 7.8    Higher Education Loan Program (HELP) weekly tax table**

Schedule 11 **Pay as you go (PAYG) withholding**                    NAT 2173

# Higher Education Loan Program weekly tax table

Including statement of formulas for calculating weekly and monthly withholding

**!** FOR PAYMENTS MADE ON OR AFTER
1 JULY 2013 TO 30 JUNE 2014

**!** Do not withhold any amount for HELP from lump sum termination payments.

**WHO SHOULD USE THIS TABLE?**
You should use this table if you make weekly payments and your payee has given you a *Tax file number declaration* (NAT 3092) or *Withholding declaration* (NAT 3093) and they answered **yes** to the question 'Do you have an accumulated Higher Education Loan Program (HELP) debt?'.

If your payee has claimed the tax-free threshold, use this table if they have:
- weekly income of $986 or more
- not applied for an exemption or reduction of the Medicare levy due to low family income on a *Medicare levy variation declaration* (NAT 0929).

If your payee has not claimed the tax-free threshold, use this table if their weekly income is $636 or more.

You must withhold the HELP component from all your payee's earnings, including taxable allowances, bonuses and commissions.

**>** For a full list of tax tables, visit our website at **ato.gov.au/taxtables**

Alternatively, our calculator can help you work out the correct amount of tax to withhold from payments to most payees. To access the calculator, visit our website at **ato.gov.au/taxwithheldcalculator**

**!** This document is a withholding schedule made by the Commissioner of Taxation in accordance with sections 15-25 and 15-30 of schedule 1 to the *Taxation Administration Act 1953*. It applies to withholding payments covered by Subdivisions 12-B (except sections 12-50 and 12-55), 12-C (except sections 12-85 and 12-90) and 12-D of schedule 1.

**Australian Government**
**Australian Taxation Office**

NAT 2173-05.2013

**Figure 7.8**

### Can you use a formula?

The withholding amounts shown in this table can be expressed in a mathematical form.

If you have developed your own payroll software package, you can use the formulas and component rates outlined below.

The formulas comprise linear equations of the form **y = ax**, where:

- **y** is the weekly HELP component
- **x** is the weekly earnings expressed in whole dollars plus 99 cents
- **a** is the value of the component rate as shown in the following tables.

#### Tax-free threshold claimed or foreign resident

| Weekly earnings – x $ | | | Component rate – a % |
|---|---|---|---|
| 0 | to | 985.99 | 0.0 |
| 986.00 | to | 1,098.99 | 4.0 |
| 1,099.00 | to | 1,210.99 | 4.5 |
| 1,211.00 | to | 1,274.99 | 5.0 |
| 1,275.00 | to | 1,369.99 | 5.5 |
| 1,370.00 | to | 1,483.99 | 6.0 |
| 1,484.00 | to | 1,561.99 | 6.5 |
| 1,562.00 | to | 1,718.99 | 7.0 |
| 1,719.00 | to | 1,831.99 | 7.5 |
| 1,832.00 | and | over | 8.0 |

#### No tax-free threshold claimed

| Weekly earnings – x $ | | | Component rate – a % |
|---|---|---|---|
| 0 | to | 635.99 | 0.0 |
| 636.00 | to | 748.99 | 4.0 |
| 749.00 | to | 860.99 | 4.5 |
| 861.00 | to | 924.99 | 5.0 |
| 925.00 | to | 1,019.99 | 5.5 |
| 1,020.00 | to | 1,133.99 | 6.0 |
| 1,134.00 | to | 1,211.99 | 6.5 |
| 1,212.00 | to | 1,368.99 | 7.0 |
| 1,369.00 | to | 1,481.99 | 7.5 |
| 1,482.00 | and | over | 8.0 |

### HOW TO WORK OUT THE MONTHLY COMPONENT

To work out the monthly component, you must:

1 Work out the total monthly earnings. If the result is an amount ending in 33 cents, add 1 cent (so the amount ends in 34 cents).

2 Multiply this amount by 12 and then divide the result by 52 to obtain the weekly gross amount. Ignore any cents in the result and add 99 cents.

3 Calculate the rounded weekly HELP component applicable to the weekly equivalent of earnings by applying the above formula.

4 Multiply this amount by 52 and then divide by 12 to obtain the monthly HELP component.

> **!** Add the monthly HELP component to the monthly withholding amount.

> **➤** *Monthly withholding table* (NAT 1007) and *Higher Education Loan Program monthly withholding table* (NAT 2186) are available on our website at **ato.gov.au/taxtables**

### ROUNDING OF COMPONENT AMOUNTS

Component amounts calculated as a result of applying the above formulas should be rounded to the nearest dollar. Results ending in 50 cents are rounded to the next higher dollar.

#### EXAMPLE

> The payee has claimed the tax-free threshold and has weekly earnings of $1,018.62.
>
> HELP component = $1,018.99 × 4.0% = $41.00 rounded to the nearest dollar.

### HOW TO WORK OUT THE WITHHOLDING AMOUNT

To work out the amount you need to withhold, you must:

1 Use the *Weekly tax table – including instructions for calculating monthly and quarterly amounts* (NAT 1005) to calculate the weekly withholding amount for your payee's earnings, allowing for any tax offsets claimed.

2 Use this HELP weekly tax table to calculate the HELP component to withhold.

3 Add the HELP component to the withholding amount. Withhold this amount from your payee's earnings.

4 If your payee also has a Financial Supplement debt, add the Student Financial Supplement Scheme (SFSS) component (calculated using the SFSS tax tables) as well as the HELP component to the amount to withhold. Withhold the result from your payee's earnings.

### HOW TO FIND THE HELP COMPONENT IN THE TABLE

Find your payee's weekly earnings in column 1 (ignoring any cents) and use the appropriate column to find the HELP component.

Use column 2 if your payee is either:

- claiming the tax-free threshold
- a foreign resident

Use column 3 if your payee is not claiming the tax-free threshold.

#### EXAMPLE

> The payee has claimed the tax-free threshold and has weekly earnings of $1,009.54. Ignoring cents, find $1,009 in column 1. The HELP component in column 2 is $40.00.

### ACCOUNTING SOFTWARE

Software written in accordance with the formulas in this schedule should be tested for accuracy against the table on the following pages. You should only use the software if it produces the exact amounts shown in the table.

Figure 7.8

## HELP WEEKLY TAX TABLE

| Weekly earnings 1 $ | Tax-free threshold weekly component 2 $ | No tax-free threshold weekly component 3 $ | Weekly earnings 1 $ | Tax-free threshold weekly component 2 $ | No tax-free threshold weekly component 3 $ | Weekly earnings 1 $ | Tax-free threshold weekly component 2 $ | No tax-free threshold weekly component 3 $ | Weekly earnings 1 $ | Tax-free threshold weekly component 2 $ | No tax-free threshold weekly component 3 $ |
|---|---|---|---|---|---|---|---|---|---|---|---|
| 636 | — | 25.00 | 716 | — | 29.00 | 796 | — | 36.00 | 876 | — | 44.00 |
| 637 | — | 26.00 | 717 | — | 29.00 | 797 | — | 36.00 | 877 | — | 44.00 |
| 638 | — | 26.00 | 718 | — | 29.00 | 798 | — | 36.00 | 878 | — | 44.00 |
| 639 | — | 26.00 | 719 | — | 29.00 | 799 | — | 36.00 | 879 | — | 44.00 |
| 640 | — | 26.00 | 720 | — | 29.00 | 800 | — | 36.00 | 880 | — | 44.00 |
| 641 | — | 26.00 | 721 | — | 29.00 | 801 | — | 36.00 | 881 | — | 44.00 |
| 642 | — | 26.00 | 722 | — | 29.00 | 802 | — | 36.00 | 882 | — | 44.00 |
| 643 | — | 26.00 | 723 | — | 29.00 | 803 | — | 36.00 | 883 | — | 44.00 |
| 644 | — | 26.00 | 724 | — | 29.00 | 804 | — | 36.00 | 884 | — | 44.00 |
| 645 | — | 26.00 | 725 | — | 29.00 | 805 | — | 36.00 | 885 | — | 44.00 |
| 646 | — | 26.00 | 726 | — | 29.00 | 806 | — | 36.00 | 886 | — | 44.00 |
| 647 | — | 26.00 | 727 | — | 29.00 | 807 | — | 36.00 | 887 | — | 44.00 |
| 648 | — | 26.00 | 728 | — | 29.00 | 808 | — | 36.00 | 888 | — | 44.00 |
| 649 | — | 26.00 | 729 | — | 29.00 | 809 | — | 36.00 | 889 | — | 44.00 |
| 650 | — | 26.00 | 730 | — | 29.00 | 810 | — | 36.00 | 890 | — | 45.00 |
| 651 | — | 26.00 | 731 | — | 29.00 | 811 | — | 37.00 | 891 | — | 45.00 |
| 652 | — | 26.00 | 732 | — | 29.00 | 812 | — | 37.00 | 892 | — | 45.00 |
| 653 | — | 26.00 | 733 | — | 29.00 | 813 | — | 37.00 | 893 | — | 45.00 |
| 654 | — | 26.00 | 734 | — | 29.00 | 814 | — | 37.00 | 894 | — | 45.00 |
| 655 | — | 26.00 | 735 | — | 29.00 | 815 | — | 37.00 | 895 | — | 45.00 |
| 656 | — | 26.00 | 736 | — | 29.00 | 816 | — | 37.00 | 896 | — | 45.00 |
| 657 | — | 26.00 | 737 | — | 30.00 | 817 | — | 37.00 | 897 | — | 45.00 |
| 658 | — | 26.00 | 738 | — | 30.00 | 818 | — | 37.00 | 898 | — | 45.00 |
| 659 | — | 26.00 | 739 | — | 30.00 | 819 | — | 37.00 | 899 | — | 45.00 |
| 660 | — | 26.00 | 740 | — | 30.00 | 820 | — | 37.00 | 900 | — | 45.00 |
| 661 | — | 26.00 | 741 | — | 30.00 | 821 | — | 37.00 | 901 | — | 45.00 |
| 662 | — | 27.00 | 742 | — | 30.00 | 822 | — | 37.00 | 902 | — | 45.00 |
| 663 | — | 27.00 | 743 | — | 30.00 | 823 | — | 37.00 | 903 | — | 45.00 |
| 664 | — | 27.00 | 744 | — | 30.00 | 824 | — | 37.00 | 904 | — | 45.00 |
| 665 | — | 27.00 | 745 | — | 30.00 | 825 | — | 37.00 | 905 | — | 45.00 |
| 666 | — | 27.00 | 746 | — | 30.00 | 826 | — | 37.00 | 906 | — | 45.00 |
| 667 | — | 27.00 | 747 | — | 30.00 | 827 | — | 37.00 | 907 | — | 45.00 |
| 668 | — | 27.00 | 748 | — | 30.00 | 828 | — | 37.00 | 908 | — | 45.00 |
| 669 | — | 27.00 | 749 | — | 34.00 | 829 | — | 37.00 | 909 | — | 45.00 |
| 670 | — | 27.00 | 750 | — | 34.00 | 830 | — | 37.00 | 910 | — | 46.00 |
| 671 | — | 27.00 | 751 | — | 34.00 | 831 | — | 37.00 | 911 | — | 46.00 |
| 672 | — | 27.00 | 752 | — | 34.00 | 832 | — | 37.00 | 912 | — | 46.00 |
| 673 | — | 27.00 | 753 | — | 34.00 | 833 | — | 38.00 | 913 | — | 46.00 |
| 674 | — | 27.00 | 754 | — | 34.00 | 834 | — | 38.00 | 914 | — | 46.00 |
| 675 | — | 27.00 | 755 | — | 34.00 | 835 | — | 38.00 | 915 | — | 46.00 |
| 676 | — | 27.00 | 756 | — | 34.00 | 836 | — | 38.00 | 916 | — | 46.00 |
| 677 | — | 27.00 | 757 | — | 34.00 | 837 | — | 38.00 | 917 | — | 46.00 |
| 678 | — | 27.00 | 758 | — | 34.00 | 838 | — | 38.00 | 918 | — | 46.00 |
| 679 | — | 27.00 | 759 | — | 34.00 | 839 | — | 38.00 | 919 | — | 46.00 |
| 680 | — | 27.00 | 760 | — | 34.00 | 840 | — | 38.00 | 920 | — | 46.00 |
| 681 | — | 27.00 | 761 | — | 34.00 | 841 | — | 38.00 | 921 | — | 46.00 |
| 682 | — | 27.00 | 762 | — | 34.00 | 842 | — | 38.00 | 922 | — | 46.00 |
| 683 | — | 27.00 | 763 | — | 34.00 | 843 | — | 38.00 | 923 | — | 46.00 |
| 684 | — | 27.00 | 764 | — | 34.00 | 844 | — | 38.00 | 924 | — | 46.00 |
| 685 | — | 27.00 | 765 | — | 34.00 | 845 | — | 38.00 | 925 | — | 51.00 |
| 686 | — | 27.00 | 766 | — | 35.00 | 846 | — | 38.00 | 926 | — | 51.00 |
| 687 | — | 28.00 | 767 | — | 35.00 | 847 | — | 38.00 | 927 | — | 51.00 |
| 688 | — | 28.00 | 768 | — | 35.00 | 848 | — | 38.00 | 928 | — | 51.00 |
| 689 | — | 28.00 | 769 | — | 35.00 | 849 | — | 38.00 | 929 | — | 51.00 |
| 690 | — | 28.00 | 770 | — | 35.00 | 850 | — | 38.00 | 930 | — | 51.00 |
| 691 | — | 28.00 | 771 | — | 35.00 | 851 | — | 38.00 | 931 | — | 51.00 |
| 692 | — | 28.00 | 772 | — | 35.00 | 852 | — | 38.00 | 932 | — | 51.00 |
| 693 | — | 28.00 | 773 | — | 35.00 | 853 | — | 38.00 | 933 | — | 51.00 |
| 694 | — | 28.00 | 774 | — | 35.00 | 854 | — | 38.00 | 934 | — | 51.00 |
| 695 | — | 28.00 | 775 | — | 35.00 | 855 | — | 39.00 | 935 | — | 51.00 |
| 696 | — | 28.00 | 776 | — | 35.00 | 856 | — | 39.00 | 936 | — | 52.00 |
| 697 | — | 28.00 | 777 | — | 35.00 | 857 | — | 39.00 | 937 | — | 52.00 |
| 698 | — | 28.00 | 778 | — | 35.00 | 858 | — | 39.00 | 938 | — | 52.00 |
| 699 | — | 28.00 | 779 | — | 35.00 | 859 | — | 39.00 | 939 | — | 52.00 |
| 700 | — | 28.00 | 780 | — | 35.00 | 860 | — | 39.00 | 940 | — | 52.00 |
| 701 | — | 28.00 | 781 | — | 35.00 | 861 | — | 43.00 | 941 | — | 52.00 |
| 702 | — | 28.00 | 782 | — | 35.00 | 862 | — | 43.00 | 942 | — | 52.00 |
| 703 | — | 28.00 | 783 | — | 35.00 | 863 | — | 43.00 | 943 | — | 52.00 |
| 704 | — | 28.00 | 784 | — | 35.00 | 864 | — | 43.00 | 944 | — | 52.00 |
| 705 | — | 28.00 | 785 | — | 35.00 | 865 | — | 43.00 | 945 | — | 52.00 |
| 706 | — | 28.00 | 786 | — | 35.00 | 866 | — | 43.00 | 946 | — | 52.00 |
| 707 | — | 28.00 | 787 | — | 35.00 | 867 | — | 43.00 | 947 | — | 52.00 |
| 708 | — | 28.00 | 788 | — | 36.00 | 868 | — | 43.00 | 948 | — | 52.00 |
| 709 | — | 28.00 | 789 | — | 36.00 | 869 | — | 43.00 | 949 | — | 52.00 |
| 710 | — | 28.00 | 790 | — | 36.00 | 870 | — | 44.00 | 950 | — | 52.00 |
| 711 | — | 28.00 | 791 | — | 36.00 | 871 | — | 44.00 | 951 | — | 52.00 |
| 712 | — | 29.00 | 792 | — | 36.00 | 872 | — | 44.00 | 952 | — | 52.00 |
| 713 | — | 29.00 | 793 | — | 36.00 | 873 | — | 44.00 | 953 | — | 52.00 |
| 714 | — | 29.00 | 794 | — | 36.00 | 874 | — | 44.00 | 954 | — | 53.00 |
| 715 | — | 29.00 | 795 | — | 36.00 | 875 | — | 44.00 | 955 | — | 53.00 |

SCHEDULE 11 HIGHER EDUCATION LOAN PROGRAM WEEKLY TAX TABLE

3

## Figure 7.8

### HELP WEEKLY TAX TABLE

| Weekly earnings 1 $ | Tax-free threshold weekly component 2 $ | No tax-free threshold weekly component 3 $ | Weekly earnings 1 $ | Tax-free threshold weekly component 2 $ | No tax-free threshold weekly component 3 $ | Weekly earnings 1 $ | Tax-free threshold weekly component 2 $ | No tax-free threshold weekly component 3 $ | Weekly earnings 1 $ | Tax-free threshold weekly component 2 $ | No tax-free threshold weekly component 3 $ |
|---|---|---|---|---|---|---|---|---|---|---|---|
| 956 | — | 53.00 | 1036 | 41.00 | 62.00 | 1116 | 50.00 | 67.00 | 1196 | 54.00 | 78.00 |
| 957 | — | 53.00 | 1037 | 42.00 | 62.00 | 1117 | 50.00 | 67.00 | 1197 | 54.00 | 78.00 |
| 958 | — | 53.00 | 1038 | 42.00 | 62.00 | 1118 | 50.00 | 67.00 | 1198 | 54.00 | 78.00 |
| 959 | — | 53.00 | 1039 | 42.00 | 62.00 | 1119 | 50.00 | 67.00 | 1199 | 54.00 | 78.00 |
| 960 | — | 53.00 | 1040 | 42.00 | 62.00 | 1120 | 50.00 | 67.00 | 1200 | 54.00 | 78.00 |
| 961 | — | 53.00 | 1041 | 42.00 | 63.00 | 1121 | 50.00 | 67.00 | 1201 | 54.00 | 78.00 |
| 962 | — | 53.00 | 1042 | 42.00 | 63.00 | 1122 | 51.00 | 67.00 | 1202 | 54.00 | 78.00 |
| 963 | — | 53.00 | 1043 | 42.00 | 63.00 | 1123 | 51.00 | 67.00 | 1203 | 54.00 | 78.00 |
| 964 | — | 53.00 | 1044 | 42.00 | 63.00 | 1124 | 51.00 | 67.00 | 1204 | 54.00 | 78.00 |
| 965 | — | 53.00 | 1045 | 42.00 | 63.00 | 1125 | 51.00 | 68.00 | 1205 | 54.00 | 78.00 |
| 966 | — | 53.00 | 1046 | 42.00 | 63.00 | 1126 | 51.00 | 68.00 | 1206 | 54.00 | 78.00 |
| 967 | — | 53.00 | 1047 | 42.00 | 63.00 | 1127 | 51.00 | 68.00 | 1207 | 54.00 | 79.00 |
| 968 | — | 53.00 | 1048 | 42.00 | 63.00 | 1128 | 51.00 | 68.00 | 1208 | 54.00 | 79.00 |
| 969 | — | 53.00 | 1049 | 42.00 | 63.00 | 1129 | 51.00 | 68.00 | 1209 | 54.00 | 79.00 |
| 970 | — | 53.00 | 1050 | 42.00 | 63.00 | 1130 | 51.00 | 68.00 | 1210 | 54.00 | 79.00 |
| 971 | — | 53.00 | 1051 | 42.00 | 63.00 | 1131 | 51.00 | 68.00 | 1211 | 61.00 | 79.00 |
| 972 | — | 54.00 | 1052 | 42.00 | 63.00 | 1132 | 51.00 | 68.00 | 1212 | 61.00 | 85.00 |
| 973 | — | 54.00 | 1053 | 42.00 | 63.00 | 1133 | 51.00 | 68.00 | 1213 | 61.00 | 85.00 |
| 974 | — | 54.00 | 1054 | 42.00 | 63.00 | 1134 | 51.00 | 74.00 | 1214 | 61.00 | 85.00 |
| 975 | — | 54.00 | 1055 | 42.00 | 63.00 | 1135 | 51.00 | 74.00 | 1215 | 61.00 | 85.00 |
| 976 | — | 54.00 | 1056 | 42.00 | 63.00 | 1136 | 51.00 | 74.00 | 1216 | 61.00 | 85.00 |
| 977 | — | 54.00 | 1057 | 42.00 | 63.00 | 1137 | 51.00 | 74.00 | 1217 | 61.00 | 85.00 |
| 978 | — | 54.00 | 1058 | 42.00 | 64.00 | 1138 | 51.00 | 74.00 | 1218 | 61.00 | 85.00 |
| 979 | — | 54.00 | 1059 | 42.00 | 64.00 | 1139 | 51.00 | 74.00 | 1219 | 61.00 | 85.00 |
| 980 | — | 54.00 | 1060 | 42.00 | 64.00 | 1140 | 51.00 | 74.00 | 1220 | 61.00 | 85.00 |
| 981 | — | 54.00 | 1061 | 42.00 | 64.00 | 1141 | 51.00 | 74.00 | 1221 | 61.00 | 86.00 |
| 982 | — | 54.00 | 1062 | 43.00 | 64.00 | 1142 | 51.00 | 74.00 | 1222 | 61.00 | 86.00 |
| 983 | — | 54.00 | 1063 | 43.00 | 64.00 | 1143 | 51.00 | 74.00 | 1223 | 61.00 | 86.00 |
| 984 | — | 54.00 | 1064 | 43.00 | 64.00 | 1144 | 52.00 | 74.00 | 1224 | 61.00 | 86.00 |
| 985 | — | 54.00 | 1065 | 43.00 | 64.00 | 1145 | 52.00 | 74.00 | 1225 | 61.00 | 86.00 |
| 986 | 39.00 | 54.00 | 1066 | 43.00 | 64.00 | 1146 | 52.00 | 75.00 | 1226 | 61.00 | 86.00 |
| 987 | 40.00 | 54.00 | 1067 | 43.00 | 64.00 | 1147 | 52.00 | 75.00 | 1227 | 61.00 | 86.00 |
| 988 | 40.00 | 54.00 | 1068 | 43.00 | 64.00 | 1148 | 52.00 | 75.00 | 1228 | 61.00 | 86.00 |
| 989 | 40.00 | 54.00 | 1069 | 43.00 | 64.00 | 1149 | 52.00 | 75.00 | 1229 | 61.00 | 86.00 |
| 990 | 40.00 | 55.00 | 1070 | 43.00 | 64.00 | 1150 | 52.00 | 75.00 | 1230 | 62.00 | 86.00 |
| 991 | 40.00 | 55.00 | 1071 | 43.00 | 64.00 | 1151 | 52.00 | 75.00 | 1231 | 62.00 | 86.00 |
| 992 | 40.00 | 55.00 | 1072 | 43.00 | 64.00 | 1152 | 52.00 | 75.00 | 1232 | 62.00 | 86.00 |
| 993 | 40.00 | 55.00 | 1073 | 43.00 | 64.00 | 1153 | 52.00 | 75.00 | 1233 | 62.00 | 86.00 |
| 994 | 40.00 | 55.00 | 1074 | 43.00 | 64.00 | 1154 | 52.00 | 75.00 | 1234 | 62.00 | 86.00 |
| 995 | 40.00 | 55.00 | 1075 | 43.00 | 65.00 | 1155 | 52.00 | 75.00 | 1235 | 62.00 | 87.00 |
| 996 | 40.00 | 55.00 | 1076 | 43.00 | 65.00 | 1156 | 52.00 | 75.00 | 1236 | 62.00 | 87.00 |
| 997 | 40.00 | 55.00 | 1077 | 43.00 | 65.00 | 1157 | 52.00 | 75.00 | 1237 | 62.00 | 87.00 |
| 998 | 40.00 | 55.00 | 1078 | 43.00 | 65.00 | 1158 | 52.00 | 75.00 | 1238 | 62.00 | 87.00 |
| 999 | 40.00 | 55.00 | 1079 | 43.00 | 65.00 | 1159 | 52.00 | 75.00 | 1239 | 62.00 | 87.00 |
| 1000 | 40.00 | 55.00 | 1080 | 43.00 | 65.00 | 1160 | 52.00 | 75.00 | 1240 | 62.00 | 87.00 |
| 1001 | 40.00 | 55.00 | 1081 | 43.00 | 65.00 | 1161 | 52.00 | 76.00 | 1241 | 62.00 | 87.00 |
| 1002 | 40.00 | 55.00 | 1082 | 43.00 | 65.00 | 1162 | 52.00 | 76.00 | 1242 | 62.00 | 87.00 |
| 1003 | 40.00 | 55.00 | 1083 | 43.00 | 65.00 | 1163 | 52.00 | 76.00 | 1243 | 62.00 | 87.00 |
| 1004 | 40.00 | 55.00 | 1084 | 43.00 | 65.00 | 1164 | 52.00 | 76.00 | 1244 | 62.00 | 87.00 |
| 1005 | 40.00 | 55.00 | 1085 | 43.00 | 65.00 | 1165 | 52.00 | 76.00 | 1245 | 62.00 | 87.00 |
| 1006 | 40.00 | 55.00 | 1086 | 43.00 | 65.00 | 1166 | 53.00 | 76.00 | 1246 | 62.00 | 87.00 |
| 1007 | 40.00 | 55.00 | 1087 | 44.00 | 65.00 | 1167 | 53.00 | 76.00 | 1247 | 62.00 | 07.00 |
| 1008 | 40.00 | 55.00 | 1088 | 44.00 | 65.00 | 1168 | 53.00 | 76.00 | 1248 | 62.00 | 87.00 |
| 1009 | 40.00 | 56.00 | 1089 | 44.00 | 65.00 | 1169 | 53.00 | 76.00 | 1249 | 62.00 | 87.00 |
| 1010 | 40.00 | 56.00 | 1090 | 44.00 | 65.00 | 1170 | 53.00 | 76.00 | 1250 | 63.00 | 88.00 |
| 1011 | 40.00 | 56.00 | 1091 | 44.00 | 66.00 | 1171 | 53.00 | 76.00 | 1251 | 63.00 | 88.00 |
| 1012 | 41.00 | 56.00 | 1092 | 44.00 | 66.00 | 1172 | 53.00 | 76.00 | 1252 | 63.00 | 88.00 |
| 1013 | 41.00 | 56.00 | 1093 | 44.00 | 66.00 | 1173 | 53.00 | 76.00 | 1253 | 63.00 | 88.00 |
| 1014 | 41.00 | 56.00 | 1094 | 44.00 | 66.00 | 1174 | 53.00 | 76.00 | 1254 | 63.00 | 88.00 |
| 1015 | 41.00 | 56.00 | 1095 | 44.00 | 66.00 | 1175 | 53.00 | 76.00 | 1255 | 63.00 | 88.00 |
| 1016 | 41.00 | 56.00 | 1096 | 44.00 | 66.00 | 1176 | 53.00 | 77.00 | 1256 | 63.00 | 88.00 |
| 1017 | 41.00 | 56.00 | 1097 | 44.00 | 66.00 | 1177 | 53.00 | 77.00 | 1257 | 63.00 | 88.00 |
| 1018 | 41.00 | 56.00 | 1098 | 44.00 | 66.00 | 1178 | 53.00 | 77.00 | 1258 | 63.00 | 88.00 |
| 1019 | 41.00 | 56.00 | 1099 | 49.00 | 66.00 | 1179 | 53.00 | 77.00 | 1259 | 63.00 | 88.00 |
| 1020 | 41.00 | 61.00 | 1100 | 50.00 | 66.00 | 1180 | 53.00 | 77.00 | 1260 | 63.00 | 88.00 |
| 1021 | 41.00 | 61.00 | 1101 | 50.00 | 66.00 | 1181 | 53.00 | 77.00 | 1261 | 63.00 | 88.00 |
| 1022 | 41.00 | 61.00 | 1102 | 50.00 | 66.00 | 1182 | 53.00 | 77.00 | 1262 | 63.00 | 88.00 |
| 1023 | 41.00 | 61.00 | 1103 | 50.00 | 66.00 | 1183 | 53.00 | 77.00 | 1263 | 63.00 | 88.00 |
| 1024 | 41.00 | 61.00 | 1104 | 50.00 | 66.00 | 1184 | 53.00 | 77.00 | 1264 | 63.00 | 89.00 |
| 1025 | 41.00 | 62.00 | 1105 | 50.00 | 66.00 | 1185 | 53.00 | 77.00 | 1265 | 63.00 | 89.00 |
| 1026 | 41.00 | 62.00 | 1106 | 50.00 | 66.00 | 1186 | 53.00 | 77.00 | 1266 | 63.00 | 89.00 |
| 1027 | 41.00 | 62.00 | 1107 | 50.00 | 66.00 | 1187 | 53.00 | 77.00 | 1267 | 63.00 | 89.00 |
| 1028 | 41.00 | 62.00 | 1108 | 50.00 | 67.00 | 1188 | 54.00 | 77.00 | 1268 | 63.00 | 89.00 |
| 1029 | 41.00 | 62.00 | 1109 | 50.00 | 67.00 | 1189 | 54.00 | 77.00 | 1269 | 63.00 | 89.00 |
| 1030 | 41.00 | 62.00 | 1110 | 50.00 | 67.00 | 1190 | 54.00 | 77.00 | 1270 | 64.00 | 89.00 |
| 1031 | 41.00 | 62.00 | 1111 | 50.00 | 67.00 | 1191 | 54.00 | 77.00 | 1271 | 64.00 | 89.00 |
| 1032 | 41.00 | 62.00 | 1112 | 50.00 | 67.00 | 1192 | 54.00 | 78.00 | 1272 | 64.00 | 89.00 |
| 1033 | 41.00 | 62.00 | 1113 | 50.00 | 67.00 | 1193 | 54.00 | 78.00 | 1273 | 64.00 | 89.00 |
| 1034 | 41.00 | 62.00 | 1114 | 50.00 | 67.00 | 1194 | 54.00 | 78.00 | 1274 | 64.00 | 89.00 |
| 1035 | 41.00 | 62.00 | 1115 | 50.00 | 67.00 | 1195 | 54.00 | 78.00 | 1275 | 70.00 | 89.00 |

4

SCHEDULE 11 HIGHER EDUCATION LOAN PROGRAM WEEKLY TAX TABLE

## Figure 7.8

### HELP WEEKLY TAX TABLE

| Weekly earnings 1 $ | Tax-free threshold weekly component 2 $ | No tax-free threshold weekly component 3 $ | Weekly earnings 1 $ | Tax-free threshold weekly component 2 $ | No tax-free threshold weekly component 3 $ | Weekly earnings 1 $ | Tax-free threshold weekly component 2 $ | No tax-free threshold weekly component 3 $ | Weekly earnings 1 $ | Tax-free threshold weekly component 2 $ | No tax-free threshold weekly component 3 $ |
|---|---|---|---|---|---|---|---|---|---|---|---|
| 1276 | 70.00 | 89.00 | 1356 | 75.00 | 95.00 | 1436 | 86.00 | 108.00 | 1516 | 99.00 | 121.00 |
| 1277 | 70.00 | 89.00 | 1357 | 75.00 | 95.00 | 1437 | 86.00 | 108.00 | 1517 | 99.00 | 121.00 |
| 1278 | 70.00 | 90.00 | 1358 | 75.00 | 95.00 | 1438 | 86.00 | 108.00 | 1518 | 99.00 | 122.00 |
| 1279 | 70.00 | 90.00 | 1359 | 75.00 | 95.00 | 1439 | 86.00 | 108.00 | 1519 | 99.00 | 122.00 |
| 1280 | 70.00 | 90.00 | 1360 | 75.00 | 95.00 | 1440 | 86.00 | 108.00 | 1520 | 99.00 | 122.00 |
| 1281 | 71.00 | 90.00 | 1361 | 75.00 | 95.00 | 1441 | 87.00 | 108.00 | 1521 | 99.00 | 122.00 |
| 1282 | 71.00 | 90.00 | 1362 | 75.00 | 95.00 | 1442 | 87.00 | 108.00 | 1522 | 99.00 | 122.00 |
| 1283 | 71.00 | 90.00 | 1363 | 75.00 | 95.00 | 1443 | 87.00 | 108.00 | 1523 | 99.00 | 122.00 |
| 1284 | 71.00 | 90.00 | 1364 | 75.00 | 96.00 | 1444 | 87.00 | 108.00 | 1524 | 99.00 | 122.00 |
| 1285 | 71.00 | 90.00 | 1365 | 75.00 | 96.00 | 1445 | 87.00 | 108.00 | 1525 | 99.00 | 122.00 |
| 1286 | 71.00 | 90.00 | 1366 | 75.00 | 96.00 | 1446 | 87.00 | 109.00 | 1526 | 99.00 | 122.00 |
| 1287 | 71.00 | 90.00 | 1367 | 75.00 | 96.00 | 1447 | 87.00 | 109.00 | 1527 | 99.00 | 122.00 |
| 1288 | 71.00 | 90.00 | 1368 | 75.00 | 96.00 | 1448 | 87.00 | 109.00 | 1528 | 99.00 | 122.00 |
| 1289 | 71.00 | 90.00 | 1369 | 75.00 | 103.00 | 1449 | 87.00 | 109.00 | 1529 | 99.00 | 122.00 |
| 1290 | 71.00 | 90.00 | 1370 | 82.00 | 103.00 | 1450 | 87.00 | 109.00 | 1530 | 100.00 | 122.00 |
| 1291 | 71.00 | 90.00 | 1371 | 82.00 | 103.00 | 1451 | 87.00 | 109.00 | 1531 | 100.00 | 123.00 |
| 1292 | 71.00 | 91.00 | 1372 | 82.00 | 103.00 | 1452 | 87.00 | 109.00 | 1532 | 100.00 | 123.00 |
| 1293 | 71.00 | 91.00 | 1373 | 82.00 | 103.00 | 1453 | 87.00 | 109.00 | 1533 | 100.00 | 123.00 |
| 1294 | 71.00 | 91.00 | 1374 | 82.00 | 103.00 | 1454 | 87.00 | 109.00 | 1534 | 100.00 | 123.00 |
| 1295 | 71.00 | 91.00 | 1375 | 83.00 | 103.00 | 1455 | 87.00 | 109.00 | 1535 | 100.00 | 123.00 |
| 1296 | 71.00 | 91.00 | 1376 | 83.00 | 103.00 | 1456 | 87.00 | 109.00 | 1536 | 100.00 | 123.00 |
| 1297 | 71.00 | 91.00 | 1377 | 83.00 | 103.00 | 1457 | 87.00 | 109.00 | 1537 | 100.00 | 123.00 |
| 1298 | 71.00 | 91.00 | 1378 | 83.00 | 103.00 | 1458 | 88.00 | 109.00 | 1538 | 100.00 | 123.00 |
| 1299 | 71.00 | 91.00 | 1379 | 83.00 | 103.00 | 1459 | 88.00 | 109.00 | 1539 | 100.00 | 123.00 |
| 1300 | 72.00 | 91.00 | 1380 | 83.00 | 104.00 | 1460 | 88.00 | 110.00 | 1540 | 100.00 | 123.00 |
| 1301 | 72.00 | 91.00 | 1381 | 83.00 | 104.00 | 1461 | 88.00 | 110.00 | 1541 | 100.00 | 123.00 |
| 1302 | 72.00 | 91.00 | 1382 | 83.00 | 104.00 | 1462 | 88.00 | 110.00 | 1542 | 100.00 | 123.00 |
| 1303 | 72.00 | 91.00 | 1383 | 83.00 | 104.00 | 1463 | 88.00 | 110.00 | 1543 | 100.00 | 124.00 |
| 1304 | 72.00 | 91.00 | 1384 | 83.00 | 104.00 | 1464 | 88.00 | 110.00 | 1544 | 100.00 | 124.00 |
| 1305 | 72.00 | 91.00 | 1385 | 83.00 | 104.00 | 1465 | 88.00 | 110.00 | 1545 | 100.00 | 124.00 |
| 1306 | 72.00 | 91.00 | 1386 | 83.00 | 104.00 | 1466 | 88.00 | 110.00 | 1546 | 101.00 | 124.00 |
| 1307 | 72.00 | 92.00 | 1387 | 83.00 | 104.00 | 1467 | 88.00 | 110.00 | 1547 | 101.00 | 124.00 |
| 1308 | 72.00 | 92.00 | 1388 | 83.00 | 104.00 | 1468 | 88.00 | 110.00 | 1548 | 101.00 | 124.00 |
| 1309 | 72.00 | 92.00 | 1389 | 83.00 | 104.00 | 1469 | 88.00 | 110.00 | 1549 | 101.00 | 124.00 |
| 1310 | 72.00 | 92.00 | 1390 | 83.00 | 104.00 | 1470 | 88.00 | 110.00 | 1550 | 101.00 | 124.00 |
| 1311 | 72.00 | 92.00 | 1391 | 84.00 | 104.00 | 1471 | 88.00 | 110.00 | 1551 | 101.00 | 124.00 |
| 1312 | 72.00 | 92.00 | 1392 | 84.00 | 104.00 | 1472 | 88.00 | 110.00 | 1552 | 101.00 | 124.00 |
| 1313 | 72.00 | 92.00 | 1393 | 84.00 | 105.00 | 1473 | 88.00 | 111.00 | 1553 | 101.00 | 124.00 |
| 1314 | 72.00 | 92.00 | 1394 | 84.00 | 105.00 | 1474 | 88.00 | 111.00 | 1554 | 101.00 | 124.00 |
| 1315 | 72.00 | 92.00 | 1395 | 84.00 | 105.00 | 1475 | 89.00 | 111.00 | 1555 | 101.00 | 124.00 |
| 1316 | 72.00 | 92.00 | 1396 | 84.00 | 105.00 | 1476 | 89.00 | 111.00 | 1556 | 101.00 | 125.00 |
| 1317 | 72.00 | 92.00 | 1397 | 84.00 | 105.00 | 1477 | 89.00 | 111.00 | 1557 | 101.00 | 125.00 |
| 1318 | 73.00 | 92.00 | 1398 | 84.00 | 105.00 | 1478 | 89.00 | 111.00 | 1558 | 101.00 | 125.00 |
| 1319 | 73.00 | 92.00 | 1399 | 84.00 | 105.00 | 1479 | 89.00 | 111.00 | 1559 | 101.00 | 125.00 |
| 1320 | 73.00 | 92.00 | 1400 | 84.00 | 105.00 | 1480 | 89.00 | 111.00 | 1560 | 101.00 | 125.00 |
| 1321 | 73.00 | 93.00 | 1401 | 84.00 | 105.00 | 1481 | 89.00 | 111.00 | 1561 | 102.00 | 125.00 |
| 1322 | 73.00 | 93.00 | 1402 | 84.00 | 105.00 | 1482 | 89.00 | 119.00 | 1562 | 109.00 | 125.00 |
| 1323 | 73.00 | 93.00 | 1403 | 84.00 | 105.00 | 1483 | 89.00 | 119.00 | 1563 | 109.00 | 125.00 |
| 1324 | 73.00 | 93.00 | 1404 | 84.00 | 105.00 | 1484 | 97.00 | 119.00 | 1564 | 110.00 | 125.00 |
| 1325 | 73.00 | 93.00 | 1405 | 84.00 | 105.00 | 1485 | 97.00 | 119.00 | 1565 | 110.00 | 125.00 |
| 1326 | 73.00 | 93.00 | 1406 | 84.00 | 106.00 | 1486 | 97.00 | 119.00 | 1566 | 110.00 | 125.00 |
| 1327 | 73.00 | 93.00 | 1407 | 84.00 | 106.00 | 1487 | 97.00 | 119.00 | 1567 | 110.00 | 125.00 |
| 1328 | 73.00 | 93.00 | 1408 | 85.00 | 106.00 | 1488 | 97.00 | 119.00 | 1568 | 110.00 | 126.00 |
| 1329 | 73.00 | 93.00 | 1409 | 85.00 | 106.00 | 1489 | 97.00 | 119.00 | 1569 | 110.00 | 126.00 |
| 1330 | 73.00 | 93.00 | 1410 | 85.00 | 106.00 | 1490 | 97.00 | 119.00 | 1570 | 110.00 | 126.00 |
| 1331 | 73.00 | 93.00 | 1411 | 85.00 | 106.00 | 1491 | 97.00 | 119.00 | 1571 | 110.00 | 126.00 |
| 1332 | 73.00 | 93.00 | 1412 | 85.00 | 106.00 | 1492 | 97.00 | 119.00 | 1572 | 110.00 | 126.00 |
| 1333 | 73.00 | 93.00 | 1413 | 85.00 | 106.00 | 1493 | 97.00 | 120.00 | 1573 | 110.00 | 126.00 |
| 1334 | 73.00 | 93.00 | 1414 | 85.00 | 106.00 | 1494 | 97.00 | 120.00 | 1574 | 110.00 | 126.00 |
| 1335 | 73.00 | 94.00 | 1415 | 85.00 | 106.00 | 1495 | 97.00 | 120.00 | 1575 | 110.00 | 126.00 |
| 1336 | 74.00 | 94.00 | 1416 | 85.00 | 106.00 | 1496 | 97.00 | 120.00 | 1576 | 110.00 | 126.00 |
| 1337 | 74.00 | 94.00 | 1417 | 85.00 | 106.00 | 1497 | 97.00 | 120.00 | 1577 | 110.00 | 126.00 |
| 1338 | 74.00 | 94.00 | 1418 | 85.00 | 106.00 | 1498 | 97.00 | 120.00 | 1578 | 111.00 | 126.00 |
| 1339 | 74.00 | 94.00 | 1419 | 85.00 | 106.00 | 1499 | 97.00 | 120.00 | 1579 | 111.00 | 126.00 |
| 1340 | 74.00 | 94.00 | 1420 | 85.00 | 107.00 | 1500 | 98.00 | 120.00 | 1580 | 111.00 | 126.00 |
| 1341 | 74.00 | 94.00 | 1421 | 85.00 | 107.00 | 1501 | 98.00 | 120.00 | 1581 | 111.00 | 127.00 |
| 1342 | 74.00 | 94.00 | 1422 | 85.00 | 107.00 | 1502 | 98.00 | 120.00 | 1582 | 111.00 | 127.00 |
| 1343 | 74.00 | 94.00 | 1423 | 85.00 | 107.00 | 1503 | 98.00 | 120.00 | 1583 | 111.00 | 127.00 |
| 1344 | 74.00 | 94.00 | 1424 | 85.00 | 107.00 | 1504 | 98.00 | 120.00 | 1584 | 111.00 | 127.00 |
| 1345 | 74.00 | 94.00 | 1425 | 86.00 | 107.00 | 1505 | 98.00 | 120.00 | 1585 | 111.00 | 127.00 |
| 1346 | 74.00 | 94.00 | 1426 | 86.00 | 107.00 | 1506 | 98.00 | 121.00 | 1586 | 111.00 | 127.00 |
| 1347 | 74.00 | 94.00 | 1427 | 86.00 | 107.00 | 1507 | 98.00 | 121.00 | 1587 | 111.00 | 127.00 |
| 1348 | 74.00 | 94.00 | 1428 | 86.00 | 107.00 | 1508 | 98.00 | 121.00 | 1588 | 111.00 | 127.00 |
| 1349 | 74.00 | 94.00 | 1429 | 86.00 | 107.00 | 1509 | 98.00 | 121.00 | 1589 | 111.00 | 127.00 |
| 1350 | 74.00 | 95.00 | 1430 | 86.00 | 107.00 | 1510 | 98.00 | 121.00 | 1590 | 111.00 | 127.00 |
| 1351 | 74.00 | 95.00 | 1431 | 86.00 | 107.00 | 1511 | 98.00 | 121.00 | 1591 | 111.00 | 127.00 |
| 1352 | 74.00 | 95.00 | 1432 | 86.00 | 107.00 | 1512 | 98.00 | 121.00 | 1592 | 112.00 | 127.00 |
| 1353 | 74.00 | 95.00 | 1433 | 86.00 | 108.00 | 1513 | 98.00 | 121.00 | 1593 | 112.00 | 128.00 |
| 1354 | 75.00 | 95.00 | 1434 | 86.00 | 108.00 | 1514 | 98.00 | 121.00 | 1594 | 112.00 | 128.00 |
| 1355 | 75.00 | 95.00 | 1435 | 86.00 | 108.00 | 1515 | 99.00 | 121.00 | 1595 | 112.00 | 128.00 |

SCHEDULE 11 HIGHER EDUCATION LOAN PROGRAM WEEKLY TAX TABLE                    5

**Figure 7.8**

## HELP WEEKLY TAX TABLE

| Weekly earnings 1 $ | Tax-free threshold weekly component 2 $ | No tax-free threshold weekly component 3 $ |
|---|---|---|
| 1596 | 112.00 | 128.00 |
| 1597 | 112.00 | 128.00 |
| 1598 | 112.00 | 128.00 |
| 1599 | 112.00 | 128.00 |
| 1600 | 112.00 | 128.00 |
| 1601 | 112.00 | 128.00 |
| 1602 | 112.00 | 128.00 |
| 1603 | 112.00 | 128.00 |
| 1604 | 112.00 | 128.00 |
| 1605 | 112.00 | 128.00 |
| 1606 | 112.00 | 129.00 |
| 1607 | 113.00 | 129.00 |
| 1608 | 113.00 | 129.00 |
| 1609 | 113.00 | 129.00 |
| 1610 | 113.00 | 129.00 |
| 1611 | 113.00 | 129.00 |
| 1612 | 113.00 | 129.00 |
| 1613 | 113.00 | 129.00 |
| 1614 | 113.00 | 129.00 |
| 1615 | 113.00 | 129.00 |
| 1616 | 113.00 | 129.00 |
| 1617 | 113.00 | 129.00 |
| 1618 | 113.00 | 130.00 |
| 1619 | 113.00 | 130.00 |
| 1620 | 113.00 | 130.00 |
| 1621 | 114.00 | 130.00 |
| 1622 | 114.00 | 130.00 |
| 1623 | 114.00 | 130.00 |
| 1624 | 114.00 | 130.00 |
| 1625 | 114.00 | 130.00 |
| 1626 | 114.00 | 130.00 |
| 1627 | 114.00 | 130.00 |
| 1628 | 114.00 | 130.00 |
| 1629 | 114.00 | 130.00 |
| 1630 | 114.00 | 130.00 |
| 1631 | 114.00 | 131.00 |
| 1632 | 114.00 | 131.00 |
| 1633 | 114.00 | 131.00 |
| 1634 | 114.00 | 131.00 |
| 1635 | 115.00 | 131.00 |
| 1636 | 115.00 | 131.00 |
| 1637 | 115.00 | 131.00 |
| 1638 | 115.00 | 131.00 |
| 1639 | 115.00 | 131.00 |
| 1640 | 115.00 | 131.00 |
| 1641 | 115.00 | 131.00 |
| 1642 | 115.00 | 131.00 |
| 1643 | 115.00 | 132.00 |
| 1644 | 115.00 | 132.00 |
| 1645 | 115.00 | 132.00 |
| 1646 | 115.00 | 132.00 |
| 1647 | 115.00 | 132.00 |
| 1648 | 115.00 | 132.00 |
| 1649 | 115.00 | 132.00 |
| 1650 | 116.00 | 132.00 |
| 1651 | 116.00 | 132.00 |
| 1652 | 116.00 | 132.00 |
| 1653 | 116.00 | 132.00 |
| 1654 | 116.00 | 132.00 |
| 1655 | 116.00 | 132.00 |
| 1656 | 116.00 | 133.00 |
| 1657 | 116.00 | 133.00 |
| 1658 | 116.00 | 133.00 |
| 1659 | 116.00 | 133.00 |
| 1660 | 116.00 | 133.00 |
| 1661 | 116.00 | 133.00 |
| 1662 | 116.00 | 133.00 |
| 1663 | 116.00 | 133.00 |
| 1664 | 117.00 | 133.00 |
| 1665 | 117.00 | 133.00 |
| 1666 | 117.00 | 133.00 |
| 1667 | 117.00 | 133.00 |
| 1668 | 117.00 | 134.00 |
| 1669 | 117.00 | 134.00 |
| 1670 | 117.00 | 134.00 |
| 1671 | 117.00 | 134.00 |
| 1672 | 117.00 | 134.00 |
| 1673 | 117.00 | 134.00 |
| 1674 | 117.00 | 134.00 |
| 1675 | 117.00 | 134.00 |
| 1676 | 117.00 | 134.00 |
| 1677 | 117.00 | 134.00 |
| 1678 | 118.00 | 134.00 |
| 1679 | 118.00 | 134.00 |
| 1680 | 118.00 | 134.00 |
| 1681 | 118.00 | 135.00 |
| 1682 | 118.00 | 135.00 |
| 1683 | 118.00 | 135.00 |
| 1684 | 118.00 | 135.00 |
| 1685 | 118.00 | 135.00 |
| 1686 | 118.00 | 135.00 |
| 1687 | 118.00 | 135.00 |
| 1688 | 118.00 | 135.00 |
| 1689 | 118.00 | 135.00 |
| 1690 | 118.00 | 135.00 |
| 1691 | 118.00 | 135.00 |
| 1692 | 119.00 | 135.00 |
| 1693 | 119.00 | 136.00 |
| 1694 | 119.00 | 136.00 |
| 1695 | 119.00 | 136.00 |
| 1696 | 119.00 | 136.00 |
| 1697 | 119.00 | 136.00 |
| 1698 | 119.00 | 136.00 |
| 1699 | 119.00 | 136.00 |
| 1700 | 119.00 | 136.00 |
| 1701 | 119.00 | 136.00 |
| 1702 | 119.00 | 136.00 |
| 1703 | 119.00 | 136.00 |
| 1704 | 119.00 | 136.00 |
| 1705 | 119.00 | 136.00 |
| 1706 | 119.00 | 137.00 |
| 1707 | 120.00 | 137.00 |
| 1708 | 120.00 | 137.00 |
| 1709 | 120.00 | 137.00 |
| 1710 | 120.00 | 137.00 |
| 1711 | 120.00 | 137.00 |
| 1712 | 120.00 | 137.00 |
| 1713 | 120.00 | 137.00 |
| 1714 | 120.00 | 137.00 |
| 1715 | 120.00 | 137.00 |
| 1716 | 120.00 | 137.00 |
| 1717 | 120.00 | 137.00 |
| 1718 | 120.00 | 138.00 |
| 1719 | 129.00 | 138.00 |
| 1720 | 129.00 | 138.00 |
| 1721 | 129.00 | 138.00 |
| 1722 | 129.00 | 138.00 |
| 1723 | 129.00 | 138.00 |
| 1724 | 129.00 | 138.00 |
| 1725 | 129.00 | 138.00 |
| 1726 | 130.00 | 138.00 |
| 1727 | 130.00 | 138.00 |
| 1728 | 130.00 | 138.00 |
| 1729 | 130.00 | 138.00 |
| 1730 | 130.00 | 138.00 |
| 1731 | 130.00 | 139.00 |
| 1732 | 130.00 | 139.00 |
| 1733 | 130.00 | 139.00 |
| 1734 | 130.00 | 139.00 |
| 1735 | 130.00 | 139.00 |
| 1736 | 130.00 | 139.00 |
| 1737 | 130.00 | 139.00 |
| 1738 | 130.00 | 139.00 |
| 1739 | 130.00 | 139.00 |
| 1740 | 131.00 | 139.00 |
| 1741 | 131.00 | 139.00 |
| 1742 | 131.00 | 139.00 |
| 1743 | 131.00 | 140.00 |
| 1744 | 131.00 | 140.00 |
| 1745 | 131.00 | 140.00 |
| 1746 | 131.00 | 140.00 |
| 1747 | 131.00 | 140.00 |
| 1748 | 131.00 | 140.00 |
| 1749 | 131.00 | 140.00 |
| 1750 | 131.00 | 140.00 |
| 1751 | 131.00 | 140.00 |
| 1752 | 131.00 | 140.00 |
| 1753 | 132.00 | 140.00 |
| 1754 | 132.00 | 140.00 |
| 1755 | 132.00 | 140.00 |
| 1756 | 132.00 | 141.00 |
| 1757 | 132.00 | 141.00 |
| 1758 | 132.00 | 141.00 |
| 1759 | 132.00 | 141.00 |
| 1760 | 132.00 | 141.00 |
| 1761 | 132.00 | 141.00 |
| 1762 | 132.00 | 141.00 |
| 1763 | 132.00 | 141.00 |
| 1764 | 132.00 | 141.00 |
| 1765 | 132.00 | 141.00 |
| 1766 | 133.00 | 141.00 |
| 1767 | 133.00 | 141.00 |
| 1768 | 133.00 | 142.00 |
| 1769 | 133.00 | 142.00 |
| 1770 | 133.00 | 142.00 |
| 1771 | 133.00 | 142.00 |
| 1772 | 133.00 | 142.00 |
| 1773 | 133.00 | 142.00 |
| 1774 | 133.00 | 142.00 |
| 1775 | 133.00 | 142.00 |
| 1776 | 133.00 | 142.00 |
| 1777 | 133.00 | 142.00 |
| 1778 | 133.00 | 142.00 |
| 1779 | 133.00 | 142.00 |
| 1780 | 134.00 | 142.00 |
| 1781 | 134.00 | 143.00 |
| 1782 | 134.00 | 143.00 |
| 1783 | 134.00 | 143.00 |
| 1784 | 134.00 | 143.00 |
| 1785 | 134.00 | 143.00 |
| 1786 | 134.00 | 143.00 |
| 1787 | 134.00 | 143.00 |
| 1788 | 134.00 | 143.00 |
| 1789 | 134.00 | 143.00 |
| 1790 | 134.00 | 143.00 |
| 1791 | 134.00 | 143.00 |
| 1792 | 134.00 | 143.00 |
| 1793 | 135.00 | 144.00 |
| 1794 | 135.00 | 144.00 |
| 1795 | 135.00 | 144.00 |
| 1796 | 135.00 | 144.00 |
| 1797 | 135.00 | 144.00 |
| 1798 | 135.00 | 144.00 |
| 1799 | 135.00 | 144.00 |
| 1800 | 135.00 | 144.00 |
| 1801 | 135.00 | 144.00 |
| 1802 | 135.00 | 144.00 |
| 1803 | 135.00 | 144.00 |
| 1804 | 135.00 | 144.00 |
| 1805 | 135.00 | 144.00 |
| 1806 | 136.00 | 145.00 |
| 1807 | 136.00 | 145.00 |
| 1808 | 136.00 | 145.00 |
| 1809 | 136.00 | 145.00 |
| 1810 | 136.00 | 145.00 |
| 1811 | 136.00 | 145.00 |
| 1812 | 136.00 | 145.00 |
| 1813 | 136.00 | 145.00 |
| 1814 | 136.00 | 145.00 |
| 1815 | 136.00 | 145.00 |
| 1816 | 136.00 | 145.00 |
| 1817 | 136.00 | 145.00 |
| 1818 | 136.00 | 146.00 |
| 1819 | 136.00 | 146.00 |
| 1820 | 137.00 | 146.00 |
| 1821 | 137.00 | 146.00 |
| 1822 | 137.00 | 146.00 |
| 1823 | 137.00 | 146.00 |
| 1824 | 137.00 | 146.00 |
| 1825 | 137.00 | 146.00 |
| 1826 | 137.00 | 146.00 |
| 1827 | 137.00 | 146.00 |
| 1828 | 137.00 | 146.00 |
| 1829 | 137.00 | 146.00 |
| 1830 | 137.00 | 146.00 |
| 1831 | 137.00 | 147.00 |
| 1832 | 147.00 | 147.00 |

❗ If the payee's weekly earnings are more than $1,832, the HELP component is $147 plus 8 cents for each $1 of weekly earnings over $1,832. Amounts calculated should be rounded to the nearest dollar.

**PUBLISHED BY**

Australian Taxation Office, Canberra, May 2013
JS 27904

**OUR COMMITMENT TO YOU**

We are committed to providing you with accurate, consistent and clear information to help you understand your rights and entitlements and meet your obligations. If you feel that this publication does not fully cover your circumstances, or you are unsure how it applies to you, you can seek further assistance from us.

We regularly revise our publications to take account of any changes to the law, so make sure that you have the latest information. If you are unsure, you can check for more recent information on our website at **ato.gov.au** or contact us.

This publication was current at **May 2013**.

Figure 7.9    Medicare levy variation declaration form

**Australian Government**

**Australian Taxation Office**

# Medicare levy variation declaration form

- Refer to the Instructions to help you complete this declaration.
- Print neatly in BLOCK LETTERS and use a black or dark blue pen.
- Print ☒ in the appropriate boxes.

> ❗ The information in the completed *Medicare levy variation declaration* form must be treated as sensitive.

## Section A: **Payee's declaration**

> ❯ To be completed by payee.

**1   What is your tax file number (TFN)?**

> ❯ See 'Privacy' on the inside front cover of the instructions.

**2   What is your name?**

Title:   Mr ☐   Mrs ☐   Miss ☐   Ms ☐   Other ☐

Family name

Given names

**3   What is your home address?**

Street address

Suburb/town                                State/Territory ▼    Postcode

**4   Do you want your payer to increase the amounts withheld from you to cover the Medicare levy surcharge?**

No ☐ Go to question 5.    Yes ☐ Select one of the following rates

1% ☐   1.25% ☐   1.5% ☐

If you want to make other variations using this form, go to question 5. Otherwise, sign and date the declaration and give it to your payer.

**5   Do you qualify for a Medicare levy exemption?**

No ☐ Go to question 8.    Yes ☐

**6   Do you want to claim a full exemption from the Medicare levy?**

No ☐    Yes ☐ Go to question 9.

**7   Do you want to claim a half levy exemption from the Medicare levy?**

No ☐    Yes ☐ Go to question 9.

**8   Do you want to claim a Medicare levy reduction?**

No ☐    Yes ☐

**9   Do you have a spouse?**

No ☐    Yes ☐

> ❯ For a definition of spouse, see Definitions on page 5.

**10   Is the combined weekly income of you and your spouse, or your income as a sole parent, less than the relevant amount in table A on page 1?**

No ☐    Yes ☐

**11a   Do you have an accumulated Higher Education Loan Program (HELP) debt?**

No ☐    Yes ☐ If you also answered **yes** at question 10, you are exempt from having additional PAYG amounts for HELP withheld from payments to you.

**11b   Do you have an accumulated Financial Supplement debt?**

No ☐    Yes ☐ If you also answered **yes** at question 10, you are exempt from having additional PAYG amounts for Financial Supplement debts withheld from payments to you.

**12   Do you have dependent children?**

No ☐ Sign and date the declaration.    Yes ☐ How many? [    ]

> ❯ For a definition of dependent children, see Definitions on page 5.

NAT 0929-07.2013                **Sensitive** (when completed)

**Figure 7.9**

**DECLARATION BY PAYEE**

*I declare that the information I have given on this form is true and correct.*

⊖ The tax laws impose heavy penalties for giving false or misleading statements.

Signature of payee

Date [ ][ ]/[ ][ ]/[ ][ ][ ]
Day / Month / Year

❷ Give your completed declaration to your payer.

## Section B: **Payer's declaration**

❗ The information in the completed *Medicare levy variation declaration* form must be treated as sensitive.

❷ To be completed by payer.

**YOUR DETAILS**

1  **What is your Australian business number (ABN) (or your withholding payer number if you are not in business)?**

2  **What is your registered business name or trading name (or your individual name if you are not a business)?**

❷ HOW MUCH SHOULD YOU WITHHOLD?

A **yes** answer at question 4 will require increasing the amount you withhold by 1%, 1.25% or 1.5% of the payee's gross earnings.

A **yes** answer at questions 6, 7 or 8 will require the special *Medicare levy adjustment weekly tax table* (NAT 1010) to calculate the correct amount to withhold.

A **yes** answer at question 10 will require the special *Medicare levy adjustment weekly tax table* (NAT 1010) to calculate the correct amount to withhold. If the payee also has a HELP or Financial Supplement debt, do not withhold additional amounts to cover the HELP or Financial Supplement repayment.

**DECLARATION BY PAYER**

*I declare that the information I have given on this form is true and correct.*

⊖ The tax laws impose heavy penalties for giving false or misleading statements.

Signature of payer

Date [ ][ ]/[ ][ ]/[ ][ ][ ]
Day / Month / Year

❷ If you need copies of our publications, including the *Medicare levy variation declaration* (NAT 0929), the *Tax file number declaration* (NAT 3092), PAYG withholding tax tables or *Medicare levy adjustment weekly tax table* (NAT 1010), you can:
■ visit our website at **ato.gov.au**
■ phone us on **1300 720 092** between 8.00am and 6.00pm, Monday to Friday.

| **Print form** | **Save form** | **Reset form** |

**STORING AND DISPOSING OF MEDICARE LEVY VARIATION DECLARATIONS**

The information in the completed *Medicare levy variation declaration* form must be treated as sensitive. Once you have completed, signed and dated the declaration, you should file it. **Do not send it to us.**

Under the TFN guidelines in the *Privacy Act 1988*, you must use secure methods when storing and disposing of TFN information. Under tax laws, if a payee submits a new *Medicare levy variation declaration* or leaves your employment, you must still keep this declaration for the current and next financial year.

❗ Do not send this declaration form to us.

**Sensitive** (when completed)

**Figure 7.10     Calculation of PAYG withholding**

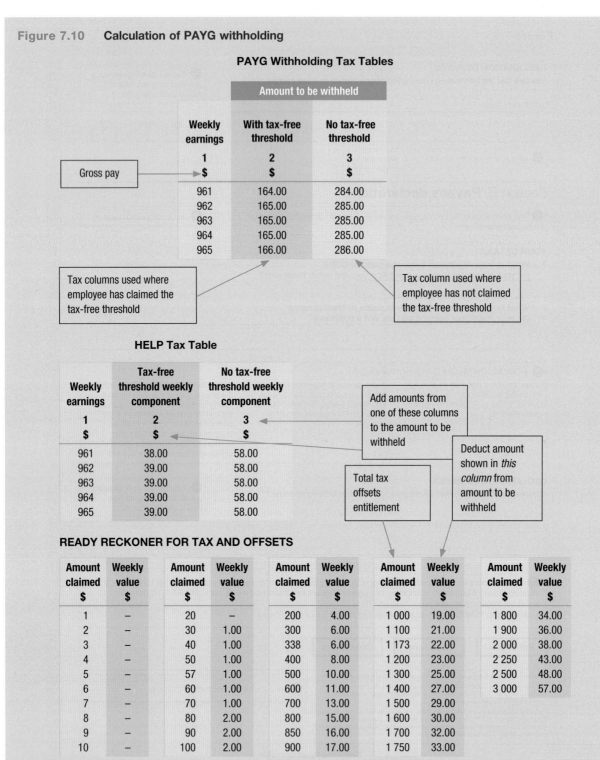

**PAYG Withholding Tax Tables**

| Weekly earnings | Amount to be withheld | |
| | With tax-free threshold | No tax-free threshold |
| 1 | 2 | 3 |
| $ | $ | $ |
| 961 | 164.00 | 284.00 |
| 962 | 165.00 | 285.00 |
| 963 | 165.00 | 285.00 |
| 964 | 165.00 | 285.00 |
| 965 | 166.00 | 286.00 |

Gross pay

Tax columns used where employee has claimed the tax-free threshold

Tax column used where employee has not claimed the tax-free threshold

**HELP Tax Table**

| Weekly earnings | Tax-free threshold weekly component | No tax-free threshold weekly component |
| 1 | 2 | 3 |
| $ | $ | $ |
| 961 | 38.00 | 58.00 |
| 962 | 39.00 | 58.00 |
| 963 | 39.00 | 58.00 |
| 964 | 39.00 | 58.00 |
| 965 | 39.00 | 58.00 |

Add amounts from one of these columns to the amount to be withheld

Total tax offsets entitlement

Deduct amount shown in *this column* from amount to be withheld

**READY RECKONER FOR TAX AND OFFSETS**

| Amount claimed $ | Weekly value $ | Amount claimed $ | Weekly value $ | Amount claimed $ | Weekly value $ | Amount claimed $ | Weekly value $ | Amount claimed $ | Weekly value $ |
|---|---|---|---|---|---|---|---|---|---|
| 1 | – | 20 | – | 200 | 4.00 | 1 000 | 19.00 | 1 800 | 34.00 |
| 2 | – | 30 | 1.00 | 300 | 6.00 | 1 100 | 21.00 | 1 900 | 36.00 |
| 3 | – | 40 | 1.00 | 338 | 6.00 | 1 173 | 22.00 | 2 000 | 38.00 |
| 4 | – | 50 | 1.00 | 400 | 8.00 | 1 200 | 23.00 | 2 250 | 43.00 |
| 5 | – | 57 | 1.00 | 500 | 10.00 | 1 300 | 25.00 | 2 500 | 48.00 |
| 6 | – | 60 | 1.00 | 600 | 11.00 | 1 400 | 27.00 | 3 000 | 57.00 |
| 7 | – | 70 | 1.00 | 700 | 13.00 | 1 500 | 29.00 | | |
| 8 | – | 80 | 2.00 | 800 | 15.00 | 1 600 | 30.00 | | |
| 9 | – | 90 | 2.00 | 850 | 16.00 | 1 700 | 32.00 | | |
| 10 | – | 100 | 2.00 | 900 | 17.00 | 1 750 | 33.00 | | |

If the exact offset amount claimed is not shown in the ready reckoner, add the values for an appropriate combination
Example: Tax offsets of $425 claimed. Add values of $400, $20, and $5 = $8.00 + $0.00 + $0.00 = $8.00.
　　　　Therefore, reduce the amount to be withheld by $8.00.

**Figure 7.11    Business Activity Statement**

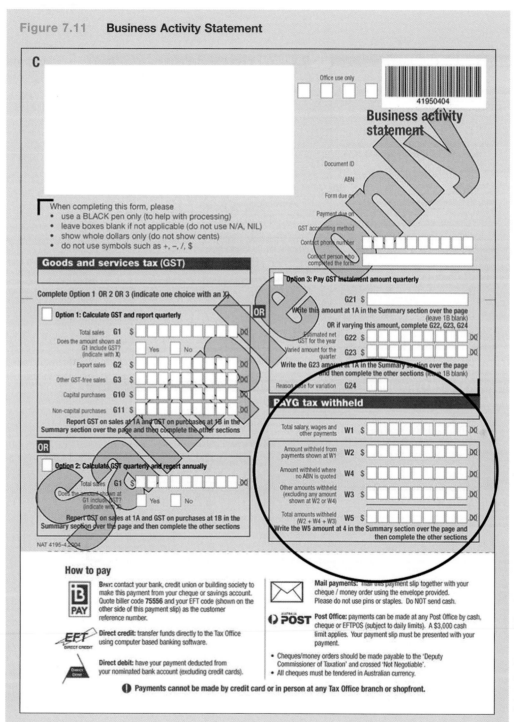

Figure 7.11

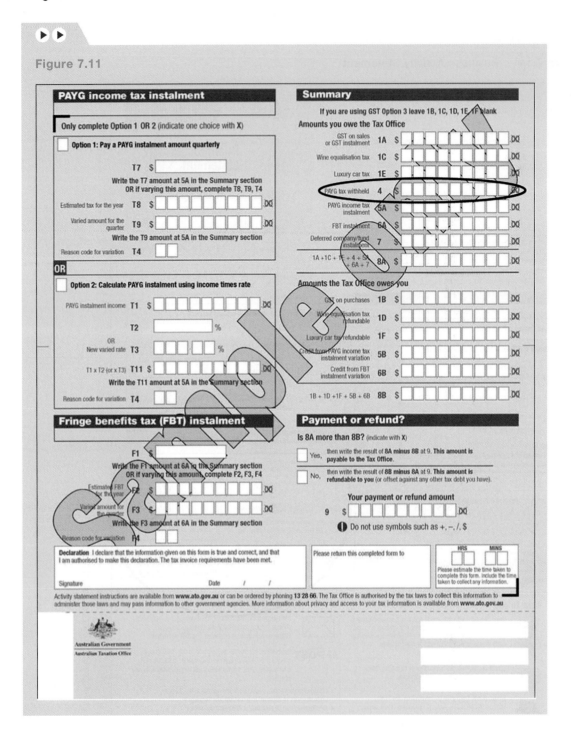

**Figure 7.12     PAYG payment summary — individual non-business**

## Summary

What have you covered in this chapter?

◆ Details of the employee records and controls necessary in a typical payroll system

◆ Calculations for weekly net pays for employees, taking into account starting and finishing time each day, overtime, paid leave, unpaid leave, employee deductions (union fees, medical benefits, superannuation) and PAYG withholding

◆ Preparation of entries for the weekly payroll in relevant employee and other records

◆ Preparation of entries for the payment of balances of PAYG withholding and employee deduction liability accounts created from the payroll

◆ Completing all journal and General Ledger entries arising from payroll transactions

◆ Employer's responsibilities in relation to PAYG withholding, payroll tax, workers' compensation and superannuation guarantee

◆ Review the internal controls procedures for payroll

# INDEX